10 倍速提升字彙力

5大考試
單字速記手冊 2011

Building Vocabulary for
iBT, SAT, GRE, TOEIC, GEPT

Dr. Park Jong Hwa 著

PEARSON

Longman 朗文

編者序

亞洲各國的英語學習者，經常花費許多時間和精力在記憶單字上。抱著字典逐頁逐字背誦者不在少數。在以往，這不失為累積單字量的一種方式，但在講求效率及方法的今天，語言學習也必須順應潮流，朝更經濟、有效的方向前進。有鑒於此，本書整理出一套有效的單字記憶方式，幫助讀者省時省力地快速累積字彙量。

首先篩選出 iBT, SAT, GRE, TOEIC, GEPT 國內五大考試的三千頻出單字，再配合單字特性運用以下四種快速記憶方式與深廣並蓄的例句，達到最大的學習效果。

❶「Z 字型拆解記憶法」：利用構詞法拆解單字，讓讀者以口訣方式記下字首、字根或字尾的意思，再如 Z 字型般由一個詞素搭配另一詞素，向下延伸學習。如下例（ana-, syn-, hypo- 為字首，chron, thesis 為字根）：

> **anachron**ism
>
> **synchron**ize
>
> **syn**thesist
>
> **hypo**thesis
>
> ...
>
> ...

❷「熟字聯想新字記憶法」：顧名思義就是利用已知單字的發音、意義、字型或情境等來連結難字的字義，藉以強化印象而不易忘記。

❸「詞素家族記憶法」：由 a-z 表列出字首、字根或字尾這三大詞素的意義後，再分別臚列具相同詞素的單字一起學習。熟悉這種記憶方式，日後在閱讀句子或文章時遇到生字，即可據依此原則並參酌上下文後推知字義。

❹「主題式記憶法」：分成校園學術篇與日常生活篇，前者網羅學生經常觸及的校園生活及課業學習之相關字彙，並適時穿插不同學術領域的專業用語，極具學習價值。後者則是鎖定日常生活頻用詞彙，並輔以高實用性例句，對於參與全民英檢等考試有很大的幫助。

用最有有效的方法記住最有效的考試字量，是研讀本書最大的好處。請讀者一定要自我督促，配合書中規劃的日程學習，如此定能在 iBT, SAT, GRE, TOEIC, GEPT 五大考試上獲得好成績。

本書結構

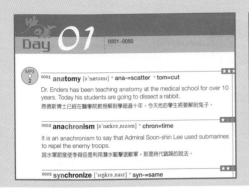

Vocabulary

本書收錄的單字,皆為iBT, SAT, GRE, TOEIC, GEPT五大考試中的高頻率單字(以★標示頻率高低,由五星至一星,頻率遞減)。每個單字同時以英英及英漢兩種方式做解釋,讀者可一併學到其他的英文同義說法,累積更多字量。至於搭配的例句,取材廣泛,摘自知名文學作品、醫學、經濟論述、日常活動等等,不但可理解單字用法,且能逐步增進閱讀能力。

Chapter

全書共分成五章,配合單字特性使用不同的記憶方式,並貼心規劃學習日程。讀者若能按部就班,認真研習,除可於短時間內記憶三千個有效考用單字外,還可運用本書所教導的快速記憶方式擴增其他領域的字彙。

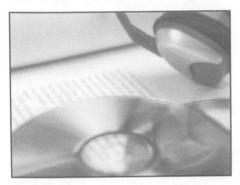

Mp3

讀者可以利用MP3做聽力及跟讀的雙重練習,一方面提升英語耳力,同時學會正確發音,而這是單字學習上極為重要的部分。

Tea Time

簡要介紹起源於某些神話、小說或軼事的單字,讓讀者在輕鬆無負擔的情境下學習一些衍生字。

Review Test

配合每天(Day)的學習，一共有五十六個Review Test，主要是針對單字的字義和拼字作練習，以檢核學習成效。

Review Test 01

Complete each word by filling in the blank with proper spellin meaning as suggested. Then please write the meaning of each

1. 分析	= a n a _ _ _ _	11. effusive
2. 綜合體	= s y n _ _ _ _ _ _	12. transfusion
3. 時代錯誤	= a n a _ _ _ _ _ _ _ _	13. proscribe
4. 動物標本製作	= _ _ _ _ d e r m y	14. convention
5. 假設	= _ _ _ _ t h e s i s	15. circumscribe
6. 生態學	= e c o _ _ _ _	16. deduct
7. 敵手	= _ _ _ a g o n i s t	17. suspend
8. 全神貫注	= _ _ _ c e n t r a t e	18. introduction

Practice Test

每經過四天的學習，就會有一個Practice Test，接在Review Test之後。除了測試之前篇幅中重要單字的字義和拼字外，更重要的是測試延伸學到的同義字。此外還提供一篇內容有趣的中長篇文章，要求讀者讀後回答問題。

Practice Test 01

The highlighted word is closest in meaning to which of the follo

1. In the early history of the United States, a nationwide political con advent of American hotels.

(A) assembly　　　　　　　　　(B) transfusion

(C) recession　　　　　　　　　(D) secession

2. It is said that an introverted person needs less space for living.

(A) assiduous　　　　　　　　　(B) attentive

Actual Test

在每章的最後有一個Actual Test，摘錄兩篇文章，文中某些單字加註記號，要求讀者在讀完全文後回答字義題。讀者藉由實際解題的過程，一者可了解自己到底記憶了多少單字，二者學會如何由構詞法及上下文去推知單字的意思。

Actual Test

Passage 1

The Titanic

At 2:20 a.m. on April 15, 1912, the White Star Line's "Unsinkable" the most gigantic and luxurious sea liner in the world, sank into the gla Atlantic. The disaster took a heavy toll of 1,500 lives - the greatest n maritime catastrophe in peacetime history.

On her doomed maiden voyage from Southampton to New York, th speeding through dark, smooth seas at 22.5 knots. The White Star Line's record for crossing the Atlantic in the shortest time accelerated the ship

Answers

為幫助讀者理解，並節省時間與精力，書中的每一道練習題及文章都附上中譯，並加註答案，提供讀者核對。

Chapter 1

Review Test_01

❶ 第1到10題為「拼字題」，請根據中文意思完成英文拼字填空。第11到20題為「釋義題」，請根據英文字彙寫出中文意思。

解答 | 1. analysis 2. synthesis 3. anachronism 4. taxidermy 5. hypothesis 6. ecology 7. antagonist 8. concentrate 9. recession 10. retract 11. 過度熱情的，情感洋溢的 12. 輸血 13. 禁止 14. 會議，大會 15. 限制，受限於~ 16. 扣除（額），減除（額）17. 懸掛，吊掛 18. 前言，序曲 19. 推翻，顛覆 20. 勤勉的，勤奮的

10. distribute　11.
12. 回到，回想　1
14. 禁止，使不可能
15. 呼氣，吐氣，呼
17. 冷淡，漠不關心
滔滔不絕地，滔

❷ 請根據句意，從底下四個句子的字彙。
21. 美國黃石國家公園以間歇泉。
(A) 怡然自得的 (B) 閒

22. 部長試圖介入以調停
(A) 退卻 (B) 解放奴隸

解答 | 21. (B) 22. (D)

❸ 請根據句意，從底下四個字意題的字彙。
23. 從事園藝必定會耗去
(A) 痠疼的 (B) 汗水

Contents

代號說明

n. 名詞

v. 動詞

a. 形容詞

ad. 副詞

字母後加–者代表字首

字母前加–者代表字尾

未加者代表字根

Building Vocabulary for
iBT, SAT, GRE, TOEIC, GEPT

12天

CHAPTER

01 02 03

Ｚ字型拆解記憶法

0001~0600

y taxonomy economic ecology biology antibiotic antagonist egoist egocentri
ansitory transfusion effusive exhibition prohibitive proscribe circumscrib
nt deduction introduction introverted subvert subside assiduous assemb
s congressman convivial survive resurrection recede intercede intermitte
act distribute attribute attraction intractable inadvertent revert resun
tipathy apathy atheism pantheism pandemonium insane interminab
temporize extort retort reject eject elaborate collaborate collective eclect
mplicated composite preposition prescience omniscient omnivoro
ve perverseness perceive deceive deciduous decadent delinquent relinquis

04 05 Answers

pithet hypothetical hypocritical economical astronomical disaster dispers
inate delimit deflate inflate innovation renovation retribution contribu
fer prefer preface artifact artisan partisan impart impetus compete compre
ntrovertible contretemps extemporaneous explode implode impel propell
ovocation prognosis diagnose diathermy thermoplastic protoplasm protozoa
it forfeit foreign sovereign superstition prostitution prognosticate recogni
nflict infect effective effort afford adduce deducible anatomy anachronis
ecology biology antibiotic antagonist egoist egocentric concentrate congrega
hibition prohibitive proscribe circumscribe circumvent convention conduct
l subvert subside assiduous assemble dissemble disposal depose deceptic
urrection recede intercede intermittent manumit emancipate elude prelud
inadvertent revert resume unassuming unprejudiced preclude exclude exha
sane interminably exterminate expire perspiration perspicacious conspicuo

MP3 2

0001 anatomy [ə`nætəmɪ] * ana-=scatter * tom=cut ★★★☆☆

Dr. Enders has been teaching anatomy at the medical school for over 10 years. Today his students are going to dissect a rabbit.

恩德斯博士已經在醫學院教授解剖學超過十年，今天他的學生將要解剖兔子。

解剖學，動植物解剖結構
n. the science of the bodily structure of animals and plants

0002 anachronism [ə`nækrə,nɪzəm] * chron=time ★☆☆☆☆

It is an anachronism to say that Admiral Soon-shin Lee used submarines to repel the enemy troops.

說水軍節度使李舜臣是利用潛水艇擊退敵軍，那是時代錯誤的說法。

時代錯誤
n. the attribution of a custom, event, etc. to a period to which it does not belong

---

0003 synchronize [`sɪŋkrə,naɪz] * syn-=same ★★☆☆☆

The two swimmers had trained for years to synchronize their movements while dancing in the water.

兩位水上芭蕾泳者經過多年訓練，為的是在水中表演時動作能夠協調一致。

使同時發生 / 使協調一致
v. cause to occur at the same time / occur at the same time; coincide

---

0004 synthesis [`sɪnθəsɪs] * thesis=set ★★★★☆

The beliefs of most people in the small country were a synthesis of Buddhism and Confucianism. Their beliefs showed some common characteristics of the two beliefs.

該小國大多數人民的信仰是佛教和儒教的綜合體。從他們的信仰中可看出這兩種教義的某些共同特色。

綜合體，混合體，合成物
n. combination; composition; union; amalgamation; unification; mixture; concoction

---

0005 hypothesis [haɪ`pɑθəsɪs] * hypo-=under, low ★★★☆☆

In order to determine the cause of something we often form a hypothesis, on which we base our argument.

為了確定某事物的起因，我們常會先建立一個假設，作為我們論點的依據。

假設，前提
n. supposition; assumption

0006 hypodermic [,haɪpə`dɜmɪk] * derm=skin ★★☆☆☆

A hypodermic syringe is a medical instrument which is used to inject a drug under a person's skin.

皮下注射器是用於將藥液注射到病患皮下組織的醫療器具。

皮下的
a. of or relating to the area beneath the skin

0007 taxidermy [`tæksə,dɜmɪ] * taxi-=arrange ★☆☆☆☆

He had always loved taxidermy, and when he died, his house looked like a silent and eerie zoo.

他向來酷愛製作動物標本，當他去世時，住家就像座令人毛骨悚然的無聲動物園。

剝製技術，動物標本製作
n. the art of preparing, stuffing and mounting the skins of animals with lifelike effect

---

0008 taxonomy [tæks`ɑnəmɪ] * nom=manage; law ★☆☆☆☆

Taxonomy is the classification and naming of things, such as animals and plants in groups.

分類學是針對事物進行分門別類和命名，例如成群的動物和植物等。

分類學
n. the science of the classification of living and extinct organisms

0009 economic [ˌikəˈnɑmɪk] * eco-=house, living ★★★★★

There are many problems that plague our nation at this time, but the economic problems probably top the list of things to be corrected first.

此刻有許多問題困擾著我們國家，然而經濟課題或許是最需要優先導正的。

經濟學的，經濟上的，金融的
a. of or relating to economics; financial; fiscal; pecuniary; monetary

---

0010 ecology [ɪˈkɑlədʒɪ] * -logy=study ★★★★★

The Antarctic Treaty nations drew up plans on how to preserve the frozen continent's unique ecology.

南極公約的締約國起草數項計畫，以保存極地特有的生態環境。

生態學，生態環境，生態工程學
n. study of ecosystems; ecological engineering

0011 biology [baɪˈɑlədʒɪ] * bio-=living ★★★★★

Biology, which includes botany and zoology, is the scientific study of plants and animals.

生物學包含植物學和動物學，是研究動、植物的一門科學。

生物學
n. science of organisms, ecology, natural science or history

0012 antibiotic [ˌæntɪbaɪˈɑtɪk] * anti-=against ★★★★☆

Doctor Smith prescribed an antibiotic for me in order to kill the bacteria that I had come in contact with.

史密斯醫師開了一劑抗生素給我，以殺死我體內的細菌。

抗生素
n. any of various substances produced by microorganisms or made synthetically, which inhibit the growth of bacteria and other microorganisms

---

0013 antagonist [ænˈtægəˌnɪst] * -ist-=perso ★★★☆☆

Most movies are quite predictable because in almost every case the antagonist loses in the end.

大部分電影都相當容易預測結局，因為幾乎每一次敵對者最後都輸了。

敵手，敵對者
n. adversary; opponent; contender; competitor

0014 egoist [ˈigoɪst] * ego-=I ★★★★☆

James Brooks is considered by many around him to be an egoist. They don't expect him to help others.

詹姆斯·布魯克斯身邊許多朋友都認為他是個自私的傢伙。他們不指望他會幫助其他人。

自私自利者
n. an egoistic person

0015 egocentric [ˌigoˈsɛntrɪk] * centr=center ★★☆☆☆

It is very difficult to work with egocentric people because they only think of themselves.

要和以自我為中心的人一起工作是很困難的，因為他們只會想到自己。

自我中心的
a. self-centered

0016 concentrate [ˈkɑnsn̩ˌtret] * con-=at one place ★★★★★

I couldn't concentrate on my studies because my neighbor's ugly bulldog kept barking all through the night.

我無法全神貫注於我的學習，因為鄰居的討厭惡犬整晚叫個不停。

全神貫注於～，集中注意力於～
v. think intensely; be engrossed in; give exclusive attention to; brood over

0017 **congregate** [ˋkɑŋgrɪˌget] * greg=gather ★★★★☆

As I was walking through the open market, I saw many people congregate in the middle of the street in order to see the fight that broke out between two merchants.

當我漫步在露天市場，看到許多人聚集在街道中觀看兩名小販打鬥。

聚集，集結
v. *convene; gather*

0018 **segregate** [ˋsɛgrɪˌget] * se-=separate ★★★★☆

In the past, some high schools in my country used to segregate boys and girls. These days many schools have co-ed systems.

過去我國有些中學習慣將男女學生隔離，如今許多學校都實施男女同校制。

隔離，使隔開，使分離
v. *isolate; divide; separate; split up*

0019 **secession** [sɪˋsɛʃən] * cess=go ★★★☆☆

The leader's secession from the union was imitated by many other members. As a result, the union almost became dismembered.

工會領袖的退出使得許多成員起而效尤，結果幾乎導致工會瓦解。

退出，脫離
n. *withdrawal; retraction; departure*

0020 **recession** [rɪˋsɛʃən] * re-=back ★★☆☆☆

During the recession Tim's business remained stagnant. He decided to take drastic measures to boost his sagging sales.

提姆的生意在經濟衰退期持續不景氣。他決定採取激烈手段來提振下滑的營業額。

經濟衰退（期），不景氣，蕭條
n. *depression; decline*

0021 **retract** [rɪˋtrækt] * tract=draw ★★★★☆

I didn't mean to offend you. I'd like to retract my statement. I must have been out of my mind at that time.

我不是存心要冒犯你，所以我想要撤回供述，當時我一定是瘋了。

撤銷，撤回
v. *withdraw; draw away; take in*

0022 **extract** [ɪkˋstrækt] * ex-=out ★★★★★

I had wanted to have my cavity filled in. But the dentist checked the decayed tooth and decided to extract it. He told me that I should have come earlier.

我原本想把蛀牙補一補就好，但牙醫檢查後決定拔除。他說我應該早點來看醫生。

（使勁地）拔出，抽出
v. *remove; take out; pluck out; extricate*

0023 **exit** [ˋɛgzɪt] * it=go ★★★★★

The championship game was such a disappointment that halfway through the fourth quarter people began heading for the exits because it was obvious who was going to win.

那場總冠軍賽令人大為掃興，第四節比賽才到一半，觀眾就紛紛離去，因為比賽勝負明顯已定。

出口
n. *way out; outlet*

0024 transitory [`trænsə,tɔrɪ] * trans-=pass through   ★★★★☆

Our director explained that our stay in these offices would be transitory, and we would soon move to a new workplace.

總監解釋我們在這些辦公室工作將是短暫的，不久就會遷往新的工作場所。

短暫的
a. *not permanent; transient; fleeting; ephemeral*

0025 transfusion [træns`fjuʒən] * fus=water   ★★★☆☆

By evening the patient's condition became worse. The doctor told his parents that he needed an immediate transfusion.

病患的情況到了傍晚開始惡化，醫生告訴病患家屬需要立即輸血。

輸血
n. *blood exchange*

MP3
3

0026 effusive [ɛ`fjusɪv] * ef-, ex-=out   ★★☆☆☆

Shoppers often get embarrassed by a dealer's effusive welcome. Therefore I sometimes wish that there would be no clerk at a store.

購物者有時會因商家過度熱情歡迎而感到尷尬，因此我有時真希望店裡沒有店員招呼我。

過度熱情的，情感洋溢的
a. *gushing; exuberant; profuse; lavish*

0027 exhibition [ˌɛnsə`bɪʃən] * hibit=hold   ★★★★★

Cathy was so proud when she learned that her picture was chosen among those of her classmates to represent her school in the exhibition that would be held in the mall.

凱西得知她的畫作從其他同學作品中脫穎而出時感到十分驕傲。她的作品將代表學校陳列在展覽會大廳中。

展覽會，展覽
n. *show; fair; presentation*

0028 prohibitive [pro`hɪbɪtɪv] * pro-=in advance   ★★★★★

Jack really liked taking photographs, and he wanted to buy a Hasselblad, a medium-format camera which uses 120mm film. However, he found that the price was prohibitive.

傑克非常喜歡攝影，他想購買一台使用 120mm 底片的哈蘇中片幅相機，但是他發現價格太貴了。

禁止的 /（費用或價格）過高的
a. *prohibiting; restraining; suppressive; repressive / too expensive*

0029 proscribe [pro`skraɪb] * scrib=draw a line   ★★★★☆

The poor farmer was arrested for growing opium poppies. He didn't know that growing them was proscribed by law.

那名窮困的農民因為種植罌粟花而遭到逮捕。他並不知道種植罌粟花是法律所禁止的事。

禁止
v. *forbid; interdict; prohibit; ban*

0030 circumscribe [ˌsɝkəm`skraɪb] * circum-=around   ★★★☆☆

Helen Keller's physical activities were severely circumscribed by her deafness and blindness. However, she tried to overcome these obstacles.

海倫·凱勒的身體活動因聾盲受到極大限制，然而她卻盡力克服這些障礙。

限制，受限於～
v. *limit; bound; confine; restrict; restrain*

0031 circumvent [ˌsɜkəmˈvɛnt] * vent=go, come ★★★☆☆

It was found that the company had circumvented the VAT secretly. At last the company had to pay a heavy fine as well as the tax.

該公司被發現暗中規避加值稅，最後不但要付出高額罰金，還要補繳稅額。

規避（法規等）／以智取勝
v. *evade / outwit*

0032 convention [kənˈvɛnʃən] * con-=together ★★★★★

At the international trade convention, he met businessmen from many different countries. From them he got some ideas about the business trends of many countries.

在國際商務會議中，他遇到來自許多不同國家的商務人士，並從他們身上了解許多國家的商業發展趨勢。

會議，大會／習俗，慣例
n. *assembly; gathering; congregation; congress; convocation / custom*

0033 conductor [kənˈdʌktə] * duct=draw ★★★★★

David has worked for several years as a train conductor and has had many close calls while at the controls.

大衛已經當了好幾年的火車車掌，在控制室裡也歷經許多千鈞一髮的驚險場面。

領導者，管理者／車掌
n. *guide; director / a person who collects fares in a bus, etc.*

0034 deduct [dɪˈdʌkt] * de-=down ★★★★☆

We are in the final stages of negotiations and the buyer has stated that he will sign the contract if we deduct $10,000 from the originally quoted price.

我們進行到談判的最後階段，買主宣稱如果我們願意從原始報價中再減除一萬美元，他就會簽署合約。

扣除，減除
v. *subtract; take away; reduce*

0035 despise [dɪˈspaɪz] * spis=see ★★★★★

The union leader was often despised by the union members. He was considered a chicken.

該工會領袖時常受到工會會員鄙視，並被當成懦夫。

鄙視，看不起，輕視
v. *scorn; disdain; hold in contempt; look down upon*

0036 suspicion [səˈspɪʃən] * sus-, sub-=down ★★★★★

JEALOUSY never allows reason to judge things as they really are. Jealous people see things through an inverted looking glass, which turns small things large, dwarfs into giants and suspicions into truths.
── Cervantes

猜忌從不容許以理性來判斷事物本來的樣貌。猜忌者透過虛構的鏡子來看待事物，因此把小事化大、視侏儒為巨人，並將猜疑當成事實。
──（西班牙小說家）塞凡提斯

猜疑，懷疑
n. *mistrust; distrust; doubt*

0037 suspend [səˈspɛnd] * pend=hang ★★★★☆

The climber found a rope suspended from the top of the cliff. But he wasn't sure if the rope was strong enough.

攀岩者發現有條繩索從懸崖頂端吊掛下來，但不確定繩索是否夠牢固。

懸掛，吊掛
v. *hang; dangle*

0038 dependent [dɪˋpɛndənt] * de-=down ★★★★★

Jimmy was fortunate that his parents didn't declare him as dependent on their tax return, because he was able to apply for and receive a government grant that paid for all of his schooling.

吉米非常幸運，由於雙親並未在納稅申報書上將他列為受扶養親屬，因此他得以申請並獲得政府補助以支付所有學業開銷。

從屬的，隸屬的 / 受扶養者，受扶養親屬
a. contingent; subject /
n. a person who depends on someone else

0039 deduction [dɪˋdʌkʃən] * duct=draw ★★★★☆

I was pleasantly surprised to find that the outfit I wanted to buy was on sale with a 50% deduction off the original price.

我驚喜地發現我想買的衣服正在進行半價特惠促銷。

扣除（額），減除（額）
n. subtraction; removal; curtailment

0040 introduction [ˌɪntrəˋdʌkʃən] * intro-=into ★★★★★

Many people dispense with reading the introduction when they read books. But the introduction is an important part which tells the reader all about the book.

許多人在看書的時後都會略過前言，但那是很重要的部分，它告訴讀者關於這本書的全貌。

前言，序曲
n. preface; foreword; prelude

0041 introverted [ˋɪntrəˏvɜtɪd] * vert=turn ★★★★☆

Recent studies have shown that an aggressive, outgoing person needs more living space than a passive, introverted person.

近來的研究報告指出，一個積極進取又外向的人，其實比不喜交際又內向的人需要更多生活空間。

個性內向的，不喜交際的
n. uncommunicative; shy

0042 subvert [səbˋvɜt] * sub-=down ★★★★☆

The rebels were arrested for trying to subvert the government. Eventually, they were convicted of treason.

造反者因試圖推翻政府遭到逮捕，最後被判叛國罪。

推翻，顛覆
v. overthrow; overturn

0043 subside [səbˋsaɪd] * sid=sit ★★★☆☆

Whenever he subsided into affection, he called me Pip, and whenever he relapsed into politeness he called me Sir.

Great Expectations —— Charles Dickens

每當他陷入熱情時，就稱呼我為「皮普」；而當他又開始客氣起來時，則尊稱我為「先生」。

——《孤星血淚》（英國小說家）狄更斯

陷入
v. sink down; descend; decline; fall in; slump

0044 assiduous [əˋsɪdʒʊəs] * as-, ad-=to ★★★☆☆

Shane is a particularly assiduous worker who always strives for perfection. So it is natural that he should be promoted.

尚恩是個特別勤勉的工作者，總是盡全力做到最好，自然應該得到升職。

勤勉的，勤奮的
a. attentive; diligent

0045 assemble [əˋsɛmbḷ] * sembl=appearance ★★★★★

The machine came in a box and there were so many parts that it took me three hours to assemble all of them.

這部機器送來時是裝在箱子裡的，而且裡面有好多零件，我花了三個鐘頭才把它組裝完畢。

組裝，裝配 / 召集，聚集
v. construct; put together; set up / gather together; convene; congregate

0046 dissemble [dɪˋsɛmbl] * dis-=scatter, different ★★★☆☆

Chuck doesn't seem to be outspoken. He usually dissembles his true thoughts. So I think I will have to tell him that he should tell me as it is.

查克似乎並不坦率，總是隱藏自己真正的想法。所以我想我必須告訴他應該要跟我說實話。

隱瞞，隱藏，掩飾
v. conceal; camouflage; feign; disguise

0047 disposal [dɪˋspozl] * pos=put ★★★★☆

The residents of the area where a nuclear power plant is going to be built are concerned about the disposal of nuclear waste.

住在核能發電廠預定地附近的居民擔心核廢料處理問題。

處理，處置
n. disposition; the act of disposing of something

0048 depose [dɪˋpoz] * de-=down, under ★★★☆☆

The king discovered that one of the military commanders was planning to depose him. The king arrested him and put him to death.

國王發現一名軍事指揮官正計畫廢除王位，所以將他逮捕並處以死刑。

罷免，廢除（王位等）/ 宣示作證
v. remove from office; dethrone / bear witness, esp. on oath in court

---

0049 deception [dɪˋsɛpʃən] * cept=take ★★★☆☆

Everyone in our village knows that Paul the miser obtained almost all of his money through deception.

村裡每個人都知道，守財奴保羅是以詐欺手段得到他絕大多數的財富。

詐欺，欺騙
n. the act or an instance of deceiving; trick; sham

0050 susceptible [səˋsɛptəbl] * sus-, sub-=down ★★★★★

People with the HIV virus are more susceptible to serious infection.

愛滋病患很容易受到嚴重感染。

易受影響的，易受感染的
a. exposed to; liable to; prone to; subject to; vulnerable to

---

Tea Time... ☕

<Greek myth> Tantalos
The Mythical king of Phrygia who was condemned to stand in water that receded when he tried to drink it and was under branches that drew back when he tried to pick the fruit.

〈希臘神話〉坦塔洛斯
在希臘神話中，宙斯之子佛里幾亞國王坦塔洛斯因洩露天機而被眾神懲罰，他站在水中，頭上懸著果樹枝。當他想要喝水時，水就退去；而當他想要摘食果實時，樹枝就縮回。（註：本字常用來形容「渴望的事物雖然近在眼前卻無法得到的痛苦」。）

❖ **tantamount** [ˋtæntəˏmaʊnt] *a. equivalent; equal* │ 等同於～的，相等的
His boss's request was tantamount to an order to Jack, who had no choice but to accept it. He had to deliver a speech in place of his boss.
對傑克而言，上司的要求就是命令，除了接受之外別無選擇。所以他必須代替上司發表演說。

❖ **tantalizing** [ˋtæntlˏaɪzɪŋ] *a. teasing* │ 誘人的，逗弄人的
The smells coming out of the fried chicken shop were so tantalizing that I sometimes went in and bought some.
從炸雞店傳來的香味是如此誘人，我有時會走進去買一些炸雞來吃。

1

Complete each word by filling in the blank with proper spelling so that it has the same meaning as suggested. Then please write the meaning of each word in Chinese.

1. 分析 = ana_lyze_
2. 綜合體 = syn_thesis_
3. 時代錯誤 = ana_chronism_
4. 動物標本製作 = _taxy_dermy
5. 假設 = _hypo_thesis
6. 生態學 = eco_logy_
7. 敵手 = _an_tagonist
8. 全神貫注 = _con_centrate
9. 經濟衰退 = _re_cession
10. 撤銷 = re_tract_

11. effusive = _____
12. transfusion = _____
13. proscribe = _____
14. convention = _____
15. circumscribe = _____
16. deduct = _____
17. suspend = _____
18. introduction = _____
19. subvert = _____
20. assiduous = _____

2

Choose a word that best completes the sentence.

21. We can hardly find a baby who cries or yells when a mosquito inserts its blood sucking needle into its skin, nor do we find a baby who does not cry or yell when a nurse inserts a(n) _____ syringe into its skin.

    (A) hypodermic   (B) transitory   (C) unprejudiced   (D) retrospective

22. We should _____ when solving a math problem; otherwise we may make a mistake.

    (A) extract   (B) circumvent   (C) evade   (D) concentrate

23. Where is the _____ of this outlet? I think I am lost.

    (A) depression   (B) exit   (C) hypothesis   (D) anatomy

3

The highlighted word is closest in meaning to which of the following?

24. Movies are quite predictable. Many moviegoers know what will happen to the protagonist and his antagonist when they see the beginning of a movie. They insist that they do not have to see the whole thing.

    (A) enemy   (B) egoist   (C) dependent   (D) conductor

25. We are going to kick in some money for Jane's wedding gift: 10 dollars from each person. This amount of money will be automatically deducted from your salary.

    (A) expired   (B) subtracted   (C) segregated   (D) congregated

0051 suspect [sə`spɛkt] * spect=see ★★★★★

The stranger was willing to take us from the zoo to the parking lot. At first we suspected his motives. But he said that he had been driving his car for more than 30 minutes looking for a parking space and wanted to take ours.

那位陌生人願意從動物園載我們到停車場。起初我們懷疑他的動機,但他說為了找停車位已經繞了半小時以上,所以願意載我們。

嫌犯,可疑份子 / 懷疑,猜疑
n. a suspected person /
v. disbelieve; mistrust;
distrust; be suspicious of

0052 retrospective [ˌrɛtrə`spɛktɪv] * retro-=backward ★★★☆☆

Mr. Thomas nodded his head retrospectively two or three times, and actually let out a sigh.

湯瑪斯先生回顧地點了兩三次頭,接著嘆了一口氣。

懷舊的,回顧的 / 回顧展
a. looking back on or dealing with the past / *n.* a retrospective exhibition

0053 retrogress [ˌrɛtrə`grɛs] * gress=go ★★★☆☆

Once he had been released from the psychological ward, he tried to live normally, but it was only a matter of days before he began to retrogress to the earliest stages.

當他從精神病院釋放出來後,試著過正常人的生活,但是不到幾天光景,就又倒退回原來的樣子。

倒退,逆行 / 退化,退步
v. go back; move backwards / deteriorate

0054 congressman [`kɑŋgrəsmən] * con-=together ★★★★★

His first act after being elected a congressman was to draft a law concerning gun control. He thought that there were too many criminals using guns.

他當選國會議員後,第一步就是草擬槍械管制法案,因為他認為有太多槍械罪犯。

國會議員
n. lawmaker; representative

0055 convivial [kən`vɪvɪəl] * viv=life ★★★★☆

Mr. Smith is a very convivial person. He is very friendly and fond of chatting, merry-making and drinking with others.

史密斯先生是個非常怡然自得的人,他非常友善,喜歡聊天和製造歡樂,並與他人開懷暢飲。

怡然自得的,愉快的
a. fond of good company; sociable and lively

0056 survive [sə`vaɪv] * sur-=up; better than ★★★★★

Only five people survived the air crash. Everyone else was killed. But people thought that it was a miracle that there were survivors.

只有五人從空難中生還,其他人都喪命了。大家認為有生還者是奇蹟。

倖存,從～中生還,比～長命
v. continue to live; last; pull through; outlive

0057 resurrection [ˌrɛzə`rɛkʃən] * re-=again; back ★★☆☆☆

復活，復甦
n. the act or an instance of rising from the dead

Christians believe in the Holy Spirit, the Holy Catholic Church, the communion of saints, the forgiveness of sins, the resurrection of the body, and the life everlasting.

基督徒相信聖靈，相信聖而公之教會，相信諸聖相通，相信罪能赦免，相信肉身復活，相信永生。（譯註：這段文字出自 Apostles' Creed《使徒信經》）

0058 recede [rɪ`sid] * -cede=go ★★★★☆

後退，退潮，退卻
v. ebb; move back; shrink back; retreat; diminish; lessen

As the tide receded, many children went out on the beach to collect shells. But their parents had told them that the tide would rush in within two hours.

當潮水退卻後，許多孩童走出來到海灘上撿拾貝殼，但父母告誡他們兩個小時內會再出現漲潮。

0059 intercede [ˌɪntə`sid] * inter-=between ★★★★☆

仲裁，調停
v. interpose; intervene; plead

Trying to help settle their differences, the minister interceded between the union and the management.

為了解決雙方的歧見，部長介入調停工會和領導階層。

0060 intermittent [ˌɪntə`mɪtn̩t] * mit=send ★★★★☆

間歇的，斷續的
a. occurring at intervals; sporadic; on-off; fitful; periodic

Dr. Johnson in his dictionary defines a kiss as "a salute given by joining the lips," which may be accepted as the minimum of definition; a more intimate one is, "a prolonged pressing of mouth against mouth with slight intermittent movements."

The Natural History of a Kiss —— E. Royston Pike

約翰森博士在其著作《英語字典》中，將「親吻」定義為「以唇相接作為致意」，這句話可視為最低限度的定義。另外還有一個更為親密的定義為：「唇與唇長時間的貼壓，並帶著些微間歇的動作」。

——《親吻的自然史》（英國作家）E・羅依斯頓・派克

0061 manumit [ˌmænjə`mɪt] * man-=hand ★★☆☆☆

解放奴隸
v. set a slave free

In these excursions he was usually accompanied by an old negro, called Jupiter, who had been manumitted before the reverses of the family.

The Gold-bug —— Edgar A. Poe

每回出遊時，他身邊總是跟著一個名叫丘比特的老黑人；其實在家道中落前，丘比特就已經獲得解放。

——《金甲蟲》（美國作家）愛倫坡

0062 emancipate [ɪ`mænsəˌpet] * e-=out ★★★☆☆

解放，使不受束縛，釋放
v. release; liberate; deliver; loose; free; let go; set free; unshackle; unchain

A writer must read the masters in order to grasp their technique. At first he may imitate them; then, progressively, he will emancipate himself.

作家必須閱讀大師經典作品以掌握其寫作技巧。起初或許只能模仿，但漸漸地就能夠盡情發揮。

0063 elude [ɪˋlud] * lud=play ★★★☆☆

I couldn't remember his name. It eluded me for a while. Therefore I tried to stay away from him, trying to remember his name.

我想不起他的名字，一時之間難倒了我，於是我試著離他遠一點並努力回想他的名字。

使困惑，難倒
v. evade; escape; avoid; dodge; slip

0064 prelude [ˋprɛljud] * pre-=before ★★★★★

Our present problem may be the prelude to a vast upheaval which we cannot hope to understand. We have to answer out of our ignorance, and as well as we can. And to my limited outlook, Hitler's Germany is the villain.

Culture and Freedom —— E. M. Forster

當前的問題也許是我們無法了解的大動亂序幕。即使出於無知，我們必須能夠回應當前問題。就我個人淺薄的看法，我認為希特勒所領導的納粹德國是為惡之徒。

——《文化與自由》（英國作家）福斯特

前奏，序幕 / 前言
n. an introductory piece of music / foreword

0065 precocious [prɪˋkoʃəs] * coc=cook ★★★★★

We know from child psychology that a child may be intellectually extremely precocious, whilst the development of his moral or temperamental qualities have been arrested at an infantile stage.

Rational and Irrational Elements of Contemporary Society —— Karl Mannheim

從兒童心理學中我們知道，孩童可能在智力上極度早熟，然而在道德、心理或人格特質上的發展卻仍受阻於幼稚階段。

——《社會理智與非理智成分》（德國知識社會學家）卡爾·曼海姆

早熟的，早慧的 / 過早發育的
a. prematurely developed

0066 concoct [kənˋkɑkt] * con-=together ★★★★☆

The absentee concocted some excuse about having had to visit a sick friend. In fact he went hiking with his friend.

缺席者編造一些藉口，說自己必須去探望生病的友人，但事實上是跟朋友去健行。

編造，捏造 / 混合調製
v. invent; make by mixing ingredients; cook up

0067 contract [ˋkɑntrækt] * tract=draw ★★★★★

I have to look over the contract very carefully before I sign it because there might be something in it that I might not fully agree with.

我在簽署合約前必須非常仔細地檢查一遍，因為合約上也許會有一些我並不完全同意的內容。

合約，契約 / 使縮小，使變小
n. a written or spoken agreement / *v.* diminish; reduce; shrink; dwindle

0068 distract [dɪˋstrækt] * dis-=away ★★★★☆

People in the East will not take on two jobs if they can pay their bills with one, for two jobs consume their time and distract their skills.

East and West —— Pearl Buck

在西方世界裡，如果從事一份工作的薪水就足以過活，人們不會去找兩份工作來做，因為同時做兩份工作不但會耗盡他們的時間，也會分散其熟練度。

——《東方與西方》（美國小說家暨諾貝爾文學獎得主）賽珍珠

分散（心思、注意力等），轉移，使困擾，使混亂
v. bewilder; puzzle; divert; addle; draw the attention of

0069 distribute [dɪ`strɪbjut] * tribut=give

Food and clothing were distributed to the flood victims, who were in desperate situations. The flood was one of the greatest in recorded history.

食物和衣服分發給處境危急的水患受災戶，這次水患是史上最嚴重的災害之一。

分發，分配
v. allot; pass out; apportion

0070 attribute [ə`trɪbjut] * at-, ad-=to

My professor has so many different talents and abilities that it is almost impossible to list all of his attributes.

我的教授有太多不同的才藝和技能，幾乎不可能將他的才能全部列舉出來。

特性，才能，特質 / 歸因於
n. quality; character; characteristic; feature; trait; property / *v.* ascribe; impute

0071 attraction [ə`trækʃən] * tract=draw

Research into communication encounters suggests that attraction is not haphazard but rather is shaped and strengthened by six factors; these factors are nearness and exposure, similarity, physical attractiveness, status and competence, social adjustment, and rhetorical sensitivity.

Interpersonal Attraction —— R. S. Ross

針對溝通互動者的研究指出，吸引力並非隨意發生的，而是透過六個因素強化得出的，這六大因素分別是：親近與接觸、相似性、身體吸引力、地位與能力、社會適應，以及語藝敏感度。

—— 《人際之間的吸引力》（澳洲社會主義者）R · S · 羅斯

吸引力，吸引
n. the act or power of attracting; attractiveness; attractive force

0072 intractable [ɪn`træktəbļ] * in-=not

Nancy is such an intractable child. She is so obstinate that it is difficult for her teacher to control her.

南西是個非常倔強的孩子，她是如此固執，以至於連學校老師也很難管理她。

倔強的，固執的
a. stubborn; obstinate; perverse; bullish; wayward; mulish; headstrong

0073 inadvertent [ˌɪnəd`vɝtņt] * vert=turn

The tragedy in all of this is the fact that everything was nothing more than an inadvertent mistake.

悲劇的起因完全是因為一個粗心大意的錯誤。

疏忽的，不注意的
a. unintentional; unintended; unpremeditated; accidental

0074 revert [rɪ`vɝt] * re-=back

My thoughts reverted to Zenobia. It could only be her wealth which Hollingsworth was appropriating so lavishly.

The Blithedale Romance —— Nathaniel Hawthorne

我的思緒回到季諾碧雅身上。霍林斯沃思如此大剌剌地盜用的可能就是她的財產了。

—— 《快樂谷傳奇》（美國小說家）霍桑

回到，回想
v. return to; go back to; relapse into

0075 resume [rɪˋzum] * sume=take ★★★★★

Why don't we stop now, and resume after a 5-minute break? My stomach keeps on growling, so I think I'll have to go grab a bite.

我們何不現在暫停一下，五分鐘後再重新開始呢？我的肚子一直咕嚕咕嚕叫，我想得趕快找點東西吃。

重新開始，再繼續
v. *begin again; recommence; reopen*

MP3 5

0076 unassuming [ˌʌnəˋsjumɪŋ] * un-=not, as-, ad-=in advance ★★☆☆☆

Now when the income was shrunk to $20, the letters of "Dillingham" looked blurred, as though they were thinking seriously contracting to a modest and unassuming letter 'D'.

The Gift of the Magi ── O. Henry

當收入縮減到二十美元時，「狄林罕」這幾個字母看起來也變得模糊不清，彷彿它們正在認真思考，想要縮小成一個謙虛而不出風頭的字母 D。

──《聖誕禮物》（美國小說家）歐‧亨利

謙虛的，不出風頭的
a. *not arrogant; modest; humble*

0077 unprejudiced [ʌnˋprɛdʒədɪst] * pre-=before / jud=judge ★★★☆☆

We found the senior citizens group to be the most unprejudiced of all our fund-raising organizations as they treated all the various ethnic groups equally.

我們發現老人團體是我們所有募款機構中最沒有成見的，因為他們公平對待不同種族的群體。

公平的，沒有成見的
a. *not prejudiced; unbiased; impartial; just; fair; square; objective; disinterested*

0078 preclude [prɪˋklud] * clud=hold; boundary ★★★☆☆

His final argument was designed to preclude any further discussion, and when he finished speaking, the entire room was silent and no one dared to say anything.

他的最後論據是禁止任何進一步的討論，所以當他說完話，全場一片靜默，沒人敢再出聲。

禁止，使不可能，阻止
v. *bar; ban; enjoin; prevent; exclude; prohibit; debar; impede; inhibit; hamper; clog*

0079 exclude [ɪkˋsklud] * ex-=out ★★★★★

Nick couldn't exclude the possibility that he would be fired because of his mistake. So he wasn't surprised when he got a pink slip the next day.

尼克並不排除因個人錯誤而被解雇的可能性。所以當他隔天拿到解雇通知時並不覺得意外。

將～排除在外
v. *eliminate; leave out; rule out; except; preclude; blot out; delete; white out; obliterate*

0080 exhale [ɛksˋhel] * hale=breathe ★★★★☆

When I went to see the doctor, he put his stethoscope on my chest and said, "Now, please inhale and then exhale."

我去看醫生時，醫生把聽診器放在我胸上，然後對我說：「現在請先吸氣，然後吐氣。」

呼氣，吐氣，呼出
v. *breathe out; puff out; blow out*

0081 inhale [ɪn`hel] * in-=in ★★★★☆

Sam smokes about two packs of cigarettes a day and claims it isn't harmful to his health because he doesn't inhale.

山姆一天大約抽兩包煙，但他宣稱這對他的健康無害，因為他並未將香煙吸入肺中。

吸入，吸氣
v. *breathe in; take a breath*

0082 intoxicated [ɪn`tɑksəˌketɪd] * tox=poison ★★★★☆

One night, returning home, much intoxicated from one of my haunts about town, I fancied that the cat avoided my presence. I seized him.

The Black Cat —— Edgar A. Poe

某晚我在城裡一家常去的酒吧喝得酩酊大醉，回到家後覺得這隻貓躲著我，於是一把抓住牠。

——《黑貓》愛倫坡

喝醉的，酒醉的
a. *drunk; inebriated*

0083 antitoxin [ˌænti`tɑksɪn] * anti-=against ★★★☆☆

The government spends millions of dollars a year to support antitoxin research in hopes that someday scientists might come up with an effective way to fight cancer.

政府一年花費數百萬元資助抗毒素研究，希望有朝一日科學家能提出對抗癌症的有效方法。

抗毒素
n. *an antibody that counteracts a toxin*

0084 antipathy [æn`tɪpəθɪ] * -pathy=feel ★★★★☆

After Peggy found out that it was I who kept slandering her behind her back, she had a strong antipathy towards me and refused to talk to me.

佩姬發現是我一直在暗中造謠中傷後，對我產生極大反感，並拒絕和我講話。

反感，厭惡
n. *aversion; dislike*

0085 apathy [`æpəθɪ] * a-=no ★★★★☆

She fell in love with him, but because of his apathy toward her, she soon lost interest in him. She found that he was the antithesis of what she believed an ideal man had to be.

她愛上他，然而由於他冷淡以對，使她很快失去興趣。她發現他和自己認為的理想男子正好相反。

冷淡，漠不關心
n. *nonchalance; callousness; indifference*

0086 atheism [`eθɪˌɪzəm] * the(o)=god ★★★☆☆

Atheism is the belief that there is no God. But it requires a whole lifetime of continuous prosperity or courage to face all the hard times in life.

無神論相信神不存在，但這種信仰需要終其一生永保成功，或具有面對人生所有難關的勇氣。

無神論，不信神
n. *the theory or belief that God does not exist*

0087 pantheism [ˈpænθiˌɪzəm] * pan-=all ★☆☆☆☆

Pantheism is the belief in having many spirits or gods that control all facets of existence. Those with the belief are apt to believe there is a god even in a rock.

泛神論相信有許多神靈支配著世間萬物的存在，他們甚至相信連石頭裡也有神靈。

泛神論
n. *the belief that God is identifiable with the forces of nature and with natural substances*

0088 pandemonium [ˌpændɪˈmonɪəm] * ium=place ★★☆☆☆

Pandemonium reigned when the roof collapsed and everyone tried to leave through the main door at once.

屋頂倒塌時現場陷入一片混亂，大家立刻擠向大門，試圖逃離現場。

大混亂
n. *uproar; utter confusion; disorder; bedlam; chaos*

0089 sanatorium [ˌsænəˈtorɪəm] * san-=health ★☆☆☆☆

The medic thought that if he kept working in the sanatorium he would eventually end up there, not in a position of responsibility, but as a patient.

那名醫生認為如果繼續在療養院工作下去，最後一定會終老於此，不是基於醫生職責，而是自己也變成病患。

（精神病患、酗酒者等）療養院
n. *infirmary; an establishment for the treatment of invalids*

0090 insane [ɪnˈsen] * in-=not ★★★☆☆

Father grinned and winked at his visitor. Joe Kane decided that the man who confronted him was mildly insane but harmless.

The Egg —— Sherwood Anderson

父親對著訪客露齒而笑卻又眨眼示意，喬‧肯恩因此相信，站在他眼前的這位男子有一點精神錯亂，但不會傷人。

——《雞蛋》（美國短篇小說家）薛伍德‧安德森

精神錯亂的，瘋狂的
a. *mad; maniacal; lunatic; demented; crazy; out of one's mind*

0091 interminably [ɪnˈtɜmənəblɪ] * termin=end ★★★☆☆

The Minnesota winter usually prolongs interminably and it is almost May when the winds become soft.

明尼蘇達州的冬天通常漫長得無邊無際，和煦的風幾乎要到五月才開始吹拂。

漫無止境地，冗長地
ad. *endlessly; unceasingly; continually; uninterruptedly; persistently; relentlessly; round the clock; constantly*

0092 exterminate [ɪkˈstɜməˌnet] * ex-=out ★★★★☆

We learned that our house was filled with termites, so we had to spend a lot of money to have a pest control company come and exterminate them.

我們得知住家長滿白蟻，因此須花費大筆金錢請害蟲防治公司來滅蟲。

消滅，根除，滅絕
v. *destroy; eradicate; uproot; extirpate; annihilate; wipe out; obliterate; put an end to; terminate; liquidate*

0093 expire [ɪkˈspaɪr] * spire=breathe ★★★★☆

My driver's license expires next month. So, I think I'll have to have it renewed before the end of this month.

我的駕照下個月就過期了，所以我想我必須趕在本月底前把駕照換新。

期滿失效，過期 / 吐氣 / 死亡
v. *come to an end; become void / exhale / die*

0094 perspiration [ˌpɝspəˈreʃən] * per-=through ★★★★☆

It was a hot noon in July; and his face, lustrous with perspiration, beamed with barbaric good humor.

Billy Budd, Sailor —— Herman Melville

那是個炎熱的七月中午，他的臉龐閃爍著汗珠的光澤，並帶著粗獷的開心笑容。

—— 《水手比利‧巴德》（美國作家）赫爾曼‧梅爾維爾

汗水
n. *sweat; sweating*

0095 perspicacious [ˌpɝspɪˈkeʃəs] * spic=see ★★★★☆

The professor's remarks about the novel were very perspicacious. His students learned something they had never thought about.

教授對於這本小說的評論極具洞察力，他的學生藉此學到一些從不曾想到的知識。

富有洞察力的，敏銳的
a. *shrewd; astute; discerning*

0096 conspicuous [kənˈspɪkjʊəs] * con-=together ★★★★★

Jane's red hair made her conspicuous. I could spot her in the audience pretty easily because of her red hair.

珍的紅髮十分引人注目。因為她的紅頭髮，我可以輕易在觀眾裡發現她。

引人注目的，明顯易見的
a. *outstanding; obvious; striking; evident; marked; manifest; distinct; prominent; preeminent; noticeable*

0097 contemporary [kənˈtɛmpəˌrɛrɪ] * tempor=moment ★★★★★

I love the way you have decorated your house with all of these modern colors and in this contemporary style.

我喜歡你的居家裝飾方式，既充滿摩登色彩，又富有當代風格。

當代的，現代的 / 同時代的
a. *modern; up-to-date; advanced / concurrent*

0098 extemporize [ɪkˈstɛmpəˌraɪz] * ex-=out ★★★☆☆

As the music came fresher on their ears, they danced to its cadence, extemporizing new steps and attitudes.

The Marble Faun —— Nathaniel Hawthorne

當旋律更加清晰地傳入他們耳中時，他們隨著節奏起舞，即興跳出嶄新舞步和舞姿。

—— 《大理石牧神》霍桑

即興表演（演說），即席做出～
v. *improvise; compose or produce without preparation*

0099 extort [ɪkˈstɔrt] * tort=twist ★★★★☆

The blackmailer tried to extort a large sum of money from the rich widow. He insisted that her dead husband had owed him money and that she should pay back the money.

勒索者試圖向有錢寡婦敲詐大筆金錢。他堅稱寡婦死去的先生欠他錢，她必須代為償還。

勒索，敲詐
v. *obtain by force; exact*

0100 retort [rɪˋtɔrt] * re-=against

His secretary hardly ever speaks of herself except when compelled, and never defends herself with a mere retort.

他的祕書除非迫不得已，否則鮮少提及自己的事；甚至不曾以一個小小反駁來為自己辯護。

★★★★★

反駁，頂嘴 / 反駁，反擊
n. *rebuttal; counterblast; sharp reply; pointed answer /*
v. *rebut; contradict*

Tea Time... ☕

<Medieval story> Curfew (cover+fire)

In the Middle Ages, a regulation causing a bell to be rung every evening at a certain time as a signal for people to cover fires, put out lights, and retire to their homes.

〈中古世紀故事〉晚鐘熄燈令（加蓋於爐火上）
在中古世紀時期，根據規定，每天晚上在某一特定時間會以鐘響作為信號，告訴大家必須將爐火加蓋，並熄滅燈火，準備就寢。（註：curfew 一字帶有「熄燈令」或「禁止夜間外出」之意。）

❖ **curfew** [ˋkɝfju] **n.** *a time set as a deadline beyond which inhabitants may not appear on the streets* │ 宵禁

Highway robberies took place every night. The government decided to impose 11 o'clock curfews.

攔路搶劫案每晚都發生，因此政府下令每晚十一點實施宵禁。

1

Complete each word by filling in the blank with proper spelling so that it has the same meaning as suggested. Then please write the meaning of each word in Chinese.

1. 懷疑 = s u s p e c t
2. 懷舊的 = r e t r o s p e c t i v e
3. 怡然自得的 = c o n v i v i a l
4. 復活 = r e s u r r e c t i o n
5. 退卻 = r e c e d e
6. 間歇的 = i n t e r _ _ _ t e n t
7. 使困惑 = e _ _ _ e
8. 早熟的 = p r e _ _ _ i o u s
9. 分散注意力 = d i s t r a c t
10. 分發 = d i s _ _ _ _ _ _ _

11. intractable = _____
12. revert = _____
13. unprejudiced = _____
14. preclude = _____
15. exhale = _____
16. antitoxin = _____
17. apathy = _____
18. pandemonium = _____
19. interminably = _____
20. expire = _____

2

Choose a word that best completes the sentence.

21. **Yellowstone Park is famous for its _____ springs, or geysers.**
    (A) convivial (B) intermittent (C) retrospective (D) precocious

22. **The minister tried to _____ between the union and management.**
    (A) recede (B) manumit (C) retrogress (D) intercede

3

The highlighted word is closest in meaning to which of the following?

23. **Gardening necessitates much water, mostly in the form of perspiration .**
    (A) sanatorium (B) sweat (C) apathy (D) attraction

24. **Mrs. Brown boasted that her son was a precocious genius by saying that he was able to walk when he was 10 months old. Mrs. White told her that her son ordered her to carry him at that age.**
    (A) prematurely developed (B) fond of good company
    (C) occurring at intervals (D) round the clock

25. **The pupils of our eyes contract when they are exposed to light.**
    (A) preclude (B) elude (C) attribute (D) shrink

0101 reject [rɪ`dʒɛkt] * -ject=shoot ★★★★★

The manager rejected his subordinate's idea without a trial. However one month later his rival company put out a novel product based on a similar idea.

經理試都不試就駁回屬下的點子，但一個月後對手公司卻根據類似點子推出一項新奇商品。

駁回，否決，拒絕
v. refuse; decline; turn down; shrug off; repudiate

0102 eject [ɪ`dʒɛkt] * e-=out ★★★★☆

The volcano began to eject lava and ash. Only then did the residents begin to pay attention to the volcanologists' warning.

火山開始噴出岩漿和火山灰，至此居民才開始注意到火山學家的警告。

噴出（液體或煙等），射出，
v. discharge; emit; spew; spout; exude

0103 elaborate [ɪ`læbərɪt] * labor=work ★★★★☆

The two bank robbers were very particular in the way they prepared their elaborate plans for doing the job.

那兩名銀行搶匪的特殊之處，在於他們備妥精心籌劃的搶劫計畫。

精心籌劃的
a. intricate; sophisticated

0104 collaborate [kə`læbə͵ret] * col-=together ★★★★★

The expert on Korea and the expert on America decided to get together and collaborate in writing a book on Korean-American relations.

美韓兩國的專家決定聚在一起，共同撰寫一本關於美韓雙邊關係的書籍。

共同合作，合著
v. work together; join forces; cooperate; unite

0105 collective [kə`lɛktɪv] * lect=choose ★★★★★

The vice president embezzled the collective assets of his corporation. At last he was accused of misappropriation.

副總裁盜用公司名下的共同資產，最後被控侵吞。

共同的，集體的
a. combined; aggregated; cumulative; composite

0106 eclectic [ɪk`lɛktɪk] * ec-, ex-=out ★★★★☆

The members of the special team were quite eclectic. All of them were experts from various fields.

這個特殊團隊的成員十分兼容並蓄，全是來自各種不同領域的專家。

兼容並蓄的，折衷的
a. derived from various sources

0107 eccentric [ɪk`sɛntrɪk] * centr=center ★★★★☆

She has never been known to be a person who follows the crowd and is considered to be a very eccentric person in her neighborhood.

她向來以不流俗聞名，鄰居們都認為她是個非常古怪的人。

（人或行為等）古怪的，反常的
a. peculiar; odd; weird; outlandish; extraordinary

0108 concentration [͵kɑnsn̩`treʃən] * con-=at one place ★★★★★

Solving a math problem requires intense concentration. I often make a mess. Math is a mass of mysteries for me.

進行數學解題時需要非常全神貫注，我總是弄得一團糟。對我而言數學是一團難解之謎。

全神貫注 / 集結軍力
n. close attention / strength

0109 converge [kən`vɝdʒ] * verg=turn ★★★★☆

Rays of light which pass through a convex lens converge into one point. Using this we can burn a piece of paper.

光束透過凸透鏡聚合成一點，我們可利用這個原理來燃燒紙張。

使集於一點，使集中
v. come together; meet

0110 divergent [daɪ`vɝdʒənt] * di-=away ★★★☆☆

The U.S. is a country where there are widely divergent ethnic and religious groups, so it is usually referred to as a melting pot.

美國是一個容納不同種族和信仰的國家，因此一般都將美國稱為大熔爐。

分歧的 / 差異的
a. separate; splitting off / different; disagreeing; conflicting

---

0111 digestion [də`dʒɛstʃən] * gest-=stomach ★★★★★

I can eat anything and do not get sick because I have very good digestion. That's why I've got the nickname "Vacuum."

我因為有非常好的消化能力，吃任何食物都不會生病。這就是為什麼我的綽號叫做「吸塵器」。

消化能力，消化作用，消化
n. the process of digesting

0112 indigestion [ˌɪndə`dʒɛstʃən] * in-=not ★★★★☆

Don't eat your food so quickly. I'm afraid you'll get indigestion. Please try to chew the food long enough.

吃東西不要太快，我擔心你會消化不良。請盡量用夠長的時間咀嚼食物。

消化不良
n. dyspepsia; difficulty in digesting food

0113 inexplicable [ɪn`ɛksplɪkəbl] * plic=fold ★★★★☆

Most of the theories concerning UFO's are inexplicable. There are many people who insist that they have seen UFO's, but there is no conclusive evidence.

多數關於幽浮的理論都是無法解釋的，許多人堅稱看到幽浮，但卻沒有確切證據。

無法解釋的，不可思議的
a. unexplainable; unfathomable; insolvable; incomprehensible; perplexing; insoluble

---

0114 complicated [`kɑmplə͵ketɪd] * com-=together ★★★★★

Of all forms of symbolism, language is the most highly developed, most subtle and most complicated.

Language as Symbolism —— S. Hayakawa

在所有象徵性符號的表現形式中，語言是最為高度發展的形式，同時也是最精妙、最複雜的。

——《作為象徵符號的語言》（日裔美籍語意學家）早川教授

複雜的，難懂的
a. complex; intricate; entangled; knotty

0115 composite [kəm`pɑzɪt] * posit=put ★★★★☆

Pablo Picasso often made a composite drawing of two faces. In some of his drawings we can see both the front and the side of a person's face.

西班牙畫家畢卡索經常以合成畫風表現兩個臉龐。在他的部分畫作中，我們可以同時看到一個人臉龐的正面和側面。

合成的，混成的
a. combined; compound; blended

0116 preposition [ˌprɛpə`zɪʃən] * pre-=before ★★★★★

A position of an object can be described by a preposition, such as 'above,' 'in' or 'under,' which is usually placed before a noun or pronoun.

一物的位置可用介系詞來描述，如「在～之上」、「在～之中」或「在～之下」等。介系詞通常置於所描述的名詞或代名詞的前面。

介系詞
n. a word governing a noun or pronoun and expressing a relation to another word

0117 prescience [ˈprɛʃɪəns] * science=know ★★☆☆☆

預知
n. foreknowledge; foresight

Prescience is not accepted as fact by scientists, but many people believe in it and consult fortune tellers or psychics when they have a major decision to make.

科學家並不承認預知是一項事實，然而許多人都相信它，當他們需要做出重大決定時，會求助算命師或靈媒。

0118 omniscient [ɑmˈnɪʃənt] * omni-=all ★☆☆☆☆

無所不知的，全知的
a. knowing everything or much

Even professors cannot be expected to know everything. They are not omniscient. There can be many things even professors do not know.

即使是教授也不能期望他們知道所有事，他們並不是無所不知的。有許多事就算是教授也不知道。

0119 omnivorous [ɑmˈnɪvərəs] * vor=throat ★★★★☆

（動物）雜食的
a. feeding on many kinds of food, esp. on both plants and flesh

Humans are naturally omnivorous, meaning that they can consume both; meat and plants.

人類天生就是雜食的，也就是說，人類可以同時吃肉類和蔬果類食物。

0120 herbivore [ˈhɝbɪˌvɔr] * herb-=plant ★★★★☆

草食性動物
n. an animal that feeds on plants

A cow is a herbivore because it only eats plants. A cow gives us meat but does not eat meat.

只吃植物的牛屬於草食性動物。牛提供肉類來源給人類食用，但本身不吃肉。

0121 herbicide [ˈhɝbɪˌsaɪd] * cid=cut ★★★★☆

除草劑
n. a substance toxic to plants and used to destroy unwanted vegetation

Herbicides have proven to be very helpful in reducing the amount of unwanted plants as well as improving the production of agricultural products, but there are many who are concerned about the ill effects from eating foods that have been treated by herbicides.

除草劑經證實可有效清除有害植物或雜草，同時也可提高農作物生產力。然而許多人擔心食用噴灑過除草劑的食物所帶來的不良影響。

0122 decide [dɪˈsaɪd] * de-=down ★★★★★

決定
v. determine; resolve; settle; make up one's mind

I've been offered a good job for more money, but if I take it I will have to move, which I really don't want to do. I'm having a hard time trying to decide if I should take the job.

我得到一份薪水較高的好工作，如果接受就必須搬家，但我實在不想。我很難決定是否要接受這份工作。

0123 deplore [dɪˈplɔr] * plore=shout ★★★★☆

譴責，強烈反對
v. lament; mourn; bemoan; bewail; grieve for

Mrs. Jones has actively deplored the use of drugs and alcohol ever since the day her daughter was injured by a drunk driver.

自從瓊斯太太的女兒被酒駕者撞傷的那天起，她便強烈譴責服用藥物和酒精。

0124 implore [ɪm`plor] * im-=in ★★★★☆

Now that the risk of contracting the HIV virus is so high, many medical experts are imploring homosexuals to take blood tests.

既然感染愛滋病的風險如此之高，許多醫療專家因此懇求同性戀者接受血液檢查。

懇求
v. beg; beseech; entreat; plead with; supplicate

0125 immersion [ɪ`mɝʃən] * mers, merg=plunge ★★★★☆

Some churches baptize their members by sprinkling water on the top of their heads, while other churches baptize their members by immersion.

部分教會為教徒施洗的方式是將水灑在受洗者的頭頂上，另外有些教會則採用浸禮方式。

浸禮
n. the act or an instance of immersing

MP3
7

0126 submerge [səb`mɝdʒ] * sub-=down ★★★★★

The submarine submerged into the depths of the water when a fighter plane appeared. It remained in the deep water until the plane disappeared.

戰機迫近時潛水艇即潛入海底，並一直保持深水潛航直到戰機消失為止。

（潛水艇等）潛航，沉入水中
v. plunge; go under water; immerse; sink; dive

0127 subversive [səb`vɝsɪv] * vers=turn ★★★☆☆

The subversive person contrived to turn the demonstration into a riot. But most people did not support his intention to overthrow the government.

那名滋事份子圖謀將示威活動變成一場暴動，然而大多數民眾都不支持他推翻政府的意圖。

破壞的，滋生事端的
a. revolutionary; seditious

0128 perverseness [pɚ`vɝsnɪs] * per-=perfect ★★★☆☆

And then came, as if to my final and irrevocable overthrow, the spirit of perverseness. Of this spirit philosophy takes no account.

The Black Cat —— Edgar A. Poe

接著到來的是頑強的靈魂，彷彿是我最終的、無可挽回的毀滅。這樣的靈魂卻是哲學所忽略的。

—— 《黑貓》愛倫坡

剛愎，執拗，頑強
n. being stubborn

0129 perceive [pɚ`siv] * -ceive=catch, take ★★★★★

Even if we cannot at once perceive anything good in a book which has been admired and praised for hundreds of years, we may be sure that by trying, by studying it carefully, we will at last be able to feel the reason of this admiration and praise.

On Reading —— Lafcadio Hearn

即使我們無法馬上領略一本書數百年來受人欣賞和讚頌的可貴之處，只要試著仔細閱讀，最後必定能了解箇中原因。

—— 《談閱讀》（日本文學家）小泉八雲

了解，察覺，意識到
v. notice; be aware of; discern / observe; see

0130 deceive [dɪ`siv] * de-=down ★★★★★

She bought a diamond ring while taking an overseas trip but years later she found that she had been deceived. It was not a real diamond.

她在海外旅遊時買了一只鑽石戒指，但幾年後才發現自己被騙了，原來那並不是真正的鑽石。

蒙蔽，欺騙
v. mislead; delude; trick; fool; cheat; swindle; defraud

0131 deciduous [dɪˈsɪdʒʊəs] * cid=fall ★★★☆☆

Oaks are not evergreen trees but deciduous ones that drop their leaves every fall and grow them back every spring.

橡樹不是常綠樹而是落葉林木，每到秋天葉片就會掉落，直到來年春天才又長出新葉。

落葉性的
a. shedding leaves annually

0132 decadent [ˈdɛkədn̩t] * de-=down ★★★★☆

His 85-year-old grandmother's health deteriorated and she is now in a decadent state in a hospital.

他八十五歲祖母的健康每況愈下，現在病入膏肓躺在醫院裡。

衰敗的，衰微的，頹廢的
a. debased; degenerating; corrupt

0133 delinquent [dɪˈlɪŋkwənt] * linq=give up ★★★★☆

The juvenile delinquent was released from custody. He had been given a 3 day detention for stealing.

少年犯從拘留所中獲得釋放，他因偷竊被拘禁三天。

犯過者，犯罪者
n. misdoer; wrongdoer

0134 relinquish [rɪˈlɪŋkwɪʃ] * re-=away ★★★★☆

Those who hold the reins of power are often loath to relinquish them. Power has a certain sort of attraction which defies clear explanation.

掌權者通常不願意讓出權力，權力帶有某種無法清楚解釋的吸引力。

讓渡，放棄
v. abandon; renounce; dismiss; lay aside; discard; yield; give up; let go; waive

---

0135 repel [rɪˈpɛl] * -pel=drive ★★★★☆

During the Korean Civil War we were able to repel the attacking enemy thanks to the help of allied forces.

在韓國內戰期間，幸虧我們得到盟軍協助，才得以擊退進攻的敵軍。

擊退，趕走
v. push back; force back; repulse; dispel; disperse; chase away

---

0136 dispel [dɪˈspɛl] * dis-=away ★★★★★

In some countries the police use water guns, while others tear gas, but in many both of them are used to dispel demonstrators.

在某些國家警方用水柱驅散示威群眾，另外有些國家使用催淚瓦斯。然而許多國家兼用兩者來驅離示威者。

驅散，驅逐，驅離
v. scatter; drive away by scattering; expel; repel; banish

0137 dissimulation [dɪˌsɪmjəˈleʃən] * simul=same ★☆☆☆☆

The manager told his subordinates that he knew that he would be fired, but in front of the boss he pretended that he did not know this fact. He continued to curry favor with the boss. Others could not put up with his dissimulation.

經理告訴屬下們他知道自己將被解雇。但在上司面前卻佯裝不知情，繼續巴結老闆，旁人都無法忍受他的虛偽。

虛偽，偽善
n. hypocrisy; deception; double-dealing

0138 assimilate [əˈsɪmlˌet] * as-, ad-=to ★★★☆☆

The foreign worker population should try to be assimilated into the local culture. Otherwise they will have difficulty living within the local community.

外籍工作人口應該試著融入當地文化，否則和本地社群共同居住時會有困難。

理解 / 使同化，使融入
v. absorb (information, etc.) into the mind / cause to resemble

0139 associate [əˈsoʃɪˌet] * soci=gather ★★★★★

Those two got into a large argument over money, and they haven't associated with each other for months now.

他們倆因金錢陷入激烈爭執，現在已經幾個月沒聯絡了。

交往，往來 / 使互相關聯
v. consort; mingle / correlate

0140 dissociate [dɪˈsoʃɪˌet] * dis-=away ★★★★★

Despite all of our efforts to befriend Mary, she dissociated herself from us in any way she could.

儘管我們盡全力和瑪麗交朋友，她依然用盡各種方式和我們斷絕關係。

使斷絕關係，使分離
v. disconnect; estrange; sever; break off with

0141 dislocate [ˈdɪsloˌket] * loca=place ★★★★☆

While he was trying to ski down a slope that was beyond his ability, Lorne dislocated his shoulder.

洛恩試著滑下超過他能力所及的斜坡，肩膀因此脫臼。

使脫臼 / 使混亂
v. put out of joint / disconnect; disengage

0142 allocate [ˈæləˌket] * al-, ad-=to ★★★★☆

I'm sorry. I have no influence on the way the funds are allocated to each one of the departments.

很抱歉，我無法左右資金如何分配到各部門。

分配，分派
v. allot; assign; apportion

0143 alluvial [əˈluvɪəl] * luv=water ★☆☆☆☆

There was an alluvial deposit left on the road following the flood and it caused a very long delay in traffic.

水災過後道路上還留有淤積的泥沙沉澱物，導致交通嚴重堵塞。

淤積的，沖積的
a. of or relating to alluvium

0144 diluvial [dɪˈluvɪəl] * di-=away ★☆☆☆☆

When the dam burst and the lake flowed over the small town the diluvial damage was severe. The Red Cross hurriedly set up a rescue operation.

水壩潰堤時大水氾濫並淹沒小鎮，導致洪水災情慘重。紅十字會倉促地成立救援組織。

洪水的
a. of a flood

0145 digest [daɪˈdʒɛst] * gest=stomach ★★★★★

You should always wait until you digest your food before you go swimming because you may get severe cramps if you go swimming with a full stomach.

你應該等到食物消化完後再去游泳，如果一吃飽就去游泳胃部可能會嚴重痙攣。

消化
v. assimilate; convert into an absorbable form

0146 congestion [kənˈdʒɛstʃən] * con-=together ★★★★☆

The reason I got here so late was that there was terrible traffic congestion. I had to spend a couple of hours stuck in traffic.

我之所以遲到這麼久是因為遇到嚴重交通阻塞，被困在車陣中好幾個鐘頭。

(交通) 阻塞，(都市) 擁擠
n. jam; crowding; overcrowding; mess; bottleneck

0147 constitution [ˌkɑnstəˈtjuʃən] * stit=set ★★★★☆

憲法
n. *governing charter*

It is because of the constitution that their country is able to remain one of the freest countries in the world.

正因為這部憲法的存在，他們才能成為世界上最自由的國家之一。

0148 substitute [ˈsʌbstəˌtut] * sub-=under ★★★★★

替代，替換，代用
v. *exchange; fill in*

Many people, instead of saying "died," often substitute such an expression as "passed away," "departed" and "went west."

許多人提到「死亡」字眼時，經常以「去世」、「逝世」或「歸西」等措辭來代換。

0149 subscribe [səbˈskraɪb] * scrib=write ★★★★☆

訂閱／認捐
v. *have a subscription / pledge money; promise to contribute*

What kind of newspaper or magazine do you subscribe to? Can you recom-mend one for me? I cannot choose one among so many types.

請問你訂閱什麼報紙或雜誌，可以推薦給我嗎？我無法在這麼多報章雜誌中選出一種來。

0150 conscript [kənˈskrɪpt] * con-=together ★★★★☆

徵召士兵，新兵
n. *a person enlisted by conscription*

The conscripts who had just completed basic military training goose-stepped forward as the drums rolled.

鼓聲隆隆作響時，甫完成基本軍事訓練的徵召士兵踢著正步前進。

Tea Time... ☕

<Roman legend> Pyrrhic victory	〈羅馬傳奇故事〉皮拉斯王的勝利
From the victory of Pyrrhus, king of Epirus, over the Romans (279 B.C.) He fought against the Romans with 25,000 soldiers and 20 elephants. He got a victory, but he lost almost three quarters of his soldiers.	西元前二七九年，伊庇魯斯國王皮拉斯以兩萬五千名士兵和二十頭大象的軍力擊敗羅馬人，取得勝利。他雖戰勝但卻失掉將近四分之三的兵力。（註：本詞常用來形容「付出重大犧牲所換取的勝利」，也就是「得不償失」。）

❖ **Pyrrhic victory** [ˌpɪrɪk ˈvɪktərɪ] ***n.*** *victory achieved at such great cost that it is nearly a defeat* |
得不償失，以重大犧牲換取的勝利

It was a Pyrrhic victory. Even though we won the basketball game, four of our players got injured.

這真是得不償失。雖然我們贏了這場籃球比賽，但共有四名球員因此受傷。

1 Complete each word by filling in the blank with proper spelling so that it has the same meaning as suggested. Then please write the meaning of each word in Chinese.

1. 合著	= _ _ _ l a b o r a t e	11. herbicide	= _____
2. 兼容並蓄的	= e c _ _ _ _ _ _	12. decide	= _____
3. 精心籌劃的	= e _ _ _ _ _ a t e	13. immersion	= _____
4. 徵召士兵	= c o n _ _ _ _ _ _	14. subversive	= _____
5. 洪水的	= _ _ _ u v i a l	15. perceive	= _____
6. 使集於一點	= c o n _ _ _ _ e	16. deciduous	= _____
7. 差異的	= _ _ v e r g e n t	17. relinquish	= _____
8. 無法解釋的	= i n e x _ _ _ _ a b l e	18. dissimulation	= _____
9. 介系詞	= _ _ _ p o s i t i o n	19. associate	= _____
10. 雜食的	= o m n i _ _ _ o u s	20. alluvial	= _____

2 Choose a word that best completes the sentence.

21. A rosemary is often _____ with remembrance, for its leaf remains green long after it is picked.

    (A) subversive   (B) deciduous   (C) associated   (D) decadent

22. Cows are _____ . It is said that they go crazy, ending up with mad cow disease if they are fed meat.

    (A) herbivores   (B) delinquents   (C) dissimulation   (D) immersion

23. My brother thinks that any food that has not expired is good for the health. I think that he is able to _____ everything he eats.

    (A) digest   (B) dissociate   (C) allocate   (D) dispel

3 The highlighted word is closest in meaning to which of the following?

24. Farmer Green sprayed herbicides instead of insecticides. All of his tomato plants wilted and died.

    (A) feeding on many kinds of foods   (B) the act of immersing
    (C) substances toxic to plants   (D) animals that feed on plants

25. Traffic congestion on a highway can be caused by a single disabled car.

    (A) converge   (B) conscript   (C) immersion   (D) jams

MP3
8

0151 concave [ˌkɑnˈkev] * cave=cave ★★★★☆

A telescope consists of a concave lens and a convex lens and it is used for seeing an object in the distance.

望遠鏡由凹透鏡和凸透鏡構成，可用來觀看遠處物體。

凹面的，凹形的，凹的
a. curving inward; sunken; indented

0152 excavate [ˈɛkskəˌvet] * ex-=out ★★★★★

A good writer is wise in his choice of subjects, and exhaustive in his accumulation of materials. A good writer must have an irrepressible confidence in himself and in his ideas. Good writers know how to excavate significant facts from masses of information.

—— Ernest Hemingway

一位優秀的作家不但會慎選寫作題材，同時也會毫無遺漏地累積寫作資料。優秀作家必須對自己和自己的構想有絕對信心，並知道如何從大量資訊中挖掘出具有意義的真相。

—— （美國小說家暨諾貝爾文學獎得主）海明威

挖掘，挖出
v. dig out; scoop out; unearth; uncover; remove

0153 expatriate [ɛksˈpetrɪˌet] * pater=father(land) ★★★★☆

During World War II, a lot of German expatriates settled in many other countries. Many of them chose the United States.

在第二次世界大戰期間，有許多流亡海外的德國人到其他國家定居，其中許多人選擇了美國。

寓居國外者，流亡海外者
n. exile; refugee; outcast; deported person

0154 patriarchal [ˌpetrɪˈɑrkl] * arch=first, head ★★★☆☆

A patriarchal society which is ruled by men is no longer possible in this highly complex modern society.

由男性掌控的父系社會，在今日高度複雜的現代化社會中已變得不可能。

父權的，父系的
a. of or relating to patriarchy

0155 monarch [ˈmɑnək] * mon-=one ★★★★★

A political community is possible in which the governor is limited; in which sovereignty ultimately pertains not to the monarch, as opposed to those whom he governs, but to the people as a whole.

Rocke's Political Theory —— Richard I. Aaron

唯有統治者的權力受到限制，政治社群才有形成的可能；統治權最終並不從屬於被統治者反對的世襲君王，而是屬於全體人民所有。

—— 《洛克的政治理論》（威爾斯哲學家）理查·亞倫

世襲君王
n. hereditary sovereign

0156 monorail [ˈmɑnəˌrel] * rail=rail ★★☆☆☆

One can have a tour of Disneyland on a monorail. Small trains run on a track consisting of a single rail.

人們可搭乘單軌列車遊迪士尼樂園。有小火車行駛於單一軌道鐵軌上。

單軌鐵路
n. a railway in which the track consists of a single rail

0157 derail [dɪˈrel] * de-=down ★★☆☆☆

The horrible accident was caused by the derailed bullet train. Investigators are inspecting what caused the train to leave the rails.

這起可怕意外是肇因於一列出軌的高速子彈列車，調查人員正在調查列車脫軌原因。

使（火車等）出軌
v. cause a train to leave the rails

0158 degradation [ˌdɛgrəˈdeʃən] * grad=go ★★★★☆

We human beings should do our utmost to fight pollution and environmental degradation. We should use more of the renewable energy sources.

人類應盡全力對抗空氣污染和環境品質的降低。我們應盡量使用再生能源資源。

下降，降低，退步
n. *degeneration;*
deterioration; corruption;
depravity

0159 upgrade [ˈʌpˌgred] * up-=up ★★★★★

This archaic computer needs an upgrade. But I am not sure if you will be able to find the parts used for this computer.

這部老舊電腦需要升級，但我不確定你是否能找到這部電腦使用的零件。

升級，晉升 / 使升級，提升
n. *improvement; promotion /*
v. *raise in rank*

0160 upsurge [ʌpˈsɝdʒ] * surg=surge ★★★★☆

Since this town became a city, crime has upsurged. Now the police and educational authorities are preparing an educational program to reduce crime rates.

自從這個小鎮變成都市後犯罪活動也增加了。現在警方和教育當局正在籌劃一項教育課程，以降低犯罪率。

高漲，急遽上升 / 增加
n. *an upward surge /*
v. *increase*

0161 resurgent [rɪˈsɝdʒənt] * re-=again ★★★★☆

In Poland the communist party is a resurgent political force. They are gaining more and more momentum.

在波蘭，共產黨是復甦的政治勢力，共產黨員的聲勢日益壯大。

復甦的，再起的
a. *rising again*

0162 regenerate [rɪˈdʒɛnəˌret] * gener=class ★★★★★

Sir Winston Churchill aimed to regenerate British industry. The Second World War left England devastated.

邱吉爾爵士打算重建英國產業。第二次世界大戰重創了英國。

重建，使更生
v. *restore; generate again*

0163 degenerate [dɪˈdʒɛnəˌret] * de-=down ★★★★★

Too much liberty is apt to degenerate into lawlessness. However, too much pressure leads to tyranny.

太多自由容易淪為目無法紀，然而太多壓迫則會導致暴政。

墮落，淪落為～
v. *decline; deteriorate;*
decay; worsen; degrade;
backslide

0164 decrepit [dɪˈkrɛpɪt] * crep=sound ★★★★★

Pam's grandmother had been in the hospital for several years. Last week the poor decrepit soul peacefully passed away.

潘的祖母在醫院住了好幾年，上周這位可憐的老婦安詳去世了。

衰老的，老朽的
a. *aged; old*

0165 discrepancy [dɪˈskrɛpənsɪ] * dis-=different ★★★★☆

There was a great discrepancy between what the first son said he did and what his younger brother told their parents.

大兒子宣稱自己所做的事和弟弟告訴雙親的內容間有極大矛盾。

不一致，不符，矛盾
n. *difference; inconsistency;*
disparity; divergence

0166 **discompose** [ˌdɪskəm`poz] * pos=put

The sign said that items could be returned without the receipt, but when Nancy tried to return the dress the employee gave her a real hard time and she was visibly discomposed.

招牌上說不用憑發票也可以換貨，然而南西想退回洋裝時，店員一直刁難，使她顯得很慌亂。

使慌亂，使不安，使心慌
v. disturb; agitate

0167 **repose** [rɪ`poz] * re-=back

My father loves to come back home after his work and repose in front of the television. He always has a remote control in his hand.

我父親喜歡在工作結束後回到家在電視機前休息，他總是手握遙控器。

休息／使休息
n. rest / v. take a rest

0168 **remission** [rɪ`mɪʃən] * mis=send

When the doctors announced that her cancer was in remission all the grandchildren went to the hospital to visit her.

當醫生宣布她的癌症病情已暫時緩和下來時，所有子孫輩都前往醫院探視。

（痛苦或疾病等暫時的）減輕，緩和／（刑罰或稅金等的）減免，寬恕
n. diminution of force, effect or degree (esp. of disease or pain) / exoneration; forgiveness

---

0169 **intermission** [ˌɪntə`mɪʃən] * inter-=between

At the first intermission of the play many patrons left the theater in disgust because the story made no sense at all, yet the newspapers had called it a masterpiece.

許多觀眾在第一次幕間休息時便不滿地離場，因為故事情節太離譜，但報紙卻稱它是一大傑作。

換幕時間，幕間休息
n. interruption; interlude; break

0170 **interfere** [ˌɪntə`fɪr] * fer=put, carry

Since he was a child he has always been taught not to interfere with the adults when they are talking.

當他還小的時候，大人總是教育他，不要打斷大人的談話。

干擾，妨礙
v. meddle; obstruct; get in the way of; barge in; intercede; interpose; horn in; butt in; intrude; poke one's nose in

---

0171 **infer** [ɪn`fɝ] * in-=in

He never really came right out and said it, but it was obvious that he was inferring that I was not qualified.

他從來不曾明說，但很明顯是在暗示我無法勝任。

推測，推論／暗示
v. deduce; surmise / imply

0172 **interment** [ɪn`tɝmənt] * ter=earth, soil

The place of Catherine's interment, to the surprise of the villagers, was neither in the chapel, under the carved monument of the Lintons, nor yet by the tombs of her own relations, outside.

Wuthering Heights —— Emily Bronte

出乎村民意料的是，凱瑟琳所葬之處既非林頓家族雕刻紀念碑下的小禮拜堂，也不是莊園外娘家親戚的墳墓旁。

—— 《咆哮山莊》（英國文學家）艾蜜莉．勃朗特

埋葬
n. burial

0173 Mediterranean [ˌmɛdətəˈrenɪən] * medi-=middle ★★★★★

Her trip to the Mediterranean included visits to Greece, Italy, Israel and Egypt but not to Morocco, which is where she wanted to go for her honeymoon.

她的地中海之旅包括遊覽希臘、義大利、以色列和埃及，但是不含她想去度蜜月的摩洛哥。

地中海
n. *the sea bordered by S. Europe, SW Asia and N. Africa*

0174 medieval [ˌmidɪˈivəl] * eval=age ★★★★★

In medieval Europe, heroes rode large white horses and rescued damsels in distress while the kings and queens feasted and the peasants starved.

在中古世紀的歐洲，英雄騎著白馬拯救少女於危難中，國王和王后整天設宴享受，農民們則經常挨餓。

中古世紀的
a. *of the Middle Ages*

0175 coeval [koˈivl] * co-=together ★☆☆☆☆

Coeval artifacts come from the same time period, and are used to compare the differences between civilizations throughout history.

同時代的手工藝品來自同一時期，可用來比較文明和歷史等各方面差異。

同時代（年代、時期）的
a. *living or existing at the same epoch*

MP3
9

0176 coalesce [ˌkoəˈlɛs] * ale=grow ★★★☆☆

It is interesting that even though a husband and a wife are two totally different people, the longer they are married, the more they coalesce into one harmonized unit.

很有趣的是，即使丈夫和妻子是兩個完全不同的人，結婚時間愈久，兩人就愈加融為和諧一體。

結合，聯合
v. *grow together; merge; combine*

0177 adolescence [ˌædlˈɛsn̩s] * ad-=to ★★★★★

Adolescence means 'growing up' and strictly speaking, should apply to a child from birth to maturity.

青春期意謂著「成長」，嚴格來說，這個詞只適用於孩童從出生到成熟的期間。

青春期
n. *puberty*

0178 adhesive [ədˈhisɪv] * hes=stick ★★★★★

Adhesive is used to bond two things together and is very useful to keep around the house. But one of the problems is that some adhesives do not work well.

可將兩物黏合的黏著劑是居家必備的實用工具。但是有個麻煩，那就是部分黏著劑黏性不佳。

有黏性的 / 黏著劑，黏膠
a. *sticky /* **n.** *an adhesive substance, esp. one used to stick other substances together; glue*

0179 cohesion [koˈhiʒən] * co-=together ★★★★★

For years, scientists have been trying to discover the mysteries of chemical cohesion in hopes of developing new and improved ways to bond things together.

科學家多年來一直試圖解開化學分子凝聚力的謎團，希望能藉此發展出結合物體的改良新法。

（分子間的）凝聚力
n. *the act or condition of sticking together; a tendency to cohere*

0180 cohere [koˋhɪr] * here=stick ★★★★★

Sentences that do not cohere are hard to understand. Reading such sentences is just like reading two different scraps from different newspapers pasted together.

前後不連貫的句子是難以理解的，閱讀這類句子就像是在讀不同報紙剪下來的兩篇不同剪報一樣。

黏著，附著 / 前後連貫，前後一致
v. stick together; glue; consolidate; congeal / be consistent; be related

0181 inherent [ɪnˋhɪrənt] * in-=in ★★★★★

Now that you are appointed as a public officer, you must not forget the duties inherent in a public office.

既然你已被任命為公職人員，就不應忘記這份公職本身應有的責任。

固有的，與生俱來的
a. essential; intrinsic; ingrained

0182 invasion [ɪnˋveʒən] * vas=go ★★★★★

On October 30, 1938, thousands of Americans in the New York area were terror-stricken by a radio broadcast describing an invasion from Mars.

Crowds —— Meyer J. Nimkoff

一九三八年十月三十日，成千上萬名紐約地區的美國人因為聽到廣播敘述火星人入侵而飽受驚嚇。

——《人群》（美國作家）梅爾·林姆科夫

侵略，入侵
n. encroachment; breach; intrusion; infringement; trespass; overstepping

0183 pervasive [pəˋvesɪv] * per-=through ★★★★☆

A skunk came into the garage and the nasty smell of its gas was very pervasive and offensive, so no one was able to breathe.

一隻臭鼬闖進花園散發出難聞的惡臭，臭味四處瀰漫且令人作嘔，大家都無法呼吸。

遍布的，瀰漫的
a. pervading; able to pervade; penetrating; permeating; widespread

0184 percussion [pəˋkʌʃən] * cuss=strike ★★★★★

George's specialty was percussion. He had natural rhythm, and an understanding of beat and timing.

喬治的專長是打擊樂，他的節奏感是與生俱來的，而且對於敲擊和時間的掌握也很有領悟力。

打擊樂 / 打擊樂器組
n. the playing of music by striking instruments with sticks, etc. / the section of such instruments in an orchestra

0185 concussion [kənˋkʌʃən] * con-=together ★★★★☆

Other than a slight concussion, there were no other serious injuries sustained to his head when he fell off his bike.

他跌下自行車時，除了輕微的腦震盪外，頭部沒有其他嚴重傷害。

腦震盪
n. temporary unconsciousness or incapacity due to injury to the head

0186 conglomeration [kənˋglɑməˋreʃən] * glomer=globe ★★★★☆

His business started many years ago as a very small cement company, but through years of hard work and sacrifice, he has nurtured it into a diversified and successful conglomeration.

許多年前他的事業剛起步時，只是一家小小的水泥公司，然而經過多年辛勤工作和犧牲奉獻，他已經將自己的事業打造為成功的多元化集團企業。

團塊 / 複合企業，集團企業
n. agglomerate / organization

0187 agglomerate [əˋglɑməˏret] * ag-, ad-=to ★★★★☆

The people agglomerated in the center of the room in order to leave room on the edges to set up chairs.

人們聚集在房間中央，以便騰出四周空間擺放椅子。

聚結，結塊 / 積聚 / 團塊
v. collect into a mass /
v. accumulate /
n. conglomeration

0188 adequate [ˋædəkwɪt] * equ-=equal ★★★★★

適當的，足以勝任的 / 足夠的，充足的
a. suitable; proper; fitting / sufficient; enough

When I entered the classroom, the exam had already started. Therefore I did not have adequate time to finish the test.
我進入教室時考試已經開始，因此沒有足夠時間做完測驗。

0189 equanimity [ˌikwəˋnɪmətɪ] * anim=mind ★★★★☆

平靜，鎮定
n. mental composure; evenness of temper

With an air of unassailable equanimity, she walked into her department manager's office to ask for a raise and a promotion.
她懷著堅定而平靜的心情走進部門經理辦公室，要求升職和加薪。

0190 unanimous [juˋnænəməs] * un-=one ★★★★★

意見一致的，全體無異議的
a. all in agreement

The jury's decision was unanimous as they all voted 'guilty' in the murder trial of the serial killer.
陪審團的判決一致，針對連續殺人犯的謀殺罪審判全部投以「有罪」。

0191 unilateral [ˌjunɪˋlætərəl] * lateral-=side ★★★★☆

單方面的，片面的
a. one-sided

Unilateral views are those which come from only one of the parties concerned and they are often found to be prejudiced.
只來自當事者其中一方的見解，稱為單方面的見解，這類見解通常帶有偏見。

0192 multilateral [ˌmʌltɪˋlætərəl] * multi-=many ★★★★☆

多邊的，多國之間的
a. having many sides; various

The three countries signed a multilateral treaty after the war was concluded and everyone felt safe once more.
三個國家在戰後共同簽署一項多邊協定，此舉讓彼此都感到更安全。

0193 multilingual [ˌmʌltɪˋlɪŋgwəl] * lingu=language ★★★★★

使用多國語言的 / 說多國語言的
a. in or using several languages

It is best to be multilingual if you are going to live in a place like Hong Kong, especially in languages such as Mandarin, Cantonese, English and Japanese.
如果要居住在類似香港這樣的地方，會說多國語言是最好不過的，特別是會說中文普通話、廣東話、英語和日語。

0194 bilingual [baɪˋlɪŋgwəl] * bi-=two ★★★★★

會說兩種語言的，雙語的 / 兩種語言並用的
a. able to speak two languages / spoken or written in two languages

Bilingual college students have a distinct advantage when looking for a job because employers are looking to hire people who can speak a second language.
雙語院校學生求職時具有明顯優勢，因為雇主也在尋覓能說第二外國語的人才。

0195 bigamy [ˋbɪgəmɪ] * gam=marriage ★☆☆☆☆

重婚，重婚罪
n. the crime of marrying when one is lawfully married to another person

Finding that he was still married to another woman, his second wife charged him with bigamy and he went to jail.
第二任妻子發現他和另一名女子仍有婚約時，控告他重婚罪，使他銀鐺入獄。

0196 misogamist [mɪˈsɑgəmɪst] * mis-=hate ★☆☆☆☆

James seems to be a misogamist. He really doesn't want to get married. The best way to drive him away is to start talking about marriage.

詹姆士似乎是個厭惡婚姻者，他完全不想結婚。想要讓詹姆士轉身離去的最好辦法就是在他面前談論婚姻。

厭惡婚姻者
n. a person who hates marriage

0197 misanthrope [ˈmɪsənˌθrop] * anthropo=human being ★★★★☆

While doing his business he had been repeatedly deceived by many people around him. He ended up being a misanthrope, and avoided meeting people.

在他經營事業的過程中曾多次被許多身邊的人欺騙，最後他變得討厭與人交往，總是避免認識他人。

討厭與人交往者，憎恨人類者
n. a person who hates mankind

0198 anthropologist [ˌænθrəˈpɑlədʒɪst] * -ist=person ★★★★★

The pioneer English anthropologist E.B.Tylor described a kiss as "salute by tasting."

The Natural History of a Kiss —— E. Royston Pike

英國人類學家先驅 E・B・泰勒曾將「親吻」描述成「以嘗味致意」。

—— 《親吻的自然史》E・羅依斯頓・派克

人類學家
n. a person whose field of study is anthropology

0199 dermatologist [ˌdɝməˈtɑlədʒɪst] * derm-=skin ★★★★☆

Because Jane noticed some red spots on her back, she called a dermatologist to make an appointment.

珍因為留意到背上有些紅色斑點，於是打電話給皮膚科醫師約診。

皮膚科醫師
n. skin doctor

0200 epidermis [ˌɛpəˈdɝmɪs] * epi-= on ★★★★☆

Many doctors will tell you that it is very important to protect the epidermis from the sun's rays because sunburns can cause skin cancer.

許多醫生都指出，保護人體表皮組織不受太陽輻射的照射是非常重要的，因為曬傷會導致皮膚癌。

（解剖學）表皮，上皮，外皮
n. outer layer of the skin

Tea Time... ☕

<From the name of an electrician> **Galvanism** **This word stems from Luigi Galvani, an Italian electrician.**	〈來自一位電流學家之名〉直流電 本字起源自十八世紀義大利解剖學暨電流學家路易吉・賈法尼的姓 Galvani。（註：後世將所有和電流、電位相關的單字都冠上 galvani- 或 galvan-。

❖ **galvanize** [ˈgælvəˌnaɪz] *v. stimulate / coat iron with zinc* | 激勵 / 電鍍

I cheered my nephew up. He had been totally dejected after he failed the job interview. After I persuaded him to start his own business, he seemed to be galvanized.

我安慰工作面談失敗後極度沮喪的姪子。在我說服他發展個人事業後，他似乎獲得激勵。

1

Complete each word by filling in the blank with proper spelling so that it has the same meaning as suggested. Then please write the meaning of each word in Chinese.

1. 挖掘   = e x _ _ _ _ _ _
2. 凹的   = _ _ _ c a v e
3. 升級   = _ _ g r a d e
4. 墮落   = d e _ _ _ _ _ a t e
5. 流亡海外者 = _ _ p a t r i a t e
6. 世襲君王   = _ _ _ a r c h
7. 降低   = d e _ _ _ _ a t i o n
8. 高漲   = u p _ _ _ _ e
9. 復甦的   = _ _ s u r g e n t
10. 衰老的   = d e _ _ _ _ i t

11. repose   = _____
12. interfere   = _____
13. interment   = _____
14. medieval   = _____
15. adolescence   = _____
16. cohesion   = _____
17. inherent   = _____
18. invasion   = _____
19. concussion   = _____
20. adequate   = _____

2

Choose a word that best completes the sentence.

21. **My uncle was never a good driver because of his _____ carelessness.**
    (A) medieval   (B) inherent   (C) decrepit   (D) resurgent

22. **In the countries where there was the _____ feudal system, people drive on the left.**
    (A) medieval   (B) adhesive   (C) bilingual   (D) multilingual

3

The highlighted word is closest in meaning to which of the following?

23. **All of my classmates were unanimous in wanting the party. Everybody was excited.**
    (A) inherent   (B) consistent   (C) adequate   (D) pervasive

24. **A woman ran into a hospital with a mug stuck to her hand. She said that she was trying to fix the broken cup with adhesive .**
    (A) glue   (B) invasion   (C) percussion   (D) adolescence

25. **My father is playing a multilateral role at home; a cook, a baby-sitter, a seamstress and a chiropractor for my Mom.**
    (A) various   (B) coeval   (C) bigamy   (D) agglomerate

1 The highlighted word is closest in meaning to which of the following?

1. In the early history of the United States, a nationwide political convention led to the advent of American hotels.
   (A) assembly
   (B) transfusion
   (C) recession
   (D) secession

2. It is said that an introverted person needs less space for living.
   (A) assiduous
   (B) attentive
   (C) uncommunicative
   (D) egoistic

3. The man was introverted and could not control himself.
   (A) intractable
   (B) drunk
   (C) precocious
   (D) unassuming

4. The new neighbor who has moved into my neighborhood is quite an eccentric person.
   (A) collective
   (B) elaborate
   (C) eclectic
   (D) peculiar

5. I have been suffering from indigestion. I think my stomach has a serious problem.
   (A) concentration
   (B) antipathy
   (C) dyspepsia
   (D) atheism

Chapter

1
2
3
4
5

2 Please answer the following questions.

Salmon

When Pacific salmon reach six years of age, they set out to mate. This involves making an upriver swim to revert to their place of birth, in the headwaters of North American rivers. Driven by scent, the salmon instinctively swim some 2,400 kilometers to reach their destination.

The travel upstream is one filled with treacherous obstacles. Many expire , falling prey to bears and other predators, while others do not survive the exhausting journey against rough currents.

The ones that eventually do make it, make nests in the waterbed by scooping out gravel to prepare for the thousands of eggs that they will lay. Once the eggs have been laid, the salmon die collectively from exhaustion, having interminably continued the yearly cycle of birth.

6. The word revert is closest in meaning to which of the following?

(A) depose (B) return

(C) suspect (D) despise

7. The word expire is closest in meaning to which of the following?

(A) die (B) deduct

(C) proscribe (D) circumvent

8. The word survive is closest in meaning to which of the following?

(A) recede (B) dissemble

(C) endure (D) retract

9. The word collectively is closest in meaning to which of the following?

(A) all together (B) prone to

(C) prematurely (D) unintentionally

10. The word interminably is closest in meaning to which of the following?

(A) effusively (B) endlessly

(C) intermittently (D) inadvertently

MP3 10

0201 epithet [ˈɛpəˌθɛt] * thet=set
★☆☆☆☆

"Six Fingers" Louie gained that particular epithet because he had lost two fingers on each hand during one of his many criminal activities.

「六指」路易之所以得到這個特別綽號，是因為在某次犯罪活動中雙手各失去兩隻手指。

綽號，稱號
n. an adjective or other descriptive word expressing a quality or attribute, esp. used with or as a name

0202 hypothetical [ˌhaɪpəˈθɛtɪkl̩] * hypo-=under
★★★☆☆

The misunderstanding occurred because the scientist was actually talking about a hypothetical situation, but his students thought that it really did happen.

誤解產生的原因在於事實上科學家是在談論一個假設情況，然而學生們卻以為確有其事。

假設的，假定的
a. suppositional

0203 hypocritical [ˌhɪpəˈkrɪtɪkl̩] * -cal=ending for an adjective
★★★☆☆

The American writer Nathaniel Hawthorne harshly criticized the Puritans' hypocritical attitudes toward sins.

美國作家霍桑嚴厲批判清教徒對於罪惡的偽善態度。

虛偽的，偽善的，偽善者的
a. deceitful; sanctimonious

0204 economical [ˌikəˈnɑmɪkl̩] * nom=manage
★★★★★

Transforming the unused garage into a playroom was an economical use of interior space. The children were so happy about their father's decision.

將未使用的車庫改裝成遊戲室可節省內部空間。孩子們對父親的決定感到非常開心。

節省的，節約的
a. provident; sparing; frugal

0205 astronomical [ˌæstrəˈnɑmɪkl̩] * aster-=star
★★★★★

I don't ever shop at that store because I can't afford their astronomical prices. An unsubstantial-looking suit is more than 1,000 dollars.

我從不曾在那家商店購物，因為負擔不起高價位。一套中看不中穿的西裝竟然要價超過一千美元。

King Sejong's comprehensive interest in astronomical science resulted in a sun-dial, a water clock, celestial globes, astronomical maps, etc.

朝鮮王朝世宗大王對天文科學的廣泛興趣，結果帶來了日晷、自擊漏水鐘、渾天儀，以及天文天體圖等。

（數量）龐大的／天文（學）的
a. of or relating to astronomy

0206 disaster [dɪˈzæstə] * dis-=away
★★★★★

Many scientists have expressed serious concern about the possibility of a nuclear disaster as more and more nations come to have nuclear weapons.

許多科學家對發生核子大災難的可能性深表憂慮，因為有愈來愈多國家自擁核子武器。

（突然的）大災難，大災禍
n. misfortune; catastrophe; mishap; calamity

0207 disperse [dɪˈspɜs] * sper=scatter
★★★★★

The police tried to disperse the crowd at the scene of the accident but some of them refused to leave.

警方試圖驅散意外發生現場的人群，然而有些民眾不願離去。

驅散，疏散
v. scatter; distribute; diffuse; dissipate; disband

0208 prosperous [`prɑspərəs] * pro-=forward ★★★★★

There are some people who say that oftentimes a war is prosperous, but it is only true for the victor.

有些人說戰爭往往是有利的，但這句話只有站在勝利者的立場來說是正確的。

有利的，繁榮的
a. *flourishing; thriving; booming*

0209 proponent [prə`ponənt] * pon=put ★★★★☆

As a proponent of peace and prosperity, he was against the war and tried as hard as he could to bring it to an end.

作為和平與繁榮的擁護者，他是反對戰爭的，並試著盡全力結束戰事。

擁護者，支持者
n. *supporter; upholder; backer; advocate; patron*

0210 exponent [ɪk`sponənt] * ex-=out ★★★★☆

I can do simple math problems, but when I get into multiplying numbers with exponents, I get really confused.

我可以處理簡單數學問題，不過碰到乘冪數字相乘時，就真的很混亂。

（數學的）指數，冪／（學說）擁立者，典型代表人物
n. *index / proponent; representative*

0211 explicit [ɪk`splɪsɪt] * plic=fold ★★★★★

The boss left explicit instructions not to disturb him, but his secretary knocked on his door and woke him up.

老闆下達明確指示不希望有人打擾，但秘書還是敲門吵醒他。

明確的，清楚的
a. *clear; plain; manifest; unmistakable; distinct*

0212 implicit [ɪm`plɪsɪt] * im-=in ★★★★★

Mr. Brown naively thought that they had an implicit understanding about their negotiation, but as it turned out, his partner had very different opinions.

伯朗先生天真地以為雙方對談判已達成默認共識，然而結果卻是合夥人有非常不同的意見。

默認的，隱含的，不言明的
a. *indirect; implied*

0213 immigrate [`ɪmə,gret] * -migrate=move into ★★★★★

There are a lot of foreigners who have immigrated to America and begun businesses there and are doing very well now.

許多外國人移民到美國並開始在當地做生意，現在也經營得很成功。

（自國外）移民
v. *come as a permanent resident to a country other than one's native land*

0214 emigrate [`ɛmə,gret] * e-=out ★★★★★

The young history teacher emigrated from Japan. He decided to move out of his country because he believed that it was not right to teach students distorted information.

年輕的歷史老師是從日本移民過來的，他之所以決定搬離日本，是因為他認為在當地教導學生曲解的歷史資訊是錯誤的。

移居，移民
v. *leave one's own country to settle in another*

0215 eliminate [ɪ`lɪmə,net] * lim=limit ★★★★★

As the tournament went on, Karen was able to eliminate all of the other competitors and she won the National Wrestling Championship.

隨著錦標賽持續進行，凱倫淘汰了其他所有競爭對手，並拿下全國摔角比賽冠軍。

淘汰，排除
v. *remove; get rid of; eradicate; obliterate; liquidate*

0216 delimit [dɪˋlɪmɪt] * de-=down ★★☆☆☆

This chapter delimits my area of research. This research is confined to the cause of global warming.

本章界定了我的研究範圍，並侷限在地球暖化成因上。

劃定界限，限定
v. determine the limits of; restrict

0217 deflate [dɪˋflet] * -flate=blow ★★★☆☆

The pilot whose plane went down in the ocean managed to survive the initial crash and inflate a life raft, but after a few hours his raft deflated when the Coast Guard located him.

墜海飛機的駕駛在飛機往下墜時便設法逃生，同時將橡皮救生艇充氣，但是幾個小時後海岸防衛隊找到他時，救生艇已經漏氣了。

放出（輪胎、氣球等的）空氣
v. let air or gas out of

0218 inflate [ɪnˋflet] * in-=in ★★★★★

It was difficult for me to inflate my float tube. However hard I tried to blow it up, it didn't expand. At last I found out that it was punctured.

我很難把浮艇充氣，無論多麼努力地試著充氣，它就是不膨脹。最後才發現原來它破了。

充氣，使膨脹
v. blow up; pump up; distend; expand; swell

0219 innovation [ˌɪnəˋveʃən] * nov=new ★★★★★

Without technical innovations, a breakthrough in this country's economy seems unlikely.

這個國家欠缺科技創新，似乎不太可能有經濟上的突破。

創新
n. modernization

0220 renovation [ˌrɛnəˋveʃən] * re-=again ★★★★★

Sophisticated scientific and technological renovations are needed to reduce air pollution. Heavily polluted air sears our eyes and blackens our lungs.

降低空氣污染需要精密科技上的革新。嚴重污染的空氣不但會讓我們的雙眼乾澀，還會導致肺部變黑，影響肺臟功能。

革新
n. restoration

0221 retribution [ˌrɛtrəˋbjuʃən] * tribut=give ★☆☆☆☆

Some claim that the despot's death was divine retribution for his evil deeds. He had ordered the death of more than a hundred people.

有些人宣稱這名獨裁者之所以走上絕路，是因其惡行而遭天譴。他曾下令殺害一百多名民眾。

報應，天譴
n. retaliation; revenge

0222 contribute [kənˋtrɪbjut] * con-=together ★★★★★

The pop singer wanted to contribute to the Olympic team. He organized and put on a fund-raising dinner and donated the proceeds to the athletes.

這位流行歌手想要捐助奧林匹克代表隊，於是組織募款餐會並上台表演，接著將募款所得捐贈給運動員。

捐助，捐獻
v. donate; give; grant

0223 consummate [ˋkɑnsəˌmet] * sum=sum ★★★★★

Margaret Mitchell had devoted to *Gone with the Wind* many years of her short life and had acquired consummate skill.

美國作家瑪格麗特‧米契爾為了《飄》這部小說奉獻了短暫生命中的許多光陰，同時累積了熟練的寫作技巧。

熟練的，完美的
a. complete; perfect

0224 **summa cum laude** [ˌsʌməˌkʌm ˈlɔdɪ] * laud=praise

★☆☆☆☆

I never went to collage. I shall always regret the fact. I don't think I should have a cent more to my name today if I had been graduated from Harvard, summa cum laude.

I Never Went to College ── Calvin Kinney

我未曾上過大學,並將永遠為此事實後悔。然而即使以最高榮譽畢業於哈佛大學,我也不認為今天可以獲得超過我應得的任何一分錢。

──《我未曾上過大學》凱文‧肯尼

以最高榮譽(記載在畢業證書等的文字)
a. of the highest standard; with the highest distinction

0225 **applaud** [əˈplɔd] * ap-, ad-=to

★★★★☆

I went to the television station to see the live taping of a show and was surprised when the director instructed the audience when to applaud and when not to.

我到電視台參觀現場錄影秀,卻驚訝地發現導演指揮觀眾何時要鼓掌喝采,何時要保持安靜。

鼓掌喝采
v. give a person a big hand; clap in approval

0226 **adorn** [əˈdɔrn] * orn=embellish

★★★★☆

Many rich people adorn themselves with gold and jewels. They believe that they will look more attractive if they decorate themselves with the stuff.

許多有錢人喜歡配戴金飾和珠寶,他們相信如果用這些東西來裝飾自己會看起來更具吸引力。

配戴,使生色
v. mbellish; decorate

0227 **ornament** [ˈɔrnəmənt] * -ment=ending for a noun

★★★★☆

The nurse chose not to wear any jewelry since she felt that any expensive ornament would be inappropriate while she was working in such a poor country.

護士選擇不配戴任何珠寶首飾,因為她覺得既然是在如此貧窮的鄉間工作,任何高價飾品都是不恰當的。

裝飾(品)
n. decoration; accessory

0228 **confinement** [kənˈfaɪnmənt] * fin=boundary

★★★★☆

Prisoner Ted was the instigator in the fight between the two inmates and therefore was assigned to two weeks in solitary confinement.

囚犯泰德因教唆獄中兩群囚犯互鬥,被判處兩周的單獨監禁。

監禁,禁閉,拘禁
n. captivity; detention

0229 **definition** [ˌdɛfəˈnɪʃən] * de-=down

★★★★★

I couldn't really understand what Steve was trying to say because I didn't know his definition of the words that he was using.

我真的不懂史帝夫想說些什麼,因為我不明白他的遣辭用句定義。

定義
n. description; clarification; demarcation

0230 **defer** [dɪˈfɝ] * fer=carry, put

★★★★☆

She always had to defer to her father's wishes, whether or not she agreed with him. He wishes that she would be back home no later than 8 o'clock in the evening.

她總是必須服從父親的期望,無論她是否贊同他的意見。父親希望她能在晚上八點前返家。

服從,順從 / 延緩,延期
v. bow; yield; acquiesce; accede / postpone; delay

0231 prefer [prɪ`fɝ] * pre-=before

★★★★★

Peggy prefers hamburgers to delicate French cuisine. No wonder why she has a weight problem.

佩姬偏愛漢堡而不喜歡吃精緻的法國菜餚，難怪她有體重增加的問題。

偏愛，比較喜歡，寧願
v. *favor; like better*

0232 preface [`prɛfɪs] * fac=make

★★★★★

An author usually acknowledges his purpose in the preface of his book. Therefore, it is important to read it to understand the author's intention.

作者經常會在自己書中的序言表明寫作目的，因此為了掌握作者的寫作意圖，閱讀序言是很重要的。

序言
n. *introduction; foreword; prologue; preamble*

0233 artifact [`ɑrtɪ,fækt] * art-=art, skill

★★★★★

Korea has a lot of excellent artifacts handed down from Koryo times, almost all of them excavated from tombs.

韓國有許多自高麗時代傳承下來的精緻手工藝品，絕大多數都是從古墓中挖掘出來的。

（古代的）手工藝品
n. *a product of prehistoric or aboriginal workmanship*

0234 artisan [`ɑrtəzn̩] * san=person

★★★★☆

My uncle is a good artisan and builds shelves better than anyone I know. I have been using a shelf he made for me 3 years ago.

我的舅舅是非常優秀的工匠，他製作的書架比任何人都要好，我現在所用的書架就是他三年前為我做的。

工匠，手藝師傅，技工
n. *a skilled worker*

0235 partisan [`pɑrtəzn̩] * parti-=party

★☆☆☆☆

Partisan politics is a very confusing system of government since everyone must choose a side to support, but yet everyone has to work together to achieve harmony.

政黨政治是一套相當令人混淆的政治系統，因為它要求每個人都必須選邊站，但又必須和他人合作以求和諧。

黨派的／黨人，（黨派等的）強硬支持者
a. *of or characteristic of partisans /* **n.** *a strong, esp. unreasoning, supporter of a party*

0236 impart [ɪm`pɑrt] * im-=in, on

★★☆☆☆

Since the chairman was getting older he was starting to think about preparing for death. He sat down and prepared his will and decided how he was going to impart his belongings to his children.

由於董事長日益衰老，他開始思考如何規劃身後事。他著手草擬遺囑並決定如何將財產分給子女。

分給，給予
v. *transmit; convey*

0237 impetus [`ɪmpətəs] * pet=force, strive

★★★★☆

The grant for building a new playground at that school gave impetus to both the teachers and students.

在該校建造新操場的政府補助，鼓舞了師生們的士氣。

促進，刺激，鼓動
n. *impulse; driving force; stimulus; incentive; drive*

0238 compete [kəm`pit] * com-=together

★★★★★

Competition can be a very good thing because the best is brought out in us when we compete with other people.

競爭可以是件非常好的事，因為透過和他人之間的相互競爭，可以激發出我們最好的表現。

競爭，對抗
v. *ontend; vie; struggle; fight; battle*

0239 compress [kəm`prɛs] * press-=press ★☆☆☆☆

The blacksmith got a third-degree burn on his arm and applied a cold compress to the burnt area and it felt much better.

鐵匠的手臂受到三級燒傷，燒傷的傷口敷上冷壓布後他感覺好多了。

壓縮，壓緊／（壓貼在傷口以止血或退燒的）壓布，繃帶
v. press / *n.* a pad pressed on part of the body to relieve inflammation, stop bleeding, etc.

0240 depressed [dɪ`prɛst] * de-=down ★★★☆☆

You look depressed. Cheer up. I'm sure you'll pass the exam, because you have been studying hard for long enough.

你看起來十分消沉，開心點。我相信你考試一定會及格，因為你已經花了很多時間溫書。

沮喪的，消沉的
a. dispirited

0241 deficient [dɪ`fɪʃənt] * fic=make, do ★★★☆☆

Whenever I get a canker sore, I know that my body is vitamin B deficient and so I take some vitamins to replenish my body.

每當我口腔潰瘍，就知道自己的身體缺乏維生素 B，我會補充一些維他命。

不足的，缺乏的
a. incomplete; faulty; impaired; flawed; inadequate; insufficient

0242 magnificent [mæg`nɪfəsṇt] * magn-=big ★★★☆☆

"Leaves. On the ivy vine. When the last one falls I must go, too. I've known that for three days. Didn't the doctor tell you?" "Oh, I never heard of such nonsense," complained Sue, with magnificent scorn.

The Last Leaf —— O. Henry

「藤蔓上的葉子啊，當最後一片藤葉掉落時，也是我生命走到盡頭的時候。三天前我就知道會是這個結局，難道醫生沒有告訴妳嗎？」蘇以充滿嘲弄的語氣抱怨道：「噢，我沒聽過這種胡說八道的話。」

——《最後一片藤葉》歐·亨利

莊嚴的，壯麗的，大的
a. grand; impressive; stately

0243 magniloquent [mæg`nɪləkwənt] * log=words, say ★★☆☆☆

Bernard often uses magniloquent words and phrases obliquely and most often leaves us confused.

伯納德經常轉彎抹角使用誇張字詞，而且總是讓我們感到困惑。

誇張的，誇大的，吹牛的
a. boastful; grandiose in speech

0244 eloquent [`ɛləkwənt] * e-=out ★★★★☆

In a very eloquent speech, the President promised that there wouldn't be new taxes in the coming year.

總統以十分具有說服力的演說，承諾來年不會加稅。

（口才或文章）動人的，具有說服力的
a. rhetorical; convincing; cogent; persuasive

0245 evince [ɪ`vɪns] * vinc=go ★★★★☆

A dog usually evinces its dislike of strangers by growling. I wish my dog would only growl instead of biting a stranger at first sight.

狗總是以咆哮來表現對陌生人的厭惡，我真希望我的狗在看到陌生人的第一眼時，只要吼叫就好，不要咬人。

表現出（情感等）
v. indicate; make evident; demonstrate

0246 invincible [ɪn`vɪnsəbḷ] * in-=not ★★★☆☆

Many thought Spain was invincible until the loss of her mighty Armada. Queen Elizabeth I defeated the Armada.

在西班牙喪失強大無敵艦隊前，許多人認為她是無法征服的。無敵艦隊最後被英國女王伊麗莎白一世擊敗。

無敵的，無法征服的
a. *unconquerable; unbeatable; indomitable; insuperable; unassailable; impregnable*

0247 incontrovertible [ˌɪnkɑntrə`vɝtəbḷ] * contr=against ★★★★☆

The prosecuting attorney had collected so much incontrovertible evidence that he knew he would have an open-and-shut case before he set foot in the court room.

檢察官已蒐集到許多不容置疑的證據，他知道當自己踏入法庭時手上握有明顯易斷的案件。

不容置疑的，沒有爭辯餘地的
a. *indisputable; indubitable; undeniable; unquestionable*

0248 contretemps [`kɑntrətɑn] * tempo=moment ★☆☆☆☆

It was quite a great contretemps for Jason to spill pumpkin soup on the president's wife at the company party.

對傑生來說，在公司宴會上把南瓜湯灑到總裁夫人身上，真是件天大窘事。

窘困之事，不幸的意外
n. *misfortune; an unexpected mishap*

0249 extemporaneous [ɪkˌstɛmpə`renɪəs] * ex-=out ★★☆☆☆

William is an extemporaneous, wild and crazy guy who does things right off the top of his head that no one else would think of doing.

威廉是個隨興所至的狂野傢伙，總是想到什麼就立刻去做，而那些事是其他人想都沒想過的。

隨興而至的，即席的
a. *impromptu; improvised; extemporized; extempore; unprepared; ad lib*

0250 explode [ɪk`splod] * plod-=burst ★★★☆☆

The game was tied with 5 seconds left on the clock and George caused the crowd to explode when he shot the ball from half court and sank the game-winning basket right at the buzzer.

比賽距離終場還有五秒鐘，雙方戰成平手，喬治在半場線上跳投長射，觀眾群情激動，這記致勝之球在終場鈴響時投進。

使激發（情感等），爆炸
v. *blow up; go off; burst; detonate; erupt*

Tea Time... ☕

<Ancient philosophy>
Quintessence
In ancient philosophy quintessence, known as the fifth essence, was supposed to be the constituent matter of the heavenly bodies, the others being air, fire, earth, and water.

〈古代哲學思想〉純質，精髓
在古代哲學思想中，純質又稱為第五元素，是構成宇宙的五大元素之一，其他四者為氣、火、土、水。

❖ **quintessence** [kwɪn`tɛsn̩s] **n.** *the most essential part of any substance; core; nub* │ 典型，代表

Adolf Hitler, although he was a political genius, was the quintessence of evil in the twentieth century.

希特勒雖然是政治天才，但同時也是二十世紀邪惡的代表。

1

Complete each word by filling in the blank with proper spelling so that it has the same meaning as suggested. Then please write the meaning of each word in Chinese.

1. 綽號	= _ _ _ t h e t	11. emigrate	= _____
2. 假設的	= _ _ _ _ t h e t i c a l	12. delimit	= _____
3. 莊嚴的	= _ _ _ _ _ f i c e n t	13. inflate	= _____
4. 驅散人群	= _ _ s p e r s e	14. retribution	= _____
5. 擁護者	= _ _ _ p o n e n t	15. consummate	= _____
6. 革新	= _ _ n o v a t i o n	16. adorn	= _____
7. 節省的	= e c o _ _ _ i c a l	17. confinement	= _____
8. 大災難	= _ _ _ a s t e r	18. explode	= _____
9. 有利的	= _ _ _ s p e r o u s	19. artisan	= _____
10. 默認的	= _ _ p l i c i t	20. impart	= _____

2

Choose a word that best completes the sentence.

21. Mr. Brown has keen business acumen, and therefore his business has been

  _____.

(A) prosperous   (B) explicit   (C) depressed   (D) implicit

22. The archaeologist has excavated many _____ from the ancient tomb.

(A) artifacts   (B) partisans   (C) artisans   (D) proponents

23. A tsunami _____ in Southeast Asia claimed tens of thousands of lives.

(A) exponent   (B) innovation   (C) disaster   (D) preface

3

The highlighted word is closest in meaning to which of the following?

24. On the second day of camping: "Hey, kids, which would you `prefer` on your bread, butter with sand or honey with ants?

(A) like better   (B) make evident   (C) blow up   (D) pump up

25. Jane looked `depressed` when she was stepping out of the examination room. Her friends tried to cheer her up.

(A) dispirited   (B) deficient   (C) magnificent   (D) eloquent

MP3 12

0251 implode [ɪm`plod] * im-=in   ★★☆☆☆

The Russian submarine sank to the bottom of the ocean and the resulting pressure of the water caused it to implode, unfortunately killing everyone aboard.

俄國潛艇沉到海底，水壓使潛艇內爆，潛艇上所有人員都不幸罹難。

內爆，向內聚爆
v. burst inwards

0252 impel [ɪm`pɛl] * pel=drive   ★★★★★

One of the common denominators among champions is that they all have an aggressive coach or trainer behind them impelling them to do their best all the time.

優勝者的共同點之一在於他們背後都有一位非常積極進取的教練或訓練師，能夠激勵他們不斷追求最佳表現。

驅使，激勵
v. drive forward; propel; force

0253 propeller [prə`pɛlə] * pro-=forward, beforehand   ★★★★★

Old fashioned planes used at least one propeller to power their flight, but nowadays jets use stronger engines.

舊式飛機要靠至少一個推進器才能發動，現在的噴射機則使用較強的飛行引擎。

推進器，螺旋槳
n. a revolving shaft with blades, esp. for propelling a ship or aircraft

0254 protection [prə`tɛkʃən] * tect=cover   ★★★★★

Police protection was requested by the witness. He was afraid of any form of retaliation from the defendant.

證人要求警方保護，因為他擔心來自被告的任何報復行為。

保護，庇護
n. care; guardianship; custody; preservation

0255 detect [dɪ`tɛkt] * de-=away   ★★★★★

Christopher said that he had not been drinking, but the police officer detected alcohol on his breath by administering the breathalyzer test to him.

克里斯多夫表示他並沒有飲酒，但警方用酒測器檢測出他的呼吸中含有酒精。

發現，查出，看穿
v. uncover; find out; discover; notice; spot

0256 detach [dɪ`tætʃ] * tach=touch   ★★★★☆

Some insects, while in the nymph stage of development, attach themselves to rocks on the bottom of the stream and when they are ready to hatch, they detach themselves, float to the surface, dry their newly developed wings and fly away.

有些昆蟲在成蛹階段會先依附在溪流底的岩石上。當牠們準備好孵化時才跟蛹分離，順勢漂浮在水面上，等到新生羽化的翅膀乾了就可以飛離水面。

分開，分離
v. separate; disjoin; disengage; disconnect; cut off

0257 attaché [ˌætə`ʃe] * at-, ad-=near   ★☆☆☆☆

John enjoys his job as an attache to the ambassador because of the opportunities to travel and see the world.

約翰很喜歡大使隨行人員的工作，因為可藉此機會遍覽世界各地。

大使隨行人員
n. a person appointed to an ambassador's staff usu. with a special sphere of activity

Chapter

1
2
3
4
5

0258 **attain** [əˋten] * -tain=hold ★★★★★

It has taken many years of persistent study and dedication to attain enough knowledge to do my business.

要做我這一行需要歷經多年不間斷的學習和奉獻，以獲得足夠的專業知識。

獲得，達到（目的或願望等）
v. *gain; accomplish*

0259 **contain** [kənˋten] * con-=together ★★★★★

You should read this book because it contains a lot of additional information of what you are studying in school.

你應該閱讀這本書，因為書中包含許多在校學習的額外資訊。

包含，含有
v. *hold; include; comprise; lodge*

0260 **collateral** [kəˋlætərəl] * lateral=side ★★★★☆

I didn't want to but I had to offer my house as collateral for the business loan because I didn't have other assets that qualified me for the loan.

我雖然不願意，但還是必須把我的房子作為抵押擔保以取得企業融資貸款，因為我沒有其他可用來借貸的資產。

抵押擔保 / 並行的 / 附帶的
n. *security* / **a.** *parallel* / *additional*

0261 **equilateral** [ˌikwəˋlætərəl] * equi-=equal ★★★☆☆

The three sides of an equilateral triangle measure the same. A triangle that has only two sides equal in length is called an isosceles triangle.

等邊三角形的三邊量起來是等長的，至於兩邊等長、但第三邊不等長的三角形則稱為等腰三角形。

等邊的
a. *having all its sides equal in length*

0262 **equivocal** [ɪˋkwɪvəkḷ] * voc=call ★★★★☆

Sam's essay was filled with equivocal points so the teacher was certain that he had not done all the required reading and was trying to pretend he had.

山姆的論文裡充滿了模稜兩可的觀點，老師因此相信他並未讀完所有指定教材，卻試圖假裝已讀完。

模稜兩可的，含糊不清的
a. *of double or doubtful meaning; ambiguous; indistinct; confused; uncertain*

0263 **provocation** [ˌprɑvəˋkeʃən] * pro-=before ★★★★☆

After much provocation and many insults, not to mention a punch or two, the Champion was forced to beat up his would-be robbers.

經過一連串挑釁和羞辱，同時還挨了一、兩拳後，冠軍得主被迫出手痛毆打算搶劫他的搶匪。

挑釁，激怒
n. *incitement; instigation*

0264 **prognosis** [prɑgˋnosɪs] * gno=know ★★★☆☆

The doctor's prognosis should be re-evaluated through a more thorough examination. So please don't be so depressed.

醫生要經過更詳細的檢查才能重新評估預後情形，所以請不要太沮喪。

（醫師根據經驗判斷疾病發展情況的）預後
n. *forecast; prognostication*

0265 **diagnose** [ˌdaɪəgˋnos] * dia-=through ★★★★☆

The doctor diagnosed Raymond's case as pneumonia. But after a closer examination it was found that he was suffering from tuberculosis (T.B.).

醫師原本診斷雷蒙得了肺炎，但經過更仔細的檢查後發現其實他感染了肺結核。

診斷
v. *make a diagnosis of a disease from its symptoms*

0266 diathermy [ˈdaɪəˌθɝmɪ] * therm=heat ★☆☆☆☆

Diathermy is a very useful and therapeutic way of warming parts of the body using electromagnetic energy.

利用電磁讓身體暖和起來的電療是很有效的治療方式。

電療
n. the application of high frequency electric currents to produce heat in the deeper tissues of the body

---

0267 thermoplastic [ˌθɝmoˈplæstɪk] * plast-=form ★★☆☆☆

The use of thermoplastic items, like Styrofoam, which is solid when cool, but soft when it is hot, allows for great convenience of shape and size.

聚苯乙烯等可熱塑物料具有冷硬熱軟的性質，很適合用來塑造特定形狀和尺寸。

熱塑性的，（塑料等）可熱塑的
a. (of a substance) that becomes plastic on heating

0268 protoplasm [ˈprotəˌplæzəm] * proto-=first ★★★★★

A drop of protoplasm holds within itself the germ of life. Even if we put all of the material of all the world's people in one place, it would be less than a spoonful.

單單一小滴原生質就蘊含生命的起源。即使把全世界人類都集中在一起，也不會超過一匙的量。

原生質
n. the material comprising the living part of a cell

0269 protozoan [ˌprotəˈzoən] * zo=animal ★★★★☆

Any one of the single-celled microscopic organisms that some believe are the original form of life are called protozoan.

一些人相信單細胞微小有機體是生命最原始的形式，他們稱為原生動物。

原生動物
n. unicellular and microscopic organism of the subkingdom protozoa

---

0270 zoology [zoˈɑlədʒɪ] * -logy-=study ★★★★★

Zoology is the scientific study of various kinds of animals and is one of the important fields of biology.

動物學是研究各種動物的一門科學，也是相當重要的生物學分支之一。

動物學
n. the scientific study of animals

0271 morphology [mɔrˈfɑlədʒɪ] * morpho-=form ★★★☆☆

Morphology is a field of linguistics and is mainly concerned with the forms of words.

形態學屬於語言學的範疇，主要在探討字詞的形態變化。

（語言）形態學
n. the system of forms in a language

0272 amorphous [əˈmɔrfəs] * a-=no ★★★☆☆

Air is one of the most common amorphous substances known to man. It has no definite form.

眾所周知，本身沒有確切形狀的空氣是最普遍的無定形物質之一。

無定形的，難以歸類的
a. shapeless; having neither definite form nor structure

0273 abyss [əˈbɪs] * -byss=base ★★★★★

Some abysses at the bottom of the ocean are so deep and dark that scientists have a hard time gathering helpful information.

有些位於海洋深處的深淵既深又暗，使科學家很難收集有用資訊。

深淵
n. unfathomable depths; bottomless chaos

1

2

3

4

5

0274 abase [ə`bes] * a-=to ★★★☆☆

Before meeting Jimmy, I thought I was a good tennis player, but I felt abased after watching his flawless match.

遇到吉米前我以為自己是很棒的網球選手，等到看過他無懈可擊的比賽後，才覺得自己被比下去。

降低（地位、身份、階級等），使卑下
v. *degrade; humiliate*

0275 aver [ə`vɜ] * ver=truth ★★★☆☆

The witness averred the story told by the defendant and as a result the defend-ant was set free.

由於證人證實被告所言屬實，結果被告獲得無罪釋放。

確言（某事的真實性），（法律上的）證實
v. *affirm; assert; declare*

MP3 13

0276 verdict [`vɜdɪkt] * dict=say ★★★★☆

The twelve members of the jury couldn't reach a verdict. They were not sure whether the defendant was innocent or guilty.

陪審團十二名成員無法達成判決。他們無法確定被告是無辜或有罪的。

（法庭陪審團的）判決，裁決
n. *decision; judgment; sentence*

0277 indict [ɪn`daɪt] * in-=in ★★★★☆

The union leader who had been leading the national union was indicted for violating national security laws.

全國工會領袖因違反國家安全法遭到起訴。

起訴
v. *accuse; charge; prosecute*

0278 insurrection [ˌɪnsə`rɛkʃən] * sur-=up ★★☆☆☆

The rebels' insurrection spread into a civil war. However at the last moment the uprising was put down by the government.

造反者的暴動發展為內戰，最後被政府弭平。

暴動，叛亂
n. *rebellion; uprising*

0279 surfeit [`sɜfɪt] * feit=do, make ★★★☆☆

There was a surfeit amount of food at the banquet and no one could eat it all, try as they might.

宴會上的食物太多沒人吃得完，大家只能盡量吃。

暴飲暴食 / 過度，過多
n. *an excess in eating / excess; glut; plethora; surplus; oversupply*

0280 forfeit [`fɔrfɪt] * for-=outdoors ★★★☆☆

He was a very popular businessman in his community and was given the chance to run for that state's senatorial seat. Later he was forced to forfeit his reputation because of a certain rumor.

他在商界富有盛名並獲得角逐州參議員席次的機會，但後來因某項傳聞失去聲望。

（因犯罪、受罰等而）喪失，失去（權利、名譽等）
v. *lose the right to; be deprived of*

0281 foreign [`fɔrɪn] * reign=reign ★★★★★

I think that it is very important that everyone have an opportunity to live in a foreign country so that he can see how different people of the world really are.

我認為人人有旅居海外的機會是很重要的，如此一來就可以見證世上的人民是多麼的不同。

外國的 / 異國的，外來的
a. *alien; overseas; external / outlandish; exotic*

0282 sovereign [ˈsɑvrɪn] * sover-, super-=top ★★★☆☆

元首，最高統治者
n. *supreme ruler; monarch*

Queen Elizabeth I was the sovereign who conquered the Invincible Armada and proved the power of the English navy.

伊麗莎白一世女王是戰勝西班牙無敵艦隊的英國最高統治者，並證明英國海軍艦隊的實力。

0283 superstition [ˌsupəˈstɪʃən] * stit=stand ★★★☆☆

迷信，迷信行為
n. *credulity regarding the supernatural*

Superstition is incompatible with the scientific tradition. Beliefs in supernatural beings cannot be explained by science.

迷信和科學慣例是相互矛盾的，對超自然存在的信仰無法用科學解釋。

0284 prostitution [ˌprɑstəˈtuʃən] * pro-=before ★☆☆☆☆

賣淫
n. *whoredom*

Some believe that prostitution serves a necessary but unwanted function in society. They insist that without whoredom a society would have higher crime rates.

有些人相信賣淫為社會群體滿足必要但不樂見的目的。這些人堅稱若少了賣淫，社會犯罪率會更高。

0285 prognosticate [prɑgˈnɑstɪˌket] * gno, cogno=know ★☆☆☆☆

預告，預知
v. *foretell; foresee; prophesy*

The early arrival of winter birds prognosticated an early winter. In the middle of October the temperature plummeted to below freezing.

早到的冬季候鳥預告了早冬的來臨，十月中旬氣溫便一路下滑到零度以下。

0286 recognize [ˈrɛkəgˌnɑɪz] * re-=again ★★★★★

認出，認識
v. *identify (a person or thing) as already known; realize*

I didn't recognize the man whom I had met the day before. I think I have an extremely poor memory.

我未能認出前一天遇到的男子，我想我的記性真的很差。

0287 regenerate [rɪˈdʒɛnəˌret] * gen=birth ★★★★★

使（生物組織等）再生
v. *generate again; improve*

An iguana chooses to sever part of its tail when it is inevitable, but it is able to regenerate its lost tail.

蜥蜴遇到無法避免的情況時會斷尾求生，但能再生出失去的尾巴。

0288 progenitor [proˈdʒɛnətɚ] * pro-=beforehand, before ★★★★☆

（人、動物等的）祖先
n. *ancestor; predecessor; forerunner; precursor; antecedent*

After he claimed the throne for himself, he became the progenitor of a line of kings that ruled the small country for several hundred years.

他聲稱王位歸其所有後，便成為統治小國達數百年之久的王室直系祖先。

0289 protrude [proˈtrud] * trud=thrust; stick ★★★★☆

使突出，使伸出
v. *stick out; jut out; project; thrust out; poke out*

The doctor said that it was necessary to operate to correct the position of the visibly protruding bone.

醫生表示須開刀導正明顯突出的骨頭部位。

0290 extrude [ɛk`strud] * ex-=out ★☆☆☆☆

It had been rude of them to say so but it was true; her nose did extrude from her face more than was considered usual.

他們這麼說固然無禮卻也是事實，她的鼻子真的不正常突起。

突出
v. *thrust out*

0291 extortionate [ɪk`stɔrʃənɪt] * tort=twist ★★☆☆☆

The extortionate Chief Accountant was fired, charged with embezzlement and imprisoned for life after it was discovered that he had been stealing from the city treasury for nearly twenty years.

貪婪會計長被發現盜用都市公庫經費近二十年後，遭到免職並被控侵吞公款，最後獲判終生監禁。

（人或行為等）強索的，勒索的，貪婪的
a. *rapacious*

0292 affectation [ˌæfɛk`teʃən] * af-, ad-=to, fec=do, make ★★★☆☆

Even though Todd was from America, he spoke with a British accent, which was only one affectation that annoyed his friends.

陶德雖來自美國卻操著一口英國腔，這種裝腔作勢是讓友人們唯一感到不快的事。

裝模作樣，矯揉造作，裝腔作勢
n. *pretension; false display; airs*

0293 affliction [ə`flɪkʃən] * flict=strike ★★★★★

A study showed that there was a relationship between the amount of love or affection shown to an injured animal and the rate at which the animal recovers from its affliction.

一項研究指出，當動物受傷時人類付出的疼愛和關心，與牠從痛苦中復原的速度之間具有某種程度的關連。

（身心的）痛苦，折磨
n. *hardship; misery; misfortune; distress; ordeal; trial; tribulation; torture; adversity; suffering; agony*

0294 inflict [ɪn`flɪkt] * in-=in ★★★★★

Barbara couldn't help but inflict pain on the man who had lied and broken her heart. She felt it was justified.

芭芭拉不得不傷害欺騙她又讓她傷心的男子，她覺得這麼做理由正當。

給予（打擊、痛苦等），施以（懲罰、判刑等），使遭受（損傷等）
v. *impose suffering on*

0295 infect [ɪn`fɛkt] * fect=do, make ★★★★★

Most people say that you can't get the HIV virus through kissing, but no one really knows exactly how you can be infected with the virus.

多數人說接吻不會感染愛滋病毒，但是沒人真的知道到底怎樣會被傳染。

（醫學上的）傳染，感染
v. *affect a person with disease*

0296 effective [ə`fɛktɪv] * ef-, ex-=out ★★★★★

The goal of this policy is to decrease the traffic accidents in this city, but un-fortunately, the policy has not been very effective.

這項政策的目的在於降低都市交通意外，不幸的是並非十分有效。

有效的，有作用的
a. *having a desired effect; efficacious; effectual*

0297 **effort** [`ɛfət] * fort=force ★★★★★

努力，成果
n. endeavor; try; attempt

We made an effort to arrive on time, but there was a terrible traffic jam on the way here. We were stuck in traffic more than 30 minutes.

我們盡量準時到達但路上卻出現可怕大塞車，害我們塞在車陣裡超過半小時。

0298 **afford** [ə`ford] * af-, ad-=to ★★★★★

力足以～，～得起
v. have the money for

Now we can afford the utility vehicle. We have saved our pennies for more than a couple of years.

這幾年來我們一直努力存下每一分錢，所以現在供得起多功能休旅車了。

0299 **adduce** [ə`dus] * duce=draw ★★★★☆

引用
v. cite as an instance or as proof or evidence

Jack was able to adduce Shakespeare during a debate over Macbeth at his university, which truly impressed his professor who believed that he hadn't done his homework.

傑克在一場關於馬克白的大學辯論會上引用莎士比亞的話，讓以為傑克沒做好會前準備工作的教授印象深刻。

0300 **deducible** [dɪ`djusəbl] * de-=down ★★★★☆

可推論的，可推斷的
a. can be inferred

This is not a deducible problem. We have to come to a solution based on the facts as they present themselves.

這不是一個推論式問題，我們須根據客觀事實得出解決方案。

Tea Time...

<French story> Chauvinism
After Nicholas Chauvin, a devoted soldier and overzealous supporter of Napoleon Bonaparte.

〈法國歷史故事〉盲目愛國精神
本字源自狂熱支持拿破崙的法國虔誠士兵尼古拉‧沙文。
（註：後世將此字引申為著名的「沙文主義」一詞，用來表示對自己所屬的國家、民族、團體或性別過於自傲，而以帶有偏見的自大眼光輕視其他族群。）

❖ **chauvinist** [`ʃovɪnɪst] *n. a person displaying chauvinism* | 沙文主義者

We call Mr. Morris a male chauvinist because he believes that a man is better than a woman and a woman has to be subordinate to a man.

我們稱莫里斯先生為男性沙文主義者，因為他認為男性比女性優越，女性應該服從男性。

Review Test 06

1 Complete each word by filling in the blank with proper spelling so that it has the same meaning as suggested. Then please write the meaning of each word in Chinese.

1. 驅使　　　　＝ __p e l
2. 引用　　　　＝ a d _ _ _ _
3. 買得起　　　＝ a f _ _ _ _
4. 有效的　　　＝ e f _ _ _ t i v e
5. 感染　　　　＝ __f e c t
6. 保護　　　　＝ p r o _ _ _ _ i o n
7. 大使隨行人員＝ __t a c h é
8. 抵押擔保品　＝ c o l _ _ _ _ _ _ _
9. 等邊的　　　＝ _ _ _ _ l a t e r a l
10. 挑釁　　　　＝ _ _ _ v o c a t i o n

11. diathermy　　＝ _____
12. protoplasm　 ＝ _____
13. zoology　　　＝ _____
14. amorphous　 ＝ _____
15. verdict　　　＝ _____
16. insurrection 　＝ _____
17. superstition　＝ _____
18. regenerate　 ＝ _____
19. progenitor　 ＝ _____
20. extortionate　＝ _____

2 Choose a word that best completes the sentence.

21. **An experienced aviator said to a novice, "A _____ is like an electric fan. If it stops, you will start to sweat."**

    (A) collateral　　　(B) propeller　　　(C) verdict　　　(D) protozoan

22. **Please never mention her _____ chin. I am afraid she will be mad.**

    (A) protruding　　　(B) recognizing　　　(C) forfeiting　　　(D) indicting

3 The highlighted word is closest in meaning to which of the following?

23. **The tectonic plates which carry heavy ocean floors sink down to the abyss when plates collide.**

    (A) bottomless depth　　(B) insurrection　　　(C) abase　　　(D) generate again

24. **It is said that hot tea is very effective in preventing a cold.**

    (A) deducible　　　(B) extortionate　　　(C) thermoplastic　　　(D) efficacious

25. **Judge Smith could not reach a verdict . At last he decided to postpone the session.**

    (A) decision　　　(B) progenitor　　　(C) surfeit　　　(D) rebellion

MP3
14

0301 destitution [ˌdɛstə`tjuʃən] * stit=stand ★★★★☆

窮困，貧乏
n. poverty; need; indigence

It was really something to go to the country and see the destruction of the land and the properties as well as the destitution of the people that has been caused by the civil war that has lingered for seven years in that country.

到該國看看七年內戰對土地和屋舍造成的毀壞，以及給人民帶來的窮困，是極具意義的。

0302 constituent [kən`stɪtʃuənt] * -ent=person, thing ★★★★☆

選舉人／組成要素
n. a person who appoints another as agent; a component part

In their country the number of constituents that each state is allowed during an election is determined by the population of that state.

在他們的國家，各州在選舉期間依法可有多少選舉人票，是根據該州人口來決定的。

0303 resident [`rɛzədənt] * sid=sit ★★★★★

居民，居住者
n. dweller; inhabitant; citizen; denizen; occupant

The exodus of rural residents in search of higher incomes was a usual phenomenon in our country in the 1970's.

我國七○年代農業人口普遍移居海外以追求更高收入。

0304 preside [prɪ`zaɪd] * pre-=before ★★★★★

主持，擔任會議主席
v. be in a position of authority, esp. as the chairperson or president of a meeting; supervise

Mr. Algier does not like to preside over a wedding because he's always nervous before the public.

阿爾吉爾先生不喜歡主持婚禮儀式，因為他在公開場合很容易緊張。

0305 precise [prɪ`saɪs] * cis=cut ★★★★★

精確的，準確的
a. exact; accurate; correct

Jack Ericson gave the carpenter precise measurements, but the carpenter still didn't make the cabinet correctly and it didn't fit in his kitchen.

傑克・艾利克森把櫥櫃的精確尺寸交給木工師傅，但師傅仍沒有準確做出櫥櫃，不合傑克家的廚房尺寸。

0306 circumcise [`sɝkəmˌsaɪz] * circum-=around ★☆☆☆☆

割包皮
v. cut off the foreskin, as a Jewish or Muslim rite or a surgical operation

In the past, most doctors felt very strongly that newborn males needed to be circumcised, but nowadays, because of improved hygiene many doctors are becoming more lax about circumcision.

過去多數醫生都堅持新生男嬰需割包皮。時至今日因衛生條件改善，許多醫生對割包皮的必要性已不再堅持。

0307 circumlocution [ˌsɝkəmlo`kjuʃən] * loc=words, say ★★☆☆☆

婉轉說法，委婉用語
n. a roundabout expression; periphrasis; euphemism

There are many circumlocutions about money matters: "We would appreciate your early attention to this matter," or "May we look forward to an early remittance?"

談論金錢有許多委婉用法，例如：「如能盡速關照此事，我等將深表感激」或「祈盼盡快匯款」等。

0308 grandiloquent [græn`dɪləkwənt] * grand-=big ★★☆☆☆

Since the politician was famous, people forgave him his grandiloquent speaking style, but his fame didn't stop people from thinking he was a liar.

政治人物的高知名度使大家原諒他誇大其辭的說話方式，但仍不免視他為說謊者。

（言論）誇張的，誇大其辭的
a. *pompous; bombastic; ostentatious; pedantic; ornate; showy*

0309 aggrandize [ə`græn͵daɪz] * ag-, ad-=to ★★★☆☆

A good business plan is almost sure to aggrandize a business and ultimately leads to success.

好的企業經營計畫幾乎一定會擴大企業版圖，最後也能帶來成功。

擴大（企業版圖等），提高（個人地位、國家重要性等）
v. *increase the power, rank or wealth; cause to appear greater than is the case*

0310 aggressive [ə`grɛsɪv] * gress=go ★★★★★

My badminton trainer is too aggressive for me to talk to. She often shouts at me with her eyes wide open.

我的羽球教練太有衝勁以致很難溝通，她常瞪大眼睛對我大吼大叫。

好戰的，好鬥的 / 有衝勁的，積極進取的
a. *combative; antagonistic; warlike; belligerent; bellicose; pugnacious / offensive; hostile; unfriendly*

0311 degression [dɪ`grɛʃən] * de-=down ★★☆☆☆

Even with the governmental support, the company could not stop its degression. At last they decided to close down several factories.

那家公司雖有政府支持仍無法避免縮減規模，最後決定關掉數間工廠。

下降，減量
n. *reducing in amount*

0312 demolish [dɪ`mɑlɪʃ] * mol=powder, soft ★★★★★

He had too much to drink at a party and got in a terrible accident when he was driving home. He completely demolished his brand new car.

他在宴會上喝太多酒，打道回府時出了可怕的交通意外，把自己的新車完全撞壞了。

毀壞 / 拆除（建築物等）
v. *tear down; pull down; raze; destroy*

0313 mollify [`mɑlə͵faɪ] * -fy-=make ★★★★☆

In an attempt to mollify her husband's anger, she cooked him his favorite meal and then suggested that they go out to a movie.

她為了安撫先生的怒氣，下廚做了他最喜歡的料理，然後建議兩人一起出去看電影。

安撫，使鎮靜，使緩和
v. *calm; moderate; appease; pacify; soften; reduce the severity of*

0314 mortifying [`mɔrtəfaɪɪŋ] * mort-=death ★★☆☆☆

There were many mortifying setbacks while he was doing his business. However each time he faced difficulties with courage.

他在創業過程曾遇到許多令人氣餒的挫折，但仍以勇氣面對每個難關。

令人感到屈辱的，叫人生氣的
a. *humiliating; shameful*

0315 postmortem [͵post`mɔrtəm] * post-=after ★★☆☆☆

The doctor decided, upon completing the postmortem, that the death was accidental, and not the result of poisoning.

法醫相驗後確認死因是出於意外而非中毒。

驗屍
n. *autopsy; coroner's inquest*

0316 **postdate** [ˌpostˋdet] * date=date ★★☆☆☆

Even though the contract was written on July 25th, it was postdated one week later so that the date would correspond to the actual signing of the deal.

合約雖然是在七月二十五日擬好的，但為了吻合實際簽約日相，所以把日期填遲一個禮拜。

（在書信、支票、文件等上）填遲日期
v. assign a date later than the actual one to (a document, event, etc.)

0317 **antedate** [ˌæntɪˋdet] * ante-=before ★★☆☆☆

He instructed his secretary to antedate the letter by a few days. So the secretary had to put an earlier date.

他指示祕書在信裡填寫提早幾天的日期，所以祕書必須填上一個較早日期。

（在書信、支票、文件等上）填早日期
v. assign an earlier date; exist or occur at a date earlier than

---

0318 **antechamber** [ˋæntɪˌtʃembɚ] * chamber=chamber ★☆☆☆☆

Every time I go to see Mr. Jones at his office, I have to wait for at least 20 minutes in the antechamber before I can speak with him.

每當我到瓊斯先生的辦公室見他，都得在來賓接待室等上至少二十分鐘才能跟他講到話。

來賓接待室，前廳
n. anteroom

0319 **bicameral** [baɪˋkæmərəl] * bi-=two ★★★☆☆

A bicameral legislature, such as the House of Representatives and the Senate in the United States, is a very effective way to govern a nation as well as guard against an authoritarian takeover.

如美國參、眾院的兩院制立法機關，既能有效治理國家又能防止獨裁主義專權。

（政府制度上）有兩個議院的，兩院制的
a. having two chambers

0320 **bilateral** [baɪˋlætərəl] * lateral=side ★★★★☆

Head delegations from the countries are now at the negotiation tables in the first round of bilateral talks, the results of which are hoped to be the beginning of improved relations between the two nations.

兩國首席代表團現正就坐談判桌前，展開第一回合的雙邊會談，希望藉此作為改善兩國關係的開端。

雙邊的，有兩邊的
a. of or with two sides

0321 **quadrilateral** [ˌkwɑdrəˋlætərəl] * quadri-=four ★★★☆☆

The party was held in the small quadrilateral park, which was framed by two dormitory buildings, a classroom building and the main cafeteria, at the university.

舞會在大學校園的小型四邊形公園舉行，四周分別有兩棟學生宿舍、一幢教學大樓及師生餐廳。

四邊形的
a. having four sides

0322 **quarterfinal** [ˌkwɔrtɚˋfaɪnl] * fin=boundary, end ★☆☆☆☆

In order to pass on to the semifinal competition, she had to be one of the top three finalists in one of the quarterfinal competitions.

她為了打入準決賽須在半準決賽中拿下前三強。

半準決賽（的）
n. a. (of) a match or round preceding the semifinal

0323 **confine** [kən`faɪn] * con-=together, at one place ★★★★★

Because the girl was crippled, she was confined to a wheelchair. She had so much difficulty going outdoors.

女孩因為殘廢，活動範圍受限於輪椅可到之處，要到戶外常有諸多不便。

限制 / 監禁
v. restrict / imprison

0324 **concubine** [`kɑŋkjʊˌbaɪn] * cub=lie, lay ★☆☆☆☆

Mrs. Scott is terribly upset to find that her husband has a second apartment and a concubine that he regards as his second wife.

史考特太太很難過地發現先生有第二個住所和他視為第二任妻子的小老婆。

小老婆，姨太太
n. a secondary wife

0325 **incubator** [`ɪnkjəˌbetə] * in-=in ★★★★★

Incubators, which are used for rearing small, weak babies born prematurely, are essential apparatuses at a maternity hospital.

用來照料早產虛弱嬰兒的保溫箱，是產科醫院不可或缺的醫療設備。

（早產兒的）保溫箱，保育器
n. an apparatus used to provide a suitable temperature and environment for a premature baby or one of low birth-weight

MP3 15

0326 **insidious** [ɪn`sɪdɪəs] * sid=sit ★★★★☆

Even the most renowned doctor could not prescribe a cure for this insidious disease. He did not know what exactly caused the disease.

就算最有名的醫生也無法為這種潛伏疾病開立藥方。他不知道真正的病因是什麼。

（疾病等）暗中潛伏的
a. inconspicuous but harmful; treacherous

0327 **dissident** [`dɪsədənt] * dis-=away ★★★★☆

The vice president is known as the dissident because he never seems to be able to agree with anyone else.

副總統以唱反調者聞名，因為他似乎從來不曾和任何人的意見一致過。

唱反調者，持異議者
n. dissenter; protester

0328 **dissuade** [dɪ`swed] * suade=sweet ★★★★☆

His only daughter was determined to study abroad but he didn't think it would be a good idea and did everything he could to dissuade her.

他唯一的女兒決定要出國念書，但他不認為這是個好主意，於是盡一切可能勸阻。

暴飲暴食 / 過度，過多
v. discourage; persuade against

0329 **persuade** [pə`swed] * per-=perfect ★★★★★

Finally, after a long argument, we were able to persuade them. They finally allowed us to camp overnight in the forest.

經過長時間的爭論，最後總算能夠說服他們，允許我們在森林裡露營一夜。

說服，勸服
v. induce; importune; prompt; convince

0330 **peruse** [pə`ruz] * use=use ★★★★☆

Bill was going to peruse the report before he read it aloud in class, but he forgot, and so he looked like a fool when he kept on stuttering.

比爾原本打算先精讀報告接著才在全班面前大聲朗讀，但他忘了，於是當場結巴像個傻瓜。

細讀，精讀
v. read or study thoroughly; examine carefully

0331 abuse [ə`bjus] * ab-=off ★★★★☆

Her parents were found guilty of gross neglect and abuse. The police detected some bruising on the back of the girl.

女孩雙親被控重大過失和虐待，並獲判有罪。警方在女孩背上發現一些瘀傷。

虐待／濫用（權勢、語言等）
n. maltreatment; battering; beating; violation / misuse; addiction

---

0332 aboriginal [ˌæbə`rɪdʒənḷ] * ori=birth, origin ★★★★☆

Darwin's theory of evolution is based on the idea that man developed to this current state over millions of years from an aboriginal form.

達爾文進化論的基本觀點在於人類是從數百萬年前的原始外貌演化到今日的狀態。

原始的
a. native; original

0333 abortive [ə`bɔrtɪv] * ab-=away ★★★★☆

The military attempted to rescue the prisoner of war but they will have to try again later because it was an abortive effort.

軍方企圖營救戰俘，但因這次行動失敗所以必須再試一次。

沒有結果的，失敗的
a. fruitless; unsuccessful

0334 absolve [əb`zɑlv] * solv=solve, release ★★★★★

The court absolved him from any wrongdoings and allowed him to go free. He could enjoy real freedom.

法官宣布赦免他一切罪行並准其自由離開，他可以享有真正的自由。

宣布赦免（罪過等），免除（責任等）
v. set free from blame or obligation; pardon

0335 insolvent [ɪn`sɑlvənt] * in-=not ★★★★☆

Although Chris had once been rich, his bad luck at the roulette tables in Las Vegas had left him insolvent and homeless.

克里斯雖曾一度非常富有，但他在賭城輪盤賭桌上的壞運氣讓他破產且無家可歸。

無力清償債務的，破產的
a. unable to pay one's debts; bankrupt; broke

0336 indolence [`ɪndələns] * dole=sorrow ★★★★☆

A 'couch potato' is someone who lies about in indolence on a sofa and watches television or video movies all day and never exercises either his mind or his body.

「沙發馬鈴薯」指整天懶散躺在沙發上看電視或電影錄影帶、既不動腦也不運動的人。

懶惰，懶散
n. laziness; slothfulness; inertia; sluggishness

0337 condole [kən`dol] * con-=together ★★★★☆

I condoled with Mr. Mechem on his wife's death. He was overwhelmed with sorrow and even gave up eating food.

我慰問麥克翰先生喪妻之痛。他深感悲痛，甚至茶飯不思。

弔唁，慰問
v. sympathize; commiserate

0338 concurrent [kən`kɝənt] * cur=occur ★★★★☆

The fair is fun to go to but it is difficult to take in everything because there are so many concurrent events going on.

這場博覽會非常有趣，只是很難將一切盡收眼底，因為有太多活動同時進行中。

同時進行的，同步的
a. simultaneous

0339 recurrence [rɪ`kɝəns] * re-=again ★★★☆☆

We flood victims should take measures to prevent the recurrence of similar disasters next summer.

我們這些水患受災戶應採取行動防止明年夏天再度發生類似災禍。

再發生，重現
n. repetition

0340 resurge [rɪ`sɝdʒ] * surge=wave ★★★☆☆

Country music resurged in the 1980's after being quite unpopular with young people during the 1960's and 1970's.

六○和七○年代盛行的鄉村音樂相當不受年輕人歡迎，但八○年代卻再度復活。

復活，再起（思想、信仰、風潮等）
v. rise again; revive

0341 insurgent [ɪn`sɝdʒənt] * in-=in ★★★★☆

He had been a famous insurgent who had led many demonstrations against the government's unjust policies but he had never managed to actually change anything.

他是知名反對份子，曾多次帶領群眾展開示威活動抗議政府不公平的政策，但他從未真正設法改變任何事。

反對份子，暴動者 / 暴動的
n. rebel; mutineer /
a. rebellious

0342 innate [ɪ`net] * nat=birth ★★★★☆

Many people think that the ability to learn a language is innate rather than acquired. Those people without a natural ability tend to give up learning a foreign language.

許多人認為學習語言的能力是天生而非後天養成的。沒有先天能力者容易放棄學習外國語言。

天生的，天賦的，與生俱來的
a. inborn; natural

0343 connatural [kə`nætʃərəl] * con-=together ★★★☆☆

Lenny seemed to have a connatural ability to understand music and so his parents sent him to piano lessons when he was only four years old.

藍尼在音樂理解上似乎有種天生能力，所以四歲時雙親就送他去上鋼琴課。

先天的，固有的，天生的
a. innate

0344 constitute [`kɑnstə,tut] * stit=stand ★★★★★

Fifty states constitute the United States. Two of them, Alaska and Hawaii are separated from the other 48 states.

美國由五十州組成，其中阿拉斯加和夏威夷這兩州不在美國本土。

組成（整體），構成
v. be the components of;
make up; form

0345 institution [,ɪnstə`tjuʃən] * in-=on ★★★★★

The insurance salesperson hopes to work for an institution with a better insurance package. He has found that his company's package does not satisfy consumers.

保險業務員希望能在提供較佳保險計畫的組織工作，因為他發現自己公司的配套產品無法讓客戶滿意。

機關，組織 / 創立
n. establishment; formation;
organization

0346 inscribe [ɪnˈskraɪb] * scrib=write

★★★☆☆

雕刻，題寫
v. write or carve (words etc.)

The author inscribed a brief message on the first page of his novel which he gave as a gift to his niece on her birthday.
作者在他小說的首頁題寫一段簡短文字，作為送給姪女的生日禮物。

0347 prescribe [prɪˈskraɪb] * pre-=before

★★★★★

開立藥方，提供醫囑 / 指示
v. advise the use of (a medicine etc.) / ordain; order; decree; stipulate

The doctor has prescribed for him a medicine to cure his heart disease. He has also told him that it is important for him to take the medicine according to the instruction.
醫生開立藥方治療他的心臟病，同時囑咐他依照指示服藥是很重要的。

0348 premise [ˈprɛmɪs] * mis=send

★★★★☆

前提，假設
n. assumption; proposition; hypothesis; assertion; supposition; surmise

He based his premise on what was given to him by his colleagues, but it was incorrect and when he submitted his report, his superiors laughed at him.
他根據同事提供的資訊作為假設前提，但其實那是不正確的。因此在提交報告時受到上司嘲笑。

0349 emissary [ˈɛməˌsɛrɪ] * e-=out

★★★☆☆

特務，間諜 / 密使，特使
n. a person sent on a special mission; envoy

It is not now known, nor will it ever exactly be known, how many emissaries the KGB had placed in the United States during the cold war.
目前非但不清楚前蘇聯國家安全委員會曾在冷戰期間安排多少特務到美國活動，未來也未必能確切知道。

0350 educe [ɪˈdjus] * -duce=draw

★★★☆☆

引出，導出 / 推斷，演繹
v. bring out or develop from latent or potential existence; derive

Paul has become a valued employee at our company because of his ability to educe from a situation the correct action to take in order to solve the problem.
保羅成為我們公司相當重要的員工，因為他能從現實狀況中推斷並採取正確行動，以解決問題。

Tea Time... ☕

<Roman myth> Bacchus
A Roman god of wine and revelry.

〈羅馬神話〉巴克斯酒神
羅馬神話中專司飲酒和狂歡的神祇。
（註：後世將所有和飲酒作樂、狂歡嬉鬧有關的字詞字首都冠以 bacch-。）

❖ **bacchanalian** [ˌbækəˈnelɪən] *a. riotous; roistering* | 飲酒作樂的，狂歡嬉鬧的

Vikings, after a long sea journey, enjoyed a bacchanalian gathering where women and wines were a must.
北歐海盜維京人結束長途航海旅程後必定齊聚一堂，享受醇酒美人的狂歡盛宴。

1

Complete each word by filling in the blank with proper spelling so that it has the same meaning as suggested. Then please write the meaning of each word in Chinese.

1. 導出 = _ d u c e
2. 假設前提 = p r e _ _ _ _
3. 開立藥方 = p r e _ _ _ _ _ _
4. 題寫 = _ _ s c r i b e
5. 組成 = _ _ _ s t i t u t e
6. 窮困 = d e _ _ _ _ u t i o n
7. 精確的 = p r e _ _ _ e
8. 受限於 = _ _ _ _ _ _ s c r i b e
9. 委婉用語 = c i r c u m _ _ _ u t i o n
10. 有衝勁的 = a _ _ _ _ _ _ i v e

11. mortifying = _____
12. postmortem = _____
13. antechamber = _____
14. bilateral = _____
15. quadrilateral = _____
16. confine = _____
17. dissuade = _____
18. peruse = _____
19. aboriginal = _____
20. absolve = _____

2

Choose a word that best completes the sentence.

21. **One of the main purposes of education is to _____ latent talents.**

    (A) antedate   (B) mollify   (C) educe   (D) dissuade

22. **The city has decided to _____ the dilapidated building and build a new one.**

    (A) moderate   (B) demolish   (C) persuade   (D) peruse

23. **The minister did not like to _____ over a wedding. So when young people began to talk about marriage, he tried to talk about something else.**

    (A) confine   (B) absolve   (C) preside   (D) condole

3

The highlighted word is closest in meaning to which of the following?

24. **The owner of the business went** insolvent **because of financial difficulties.**

    (A) concurrent   (B) innate   (C) bankrupt   (D) simultaneous

25. **Mrs. Jones tried to** mollify **her morning sickness by trying some roast ginger, because one of her relatives told her that it was effective.**

    (A) destroy   (B) soften   (C) postdate   (D) aggrandize

MP3
16

0351 reduce [rɪ`dus] * re-=down ★★★★★

Microfilm can hold a lot of information in a small space. The image is stored in a reduced form. So it is possible for us to store a lot of information.
顯微膠片可將大量資訊容納在極小空間裡，由於以簡化形式儲存影像，所以可保存大量資訊。

減少，減縮／降低，簡化
v. make or become smaller or less; decrease; diminish; abate; lessen; let up; moderate

0352 retrench [rɪ`trɛntʃ] * trench=cut ★★☆☆☆

The company retrenched by eliminating half of the workers. They had not been able to meet the expenses.
該公司無法償付支出費用，於是裁掉一半人力以縮減開支。

縮減，削減／刪除，省略
v. reduce the amount of; cut down expenses; abridge; shorten

0353 entrench [ɪn`trɛntʃ] * en-=in ★★★☆☆

My guidance professor's ideas got deeply entrenched in my philosophy. His teaching helped me a lot.
指導教授的見解深烙在我的人生觀裡，他的教育帶給我許多幫助。

確立，使深留在（腦海、記憶）中／侵占
v. fix; establish; embed; root / encroach; trespass; intrude; make inroads; infringe; invade

0354 enjoin [ɪn`dʒɔɪn] * join=join ★★★☆☆

The General enjoined the sergeant to fill out a report explaining in exact detail what had caused the problem.
陸軍上將命令中士呈交報告，詳細解釋造成問題的真正原因。

命令，吩咐／禁止
v. command; order / prohibit a person by order

0355 conjoin [kən`dʒɔɪn] * con-=together ★★☆☆☆

Even though the prisoners were conjoined together with handcuffs for transport, two of them managed to escape anyway.
囚犯在押解過程中雖以手銬相連，但仍有兩名人犯企圖逃脫。

聯合，結合
v. combine; join

0356 congratulation [kən,grætʃə`leʃən] * grat=pleasure; gratitude ★★★★★

The newly married couple received a pretty card which read, "Heartiest congratulations to you both!"
新婚夫妻收到一張精美賀卡，上面寫著：「由衷祝福兩位！」

祝辭，賀辭
n. expression of pleasure and good wishes

0357 ingrate [`ɪngret] * in-=not ★★★★☆

I have yet to witness him thank anyone for anything and I consider him to be the biggest ingrate I have ever seen.
我沒見過他為了任何事感激別人，我認為他是我見過最忘恩負義的人。

忘恩負義者
n. an ungrateful person

0358 incessantly [ɪn`sɛsntlɪ] * cess=cease ★★★★★

The office worker couldn't get my report done because one of her colleagues chattered incessantly.
辦公室職員無法完成我要的報告，因為她的同事一直喋喋不休。

不斷地，不停地
ad. endlessly; unceasingly

0359 deceased [dɪ`sist] * de-=down ★★★★★

David's parents are deceased. He is an orphan. So the authorities are looking for a foster family for him.

孤兒大衛的父母雙亡，有關當局正在為他尋找收養家庭。

已故的，已死亡的
a. dead

0360 depreciate [dɪ`priʃɪˌet] * preci=price ★★★★☆

Computers depreciate rapidly. Two-thousand dollars' worth of computers are worth less than one thousand dollars within a year of purchase.

電腦迅速跌價，價值兩千美元的電腦在買進一年內只剩下不到一千美元價值。

貶值，跌價／輕視，貶低
v. diminish in value / disparage; belittle; underestimate; deride

---

0361 appreciate [ə`priʃɪˌet] * ap-, ad-=to ★★★★★

Koryo pottery is something which the Korean people justly take pride in, and which the world has come to appreciate and admire.

高麗陶器是韓國人引以為傲的成就，並日漸受到世人讚賞。

We should always remember that it is very important to appreciate the nice things that we enjoy in our lives, because there are many people who can't have the things that we so often take for granted.

我們應時時牢記領略生命中種種美好是很重要的，因為許多人無法擁有我們視為理所當然之物。

增值，大漲／體會，領略／欣賞，賞識
v. esteem highly; value; cherish; admire; treasure; respect / understand; comprehend; recognize; perceive / enjoy

---

0362 append [ə`pɛnd] * pend=han ★★★★★

Tim appended a list of errors to the end of the report for quick reference. However even in his list he made some typos.

提姆在報告最後附上一份勘誤表作為快速查閱之用，但其中仍有一些打字錯誤。

附上，附加，增補
v. attach; affix; add; tack

0363 impending [ɪm`pɛndɪŋ] * im-=on ★★★★★

Even though Richard Kingsley was released on bail and had six weeks before the trial began, he simply could not get the impending charges out of his mind.

理查‧金斯利雖已獲保釋且距離下次開庭審理還有六周，但他就是無法忘記即將到來的指控。

逼近的，即將到來的
a. imminent; approaching; close at hand; near at hand; forthcoming; in the offing

---

0364 impugn [ɪm`pjun] * pugn=fight ★★★★☆

The witness presented some very powerful facts in favor of the accused but the prosecuting attorney, to his credit, impugned the motives of the accused and eventually won the case.

證人提出對被告有利的有效事證，但檢察官基於其可信度對被告動機表示懷疑，最後打贏官司。

抨擊，對～表示懷疑
v. challenge; call in question

0365 inexpugnable [ˌɪnɪks`pʌgnəbl] * ex-=out ★★★☆☆

The champion has knocked out thirty-two opponents in a row and is now thought to be inexpugnable.

冠軍優勝者已接連擊敗三十二名對手，現在被視為是無敵的。

無敵的，無法征服的
a. invincible

0366 extraction [ɪk`strækʃən] * tract=draw ★★★☆☆

拔牙，拔取 / 後裔，家世

n. *removal; extrication; uprooting; pulling / lineage; pedigree; blood; stock*

The extraction of a tooth without the use of anaesthesia is always a horrible and painful experience.

沒有麻醉就直接拔牙是既恐怖又痛苦的經驗。

0367 retractable [rɪ`træktəbl] * re-=again; back ★★★☆☆

可取消的，可撤回的

a. *that can be revoked*

I wonder if our contract is retractable. I'm afraid I'll not be able to raise the necessary funds. Do I lose my deposit if I annul the contract?

我想知道是否可取消合約，因為我擔心籌不到所需資金。如果取消的話，會拿不回保證金嗎？

0368 recumbent [rɪ`kʌmbənt] * cumb=lie ★★☆☆☆

斜倚的，橫臥的

a. *lying down*

A recumbent position is the most comfortable for sleeping yet still many students sleep while sitting at their desks.

橫躺是最舒服的睡覺姿勢，但許多學生就算坐在書桌前也能睡著。

0369 succumb [sə`kʌm] * sub-=under ★★★★★

屈服於，屈從

v. *yield; give in; give way; surrender; cave in; capitulate; submit*

The spinster tried for years to win him over, and when she finally asked him to marry her, he had no choice but to succumb to her wishes.

已過適婚年齡的未婚女子多年來一直試圖說服他結婚。當她終於開口求婚，他除了屈服外別無選擇。

0370 subsidiary [səb`sɪdɪˌɛrɪ] * sid=sit ★★★★☆

副業的，次要的

a. *ancillary; auxiliary; additional; supplementary; accessory; subordinate*

Writers nowadays spend too much energy on the subsidiary activities of talking and making money, which leaves them too little time for serious writing.   *Advice to a Young Man* —— Ernest Hemingway

現在的作家花費太多精力在談話或賺錢等副業上，因此沒有太多時間認真寫作。

——《給年輕人的評言》海明威

0371 residue [`rɛzəˌdu] * re-=again ★★★★★

殘留物，剩餘，渣滓

n. *remainder; leftovers; remains; excess*

New forms of dish soap leave behind less sticky residue, which is something many housewives are happy about.

新式洗碗精使用後的黏稠殘留物較少，讓家庭主婦們感到滿意。

0372 respite [`rɛspɪt] * spi=see ★★★☆☆

暫時休息，暫止 / 給予緩刑，使有喘息機會

n. *intermission; interruption /* **v.** *reprieve*

There was no respite from the abuse and taunts that the office manager heard every day because people didn't understand him or his way of thinking.

每天傳到辦公室經理耳中的辱罵和嘲弄從未停過，因為大家不了解他本人和他的思考模式。

0373 despite [dɪ`spaɪt] * de-=down ★★★★★

惡意，侮辱 / 不顧，不管

n. *malice; hatred /* **prep.** *in spite of; notwithstanding; regardless of; in defiance of*

My brother is unruly. He keeps doing dangerous things despite all my warnings. I wish that he were as good as gold.

弟弟很任性，總是不顧我的告誡總是做些危險事，真希望他乖一點。

0374 depletion [dɪ`pliʃən] * ple(t)=fill ★★★★☆

Acid rain that is destroying our forests, the devastating green house effect, urban crowding, traffic congestion, ground water contamination and depletion, toxic waste and garbage; all these grave problems warn us that we should take action to halt the growth of our population.

破壞森林的酸雨、毀滅性溫室效應、擁擠的都市人口、交通壅塞、地下水污染與枯竭，以及有毒廢棄物與垃圾等重大問題，在在警告我們應該要採取行動以抑制人口成長。

枯竭，耗盡
n. consumption; exhaustion

0375 supplement [`sʌpləmənt] * sup-, sub-=under ★★★★★

This newspaper has a weekly supplement that offers free English lessons. Once a week the newspaper has a few more pages.

這份報紙附有每周一期的增刊，專門提供免費英文學習課程，所以每周會有一天多出幾個版面。

增刊，增補
n. addition; appendage; adjunct; addendum; appendix

0376 subsist [səb`sɪst] * sist=stand ★★★★☆

The poor family subsisted on charity. Without the help from the organization they could not have survived.

貧窮家庭靠慈善團體接濟，沒有該組織的幫助就無法生存。

維持生活，過日子
v. keep oneself alive; exist

0377 consistent [kən`sɪstənt] * con-=at one place ★★★★★

He joined an amateur golf tournament, and he could have won, but he wasn't consistent enough in his shots.

他參加高爾夫球業餘錦標賽本來會獲勝，但揮杆擊球不夠平穩。

堅定不移的，平穩的 / 前後一致的
a. constant; steady; unswerving / harmonious; compatible

0378 constellation [ˌkɑnstə`leʃən] * stella=star ★★★★☆

The astronomer loves to watch the stars at night and see how many constellations he can see at any given time.

天文學家最愛觀看夜晚星空，看看能看見多少星座。

星座，星群
n. a group of fixed stars

0379 interstellar [ˌɪntɚ`stɛlɚ] * inter-=between ★★★★☆

Stars are the products of condensation which occurs in the dense interstellar gas clouds.

星星是由稠密的星際雲氣冷凝而成的產物。

星與星之間的，星際的
a. occurring or situated between stars

0380 interlude [`ɪntɚˌlud] * lud=play ★★★★★

Her job had always been to provide a musical interlude between acts at the theater, but with the invention of recorded music, she soon lost her job.

她的工作一直是在戲劇幕間提供音樂插曲，但錄音樂曲問世後她很快就失業了。

幕間表演，幕間插曲，換幕時間
n. a pause between the acts of a play; interval; intermission; pause; interruption; hiatus

0381 delude [dɪ`lud] * de-=down ★★★★★

The hardest thing about hunting with a bow and arrow is deluding the animal into thinking that you too are an animal.

弓箭狩獵最難之處在於欺騙動物拿著弓箭的你跟牠一樣都是動物。

欺騙，迷惑
v. deceive; mislead; fool; hoax; trick; swindle; double-cross; take in

0382 demise [dɪ`maɪz] * mis=send ★★☆☆☆

Poverty among the people created the demise of communism in the Soviet Union and East Germany.
民眾的窮困導致前蘇聯和東德境內共產主義的滅亡。

死亡，消滅，滅亡
n. death

0383 submissive [səb`mɪsɪv] * sub-=under ★★★★☆

Be firm but not aggressive; be polite but not submissive.
做個堅定而非激進、有禮而非順從的人。

順從的，柔順的，服從的
a. humble; obedient; yielding; deferential; compliant; acquiescent; tractable; amenable; docile; meek

0384 subsume [səb`sum] * -sume=take ★★★☆☆

Crocodiles are subsumed in the class of reptiles together with turtles, snakes and extinct dinosaurs.
鱷魚和海龜、蛇、絕種恐龍一樣，都屬於爬蟲類動物綱。

包含在（規則、範圍等）內
v. include in a rule, class, category, etc.

0385 presume [prɪ`zum] * pre-=before ★★★★★

One might presume that someone who lived in America for a long time could speak English perfectly, but as often as not, this is incorrect.
也許有人會假定長期住在美國的人就一定能說流利英語，但這種推斷往往不正確。

假定，推斷
v. assume; take for granted; suppose; surmise; infer; postulate

0386 precede [prɪ`sid] * cede=go ★★★★★

The invited lecturer preceded her lecture with an amusing anecdote. She wanted to build a kind of natural rapport.
客座講師在演講開始前先透露一則有趣軼事，她希望營造自然和諧的氣氛。

置於～之前 / 前導
v. come or go before; lead; pave the way for / herald; usher in; introduce

0387 antecedent [ˌæntə`sidn̩t] * ante-=before ★★★☆☆

Professor Watson is my antecedent who came to this college before me and taught me a lot of things he knew.
華生教授是比我更早進入這所學院的前輩，教我許多他知道的事。

在前的，在先的 / 前例，前輩
a. pervious; prior; earlier; preceding / *n.* ancestor; predecessor

0388 antenatal [ˌæntɪ`netl̩] * nat=birth ★★★☆☆

Mrs. Smith, who is expecting a baby, is going for her antenatal this morning. She wants her husband to accompany her.
有孕在身的史密斯太太今早要到醫院進行產前檢查，她希望先生陪同前往。

出生前的 / 產前檢查
a. existing or occurring before birth / *n.* medical examination of a pregnant woman

0389 postnatal [ˌpost`netl̩] * post-=after ★★★☆☆

Postnatal care for women is vital to the health and recovery of both the mother and the newborn and should be a priority in all hospital budget discussion.
婦女產後保健對母親和新生嬰兒的健康和復原都至關重要，因此應作為所有醫院預算討論的最優先事項。

出生後的，產後的
a. relating to the period after childbirth

0390 postgraduate [post`grædʒʊɪt] * graduate=grad(=go, step)+ ate(=person) ★★★★★

My roommate James has decided to continue studying and get a postgraduate degree in engineering.
我的室友詹姆斯決定繼續攻讀工程學碩士學位。

研究所的 / 研究生
a. carried on after taking a first degree

0391 undergraduate [ˌʌndə`grædʒʊɪt] * under-=under ★★★★★

The undergraduates sat in the back while the graduate students were seated at the front of the auditorium.
大學部學生坐在禮堂後方座位，研究生則坐在前方。

大學部學生
n. a student at a university who has not yet taken a first degree

0392 underexposed [`ʌndərɪk`spozd] * expose=ex(=out)+ pose(=to put) ★★★☆☆

So many of the photographs were underexposed that the photographer had difficulty making distinctions between the horses and the cows.
由於太多照片感光不足，使攝影師很難分辨馬群和牛群的不同。

曝光不足的，感光不足的
a. exposed with insufficient light

0393 overexpose [`ovərɪk`spoz] * over-=over ★★★☆☆

They wanted their daughter to experience the world but they didn't want to overexpose her to the dangers and problems that people make for themselves.
他們希望女兒體驗一切，但不想讓她過度暴露在他人自找的危險和問題下。

使曝光過度，使過度接觸到～，過度暴露在～之下
v. expose too much

0394 overvalue [ˌovə`vælju] * value=worth ★★★★☆

You should be careful not to overvalue yourself. Overrating oneself often brings on overconfidence.
你應小心不要高估自己，對自己評價過高往往招來自負。

高估，過於重視
v. value too highly

0395 invaluable [ɪn`væljəbl] * in-=not ★★★★★

The jewelry that Jane has lost is invaluable. Furthermore it was borrowed from her friend Nancy.
珍遺失的珠寶非常貴重，更糟的是那是向友人南西借來的。

無價的，非常貴重的
a. priceless; precious; costly; valuable; expensive

0396 ineluctable [ˌɪnɪ`lʌktəbl] * luct=lock ★★★★☆

Traffic jams are ineluctable on a holiday weekend. People often think it is natural for them to spend a long time stuck in traffic.
假日塞車難免，人們總認為花很長時間塞在車陣中是很自然的。

無可避免的，難免的
a. not to be avoided; inevitable

0397 reluctant [rɪ`lʌktənt] * re-=against ★★★★★

An introverted person's action is usually marked by hesitance, as if he is reluctant to commit himself to anything.
內向的人行事常表現出遲疑，好像不願意承諾任何事一樣。

不情願的，勉強的，遲疑的
a. unwilling; disinclined; hesitant; loath; averse; opposed

0398 relent [rɪˋlɛnt] * lent=bend ★★★★★

At first Miss Lee's father wouldn't let her study abroad, but at the last moment he relented somewhat.
李小姐的父親起初不讓她出國念書，但最後態度有點軟化。

使心軟，使動惻隱之心
v. relax; soften; yield; melt; succumb; show pity

0399 relentless [rɪˋlɛntlɪs] * -less-=without ★★★★★

The police pursued the criminal relentlessly and finally caught him. They had been chasing him for over a year.
警方鍥而不捨地緝拿罪犯，最後終於將他逮捕到案，前後共花了一年多時間。

冷酷無情的／鍥而不捨的
a. unyielding; inexorable; dogged; implacable; inflexible; rigid; obstinate; adamant; determined; ruthless

---

0400 faultless [ˋfɔltlɪs] * fault=err, deceive ★★★★☆

The audience was deeply impressed by the faultless rendition of the musicians, who received a long standing ovation.
音樂家無懈可擊的表演讓觀眾深受感動，紛紛起立鼓掌良久。

完美無缺的，無懈可擊的，零缺點的
a. flawless; immaculate; perfect; exemplary; irreproachable

Tea Time... ☕

<From the name of a book>
Utopia
An imaginary island described in a book of the same name by Sir Thomas More (1516) as having a perfect political and social system.

〈出自書名〉烏托邦
本字源自英國作家暨社會主義者湯瑪斯‧摩爾爵士在一五一六年出版的同名著作《烏托邦》，書中描述一個具有完美政府與社會制度的理想島國。（註：本字原意是指內含一切至美至善的理想國度，後世將此字引申為「理想國」或「理想社會」，也暗指「不可能實現的完美事物」。）

❖ **utopian** [juˋtopɪən] *a.* characteristic of utopia; idealistic │ 烏托邦式的，理想的，不可能實現的

Pilgrims wished to build utopian communities in the new world. They really wanted religious independence.
英國清教徒希望在新世界建立一個理想社會，並迫切渴望爭取宗教自主。

1 Complete each word by filling in the blank with proper spelling so that it has the same meaning as suggested. Then please write the meaning of each word in Chinese.

1. 鍥而不捨的 = r e _ _ _ _ l e s s
2. 不情願的 = r e _ _ _ _ a n t
3. 無懈可擊的 = f a u l t _ _ _ _
4. 高估 = _ _ _ _ v a l u e
5. 使過度接觸 = o v e r e x _ _ _ _
6. 確立 = _ _ t r e n c h
7. 縮減開支 = r e _ _ _ _ _ _
8. 命令 = _ _ _ j o i n
9. 不停地 = i n _ _ _ _ a n t l y
10. 跌價 = d e _ _ _ _ _ a t e

11. append = _____
12. impending = _____
13. impugn = _____
14. inexpugnable = _____
15. subsidiary = _____
16. residue = _____
17. depletion = _____
18. subsist = _____
19. constellation = _____
20. delude = _____

2 Choose a word that best completes the sentence.

21. Mr. Baker was extremely angry when he found that his daughter got back home too late. But later he _____ somewhat.
    (A) relented   (B) assumed   (C) confirmed   (D) depended

22. The husband could not help but _____ to his wife's wishes. She had wanted to move to a big city.
    (A) succumb   (B) supplement   (C) subsume   (D) precede

3 The highlighted word is closest in meaning to which of the following?

23. During the 10-minute interlude between the second and the third acts, Jack went out to buy some drinks.
    (A) constellation   (B) overexpose   (C) postgraduate   (D) interruption

24. Mosquitoes were bugging the campers so relentlessly that they could not sleep a wink.
    (A) flawlessly   (B) permanently   (C) previously   (D) doggedly

25. We human beings should conserve energy; otherwise the depletion of natural resources might become an unwelcome visitor.
    (A) supplement   (B) respite   (C) exhaustion   (D) residue

Practice Test 02

1 The highlighted word is closest in meaning to which of the following?

1. His business has been prosperous since he admitted a new system of assembly lines.

   (A) explicit

   (B) flourishing

   (C) implicit

   (D) consummate

2. After the examination the student felt depressed because he could not solve any of the complicated math problems.

   (A) deficient

   (B) magnificent

   (C) dispirited

   (D) extemporaneous

3. After signing the contract he decided not to buy the property. He forfeited his deposit.

   (A) recognized

   (B) lost

   (C) indicted

   (D) averred

4. Superstitious people are reluctant to walk under a ladder. They believe that it may bring bad luck.

   (A) unwilling

   (B) ineluctable

   (C) invaluable

   (D) postnatal

5. He had no alternative but to succumb to his wife's wishes. She has insisted on buying a sports car.

   (A) supplement

   (B) subsist

   (C) yield

   (D) impugn

2 Please answer the following questions.

Earthquakes

Earthquakes take place almost continuously. However, most of them are not destructive. Slight earthquakes, which are often called tremors by seismologists, can be detected only by highly sensitive devices called seismographs. However, tremendous shuddering of the earth is far from rare. A really violent earthquake takes place at least once a year in some parts of the world. The most magnificent earthquakes are usually related to ruptures of the earth's crust, which are also called faults. Great earthquakes demolish cities, break dams, and cause volcanoes to erupt. They can even make a lake disappear. On average, earthquakes claim approximately 10,000 lives annually. As cities expand to house an ever-increasing population, losses of life and property linked to earthquakes are expected to soar. So much so that many nations are making efforts to improve methods of detection and to enhance warning systems, while trying to construct stronger buildings, bridges and dams. In fact, many environmentalists try to dissuade scientists from conducting underground nuclear weapon tests in that they might irritate our sensitive and invaluable globe.

6. The word **magnificent** is closest in meaning to which of the following?
   (A) relentless
   (B) gigantic
   (C) eloquent
   (D) consummate

7. The word **demolish** is closest in meaning to which of the following?
   (A) evince
   (B) inflate
   (C) destroy
   (D) detach

8. The word **efforts** is closest in meaning to which of the following?
   (A) partisans
   (B) prefaces
   (C) endeavors
   (D) artifacts

9. The word **dissuade** is closest in meaning to which of the following?
   (A) supplement
   (B) subsist
   (C) append
   (D) prevent

10. The word **invaluable** is closest in meaning to which of the following?
    (A) precious
    (B) innate
    (C) retractable
    (D) impending

MP3
18

0401 default [dɪ`fɔlt] * de-=down ★★★★★

The young couple was very excited when they bought and moved into their first house, but their dreams were shattered when they defaulted on their mortgage payments and lost their house.

這對年輕夫妻買下首棟房子並遷入定居後深感興奮，等到拖欠房貸失去房子，美夢也因此破碎。

不履行（職責、債務等），拖欠 / 不履行，拖欠
n. failure; fault; neglect; dereliction; negligence; lapse; oversight / v. disregard

---

0402 depend [dɪ`pɛnd] * pend=hang ★★★★★

Living a healthy life depends on whether you exercise, in which environments you live and what kind of food you eat.

生活要健康，取決於是否運動、生活環境如何，以及飲食選擇。

取決於～ / 信賴，依靠
v. be contingent on; be determined by; hinge on; pivot on / rely on; bank on; count on; rest on

---

0403 perpendicular [ˌpɝpən`dɪkjələ] * per-=perfect ★★★★☆

A line which is perpendicular to a horizontal line is called vertical.

垂直於水平線的直線稱為垂直線。

垂直的 / 陡峭的，險峻的
a. at right angles to; at 90 degrees to / erect; upright; vertical; plumb

---

0404 persecute [`pɝsɪˌkjut] * sec=follow ★★★☆☆

When the English started to persecute the protestants, they decided to head for America on a ship named the Mayflower.

當英國人開始迫害新教徒，他們便決定搭乘五月花號前往美國。

（以宗教、信仰、政治主張等為由加以）迫害
v. oppress; maltreat; abuse; molest; afflict; martyr; torture

---

0405 consecutive [kən`sɛkjutɪv] * con-=together ★★★★☆

The sprinter has set a goal to run for three consecutive days and he's going to do his best to run everyday and accomplish his goal.

短跑選手定下連跑三天的目標，他每天都將全力以赴達成目標。

連續不斷的
a. successive; following continuously

0406 confirm [kən`fɝm] * firm=firm ★★★★★

I need to call the travel agent to confirm my flight reservation. Last year I couldn't travel because an airline cancelled my flight.

我必須打給旅行社確認預訂的機票。去年因航空公司取消航班，害我無法出遊。

確認，證實
v. affirm; ensure; guarantee

0407 infirmary [ɪn`fɝmərɪ] * in-=in ★★★☆☆

The grandmother's health has been deteriorating for the past several years and she is now so weak that the family has decided to put her in an infirmary.

過去幾年來祖母的健康情況日趨惡化，現在十分虛弱，家人決定送她到醫療中心。

醫務室，診療所，醫院
n. hospital; health center; clinic

0408 inoculate [ɪn`ɑkjəˌlet] * ocul=eye ★★★☆☆

The owner of the pedigree pet dog inoculated his dog against a disease before taking it on his journey.

狗主帶純種狗一起旅遊前，有先帶牠去預防接種。

接種疫苗，給予預防接種
v. inject

0409 binoculars [bɪˋnɑkjələs] * bi-=two ★★★☆☆

Binoculars are used for looking at distant objects, which otherwise might not be clearly visible.

雙筒望遠鏡可用來觀看可能無法看清楚的遠處目標。

雙筒望遠鏡
n. an optical instrument with a lens for each eye, for viewing distant objects

0410 bicentennial [ˌbaɪsɛnˋtɛnɪəl] * enni=year ★★★☆☆

During the 200th anniversary of the founding of the United States there were bicentennial parties and celebrations all year long.

美國建國兩百周年紀念期間,全年無休進行兩百年才舉辦一次的派對和慶祝活動。

每兩百年發生一次的,存續兩百年之久的
a. lasting two hundred years or occurring every two hundred years

0411 perennial [pəˋrɛnɪəl] * per-=through ★★★★★

No living thing on earth could enjoy a perennial lifespan; all of them face death after all. They are mortal.

地球上沒有任何生物可享有永恆壽命,所有生物終究會面臨死亡,大家都是會死的。

永久的/終年的,長年的
a. lasting several years / lifelong; enduring; persistent; endless; imperishable; perpetual; eternal; immortal; permanent

0412 perturb [pəˋtɝb] * turb=disorder ★★★★★

Maggie knew that it would perturb her husband to go out with her friends, but she did it anyway.

瑪姬知道和友人一起外出會讓丈夫感到困擾,但她不管三七二十一還是出門了。

使不安,使煩惱,使困擾
v. upset; agitate; disconcert

0413 disturb [dɪˋstɝb] * dis-=away, scatter ★★★★★

Tom's father specifically warned him not to disturb his mother while she was sleeping. He got into a lot of trouble when he went bursting into her room and woke her up.

爸爸特別警告湯姆別去打擾熟睡的媽媽,當他闖入房間吵醒媽媽後便挨了一頓罵。

打擾,擾亂
v. agitate; ruffle; unsettle

0414 dissect [dɪˋsɛkt] * sect=cut ★★★☆☆

Robert didn't like biology classes during his high school days because he didn't like to dissect frogs, worms and other things.

高中時羅伯特很不愛上生物課,因為他不喜歡解剖青蛙、蚯蚓,以及其他生物。

切開,解剖/詳細研究
v. cut into pieces; analyze

0415 resect [rɪˋsɛkt] * re-=away ★★☆☆☆

Once they discovered the malignant tumor, the doctors were able to resect it and the patient was cured.

醫生一發現癌細胞腫瘤便動手術切除,病患因此痊癒。

(外科手術)切除,割掉
v. cut out part of

0416 repulse [rɪˋpʌls] * puls-=drive, force ★★★☆☆

The allies were able to repulse almost all attacks that the Nazis launched and they reclaimed Paris.

同盟國聯軍幾乎瓦解納粹所有攻勢並收復巴黎。

擊敗,驅逐,瓦解敵軍攻勢
v. repel; drive back; ward off; beat off

0417 impulse [`ɪmpʌls] * im-=in ★★★★★

衝動，一時衝動
n. the act or an instance of impelling; push; impetus

Just before dying in the electric chair the convicted murderer stated that everything he did was due to impulses that he had had ever since he was a little child.

獲判有罪的殺人犯臨刑前坐在電椅上，宣稱自己的所作所為是源自小時候就有的衝動。

0418 implicate [`ɪmplɪ͵ket] * plic=fold ★★★★★

牽連，連累，涉及
v. incriminate; inculpate; involve; embroil; associate

As an innocent bystander, I had nothing to do with the cause of the accident, but it didn't take long for the driver of the car to implicate me in the incident in an attempt to get out of the mess he had created for himself.

作為無辜旁觀者的我跟這起意外毫無關連，但不久汽車駕駛就把我牽連進去，因為他企圖開脫自己製造的大麻煩。

0419 accomplice [ə`kɑmplɪs] * ac-, ad-=to ★★★★☆

共犯，同謀，幫兇
n. confederate; conspirator; abettor; partner in crime

Even though she was not directly involved in the crime, the police arrested her as an accomplice to the crime.

她雖未直接涉入那起犯罪活動，警方仍以共犯將她逮捕。

0420 accelerate [ək`sɛlə͵ret] * celera=hasten ★★★★★

加速，促進
v. increase speed; quicken

Rapid economic growth and industrialization have accelerated urbanization in that country. Rapid increases in urban population have brought about a decrease in the rural population.

快速的經濟成長和工業化進展加速該國都市化發展，都市人口的快速增加也導致農業人口減少。

0421 decelerate [di`sɛlə͵ret] * de-=do the opposite of ★★★★★

減速
v. reduce speed; make slower

Three people were killed in the crash and the police determined that the car was traveling at about 80 miles an hour and that the driver did not have time to decelerate.

汽車對撞意外共造成三人喪生。警方判定肇事車輛是以每小時八十英哩的速度前進，因此駕駛沒有時間減速。

0422 desist [dɪ`zɪst] * sist=stand ★★★★☆

停止
v. cease; abstain

Many of the volunteers who were working for the candidate were shocked to hear of his resignation and desisted their work immediately.

許多為該候選人工作的志工得知他退選而感到震驚，立刻停下手邊的工作。

0423 persist [pə`zɪst] * per-=through, perfect ★★★★★

堅持
v. stand firm; be steadfast; persevere

The farmers of the country persisted doggedly in their campaign against grain imports, which they believed would deliver a lethal blow to agriculture.

該國農民反對穀物進口並堅持抗爭到底，他們認為這會對本土農業帶來致命一擊。

0424 pertain [pə`ten] * tain=hold ★★★★★

He had no idea what the office memo was supposed to pertain to. He read it and then threw it away.

他不知道那份公司買賣備忘錄是關於什麼，於是看過後就把它丟了。

有關，關於，附屬
v. concern; have relation to; apply to; relate to; appertain to

0425 retain [rɪ`ten] * re-=again ★★★★★

No sagacious man will long retain his sagacity, if he lives exclusively among reformers and progressive people.

The Blithedale Romance —— Nathaniel Hawthorne

睿智的人如果將自己置外於改革者和進取者之列，就不可能永保智慧。

—— 《快樂谷傳奇》霍桑

保有，保持
v. keep possession of; hold on to; reserve; preserve

0426 recipient [rɪ`sɪpɪənt] * cip=take ★★★☆☆

The new manager of the notoriously difficult department has become the recipient of much criticism despite his hard work.

以營運困難聞名的部門新任經理雖努力工作，仍遭到諸多批評。

接受者
n. receiver; beneficiary; a person who receives something

0427 incipient [ɪn`sɪpɪənt] * in-=in ★★★☆☆

It is reported that hot tea is effective to break an incipient cold. So please drink some hot tea if you feel like you are coming down with a cold.

據說熱茶對制伏初期感冒很有效，所以覺得自己快感冒時請多喝熱茶。

初期的，早期的
a. beginning; initial

0428 incisive [ɪn`saɪsɪv] * cis=cut ★★★★☆

The screen writer pitched his new script to the producer who said that he had decided to go ahead and produce the movie because the script was written in an incisive way.

編劇將寫好的新劇本交給決定據此開拍新電影的製片，因為它是以犀利尖刻的筆調寫成的。

犀利的，敏銳的，尖刻的
a. sharp; keen; acute; piercing

0429 excise [ɛk`saɪz] * ex-=out ★★★★★

The smokers protested the heavy excise levied on tobacco products.

吸煙者反對針對菸草製品徵收高額貨物稅。

刪除，切除 / 貨物稅
v. cut out / **n.** tax

0430 exaction [ɪg`zækʃən] * act=act, do ★★★☆☆

The miser was infamous for his exaction abilities, and the persons who owed him money had good reason to be scared if they couldn't pay on time.

這個守財奴的勒索能力惡名昭彰，欠錢者如果沒有準時還錢都會感到很害怕。

勒索，強取，搾取
n. the act or an instance of exacting

0431 transaction [trænz`ækʃən] * trans-=across, over ★★★★★

Coins are adequate for small transactions, while paper notes are used for general business. *Money and Banking* — Tom McArthur

硬幣適用於小額交易，至於紙幣則用於一般買賣。

—— 《貨幣與銀行業務》湯姆‧麥克阿瑟

交易，買賣
n. deal; dealing; negotiation

0432 transmute [træns`mjut] * mut=change ★★★☆☆

At last the chemist transmuted the gas which he was experimenting with into liquids, completing his work.
最後化學家把正在實驗的氣體變成液態物，完成實驗工作。

改變（性質、外觀等）
v. transform

0433 commute [kə`mjut] * com-=together ★★★★★

It's ironic that people complain about the traffic congestion but at the same time they are not willing to commute to work with a car pool.
諷刺的是人們總是抱怨塞車，但同時卻不願以共乘方式通勤上班。

通勤
v. travel to and from one's daily work; transpose

0434 commotion [kə`moʃən] * mot=move ★★★★☆

The secretary heard a large commotion outside in the lounge area and when she went to see what the noise was, she found out that two directors of the board were fighting each other over the dividend.
秘書長聽到外面休息室傳來嘈雜喧鬧聲，外出查看才發現原來是兩位董事為了股利問題爭執不下。

騷動，喧鬧／暴動，暴亂
n. noise; disorder; disturbance; outburst

0435 promote [prə`mot] * pro-=forward ★★★★★

Vitamin A, which is found in carrots, sweet potatoes, milk and liver, helps promote good eyesight.
胡蘿蔔、蕃薯、牛乳和肝臟內富含的維他命 A 可增進視力。

增進，促進／擢陞，拔擢，升級
v. help forward; encourage; support actively / advance or raise a person to a higher office, rank, etc.

0436 procession [prə`sɛʃən] * cess=go ★★★★☆

Many cried as the funeral procession passed by. The president who had been greatly respected was assassinated by a young man.
喪葬隊伍經過時許多人都傷心地哭了。深受人民敬仰的總統遭到一名年輕人暗殺。

行列，隊伍
n. parade; march; train

0437 recess [risɛs] * re-=back ★★★☆☆

The court which stood in recess while the jury deliberated their decision resumed its session thirty minutes later.
法庭裁示休庭，三十分鐘後將再度開庭，陪審團目前正就判決展開商議。

休會，休庭／山脈凹陷處，壁龕
n. rest; interlude; break / niche; hollow; bay

0438 recondite [`rɛkənˌdaɪt] * cond, scond=hide ★★☆☆☆

Many of Gautama Siddhartha's teachings are thought to be recondite and difficult to understand.
釋迦牟尼悉達多的許多教義，被公認是深奧而難以理解的。

深奧的，不易懂的
a. abstruse; obscure; esoteric; opaque; enigmatic

0439 ensconce [ɛn`skɑns] * en-=in ★☆☆☆☆

After a long day at the office, he was looking forward to going home and being able to ensconce himself in his favorite chair and watch movies.
結束一天漫長的工作後，他希望趕快回家並安坐在最喜歡的椅子上看電影。

安置，安坐於～／使隱藏
v. establish or settle comfortably, safely, or secretly

0440 entomology [ˌɛntəˈmɑlədʒɪ] * tom=cut ★★★★☆

My friend Jim had always been interested in insects so he studied entomology when he went to college.

友人吉姆一向對昆蟲很感興趣，所以上大學時選擇研究昆蟲學。

昆蟲學
n. the study of the forms and behavior of insects

0441 epitome [ɪˈpɪtəmɪ] * epi-=on ★★★★☆

The epitome of the novel did not do justice to the complexity of the story and so no one ever bought the book.

那本小說的節錄無法充分表達故事的錯綜複雜性，所以沒有人想買書來看。

縮影，典型 / 摘要，大綱
n. embodiment; incarnation; personification; essence / summary; outline; synopsis

---

0442 epidemic [ˌɛpəˈdɛmɪk] * dem=people ★★★★☆

In the 14th century, there was a severe epidemic, which is known as the Black Death, in Europe.

十四世紀的歐洲有一種非常嚴重的流行性疾病，稱之為黑死病。

流行性疾病，傳染性疾病 / 流行，盛行
n. plague; pestilence; disease; outbreak; scourge / a. widespread; rampant; ubiquitous; prevalent

---

0443 demagogue [ˈdɛməˌgɑg] * -gogue=leader ★★★☆☆

The presidential candidate's mastery of the English language, his suave presence in front of the masses and his ability to convince people that he really can make a difference have led some political analysts to dub him the greatest demagogue of this century.

該總統候選人在英語遣辭用句上的精練度、面對群眾的優雅姿態，以及說服群眾相信的確能做出改變的能力，讓部分政治分析家封他為本世紀最偉大的民心煽動者。

煽動民心的政客，群眾煽動家
n. agitator

0444 pedagogue [ˈpɛdəˌgɑg] * ped-=child ★★★☆☆

The Queen sent her son to a famous pedagogue so that he would have the best education and become the smartest man in the land.

女王將王子送到知名教育家那裡去學習，如此一來就能受到最好教育，並成為全國最聰明的人。

教育家，教師
n. schoolmaster; teacher

0445 orthopedist [ˌɔrθəˈpidɪst] * ortho-=correct ★★★★☆

She was fascinated with orthopedics and studied very hard to become an orthopedist. Later she helped her young niece who was born with a deformity.

她對整形外科很著迷，於是用功念書成為整形外科醫師，後來還為患有先天畸形的小姪女進行手術。

整形外科醫師
n. a doctor who corrects deformities of bones or muscles in children

---

0446 orthography [ɔrˈθɑgrəfɪ] * graph=writing ★★★★☆

Bob's skills in orthography were weak, which prevented him from ever becoming a great writer.

鮑伯的正確拼字能力很差，因此無法成為偉大作家。

正確拼字法，正確拼字
n. correct or conventional spelling

0447 telegraph [ˈtɛləˌgræf] * tele-=far ★★★★☆

The invention of the telegraph was credited to Samuel F. B. Morse and it revolutionized the communications industry.

由山繆爾‧F‧B‧摩斯發明的電報徹底改革了通訊產業。

電報
n. a system of or device for transmitting messages or signal over a distance

0448 **telepathy** [tə`lɛpəθɪ] * -pathy-=feel

★★★★☆

心電感應

n. the supposed communication of thoughts or ideas other than by the known senses

Whether or not you believe in telepathy, it has been proven in specific situations, in laboratories and in real life.

無論你是否相信心電感應，它在某些特殊狀況、實驗研究室和現實生活中，都經證實是確實存在的。

0449 **sympathize** [`sɪmpə͵θaɪz] * sym-=same

★★★★★

同情，憐憫，有同感

v. have pity for; condole with; commiserate

Even though such a horrible accident had never befallen him, he could sympathize with the pain that his neighbor had gone through.

這場可怕的意外雖未降臨在他身上，他對鄰居所經歷的痛苦仍深表同情。

0450 **symposium** [sɪm`pozɪəm] * pos=put

★★★★★

研討會，座談會，專題討論會

n. conference; meeting

The leaders who represented the two nations met at a symposium to discuss the issue of wartime military control.

兩國領袖代表齊聚在研討會上共同商討戰時軍事管制議題。

𝒯ea 𝒯ime... ☕

<Greek legend> Trojan horse
A huge, hollow wooden horse filled with Greek soldiers and left at the gates of Troy: when it was brought into the city, the soldiers came out at night and opened the gates to the Greek army, which destroyed the city.

〈來自希臘神話〉特洛伊木馬
希臘城邦聯軍將一隻腹中挖空滿載希臘士兵的大木馬留在特洛伊城城門前，特洛伊人將它拉進城內，當晚木馬裡的士兵殺出，打開城門迎接希臘聯軍，最後摧毀特洛伊城。
（註：本詞原意是指在特洛伊戰爭中希臘軍隊用來攻入特洛伊城的工具，也就是一隻偽裝木馬。後世將此詞引申為「偽裝潛入敵國或競爭對手公司以進行破壞工作的破壞份子」。）

❖ **Trojan Horse** [`trodʒən hɔrs] *n. any person, group, or thing that seeks to subvert a nation, organization, etc. from within* │ 破壞份子，顛覆份子

Our most trusted colleague was, in fact, a Trojan Horse. He was at last accused of industrial spying.

我們最信任的同事事實上是個破壞份子，最後被控商業間諜罪。

1 Complete each word by filling in the blank with proper spelling so that it has the same meaning as suggested. Then please write the meaning of each word in Chinese.

1. 交易 = _ _ _ _ _ a c t i o n
2. 通勤 = _ _ _ m u t e
3. 喧鬧 = c o m _ _ _ i o n
4. 休庭 = _ _ c e s s
5. 昆蟲學 = e n _ _ _ o l o g y
6. 流行性疾病 = e p i _ _ _ i c
7. 研討會 = _ _ _ p o s i u m
8. 拖欠 = _ _ f a u l t
9. 迫害 = p e r _ _ _ u t e
10. 連續不斷的 = _ _ _ s e c u t i v e

11. inoculate = _____
12. perennial = _____
13. perturb = _____
14. dissect = _____
15. repulse = _____
16. implicate = _____
17. decelerate = _____
18. pertain = _____
19. recipient = _____
20. incisive = _____

2 Choose a word that best completes the sentence.

21. The department manager was _____ to a general manager. So we congratulated him.
   (A) excised   (B) persecuted   (C) promoted   (D) depended

22. I'm calling to _____ my flight reservation.
   (A) sympathize   (B) ensconce   (C) confirm   (D) encourage

23. Grandmother peeled the peach and _____ the wormy part.
   (A) retained   (B) transmuted   (C) reserved   (D) excised

3 The highlighted word is closest in meaning to which of the following?

24. When refreshments were delivered to the military compound on the battlefield, there was a large commotion among soldiers.
   (A) recess   (B) outburst   (C) recipient   (D) entomology

25. The marine corps could repulse the enemy troops who invaded along the border.
   (A) resect   (B) repel   (C) pertain   (D) desist

MP3
20

0451 deposit [dɪ`pazɪt] * de-=down

★★★★★

If you make it a habit to deposit money into the bank every month, it won't take long to build up good savings.

如果你每個月都習慣把錢存到銀行，不用多久就會有一筆高額存款。

放下，放置 / 儲存
v. *put; place; set down; give as partial payment*

0452 deviate [`divɪ,et] * via=way

★★★★☆

Many successful people will tell you that the key to success is to set a goal and not to deviate from it.

許多成功者都說成功的祕訣是先設定一個目標，然後全力以赴不違背初衷。

違背，脫離
v. *stray; wander; turn aside; go astray*

0453 previous [`privɪəs] * pre-=before

★★★★★

Since William Collins had a previous engagement, he was unable to attend the boss's farewell dinner.

威廉‧柯林斯因事先有約，因此未能參加老闆的餞別晚宴。

先前的，以前的
a. *prior; preceding; earlier; foregoing; former*

0454 premature [ˌprimə`tjur] * mature=to grow up

★★★★★

It was premature of the manager to resign from the company since he hadn't exhausted all the avenues of action available to him.

經理太早向公司遞出辭呈，因為他尚未用盡所有可行方法。

過早的
a. *too soon; too early; untimely*

0455 immature [ˌɪmə`tjur] * im-=not

★★★★★

Girls usually mature faster than boys. A lot of girls date boys who are older than them, because they think boys of their age are too immature.

女孩通常比男孩早熟，所以會跟比自己年紀大的男孩約會，她們認為同齡男孩太不成熟。

不成熟的，幼稚的
a. *undeveloped; unfledged; raw; pubescent*

0456 immensely [ɪ`mɛnslɪ] * mens=measure

★★★★★

She doesn't like him very much and even though it's not nice to wish bad on anyone, she was immensely happy to hear he was having financial difficulties.

雖然不該希望別人遭遇不幸，但因為她很討厭他，所以聽說他面臨財務困難就感到很高興。

非常地，極大地
ad. *very much; highly*

0457 commensurate [kə`mɛnʃərɪt] * com-=together

★★★★☆

I am very happy that Lisa has been chosen as vice president of the company because she is a capable person and her abilities are commensurate with the position.

我很高興麗莎獲選為公司副總裁，因為她很能幹且能力與職務相稱。

相稱的，等量的
a. *proportionate*

0458 compassion [kəm`pæʃən] * passion=feel

★★★★☆

The Buddhist ideal is that of passionless benevolence. The Christian ideal is that of compassion.

佛教徒的信念是不動情的慈悲，基督徒的信念則是憐憫。

憐憫
n. *pity; sympathy*

0459 dispassionate [dɪsˋpæʃənɪt] * dis-=not, away ★★★☆☆

Considering the fact that Jim won 10 million dollars in the lottery and he is still in his right mind, he is extremely dispassionate.

吉姆就算中了一千萬美元的樂透彩券仍保持理智，可見他非常冷靜。

不為情感所動的，冷靜的
a. free from passion; calm; impartial; composed; self-possessed; sober; equanimous; placid; serene

---

0460 disrupt [dɪsˋrʌpt] * rupt=break ★★★☆☆

I would have enjoyed myself at the theater, but a lady and her kid sitting in front of me kept coming in and out and they disrupted the whole play.

我本來能好好在戲院欣賞表演，但有個女士帶著孩子坐在我前方不停進進出出，擾亂整場演出。

使中斷，使混亂
v. interrupt the flow or continuity of; bring disorder to; shatter

---

0461 eruption [ɪˋrʌpʃən] * e-=out ★★★★★

Scientists watched the mountain for many years and tried to predict when it would erupt but they never imagined that it could have been such a devastating eruption.

多年來科學家觀測那座山並試圖預測爆發時間，但萬萬想不到那是一場極具毀滅性的火山爆發。

爆發，噴出
n. outbreak; outburst; emission; discharge

0462 erase [ɪˋres] * ras=scrape ★★★★★

Some teachers do not erase the board after they finish their class. Then the onerous work is usually turned over to the other teachers who teach the following class.

有些老師上完課不會擦黑板，於是這項繁重工作總落到下一位來上課的老師頭上。

擦掉
v. rub out; obliterate; remove all traces of; efface; delete; blot out; cross out

---

0463 abrasion [əˋbreʒən] * ab-=away ★★★★☆

The parents were convicted of child abuse because their son's teacher at school noticed abrasions on the child's arm and reported the fact to social services.

那對父母因虐待兒童被判有罪，因為學校老師在他們的兒子手臂上發現擦傷並向社服中心舉報。

擦傷／磨損，侵蝕
n. the scraping or wearing away / erosion

0464 abduct [əbˋdʌkt] * duc(t)=draw ★★★★☆

In the U.S. many parents grieve each year while desperately trying to locate their abducted children.

在美國每年有許多父母懷著悲傷拼命尋找自己被綁架的孩子。

綁架，誘拐
v. kidnap; carry off; take away

0465 education [ˌɛdʒəˋkeʃən] * e-=out ★★★★★

People who have received a university education may be intelligent but they aren't always smart or wise.

受過大學教育的人可能智商高，但不一定是聰明或有智慧的。

教育
n. schooling; instruction; teaching

0466 **erode** [ɪˋrod] * rod=scrape, rub ★★★★★

To many it looked like the house collapsed for no apparent reason, but in fact the ground began to erode several years earlier.

許多人覺得那棟房屋看來似乎無明顯原因就倒塌，事實上這塊土地早在幾年前就開始受到侵蝕。

侵蝕
v. wear away; gnaw away; corrode

0467 **corrode** [kəˋrod] * cor-=together ★★★★☆

It is important to regularly clean your battery terminals because the acid from the battery causes them to corrode very quickly.

定期檢查電池接頭是很重要的，因為電池內的酸性電解液容易使接頭快速腐蝕。

腐蝕，侵蝕
v. wear away, esp. by chemical action; be worn away; decay

0468 **corrupt** [kəˋrʌpt] * rupt=break ★★★★★

When it was discovered that the President was a very corrupt man, there was a revolution and a new government was established in its place.

大家發現其實總統非常腐敗貪污時，革命運動便興起，新政府也跟著取而代之。

道德淪喪的，腐敗貪污的
a. morally depraved; rotten; evil; wicked; corrupted

0469 **interrupt** [ˌɪntəˋrʌpt] * inter-=between ★★★★★

The newcomer was a very annoying person to debate with because he continually interrupted whoever was speaking and never let them finish what they were going to say.

跟新來的人討論事情很令人生厭，因為他一直打斷別人講話，從不讓人把話說完。

打斷，插嘴，使中斷
v. break in on; intrude into; butt in on; barge in on; disrupt

---

0470 **intercept** [ˌɪntəˋsɛpt] * cept=catch, take ★★★★☆

The spy was able to intercept the messenger who was delivering news of the deployment of enemy troops along the border to the king, and thus the king was unprepared for the assault on his land.

間諜攔截到正要將敵軍邊境部署消息傳達給國王的傳令兵，於是國王對攻擊行動毫無應戰準備。

攔截，截獲，竊聽
v. stop; halt; interrupt; block

0471 **exception** [ɪkˋsɛpʃən] * ex-=out ★★★★★

If you don't treat others with respect, almost without exception you will have a very difficult time getting along with people wherever you go.

如果你無法尊重他人，無論走到哪裡都很難和他人好好相處。

例外，除外
n. an instance that does not follow a rule

0472 **excursion** [ɪkˋskɝʒən] * curs=run ★★★☆☆

Last spring my class made an interesting excursion to Rome, one of the richest repositories of ancient history and arts.

去年春天我們班到富藏古代歷史和藝術寶庫的羅馬，展開一場有趣的短程旅行。

遠足，短程團體旅行
n. a short journey; outing; trip

0473 incursion [ɪnˈkɝʃən] * in-=in ★★★★☆

I heard reports on the evening news about the incursions that the Bosnians were carrying out on the Muslims in the former Yugoslavia.

我從晚間新聞報導中得知波士尼亞人襲擊前南斯拉夫境內的回教徒。

入侵，襲擊
n. *invasion; attack; assail; assault; raid; charge; onslaught*

0474 infuse [ɪnˈfjuz] * fus=water ★★★★☆

The English teacher has been trying for the last three years to infuse into his students the proper way to learn English, but he hasn't been very effective.

過去三年來英文老師一直試著灌輸學生學習英文的正確方法，但並非十分奏效。

灌輸，傾注
v. *imbue; pervade*

0475 profusion [prəˈfjuʒən] * pro-=forward ★★★★★

When the television network announced that they were canceling the show, there was such a profusion of protest letters that eventually the decision was reversed.

當電視台宣布要停播節目，大量抗議信件湧入電視台，最後該決定被取消了。

大量，豐富
n. *abundance; bounty; plenty; copiousness; glut; surplus*

MP3 21

0476 protract [proˈtrækt] * tract=draw ★★★★★

In order to protract the diplomatic discussions, the ambassador continued to ask complicated questions and demand detailed answers.

為了延長外交會談時間，大使繼續詢問複雜問題並要求鉅細靡遺的答覆。

延長，拖長
v. *lengthen; prolong; elongate*

0477 contraction [kənˈtrækʃən] * con-=together ★★★★☆

Jim was writing a paper and there wasn't enough room on the line to finish the sentence, so he used some contractions.

吉姆正在撰寫報告，但沒有足夠空間寫完最後一句，於是就使用縮寫字。

縮寫
n. *abbreviation*

0478 conference [ˈkɑnfərəns] * fer=carry, put ★★★★★

I'm sorry but Mr. Smith is in a conference right now and is not available, but I will tell him you called and have him get in touch with you as soon as possible.

很抱歉，史密斯先生正在開會所以無法接聽電話。我會轉告他您的來電，並請他盡快與您聯絡。

會議
n. *meeting; convention; symposium; congress; seminar; forum; colloquium*

0479 vociferous [voˈsɪfərəs] * voc-=shout, call ★★★☆☆

Many citizens wish that political parties would forgo vociferous wrangling and get along harmoniously with each other.

許多市民希望不同政黨能摒棄大吼大叫的爭辯並和諧相處。

大聲喊叫的，大吼大叫的
a. *noisy; clamorous*

0480 invocation [ˌɪnvəˈkeʃən] * in-=in ★★☆☆☆

As the drought continued, the priest of the tribe decided to perform an invocation to its god, or a rain ritual.

隨著乾旱持續，部落祭司決定進行祈雨儀式向神靈祈禱。

祈禱
n. *litany; obsecration; prayer*

0481 infection [ɪnˋfɛkʃən] * fec(t)=do, make ★★★★★

Especially in summer the health authorities are very much concerned about various forms of infections.

衛生當局特別關注各類傳染病的夏季感染疫情。

傳染，傳染病
n. the process of infecting or state of being infected; disease

0482 affection [əˋfɛkʃən] * af-, ad-=near ★★★★★

Daughters usually turn to their mothers for affection and companionship and oftentimes vice versa.

女兒通常向母親尋求鍾愛與陪伴，做母親的往往也向女兒尋求相同的情感慰藉。

鍾愛，親愛
n. love

0483 affinity [əˋfɪnətɪ] * fin=boundary, end ★★★★☆

After more than ten years of working together Jim and Kirk developed an affinity that would last a lifetime.

吉姆和柯克一起工作超過十年後，建立了足以維持一輩子的密切關係。

密切關係 / 相似性，同類性
n. friendliness; fondness; liking; rapport; attraction / similarity; similitude

0484 definitive [dɪˋfɪnɪtɪv] * de-=down ★★★★☆

I can understand that my answer will be treated as definitive. So I think I'll have to be careful in giving my answer and I won't change my mind.

我明白自己的答覆具有決定性的影響力，因此我認為我必須小心回答且不會改變我的心意。

決定性的，最後的，絕對的
a. decisive; final; absolute

0485 denounce [dɪˋnauns] * -nounce=report, tell ★★★★☆

Even though he had been a staunch believer in Buddhism for most of his life, upon the death of his wife, he denounced Buddhism and other forms of religion altogether.

雖然他終其一生都是虔誠佛教徒，但妻子去世後卻公然抨擊佛教信仰和其他宗教。

公然抨擊，當眾指責
v. condemn; criticize; censure; vilify; accuse

0486 announce [əˋnauns] * an-, ad-=to ★★★★★

Jack announced his engagement so that everyone could know about it. He was soon overwhelmed with congratulatory notes and e-mails.

傑克向大家宣布訂婚消息，接著立刻收到許多令他大為感動的恭賀信函和電子郵件。

宣布
v. proclaim; declare; disseminate; give out; disclose; reveal

0487 annihilate [əˋnaɪəˏlet] * nihil-=zero ★★★★☆

The king hoped to annihilate his enemies but they proved to be too strong for him to overcome.

國王希望徹底消滅自己的敵人，但事實證明敵人太強無法征服。

徹底消滅，殲滅
v. wipe out; exterminate; liquidate; eradicate; extirpate

0488 nihilism [ˋnaɪəlˏɪzəm] * -ism=ideology ★☆☆☆☆

Simon's university major was philosophy, particularly 'nihilism,' which made him a very boring person to talk to since he believed that nothing really existed.

賽門在大學主修哲學，特別是「虛無主義」，結果使他變得言語無趣，因為他相信沒有任何事物是真正存在的。

虛無主義
n. disbelief in anything

0489 feminism [ˈfɛməˌnɪzəm] * femin-=woman ★★★☆☆

Korean women are slowly changing the social status of women in Korean society and the feminism issue is rapidly gaining momentum.

韓國婦女正慢慢改變自己在國內的社會地位，女權運動議題的聲勢也快速增強中。

女權運動，男女平等主義
n. the advocacy of women's rights on the ground of the equality of the sexes

0490 effeminate [əˈfɛmənɪt] * ef-, ex-=out ★☆☆☆☆

Many surveys have shown that men with effeminate traits are much more likely to have homosexual tendencies than more masculine men.

許多研究顯示，娘娘腔的男子比富有男子氣概的可能更具有同性戀傾向。

娘娘腔的，無男子氣概的
a. unmanly; unmasculine; womanish

0491 efficacious [ˌɛfəˈkeʃəs] * fic=do, make ★★★★☆

Screaming, shouting and crying are very efficacious ways of gaining people's attention, but not their favor.

尖叫、大喊和哭鬧是引起別人注意的極有效方式，但同時也是他人不樂見的。

有效的，靈驗的
a. effectual; effective; productive; serviceable

0492 nonfiction [nɑnˈfɪkʃən] * non-=not ★★★★☆

His work was a masterpiece of nonfiction that for the first time told the story of what really happened to J.F.K. and his assassins, but only a few people believed him.

他的作品是非小說類文學傑作，首度揭露美國前總統甘迺迪及其暗殺者的真實內幕，但只有少數人相信。

（歷史、傳記、遊記等）非小說類散文文學
n. literary work other than fiction

0493 nonconformist [nɑnkənˈfɔrmɪst] * form=form ★☆☆☆☆

The three men had certain nonconformist views, such as having long hair dyed in many different colors, which prohibited them from having one of those boring old office jobs they didn't really want anyway.

那三名男子有某些違背傳統的觀點，例如頂著一頭五顏六色的長髮。所以他們找不到坐辦公桌的工作，不過他們也不想要就是了。

不遵從傳統觀念者，不墨守成規者
n. a person who does not conform to a prevailing principle; renegade; heretic; dissenter

0494 deformity [dɪˈfɔrmətɪ] * de-=down ★★★★☆

Despite their hopes of having a perfectly normal baby, their child was born with a severe deformity of the left foot.

儘管他們想要一個正常健康的嬰孩，寶寶一生下來仍帶有嚴重的左腳殘障。

身體畸形，殘缺，殘障
n. the state of being deformed; disfigurement

0495 detract [dɪˈtrækt] * tract, treat=draw ★★★☆☆

The peeling walls detract from the beauty of the hotel building. It is in disrepair and needs renovating.

斑駁的牆壁減損了飯店建物的美，這面年久失修的牆需要修繕一番。

減損，降低
v. reduce; diminish; lower

0496 **retreat** [rɪ`trit] * re-=back ★★☆☆☆

The general ordered a retreat when he knew that there was no way they could win the battle.

當將軍發現不可能打贏這場戰爭，便命令士兵撤退。

撤退
n. strategic withdrawal; falling back; evacuation; flight; getaway; escape

0497 **relapse** [rɪ`læps] * -lapse=glide, fall ★★★☆☆

Hamilton is very uncommunicative and shy. At the meeting, he murmured something and soon relapsed into silence.

漢彌爾頓非常害羞寡言，他在會議上低語幾句，又立刻陷入沉默。

重新陷入，故態復萌
v. fall back; slip back; sink back; revert; backslide; retrogress

0498 **elapse** [ɪ`læps] * e-=out ★★★☆☆

How much time has elapsed since the test began? I'll be in big trouble if I am not allowed to enter the examination room.

考試開始了多久？如果我不能進考場就糟了。

光陰逝去，時間過去
v. pass by; glide by; lapse; slip away

0499 **edict** [`idɪkt] * dict=say, words ★★☆☆☆

The king issued an edict which many of his subjects didn't like but were forced to obey. He prohibited all forms of alcohol in his land.

國王頒布禁止所有酒類在國內流通的敕令，許多臣民不願接受卻只能被迫服從。

詔書，聖旨，敕令，布告
n. decree; proclamation; ordinance; mandate; manifesto; enactment

0500 **unpredictable** [ˌʌnprɪ`dɪktəbl̩] * pre-=beforehand ★★★★☆

Her unpredictable actions, although entertaining, made us nervous as we never knew what to expect.

她出人意表的行為雖極具娛樂效果，但還是讓我們很緊張，因為不知道接下來會發生什麼事。

不可預料的，出乎意料的
a. not predictable; not foreseeable; unstable; fitful; mercurial; capricious; whimsical

---

Tea Time... ☕

<Music history> Gamma

After gamma, name used by Guido d'Arezzo for the lowest note of his scale.

〈來自音樂歷史〉希臘文字母中的第三個字母
本字源自義大利中世紀音樂理論家奎多‧達雷佐首創音階法的最低音音符。（註：本字原為希臘文字母中的第三個字母。達雷佐是現代樂譜記號和唱名法的創始者，其首創的音階法為五線譜奠定基礎。後世從本字衍生出 gamut，原指「樂理上的全音階或全音域」，引申為「全部、整個範圍」。）

❖ **gamut** [`gæmət] *n.* the entire range | 全部，整個範圍

The contemporary musician's interest in music runs the gamut. He likes everything from choral to jazz.

現代音樂家的音樂興趣十分廣泛，從聖歌到爵士樂都喜歡。

1 Complete each word by filling in the blank with proper spelling so that it has the same meaning as suggested. Then please write the meaning of each word in Chinese.

1. 侵蝕	= _ r o d e		11. deviate	=	_____
2. 灌輸	= i n _ _ _ e		12. retreat	=	_____
3. 縮寫	= _ _ _ t r a c t i o n		13. commensurate	=	_____
4. 大吼大叫的	= _ _ _ i f e r o u s		14. dispassionate	=	_____
5. 向神靈祈禱	= _ _ v o c a t i o n		15. disrupt	=	_____
6. 鍾愛	= _ _ f e c t i o n		16. eruption	=	_____
7. 儲存	= _ _ p o s i t		17. abrasion	=	_____
8. 先前的	= _ _ _ v i o u s		18. corrode	=	_____
9. 過早的	= _ _ _ m a t u r e		19. corrupt	=	_____
10. 不成熟的	= i m _ _ _ _ _ _		20. interrupt	=	_____

2 Choose a word that best completes the sentence.

21. Male emperor penguins are famous for their paternal _____. They incubate an egg for two months without eating anything.

(A) affection   (B) invocation   (C) profusion   (D) affinity

22. Grandmother's _____ illness rendered her feeble; she was bedridden for a long time.

(A) eroded   (B) commensurate   (C) intercepted   (D) protracted

3 The highlighted word is closest in meaning to which of the following?

23. The aggressor nation made an incursion into its neighboring nation.

(A) inroad   (B) excursion   (C) infection   (D) abrasion

24. The OK pest control company placed an ad in the newspaper. However, there was a typo: "Don't worry about "aunts." We'll surely annihilate them."

(A) detract   (B) relapse   (C) exterminate   (D) elapse

25. Because of the young author's premature death, his book was published posthumously.

(A) untimely   (B) impartial   (C) placid   (D) corrupt

MP3
22

0501 predecessor [ˌprɛdɪˈsɛsə] * cess=go ★★★★★

When he was elected president, his first year was spent correcting all of the foolish things his predecessor had done.

他當選為總統後，第一年任期都花在導正前總統推行的一切不明智政策。

前任，前輩，祖先
n. forerunner; antecedent; precursor

0502 process [ˈprɑsɛs] * pro-=before, forward ★★★★★

Adolescence is the process of going from childhood to maturity. Many young children at this stage experience rapid emotional and physical changes.

青春期是從幼兒期過渡到成人期的過程，許多青少年在此階段都會經歷快速心理和生理的變化。

過程
n. procedure; proceeding; passage; course

0503 propel [prəˈpɛl] * -pel=drive ★★★★★

The lifeguard used swimming fins to propel himself through the water in an effort to reach the drowning girl as quickly as possible.

救生員穿著蛙鞋在水中前進，以便盡快趕到溺水女孩身邊。

推進，推動
v. set in motion; impel; drive forward; push forward; precipitate

---

0504 compel [kəmˈpɛl] * com-=together, all ★★★★★

Poor health has compelled Jim to resign from his job. Recently he has been in a worse condition and unable to report for work.

健康不佳迫使吉姆辭去工作，近來他因健康狀況惡化而無法上班。

迫使，被迫，逼使
v. force; require; oblige; necessitate

0505 complicity [kəmˈplɪsətɪ] * plic=fold ★★★★☆

A full investigation is under way and Mr. Reed is worried because the prosecuting attorney would like to put him away for his complicity in the crime.

全面調查業已展開，瑞德先生擔心檢察官想以共謀罪將他起訴。

共謀，串通
n. partnership in a crime or wrongdoing

0506 explicate [ˈɛksplɪˌket] * ex-=out ★★★☆☆

She told one lie in an effort to explicate her desperate situation, but that only led to another lie, and then another and soon she forgot what was true and what wasn't.

她為了詳細說明自己的危險處境而說謊，接著又一再撒謊好圓謊，結果很快就忘記什麼是真相，什麼是謊言。

詳細說明，辯明
v. account for; delineate; unravel; untangle

0507 expose [ɪkˈspoz] * pos=put ★★★☆☆

Cunning is a short blanket - if you pull it over your face, you expose your feet. — Sir Walter Scott

狡猾就像一條短毛毯，如果把它拉上來蓋住臉，那麼腳就露出來了。
—— （英國歷史小說家暨詩人）華特‧史考特爵士

使暴露，露出
v. bare; uncover; show; display; exhibit; denude; divest

0508 **supposition** [ˌsʌpəˈzɪʃən] * sup-, sub-=under ★★★★★

Working on the supposition that things might actually change at the office, Mr. Mitchell tried to make as many suggestions as possible.

米歇爾先生基於辦公環境或許真能改變的假設前提，試著盡量提出許多建議。

假設
n. presumption; assumption; surmise; hypothesis

0509 **suppress** [səˈprɛs] * press=push down ★★★★★

The government of the despotic nation has a tendency to suppress all forms of individuality and creative thinking.

專制國家政府有鎮壓各種形式的個人主義和創意思維的傾向。

平定，鎮壓
v. put down; crush; squash; quell; extinguish; subdue; put an end to

0510 **depressing** [dɪˈprɛsɪŋ] * de-=down ★★★★☆

Life which is devoid of pleasure can be very depressing. However, life which is full of pleasure only can be meaningless.

沒有樂趣的人生是沉悶的，但只有歡愉的人生則是空虛的。

令人沮喪的，沉悶的
a. miserable

0511 **devour** [dɪˈvaʊr] * vo(u)r=throat ★★★★☆

Howard is such a knowledgeable man and the key to his extensive knowledge lies in the fact that he has been devouring at least three books a week since he was in high school.

霍華十分博學，他之所以有如此淵博的知識，關鍵在於高中起每周至少讀三本書。

狼吞虎嚥，吞沒 / 耽讀，諦聽
v. wolf down; gulp down; swallow up; gorge; gobble up / absorb; engulf; take in

0512 **carnivorous** [kɑrˈnɪvərəs] * carni=flesh, body ★★★★☆

A carnivorous animal is commonly called a meat-eater. A tiger, lion, cheetah and leopard are some of the well-known carnivores.

肉食性動物通常被稱為食肉者，舉凡老虎、獅子、印度豹，以及美洲豹等都是常見的食肉動物。

（動物）肉食性的 /（植物）食蟲的
a. feeding on flesh

0513 **incarnation** [ˌɪnkɑrˈneʃən] * in-=in ★★★☆☆

One of my friends Philip is the incarnation of honesty. I've never seen anyone more honest than he.

友人菲利普是誠實的化身，我從未見過比他更誠實的人。

典型，化身
n. embodiment

0514 **insect** [ˈɪnsɛkt] * sect=divide, cut ★★★★★

To everyone's surprise, the melodious sound was created by a tiny insect. It was very pleasing in the summer night.

大家都想不到那悅耳動聽的聲音是由一隻小昆蟲發出的，在夏夜裡聽來份外愉快。

昆蟲 / 蟲
n. any arthropod of the class insecta, having a head, thorax abdomen / bug

0515 **bisect** [baɪˈsɛkt] * bi-=two ★★★☆☆

The new highway bisects the village, so the village is divided into two parts. An underpass is the only passage connecting the two parts.

新建公路將村莊一分為二，村落因此被分成兩等分，地下道是聯絡兩區的唯一通道。

平分，分為兩等分，一分為二
v. divide into two parts

0516 bipartisan [baɪˋpɑrtəzn̩] * part=part, divide ★★☆☆☆

The new gun control legislation was considered bipartisan because it was supported by both the Liberal Party and the Conservative Party.

一般認為新制槍械管制條例是由兩黨人士共同支持的，因為它同時受到自由黨和保守黨的贊成。

兩黨的，兩黨人士組成的
a. of or involving two political parties

0517 depart [dɪˋpɑrt] * de-=away ★★☆☆☆

The plane was scheduled to depart at 12:00, but due to weather, the flight was delayed for three hours.

該班機原本預定在中午十二點起飛，但因天候因素延遲三小時。

起程，出發
v. leave; set out

0518 devoid [dɪˋvɔɪd] * void=empty ★★★☆☆

It may be true that ideas devoid of lucid meaning often give the strongest impulse to the further development of science.

缺乏清晰意涵的構想往往可為科學的進一步發展提供最強大的推動力。

缺乏的，沒有的
a. lacking; without; wanting

0519 avoid [əˋvɔɪd] * a-=to ★★★★★

Most troubles can be avoided, but death and taxes are inevitable.
                    Reader's Choice ── Sandra Silberstein

絕大多數的麻煩都能避免，唯有死亡和繳稅除外。
    ──《讀者的選擇》（美國西雅圖華盛頓大學應用語言學教授）珊卓拉·希柏絲坦

避免，逃避
v. evade; elude; dodge; escape; avert; sidestep; shun; eschew

---

0520 ascribe [əˋskraɪb] * scrib=write ★★★★☆

The farmers ascribed the poor harvest to the drought, which had lasted more than three months in the summer.

農民將欠收歸咎於長達三個月以上的夏季乾旱。

歸咎於，歸因於
v. attribute; assign

0521 describe [dɪˋskraɪb] * de-=down ★★★★★

It is very difficult to describe a thing to a person and make him understand unless we actually experience it, whatever it may be.

要讓別人理解我們的描述是很困難的，除非他真的經歷過此事，不管那是什麼。

形容，描述
v. explain; portray; depict; illustrate; characterize

0522 detain [dɪˋten] * tain=hold ★★★★☆

Mr. Lemonick got drunk at a party and later tried to drive home, but the police caught him and detained him overnight in jail.

雷蒙尼克先生在派對上喝醉了，後來想開車回家卻被警方攔下，並扣留在拘留所一整夜。

拘留，扣押，扣留
v. confine; hold; keep in custody; lock up

0523 sustain [səˋsten] * sus-, sub-=under ★★★★★

At irregular intervals, his relatives allowed a little pittance to the poor man to help him sustain life.

他的親戚不定時提供一些津貼給窮困者維持生計。

維持生命 / 支持，承受
v. keep alive / prop; uphold

0524 susceptive [sə`sɛptɪv] * cept=take, catch ★★★★☆

The makings of a good office manager include being susceptive to new ideas and change where necessary.

優秀辦公室經理的必要條件包括容易接受新知，並懂得通權達變。

容易接受的，易受影響的
a. concerned with the receiving of ideas

0525 concept [`kɑnsɛpt] * con-=together ★★★★★

You have to pay very close attention when watching that movie because it is based on some deep concepts.

你觀賞這部電影時要特別留意，因為它是以一些深刻觀念作為拍攝基礎的。

觀念，概念
n. idea; conception; notion; supposition

0526 conform [kən`fɔrm] * form=form ★★★★★

The outlaw refused to conform to the rules of society and was sentenced to ten years in prison for the crimes he committed.

那名罪犯拒絕遵守社會規範，最後被判處十年徒刑。

遵從（法律、準則、規範、風俗等），遵守
v. comply with; follow; observe; obey; abide by

0527 multiform [`mʌltɪfɔrm] * multi-=many ★★★★☆

Water is called a 'multiform matter' since it is commonly found in one of the three forms; ice, liquid or steam.

水被稱作「多態性物質」，因為它通常可見於冰、水或水蒸氣等三種形式中。

多種形狀的，多樣的
a. having many forms

0528 multiply [`mʌltə‚plaɪ] * -ply=fold ★★★★★

After marriage they decided to follow the Lord's teaching - to "be fruitful and multiply" - but they didn't plan on having triplets.

他們婚後決定遵從上帝的教誨「要繁衍增多」，但從未計畫要生三胞胎。

增加
v. increase in number; increase; reproduce

0529 imply [ɪm`plaɪ] * im-=in ★★★★★

Raymond didn't really come right out and say it, but he implied that he thought the leader of his own party was incompetent.

雷蒙雖不曾明講但暗示自己所屬的政黨領袖是不適任的。

暗指，暗示
v. indicate; suggest; hint; insinuate

0530 immure [ɪ`mjur] * mur=wall ★☆☆☆☆

I read the story, *The Black Cat* in which a crazy man killed a person and immured him behind a brick wall.

我讀過一篇名為《黑貓》的故事，書中描述某個瘋子殺了人，並將屍首藏在磚牆後面。

監禁，幽居
v. enclose within walls; imprison

0531 intramural [‚ɪntrə`mjurəl] * intra-=in ★★☆☆☆

Jane was first introduced to gymnastics when she was in high school as it was one of the most popular intramural sports among her classmates.

珍在高中時期首次接觸到體操，當時這是最受班上同學歡迎的校內運動之一。

校內的
a. situated or done within walls

0532 intrastate [ˌɪntrəˈstet] * state=status
★★☆☆☆

州內的
a. *within a state*

After Jane won the Best Athlete of the Year award at her high school for being an incredible gymnast, she competed in and won the Intrastate Championship.

珍在以優異體操運動員身分拿下年度高中最佳運動員獎項後，繼續比賽並榮獲州冠軍。

0533 interstate [ˌɪntəˈstet] * inter-=between
★★★☆☆

州與州之間的，州際的
a. *between states*

Jane is the High School Interstate Champion Gymnast who is planning to lead her school to victory in the National Championship.

珍是高中州際體操冠軍選手，並計畫代表學校角逐全國錦標賽冠軍。

0534 interpose [ˌɪntəˈpoz] * pos-=put
★★★☆☆

插話，提出異議 / 調停
v. *intervene / interfere*

Nick tried to keep silent, but when the argument between his parents turned to matters of his personal conduct he felt he had to interpose in order to defend himself.

尼克雖想保持沉默，但等到父母的爭執演變成對他個人行為的爭論時，便覺得必須介入為自己辯解。

0535 compose [kəmˈpoz] * com-=together
★★★★★

構成，組成
v. *constitute; form; make up*

All things are composed of atoms and molecules that are constantly moving.

所有物體都是由不斷移動的原子和分子組成的。

0536 compatible [kəmˈpætəbl] * pati=stand, endure
★★★★★

能相容的，一致的，合得來的
a. *able to coexist; well-suited; mutually tolerant; consistent*

Cats and dogs are not compatible. They are almost never friendly to each other. They tend to fight tooth and nail.

貓咪和狗合不來，彼此幾乎不能和平相處，很容易就全副武裝打起來。

0537 impatient [ɪmˈpeʃənt] * im-=not
★★★★★

沒耐心的，性急的，不耐煩的
a. *irritated; itchy; intolerant*

The teacher became impatient with his unruly student, who was continuously making noise. At last he shouted at him.

老師對不守規矩發出噪音的學生漸漸不耐煩起來，最後對著他大聲喊叫。

0538 immortal [ɪˈmɔrtl̩] * mort=death
★★★★☆

不死的，長生的
a. *undying; eternal; everlasting; imperishable; enduring*

My friend Jim has nearly died three times. He sometimes jokes of the possibility of his being immortal.

友人吉姆曾有三次瀕死經驗，有時他戲稱自己或許可以長生不死。

0539 mortician [mɔrˈtɪʃən] * -cian-=person
★★☆☆☆

殯葬業者
n. *undertaker*

The mortician is almost always a lonely man, since most of his clients are dead and everyone else complains that he charges too much for his services.

殯葬業者幾乎總是孤零零的，因為他絕大多數的客戶都死了，其他人則抱怨他收費太高。

0540 optician [ɑp`tɪʃən] * opt-=eye

★★★★☆

Her grandfather had to visit the optician every three months to get new glasses since he was slowly going blind.

她的祖母每隔三個月就必須去找配鏡師配副新眼鏡，因為她漸漸失明了。

光學儀器商，眼鏡商，配鏡師
n. *a maker or seller of optical instruments, esp. spectacles and contact lenses*

0541 optometrist [ɑp`tɑmətrɪst] * meter=measure

★★★★☆

He was an optometrist and his wife was an optician. They were a great team and opened an optical store.

他是驗光師而妻子則是配鏡師，兩人合作無間開了一家眼鏡行。

驗光師
n. *a person who practices optometry*

0542 symmetry [`sɪmɪtrɪ] * sym-=the same

★★★★★

The snowflake is often thought to be an example of perfect symmetry. However, in reality there are very few snowflakes that have perfect correspondence.

大家常認為雪花是完美對稱性的最佳實例，事實上只有極少數雪花擁有完美一致性。

對稱性 / 均衡
n. *balance / correspondence*

0543 sympathy [`sɪmpəθɪ] * -pathy=feeling

★★★★★

We felt tremendous sympathy for the bereaved family. They were extremely sorrowful over the death of their grandfather.

我們向因祖父逝世深感悲傷的喪家表達深切的哀悼之意。

同情，憐憫 / 同感，共鳴
n. *compassion; commiseration; pity / understanding*

0544 empathy [`ɛmpəθɪ] * em-=in

★★★★☆

Jack, a soldier, felt a strong empathy for his younger brother, who had many fears about entering the Army.

身為軍人的傑克對因入伍而有許多恐懼的弟弟很能感同身受。

同理心 / 移情作用，同感
n. *the power of identifying oneself mentally with a person or object of contemplation / ability to share another person's feelings, experience, etc.*

0545 employ [ɪm`plɔɪ] * -ploy=enfold, engage

★★★★★

The head of the company hopes to employ close to 150 people by the end of this year. More workers are needed to meet the increasing demand.

公司主管希望能在年底前雇用近一百五十人，因為需要更多員工來滿足與日俱增的商務需求。

雇用 / 使用，利用
v. *hire; engage / use; utilize*

0546 deploy [dɪ`plɔɪ] * de-=do the opposite of, down

★★☆☆☆

About 300,000 troops from America and its allies were deployed to the Middle East in an effort to overpower Iraq.

約有三十萬美軍的兵力和聯軍部隊部署在中東地區以擊敗伊拉克。

部署
n. *cause troops to spread out*

0547 defect [`difɛkt] * fec(t)=do, make

★★★★★

My nephew was happy to get the computer that he wanted for Christmas, but he was very disappointed to find that it had a defect and he had to wait one month for the manufacturer to correct the problem.

姪子收到想要的電腦作為聖誕禮物很開心，但失望地發現原來有瑕疵，要再等一個月送交經銷商修理。

瑕疵，缺陷
n. *flaw; fault; imperfection*

0548 perfection [pəˋfɛkʃən] * per-=thorough, perfect

★★★★☆

完美無缺，十全十美
n. *faultlessness; completion*

Judy was always seeking perfection when she went on a blind date, so she never actually met anyone she liked; everyone has faults.

每當茱蒂透過友人介紹和素未謀面的男子進行第一次約會，總想尋找十全十美的化身，因此她從未遇過任何一個喜歡的人，每個人都有缺點。

0449 perpetual [pəˋpɛtʃʊəl] * pet=strive

★★★★★

永久的，無止境的
a. *eternal; lasting; everlasting; perennial; permanent; enduring; unceasing*

Communication between races, countries and people will be a perpetual problem as there is not a common language that everyone in the world uses.

不同民族、國籍和人種的溝通，將會是永遠存在的問題，因為全球人口並未使用共同語言。

0550 competition [͵kɑmpəˋtɪʃən] * com-=together

★★★★★

競爭，競賽
n. *contention; striving; struggle*

When boys become men, the competition that they experienced in sports is now found in their work. A man is usually respected if he earns a lot of money, so men do their best to continually get ahead, trying to be better than their "friends" at work.

Men's Lives ——Len Fox

當小男孩長大成人，曾在運動比賽中經歷的競爭，現在可從工作中發現。日進斗金的男性總是受人尊敬，所以男人竭盡全力不停向前衝，試圖比「朋友們」在事業上更加功成名就。

——《男人的一生》連恩‧福克斯

Tea Time... ☕

<From the name of a hospital>
Bedlam
Popular name for the Hospital of St. Mary of Bethlehem, London, an insane asylum.

〈源自一家醫院之名〉瘋人院
本字源自倫敦一家名為聖瑪麗伯利恆的知名精神病院。（註：此院是全世界第一家專門收治精神病患的醫院，自其院名衍生出 bedlam 一字，帶有「騷亂、混亂」之意，亦指「極端混亂而嘈雜的地方」。）

❖ **bedlam** [ˋbɛdləm] **n.** *pandemonium; uproar; commotion* ｜ 混亂嘈雜之地

Upon returning home from work, Mrs. Turner found that her house was bedlam. Her three sons and all of their friends were running, jumping, rolling, and shouting. Nothing in her house was in its right place.

透納太太下班返家後發現家裡又吵又亂，三個兒子和朋友們四處跑跳，在地上翻滾並大喊大叫。屋裡沒有一樣東西是放在原位的。

1

Complete each word by filling in the blank with proper spelling so that it has the same meaning as suggested. Then please write the meaning of each word in Chinese.

1. 避免 = _ v o i d
2. 拘留 = d e _ _ _ _
3. 容易接受的 = s u s _ _ _ _ i v e
4. 多樣的 = _ _ _ _ _ f o r m
5. 增加 = m u l t i _ _ _
6. 校內的 = _ _ _ _ _ m u r a l
7. 州內的 = i n t r a _ _ _ _ _
8. 組成 = _ _ _ p o s e
9. 娘娘腔的 = _ _ f e m i n a t e
10. 有效的 = e f _ _ _ a c i o u s

11. deformity = _____
12. retreat = _____
13. unpredictable = _____
14. predecessor = _____
15. compel = _____
16. explicate = _____
17. expose = _____
18. depressing = _____
19. carnivorous = _____
20. bipartisan = _____

2

Choose a word that best completes the sentence.

21. **Mrs. Scott hurriedly prepared her husband's breakfast, but it was gone. As it turned out, their five-year-old son _____ it.**
    (A) exposed   (B) propelled   (C) devoured   (D) departed

22. **We are going to have a(n) _____ athletic meet this coming Friday.**
    (A) intramural   (B) susceptive   (C) compatible   (D) devoid

23. **Actually the old lady had hoped to go see the _____ to complain about the glasses she picked up the other day. But she entered a barbershop, barking up the wrong tree.**
    (A) defect   (B) optometrist   (C) mortician   (D) symmetry

3

The highlighted word is closest in meaning to which of the following?

24. **The diplomats from both countries wanted to set up perpetual diplomatic relations.**
    (A) itchy   (B) lasting   (C) intrastate   (D) intolerant

25. **We can avoid neither death nor the IRS.**
    (A) evade   (B) ascribe   (C) detain   (D) attribute

MP3 24

0551 accommodate [əˈkɑməˌdet] * ac-=to, near ★★★★★

This room is so commodious that it can comfortably accommodate up to one hundred people.

這間房間十分寬敞，可充分容納近百人。

留宿，容納，收容 / 使適應 / 供應
v. house; lodge; admit; have capacity for; seat / reconcile; harmonize / supply; furnish

---

0552 accuse [əˈkjuz] * -cuse=case, lawsuit ★★★★★

She accused me of stealing her purse, but I could not have stolen it because I was out of town at that time.

她指控我偷她的錢包，但我不可能這麼做，因為我當時出城了。

指控，控告，告發
v. charge; indict; impeach

0553 excuse [ɪkˈskjuz] * ex-=out ★★★★★

Sue gave some lame excuse for not being able to show up. She mumbled something for an apology, but it was incoherent.

蘇提出一些站不住腳的藉口說明為何無法出席，她含糊說著抱歉，但說辭根本前後矛盾。

辯解，藉口 / 原諒，寬恕
n. apology / **v.** forgive

0554 extend [ɪkˈstɛnd] * -tend=stretch ★★★★★

Kate extended me an invitation to go to dinner but I had prior responsibilities that I needed to attend to, so I had to politely refuse.

凱特邀請我吃晚餐，但因我事先另外有約要赴，因此只能禮貌性拒絕。

給予（恩惠等）/（時間）延長，擴大（範圍、領土等）
v. offer / lengthen; elongate; stretch out

0555 contend [kənˈtɛnd] * con-=together ★★★★★

Mr. Baker contends that the accident was not his fault. He is prepared to fight it to the end if necessary in order to prove his innocence.

貝克先生聲稱那場意外的發生並非他的錯，如有需要他準備好抗爭到底，以證明個人清白。

爭奪，競爭 / 主張，聲稱
v. fight; compete / assert; maintain; hold

0556 consume [kənˈsum] * -sume=take, eat ★★★★★

Automobiles use up a great deal of fuel reserves. The government plans to put a heavy tax on cars that are inefficient and consume a lot of gas.

汽車消耗大量燃料儲存量，政府計畫針對低效能和高耗油量的車輛課以重稅。

消耗，消費，花費 / 吃光，喝光，毀滅
v. use up; deplete / devour; gulp down; swallow

0557 assume [əˈsum] * as-, ad-=near, to ★★★★★

It was my blunder. I will assume the responsibility for the mistake that I made. I should have placed the order.

這是我的錯，我會負起相關責任。我應該要下訂單的。

擔任，承當 / 假定，以為 / 假裝
v. take over; undertake; accept / presume; suppose / pretend

0558 assent [əˈsɛnt] * sent=feel ★★★★★

The student had some points that I didn't fully agree with. It took me several hours of convincing to make him assent to my point of view.

那個學生有某些我無法完全同意的觀點，我花了好幾個鐘頭說服他同意我的看法。

贊同，同意
v. consent; agree; sanction

0559 dissent [dɪˋsɛnt] * dis-=away, different ★★★★★

There was much dissent in the ranks of the soldiers when they were told that their vacations were canceled.

全體士兵聽到休假被取消都大呼不能接受。

不同意 / 異議
v. disagree / **n.** disagreement

0560 disparity [dɪsˋpærətɪ] * par=pair ★★★★☆

Unfortunately there are some disparities between urban and rural educational systems. It is true that good educational institutions are concentrated in urban areas.

不幸的是城鄉教育體系間的確存有部分差異,優良的教育機構都集中在都市地區也是事實。

懸殊,不一致,差異
n. inequality; difference; incongruity; discrepancy

0561 compare [kəmˋpɛr] * com-=together ★★★★★

I have learned that it does little good to compare myself with other people because everyone's situations are so different that there is no equal ground from which to compare.

我學會沒必要拿自己和其他人相比,因為每個人的實際情況都不一樣,也沒有相同立足點可供比較。

比較,相比
v. estimate the similarity or dissimilarity of

0562 comfort [ˋkʌmfət] * fort=strong ★★★★★

There is nothing better than relaxing in the safety and comfort of your own home after a long hard day at the office.

結束一天漫長的工作後,再沒有比待在自己安全舒適的家裡放鬆一番更好的了。

安慰,慰問 / 慰藉,舒適
v. console; solace; soothe /
n. ease

0563 fortify [ˋfɔrtəˌfaɪ] * -fy=make; do ★★☆☆☆

As I talked to her, the lady remained aloof. She seemed to fortify herself with doubts and indifference.

我跟她說話時她還是顯得冷淡,似乎想用懷疑和冷漠把自己包圍起來。

增強,加強 / 設防,建築要塞
v. arm; defend; safeguard; protect; shield

0564 magnify [ˋmægnəˌfaɪ] * magn-=big ★★★★★

You should magnify the picture in order to show it to the public. It is so small that I think people will have to use a magnifying lens in order to see it.

你應該將照片放大好展示給大家看,它太小了要用放大鏡才能看清楚。

放大,擴大,誇張
v. enlarge; amplify; augment

0565 magnanimous [mægˋnænəməs] * anim=mind ★★★★☆

The new manager is such a magnanimous man that he'll forgive your mistake. So please don't worry.

新來的經理是個很有雅量的人,會原諒你的過失,所以請不要擔心。

寬宏大量的,有雅量的
a. generous; forgiving; tolerant

0566 animadversion [ˌænəmædˋvɜʃən] * vers=turn ★★★☆☆

The critics made several animadversions about the newly released movie because it contained so much violence.

電影評論家對那部剛上映的電影提出諸多批評,因為裡面的暴力鏡頭太多了。

批評,譴責,責難
n. censure

0567 reverse [rɪˋvɝs] * re-=back ★★★★★

To date, I have been advised to perform the following feat to cure hiccups: Bend the body backward until the head touches the floor, and whistle in reverse.

至今大家仍建議我只要將身體向後彎曲直到頭頂碰到地板，然後倒立著吹口哨，就能治療打嗝。

使顛倒，調換 / 相反，顛倒
v. *invert; overturn; turn upside down; turn over /*
n. *opposite; contrary; converse; antithesis*

0568 repeal [rɪˋpil] * peal=call, sound, drive ★★★★★

There used to be a law that allowed only men to vote in the country, but after much argument the government decided to repeal it.

過去法律只允許男性擁有投票權，但經過一連串辯論後政府決定廢止這項法律。

廢止，廢除，失效
v. *revoke; rescind; annul; invalidate; void; abrogate; abolish*

0569 appeal [əˋpil] * a-=to, in advance ★★★★★

The defendant decided to appeal to a higher court for the overturn of the stiff penalty given to him.

被告決定向更高法院上訴，以推翻原先裁定要他繳交的高額罰鍰。

上訴，訴諸，懇請
v. *plead; supplicate; solicit; entreat; beseech; implore; invoke*

0570 apprehend [ˌæprɪˋhɛnd] * -prehend=catch, take ★★★★★

After a half-an-hour high speed chase, the police were finally able to apprehend the bank robbers.

經過一場為時半小時的高速追逐後，警方終於逮捕銀行搶匪。

I'm sure that you'll pass the entrance exam. So you don't have to apprehend the outcome of the test.

我相信你一定會通過入學考試，所以不用擔心考試結果。

逮捕，緝拿 / 憂慮，恐懼
v. *arrest; seize / anticipate with uneasiness; dread*

0571 comprehend [ˌkɑmprɪˋhɛnd] * com-=all ★★★★★

At first I couldn't comprehend the concepts that my teacher was discussing in class, but after I spent a long time reading many books on the subject, I was able to fully understand what he was trying to teach.

起初我無法充分了解老師在課堂上討論的觀念，等我花許多時間閱讀相關主題書籍後，就完全明白老師想教什麼。

充分了解
v. *understand; grasp; take in; fathom; perceive; assimilate*

0572 composure [kəmˋpoʒɚ] * pos=place, put ★★★★☆

When the judge read the guilty verdict, the victim's family members lost all composure and started to jump up and down in the courtroom, disturbing the courtroom proceedings.

當法官宣讀判決時，被害者家屬失去鎮靜，開始在法庭內跳上跳下擾亂秩序。

鎮靜，沉著，泰然自若
n. *calmness; tranquility; serenity; peacefulness; placidity; self-control; equanimity; self-possession*

0573 proposal [prəˋpozl] * pro-=forward ★★★★★

Despite everyone's worries, the chairman of the board readily acceded to the proposal that was presented to him.

儘管所有人都感到擔憂，董事會主席仍迅速同意上呈給他的提案。

提案，建議
n. *offer; motion; suggestion; overture; recommendation*

0574 propulsive [prə`pʌlsɪv] * puls=drive ★★☆☆☆

The desire to learn can be such a propulsive force that many people spend their entire lives at school studying and increasing their knowledge.
學習欲可作為一股極強的推動力量，許多人終其一生在校努力學習並增加知識。

推進的，有推進力的
a. impelling; pushing; driving

0575 expulsion [ɪk`spʌlʃən] * e(x)-=out ★★☆☆☆

After his expulsion from the country he moved to Australia where he and his wife lived the remainder of their lives on a farm.
他被驅逐出境後就搬到澳洲居住，夫妻倆在農場度過餘生。

逐出，驅逐，開除
n. ejection; expelling; dismissal; discharge

MP3 25

0576 evolution [ˌɛvə`luʃən] * volu=cycle ★★★☆☆

In politics, evolution is better than revolution. Revolution can only be justified when it is made for the good of the majority.
循序漸進的政治改革比革命還要好，唯有在以群體福祉為名的前提下，革命才有其正當性。

開展，發展，演變 / 進化
n. gradual development / a process by which species develop from earlier forms

---

0577 revolution [ˌrɛvə`luʃən] * re-=back ★★☆☆☆

Credit cards have brought about a sort of revolution in our spending habits. However they are also responsible for excessive consumption.
信用卡為人們的消費習慣帶來某種程度的改革，但也要為過度消費負起責任。

大改革，大變革 / 迴轉，旋轉
n. revolt; rebellion; coup; mutiny; uprising; insurgency; insurrection; putsch; overthrow / change

---

0578 revoke [rɪ`vok] * vok=call ★★★★★

If a person continues to drink and drive, then the police should immediately revoke his driver's license.
如果一再酒醉駕車，警方將立刻吊銷駕照。

吊銷（執照等），取消（命令等），使無效
v. cancel; invalidate; annul; declare null and void; nullify; retract

---

0579 invoke [ɪn`vok] * in-=in ★★★★★

The drunken husband who had forgotten their anniversary had to invoke his angry wife's forgiveness.
酒醉丈夫忘記結婚周年紀念日，必須懇求盛怒妻子的原諒。

懇求，乞求，祈求
v. appeal

0580 incur [ɪn`kɝ] * cur=occur, happen ★★★★★

Lucy tried to free her father of his debts which were incurred through his efforts to make her a university graduate.
露西試圖使父親擺脫為了讓她念完大學而扛下的債務。

負起（債務等）蒙受（損失等），招致（危險等）
v. arouse; provoke; invite

0581 concur [kən`kɝ] * con-=together ★★★★★

Even though they had a household rule for the daughter not to date until her sixteenth birthday, her father concurred to let her go to the dance just this once.
雖然家規規定女兒必須滿十六歲才可約會，但做爸爸的還是同意她參加僅此一次的舞會。

同意，意見一致 / 同時發生
v. agree; consent / coincide; happen together

0582 convert [kən`vɜt] * vert=turn ★★★★★

The first Christian explorers always tried to convert the native people they met in the new lands they found.

第一批發現新大陸的基督教拓荒者總想改變土著們的信仰。

改變，兌換 / 使皈依
v. *change in form; modify; alter; transform; mutate; transfigure / cause a person to change beliefs*

0583 divert [daɪ`vɜt] * di-=away ★★★★☆

The tightrope walker fell into the net because his attention was diverted for a split second by a spectator in the crowd.

走鋼絲表演者跌入底下的安全網中，因為他的注意力在剎那間轉移到台下某位觀眾身上。

使轉向 / 轉移
v. *distract / switch; deflect; turn away; shift*

0584 digress [daɪ`grɛs] * gress=go ★★★★★

His research paper started out sticking to the subject but digressed a little near the end of the paper.

他的研究報告剛開始有堅守主題，但快到結尾時卻有點岔題。

離題，岔題
v. *go off the point; go off the track; ramble; drift; wander; stray; diverge; deviate*

0585 congress [`kɑŋgrəs] * con-=together, all ★★★★★

He's been a book worm his whole life and it finally paid off because he's just been elected to Congress.

他終其一生都是書蟲，但到最後一切都是值得的，因為他被選為國會議員。

立法機關，國會 / 會議，代表大會
n. *parliament / conference; meeting*

0586 confident [`kɑnfədənt] * fid=trust ★★★★☆

I am very confident that we will be able to put this deal together and make money at the same time.

我很有信心一定能完成這筆交易，同時賺大錢。

有把握的，有自信的，充滿信心的
a. *self-confident; self-assured; convinced*

0587 diffident [`dɪfədənt] * dif-, dis-=away ★★★☆☆

Pam used to be a very outgoing confident person, but ever since her divorce she has become a diffident, withdrawn person.

潘本來非常外向又有自信，但自從離婚後就變成缺乏自信而害羞的人。

缺乏自信的，膽怯的，羞怯的
a. *shy; lacking self-confidence*

0588 dispose [dɪ`spoz] * pos=put ★★★★★

Why should I be the one who always has to dispose of garbage? It is not a duty or responsibility exclusively for myself.

為什麼總是要我倒垃圾？這不該是我一個人的責任。

收拾，處理，丟棄
v. *throw away; discard; get rid of; dump; jettison*

0589 indisposed [ˌɪndɪ`spozd] * in-=no, not ★☆☆☆☆

Son: When will you be back?
Mom: Around 9 o'clock.
Son: Oh, the phone is ringing. I'll get it. ..... Mom, a salesman.
Mom: Tell him that I'm indisposed.
Son: Hello. Mom tells me that she's exposed.

不願意的，微感不適的
a. *disinclined*

兒子：妳什麼時候會回來？

母親：大概九點吧。

兒子：噢，電話響了，我去接……，媽媽，是業務員。

母親：跟他說我人不舒服。

兒子：哈囉，我媽跟我說她被攻擊了。

0590 **inalienable** [ɪn`eljənəbl] * lien=place ★☆☆☆☆

Human beings are supposed to have inalienable rights, without which humans cannot exist as independent beings.

人類應擁有不可剝奪的權利，若缺乏這些權利就無法以獨立個體存在。

不能讓與的，不可剝奪的
a. inseparable; that cannot be deprived of

0591 **purlieu** [`pɝlu] * pur-, per-=perfect, through ★☆☆☆☆

Most areas of this city are designated as residential purlieus. So the proposed factory should be located in an industrial area.

本城市大部分地區都被標明為住宅區，因此預計興建的工廠應座落於工業區。

近鄰，範圍
n. a place surrounding an area; area

0592 **perambulator** [pə`æmbjə,letə] * ambl-=walk; go ★☆☆☆☆

A perambulator is very useful, especially for a mother, but not for a baby. A baby probably wants Mom's bosom. But if she always carries her baby in her arms, she will soon have muscular arms.

對母親而言嬰兒車十分管用，但小寶寶不一定這麼想，因為他可能想要媽媽抱。如果做母親的一直把寶寶抱在懷裡，要不了多久就會雙臂肌肉發達。

嬰兒車
n. baby carriage

0593 **noctambulist** [nɑk`tæmbjə,lɪst] * -ist=person ★☆☆☆☆

Mrs. White told her friend that she had been wondering if her husband was a noctambulist. She said that her husband often got ready to go to work in the middle of the night.

懷特太太跟友人說她懷疑先生是夢遊症患者，他經常在半夜準備好要上班。

夢遊者，夢遊症患者
n. somnambulist

0594 **perfectionist** [pə`fɛkʃənɪst] * fec=do; make ★★☆☆☆

A perfectionist is a person who cannot enjoy Tchaikovsky's music or an Arnold Schwarzenegger movie without knowing how to spell their names.

一個完美主義者在不知道怎麼拼柴可斯基或阿諾‧史瓦辛格的名字前，是無法好好欣賞他們的音樂或電影的。

完美主義者
n. a person who pursues perfection

0595 **mercantilist** [`mɝkəntɪlɪst] * mercan-, mercen-=commerce, trade ★★☆☆☆

The lawmaker was considered to be a mercantilist because he always puts too much emphasis on the development of commerce and trade, even at the expense of other issues.

立法者常被視為重商主義者，因其過度強調商業貿易的發展，即使犧牲其他議題也在所不惜。

重商主義者
n. a person who believes in mercantilism

0596 mercenary [ˋmɝsn̩͵ɛrɪ] * -ary= person ★★☆☆☆

Please don't think of me as a simple mercenary. I have my own principles and don't want to be one who serves only for money.
請不要把我看成區區一個受雇傭工，我有自己的原則且不受金錢奴役。

外國傭兵，受雇傭工
n. *a soldier hired into foreign service; one that serves merely for wages*

0597 missionary [ˋmɪʃən͵ɛrɪ] * mis-= send ★★★☆☆

The modernization of my country was often instigated by the self-sacrificing services of missionaries from western countries.
西方國家傳教士自我犧牲的服務精神，常推動我國現代化發展。

傳教士
n. *a person undertaking a religious mission*

0598 commission [kəˋmɪʃən] * com-= together, all ★★★★☆

Could you do me a favor? I have a few commissions for you.
請問你能幫忙嗎？我有些任務想委託你。

委託，委任狀 / 佣金
n. *a formal written warrant / a fee paid to an agent*

0599 compote [ˋkɑmpot] * pos, post-= put ★★☆☆☆

Around a compote were some kids, whose eyes were fixed on the delicious-looking fruits.
孩子們圍著一盤糖漬水果甜點，幾雙眼睛緊盯著那盤看來美味可口的水果。

糖漬水果甜點，盛裝糖果和水果的玻璃高腳盤
n. *a bowl of glass, porcelain, or metal with a base and a stem from which compotes, fruits, nuts, or sweets are served*

0600 compost [ˋkɑmpost] * com-= together ★★☆☆☆

Farmer Green made a large amount of compost which will be used for fertilizing and conditioning his land.
農夫葛林做了大量堆肥好讓農地肥沃，並保持在最佳狀態。

混合物 / 堆肥
n. *mixture; compound / a mixture that mainly consists of organic matter*

Tea Time... ☕

<Roman myth> Bellona
The goddess of war, wife of Mars.

〈來自羅馬神話〉貝羅娜
羅馬神話中專司戰爭的女神，同時也是宙斯之子戰神馬爾斯之妻。（註：本字根據羅馬神話也可引申為像貝羅娜那樣「身材高大的美女」。其相關字 belligerence 帶有「好戰性、好鬥性」的意思。）

❖ **belligerence** [bəˋlɪdʒərəns] **n.** *belligerent attitude; aggressively hostile attitude* | 好戰，好鬥

I was thinking of taking my son fishing but because of his persistent belligerence toward his sister, I decided not to.
我本來想帶兒子去釣魚，但他不斷挑釁自己的姊姊，我決定還是算了。

1. Complete each word by filling in the blank with proper spelling so that it has the same meaning as suggested. Then please write the meaning of each word in Chinese.

1. 比較	= ___ p a r e	11. compost = _____
2. 增強	= f o r t i __ __	12. missionary = _____
3. 寬宏大量的	= m a g n ____ o u s	13. commission = _____
4. 顛倒	= __ __ v e r s e	14. mercenary = _____
5. 上訴	= __ __ p e a l	15. accommodate = _____
6. 充分了解	= ___ p r e h e n d	16. accuse = _____
7. 鎮靜	= c o m ___ u r e	17. consume = _____
8. 提案	= ___ p o s a l	18. assume = _____
9. 不同意	= ___ s e n t	19. disparity = _____
10. 安慰	= ___ f o r t	20. assent = _____

2. Choose a word that best completes the sentence.

21. In the first half our team was losing, but in the second we could _____ the score.

(A) reverse   (B) magnify   (C) assent   (D) dissent

22. These days people tend to _____ too much gasoline. Even for the shortest distance people tend to drive their vehicle.

(A) contend   (B) fortify   (C) consume   (D) lengthen

3. The highlighted word is closest in meaning to which of the following?

23. He was self-sacrificing. He was willing to assume the burden.

(A) comprehend   (B) take   (C) appeal   (D) apprehend

24. The beauty of a lady in the auditorium came to divert the speaker's attention. He began to say meaningless things.

(A) distract   (B) concur   (C) consent   (D) agree

25. After the collision the crew members of the giant sea liner tried to recover composure among the passengers aboard.

(A) calmness   (B) proposal   (C) censure   (D) overture

Practice Test 03

1

The highlighted word is closest in meaning to which of the following?

1. The police suspected that there might be some other accommodate to the crime.
- (A) impulses
- (B) binoculars
- (C) confederates
- (D) infirmaries

2. The epidemic also known as the Black Death was prevalent in Europe in the 14th century.
- (A) plague
- (B) entomology
- (C) epitome
- (D) procession

3. The eruption of Mt. Saint Helens was so massive that many surrounding areas were covered with volcanic ash.
- (A) affinity
- (B) outburst
- (C) incursion
- (D) infection

4. My friend Sam is the incarnation of kindness. I have never seen a kinder person than him.
- (A) concept
- (B) personification
- (C) mortician
- (D) optician

5. The classroom was very large and it could accomplices almost one hundred students.
- (A) admit
- (B) contend
- (C) consume
- (D) extend

2

Please answer the following questions.

Emperor Penguins

Of all animals that inhabit the earth, which one is best known for its perpetual maternal affection ? Never do we hesitate to give the answer, "A human being." However, when asked if a human being has the strongest paternal affection, many fathers ask themselves if they have been equally devoted to rearing their children. "Did I spend the whole night at the bedside together with my wife when my child developed a fever?" "Did I wake up twice or three times or even once to change diapers?" Chances are that most answers are in the negative. The incarnation of the strongest paternal affection seems to be an emperor penguin.

Emperor penguins begin mating in autumn and produce eggs two months later. Females, along with their mates, travel far inland on the Antarctic continent to lay their egg. The physical toll exacted on the female, from the burden of journeying to the nesting ground to the chore of producing the egg, is so great that the female will have lost about 20 percent of her body weight by the time she lays her egg. Little wonder then that once the egg is laid, the female will dive into the waters to feed and relax while her husband assumes the duty of incubating the egg.

The male penguin places the egg on its feet and covers it with a fold of skin on the lower belly, the feathers of which have molted away temporarily, making for a brood patch. This patch of skin consists of a rich supply of blood vessels that regulate temperature, allowing for successful incubation in a climate where temperatures may drop to as low as -60 degrees Celsius, and where winds may gust up to 150 km per hour. Without eating anything, exposed to the extreme conditions, a male penguin stoops over an egg to keep it warm for two months. After two months' painstaking work the egg finally hatches, and the male penguin, which has lost almost half of its weight, is now between 30 and 40 pounds. Then the female returns, and the male penguin, with a haggard look, hails her.

6. **The word perpetual is closest in meaning to which of the following?**
   (A) everlasting
   (B) bipartisan
   (C) carnivorous
   (D) depressing

7. **The word affection is closest in meaning to which of the following?**
   (A) feminism
   (B) profusion
   (C) composure
   (D) love

8. **The word exacted is closest in meaning to which of the following?**
   (A) fortified
   (B) converted
   (C) demanded
   (D) magnified

9. **The word assumes is closest in meaning to which of the following?**
   (A) assents
   (B) takes
   (C) compares
   (D) reverses

10. **The word exposed is closest in meaning to which of the following?**
    (A) compelled
    (B) denuded
    (C) elapsed
    (D) protracted

Actual Test

The Titanic

At 2:20 a.m. on April 15, 1912, the White Star Line's "Unsinkable" Titanic, which was then the most gigantic and luxurious sea liner in the world, sank into the glacial depths of the North Atlantic. The disaster took a heavy toll of 1,500 lives - the greatest number of casualties in a maritime catastrophe in peacetime history.

On her doomed maiden voyage from Southampton to New York, the 46,500ton vessel was speeding through dark, smooth seas at 22.5 knots. The White Star Line's eagerness to set a world record for crossing the Atlantic in the shortest time accelerated the ship and precipitated her ruin. At 11:40 p.m. on April 14, the 883-foot-long ship was on the threshold of a head-on collision with an immense iceberg. On seeing the huge iceberg ahead, the lookout on the bridge shouted a warning and all measures were taken to avoid the ominous white figure ahead, but to no avail. A 300-foot-long slash was ripped along her hull. After the accident, the key crewmen wanted to recover composure among the passengers aboard and told them that there would be no serious problems except a slight delay. Even the orchestra went on playing popular music. But as the ship's bow was settling deeper and deeper, the command to enter lifeboats was issued. Unfortunately, however, the White Star Line, which had been overconfident of the ship's invulnerability, had prepared only enough lifeboats for half the passengers aboard. Furthermore, some passengers were so overconfident that they refused to escape, believing that the giant steamer would not be in real danger. However, after the collision it took less than three hours for the giant steamer to disappear into the bottomless depths. The British steamer Carpathia, which picked up the Titanic's SOS, started for the scene of the pandemonium, and several hours later she saved 712 lives from the lifeboats.

In 1985, Dudley Foster at Woods Hole Oceanographic Institute, Massachusetts, located the sunken Titanic by sonar. One year later, the Woods Hole's submersible Alvin dived down to the Titanic at 12,000 feet below sea level, giving humans a glimpse of the ghost ship. Later in 1998 the French submersible Nautile, which can go down to 20,000 feet, carried out a historic mission. Using gigantic flotation bags which contained 30,000 gallons of diesel, people succeeded in hauling a fragmented section of the Titanic's hull weighing 8 tons back to the surface. They pulled the so-called Big Piece into the sunshine for the first time in 86 years. An analysis has revealed that bacteria is biodegrading the steel and that the steel, which is high in sulfur, is approximately one-fourth as strong as the steel with which modern ships are built. It is thought that that is why the steel could not withstand the impact of the collision. But what should be remembered is that the disaster was mainly induced by human carelessness and poor judgment. If the crewmen had not been overconfident of the ship's invulnerability, she might be afloat today. And if only the lookout had not spotted the iceberg or if only the helmsman had not turned the wheel, the Titanic would have collided with the iceberg head-on, and the Titanic, with specially designed bulkheads which would check the seawater, would have been able to struggle her way to her destination and to take shelter under the outstretched arm of the Statue of Liberty.

1. The highlighted word luxurious can be replaced by which of the following?
   (A) deluxe
   (B) hypothetical
   (C) unanimous
   (D) adequate

2. The highlighted word disaster can be replaced by which of the following?
   (A) agglomerate
   (B) invasion
   (C) catastrophe
   (D) adolescence

3. The highlighted word accelerated can be replaced by which of the following?
   (A) cohered
   (B) degenerated
   (C) hastened
   (D) excavated

4. The highlighted word immense can be replaced by which of the following?
   (A) medieval
   (B) giant
   (C) deducible
   (D) effective

5. The highlighted word composure can be replaced by which of the following?
   (A) affliction
   (B) calmness
   (C) destitution
   (D) circumlocution

6. The highlighted phrase bottomless depths can be replaced by which of the following?
   (A) abyss
   (B) edict
   (C) deformity
   (D) complicity

7. The highlighted word pandemonium can be replaced by which of the following?
   (A) defect
   (B) disparity
   (C) commotion
   (D) comfort

8. The highlighted word fragmented can be replaced by which of the following?
   (A) repealed
   (B) implied
   (C) broken
   (D) intramural

9. The highlighted word revealed can be replaced by which of the following?
   (A) conformed
   (B) shown
   (C) elapsed
   (D) retreated

10. The highlighted word induced can be replaced by which of the following?
   (A) annihilated
   (B) caused
   (C) extended
   (D) deployed

An Avalanche

Various factors, such as rapidly accumulated snow, earthquakes or even the weight of a single skier, can cause an avalanche to occur. Sometimes a small chunk of snow or ice which drops from an overhanging rock or branch of a tree can cause an avalanche. Even a bird's foot can be blamed. Also, warm weather or rain after a large amount of new snow has fallen may be the suspect. A mass of snow which is excessively overloaded with a large amount of new snow is so unstable that the delicate cohesion holding it in place can be easily broken. At first, an avalanche slab breaks off from its slope bed and slides down the mountainside. As it slides down, the slab may pick up more snow, attaining a mass of millions of tons. As its speed increases, the onrushing mass may become airborne, rushing down almost friction free on top of a cushion of air; in some cases even at a velocity of approximately 360km per hour, which is about twice that of a free-falling sky diver.

One of the most disastrous known avalanches took place in Peru in 1970, when an earthquake caused a thundering ice slide to white out the town of Yungay. Also, one of the most terrible avalanches triggered by an earthquake took place in 1910, when two trains were buried in the depths of snow near Stevens Pass in Washington. Ninety-six people could not escape the sudden killer. In the same year in Canada, a dreadful snowslide trapped railroad workers who were clearing the tracks of snow from an earlier avalanche. Sixty-two were killed.

It is now estimated that in the United States alone more than 100,000 avalanches occur annually. Unfortunately, as more and more people are venturing into steep and avalanche-active mountain areas in winter, the number of victims who are killed in avalanches has more than quadrupled since the 1950s. Backcountry sports, such as skiing, snowboarding, snowmobiling and alpine mountaineering, have allured many recreationists to dangerous avalanche areas which can be easily triggered to spill down the mountainside at the slightest slip of the adventurers. The seemingly soft and delicate appearance and feeling of snow can deceive humans. The onrushing mass of snow is so awesomely powerful that it is estimated that the impact may reach about 145 tons per square meter. The crush is generally lethal.

In history, humans who noticed the formidable power of an avalanche came to use it on the battlefield. Back in 1916, Italian and Austrian soldiers were in a fight for control of the Dolomite Mountains. Both sides noticed that they could take advantage of avalanches triggered by shell-fire. In a 48-hour battle where avalanches were taken advantage of, 18,000 soldiers were killed on both sides.

It is an irony that the battle provided an idea for modern avalanche control. Nowadays, cannons and dynamite are often employed to release overhanging accumulations of snow while they are still controllable. Without these methods, the juggernauts of powerfully descending masses of snow known as avalanches would undoubtedly claim even more victims in their glacial grip.

11. The highlighted word accumulated can be replaced by which of the following?
    (A) subsumed   (B) piled
    (C) eroded   (D) abducted

12. The highlighted word cause can be replaced by which of the following?
    (A) deviate   (B) trigger
    (C) deposit   (D) sympathize

13. The highlighted word mass can be replaced by which of the following?
    (A) heap   (B) epitome
    (C) transaction   (D) exaction

14. The highlighted word attaining can be replaced by which of the following?
    (A) gaining   (B) infusing
    (C) interrupting   (D) corroding

15. The highlighted word disastrous can be replaced by which of the following?
    (A) consecutive   (B) unpredictable
    (C) depressing   (D) catastrophic

16. The highlighted word annually can be replaced by which of the following?
    (A) impatiently   (B) yearly
    (C) perpetually   (D) magnanimously

17. The highlighted word allured can be replaced by which of the following?
    (A) attracted   (B) magnified
    (C) reversed   (D) fortified

18. The highlighted word deceive can be replaced by which of the following?
    (A) dissent   (B) delude
    (C) comfort   (D) compare

19. The highlighted word lethal can be replaced by which of the following?
    (A) fatal   (B) propulsive
    (C) confident   (D) incipient

20. The highlighted word glacial can be replaced by which of the following?
    (A) relentless   (B) antenatal
    (C) interstellar   (D) icy

Building Vocabulary for
iBT, SAT, GRE, TOEIC, GEPT

12天

CHAPTER

01

02

03

熟字聯想新字記憶法

0601~1200

y taxonomy economic ecology biology antibiotic antagonist egoist egocentr

ansitory transfusion effusive exhibition prohibitive proscribe circumscri

nt deduction introduction introverted subvert subside assiduous assemb

s congressman convivial survive resurrection recede intercede intermitte

ct distribute attribute attraction intractable inadvertent revert resum

tipathy apathy atheism pantheism pandemonium insane interminab

temporize extort retort reject eject elaborate collaborate collective eclect

nplicated composite preposition prescience omniscient omnivoro

ve perverseness perceive deceive deciduous decadent delinquent relinqui

04 | 05 Answers

thet hypothetical hypocritical economical astronomical disaster disper

inate delimit deflate inflate innovation renovation retribution contribu

fer prefer preface artifact artisan partisan impart impetus compete compre

trovertible contretemps extemporaneous explode implode impel propell

vocation prognosis diagnose diathermy thermoplastic protoplasm protozo

t forfeit foreign sovereign superstition prostitution prognosticate recogni

flict infect effective effort afford adduce deducible anatomy anachronis

ology biology antibiotic antagonist egoist egocentric concentrate congrega

ibition prohibitive proscribe circumscribe circumvent convention conduct

subvert subside assiduous assemble dissemble disposal depose deceptio

rrection recede intercede intermittent manumit emancipate elude prelu

nadvertent revert resume unassuming unprejudiced preclude exclude exha

ane interminably exterminate expire perspiration perspicacious conspicuo

MP3
26

0601 abate [ə`bet] ★★★★★ 減弱，減輕 | base
接近底部 (base)

v. make less; diminish; reduce; mitigate; decrease

The weather was so foul that we waited for the storm to abate before going outside. It had been raining cats and dogs.

天氣非常惡劣，我們要等暴風雨減弱才能外出。外面一直下著傾盆大雨。

0602 abbreviate [ə`brivɪ,et] ★★★★★ 縮寫，使省略 | brief, brevity
變簡潔 (brevity)

v. shorten; abridge

If you abbreviate something when writing documents, you make it shorter. Especially in business letters we often find shortened words or phrases.

以縮寫撰寫文件可縮短文章，特別是在商業信函裡常可看到簡化的單字或片語。

0603 aberration [,æbə`reʃən] ★★★☆☆ 反常行為，脫離常軌 | error
發生錯誤 (error) 的事

n. something not typical

My brother's generosity was an aberration. Normally he had never yielded the Play Station game to anybody.

我弟弟的慷慨是反常行為，他通常不會把 PS 遊戲機讓給別人玩。

0604 abet [ə`bɛt] ★★★★☆ 煽動，教唆，慫恿 | bait
丟出誘餌 (bait)

v. agitate; incite

Although Chris was not directly involved in committing the crime, he was arrested for abetting and aiding in the act.

克里斯雖未直接涉入這起犯罪活動，仍因教唆罪遭到逮捕。

0605 abhor [əb`hɔr] ★★★★★ 厭惡，憎惡 | horror
感到厭惡 (horror) 並遠離 (ab-)

v. detest; hate; loathe

A young woman and even a man would abhor the thought of walking alone down the alleys of New York City.

想到要獨自走在紐約暗巷中，無論是年輕女性甚至男性都會感到厭惡。

0606 abnegate [`æbnɪ,get] ★★★★☆ 拒絕，克制，放棄 | negative
加以否定 (negative) 並遠離 (ab-)

v. deny; reject; renounce

Jane's sister has abnegated any foods high in calories ever since she got on the scale last week.

珍的妹妹自從上周量過體重後就不再吃高熱量食物。

0607 abominate [ə`bɑmə,net] ★★★★☆ 厭惡，憎惡，討厭 | omen
感到不祥徵兆 (omen) 而遠離 (ab-)

v. abhor; detest; loathe intensely

The annoyed wife abominated her husband's snoring so much that she kicked him out of the bed one night while he slept.

惱怒的妻子非常厭惡先生的鼾聲，某晚甚至把熟睡的他踢下床去。

0608 acclimatize [ə`klaɪmə,taɪz] ★★★★☆ 使適應，使水土相服 | climate
在氣候 (climate) 方面接近 (ac-)

v. acclimate

One who has lived in Australia for many years and then has moved to Alaska may have a difficult time acclimatizing to the cold weather.

住在澳洲多年的人若搬到阿拉斯加州，可能會難以適應寒冷氣候。

0609 accolade [ˌækəˈled] ★★★★☆

n. honor; awar

榮譽，讚揚，榮耀

collar
領口 (collar) 上有勳章

To win an Olympic gold medal is the highest accolade for most athletes. Therefore, athletes do their best to be the top at the Olympics.

對多數運動員而言贏得奧運金牌是最高榮耀，因此在奧運會上無不全力以赴爭取冠軍。

0610 accompany [əˈkʌmpənɪ] ★★★★★

v. attend; escort

伴隨，陪伴，跟隨

company
被當成同伴 (company)

James came to the party, but he was accompanied by some lady whom I had never met. He introduced her to me.

詹姆斯帶我從未見過的女子來參加派對，並介紹我們認識。

0611 accost [əˈkɔst] ★★★☆☆

v. approach and speak to somebody

攀談，搭訕

coast; side
碰觸身體側邊
(coast; side)

As the tourist was walking along the street, a man in shaggy clothing accosted him. He was a beggar asking for some change.

觀光客走在街上遇到衣衫破舊的男子搭訕，原來是乞討零錢的乞丐。

0612 accrue [əˈkru] ★★★☆☆

v. accumulate; be added

自然增加，自然增長

grow
增加 (grow) 利息

Interest on his savings account accrued on a daily basis, but the miser was not satisfied. He tried to find a way to get greater interest.

守財奴存款帳戶裡的利息逐日增加仍不滿足，還要設法獲得更高利息。

0613 acerbic [əˈsɜbɪk] ★★★☆☆

a. acrimonious; severe / bitter / sour

尖酸刻薄的，嚴厲的

acute
強烈的 (acute) 味道

The graduate student at the thesis got upset when one of the professors was making an acerbic comment on his paper.

研究生進行畢業論文口試時，其中一名口試委員提出嚴厲批評，讓他感到很不舒服。

0614 acknowledge [əkˈnɑlɪdʒ] ★★★★★

v. confess; admit; avow

承認，認定～為真

know
向 (ac-) 知道 (know) 靠近

I acknowledge the fact that I should have tried harder to accomplish my goals. I didn't reach the required score.

我承認自己應更加努力才能達成目標。我沒有達到必修分數。

0615 acme [ˈækmɪ] ★★★★★

n. peak; pinnacle; summit

頂點，極點，極致，巔峰

acute
山頂最尖 (acute) 處

With this promotion she has received, Pam has now reached the acme of her career. She has become the general manager.

潘經過這次拔擢，達到個人事業巔峰成為總經理。

0616 acne [ˈæknɪ] ★★★★☆

n. pimple (summit of maturity)

粉刺，面皰，青春痘

acute
在發育高峰期長出來的東西

My friend Susan has a severe case of acne, and she uses every kind of skin ointment on the market with no positive results.

友人蘇珊有嚴重的青春痘問題，使用市面上各種皮膚軟膏都成效不彰。

0617 acorn [ˈeˌkɔrn]　　　　　　　　橡樹果實，橡實

corn
長出像 a 字型的果實 (corn)

n. the nut of the oak

Squirrels rely on acorns to provide food throughout the winter, and work very hard gathering them during the autumn.

松鼠靠橡樹果實作為冬天食物來源，所以整個秋天都忙著辛勤採集。

0618 acquiesce [ˌækwɪˈɛs]　　　　默認，默許，默從，同意

quiet
安靜地 (quiet) 靠近 (ac-)

v. comply tacitly; assent; consent; accede

Contrary to the expectations of the authorities, the demonstrators acquiesced to the requests of the police and returned home peacefully.

示威者出乎有關當局預料同意警方要求，全部平靜返家。

0619 acquit [əˈkwɪt]　　　　　開釋，宣告無罪，無罪釋放

quit
往 (ac-) 免除 (quit) 靠近

v. exculpate; vindicate; absolve; exonerate

As his innocence was confirmed, the prisoner was acquitted on all charges and therefore was set free.

犯人證實清白後，所有相關指控都宣告無罪並獲釋。

0620 actuate [ˈæktʃuˌet]　　　　　使行動，開動，啓動

act
做出動作 (act)

v. move; drive; impel

The president, as the guest of honor, pushed the button that actuated the first subway during the opening ceremony.

總統以貴賓身分按下按鈕並啓動開幕典禮的第一班地下鐵。

0621 acumen [əˈkjumən]　　　　　心智敏銳，聰明才智

acute
敏銳的 (acute) 能力

n. shrewdness; discernment

A man who has good acumen is a good asset to any company because of his excellent mental capabilities.

擁有聰明才智的人是公司的有利資產，因其具有優異心智能力。

0622 addendum [əˈdɛndəm]　　　　　追加，補遺，附錄

add
追加的 (add) 事物

n. thing that is to be added

This book has an addendum which is added to clarify where the author found the materials used to make his points.

這本書有一篇追加附錄，其中闡明作者證實其個人主張的資料來源。

0623 adjudicate [əˈdʒudɪˌket]　　　　　判決，裁定

judge
對 (ad-) 某事下判斷 (judge)

v. settle judicially; adjudge; sentence; rule

Judge Jones was chosen to adjudicate over the case. He had to think about various points before he reached a verdict.

瓊斯法官被選定裁決這起案件，在達成判決前須考量各種論點。

0624 adopt [əˈdɑpt]　　　　收養，領養／採用，採納，採取

option
接近 (ad-) 並選擇 (option)

v. take voluntarily (a child of other parents) one's own child / embrace; espouse

Married couples who cannot have children by natural means often choose to adopt a child born to other people.

無法自然懷孕的已婚夫妻常選擇領養他人子女。

0625 affable [`æfəbl]

和藹可親的，友善而容易親近的　★★★☆☆

a. easy to talk to; friendly; compatible

The new manager at the office is an affable person. All of his subordinates have found it easy to talk to him.

辦公室新來的經理和藹可親，所有屬下都覺得可以跟他輕鬆交談。

fable
走近 (ad-) 並講述 (fable)

MP3 27

0626 affront [ə`frʌnt]

故意當面侮辱，使難堪，公然冒犯　★★★☆☆

v. insult; confront; face in defiance; offend

When Joe, one of her English students, came up to her to argue about his grades, Mrs. Smith felt deeply affronted by his rudeness.

史密斯女士的英文班學生喬跑來理論成績，無禮態度讓她深感難堪。

front
朝向 (af-=ad-) 正面 (front)

0627 aftermath [`æftə,mæθ]

後果，餘波　★★★☆☆

n. consequence; result

In the aftermath of the hurricane there were few buildings still standing, but luckily no people were killed.

颶風過後只有少數建築物完好無缺，所幸無人傷亡。

after
之後 (after) 會出現的事物

0628 aggravate [`ægrə,vet]

使加重，使惡化　★★★★★

v. worsen; deteriorate; make worse; intensify

Blake's cough was aggravated by his heavy smoking. Therefore his wife strongly insisted that he should quit smoking.

布雷克抽太多煙導致咳嗽加劇，妻子強烈要求他戒煙。

grave, gravity
使變成更嚴重的 (grave)

0629 allay [ə`le]

使緩和，使鎮靜，使釋懷　★★★★★

v. calm; quiet; subdue; alleviate; relieve

My sister, who was three months pregnant, tried some baked ginger to allay her morning sickness.

懷孕三個月的妹妹試服烤生薑以緩和害喜現象。

lay
使安置 (lay) 在位置上

0630 allegedly [ə`lɛdʒɪdlɪ]

據聲稱地，據傳聞地　★★★★★

ad. supposedly

Loch Ness in Scotland is allegedly inhabited by a giant creature, which is nicknamed 'Nessie.' Supposedly it is said to be about 20 meters long.

據說蘇格蘭境內的尼斯湖棲息著暱稱「尼西」的巨大生物，據稱約有二十公尺長。

legend
流傳下來的傳說 (legend)

0631 amenable [ə`minəbl]

聽從的，順從的　★★★★☆

a. obedient; meek; tractable; answerable

We thought that Allan was an amenable person and could be persuaded. Instead he was not that docile.

我們以為艾倫既順從又容易被說服，但其實他沒那麼聽話。

amen
順從地跟著喊阿們 (amen)

0632 amendment [ə`mɛndmənt]

修正，改良，改善，修正案　★★★★★

n. correction

The office made some new amendments that changed the procedures in the office. They replaced some inefficient procedures.

辦公室做出新修正改變辦公流程，沒效率的都被取代了。

mend
改正 (mend)

0633 **amiss** [əˋmɪs]
a. faulty; imperfect

★★★☆☆

錯誤的，差錯的

mistake
出現錯誤 (mistake)

Something seemed to be horribly amiss. I was able to figure out what caused the problem. The figures were in the metric system instead of the imperial system.

這似乎有很大錯誤，我弄清楚問題出在哪裡了，這是公制而非英制數字。

0634 **anew** [əˋnu]
ad. again; once more; newly

★★★★☆

重新地，再一次地

new
重新 (new) 來過

After a long standing ovation, the performers began anew. The ovation seemed to give them more courage.

全場起立鼓掌良久後表演者重新開始演出，熱烈的喝采似乎為他們帶來更多鼓舞。

0635 **animate** [ˋænə͵met]
v. give vigor to; quicken

★★★★★

使活潑，使有活力，激勵，賦予生命

animal
使像動物 (animal) 般有活力

The teacher began to talk about the proposed excursion and it animated his students. There were no students dozing in class.

老師開始談到校外教學讓學生變得很有活力，沒人在課堂上打瞌睡。

0636 **annexation** [͵ænɛksˋeʃən]
n. merger

★★★★☆

併吞

connect
連結 (connect) 在一起

Iraq's invasion and annexation of Kuwait was a clear violation of the United Nations Charter. It eventually caused the invader's downfall.

伊拉克入侵並併吞科威特明顯違反聯合國憲章，此舉終將導致滅亡。

0637 **apparent** [əˋpærənt]
a. evident; obvious; manifest; patent; plain

★★★★★

明顯的，顯而易見的

appear
出現 (appear) 在眼前的

I saw Mrs. Shapiro's apparent indifference to her drunken husband's oaths. He seemed to have broken too many of his promises.

我發現夏皮洛太太對酗酒丈夫的發誓明顯漠不關心，他似乎食言太多次了。

0638 **apparition** [͵æpəˋrɪʃən]
n. specter; phantom

★★★☆☆

幽靈，鬼魂，幻影

appear
鬼神現身 (appear)

Rumor has it that some citizens of London saw apparitions of ancient kings and queens in old palaces.

謠傳有些倫敦市民在古堡看到古代帝后的鬼魂。

0639 **appease** [əˋpiz]
v. pacify; mollify; placate; ease

★★★★☆

緩和，滿足

peace
帶來和平 (peace)

When Michael returned home from work, he was very hungry. He hurriedly ate one apple to appease his hunger.

邁可下班回家後覺得很餓，於是大口吃掉一顆蘋果充饑。

0640 **appoint** [əˋpɔɪnt]
v. designate; name; nominate

★★★★★

約定，指派

point
指明 (point) 並任命

As soon as the accused makes his appearance in court and enters his plea, the judge will appoint a day in the near future as the trial date.

被告出庭並提出抗辯後，法官將近期擇日公開審理。

0641 appraise [ə`prez] ★★★★☆ 估計，估量，估價，評價

price
訂出價格 (price)

v. estimate; rate; evaluate; assess; set a value on

I bought my house for $100,000 five years ago. I am glad that it is now appraised at $120,000. But I have no intention of selling it.

五年前我用十萬美元買房子，很高興現在漲到十二萬美元，但我還是不想賣。

0642 approbation [ˌæprə`beʃən] ★★★☆☆ 批准，認可 / 讚許

prove
證明 (prove) 是好的

n. approval / praise

The people needed to get approbation from the police before they could have a demonstration against the free trade agreement.

民眾需獲警方批准才能展開示威活動，反對自由貿易協定。

0643 appropriate [ə`proprɪˌet] ★★★★★ 適當的，合適的，恰當的，相稱的

proper
適當的 (proper)

a. proper; suitable; acceptable

Kurt has a very hard time finding a girlfriend because as of yet he has not learned etiquette and the appropriate way to act around women.

柯特很難找到女友，因為他迄今仍未學會得體的待人禮節。

0644 approximately [ə`prɑksəmɪtlɪ] ★★★★★ 大約，近於

proper
proxi＝最接近地
proper＝適合的，恰當的

ad. nearly; about; all but; almost

I weigh approximately 150 pounds, but I do not know exactly how much I weigh.

我的體重差不多一百五十磅，但不知道確實數字。

0645 arboreal [ɑr`bɔrɪəl] ★★★☆☆ 棲息在樹上的

Arbor Day
植樹節 (Arbor Day)

a. living in trees or adapted for living in trees

Most kinds of apes are excellently adapted for arboreal life. They are well adapted to life in the forest.

多數猿猴都非常適應叢林樹棲生活。

0646 armament [`ɑrməmənt] ★★☆☆☆ 軍備，軍事力量

arms
武器 (arms)

n. all the military forces and equipment of a nation

One week before the beginning of the war, there was significant military activity. The enemy was moving all of its armaments to the front.

戰爭開打前一周出現重大軍事行動，敵軍將所有軍備調至前線。

0647 artful [`ɑrtfəl] ★★☆☆☆ 機靈的，計謀多端的，狡猾的

art
展露技巧 (art)

a. crafty; cunning; sly; wily

The artful teacher told his students that the forest was haunted by a grizzly bear. The students could not wander freely in the woods.

足智多謀的老師告訴學生們森林常有大棕熊出沒，所以大家都不敢在樹林裡亂跑。

0648 ascertain [ˌæsə`ten] ★★★★☆ 探查，查明

certain
確實 (certain) 相信

v. find out; determine; discover

Only after months of investigation was the detective able to ascertain enough evidence to bring murder charges against the suspect.

經過數月調查後刑警終於查出足夠證據，將嫌犯以殺人罪名定罪。

0649 assuage [əˈswedʒ]   緩和，平息，減輕 | sweet

v. *appease; pacify; soothe; relieve*

His wife was really upset because Allan forgot the anniversary. He assuaged her by doing all kinds of domestic work.

妻子因艾倫忘記結婚周年紀念日而感到很不高興，他包辦所有家務事以緩和其怒氣。

以甜蜜的 (sweet) 話語安撫

★★★★☆

0650 asinine [ˈæsn̩ˌaɪn]   愚蠢的，愚昧的 | ass

a. *silly; brainless; fatuous; foolish; unwitty*

It is simply asinine to think that anyone could jump off from a cliff as high as one hundred meters and survive.

以為任何人都可從一百公尺高的懸崖上跳下還活著，是相當愚蠢的想法。

像個笨蛋 (ass)

★★★☆☆

Tea Time... ☕

<Name of an extinct animal>	〈絕種動物〉長毛象
Mammoth	長毛象是一種已絕種大象，身上有長毛覆蓋，並長有向上彎曲的長象牙，遺骸在北美、歐洲和亞洲都有發現。（註：本字源自俄羅斯古字 mammut，原指「地底下潛伏之物」。成年長毛象的身高最多可達四點五公尺，體重更可達七公噸，儼然是個龐然大物。因此後世便將本字引申為「巨大的、龐大的」。）
Extinct elephants with a hairy skin and long tusks curving upward; remains have been found in North America, Europe and Asia.	

❖ **mammoth** [ˈmæməθ] **n.** *huge; enormous; gigantic; giant; immense; massive; gargantuan; colossal; monumental; titanic; leviathan; jumbo; stupendous* │ 巨大的，龐大的

Legend has it that Paul Bunyan, a legendary hero who created the Grand Canyon, had a mammoth blue ox. The ox was so big that it was combed with a garden rake and its footprints were so enormous that they could drown men who fell into them.

一手創造出美國大峽谷的傳奇英雄保羅‧班揚據傳有大藍牛作伴，這頭牛非常龐大，用園藝專用的耙梳頭；腳印也非常大，跌進凹洞者會被溺死。

Review Test 01

Day 01 0601~0650

Chapter

1

2

3

4

5

1 Complete each word by filling in the blank with proper spelling so that it has the same meaning as suggested. Then please write the meaning of each word in Chinese.

1. 縮寫 = a b _ _ _ _ _ _ t e
2. 厭惡 = a b _ _ _ _ a t e
3. 陪伴 = a c _ _ _ _ _ _ _
4. 承認 = a c _ _ _ _ l e d g e
5. 默認 = a c _ _ _ _ s c e
6. 使行動 = _ _ _ u a t e
7. 附錄 = _ _ _ e n d u m
8. 判決 = a d _ _ _ _ c a t e
9. 後果 = _ _ _ _ _ m a t h
10. 使惡化 = a g _ _ _ _ a t e

11. amonable – _____
12. amendment = _____
13. animate = _____
14. appease = _____
15. appropriate = _____
16. appoint = _____
17. armament = _____
18. attune = _____
19. backbone = _____
20. assuage = _____

2 Choose a word that best completes the sentence.

21. Jane had no choice but to _____ to her husband's wish. He wanted to move to the country.
    (A) acquiesce   (B) appease   (C) soothe   (D) determine

22. The department manager was trusted by the chairman and was later _____ as the general manager.
    (A) adopted   (B) abbreviated   (C) appointed   (D) acknowledged

23. Smoking has _____ his cough.
    (A) animated   (B) aggravated   (C) acquitted   (D) affronted

3 The highlighted word is closest in meaning to which of the following?

24. The girl abhorred the thought of using the scoop that the old man had just licked, even though she really liked ice cream.
    (A) loathed   (B) adjudicated   (C) attuned   (D) appraised

25. Money is not the only fuel that actuates workers.
    (A) deteriorates   (B) worsens   (C) accompanies   (D) moves

Chapter 2 + *127*

MP3 28

0651 assure [əˋʃur] ★★★★★

使確信，使放心，向～保證

sure

使確實 (sure) 相信

v. ensure; convince

The lady seemed to be determined and she assured us that she would get married to him by hook or by crook.

那位小姐似乎心意已決，向我們保證要用盡一切辦法嫁給他。

0652 attune [əˋtun] ★★★★☆

使慣於，使適合

tune

音調 (tune) 一致

v. adapt; acclimate; acclimatize

Astronauts have to attune themselves to weightless conditions in space. They are often trained in an airplane designed to create the conditions.

太空人須習慣太空無重力狀態，因此常在無重力狀態設計的飛機中受訓。

0653 avow [əˋvau] ★★★★☆

承認，坦承

vow

向 (a-=to) 某人發誓 (vow)

v. claim; declare; admit

Only after marriage did the bridegroom avow that he had been married in his twenties. The bride got extremely angry.

新郎直到婚後才坦承二十多歲時曾結過一次婚，讓新娘非常生氣。

0654 babble [ˋbæbl] ★★★☆☆

牙牙學語，口齒不清地說話

baby

如嬰兒 (baby) 般說話

v. chatter; blab; chat; prattle

His 10-month-old baby has not yet learned to say words. The baby is usually babbling away all day.

他十個月大的嬰兒還沒有學會講話，經常一整天口齒不清地牙牙學語。

0655 babysitter [ˋbebɪˌsɪtə] ★★★★☆

臨時褓姆

baby, sit

讓不安份的嬰兒 (baby) 坐 (sit) 下的人

n. a person hired to take care of a child or children

I think you'd better find a babysitter who'll look after your children while you are working if you don't want to lose your job.

你如果不想失去工作，最好找個臨時褓姆在你工作時幫忙照顧孩子。

0656 backbone [ˋbækˋbon] ★★★★★

脊椎骨，分水嶺，書脊，社會中堅

back, bone

背部 (back) 的骨頭 (bone)

n. spine; vertebra; back

John was replacing the roof on his house when he tripped on a hammer. He fell backwards off the roof, breaking his backbone.

約翰更換家中屋瓦時踩到鐵鎚而摔下屋頂，結果跌斷脊椎。

0657 backslide [ˋbækˌslaɪd] ★★★☆☆

故態復萌，墮落，退步

slide

往回 (back) 滑動 (slide)

v. lapse; relapse

The old man, who is recovering from his alcoholism, is very conscious about not backsliding into his old drinking habit.

從酗酒中走出來的老人小心翼翼不要重蹈覆轍。

0658 ban [bæn] ★★★★☆

禁止，取締，查禁

Rayban

阻擋 (ban) 光線 (ray) 的眼鏡 (Rayban) 眼鏡品牌

v. bid; inhibit; interdict; prohibit; enjoin

Domestic airlines are banned from purchasing secondhand passenger aircraft because used planes may lead to serious accidents.

國內航空公司禁止購買二手民航機，因為老舊客機可能導致重大空難。

0659 barrier [ˋbærɪə]　　　　　　　　　　　　　障礙，阻礙物，柵欄　　★★★★★

n. block; blockade; bar

The students who choose to study abroad should try to break down language barriers. They should have a relatively good command of the local language.

選擇出國念書的學生應努力打破語言障礙，才能擁有熟練的當地語言表達能力。

bar
欄杆 (bar) 等用來阻擋某物的器具 (-er)

0660 basin [ˋbesn̩]　　　　　　　　　　　　　盆地　　★★★★★

n. depression; concavity; dip; hollow

The states of Utah and Nevada are located in a great basin. To the west lies the Sierra Nevada and to the east the Rocky Mountains.

猶他和內華達兩州都位於大盆地內，西有內華達山脈，東邊則是洛磯山脈。

base
位於較深的底部 (base)

0661 bass [bes]　　　　　　　　　　　　　低音部，低音樂器　　★★★★☆

n. a low, deep sound or tone

Bass is an essential part which gives fullness and depth to the piece.

低音部是提供整首樂曲飽滿度和深度的重要部分。

base
在音層底部 (base) 的音

0662 battalion [bəˋtæljən]　　　　　　　　　　營，大隊　　★★☆☆☆

n. a large group of soldiers arrayed for battle

During the battle the commander radioed for help, requesting a battalion of men to be sent to the front.

總司令在戰役中透過無線電請求支援，要求派遣一營軍隊開往前線。

battle
負責打仗 (battle) 者

0663 batter [ˋbætə]　　　　　　　　　　　連續猛擊，重擊，搗毀　　★☆☆☆☆

v. beat; baste; thrash; belabor

When the police responded to the call, they were told that the woman had been battered by her husband.

警方接獲電話，得知該女子遭丈夫毆打。

bat
以球棒 (bat) 擊打

0664 befall [bɪˋfɔl]　　　　　　　　（尤指不幸或禍事等）降臨，發生　　★★☆☆☆

v. happen; occur; betide

In the States many people believe that if a person walks under a ladder, or sees a black cat, bad luck will befall him.

許多美國人相信若從梯子底下走過或看見黑貓，厄運就會降臨在自己身上。

fall
災難降臨 (fall)

0665 beget [bɪˋgɛt]　　　　　　　　　成為～之父，引起，招致　　★★☆☆☆

v. give birth; cause; create; lead to

Liars should have a good memory, because one lie tends to beget another and another. Later they have difficulty remembering which is a lie and which is true.

撒謊者要有很好的記憶力，因為說謊會招來一連串謊言，到後來很難記得真假。

get
得到 (get) 自己的孩子

0666 beguile [bɪˋgaɪl]　　　　　　　　　　　　　欺騙　　★★★★☆

v. deceive; betray; delude; mislead; take in; double-cross

Helen found out that her husband was having an affair and she filed for divorce because she couldn't live with a man who had beguiled her.

海倫發現先生外遇便訴請離婚，因為她無法和欺騙自己的人共同生活。

guile
用奸計 (guile) 騙人

0667 belie [bɪ`laɪ]　　　　　　　　　　　　　　　　掩飾　　★★☆☆☆

lie
給予虛假的 (lie) 印象

v. give a false impression; contradict

The woman's smile she is always wearing belies the misery she has. She lost her husband and is now alone.

女子以經常掛在臉上的笑容掩飾痛苦，失去先生的她現在形單影隻。

0668 belittle [bɪ`lɪtl]　　　　　　　　　　　　　貶損，貶低　　★★★☆☆

little
小 (little) 看人或物

v. depreciate; disparage; decry; scorn; look down upon; despise

When he first came to the party he was popular because of his jokes, but as he continued to belittle everyone in the room he soon found himself alienated.

他首次參加宴會因為會講笑話而受到歡迎，但當他繼續貶損在座所有人，很快就發現他被大家疏遠。

0669 beloved [bɪ`lʌvɪd]　　　　　　　　鍾愛的，心愛的，親愛的　　★★★★☆

love
值得愛 (love) 的

a. favorite; darling; dear

It takes many years and a lot of cherished experiences to develop a trustworthy relationship with a beloved friend.

要共度許多時光並擁有共同珍惜的經驗，才能和好友建立起值得信賴的友誼關係。

0670 benighted [bɪ`naɪtɪd]　　　　　　　愚昧無知的，未開化的　　★☆☆☆☆

night
仍像晚上 (night) 般黑暗的

a. ignorant; unenlightened; unilluminated

None of the benighted tribe members could know what it was when the explorers' helicopter landed in the village.

當探險者的直昇機降落在村落，愚昧無知的部落居民不知道那是什麼。

0671 beseech [bɪ`sitʃ]　　　　　　　　　　懇求，祈求，央求　　★★★☆☆

seek
尋求 (seek) 幫助

v. beg; appeal; entreat; invoke; plead; supplicate; implore; pray

When I was in high school, my parents beseeched me to study hard so that I could get accepted to a top university.

高中時父母懇求我用功念書以獲准進入頂尖大學就讀。

0672 beverage [`bɛvrɪdʒ]　　　　　　　　　　　　飲料，飲品　　★★★★☆

imbibe
飲用 (imbibe) 品

n. drink

I went to a wedding reception and I was impressed with the wide selection of foods and beverages that were available to eat and drink.

我來到婚宴現場，有這麼多食物和飲料可供選擇令我印象深刻。

0673 beware [bɪ`wɛr]　　　　　　　　　　　當心，提防，小心　　★★★★★

aware
察覺到 (aware) 危險

v. watch; heed; be on one's guard; notice; be cautious

The sign on the door read, "Beware of dog," so the salesman approached the house with caution.

門上牌子寫著「當心惡犬」，所以業務員小心靠近房子。

0674 bigot [`bɪgət]　　　　　　　　　　　狂熱者 / 偏執狂　　★★★☆☆

By God!
對天發誓 (By God!)

n. fanatic; enthusiast; maniac; freak / a perverse person

Senator Harris is such an arrogant bigot that it is almost impossible for other members to argue with him.

參議員哈瑞斯是個傲慢自大的偏執狂，其他參議員幾乎無法跟他爭辯。

0675 **blacken** [`blækən]

★★★★☆

使變黑

black
製造黑暗 (black)

v. *give one a black eye*

He was spouting off to someone who was bigger and stronger than he and the guy hit him in the eye, blackening it.

他被比自己高大強壯的人揍，那人揍了他眼睛一拳，四周就瘀青了。

MP3
29

0676 **blanch** [blæntʃ]

★★★★☆

使蒼白

blank
空格 (blank) 處白白的什麼都沒有

v. *turn pale; bleach; whiten*

The woman blanched at the sight of a rattlesnake. Her face was as pale as marble.

女子一看到響尾蛇就嚇得臉色發白，蒼白的臉跟大理石一樣。

0677 **bleed** [blid]

★★★★☆

流血，失血

blood
流出血 (blood) 來

v. *emit or lose blood*

He was fine after the accident until he saw that he was bleeding. Then he began to cry and went into shock.

意外發生後他本來還好，直到發現流血便開始哭喊，接著就休克了。

0678 **bliss** [blɪs]

★★★☆☆

極大的快樂，福氣，天賜的福份

bless
最大的祝福 (bless)

n. *happiness; beatitude; blessedness; blissfulness*

Many people think that money is the most important thing, and that it provides them with a life of bliss.

許多人都認為能帶來一生幸福的金錢是最重要的東西。

0679 **blithe** [blaɪð]

★★☆☆☆

歡樂的，快活的，快樂的

bless
受祝福 (bless) 而感到高興

a. *carefree; cheerful; merry*

The children who were playing blithely on the ground lost track of time. When they got ready to leave the school, it became dark.

孩子們在操場上愉快地玩得忘了時間，等準備好離開校園天色已晚。

0680 **blockade** [blɑ`ked]

★★★☆☆

封鎖，阻礙物

block
加以阻擋 (block)

n. *barrier; bar; barricade*

Despite the fact that the United Nations set up an international blockade, a ship managed to slip through the blockade and arrive at its destination unscathed.

儘管聯合國拉起一道國際封鎖線，仍有一艘船隻企圖悄悄穿越，並安全抵達目的地。

0681 **bloodshot** [`blʌd͵ʃɑt]

★★☆☆☆

充血的，血紅的

blood
充滿了血 (blood)

a. *red because the small blood vessels are swollen or broken*

I didn't sleep a wink last night, thinking of the interview. That's why my eyes are terribly bloodshot now.

我昨晚惦記面試的事整夜不曾闔眼，這正是為什麼雙眼現在嚴重充血。

0682 **blossom** [`blɑsəm]

★★★★☆

全部花朵，開花

bloom
開 (bloom) 出的花朵

n. *flower; bloom*

The city which is located at the southern part of the peninsula is famous for cherry blossoms. Many people go to the city to see the flowers.

位於半島南端的城市以櫻花聞名，許多人都前來觀賞。

0683 blunder [ˈblʌndə]　　　　　　　　　　　大錯，錯誤　　　★★★★★

n. error; slip; slipup; mistake; bungle

Sometimes she thinks that she is stupid and her life is full of blunders. She failed every entrance exam and she is now divorced.

有時她認為自己很蠢，人生也充滿錯誤。她報考的所有入學考試都以失敗告終，現在又離婚了。

blind
盲目地 (blind) 犯下大錯

0684 bombard [bɑmˈbɑrd]　　　　　　　　　　砲轟，轟炸　　　★★★★☆

v. blitz; assault with bombs or shells

They were warned by the United Nations that if they didn't pull their troops out of the country they would be bombarded.

聯合國警告他們若不從該國撤軍就要進行轟炸。

bomb
用砲彈 (bomb) 攻擊

0685 bombastic [bɑmˈbæstɪk]　　　　浮誇的，誇大的，唱高調的　　★★★★☆

a. pompous; grandiloquent; magniloquent; tumid

The candidate insisted that he could not believe his rival's bombastic claims. But personally, I did not notice any touch of pomposity in his rival's speech.

候選人堅稱對手的浮誇主張不可信，但我個人並未在其演說中看到任何自大浮誇。

bomb
說話如連珠炮般 (bomb) 狂轟

0686 bondage [ˈbɑndɪdʒ]　　　　　　奴隸身份，奴役，束縛　　★★★★☆

n. enslavement; slavery

The Exodus in the Old Testament tells us that Moses led the Children of Israel out of bondage to freedom.

《舊約聖經》中的《出埃及記》告訴我們，摩西率領以色列子民脫離奴隸身分重獲自由。

bind
被束縛住 (bind)

0687 bossy [ˈbɔsɪ]　　　　　愛指揮他人的，跋扈的，盛氣凌人的　　★★★★☆

a. domineering; haughty; cocky; overbearing

Rosa sometimes plays house with her dolls and she likes to tell them what to do and sometimes becomes quite bossy with them.

羅莎有時會跟女伴們一起玩辦家家酒遊戲，她喜歡告訴大家該怎麼做，於是變得很跋扈。

boss
像老闆 (boss) 般傲慢

0688 bourgeois [burˈʒwɑ]　　　　　　　中產階級者，資本家　　★★☆☆☆

n. middle class, usually in a pejorative sense

The communists revolted against the bourgeois, or middle-class people, and the people in higher classes.

共產主義者反對又稱中產階級的資本家及較高階層人士。

proletariat
由勞工階級 (proletariat) 做聯想

0689 bravado [brəˈvɑdo]　　　　　　　　　　虛張聲勢　　　★★☆☆☆

n. affectation; an ostentatious show of bravery

With extreme bravado, the unruly student stood against his teacher. At last the angry teacher sent him to the dean.

不守規矩的學生以激烈的虛張聲勢反抗老師，最後生氣的老師把他帶到訓導主任面前。

bravo
虛張聲勢地大叫再來一個 (bravo)

0690 breach [britʃ]　　　　　　　　　　　違反，侵害／衝破，違背

n. contravention; infraction; infringement; transgression; violation / *v.* break

The contract stated that Anne would get a 15% salary increase upon completion of her first year of work, but her boss only gave her a 5% increase. Now she is suing her company for breach of contract.

合約上明訂安做完首年工作可得十五％加薪，但上司卻只給五％。現在她控告自己任職的公司違約。

break
打破 (break) 法則

0691 breast-feed [`brɛst,fid]　　　　　　　以母乳哺乳

v. nurse; nourish; suckle

At a party, Mrs. Brown withdrew for a while to breast-feed her two month-old son. A youngster who had been watching with interest suddenly asked, "Do you eat grass too?"

伯朗太太在宴會上哺乳兩個月大的兒子時暫停了一下，因為有個年輕女子興味盎然地看著她，接著突然問道：「妳也吃草嗎？」

breast, food
以乳房 (breast) 餵養食物 (food)

0692 brochure [bro`ʃur]　　　　　　　　　　小冊子

n. pamphlet; booklet

Before their trip to the gorge, the travel agent gave them some brochures about their package tours.

到峽谷旅遊前，旅行社交給他們一些關於套裝行程的小冊子。

brooch
如胸針 (brooch) 般釘住

0693 browbeat [`brau,bit]　　　　　　　　　恫嚇，叱責

v. intimidate; bully; cow; menace; threaten

Laura's brother usually browbeats the younger children. So they don't like him and try to avoid him.

蘿拉的弟弟常叱嚇小孩子，所以孩子們不但不喜歡他還會離他遠遠的。

brow, beat
敲打 (beat) 額頭 (brow)

0694 bulge [bʌldʒ]　　　　　　　　　　　　凸塊，鼓起之處

v. swell; expand

In high school, John had a very skinny build so he decided to hit the gym and work out hard. Now he has an admirable body with bulging muscles.

高中時約翰是個瘦皮猴，所以決定到健身房好好鍛鍊。現在他擁有令人欣羨的健碩身材。

ball
如球 (ball) 狀凸起

0695 bulky [`bʌlkɪ]　　　　　笨重而不易搬運的，龐大笨重的，占地方的

a. having great bulk; large; massive

You are going to need some help with that bag because it is so bulky that it will take about three people to load it into the truck.

你需要找人幫忙搬那個袋子，它太笨重大概要三個人一起裝運到卡車上。

ball
像球 (ball) 一樣占體積

0696 bump [bʌmp]　　　　　　　　　　　　使碰撞

v. bang; collide; butt

Her spoiled son was very unruly and one day he got so angry that he bumped his head on the table.

她的驕縱兒子非常不守規矩，某天耍了很大的脾氣，頭撞到了桌子。

bumper
緩和撞擊的保險桿 (bumper)

0697 **bureaucracy** [bjuˈrɑkrəsɪ]

★★☆☆☆

官僚體制，官僚作風

bureau
政府機關局處 (bureau)

n. a system of government comprising numerous bureaus

The previous government of the nation was characterized by bureaucracy, which was extremely inefficient.

該國前任政府具有極無效率的官僚體制特色。

0698 **cache** [kæʃ]

★★★☆☆

貯藏所，隱藏處

case
裝進箱子 (case) 裡保管

n. a hiding place; repository

The husband had a cache in the corner of his room where he hid his cash. Unfortunately, however, the new vacuum his wife bought was very powerful.

丈夫在房間角落有個隱密藏錢處，不幸的是妻子新買的吸塵器十分管用。

0699 **calculus** [ˈkælkjələs]

★★★★☆

微積分

calculate
計算 (calculate) 數字

n. a system of mathematical analysis using the combined methods of differential calculus and integral calculus

I had a hard time in high school with algebra, so when I came to college, I decided to retake algebra during my freshman year and take calculus during my sophomore year.

我高中時代學代數學得很辛苦，所以上大學後決定第一年重修代數課，等到二年級再修微積分。

0700 **camaraderie** [ˌkɑməˈrɑdərɪ]

★★★☆☆

（志同道合者之間的）友誼，忠誠

comrade
夥伴 (comrade) 間的情誼

n. comradeship; friendliness; a spirit of friendly goodwill typical of comrades

There is a camaraderie among my colleagues in my office. We have worked together harmoniously for over seven years.

辦公室同事擁有志同道合的友誼，一起和諧工作超過七年。

Tea Time... ☕

<From Afghanistan> Afghan
A coverlet that is knitted or crocheted from soft woolen yarn. Such coverlets originally came from Afghanistan.

〈來自阿富汗〉阿富汗針織品
以特殊織法將柔軟羊毛紗編織成床單和被單等針織品，最早來自阿富汗。（註：由於阿富汗針織品享譽國際，所以原為形容詞的 afghan「阿富汗的」一字，也可以直接作為名詞，意指「阿富汗針織品」。）

❖ **afghan** [ˈæfgæn] *n. a knitted and sewn woolen blanket or shawl* | 阿富汗針織品，阿富汗毛毯

The blue and white afghan my mother knitted for me five years ago is still my favorite blanket.

母親五年前編織給我的藍白相間阿富汗織布，至今仍是我最愛的小毛毯。

1

Complete each word by filling in the blank with proper spelling so that it has the same meaning as suggested. Then please write the meaning of each word in Chinese.

1. 連續猛擊	= _ _ _ t e r		11. browbeat	= _____
2. 欺騙	= b e _ _ _ _ _		12. calculus	= _____
3. 貶損	= b e _ _ _ _ _ _		13. bulky	= _____
4. 懇求	= b e _ _ _ _ _		14. barrier	= _____
5. 偏執狂	= b i _ _ _		15. bulge	= _____
6. 使變黑	= _ _ _ _ _ e n		16. assure	= _____
7. 封鎖	= _ _ _ _ _ a d e		17. babble	= _____
8. 眼睛充血的	= _ _ _ _ _ s h o t		18. basin	= _____
9. 浮誇的	= _ _ _ _ a s t i c		19. backslide	= _____
10. 跋扈的	= _ _ _ _ y		20. ban	= _____

2

Choose a word that best completes the sentence.

21. **Mrs. White is looking for a _____ who will take care of her kids while she is working at the office.**

    (A) babble   (B) barrier   (C) babysitter   (D) basin

22. **A student who hopes to study abroad should try to break down the language _____.**

    (A) batter   (B) barrier   (C) battalion   (D) bass

3

The highlighted word is closest in meaning to which of the following?

23. **A woman carrying a `bulky` parcel got on the train.**

    (A) large   (B) arrogant   (C) appeal   (D) entreat

24. **Jack, a glutton, went to a restaurant which had a policy of free refills on `beverages`. When he ordered the fourth refill, the harried waitress said, "Shall I get you an IV?"**

    (A) drinks   (B) bigot   (C) maniac   (D) fanatic

25. **Please do not think that your `bossy` boss is the only employer in the world.**

    (A) pompous   (B) domineering   (C) tumid   (D) darling

MP3
30

0701 capacious [kə`peʃəs]   容量大的，寬廣的   ★★★★☆

capable
有能力的 (capable)

a. spacious; ample; commodious; roomy; wide

If we intend to ship the large machinery by boat, we will have to make sure that we secure a container capacious enough.

如果我們打算以船運方式運送大型機械，必須確定有足夠貨櫃容量。

0702 cashier [kæ`ʃɪr]   出納員，櫃檯，帳房   ★★★☆☆

cash
處理現金 (cash) 的人

n. a person hired to collect and keep a record of customers' payment, as in a store

Tom started working at the Caesar's Palace as a bell boy and worked his way up to a cashier.

湯姆從凱撒皇宮大酒店的大廳服務生做起，一路做到櫃檯人員。

0703 catholic [`kæθəlɪk]   廣泛的，普遍的 / 舊教的，天主教的   ★★★☆☆

Catholic church
天主教 (Catholic) 全世界都有

a. universal

Leonardo Da Vinci was a catholic genius; he was preeminent in almost all fields. He was a painter, architect, and scientist.

達文西是個興趣廣泛的天才，幾乎在所有領域都有卓越成就，如畫家、建築師、科學家等。

0704 cavern [`kævən]   巨大洞窟，凹洞   ★★★★☆

cave
洞窟 (cave)

n. cave

Divers are exploring a newly discovered cavern at the bottom of the ocean and have yet to determine its actual depth.

潛水者正在探索新近發現的巨大海底洞窟，實際深度尚待確認。

0705 cavity [`kævətɪ]   蛀牙，蛀洞   ★★★★☆

cave
牙齒上的洞 (cave)

n. a hollow place in a tooth

His mother would always remind him that if he didn't brush his teeth, he would have a lot of cavities.

媽媽常提醒他如果不刷牙就會有許多蛀牙。

0706 certificate [sə`tɪfəkɪt]   結業證書，畢業證書，執照   ★★★★★

certain
證明確實 (certain) 的文件

n. a written or printed statement by which a fact is formally or officially certified or attested

I signed up for a two-day self-improvement course and they gave each of the participants a very nice certificate upon completion of the class.

我報名為期兩天的自我成長課程，完成全部課程後主辦單位會發給參與者十分精緻的結業證書。

0707 certify [`sɝtə,faɪ]   證明，證實   ★★★★★

certain
證明是確鑿的 (certain)

v. declare a thing true, accurate, certain, etc.

The doctor was finally able to certify her insane when she began to rant and rave and talk to herself incoherently.

當她開始語無倫次地嚷叫和毫無條理地自言自語，醫生終於證實她患有精神失常。

0708 cessation [sɛ`seʃən]   中止，中斷，停止   ★★★★☆

cease
終止，停止 (cease)

n. end; cease; termination

The two countries were fighting fiercely. The bombardment continued without cessation.

兩國處於激烈交戰中，砲轟從未停止。

0709 chatter [ˋtʃætɚ] ★★★☆☆ 喋喋不休，嘮叨

v. chat; babble; prattle

I went to see the movie, but I couldn't hear a thing because the two people sitting behind me chattered through the whole thing.

我去看電影，但什麼都聽不到，因為後方坐的兩個人在電影放映時喋喋不休地交談。

chat
閒聊 (chat)

0710 chef [ʃɛf] ★★★☆☆ 餐廳主廚

n. head of cooks

When my uncle, a gourmet, and I went to a restaurant, the chef himself came out of the kitchen and recommended a special dish for us.

我和美食家舅舅一起到餐廳吃飯時，主廚從廚房裡走出來推薦一道特選主餐。

chief
廚房的主管 (chief)

0711 choir [kwaɪr] ★★★☆☆ 教堂唱詩班

n. organized group of singers, esp. one that performs in church services

Jane is a born singer. She is in the church choir. I am sure that she sings better than anyone else I know.

珍有一副天生的好嗓子並在教堂唱詩班唱聖歌，我確定她比我認識的任何人唱得還要好。

chorus
一起合唱 (chorus) 的團體

0712 circuitous [sɜˋkjuɪtəs] ★★★☆☆ 迂迴的，間接的

a. roundabout; indirect; devious

Some people purposely use circuitous language in order to hide their true intentions or not to hurt others' feelings.

有些人會故意用迂迴的表達方式隱藏真正意圖，或不去傷害他人情感。

circle
說話兜圈子 (circle)

0713 circulate [ˋsɜkjəˌlet] ★★★★☆ 循環，環行 / 流通，傳播，發行

v. move in a circle / be distributed to a circle or mass of readers

It took the producers of that new magazine several months of preparation before they could begin to circulate the magazine.

新雜誌製作群在發行前花了好幾個月的準備時間。

circle
繞著圓圈 (circle) 轉

0714 citadel [ˋsɪtədl] ★★★★☆ 碉堡，堡壘，要塞

n. fortress; stronghold; fortification

In early history, people used to protect their city by building citadels around the outside of the city.

在早期歷史中，人們為了保護自己居住的城市，常在四周建造護城碉堡。

city
變成要塞的城市 (city)

0715 clamber [ˋklæmbɚ] ★★★☆☆ 攀爬，爬上

v. climb with effort

The main character in that movie was captured by a murderer, but narrowly escaped death by clambering up the side of a hill to safety.

那部電影主角被兇手抓住，但攀爬山壁勉強平安逃生。

climb
往上爬 (climb)

0716 cleanser [ˋklɛnzɚ] ★★★☆☆ 清潔劑

n. any preparation for cleansing, especially a powder for scouring pots, enamel surfaces, etc.

TV shows are called "soap operas" because the earliest sponsors were mostly the makers of bath soap, laundry detergent and household cleansers.

電視連續劇之所以稱為「肥皂劇」，是因早期贊助者幾乎都是浴皂、洗衣粉、家用清潔劑製造商。

clean
使物品變乾淨 (clean) 之物

0717 climactic [klaɪˈmæktɪk] ★★☆☆☆ 最高潮的，頂點的

a. forming a climax

I really enjoyed that movie, especially the way it so cleverly built up to such a climactic ending. And the final scene was really impressive.

我很愛看那部電影，特別是它非常巧妙的營造最高潮結局，最後一幕真在讓人印象深刻。

climax
達到頂點 (climax) 的

0718 cloister [ˈklɔɪstə] ★★★☆☆ 修道院，寺院，僧院

n. convent; monastery

There are many cloisters throughout the mountains of Asian countries where buddhist monks live and worship.

亞洲各國深山遍布許多寺院，是佛教僧侶居住生活和頌經禮佛之處。

close
關閉 (close) 不准閒人進入之地

0719 clout [klaʊt] ★★☆☆☆ 敲打 / 影響力

n. blow; strike / influence

When the child kept on crying for a long time in front of a computer game room, insisting on playing computer games in there, his mother gave him a clout on the buttocks.

小孩在電腦遊戲室外頭哭鬧著想進去玩，於是媽媽打了他一下屁股。

cloth
被當成標靶的布 (cloth)

0720 collapse [kəˈlæps] ★★★★★ 倒塌 / 垮臺，崩潰，瓦解

v. disintegrate; fall to pieces; shatter; cave / n. destruction; breakup

The use of improperly mixed concrete in the building structures may lead to the collapse of the buildings.

在建築物結構體內使用不當混凝土，可能會導致建物倒塌。

lapse
一起 (col-) 跌落 (lapse)

0721 combative [kəmˈbætɪv] ★★★★★ 好戰的，好鬥的，鬥志高昂的

a. belligerent; warlike; contentious; pugnacious

The popularity of big time wrestling in the United States seems to suggest that the American people are somewhat combative in nature.

美國職業摔角運動的盛行似乎暗示其實美國人有些好鬥。

combat
喜歡戰鬥 (combat)

0722 commiserate [kəˈmɪzəˌret] ★★★★☆ 憐憫，同情

v. feel for; sympathize with

The judge commiserated with the accused as he sentenced him to prison, but he mentioned that he was confident that justice had been served in this case.

法官宣判被告入獄並表達同情之意，同時也提到對本案正義得以伸張深具信心。

misery
一起 (com-) 感受苦難 (misery)

0723 commodious [kəˈmodɪəs] ★★★★★ 寬敞的

a. spacious; roomy; ample

The commodious condominium that we stayed in during the summer vacation allowed us to kick back and relax every evening.

我們在暑假暫住的寬敞公寓，讓大家能在每天傍晚放鬆心情好好休息。

accommodate, common
可以共同 (common) 容納 (accommodate) 在一起的

0724 commonplace [`kɑmən͵ples] ★★★★★

平凡的，單調的，平淡無味的

a. prosaic; trite; cliche; stereo-typed; timeworn

As even the finest landscape, seen daily, becomes monotonous, so does the most beautiful face, unless a beautiful nature shines through it. The beauty of today becomes commonplace tomorrow.

—— Ernest Hemingway

即使是最優美的風景，如果每天看也會變得索然無味；最美麗的臉龐也是如此，除非散發美好氣質。今日的美到了明日就變得平凡。

—— 海明威

common
普通平凡的 (common)

0725 compile [kəm`paɪl] ★★★★★

搜集，編纂

v. collect information and arrange it in a book, list, report, etc.

I intend to write a book, and I am now in the process of compiling data that I will use to base my thoughts on.

我想撰寫一本書，現在正在搜集資料作為構想基礎。

pile
把東西集中在一處 (com-) 堆起來 (pile)

MP3
31

0726 complacent [kəm`plesn̩t] ★★★★☆

得意的，自滿的

a. self-complacent; self-satisfied

My father gave me some good advice when he told me that the day I became complacent in my occupation, will be the day that I stop being an effective employee.

父親告誡我，如果對自己的工作感到自滿，便不再是有效率的員工。

pleasure
對一切 (com-) 都很喜愛滿意 (pleasure)

0727 compromise [kɑmprə͵maɪz] ★★★★☆

妥協，讓步 / 和解，折衷辦法

v. settle or adjust by concessions on both sides / n. settlement

Both sides of the table were very set in their demands and neither would budge until they realized that a compromise would be much better than no deal at all.

雙方在談判桌上都相當堅持自己的要求，無人願意讓步，直到發現相互妥協比談判完全破裂還要好。

promise
一起 (com-) 做的承諾 (promise)

0728 con [kɑn] ★★★★☆

反面的 / 反對

a. against / n. a reason in opposition

There can be pros and cons concerning the use of credit cards. Credit cards have many good points, but they can cause problems if consumption is not controlled.

對信用卡使用有正反兩方意見。信用卡有許多優點，但若不節制消費就會引發許多問題。

contrary, contrast
相反的 (contrary) 意見

0729 concentrate [`kɑnsn̩͵tret] ★★★★★

全神貫注於～，集中注意力於～

v. focus one's attention exclusively on something

I tell my students everyday that if they don't concentrate on what they're trying to say when speaking English, they will have a very hard time communicating.

我經常告訴學生，如果說英文時無法全神貫注於想表達的內容，就會很難溝通。

center
集中 (center) 在一起 (con-)

0730 conciliatory [kən`sɪlɪəˌtɔrɪ]　　　安撫的，撫慰的，修好的　| reconcile
a. intended or likely to conciliate　★★★★☆　| 再次 (re-) 變親近 (concil-)

His conciliatory nature as a salesman is the main reason why Daniel is so successful in convincing the buyer to buy.

業務員丹尼爾善於安撫的個性，是能如此成功說服買家購買商品的主因。

0731 condemn [kən`dɛm]　　　譴責，指摘，責備，責難　★★★★★　| damn
v. disapprove of; censure　| 一起 (con-) 辱罵和詛咒 (damn)

Most countries of the world condemned Iraq's invasion of Kuwait as immoral and illegal. However the invader paid no attention to the criticism.

多數國家都譴責伊拉克入侵科威特的行為是非法而不道德的，但伊拉克對這些指責無動於衷。

0732 condensation [ˌkɑndɛn`seʃən]　　　冷凝，凝結　★★★★★　| dense
n. the condition of being condensed　| 一起 (con-) 變密集的 (dense)

It is difficult to see in the mirror after taking a shower, because of all the condensation on the mirror.

淋浴後很難看清鏡子裡的影像，因為上面凝結了水蒸氣。

0733 configuration [kənˌfɪgjə`reʃən]　　　結構，形狀，輪廓　★★★★☆　| figure
n. form; figure　| 具共同 (con-) 形狀 (figure)

Meteorologists forecast the weather partly by studying cloud configurations. They can foretell the changes of weather by the forms of clouds.

氣象學家觀測雲層結構以預測天氣，也就是藉由辨識雲層形狀預測天氣變化。

0734 conflagration [ˌkɑnflə`greʃən]　　　大火災，大火　★★★☆☆　| black
n. a big fire　| 一起 (con-) 變黑 (black)

When there was a conflagration in the building across the street, more than 10 fire engines came to extinguish the big fire.

對街建物發生大火時，超過十輛消防車趕來撲滅火勢。

0735 confront [kən`frʌnt]　　　面對，面臨，遭遇　★★★★★　| front
v. face; stand face to face　| 一起 (con-) 朝向正面 (front)

If you are going to succeed, you must confront your fears. You should be courageous enough to face fears instead of escaping them.

如果想成功就必須面對恐懼。要有足夠勇氣面對恐懼而不是設法逃離。

0736 congeal [kən`dʒil]　　　凝結　★★★★☆　| gel
v. solidify; coagulate; jell　| 一起 (con-) 變成凝膠狀 (gel)

The wound was so deep that it took quite a while for the blood to congeal. And more than 10 stitches were needed to close the wound.

傷口非常深，所以花了很長時間血液才凝結，另外還要縫十針以上。

0737 conifer [`kɑnəfɚ]　　　針葉樹　★★★★☆　| cone
n. type of tree that bears cones　| 帶有 (fer=carry) 毬果 (cone) 的

There are many kinds of trees where I go hunting, but the conifers are by far the most common trees on the mountain.

在我打獵之處有許多不同種類的樹木，其中又以針葉樹最常見。

0738 conjugal [`kɑndʒʊg̊l̩] ★☆☆☆☆　　　夫婦的，婚姻的，配偶的
a. having to do with marriage

Mr. and Mrs. Brown have been married for thirty years. They are still enjoying their conjugal beatitude.

伯朗夫婦已結縭三十年，至今仍享受著婚姻生活的幸福美滿。

conjunction
連結 (jug-＝connect) 在一起 (con-)

0739 connotation [ˌkɑnəˋteʃən] ★★★☆☆　　　言外之意，弦外之音，含意
n. implication

The manager is a very hard person to understand because he commonly uses strange connotations in his speech.

經理令人很難了解，因為他總在講話時提到奇怪的弦外之音。

note
共同的 (con-) 註記 (note)

0740 consolidate [kənˋsɑləˌdet] ★★★★☆　　　整合，合併
v. merge; unite; join; combine into a single unit

In order to consolidate the inventory, it will take a new storage area and several hundred man-hours of work.

為了整合庫存，需有一個新儲存區域和數百人工時數的工作量。

solid
一起 (con-) 變成固體 (solid)

0741 consternation [ˌkɑnstəˋneʃən] ★★★☆☆　　　驚恐，驚愕，驚慌失措
n. surprise and anxiety; great dismay

To his utter consternation, a policeman came up to him and grabbed him by the collar. He was shell-shocked.

讓他完全驚慌失措的是，一名警察走上前來抓住他的衣領，把他徹底嚇壞了。

stare
驚訝地注視 (stare)

0742 construe [kənˋstru] ★★★★☆　　　解釋，理解為～
v. interpret; explain the meaning of

When Emily stood there saying nothing, Shane construed her silence as a tacit consent. He thought that she accepted his proposal.

艾蜜莉站在原地不發一語時，尚恩將沉默理解為默認的同意，以為她接受求婚。

construct
在心裡建立想法 (construct)

0743 contemplate [`kɑntəmˌplet] ★★★★☆　　　思忖，思索，仔細考慮，盤算
v. consider something thoughtfully; meditate

James contemplated about the problem for several months before he decided what the best course of action would be to follow.

在詹姆斯決定接下來應採取哪些最佳行動以前，花了好幾個月思索問題。

temple
到廟裡 (temple) 冥想

0744 convict [`kɑnvɪkt] ★★★★★　　　囚犯
n. criminal; offender

Mr. Hutchison served three years in prison and is now trying to find a decent job, but it is very difficult because employers are reluctant to hire a former convict.

哈奇森先生入獄服刑三年後，現在想找份像樣工作卻很難，因位雇主們都不願雇用出獄的更生人。

conviction
定罪 (conviction) 的人

0745 corny [`kɔrnɪ] ★★★★☆　　　陳腔濫調的，老套的，陳腐的
a. old-fashioned; trite; banal; unsophisticated

Jeff is a very funny man and is invited to many parties because of his sense of humor, but personally I think his jokes are corny.

傑夫是個很有趣的人，也因幽默受邀參加許多宴會，但我個人認為他的笑話都是陳腔濫調。

corn
如倉庫中的穀物 (corn) 般老舊

0746 **correlate** [`kɔrə,let]

★★★☆☆

v. *bring into mutual relation with*

使互相關聯，使有相互關係

relation

使牽連 (relate) 在一起 (cor-)

Please try to correlate your knowledge of mathematics with that of economics. You will find a close relationship.

請試著連結數學和經濟學知識，你會發現兩者有密切關係。

0747 **correspond** [,kɔrə`spɑnd]

★★★★★

v. *communicate / conform; tally; harmonize*

通信 / 符合，一致，調和

respond

一起 (cor-) 作出相同回應 (respond)

It is too expensive to communicate over the phone when doing business overseas, so many businesses choose to correspond through e-mail.

透過電話進行國際貿易往來的開銷成本很大，因此許多生意人都選擇用電子郵件溝通。

0748 **corrugated** [`kɔrə,getɪd]

★★★☆☆

a. *rough*

起皺紋的，呈波狀的，波紋的

rough

粗糙的 (rough)

The surface of the utility pottery which the Pueblo Indians made was often corrugated, and not smooth.

普埃布羅印第安人製作的多功能陶器表面常是波狀起伏而非平滑的。

0749 **cosmopolitan** [,kɑzmə`pɑlətn̩]

★★★★☆

a. *international*

世界性的，國際性的

cosmos

全宇宙 (cosmos)

In this era of globalization, English has become a cosmopolitan language. It is very important to have a good command of English.

在全球化時代英文已成為國際性語言，因此熟練英文是非常重要的。

0750 **costly** [`kɔstlɪ]

★★★★★

a. *expensive; dear / sumptuous; lavish*

貴重的，寶貴的 / 昂貴的，代價高的

cost

花了許多費用 (cost) 的

We lost thousands of dollars and wasted a lot of time on a project that in the end turned out to be a very costly mistake.

我們在這項專案上損失數千美元並浪費大量時間，到頭來變成一項代價太高的錯誤。

Tea Time... ☕

<Greek myth> Eros

The god of love, son of Aphrodite: identified by the Romans with Cupid.

〈來自希臘神話〉愛神

希臘神話中專司愛情的天神，是主掌愛與美之女神愛芙羅黛蒂之子，相當於羅馬神話裡的愛神邱比特。（註：本字也可以引申成「性愛」，形容詞為 erotic。）

❖ **erotic** [ɪ`rɑtɪk] **a.** *of or arousing sexual feelings or desires; amatory* | 性愛的，色情的，好色的

Many erotic scenes in a film are always popular amongst the younger viewers. They often identify themselves with the protagonist.

電影性愛鏡頭總是相當受到年輕觀眾歡迎，他們常把自己當成劇中主角。

1

Complete each word by filling in the blank with proper spelling so that it has the same meaning as suggested. Then please write the meaning of each word in Chinese.

1. 平凡的	= _ _ _ _ _ _ p l a c e	
2. 妥協	= c o m _ _ _ _ _ _ _	
3. 全神貫注	= c o n _ _ _ _ _ a t e	
4. 譴責	= c o n _ _ _ _	
5. 面對	= c o n _ _ _ _ _	
6. 凝結	= c o n _ _ _ a t i o n	
7. 合併	= c o n _ _ _ _ _ a t e	
8. 思忖	= c o n _ _ _ _ _ a t e	
9. 陳腔濫調的	= _ _ _ _ y	
10. 通信	= c o r _ _ _ _ _ _ _	

11. cavern = _____
12. cavity = _____
13. certificate = _____
14. cessation = _____
15. chatter = _____
16. collapse = _____
17. combative = _____
18. commiserate = _____
19. commodious = _____
20. cleanser = _____

2

Choose a word that best completes the sentence.

21. The biggest tree in the world, the General Sherman Tree in the United States, is a _____ which bears cones.

(A) conifer   (B) connotation   (C) configuration   (D) figure

22. The directors decided to _____ the two companies into one.

(A) meditate   (B) face   (C) consolidate   (D) confront

23. Are you in the church _____? I think you are a born singer.

(A) compromise   (B) consternation   (C) offender   (D) choir

3

The highlighted word is closest in meaning to which of the following?

24. It is said that the department building collapsed because of its own weight, but I think that the alarming number of shoppers was to be blamed.

(A) disintegrated   (B) sympathize   (C) clamber   (D) climb

25. Campers are advised to play dead when they confront a bear in the woods.

(A) solidify   (B) face   (C) jell   (D) interpret

0751~0800

MP3 32

★☆☆☆☆
0751 coup [ku]   政變   **coup d'etat**
n. violent overthrow of the government   軍事政變 (coup d'etat)
The coup in the emergent nation was led by some of the military officers
who contrived to overthrow the government.
新興國家發生的政變是由圖謀推翻政府的軍事將領們領導的。

★★☆☆☆
0752 covert [ˋkovət]   半掩藏的，暗地的，隱密的   **cover**
a. concealed; hidden; stealthy; disguised; secret   用蓋子 (cover) 蓋住
Racial discrimination in the United States used to be very overt, but
nowadays it has become very covert.
美國的種族歧視行為一度非常公然明顯，但現在這些行為只在檯面下發酵。

★★★☆☆
0753 coward [ˋkauəd]   懦夫，膽怯者，膽小鬼   **cow**
n. chick; chicken   被恐嚇 (cow) 的人
My friend Tim talks as if he were the bravest man in the world, but when
it comes right down to it he is a coward through and through.
友人提姆說起話來有如全世界最勇敢的人，但遇事就成了徹頭徹尾的懦夫。

★★★☆☆
0754 cower [ˋkauə]   畏縮，屈縮身體，抖縮，蜷縮   **cow**
v. crouch; tremble; shrink; wince   給予恐嚇 (cow)
His attache cowers away whenever the irritable general shouts at him. Once
he pulled over the car to the curb and ran away when the general yelled at him.
每當易怒將軍對隨行人員大吼大叫，總讓他畏縮不前。某次將軍又怒吼，他竟把車
子停在路邊就跑了。

★★★★☆
0755 creature [ˋkritʃə]   生物   **create**
n. living being, especially an animal   被創造 (create) 出來的
That movie was about an alien creature that came to earth from outer
space and fed on humans.
那部電影是有關一個來自外太空的外星生物來到地球，以人類為食物。

★★★☆☆
0756 creed [krid]   宗教信條，教條   **credit**
n. system of beliefs or opinions, especially religious beliefs   信賴 (credit)
Any organized religion has its own creed which its followers believe in
and try to live by.
任何有系統的宗教都有供教徒信仰並奉為生活圭臬的教條。

★★☆☆☆
0757 crescent [ˋkrɛsṇt]   新月，弦月，新月狀物   **crescendo**
n. a new moon   漸漸加強的 (crescendo)
Lake Baikal in Siberia is shaped like a crescent and is the largest
freshwater lake in the world. It is estimated to contain about 20% of all
freshwater of the world.
西伯利亞境內的貝加爾湖形狀有如一彎新月，為全球最大淡水湖，估計約占全球總
淡水量的百分之二十。

★☆☆☆☆
0758 crestfallen [ˋkrɛstˌfɔlən]   垂頭喪氣的，氣餒的   **crest**
a. dejected; dispirited   冠毛 (crest) 向下垂 (fallen)
Upon hearing the news report that avian influenza was prevalent in many
parts of the nation, the owner of a chicken farm became crestfallen.
一聽到新聞報導禽流感疫情在全國四處擴散，雞舍主人便顯得垂頭喪氣。

Chapter

① ② ③ ④ ⑤

0759 criminal [`krɪmən!] ★★★★★
罪犯

n. *offender; malefactor; sinner; culprit; convict*

Even though Richard has never gone to jail or even been arrested, he is so dishonest in his business activities that many who have dealt with him in the past consider him to be a criminal.

理查雖從未入獄或被捕，但因經商非常不誠實，所以許多過去和他有生意往來的人都認為他是罪犯。

crime
犯罪 (crime)

0760 crisscross [`krɪs,krɔs] ★★★★☆
十字形，十字形交叉

n. *crossing; cross*

There are many ways to shade when doing pencil sketchings, but I think that the most effective is the crisscross pattern.

進行鉛筆素描時有許多打陰影的方式，我認為最有效的就是十字形構圖法。

cross
像十字架 (cross) 般交叉

0761 crouch [krautʃ] ★★★★☆
蹲伏，曲膝縮身

v. *cower; shrink; cringe*

The natives crouched in fear when the explorers' helicopter landed. They thought that the newcomers were gods from heaven.

探險者的直昇機降落時，原住民懷著恐懼曲膝蹲伏，以為這些新來的人是從天而降的神明。

crook
因害怕而將身子彎曲 (crook)

0762 crucify [`krusə,faɪ] ★☆☆☆☆
將某人手腳釘在十字架上處死

v. *kill somebody by nailing or tying him to a cross*

The best-known account of any crucifixion recorded in history is the one found in the Bible when the Romans crucified Jesus Christ.

關於釘死在十字架的歷史記載，最有名的是《聖經》中羅馬人將耶穌基督釘在十字架上處死。

cross
十字架 (cross)

0763 crusade [kru`sed] ★★☆☆☆
（改革或反對某事等的）運動

n. *campaign; cause; drive*

Wilma's daughter was seriously injured by a drunken driver three years ago, and she has been on a personal crusade ever since to do whatever she can to bring the drunk driving problem under control.

自從三年前威爾瑪的女兒遭酒駕者撞成重傷後，她便積極投入控管酒駕問題的個人運動。

cross
反對 (cross) 並起而改革

0764 crystallize [`krɪst!,aɪz] ★★★☆☆
使形成結晶體，使結晶

v. *form into crystals*

In elementary school I remember doing an experiment where a string was suspended in some sugar water, and sugar crystallized on the string to form a pretty crystal.

我記得國中曾做過一項實驗，將一條細線懸吊在糖水裡，吸附在線上的糖就會結成漂亮晶體。

crystal
結晶體 (crystal)

0765 cuisine [kwɪ`zin] ★☆☆☆☆
烹飪，菜餚

n. *cooking / style of cooking*

Mr. and Mrs. Smith always enjoy going to the Pier Pont restaurant because they have fine cuisine at an affordable price.

史密斯夫婦很喜歡到皮爾波特餐廳用餐，因為那裡有價格公道的精緻美食。

cook
烹調 (cook)

0766 culmination [ˌkʌlməˈneʃən]   頂點，最高潮，極點   ★★★★☆

n. consummation; perfection

Success is the culmination of hard work and opportunities. Success comes from both endless effort and chance.

成功是努力和機會的最高點，它來自努力不懈和把握良機。

column
圓柱 (column) 的頂端

0767 cyclone [ˈsaɪklon]   氣旋   ★★★★☆

n. tornado; hurricane; gale

Hurricanes, typhoons and **cyclones** may grow to more than 500 miles in diameter, while a tornado contacts a small area of land.

颶風、颱風和氣旋的影響範圍可達直徑五百英里，至於龍捲風則只接觸一小塊地面區域。

cycle
像環 (cycle) 般旋轉

0768 dally [ˈdælɪ]   延誤，浪費時間   ★★★★☆

v. delay; prolong; idle

This is a very important project and I need it completed immediately. So don't dally, and let me know as soon as it is finished.

這是非常重要的專案須盡速完成，所以不要延誤，完成後立刻告訴我。

delay
延遲 (delay)

0769 daring [ˈdɛrɪŋ]   大膽的，勇敢的，勇於冒險的   ★★★★☆

a. courageous; valiant; bold

Bungee jumping is a very exciting sport where one attaches a rubber cord to his body and jumps off a high platform, but you have to be pretty daring to try it.

高空彈跳是很刺激的運動，彈跳者先將橡皮繩索綁在身上再從高處平台跳下，要相當大膽才敢嘗試。

dare
大膽去做 (dare)

0770 deadlock [ˈdɛdˌlɑk]   僵局   ★★★★☆

n. impasse; bottleneck; stalemate

The summit began in a conciliatory manner, but unfortunately it reached a deadlock at the last moment.

高峰會在和諧氣氛中展開，最後卻不幸陷入僵局。

dead, lock
用鎖鎖 (lock) 死 (dead)

0771 dearth [dɝθ]   缺乏，缺少   ★★★☆☆

n. lack; scarcity

Myth has it that when there is a serious dearth of food, a mother pelican rips some flesh off from her chest and feeds it to her baby birds.

據傳如果缺乏食物，母鵜鶘會將胸前的肉剝下來餵食雛鳥。

dear
因為不足，所以對東西到了非常寶貝的 (dear) 程度

0772 debase [dɪˈbes]   貶低，降低   ★★★★☆

v. degrade; humiliate; lower

Two people at work got in a pretty bad argument, and they tried to debase each other during the fight.

兩名同事起了極大爭執，並在爭吵中相互貶損對方人格。

base
跌 (de-) 到最低、最基礎 (base) 的程度

0773 debilitate [dɪˈbɪləˌtet]   使衰弱   ★★★★★

v. weaken; disable; enfeeble; devitalize

My dog stopped eating and got a severe case of diarrhea, which eventually debilitated him to the point where he couldn't even lift his head off the pillow.

我的狗不吃不喝還得了嚴重腹瀉，虛弱得無法從靠墊上抬起頭來。

ability
能力 (ability) 降至底部 (de-)

0774 declare [dɪˋklɛr] ★★★★★ 申報

v. make known publicly; apprise; inform; notify; formally announce

clear
廣泛 (de-) 而明確 (clear) 地告知

When Paul went through customs he forgot to declare his brand new camcorder, and later he had a hard time when he brought it back in.

保羅通過海關時忘記申報新買的攝錄影機,後來經過千辛萬苦才贖回來。

0775 decry [dɪˋkraɪ] ★★☆☆☆ 非難,譴責,責難

v. denounce; censure

cry
低頭向下 (de-) 叫喊 (cry)

The entire nation's people decried the government's policy on real estate. The poor complained about the exorbitant price of apartment houses and the rich complained about the high taxes on apartment houses.

全國人民齊聲譴責政府的不動產政策。低收入戶埋怨公寓房價太貴,高收入戶則抱怨稅額過高。

0776 deepen [ˋdipən] ★★★☆☆ 使深

v. (cause something to) become deep or deeper

deep
使 (-en) 更深 (deep)

The original plans called for a 15-foot hole to be dug in order to pour the foundation, but we found that because of the soil content, we needed to deepen the hole by 10 feet to 25 feet deep.

最初計畫要挖掘十五英尺的深洞才能灌地基,但因土壤含量問題須再向下挖深十到二十五英尺。

0777 defendant [dɪˋfɛndənt] ★★★★☆ 被告

n. a person accused or sued in a legal case

defend
必須自我防禦 (defend) 的人 (-ant)

The judge gave a harsh sentence to the **defendant**, who decided to appeal to a higher court.

遭法官處以重刑的被告決定向高等法院提出上訴。

0778 defense [dɪˋfɛns] ★★★★★ 防禦,防衛,防守員

n. guard; protection; safeguard; shield; ward

fence
從底部 (de-) 豎起圍牆 (fence)

The Chicago Bears have one of the best defenses I've ever seen, but their offense leaves something to be desired.

芝加哥熊隊擁有我見過最佳的防守球員之一,但進攻球員的表現則差強人意。

0779 defrost [diˋfrɔst] ★★★☆☆ 除霜,解凍,退冰

v. remove ice or frost from

frost
除去 (de-) 霜 (frost)

Please don't forget to defrost this fish before you cook it. The fish has been frozen in the refrigerator.

料理這條魚前請別忘了解凍,因為放在冰箱裡的魚是冰凍的。

0780 defunct [dɪˋfʌŋkt] ★★☆☆☆ 已裁撤的,已倒閉的

v. nonexistent; no longer in effect

function
去除 (de-) 作用 (function)

As soon as there appeared a jumbo shopping mall across the street, the existing small shops became defunct.

當對街一出現大型購物商場,現有的小店面就倒閉了。

0781 deliberately [dɪˋlɪbərɪtlɪ] ★★★★★ 故意地,蓄意地 / 慎重地,謹慎地

ad. intentionally; on purpose; purposely / carefully; prudently

liberty, liberal
抑制 (de-) 放縱 (liberty) 的

On the surface everything looked like an accident, but further investigation of the woman's death revealed that she was deliberately killed by someone.

儘管表面看來像是一樁意外,但經過進一步調查後發現該女子是遭人蓄意謀殺的。

0782 delectable [dɪˋlɛktəbl̩]　　　　　愉快的，快樂的／美味可口的　| **delight**
a. delightful / delicious; savory　　　　　　　　　　　　　　　　　　　　| 臉上綻放 (de-) 光彩 (light)
The foods which were cooked by the chef himself looked very delectable.
Every participant at the banquet was ready to devour the delicious-looking
foods.
主廚料理的食物看來特別可口，每位出席盛宴的賓客都準備要大吃一頓。

★★★★★

0783 deliver [dɪˋlɪvɚ]　　　　　產下（嬰兒）／給予（打擊等）　| **liberty**
v. bear; give birth to　　　　　　　　　　　　　　　　　　　　　　　| 讓身體自由 (liberty)
Jack's wife had been admitted to the local hospital on December 31,
and the next day she delivered twins.
傑克的妻子在十二月三十一日住進當地醫院，隔天就產下雙胞胎。

★★★★☆

0784 denote [dɪˋnot]　　　　　　　　　　　　　意味／表示　| **note**
v. mean / signify　　　　　　　　　　　　　　　　　　　　　| 在紙上把東西寫 (note) 下來
The stars next to the athletes' names denote that those people have　| (de-)
received gold medals in the previous Olympics.
運動員名字旁的星號表示這些選手曾在上屆奧運會中獲得金牌。

★★★★★

0785 depict [dɪˋpɪkt]　　　　　　　描繪，描述，描寫　| **picture**
v. portray; describe　　　　　　　　　　　　　　　　　　| 在紙上把東西畫 (picture) 下
The American painter Winslow Homer, who often depicted the stormy　| 來 (de-)
sea, is now thought to be the most expensive American painter.
經常描繪驚濤駭浪的美國畫家溫斯洛・荷馬是目前公認最昂貴的美國畫家。

★★★★☆

0786 depredate [ˋdɛprɪˌdet]　　　　掠奪，劫掠，破壞，侵吞　| **predator**
v. prey upon; plunder　　　　　　　　　　　　　　　　　　| 掠奪者 (predator) 將東西搶奪
The avaricious real estate agent depredated his client by making him　| 至遠處 (de-＝away)
buy the property at a higher price than the present owner asked for. He
took the difference for himself.
貪婪的不動產經紀人侵吞客戶的錢，先叫他以高於現任屋主要求的價格購入，然後
從中竊取價差。

★★★☆☆

0787 desecration [ˌdɛsɪˋkreʃən]　　　　褻瀆神明，污辱　| **sacred**
n. profanation; blasphemy　　　　　　　　　　　　　　　　| 將神聖 (sacred) 之物弄壞
On his death bed, Jack's father mentioned that the greatest fear was　| (de-＝down)
the desecration of the family name, and he cautioned his family to live
honorable lives.
傑克的父親臨終前表示自己最大的恐懼是擔心褻瀆家族聲譽，並告誡家人要堂堂正
正做人。

★★★☆☆

0788 designate [ˋdɛzɪgˌnet]　　　　　　　指定，指名　| **sign**
v. name; denominate; entitle　　　　　　　　　　　　　　| 向下 (de-) 標示或示意 (sign)
Many species of wildlife on this land have been designated as protected
animals. Some of them are endangered species.
在這片土地上有多種野生動物被指定為保育類動物，其中有些是瀕臨絕種動物。

0789 deter [dɪˋtɝ] ★★★★☆ 阻止，使斷念

v. *dissuade; discourage; divert; prevent; block; impede; obstruct; inhibit; restrain; avert; preclude; ward off*

Good parents will do their best to deter their children from doing anything self-destructive, but the decision ultimately rests upon the individual child.

好父母會盡全力阻止子女做出自我毀滅行為，但最後仍有賴子女自行決定。

> **terror**
> 因為害怕 (terror) 而向下 (de-) 擠壓

0790 detest [dɪˋtɛst] ★★★★★ 憎惡，厭惡

v. *hate; abhor; abominate; loathe*

I will never eat with that voracious man again because I detest a person with table manners such as his.

我再也不要跟那個狼吞虎嚥的男子一起吃飯，因為我厭惡有像他這種餐桌禮儀的人。

> **taste**
> 離 (de-) 所好 (taste) 很遠

0791 devastate [ˋdɛvəsˌtet] ★★★★★ 蹂躪

v. *desolate; ravage*

The rhino species remaining in Africa are being devastated by poaching and the destruction of their natural habitats.

非洲剩餘的犀牛正因盜獵問題和自然棲息地的破壞受到蹂躪。

> **vast**
> 空間 (vast) 遭破壞 (de-)

0792 dilettante [ˌdɪləˋtæntɪ] ★★★★☆ 新手，一知半解者 / 業餘愛好者

n. *tyro; novice; beginner*

I began taking computer lessons three weeks ago, and so I'm still a dilettante at computer techniques.

我從三個禮拜前開始上電腦課，所以在電腦技術上還是新手。

> **delight**
> 對某事物感到欣喜 (delight) 的人

0793 diminish [dəˋmɪnɪʃ] ★★★★★ 減少，縮小

v. *decrease; abate; dwindle; reduce; lessen; curtail*

Even though there are still many problems in our society, the crime rate has diminished significantly since last year.

儘管我們的社會仍存有許多問題，但從去年以來犯罪率已大幅降低。

> **minimum**
> 縮到極小 (minimum)
> min (小)

0794 diminutive [dəˋmɪnjətɪv] ★★★★★ 矮小的

a. *tiny; miniature; minute; wee; teensy-weensy; teeny-weeny*

Due to his diminutive stature, Jacob could not be a basketball player. He was only five feet three inches tall.

雅各身材矮小無法成為籃球員，他只有五呎三吋高。

> **minimum**
> 非常小的 (minimum)
> min (小)

0795 discard [dɪsˋkɑrd] ★★★★★ 拋棄，丟掉，摒棄

v. *abandon; jettison; get rid of; do away with*

After several hours of discussion and an exhaustive investigation of every single possibility, the idea was discarded as being impractical at this time.

經過數小時討論並徹底研究各種可能性，最後該構想因現階段不切實際而遭到摒棄。

> **card**
> 玩牌時將不需要的牌 (card) 丟得遠遠的 (dis-)

0796 discourage [dɪsˋkɝɪdʒ] ★★★★★ 使氣餒，使打消念頭，阻止

v. *dissuade; deter; divert; restrain; prevent; inhibit*

Sam never **discourages** his daughter from doing anything she is really interested in; instead he encourages her to develop her talents whenever possible.

山姆從不阻止女兒去做任何她有興趣的事，相反地還鼓勵她盡量發揮個人才能。

> **courage**
> 將勇氣 (courage) 拋得遠遠的 (dis-)

0797 discourse [`dɪskɔrs] ★★★★☆ 交談，談話，對話

n. *expression; conversation*

discuss
討論 (discuss) 的對話

Where there is a TV set, there is no more discourse. The difference between a father on Sundays and a Buddha's image is that there is no TV set in front of the latter.

有電視的地方就沒人交談。因此每到周日，待在家的爸爸跟一尊佛像間的差別，只在於佛像面前沒電視。

0798 discreet [dɪ`skrit] ★★★★★ 謹言慎行的，謹慎的

a. *cautious; circumspect; considerate; gingerly; wary*

discern
分辨 (discern) 的能力

All of our classmates were discreet; no one said anything about our plan to have a surprise party for our teacher.

全班同學都非常謹慎，沒人說出任何關於為老師舉辦驚喜派對的計畫。

0799 disfigure [dɪs`fɪgjə] ★★★★☆ 破壞，使大為遜色，使難看

v. *deface*

figure
使外型 (figure) 變得不同 (dis-)

The landscape of this area has been disfigured by so much urbanization. Nature has been ruined to house the many people who have rushed in.

過度都市化破壞本區景觀，自然風景也遭到毀壞，取而代之的是提供湧入人潮居住的一棟棟房屋。

0800 dismember [dɪs`mɛmbə] ★★★☆☆ 分割，瓜分，瓦解，解體

v. *sunder; separate; sever*

member
分離 (dis-) 會員 (member)

The Soviet Union was finally dismembered in 1992. As a result, many small nations gained their independence.

前蘇聯終於在一九九二年解體，許多小國也因此獲得獨立。

Tea Time... ☕

<From the name of a German city> Cologne

A toilet water consisting of alcohol scented with aromatic oils. It was named for the city of Cologne in Germany.

〈來自一德國城市名〉科隆
一種含有酒精成份和薰香油氣味的花露水，是以德國的城市科隆來命名的。（註：移居德國的義大利香水大師 Johann Maria Farina 於一七零九年在德國的科隆研製調配出史上第一瓶古龍水。古龍水的全稱為 Eau de Cologne，原意是「來自科隆之水」。古龍是科隆的另一個譯音。）

❖ **cologne** [kə`lon] **n.** *eau-de-cologne or a similar scented toilet water* | 古龍水

When he goes out with Ann, John always wears his favorite cologne. He is caring about the smell of cigarettes.

約翰要和安出去約會時，總會噴上最喜歡的古龍水，因為他在意身上的菸味。

1

Complete each word by filling in the blank with proper spelling so that it has the same meaning as suggested. Then please write the meaning of each word in Chinese.

1. 暗地的   = _ _ _ _ _ t   11. defendant   = _____
2. 生物   = _ _ _ _ _ u r e   12. defrost   = _____
3. 罪犯   = _ _ _ _ i n a l   13. denote   = _____
4. 十字形   = c r i s s _ _ _ _ _   14. designate   = _____
5. 使結晶   = _ _ _ _ _ _ _ i z e   15. devastate   = _____
6. 頂點   = _ _ _ _ _ _ a t i o n   16. diminish   = _____
7. 氣旋   = _ _ _ _ o n e   17. discard   = _____
8. 大膽的   = _ _ _ i n g   18. discourage   = _____
9. 貶低人格   = d e _ _ _ _   19. disfigure   = _____
10. 使深   = _ _ _ _ e n   20. dismember   = _____

2

Choose a word that best completes the sentence.

21. When he first went to church, he had a hard time memorizing the Apostles' _____.
   (A) Creed   (B) Crucify   (C) Culmination   (D) Crusade

22. The champion _____ a fatal blow to his rival.
   (A) delivered   (B) dissuaded   (C) diverted   (D) deterred

3

The highlighted word is closest in meaning to which of the following?

23. He discouraged his wife from going on shopping expeditions.
   (A) desolated   (B) ravaged   (C) prevented   (D) detested

24. His illness debilitated him. He could not do anything because he was too weak.
   (A) dallied   (B) prolonged   (C) delayed   (D) disabled

25. Doctors and nurses discard hypodermic syringes after they use them.
   (A) get rid of   (B) ward off   (C) give birth to   (D) make known

Practice Test 01

The highlighted word is closest in meaning to which of the following?

1. It is apparent that James is enamored of Jane. He is not himself when he is in front of her.

    (A) amiss   (B) obvious   (C) beloved   (D) bossy

2. He made a big blunder . He had to order 100 computers from the computer company, but he ordered 100 printers.

    (A) mistake   (B) bondage   (C) breach   (D) bombard

3. We would greatly appreciate it if you would send us enough brochures .

    (A) bumps   (B) choirs   (C) certificates   (D) pamphlets

4. A star may collapse under its own weight if its nuclear fuel is exhausted.

    (A) commiserate   (B) clamber   (C) disintegrate   (D) condemn

5. The nation has been carrying out a crusade for energy conservation.

    (A) criminal   (B) campaign   (C) deadlock   (D) defendant

Please answer the following questions.

(Comic Tale 1)

Mr. Dunn, a timorous person by nature, had suffered from a decayed wisdom tooth for a long time but abhorred the thought of seeing a dentist. One night he tossed and turned and had to resort to some aspirin to allay the pain. The next day he called the dentist's office and made an appointment. At last he reported to the dentist's office. He took a seat and the dentist tilted his chair. Mr. Dunn sheepishly closed his eyes, trembling. The dentist looked into his mouth and exclaimed, "Wow, this is the biggest cavity that I've ever seen in my whole life!" Mr. Dunn felt humiliated as he heard the dentist repeat his exclamation, so he complained about that. However, the dentist insisted, "I mentioned your cavity only one time." The nurse standing beside the dentist added, "It was an ECHO!"

(Comic Tale 2)

Farmer Green had six kids, whose ages were from ten to twenty. One day he mustered all the kids together and demanded to know who had shoved the outhouse into the stream. He browbeat , yelled, growled, begged - of course, with no luck. At last he began to tell them an anecdote of George Washington. "Listen! Even though George Washington cut down his father's beloved cherry tree, only because he stepped forward and made his confession that he had done it, he was not only forgiven but was also praised by his father." At this moment, the youngest son stepped forward and made his confession. Hardly had Farmer Green heard the confession before he began to spank his youngest son. The son whined, "Daddy, you just told us George Washington's father forgave him because he confessed. How come you are spanking me?" Farmer Green shouted, "When George Washington was chopping down the tree, his father was not in the tree."

6. **The word** abhorred **is closest in meaning to which of the following?**
   (A) detested
   (B) abated
   (C) blanched
   (D) depreciated

7. **The word** allay **is closest in meaning to which of the following?**
   (A) alleviate
   (B) worsen
   (C) actuate
   (D) adopt

8. **The word** cavity **is closest in meaning to which of the following?**
   (A) culmination
   (B) hollow
   (C) cessation
   (D) certificate

9. **The word** browbeat **is closest in meaning to which of the following?**
   (A) bump
   (B) intimidate
   (C) collide
   (D) expand

10. **The word** beloved **is closest in meaning to which of the following?**
   (A) asinine
   (B) arboreal
   (C) bulky
   (D) favorite

MP3
34

0801 disorder [dɪs`ɔrdə] 雜亂，無秩序

★★★★★

order
沒有 (dis-) 秩序 (order)

n. confusion; chaos; disarray

John can never find anything in his room because it is always in complete disorder. Everything is in a mess.

約翰無法在房內找到任何東西，因為裡面總是凌亂不堪，所有東西都亂七八糟。

0802 disparaging [dɪ`spærədʒɪŋ] 輕視的，貶抑的，輕蔑的

★★★☆☆

pair, parallel
沒有 (dis-) 可與自己並列的一方 (pair)

a. derogatory; depreciative

I couldn't stand my colleague Chuck's disparaging remarks. He always tries to find fault with other people's work.

我無法忍受同事查克輕蔑的評論，他總是對別人的工作吹毛求疵。

0803 dispense [dɪ`spɛns] 省卻，不用，免除，不可少

★★★★☆

pence
沒有 (dis-) 用錢 (pence)

v. do without; go without; get along without

Donald thinks that he can hardly dispense with a car. He is always having a hard time catching a taxi.

唐諾認為自己簡直不能沒有自用車，因為總是很難順利招到計程車。

0804 dispirited [dɪ`spɪrɪtɪd] 沮喪的，垂頭喪氣的，無精打采的

★★★☆☆

spirit
沒有 (dis-) 精神的 (spirit)

a. dejected; depressed; downcast; blue

To my disappointment, my sister appeared dispirited when she stepped out of the examination room.

令我失望的是妹妹從考場走出來時顯得無精打采。

0805 dissertation [ˌdɪsə`teʃən] 博士論文，學術論文

★★★★★

discuss
針對某主題進行討論 (discuss)

n. thesis; treatise; monograph

Kate has been writing a doctoral dissertation on American Indian dialects for over three years. I hope that it will be finished before long.

凱特花三年以上撰寫有關美洲印第安方言的博士論文，希望她再過不久就能完成。

0806 dissolve [dɪ`zɑlv] 溶解，解除

★★★★★

solve
溶化 (solve) 散開 (dis-)

v. fuse; melt; thaw; liquefy

Honey and sugar dissolve more quickly in hot water than in cold water.

蜂蜜和糖在熱水裡比在冷水更快溶解。

0807 distraught [dɪ`strɔt] 心煩意亂的，幾乎發狂的

★★☆☆☆

distract
心情被攪亂 (distract)

a. distracted; discomposed; perturbed; agitated

The drill instructor was so distraught with fury that he couldn't think clearly. He eventually began to rave like a madman.

教練在盛怒下顯得非常心煩意亂以致無法仔細思考，最後開始像瘋子般胡言亂語。

0808 diurnal [daɪ`ɝnl̩] 白天的，晝間的

★★★☆☆

daily
日常的 (daily)

a. daily; of the daytime

As is well known, most species of scorpions are not diurnal, which means that they move along at night.

眾所周知多數蠍子都是晝伏夜出，也就是夜間才出來活動。

★★★☆☆

0809 dividend [`dɪvə‚dɛnd]　　　　　　　　　　股利，股息

n. reward; premium

A company often pays a dividend to the people who own shares. A dividend can be in the form of cash or additional shares.

企業通常會分派股息給股票持有人，至於形式則可能是現金股息或新增股份。

divide

分配 (divide)

★★★★☆

0810 docile [`dɑsl]　　　　　　聽話的，容易駕御的，馴服的

a. easily taught; meek; tractable

Jim's little sister is not so docile. Once she starts to cry, all her family members have to do every thing to stop her crying; singing, dancing, jumping, rolling and acting.

吉姆小妹不太聽話，一旦開始哭，全家人都要設法讓她不哭，無論是載歌載舞、上下跳躍、前後翻滾或表演都好。

doctor; teacher

教授 (doctor) 和老師 (teacher) 都是教導者，意指要好好聽他們說話

★★★☆☆

0811 doff [dɑf]　　　　　　　　　　丟棄，脫下

v. take off; remove

Joe doffed his leather cap and donned a helmet. And then he started the engine of his motorcycle.

喬脫下皮帽再戴上安全帽，然後發動摩托車引擎。

do, off

脫掉 (put off)

★★★☆☆

0812 dog-eared [`dɔg‚ɪrd]　　　　摺角的，用舊了的，翻爛了的

a. having the corners of many pages turned down through use

Our professor's notebook must have been used since he came to our college. The corners of the pages are dog-eared.

教授的筆記本一定是打從進學院就在使用，因為裡面的書頁都是摺角的。

dog, ear

紙的一角折成像狗 (dog) 耳朵般 (eared)

★★★☆☆

0813 dogged [`dɔgɪd]　　　　　　頑強的，固執的，頑固的

a. inflexible; relentless; rigid; persistent

The social worker persisted doggedly in his campaign for civil rights despite various sorts of difficulties.

儘管遭遇許多困難，社工人員仍在活動中頑強堅持爭取市民權利。

dog

狗 (dog) 咬著褲管不放

★★☆☆☆

0814 doggie bag [`dɔgɪ bæg]　　　（餐廳裡供顧客打包未吃完食物的）剩菜袋

n. a bag supplied to a patron of a restaurant, in which he may place leftovers to take home

Whenever I go to the restaurant, I am served such large portions that I have to ask for a doggie bag to take home what I can't eat.

每當我到餐廳用餐，菜餚份量總是很多，因此得要求餐廳提供剩菜袋，把吃不完的食物打包回家。

dog

用袋子 (bag) 裝食物餵狗 (dog)

★★★☆☆

0815 don [dɑn]　　　　　　　穿（衣），戴（帽、手套等）

v. put on; array; apparel

The two moving company workers donned white cotton gloves and began to move the heavy grand piano.

那兩家搬運公司的工人戴著白色棉質手套，開始搬運笨重的平台鋼琴。

do, on

穿上 (put on)

★★★★★

0816 dormant [`dɔrmənt]　　　蟄伏的，休眠的，潛伏的，暫停活動的

a. latent; potential; lurking; inactive

This volcano erupted in the 1990's. Since then it has lain dormant. Many volcanologists are trying to learn about the volcano.

這座火山在九〇年代爆發後便呈現休火山狀態，許多火山學家正努力研究它。

dormitory

正在宿舍 (dormitory) 睡覺 (dorm-)

0817 downcast [ˋdaʊn͵kæst] ★★★☆☆   目光低垂的，垂頭喪氣的，萎靡不振的   cast

a. dejected; depressed; dispirited

心情直落 (cast) 谷底 (down)

After the entrance examination, Judy came out of the test building. To the dismay of her parents, she seemed downcast.

入學考試結束後茱蒂走出考場，讓雙親驚愕的是她看來似乎垂頭喪氣。

0818 downfall [ˋdaʊn͵fɔl] ★★★★★   敗亡，滅亡，垮臺，下（大雪、大雨等）   down, fall

n. deterioration; atrophy; decadence; decline; degeneration

向底部 (down) 掉落 (fall)

With the downfall of the dictator, the nation was greatly democratized. Most importantly, censorship was abolished.

隨著獨裁者的滅亡，該國也極度民主化，最重要的是新聞審查制度也宣告廢止。

0819 dowry [ˋdaʊrɪ] ★★★☆☆   嫁妝   endow

n. marriage portion

娘家父親資助 (endow) 的錢

Her father was very rich, and she was given a large dowry when she got married. Her husband was really excited.

非常富有的父親在她結婚時給了一大批嫁妝，讓她先生感到非常興奮。

0820 draft [dræft] ★★★★☆   徵募，徵兵／草案，草稿   draw

v. enroll; conscript; muster / n. original plan

拉 (draw) 至軍隊／最初畫 (draw) 的設計圖

Her brother was drafted into the army last week. She said that he would continue his study after 3 years of military service.

她弟弟上周被徵召入伍，她說他打算服役三年後再繼續求學。

0821 drag [dræg] ★★★★☆   緩慢進行，拖拖拉拉   draw

v. delay; dally; dawdle; lag; loiter; tarry

在後面拼命拉著 (draw)

The meeting dragged on for more than 5 hours. Every participant except the president kept on yawning.

會議拖拖拉拉進行了超過五小時，除總裁外所有與會者都阿欠連連。

0822 drain [dren] ★★★★★   排水管，下水道／耗盡，枯竭   dry

n. pipe or channel that carries away sewage or other unwanted liquid / v. deplete

水流向排水管而變乾 (dry)／資源枯竭 (dry)

After washing your face, please do not forget to pull the plug so the water can go down the drain.

洗完臉後請不要忘了拔起塞子，讓水流入排水管。

0823 drift [drɪft] ★★★★★   漂流，飄走   drive

v. become carried or floated along

無停靠處而在水上兜轉 (drive)

The disabled fishing vessel was drifting about at the mercy of the waves. Unfortunately even the Marcorni set wasn't working.

故障漁船正隨波逐流，不幸的是連船上的無線電對講機也不管用。

0824 drip [drɪp] ★★★★☆   水滴／滴落，滴下   drop

n. drop; droplet / v. fall in drops

水滴答地落下 (drop)

During my presentation, sweat began to drip down my face to my neck, so I wiped my face with a handkerchief.

我進行簡報時汗水從臉龐滴落到脖子上，於是我就用手帕擦臉。

0825 droop [drup]　　　　　　　　　　　　★★★★☆　　枯萎，凋謝 | drop
v. wilt; wither　　　　　　　　　　　　　　　　　　　　　　　　整個向下垂 (drop)
I forgot to put the flowers she gave me into a vase. They drooped for lack of water.
我忘記將她送我的花插入花瓶中，結果花朵全因缺水而枯萎。

MP3
35

0826 drought [draʊt]　　　　　　　　　　★★★★★　　久旱，乾旱 | dry
n. dryness; dry weather　　　　　　　　　　　　　　　　　　　變乾的 (dry)
We've had a terrible spell of dry weather lately. It hasn't rained for over three months. We hope this drought will end soon.
近來可怕的乾燥天氣已持續一段時間，超過三個月沒有下雨，我們希望這場乾旱盡快結束。

0827 drove [drov]　　　　　　　　　　　★★★★☆　　畜群 | drive
n. horde; multitude; flock; herd　　　　　　　　　　　　　被驅趕 (drive) 的一群～
There on the prairie we could see a drove of oxen. They were lazily grazing in the sunshine on a spring day.
大草原上有一群牛正悠閒地在春天的陽光下吃草。

0828 dubious [`dubɪəs]　　　　　　　★★★★★　　半信半疑的，懷疑的 | doubt
a. doubtful; questionable; uncertain; dubitable　　　　　　令人起疑 (doubt) 的
This puppy's condition is so serious that I'm dubious of its survival. Its nose is dry and it is panting.
這隻小狗的狀況糟得讓我懷疑牠能否存活，牠的鼻頭不但是乾的還氣喘吁吁。

0829 duel [`duəl]　　　　　　　　　　　★★☆☆☆　　決鬥 | duet, dual
n. formal fight between two men, using swords or pistols　　　　兩人 (du-) 打鬥
The two knights who fell in love with the same lady ended up in a duel, in which both of them were seriously wounded.
兩個愛上同一位女士的騎士展開一場決鬥，最後雙雙受重傷。

0830 durable [`durəbl]　　　　　　　★★★★★　　耐久的，耐用的，持久的 | endure
a. lasting　　　　　　　　　　　　　　　　　　　　　　　　持續 (endure) 很久的
The early pioneers in America wanted trousers which were made of durable material. They made blue jeans.
美國早期拓荒者需要以耐用布料做成的褲子，最後做出了牛仔褲。

0831 duration [du`reʃən]　　　　　　★★★★★　　持續，期間，持續時間 | endure
n. term; span　　　　　　　　　　　　　　　　　　　　　　　持續 (endure) 的時間
Many people are complaining that for the duration of the previous government prices and living costs had risen up too high.
許多人抱怨在前任政府主政期間物價和生活費用都大幅提高。

0832 dweller [`dwɛlə]　　　　　　　★★★★★　　居民 | dwell
n. inhabitant; denizen; occupant; resident　　　　　　　　居住 (dwell) 的人 (-er)
City dwellers are getting more concerned about serious traffic congestion and air pollution. But they hardly consider getting rid of their car.
都市居民愈來愈關切嚴重的交通堵塞和空氣污染問題，但幾乎不曾考慮不要開車。

0833 ease [iz] ★★★★★ 減輕，緩和，使安心

v. allay; alleviate; mitigate; mollify

Grandparents might be a source of wisdom and help ease the pressures between children and their parents.

祖父母或許能成為協助子孫輩及他們的父母減輕壓力的智慧之源。

easy
使舒適 (easy)

0834 eclipse [ɪ`klɪps] ★★★★★ （天體）蝕，遮蔽／（日、月的）蝕

v. overshadow; block the light of / n. solar eclipse; lunar eclipse

In the past during a solar eclipse some Indian people shot a burning arrow into the sky to rekindle the sun.

過去出現日蝕時有些印第安人會將燃燒的箭射向空中，好讓太陽重振雄風。

clip; clippers
由外 (e-) 削掉 (clip)

0835 edible [`ɛdəbl] ★★★★★ 可食的，食用的

a. eatable; nonpoisonous; fit for human consumption

Do you happen to know whether this mushroom is edible or poisonous? Or do you know how to tell the difference?

你知道這蘑菇可以吃或有毒嗎？或是你知道如何分辨兩者的不同？

eatable
可以 (-ible) 吃的

0836 efficacy [`ɛfəkəsɪ] ★★★★★ 效力，功效，效能

n. effectiveness; efficiency

Some scientists of this institute are going to test the efficacy of a newly invented influenza vaccine.

本研究所部分科學家將測試新引進的流感疫苗功效。

efficient
向外 (ef-) 產生 (fic-) 成果

0837 effigy [`ɛfədʒɪ] ★★☆☆☆ 肖像

n. an image of a person

The revolutionists of the country made an effigy of the despotic king of the country and burned it in public.

該國革命者製作暴君肖像並當眾焚毀。

figure
從外面 (ef-) 看到的樣子 (figure)

0838 effrontery [ə`frʌntərɪ] ★★☆☆☆ 厚顏，無恥

n. impudence; insolence; audacity

One of my colleagues had the effrontery to say that I was not qualified for the task and that he was the most qualified person.

有個同事厚顏無恥地表示我沒資格做那份工作，他自己才是最有資格的。

front
抹去 (ef-＝out) 臉 (front)

0839 emasculate [ɪ`mæskjə‚let] ★★☆☆☆ 使無勢力，使柔弱

v. debilitate; unnerve; enervate; castrate

The management is considering some drastic measures to emasculate the labor union to avert a strike.

管理階層考慮採取激烈手段削弱工會勢力，使他們停止罷工。

masculine
男性氣概 (masculine) 向外 (e-) 消散

0840 embarrassed [ɪm`bærəst] ★★★★★ 窘困的，尷尬的，侷促不安的

a. agitated; discomposed; perturbed

The meeting lasted throughout the lunch period. I felt so embarrassed when my stomach was making weird noises.

會議持續整個午餐時間，我的胃一直發出古怪咕嚕聲，害我好尷尬。

bar
如棒子 (bar) 卡在中間 (em-)

0841 **embed** [ɪm`bɛd] ★★★★☆

v. entrench; ingrain

使深留，埋入，嵌進

flower bed
在花田 (flower bed) 裡 (em-) 撒下種子

A feeling of guilt became so firmly embedded in the ex-convict's mind that he could hardly get rid of it.

罪惡感深植於那名前科犯的腦海中揮之不去。

0842 **embellish** [ɪm`bɛlɪʃ] ★★★★☆

v. beautify; decorate; adorn

美化，修飾，裝飾

belle
引進 (em-) 美麗 (belle)

Susan, who was getting ready for a job interview, embellished her simple-looking suit with a pretty brooch.

蘇珊準備好參加工作面試，並用漂亮胸針裝飾樸素套裝。

0843 **embodiment** [ɪm`bɑdɪmənt] ★★★★☆

n. incarnation; personification

具體化，化身

body
併入 (em-) 整個形體 (body)

We can hardly imagine Philip treats others badly. He is always kind to everybody. He's the embodiment of kindness.

我們很難想像菲利普會待人不好，因為他不但和善待人，更是仁慈的化身。

0844 **enclose** [ɪn`kloz] ★★★★☆

v. enfold; envelop; wrap

（隨函）附寄，把（文件，票據等）封入

close
放進 (en-) 再封起來 (close)

Thank you for your letter and the enclosed travel brochure. As soon as we decide on the date of the excursion, I will contact you.

感謝您的來信和隨函附上的旅遊手冊，我們一確定旅遊日期就會立刻和您聯絡。

0845 **encompass** [ɪn`kʌmpəs] ★★★★☆

v. surround; beset / include; contain; embrace; involve

包圍，圍繞 / 包括，包含

compass
使位於 (en-) 羅盤 (compass) 之內

This English test encompasses several parts, such as vocabulary, grammar, composition and reading comprehension.

本英文測驗包含字彙、文法、作文和閱讀理解數個部分。

0846 **energize** [`ɛnəˌdʒaɪz] ★★★★★

v. strengthen; invigorate

激勵，使精力充沛

energy
使有活力 (energy)

Kelly's kind advice energized her friend Stephen in facing his responsibilities. He had been afraid of meeting the boss.

凱莉的好建議激勵友人史帝芬挑起責任，他一直害怕面對老闆。

0847 **enervate** [`ɛnəˌvet] ★★★★★

v. unnerve; castrate; emasculate; debilitate; disable; fatigue

使虛弱，使無力

nerve
膽量 (nerve) 消散

We have a long hot spell. I cannot stand such an enervating climate any more. I wish it were winter.

天氣炎熱多時，我無法再忍受這麼叫人虛弱無力的氣候，真希望現在是冬天。

0848 **enlarge** [ɪn`lɑrdʒ] ★★★★★

v. magnify; blow up; amplify

放大，擴大

large
做得 (en-) 大大的 (large)

The picture of the lake that I took was so beautiful that I decided to take it to the photo shop and have it enlarged.

我拍攝的湖景照片非常漂亮，於是決定拿到照相館放大。

0849 enlighten [ɪn`laɪtn̩] 啓迪，啓發 ★★★★★

light

給予 (en-) 光亮 (light)

v. *uplift; improve; illuminate*

Many people look to religion in order to enlighten their lives and at the same time to find true happiness.

許多人依賴宗教啓發人生，並找尋真正的快樂。

0850 enliven [ɪn`laɪvən] 使生動，使活潑 ★★★★☆

live

使 (en-) 生氣勃勃 (live)

v. *animate; vivify; invigorate; give new life to*

Spring enlivens all nature. New buds begin to appear on the branches of trees which have been leafless all winter.

春天使萬物生氣蓬勃，新芽開始從整個冬季都光禿禿的樹枝上冒出來。

Tea Time...

<Name of the author>
Machiavelli
Characterized by the political principles and methods of expediency, craftiness and duplicity advocated in Machiavelli's *The Prince*.

〈來自一作家名〉馬基維利
本字特色在於馬基維利在《君王論》裡所主張的政治理論和權謀、詭詐、欺騙之道。（註：義大利佛羅倫斯外交家馬基維利在其著名的《君王論》一書中主張政治人物為達政治目的，應不擇手段地利用政治權謀策略，即使透過偽善途徑達成目的也在所不惜，不必顧慮世俗道德和法則。後世將馬基維利之名視為「操弄權謀霸術」的同義詞，其形容詞 Machiavellian 指「馬基維利式的、在政治上不擇手段的」，另外也可指名詞「權謀家」。）

❖ **Machiavellian** [ˌmækɪə`vɛlɪən] **a.** *crafty; deceitful* │（尤指在政治上）狡猾的，詭計多端的，不擇手段的

The politician resorted to Machiavellian tactics to obtain his power in the government. He didn't mind using cunning strategies to defeat his rival in the election.

該政治人物仰賴馬基維利式的狡猾手段獲取政治勢力，且不反對在選戰中運用奸詐計謀擊敗對手。

1
Complete each word by filling in the blank with proper spelling so that it has the same meaning as suggested. Then please write the meaning of each word in Chinese.

1. 雜亂	= d i s _ _ _ _ _		11. duration	=	_____
2. 省卻	= d i s _ _ _ _ _		12. dweller	=	_____
3. 溶解	= d i s _ _ _ _ _		13. effrontery	=	_____
4. 股息	= _ _ _ _ _ _ n d		14. embarrassed	=	_____
5. 頑強的	= _ _ _ g e d		15. embed	=	_____
6. 滅亡	= d o w n _ _ _ _		16. encompass	=	_____
7. 排水管	= _ _ a i n		17. energize	=	_____
8. 久旱	= _ _ o u g h t		18. enlarge	=	_____
9. 半信半疑的	= _ _ _ i o u s		19. enlighten	=	_____
10. 耐久的	= _ _ _ _ b l e		20. enliven	=	_____

2
Choose a word that best completes the sentence.

21. During the long _____, all the land became dry and parched.

(A) herd   (B) drought   (C) multitude   (D) horde

22. In India a husband often expects his wife to bring a large _____. This money often causes trouble between a husband and wife.

(A) dowry   (B) impudence   (C) efficacy   (D) effrontery

23. A spider's silk is one of the most _____ materials on earth. Scientists are contriving to use it to make sutures, bulletproof vests, bumpers and landing cables.

(A) dubitable   (B) agitated   (C) durable   (D) uncertain

3
The highlighted word is closest in meaning to which of the following?

24. A: How could we tell edible mushrooms from poisonous ones?
    B: Quite simple. Try them and see.

(A) durable   (B) agitated   (C) poisonous   (D) eatable

25. Yellowstone Park is a giant form of dormant volcano, whose magma chamber is about 20km long and 4.5km wide.

(A) relentless   (B) dogged   (C) latent   (D) persistent

0851 enmity [`ɛnmətɪ]   ★★★★★   敵意，惡意   enemy
n. animosity; animus; antagonism; antipathy; hostility; ill will; malevolence; malice; grudge; aversion   視為敵人 (enemy)
I don't understand Jim's enmity toward me. I have been trying to make up with him, but to no avail.
我不懂吉姆對我所懷的敵意。我已試著跟他和好但完全沒用。

0852 enroll [ɪn`rol]   ★★★★☆   登記，使入學，註冊，招生   roll
v. register; become or make someone a member   寫進出席簿 (roll) 裡 (en-)
Excuse me, but is it possible for me to enroll now for next semester's early morning or late evening classes?
抱歉，請問現在還能不能註冊下學期的晨間或晚間課？

0853 entail [ɪn`tel]   ★★★★☆   使需要，使負擔   tail
v. make necessary; involve   使 (en-) 在後面拖著尾巴 (tail)
This arduous task will entail a lot of hard work. I wonder if you will be able to cope with this task.
這項艱鉅任務需要下一番苦功，我想知道你能不能應付。

0854 entrepreneur [ˌɑntrəprə`nɜ]   ★★★★☆   企業家   enterprise
n. person who starts or organizes a commercial enterprise   經營事業 (enterprise) 的人
Without his business acumen, the entrepreneur could not have succeeded in such a risky business.
那位企業家若不是因為有生意頭腦，不可能在如此高風險的商場上勝出。

0855 enumerate [ɪ`njuməˌret]   ★★★★☆   枚舉，列舉，計數   number
v. list; numerate; specify one after the other   按照數字 (number) 一個個列舉
Our teacher enumerated all the things we had to prepare for the overnight camping; flashlights, candles, blankets, sleeping bags and so forth.
老師逐一列舉我們該準備的宿營用品，包括手電筒、蠟燭、毛毯，以及睡袋等。

0856 equator [ɪ`kwetə]   ★★★★★   赤道   equal
n. imaginary line around the earth at an equal distance from the North and South Poles   將上下平均 (equal) 劃分的線
The equator is an imaginary circle around the earth that is everywhere equally distant from the two poles and divides the earth's surface into the northern and southern hemispheres.
赤道是圍繞地球的虛擬線，距離南、北兩極等長，將地球表面劃分為南、北半球。

0857 equestrian [ɪ`kwɛstrɪən]   ★★★☆☆   騎術的，騎馬的   Equus
a. of horseback riding   馬屬 (equus) 的
The jockey was well known for his equestrian skills, but at the event he broke his back when his horse fell down.
那名賽馬騎師一向以高明騎術聞名，但比賽中馬卻跌倒在地使他摔斷背脊。

0858 equilibrium [ˌikwə`lɪbrɪəm]   ★★☆☆☆   平衡，均衡，均勢   equal
n. state of being balanced   左右兩邊均等 (equal)
You should maintain enough equilibrium to ride a bicycle or a motorcycle; otherwise you could wind up in a ditch.
騎腳踏車或機車時要保持平衡，否則可能會偏向摔入溝渠。

0859 equitable [ˈɛkwɪtəbḷ] ★★★★☆

公平的，公正的，正當的

a. fair; dispassionate; impartial; just

It is natural that each partner, who has invested the same amount of money, should have an equitable share.

投資相同金額的每位合夥人擁有公平的股份是合乎常理的。

equal
平等的 (equal) 對待

0860 equivalent [ɪˈkwɪvələnt] ★★★★☆

等值的，等量的，相等的

a. equal; tantamount

One mile is almost equivalent to 1.609 km.

一英里約等於一‧六零九公里。

equal
具有相同 (equal) 價值 (value) 的

0861 erroneous [ɪˈronɪəs] ★★★☆☆

錯誤的

a. incorrect; wrong; mistaken

People once had the erroneous idea that the sun revolved round the earth. They thought that the sun was a satellite of the earth.

過去人們曾有錯誤觀念認為太陽繞著地球旋轉，以為太陽是地球的衛星。

error
引起錯誤 (error)

0862 erudite [ˈɛruˌdaɪt] ★★★☆☆

博學的，飽學的

a. learned; educated; lettered

An erudite person is someone who has studied a lot and is very scholarly. My guidance professor is a model.

博學者不但閱讀大量書籍且學識淵博，我的指導教授就是簡中翹楚。

rude
有學識的人須把無禮的 (rude) 想法丟掉 (e-)

0863 escalate [ˈɛskəˌlet] ★★★☆☆

使逐步擴大，節節升高

v. increase; intensify

Housing problems in my country have escalated in the past few years, though the government has been constructing many apartment houses.

過去幾年來政府雖建造許多公寓住宅，但我國住屋問題仍日益嚴重。

escalator
如搭乘電梯 (escalator) 而上

0864 escapade [ˌɛskəˈped] ★★☆☆☆

惡作劇，越軌行為

n. mischievous act; prank

Eric's parents were disappointed when they learned every detail of his foolish escapade. They thought that he was a good student at school.

艾瑞克的父母得知愚蠢惡作劇的所有細節後大感失望，還以為兒子在學校是好學生。

escape
做了之後要逃離 (escape) 的行為

0865 escapee [ɪˌskeˈpi] ★★☆☆☆

越獄者，逃亡者，逃脫者

n. fugitive; person who has escaped

The escapees who ran away from the prison were apprehended while they were trying to hijack a truck.

幾名越獄者試圖劫持一輛卡車時遭到逮捕。

escape
逃跑 (escape) 的人

0866 eschew [ɛsˈtʃu] ★★★☆☆

避開，戒絕，避免

v. avoid; duck; shun; elude; evade

Dr. Peterson, our English professor, deliberately tries to eschew political discussion in class, as the election is getting closer.

由於選舉將至，我們的英語教授彼得森博士刻意避開在課堂上討論政治議題。

escape
避開 (escape)

0867 estrange [ɪ`strendʒ]　　　　　　　　　　遠離，使疏遠

***v.** alienate; divide; separate; split; disaffect*

If they had had a child, the couple would not have been estranged so quickly. They used separate rooms for months.

如果那對夫妻膝下有子就不會那麼快疏遠彼此，他們分居不同房好幾個月了。

stranger
變成陌生人 (stranger) 般

0868 evacuate [ɪ`vækjʊ,et]　　　　　　　撤離，使疏散，撤退

***v.** leave or withdraw from a place because of danger*

The villagers were hurriedly evacuated to a primary school as their houses were in danger of flooding.

村民因住處遭受洪水侵襲而緊急疏散到小學。

vacant
把裡面的東西騰空 (vacant) 搬到外面 (e-)

0869 evanescent [,ɛvə`nɛsṇt]　　　　　逐漸消失的，短暫的

***a.** transient; fleeting; momentary; passing; short-lived*

A movie star's fame is often as evanescent as snowflakes on a river. It is extremely momentary.

電影明星的名聲就像漸漸消失在河中的雪花般非常短暫。

vain
向外 (e-) 消散而變空 (vacant)

0870 evaporate [ɪ`væpə,ret]　　　使蒸發，使揮發，使脫水，使消失

***v.** (cause something to) change into vapor and disappear*

Gasoline evaporates more rapidly than water, which means that gasoline changes into vapor more quickly than water.

汽油比水更快揮發，也就是說汽油比水更快蒸發。

vapor
水蒸氣 (vapor) 向外 (e-) 消散

0871 exculpate [`ɛkskʌl,pet]　　　　　使無罪，使洗清罪嫌

***a.** absolve; acquit; clear; exonerate; vindicate*

After months of a stressful trial, the suspect was finally found innocent and was exculpated from any wrongdoing whatsoever.

經過數月緊湊審判，嫌犯終於以無罪開釋，洗脫所有罪行。

culprit
使去 (ex-) 罪 (culpa-＝crime)

0872 execrable [`ɛksɪkrəbl]　　　　　惡劣的，可惡的，可憎的

***a.** very bad; terrible*

The boss was one of the most arrogant persons I've ever met. I couldn't stand his execrable manners.

老闆是我見過最自大傲慢的人之一，我無法忍受其惡劣態度。

sacred
遠離 (ex-) 神聖 (sacred) 之物

0873 exemplify [ɪg`zɛmplə,faɪ]　　　　例證，例示，作為～的例子

***v.** illustrate; instance*

My uncle was nominated as father of the year. In my opinion, he really deserves it because he exemplifies everything that being a father means.

舅舅被提名角逐年度父親獎。依我所見他應獲得這份榮譽，因為他是好爸爸的最佳例證。

example
舉例 (example) 給外面 (ex-) 看

0874 exorbitant [ɪg`zɔrbətənt]　　　　過高的，過度的，過分的

***a.** excessive; extravagant; extreme; immoderate; inordinate; towering; undue*

The cost of living in this country is exorbitant. Most people are having a hard time making ends meet.

這個國家生活費用極高，多數民眾都入不敷出。

orbit
在軌道 (orbit) 之外 (ex-) 的

0875 expenditure [ɪk`spɛndɪtʃə] ★★★★★ 　支出，開支，經費

n. *expense; cost*

After struggling for two years, Mr. Clark decided that his expenditures were too high to continue his business and he closed his office.

經過兩年慘澹經營後，克拉克先生認為開支過高無法繼續經營下去，於是決定歇業。

expense
費用 (expense)

0876 extant [ɪk`stænt] ★★★★★ 　現存的 / 尚存的

a. *existing; existent / alive*

This museum displays the earliest extant map of the Korean Peninsula. It was drawn by an ancient cartographer.

這家美術館展出現存最早由古代製圖師繪製而成的朝鮮半島地圖。

extend
向外 (ex-) 長長地延伸出去 (tant-)

0877 extracurricular [ˌɛkstrəkə`rɪkjələ] ★★★★★ 　課外的，業餘的

a. *outside the regular course of work or studies at a school or college*

Today high school students are devoting less time to extracurricular activities than they did in the past.

今日的高中生比過去的學生花費較少時間在課外活動上。

curriculum
在正規課程 (curriculum) 以外的 (extra-)

0878 extramarital [ˌɛkstrə`mærətl] ★★★☆☆ 　婚外的

a. *relating to sexual relationships outside marriage*

His wife was crushed when she found out that he was having an extramarital affair, and she applied for divorce immediately.

妻子發現他有婚外情後就崩潰了，接著立刻訴請離婚。

marriage
在婚姻 (marriage) 之外的 (extra-)

0879 facade [fə`sɑd] ★★★★☆ 　（建築物的）正面，（尤指虛有其表的）外觀

n. *the front of a building*

The facade of the cathedral was decorated with pretty mosaics and various carvings. However, in the back there were no decorations at all.

大教堂正面裝飾華麗美觀的馬賽克圖案和形形色色的雕刻，但內部卻毫無裝潢。

face
如臉 (face) 般的面向

0880 fallible [`fæləbl] ★★★★☆ 　可能犯錯的，容易犯錯的，可能有誤的

a. *faulty*

We, fallible human beings, can make a mistake from time to time. No human being is free from faults.

身為容易犯錯的人類，我們時時刻刻都在犯錯，無人能免。

fallacy
會 (-ible) 犯下錯誤 (fall) 的

0881 fanatic [fə`nætɪk] ★★★★☆ 　狂熱者，～迷

n. *zealot; bug; enthusiast; maniac*

My friend Jack is a model car fanatic. His room is full of hundreds of different kinds of model cars.

友人傑克是個模型車迷，房間裡有數以百計造型各異的模型車。

fan
熱烈支持某活動的「粉絲」(fan)

0882 fanatical [fə`nætɪkl] ★★★★☆ 　狂熱的，入迷的

a. *obsessively enthusiastic*

A fanatical person continues in an activity beyond the proper limits. He does not know when he should stop.

狂熱者會毫無節制地持續進行某項活動，不懂得適可而止。

fan
像「粉絲」般對某活動著迷的

⁰⁸⁸³ **feign** [fen] 假裝 ★★★★☆

feint
以假動作 (feint) 來偽裝

a. make a false representation; pretend

The little child feigned sleep in hopes of catching a glimpse of the tooth fairy who he believed would put a nice gift under his pillow.

小孩因為想偷看牙仙子所以裝睡。他相信仙子會把精美禮物放在他的枕頭底下。

⁰⁸⁸⁴ **ferocious** [fə`roʃəs] 兇猛的，殘忍的，野蠻的 ★★★★☆

fierce
像火 (fire) 一樣凶猛的

a. fierce; brutal

I didn't realize how ferocious a deer could be until I witnessed two deer at the zoo fighting each other. They were fighting tooth and nail.

我從不知道熊有多兇殘，直到在動物園目睹兩隻熊打鬥，簡直像拼了命地廝殺。

⁰⁸⁸⁵ **finesse** [fə`nɛs] 技巧，手腕 ★★★★☆

fine
漂亮的 (fine) 技巧

n. skill in dealing with people or situations cleverly and tactfully

Olympic athletes practice several hours a day and eventually get to the point where they can perform with such finesse as to dazzle spectators around the world.

奧運選手每天練習數小時，最後終能展現絕佳技巧並令全球觀眾驚羨不已。

⁰⁸⁸⁶ **finicky** [`fɪnɪkɪ] 好挑剔的，過分講究的 ★★★★☆

fine (small)
過於關注小細節 (fine)

a. fastidious; fussy

When Maggie was born we thought she was a very picky eater. Then her brother was born and he is even more finicky because he won't even eat what his sister would.

瑪姬出生時我們覺得她是個很挑食的孩子。接著弟弟出生了卻更挑食，因為連瑪姬肯吃的東西他都不吃。

⁰⁸⁸⁷ **flagrant** [`flegrənt] 明目張膽的，惡名昭彰的 ★★★☆☆

black
心是黑的 (black)

a. wicked; particularly bad

There are usually more flagrant fouls committed during the playoffs as compared to the regular season, because the intensity level is so high.

季後賽常出現比例行賽更多的明目張膽犯規行為，因為球員都很緊繃。

⁰⁸⁸⁸ **flamboyant** [flæm`bɔɪənt] 浮誇的，炫耀的 ★★★☆☆

flame
像火花 (flame) 般華麗的

a. ornate; ostentatious; showy

Tommy, a salesman, has been very successful in what he does and now travels the world. He carries on in one of the most flamboyant styles I have ever seen.

湯米是非常成功的業務員，現在更全球走透透。他的作風是我見過最浮誇的。

⁰⁸⁸⁹ **flammable** [`flæməbl] 易燃的，可燃的，速燃的 ★★★★☆

flame
如火花 (flame) 容易被點燃的

a. combustible; inflammable

We should never smoke in a gas station because there is too much flammable material. Experts say that even using a cell phone may be dangerous.

我們絕不能在加油站吸煙，因為裡面有太多易燃物。專家指出就連使用手機都可能造成危險。

0890 fledgling [ˋflɛdʒlɪŋ] ★★★☆☆ 菜鳥，年輕而無經驗者

n. newcomer; novice; apprentice; beginner

David graduated from Law School, got a job with a firm, and worked as a fledgling lawyer for several years until he finally learned the ropes and became a very reputable lawyer.

大衛法學院畢業後在企業做了幾年菜鳥律師，最後終於掌握箇中訣竅，成為聲名大噪的律師。

fly
翅膀硬了正要開始飛翔 (fly)

0891 fleet [flit] ★★★☆☆ 艦隊，船隊，車隊

n. group of warships, submarines, etc.

In 1962 during the Cuban Missile Crisis, the whole U.S. Naval fleet was put on red alert in anticipation of an all-out nuclear war.

一九六二年古巴飛彈危機期間，美國所有海軍艦隊都進入紅色警戒狀態，因為預料會發生全面核子大戰。

float
在海上浮行 (float) 的艦隊

0892 flout [flaʊt] ★★☆☆☆ 嘲弄，藐視，嘲笑

v. sneer; scoff; disregard

Miss Brown, who was in her forties, wanted to refuse but not to flout the bachelor's offers of marriage.

年逾四十的伯朗小姐想拒絕單身漢求婚，但不想表現得像是在嘲弄他。

flute
對經過的人吹 (flute) 口哨

0893 folly [ˋfɑlɪ] ★★☆☆☆ 蠢事，荒唐事

n. foolishness; absurdity; stupidity

I own many videos, but my favorite one is the baseball follies tape. I just love to see all of the mistakes that the players make.

我有許多錄影帶，其中最喜歡的是棒球烏龍紀錄片，我就是愛看球員們犯的所有錯誤。

fool
像傻瓜 (fool) 般的行為

0894 foolhardy [ˋful͵hɑrdɪ] ★★★★☆ 有勇無謀的，魯莽的

a. rash; reckless; impetuous

When they were foolhardy kids, Nick and Tommy would go to Lake Powell and dive off the 50-foot-cliffs that shoot up out of the lake.

尼克和湯米還是有勇無謀的孩子時常去鮑威爾湖，並從湖旁五十英尺高的懸崖跳下。

fool, hard
像傻瓜 (fool) 般熱心 (hard) 奔走

0895 foot-dragging [ˋfʊtdrægɪŋ] ★★★★☆ 遲疑不前，躊躇不決

a. unhurried; slow

The government has discarded its piecemeal and foot-dragging attitude and adopted a more comprehensive and positive stance in its open door policy.

政府在門戶開放政策上一掃漸進遲疑的態度，改採更全面積極的立場。

foot, draw
拖 (draw) 著雙腳 (foot) 到處走

0896 formation [fɔrˋmeʃən] ★★★★★ 隊形

n. particular arrangement or pattern

When birds move from one place to another for a more temperate climate they usually fly in formation.

當鳥群遷徙到較溫暖的地方時常採隊形方式飛行。

form
形成某種模樣 (form)

0897 fortuitous [fɔrˋtuətəs]

★★★☆☆

偶然的，意外的

fortune

依從命運 (fortune) 的

a. accidental; unexpected

The party was the result of the captain's fortuitous meeting with his old friend. It lasted an entire night.

船長偶遇老友後促成那場通宵達旦的派對。

0898 founder [ˋfaʊndə]

★★★☆☆

使進水沉沒

found; foundation

往底部 (foundation) 沉下

v. submerge; sink

The Titanic, which was nicknamed 'Unsinkable,' foundered to the bottom of the North Atlantic after it collided with an iceberg.

號稱「不會沉沒的」鐵達尼號撞上冰山後，沉入北大西洋海底深處。

0899 franchise [ˋfræntʃaɪz]

★★★★★

參政權，選舉權

frank

有權蓋戳記 (frank)

n. right to vote at public elections

As late as in the 19th century, women were given the franchise, or the right to vote, after many years of struggle and conflict.

經過多年努力奮鬥和矛盾衝突，女性遲至十九世紀才擁有參政權，也就是選舉權。

0900 fraternity [frəˋtɝnətɪ]

★★★★☆

兄弟關係，手足之情，友愛

brother

兄弟 (brother) 之間的情誼

n. brotherly feeling; brotherhood / group of male students at a university who form a social club

Some of the best friends that Jack made in school were the guys who were in his fraternity.

傑克和學生時代結交的許多好友有著兄弟般的手足之情。

Tea Time... ☕

<Roman myth> Cupid	〈出自羅馬神話〉邱比特
The god of love, son of Venus, usually represented as a winged boy with bow and arrow.	邱比特為羅馬神話中掌管戀愛之神，是主掌愛與美的女神維納斯之子，其形象常是手持弓箭、身上長有雙翼的男童。（註：本字原指愛神邱比特，由於調皮的他會亂射手中的戀愛之箭和憎恨之箭，所以暗喻戀愛是盲目的。其名詞 cupidity 帶有「貪婪，貪心，貪欲」之意。）

❖ **cupidity** [kjuˋpɪdətɪ] *n. greed* | 貪婪，貪心

Mr. Covington has made his millions, but he loves the feeling of making money, and his cupidity has become like a disease.

柯溫頓先生賺了數百萬元，由於熱愛賺錢，他的貪婪已經成了一種疾病。

❖ **covet** [ˋkʌvɪt] *v. long for; desire* | 垂涎，貪圖，渴望，覬覦

Jimmy coveted his brother's toys and he tried to contrive a good way to make him give them up. At last, he decided to buy him some candies.

吉米覬覦弟弟的玩具，於是設法讓他放棄那些玩具，最後還決定買糖給他吃。

1 Complete each word by filling in the blank with proper spelling so that it has the same meaning as suggested. Then please write the meaning of each word in Chinese.

1. 列舉 = e _ _ _ _ _ a t e
2. 平衡 = _ _ _ _ _ i b r i u m
3. 錯誤的 = _ _ _ _ _ e o u s
4. 惡作劇 = _ _ _ _ _ _ d e
5. 使疏遠 = e _ _ _ _ _ _ _
6. 逐漸消失的 = e _ _ _ _ s c e n t
7. 使無罪 = e x _ _ _ _ _ _ _
8. 過高的 = e x _ _ _ _ _ a n t
9. 支出 = _ _ _ _ _ _ _ t u r e
10. 容易犯錯的 = _ _ _ _ i b l e

11. extramarital = _____
12. fanatic = _____
13. ferocious = _____
14. finesse = _____
15. flamboyant = _____
16. flammable = _____
17. fledgling = _____
18. foolhardy = _____
19. formation = _____
20. fortuitous = _____

2 Choose a word that best completes the sentence.

21. Wyoming gave women the _____, or the right to vote to attract more people to come.

   (A) franchise   (B) fraternity   (C) brotherhood   (D) fleet

22. The students at this school are encouraged to participate in _____ activities after school.

   (A) extant   (B) extracurricular   (C) fallible   (D) extramarital

3 The highlighted word is closest in meaning to which of the following?

23. The solution in this container is extremely flammable . You should not smoke near here.

   (A) rash   (B) inflammable   (C) impetuous   (D) ferocious

24. Your request is almost equivalent to an order to me.

   (A) transient   (B) fleeting   (C) tantamount   (D) passing

25. We were surprised at the exorbitant amount of money we had to pay.

   (A) execrable   (B) errable   (C) extant   (D) excessive

MP3 38

0901 fraudulent [ˈfrɔdʒələnt]   詐欺的，詐騙的，不誠實的   ★★★☆☆
a. deceitful or dishonest

fraud, defraud
使用欺騙 (fraud) 手段的

The man was arrested and sentenced to five years in jail because he swindled a lot of people out of several thousand dollars by running a fraudulent advertisement in the newspaper.

男子因在報上刊登不實廣告詐騙多人數千美元而被捕，並處以五年徒刑。

0902 frigid [ˈfrɪgɪd]   嚴寒的   ★★★★☆
a. very cold

freeze
凍得 (freeze) 又冰又硬

We learned that the igloos made of bricks packed with snow and ice provided sufficient protection in a frigid region.

以磚石包裹冰雪建造而成的圓頂雪屋，可為嚴寒地區居民提供充分保護。

0903 fructify [ˈfrʌktəˌfaɪ]   使結果實，使產生成果   ★★★★☆
v. bear fruit or be fruitful

fruit
使結果實 (fruit)

All of my family members hope that this apple tree, which was planted three years ago, will fructify this fall.

所有家族成員都希望這棵三年前種植的蘋果樹能在今秋結果。

0904 fruition [fruˈɪʃən]   實現，成果，收獲   ★★★★☆
n. fulfillment of hopes, plans, etc.

fruit
結果實 (fruit)

There were many times when he just wanted to forget everything and give up, but he continued on, and all of his efforts are just now coming to fruition.

好多次他都想乾脆放棄算了，最後還是堅持下來，如今一切努力都有了回報。

0905 fulfill [fulˈfɪl]   實現，履行，完成 / 滿足   ★★★★★
v. perform something or bring something to completion / satisfy; answer

full, fill
滿滿地 (full) 填上 (fill)

His mother always had expectations of his becoming a professional football player. But he became a salesman instead and didn't fulfill his mother's expectations.

母親一直希望他能成為職業足球員，但他卻是個業務員，沒有達到母親期望。

0906 fund [fʌnd]   基金，資金，專款，財源   ★★★★★
n. sum of money saved or made available for a particular purpose

foundation
經營事業的基礎 (foundation)

Many countries nowadays believe it desirable to divert funds from armaments to economic development.

現在許多國家都相信將財源投入經濟發展比轉投入軍備更好。

0907 fundamental [ˌfʌndəˈmɛntl]   基本的，根本的，主要的   ★★★★★
a. of or forming the basis or foundation of something; essential

foundation
形成基礎 (foundation) 的

How to raise the necessary funds was one of the fundamental problems of our club. We decided to have a concert.

如何募集必要資金是俱樂部的根本問題之一，因此我們決定辦場演唱會。

0908 gainsay [gen`se] ★★☆☆☆ 否認，反駁，反對

v. contradict; deny; retort

against, say

說 (say) 出反對 (against) 意見

Now that the Democrats have control of the Senate, there are many Republicans gainsaying against many of the policies that the Democrats are trying to implement.

現在民主黨員控制了參議院，許多共和黨員起而反對民主黨想要推行的政策。

0909 gesticulate [dʒɛs`tɪkjə,let] ★★☆☆☆ 比手畫腳，比手勢

v. move the hands or arms instead of speaking

gesture

做出姿勢 (gesture)

No one stands near her while Susan tells one of her tales, since everybody knows that as she gets excited she begins to gesticulate and someone is liable to get hit in the head.

蘇珊講故事時沒人敢站在她身邊，因為大家都知道她講到興頭上就會開始比手畫腳，接著一定會打到別人的頭。

0910 ghastly [`gæstlɪ] ★★★☆☆ 可怕的，極大的，糟透了的

a. causing horror or fear; distasteful; very bad

ghost

像鬼 (ghost) 般恐怖的

Mr. Evans made a ghastly mistake when he opened a letter of credit to buy an order but didn't have the money to pay for it when the shipment arrived in customs.

伊文斯先生以信用狀訂購商品時犯了極大錯誤，貨到時卻沒有錢付訂單。

0911 gigantic [dʒaɪ`gæntɪk] ★★★★★ 巨大的，龐大的

a. immense; giant; enormous; gargantuan

giant

像巨人 (giant) 般巨大的

After the tornado, a gigantic 100-year-old oak tree lay blocking the avenue. Workers had to pull the tree out of the way.

龍捲風過後一棵樹齡百年的巨大橡樹倒在街道擋住往來交通，工人須將它拉離道路。

0912 glacier [`gleʃə] ★★★★★ 冰河

n. mass of ice, formed by snow on mountains

glass

如玻璃 (glass) 般的冰

A glacier is a mass of ice, formed by snow on mountains, moving slowly down a valley. It is interesting that a mass of ice starts to move once it becomes more than 100 feet thick.

冰河是高山冰雪結合成的大片冰川，由高山緩緩向下流至山谷。有趣的是，冰河厚度須超過一百英尺才會開始移動。

0913 glacial [`gleʃəl] ★★★★★ 冰冷的，冷冽的

a. cold; freezing; bone-chilling

glass

如玻璃 (glass) 般冰冷的

In my country in the long winter months a glacial wind blows from the north. Sometimes the wind is like a knife.

我國漫長冬季時有冷冽北風吹拂，有時寒風就像利刃般冷冽。

0914 glossy [`glɔsɪ] ★★★★☆ 有光澤的，光滑的

a. smooth and shiny

glass

如玻璃 (glass) 般發光的

You can tell the difference between stainless steel and titanium products because the stainless steel metal has a very glossy finish where the titanium does not.

不銹鋼合金和鈦製產品很容易分辨不同，前者有極光滑的拋光外層但後者沒有。

0915 glut [glʌt] ★★★★☆ 供應過剩

glutton
如貪吃者 (glutton) 般吃很多

n. surplus; overabundance

There was a glut of red pepper in the market. As a result, the price of red pepper plummeted.

市場紅椒供應過剩導致價格慘跌。

0916 grandiose [ˈgrændɪˌos] ★★★☆☆ 宏偉的，堂皇的

grand
巨大的 (grand)

a. planned on large scale

They have spent nearly a million dollars building their new estate, and so it's only natural that their open house be a grandiose occasion.

他們花了近百萬元建造新莊園，開放參觀日當天必定是一場富麗堂皇的盛會。

0917 grievous [ˈgrivəs] ★★☆☆☆ 悲痛的，悲慘的，嚴重的

grief
沉浸在悲傷 (grief) 中

a. agonizing; tragic

After the Civil War, destruction on both sides was grievous. However, the disastrous condition of the South was more severe.

美國南北戰爭結束後，戰事對雙方的破壞程度都很嚴重，但南方的悲慘情況更為劇烈。

0918 handy [ˈhændɪ] ★★★★☆ 便利的，方便的

hand
可用手 (hand) 拿著到處走

a. convenient to handle or use; useful

A telephone answering machine is very handy, but sometimes it causes great frustration when someone dials the wrong number and leaves a message.

電話答錄機非常方便，但遇到有人打錯電話來留言，就會讓人感到很失望。

0919 hardship [ˈhɑrdʃɪp] ★★★★★ 艱難，艱困，辛苦

hard
很困難的 (hard) 情況

n. rigor; adversity; trial; toil

Despite all the adversity that John has faced during his life, he has managed to overcome his hardships and become a very successful person.

儘管面對所有生活逆境，約翰仍設法克服難關成為成功人士。

0920 haughty [ˈhɔtɪ] ★★★★☆ 傲慢的，自大的

high
擺出高 (high) 姿態

a. arrogant; insolent; overbearing; domineering

If you look at a person too little while he is talking, you may appear too haughty or secretive.

如果別人在講話你卻不太以正眼看他，可能會顯得太過自大或有事隱瞞。

0921 headstrong [ˈhɛdˌstrɔŋ] ★★★★☆ 剛愎自用的，一意孤行的，頑固的

head, strong
頭部 (head) 堅硬的 (strong)

a. obstinate; bullheaded; mulish; self-willed; stubborn; willful

I have often heard people talking about my neighbor Chuck's headstrong temperament. Personally, I do not think that he is so obstinate.

我常聽大家談論鄰居查克剛愎自用的個性，但我個人並不認為他有那麼頑固。

0922 heave [hiv] ★★★★☆ 拉起（船錨等）

heavy
向上舉起重物 (heavy)

v. drag up; pull up; hoist

Heave anchor! Hoist the main sail! Now bring the ship about!

起錨！升起主帆！掉頭！

0923 heedless [`hidlɪs`]　　　　　　　　不留心的，不注意的，不在意的　　★★★★☆

a. careless; inadvertent; thoughtless; unwary; reckless; remiss

Mr. Smith is a very risky business man. He is usually heedless to the warnings and advice given by his more conservative business partners.

史密斯先生是個非常膽大冒險的生意人，對保守生意夥伴提出的警告或建議常不以為意。

heed
沒有 (-less) 傾注注意力 (heed)

0924 hefty [`hɛftɪ`]　　　　　　　　　強壯的，強而有力的　　★★★★☆

a. husky; burly; stout

Jim is a very hefty guy. I have never seen anyone more powerful than he. He is strong enough to lift a small refrigerator by himself.

吉姆非常強壯，我從沒看過比他力氣更大的人。他強壯到能獨自扛起一台小冰箱。

heavy
即使是重物 (heavy) 也能輕易舉起

0925 helm [`hɛlm`]　　　　　　　船舵／領導地位，支配權，控制權　　★★★☆☆

n. helmet / the control or leadership of an organization, government, etc.

The incumbent government was defeated in the election. The government promised to turn over its helm to the newly elected party.

現任政府在選舉中落敗，承諾會將政權交給當選政黨。

helmet
像鋼盔 (helmet) 般的

0926 henpecked [`hɛn‚pɛkt`]　　　　　　　怕老婆的，懼內的　　★★☆☆☆

a. nagged by a fussy and domineering wife

"But darling," the henpecked husband whined, "I'm doing everything I can to make you happy!"

"You don't do the one thing my first husband did to make me happy!" she yelled.

"And what's that?" the embarrassed husband asked.

"He passed away!"

懼內的先生哀鳴著：「但親愛的，我已經盡全力讓妳快樂了啊！」

妻子大叫：「有件事你沒做到，但我的第一任丈夫做到了，而且讓我很快樂！」

窘困的先生問：「是哪件事？」

妻子回道：「他死掉了！」

hen, peck
被母雞 (hen) 啄的 (pecked)

0927 hindmost [`haɪnd‚most`]　　　　　　　最後面的，最後的　　★★☆☆☆

a. farthest back; closest to the rear

My favorite cut of beef is the rump roast, which is located at the hindmost portion of the cow.

我最喜歡吃的牛肉部位是為在牛隻最後面的烤牛臀肉。

behind
最 (most) 後面的 (behind)

0928 hollow [`hɑlo`]　　　　　　　中空的，空的／凹處，洞　　★★★★☆

a. empty / n. hole; cavity

A starved fox, who saw in the hollow of an oak tree some bread and meat left there by shepherds, crept in and ate it. With his stomach distended he could not get out again.　　　　　── Aesop's Fables

一頭饑餓的狐狸發現橡樹洞中有牧羊人留下的麵包和肉片，於是悄悄爬進洞裡把食物吃光，但是因為吃得太撐，竟卡在洞裡出不來。

── 《伊索寓言》

hole
如洞 (hole) 般的

0929 horrendous [hɔ`rɛndəs`]　　　　　　　恐怖的，嚇人的，可怕的　　★★★☆☆

a. horrible; frightful

We could hear the horrendous noises of the hurricane all night long. We prayed and prayed all through the night.

我們整晚都聽到颶風可怕的呼嘯聲，於是大家徹夜不斷祈禱。

horror
可怕的 (horror)

0930 humane [hju`men]　　　合乎人道的，慈悲的，有人情味的　★★★★☆

a. charitable; benevolent; humanitarian; merciful; sympathetic

The producers of the animal movie had to be careful during its filming not to injure any of the animals, because animal advocacy groups are extremely concerned about the humane treatment of animals.

動物電影製作人拍片時要小心不讓動物受傷，因為動物保護團體非常關切動物的人道對待。

human
富有人性的 (human) 和人情味的

0931 husbandry [`hʌzbəndrɪ]　　　節約，節儉 / 農務，耕種　★★☆☆☆

n. thrift; thrifty management

In most cases husbandry has been one of the greatest virtues. It is important to economize and prepare for rainy days.

多數情況下節儉是最好的美德之一，因為儉約節流、未雨綢繆是很重要的。

husband
如一家之主 (husband) 般撙節開支

0932 icicle [`aɪsɪkl̩]　　　冰柱　★☆☆☆☆

n. a tapering, pointed, hanging piece of ice, formed by the freezing of dripping or falling water

As winter progresses the icicles hanging off my roof grow larger and larger, and some of them get so big that they reach the ground.

隨著寒冬的腳步接近，屋簷下的冰柱愈結愈大，有些甚至垂落到地面。

ice
垂掛的冰 (ice)

0933 iconoclast [aɪ`kɑnə‚klæst]　　　破除偶像崇拜者　★☆☆☆☆

n. one who destroys religious images or oppose their veneration

American writer Nathaniel Hawthorne as an iconoclast opposed the Puritans' sanctimonious beliefs.

身為破除偶像崇拜者的美國作家霍桑反對清教徒的偽善信仰。

icon
粉碎 (clast-) 偶像 (icon) 的

0934 impartial [ɪm`pɑrʃən]　　　不偏不倚的，公正無私的，正大光明的　★★★☆☆

a. fair; dispassionate; equitable; just; objective; unprejudiced; unbiased

Among our friends, Gary has been considered to be the most impartial. We often take our problems to him for an equitable judgment.

在我們這群朋友中蓋瑞是公認最公正無私的，大家常請他為各種問題提供公正判斷。

part, partial
不 (im-) 偏向某部分 (part) 的

0935 impasse [`ɪmpæs]　　　僵局 / 死路，死巷　★★☆☆☆

n. predicament; dilemma; jam / dead end; blind alley

When the terrorist took the mayor hostage, the chief of police had to admit that he was at an impasse.

恐怖分子脅持市長作為人質，警察總長承認目前陷入僵局。

pass
未 (im-) 通過 (pass) 的

0936 imperative [ɪm`pɛrətɪv]　　　必要的，緊急的　★★★★☆

a. essential; necessary; prerequisite; required; obligatory

It is imperative that you listen to every word that I tell you and do exactly as I say. If you don't, you can make a wrong move and fall off the mountain to your death.

你一定要好好聽我說的每句話並一一照辦，如果做不到就可能轉錯彎而掉下山谷致死。

emperor
皇帝 (emperor) 的命令是不能違背的

0937 imperious [ɪm`pɪrɪəs]　　　傲慢的，蠻橫的　★★★☆☆

a. bossy; domineering; overbearing; haughty

Her imperious manner befitted her position as boss, but she soon lost all her friends.

她蠻橫的態度符合老闆身分，但很快就失去所有朋友。

emperor
如皇帝 (emperor) 般高傲的

0938 impertinent [ɪmˋpɝtn̩ənt]   不切題的，不適當的 / 無禮的，魯莽的   ★★★☆☆

a. irrelevant; extraneous; inapplicable / insolent

The teacher was shocked at such impertinent behavior from a student, who was singing loudly in class, while listening to music with his MP3.

老師對學生的無禮行為感到震驚，他在上課時一邊聽 MP3，一邊大聲唱歌。

> pertain
> 不 (im-) 適切的 (pertinent)

0939 imperturbability [ˋɪmpɚ͵tɝbəˋbɪlətɪ]   沉著，冷靜，泰然自若   ★★☆☆☆

n. equanimity; calmness; composure; self-possession

Imperturbability is a very necessary quality for those people who aspire to be diplomats or ambassadors, since their positions may often require them to participate in delicate negotiations.

對嚮往成為外交官或大使的人而言冷靜沉著是必要特質，因為常須參與審慎的談判協商。

> disturb
> 使完全 (per-) 不 (im-) 混亂 (disturb)

0940 implacable [ɪmˋplækəbl̩]   毫不寬容的 / 難以平息的   ★★★☆☆

a. ruthless; merciless / relentless; grim

Their boss was an implacable man who was never satisfied with their work or their performance.

上司是個毫不留情的人，從不滿意他們的工作或表現。

> place
> 不能 (im-) 安坐 (place) 在位置上的

0941 impoverish [ɪmˋpɑvərɪʃ]   使成赤貧 / 使貧瘠   ★★★★☆

v. reduce to poverty; make very poor / deplete; drain

The couple has spent too much money on the furnishings, changing everything in their new house. I'm afraid they'll soon be impoverished.

那對夫妻在居家擺設上斥資大筆金錢好讓新居煥然一新，我真擔心他們馬上會變得一貧如洗。

> poverty
> 陷入 (im-) 貧窮 (poverty)

0942 impunity [ɪmˋpjunətɪ]   免除，免罰   ★★★★☆

n. exemption; immunity

Even though she was found guilty of the crime, the judge granted impunity to her, because he felt that she had shown sufficient remorse for the crime. He felt that further punishment would damage her chances of putting her life back together again.

她雖被判有罪但法官考量她犯後態度良好故免其罪刑，以免進一步懲處影響她重獲新生。

> punish
> 不必 (im-) 接受處罰 (punish) 的

0943 inanimate [ɪnˋænəmɪt]   無生命的，死氣沉沉的，無生氣的   ★★★★☆

a. lifeless; not endowed with life

It is believed that inanimate objects, such as a chair and a table, do not have feelings. They are lifeless things.

一般咸信桌、椅等無生命物體是沒有感情、沒有生命的東西。

> animal
> 沒有 (in-) 如動物 (animal) 般的生命力

0944 incapacitate [͵ɪnkəˋpæsə͵tet]   使不能，使無能力   ★★★★☆

v. paralyze; disable; cripple; make unable or unfit

The champion was able to incapacitate the challenger with a single punch to the throat and once more he was declared world Champion.

優勝者一拳擊在挑戰者喉嚨上將他擊倒，再度登上世界冠軍寶座。

> capable
> 使沒有 (in-) 能力 (capable)

0945 incorrigible [ɪnˈkɔrɪdʒəbl]   難以彌補的，積重難返的，無可救藥的

★★★☆☆

correct
無法 (in-) 修正 (correct)

a. *not corrigible; that cannot be corrected, improved or reformed*

Can you not understand that you were fired because of your incorrigible mistake? It cost the company thousands of dollars.
你難道不明白由於犯下難以彌補的錯誤，所以你被開除了嗎？這個錯誤害公司損失數千美元。

0946 increment [ˈɪnkrəmənt]   增加，增額

★★★☆☆

increase
增加 (increase)

n. *increase*

My colleague Jim Jordan received a great increment in his salary last week. Everyone else at the office envied him.
同事吉姆‧喬丹上周得到大筆加薪，公司所有人都妒忌他。

0947 incriminate [ɪnˈkrɪməˌnet]   控告，使負罪，牽連入罪

★★★☆☆

criminal, crime
使 (in-) 有罪 (crime)

v. *accuse; impeach; indict; charge*

After he had been arrested, the criminal decided that he didn't want to go to jail alone, and tried to incriminate every criminal he had ever known.
罪犯被補後決定不要獨自入獄，於是供出自己知道的所有罪犯。

0948 incurable [ɪnˈkjurəbl]   無法治癒的，無可救藥的

★★★★☆

cure
不能 (in-) 治療 (cure) 的

a. *irreparable; hopeless; cureless; not curable*

At first they were really worried because the doctor had mentioned that the disease their daughter had caught was incurable, but after receiving other opinions, they are confident that with the right treatment the disease is curable.
起初聽醫生說女兒的病無法根治，讓他們很擔憂。但聽取各方意見後，他們很有信心只要正確治療便可痊癒。

0949 indefatigable [ˌɪndɪˈfætɪɡəbl]   不屈不撓的 / 勤勉不懈的，頑強的

★★★☆☆

fatigue
不會 (in-) 疲勞 (fatigue) 到 跌倒 (de-)

a. *inexhaustible; tireless / assiduous; dogged; persistent; relentless; tenacious*

My tennis coach is an indefatigable person. He seems to have so much energy that he never gets tired.
我的網球教練是個不屈不撓的人，似乎有用不完的精力，永遠都不覺得累。

0950 indigent [ˈɪndədʒənt]   貧窮的

★★★★★

in, eager
陷入 (ind-＝in) 貧困 (ig＝ eager) 中

a. *poor; destitute; impoverished; needy; penniless; penurious*

The millionaire was from an indigent family. He had to support his family as soon as he graduated from high school.
百萬富翁來自貧窮家庭，高中一畢業就得養家。

Tea Time... ☕

<Greek myth> nectar The drink of the gods.	〈來自希臘神話〉神酒 希臘神話中眾神飲用的酒稱為「神酒」。（註：後世因此將此字引申為「瓊漿玉液、美酒、甘美飲料、花蜜」等。）

❖ **nectar** [ˈnɛktə] **n.** *any delicious beverage; the sweetish liquid in many flowers, used by bees for the making of honey* | 花蜜

Bees are known to collect nectar from various flowers to make honey. It is said that a bee has to travel about 25,000 times from its hive to flowers to make a pound of honey.
眾所周知蜜蜂採集多種花蜜以釀製蜂蜜。據說蜜蜂每釀製一磅蜂蜜就須在蜂巢和花朵間往返飛行兩萬五千趟。

1 Complete each word by filling in the blank with proper spelling so that it has the same meaning as suggested. Then please write the meaning of each word in Chinese.

1. 使結果實 = _ _ _ _ _ i f y
2. 達成 = f u l _ _ _ _
3. 反對 = g a i n _ _ _
4. 比手畫腳 = _ _ _ _ i c u l a t e
5. 極大的 = _ _ _ _ _ l y
6. 巨大的 = _ _ _ _ _ _ i c
7. 冰河 = _ _ _ _ _ e r
8. 有光澤的 = _ _ _ _ _ y
9. 堂皇的 = _ _ _ _ _ i o s e
10. 便利的 = _ _ _ _ y

11. glacial = _____
12. henpecked = _____
13. hollow = _____
14. humane = _____
15. impasse = _____
16. implacable = _____
17. inanimate = _____
18. incorrigible = _____
19. incriminate = _____
20. indefatigable = _____

2 Choose a word that best completes the sentence.

21. The Titanic sank into the _____ depths of the North Atlantic in April, 1912.
    (A) gigantic   (B) immense   (C) glacial   (D) slight

22. Desks and chairs are _____ things. They have no life.
    (A) destitute   (B) inanimate   (C) assiduous   (D) incorrigible

23. Birds have _____ bones because light weight is important for flight.
    (A) hollow   (B) frightful   (C) hefty   (D) hindmost

3 The highlighted word is closest in meaning to which of the following?

24. The manager was considered by many to be haughty .
    (A) arrogant   (B) careless   (C) unwary   (D) inadvertent

25. The man was from an indigent family. He made a desperate effort to make more money.
    (A) relentless   (B) destitute   (C) essential   (D) inapplicable

MP3
40

0951 indisputable [ˌɪndɪˈspjutəbl]　　　　無庸置疑的，不容懷疑的，確實的　　★★★★★
a. certain; indubitable; sure; unquestionable
The evidence against the defendant was indisputable and the judge sentenced him to five years in jail.
被告因罪證確鑿遭法官判處五年徒刑。

dispute
不能 (in-) 提出討論 (dispute) 的

0952 indubitable [ɪnˈdjubɪtəbl]　　　　不容置疑的，明白的　　★★★★★
a. indisputable; incontrovertible; undeniable; unquestionable
Her reputation as a master detective was indubitable, since she had personally solved over seventy-five murders and burglaries.
她身為刑事專家的聲望不容置疑，因為曾破獲超過七十五件殺人和搶劫案。

doubt
不能 (in-) 起疑心 (doubt) 的

0953 inert [ɪnˈɜt]　　　　非活性的，不起化學作用的　　★★★★☆
a. inactive; dull; having few or no active properties
Helium is an inert gas since it rarely reacts with other chemical elements.
氦氣是非活性氣體，幾乎不和其他化學物質起作用。

energy
沒有 (in-) 活力 (ert-＝energy) 的

0954 infallible [ɪnˈfæləbl]　　　　絕對正確的，絕對可靠的，絕對有效的　　★★★★☆
a. faultless; flawless; impeccable; certain; sure
Having lived on the island for over thirty years, Mr. White was an infallible guide and delighted in taking tourists to famous places.
已在島上居住超過三十年的懷特先生是最可靠的嚮導，而且樂意帶觀光客到各名勝景點參觀。

fallacy
沒有 (in-) 失誤 (fall;fallacy) 的

0955 infamous [ˈɪnfəməs]　　　　罪大惡極的，惡名昭彰的，聲名狼藉的　　★★★☆☆
a. notorious; vile; flagrant; sinister; wicked
He was an infamous criminal, and when he was sentenced to fifty years in prison, many of the common citizens breathed a collective sigh of relief.
罪大惡極的罪犯被判入獄服刑五十年時，許多老百姓都鬆了一口氣。

fame
沒有 (in-) 好的名聲 (fame)

0956 infantile [ˈɪnfənˌtaɪl]　　　　幼稚的，像小孩似的　　★★★★☆
a. childish; immature; puerile
Mr. Brown always acts like a child in front of his wife regardless of who is present, so she wishes he would stop his infantile behavior.
伯朗先生在妻子面前總是表現得像個孩子，完全不管當時有誰在場。妻子希望他能停止這種幼稚行為。

infant
如嬰兒 (infant) 般的

0957 infernal [ɪnˈfɜnl]　　　　地獄的　　★★★☆☆
a. hellish; diabolical; fiendish
They averred that the symbol was not mere scarlet cloth, tinged in an earthly dye-pot, but was red-hot with infernal fire.
　　　　　　　　The Scarlet Letter —— Nathaniel Hawthorne
他們堅稱那個符號不只是在世俗染缸裡染過的紅布，更是有著地獄之火的熾熱記號。
　　　　　　　　　　　　　　　　—— 《紅字》霍桑

inferior
比這個世界更差、更低下的 (inferior)

0958 infiltrate [ɪnˈfɪltret]　　　　使滲入，使滲透 / 潛入，侵入　　★★★★☆
v. penetrate; permeate / infringe; invade
Due to the geographical configuration of the many small islands, the military leaders unanimously decided to infiltrate the main island from the northeast.
軍事領袖們基於各小島的地理結構，一致決定從東北方潛入主島。

filter
使放入 (in-) 濾器 (filter) 中

0959 infinitesimal [ˌɪnfɪnəˋtɛsəml] ★★★★☆
微小的，無限小的，極小的
infinite, small
小 (small) 到沒有 (in-) 盡頭的 (fin)
a. too small to be measured; infinitely small
These crystals are powdery and infinitesimal, measuring less than 10 microns in diameter. They are invisible to the naked eye.
這些粉末狀的結晶體非常微小，直徑小於十微米，是肉眼看不見的。

0960 infirmity [ɪnˋfɝmətɪ] ★★★★★
虛弱
firm
不 (in-) 結實 (firm) 的
n. debility; decrepitude; feebleness; frailty; weakness
Old age had brought with it great infirmity to the champion's once healthy and strong body, and now he could barely lift the arm that had once thrown men nearly ten meters.
年邁使一度非常健壯的冠軍選手變得十分虛弱，現在幾乎抬不起曾徒手將人擲出十公尺外的手臂。

0961 inflammable [ɪnˋflæməbl] ★★★★☆
可燃的，易燃的
flame
裡面 (in-) 容易點燃火花 (flame) 的
a. combustible; flammable; ignitable
The solution Sam was carrying was inflammable, so that's why when he got too close to the fire it went up in flames, and he got third degree burns all over his legs.
山姆攜帶的溶液是易燃的，所以太靠近火時才會造成火勢延燒，他的腿也因此受到三度灼傷。

0962 inflammatory [ɪnˋflæməˌtɔrɪ] ★★★☆☆
激動的，煽動的
flame
點燃人們內心 (in-) 的火花 (flame)
a. incendiary; provocative; revolutionary; seditious
In the beginning, everyone's emotions seemed to be controlled, but as the discussion progressed, tempers began to fly, and in the end there were many inflammatory remarks made by all parties involved.
一開始時大家情緒似乎還算冷靜，但隨著討論繼續，情緒也隨之高漲，最後所有與會者都言辭激動。

0963 inimical [ɪnˋɪmɪkl] ★★★☆☆
有敵意的，不友善的
enemy
視為敵對 (inimi＝enemy) 的
a. hostile; unfriendly
The mountain with hoary hair appeared inimical to us human beings. The top of the mountain is covered with glaciers.
對人類而言山頂被冰河覆蓋的白頭山看來似乎不太友善。

0964 iniquity [ɪˋnɪkwətɪ] ★★★★☆
不公正，不法 / 邪惡
equal
不 (in-) 公平的 (equal) 對待
n. lack of righteousness or justice / evil; wrongdoing
Many of her self-righteous neighbors viewed her home as a den of iniquity, since it was well known that she held wild parties that had a tendency to last late into the night.
許多自以為是的鄰居都認為她家是罪惡淵藪，因為眾所皆知她常在家中舉行瘋狂派對徹夜狂歡。

0965 initial [ɪˋnɪʃəl] ★★★★★
最初的，開始的
initiative
開始的 (initiative)
a. first; earliest; original; primary
His wife's initial response to his proposal of marriage was 'No.'
妻子對他求婚的最初答覆是「不要」。

0966 initiate [ɪˋnɪʃɪˏet]　　　　發起，創始，開始　　　initiative
v. begin; commence; inaugurate; launch; start　　　具有首創精神 (initiative)
★★★★★
Our government has initiated a tax reform, and the chief beneficiaries are expected to be the workers in the lower-income bracket.
我國政府開始推動稅制革新，預料最主要的受惠者將是低收入勞工階層。

0967 inordinate [ɪnˋɔrdn̩ɪt]　　　格外的，過度的，極度的　　　ordinary
a. excessive; exorbitant; extravagant; extreme; immoderate; towering; undue　　　不是 (in-) 普通的 (ordinary)
★★★★☆
He was not a good student, and it took him an inordinate length of time to graduate from university.
他不是好學生，而且花了很長時間才從大學畢業。

0968 insatiable [ɪnˋseʃəbl]　　　貪得無厭的，不知足的，永不滿足的　　　satisfy
a. unquenchable; that cannot be satisfied or appeased　　　無法 (in-) 使之滿足的 (satisfy)
★★★★☆
The forest fire seemed insatiable as it devoured acres of trees and foliage. People could do nothing but watch it spread.
森林大火貪婪吞噬許多林木和樹葉，人們無能為力只能眼睜睜看著大火延燒。

0969 insipid [ɪnˋsɪpɪd]　　　沒有味道的，清淡的，難吃的　　　sip, sap
a. unpalatable; distasteful; tasteless　　　沒有 (in-) 汁液或水分 (sap)
★★★★☆
Christine was never able to cook as well as her mother, and so her meals were always insipid and tasteless.
克莉絲汀不像母親一樣會做菜，所以她烹煮的料理總是淡而無味又難吃。

0970 insular [ˋɪnsələ]　　　狹隘的，胸襟狹窄的，氣量小的　　　island
a. narrow-minded; limited; restricted; confined　　　島國 (island) 人民的心理
★★★★☆
Her insular attitude had made it difficult for anyone to become close to her. She died an unmarried and lonely old woman.
她心胸狹窄難以親近，最後孤老而終。

0971 insulate [ˋɪnsəˏlet]　　　隔離，使孤立，使絕緣，使隔音，使隔熱　　　island
v. isolate; segregate; separate or cover with a nonconducting material in order to prevent the passage or leakage of electricity, heat, sound, radioactive particles, etc.　　　被丟到島 (island) 上
★★★★★
Make sure the wires are insulated before using them outdoors. Otherwise the leakage of electricity may cause an accident.
在戶外使用電線須確保有效絕緣，否則一旦漏電就會釀成災害。

0972 intimidate [ɪnˋtɪməˏdet]　　　威嚇，脅迫，恐嚇　　　timid
v. browbeat; bulldoze; bully; cow; scare; frighten　　　在某人心中 (in-) 置入恐懼 (timid)
★★★★★
Bill could easily intimidate people just by his sheer size and ugliness, which is why he was such a good debt collector before he was sent to prison.
比利單憑龐大身軀和醜陋外貌就足以輕易威嚇人，這正是為什麼他在入獄前是極佳的收帳員。

0973 investigation [ɪnˏvɛstəˋgeʃən]　　　調查，審查，研究　　　FBI (Federal Bureau of Investigation)
n. inquiry; inquest; inquisition; probe; quest　　　為了找尋蛛絲馬跡 (vestige) 而展開調查 (Investigation) 的 FBI
★★★★★
The Bermuda Triangle is an area of the Atlantic Ocean where lots of ships and planes have disappeared. There have been many fruitless investigations to get convincing answers to the mysteries of the triangle.

大西洋海域中的百慕達三角洲是許多船隻和飛機的消失地,因此許多調查紛紛展開,設法為謎團提出有力答案,但卻徒勞無功。

0974 inveterate [ɪnˋvɛtərɪt] ★★★☆☆ 　　　　　根深柢固的,積習的
a. confirmed; chronic; habituated; hardened

Life in the orphanage had always been strict and severe, and lying became a way of life. By the time he finally left and found a foster family, he had become an inveterate liar.

孤兒院生活嚴苛使撒謊成了家常便飯,等他終於找到領養家庭,卻變成習慣撒謊的人。

veteran
陷入如老兵 (veteran) 般頑固舊習中

0975 irreparable [ɪˋrɛpərəbl] ★★★★☆ 　　　　　無法挽回的,不能修補的
a. irrecoverable; incurable

My cousin did irreparable damage to my computer by plugging it into an outlet with higher voltage.

表弟把我的電腦插在高壓電插座上,造成無可挽救的損壞。

repair
不能修理 (repair) 的

0976 jellyfish [ˋdʒɛlɪˌfɪʃ] ★★★☆☆ 　　水母 / 沒骨氣的人,軟弱無能者
n. any of a member of free-swimming marine coelenterates, with a body made up largely of jellylike substances and shaped like an umbrella / a weak-willed person

A jellyfish which lives in the sea has a jellylike body. Some species, despite their delicate appearance, are extremely poisonous.

身體像果凍般的水母棲息在海中,部分品種雖然外觀美麗但其實帶有劇毒。

jelly
像果凍 (jelly) 般軟溜溜的動物或人

0977 jeopardy [ˋdʒɛpədɪ] ★★★★★ 　　　　　　　危險
n. danger; hazard; peril; risk

While the climbers got lost on the mountain, their lives were in jeopardy. They did not know that there would an avalanche.

在山裡失蹤的登山客生命已陷入危險,因為不知道會有雪崩。

joke, part
把部分 (part) 問題視為玩笑 (joke) 將會出現危險

0978 jettison [ˋdʒɛtəsn̩] ★★★☆☆ 　(自飛機、船艦上) 將 (貨物、飛彈等) 投棄
v. discard; abdicate; throw away; dump

A rocket is employed to launch an artificial satellite, and is then jettisoned in space.

利用火箭發射人造衛星投棄於太空中。

jet
從尾部噴射而出的噴射引擎 (jet)

0979 jocular [ˋdʒɑkjələ] ★★★☆☆ 　　　　　滑稽的,愛開玩笑的
a. witty; facetious; humorous; jocose

A jocular attitude is often an asset to an employee in a very routine job since laughter helps to alleviate the boredom.

詼諧心態對從事例行公事的員工來說是有利條件,因為笑聲可緩和無聊氣氛。

joke
很會說笑話 (joke) 的

0980 judicial [dʒuˋdɪʃəl] ★★★★☆ 　　　　　法官的,司法的
a. of judges, law courts or their functions

The highest court of the judicial branch of the federal government, or the Supreme Court, is the highest level of authority that a judge can aspire to.

聯邦政府下轄的高等法院法官席或稱最高法院,是法官嚮往的最高權威。

judge
和法官 (judge) 有關的

0981 judicious [dʒuˈdɪʃəs]　　　　　　　　　　明智的
a. wise; prudent; sensible; sage

When the boss chose Lynn for the promotion, he knew that despite everyone else's opinion, he had made a most judicious decision, since she was the most qualified and the hardest working.

老闆升琳恩時知道不管別人說什麼這個決定都是最明智的，因為她最有資格又賣力。

★★★★★
judge
有判斷 (judge) 能力的

0982 juror [ˈdʒʊrə]　　　　　　　　　　陪審員
n. a member of a jury

Mr. Joyce was asked to serve as a member of a jury. He was sworn in, together with eleven other jurors.

喬伊斯先生受邀加入陪審團，和其他十一名陪審員一起宣誓。

★★★★★
jury
由數名陪審員 (juror) 組成的陪審團 (jury)

0983 ken [kɛn]　　　　　視野，眼界／知識範圍，理解範圍
n. the extent of one's recognition, comprehension, perception, understanding, or knowledge / grasp

Mrs. Joyce could not understand her partner's extraordinary behavior. His eccentricity is beyond her ken.

喬伊斯太太不明白先生的反常行為，他的古怪超乎理解範圍。

★★★★☆
know
理解的 (know) 範圍

0984 kernel [ˈkɝnl̩]　　　　　　　　　核心，要點
n. core; gist; nub; substance

What in the world is the kernel of your argument? I mean, I can't understand what you are talking about.

你的論證要點到底是什麼？我不懂你在說什麼。

★★★★☆
corn
像穀粒 (corn) 般重要之物

0985 kindle [ˈkɪndl̩]　　　　　　　　　　使明亮
v. light; illuminate; make bright

The bright moon kindled the countryside. We could see the roads so clearly that we needed no flashlights.

明亮的月光照亮鄉間，小路清晰得不需要手電筒。

★★★★☆
candle
使像蠟燭 (candle) 般明亮

0986 kindred [ˈkɪndrɪd]　　　　　親屬關係，血緣，家族
n. clan; folk; stock

When the farmer got together with everyone in his family, including distant cousins and their spouses, his kindred numbered nearly one hundred people.

農夫加上所有家人、遠親及其配偶，整個家族將近百人。

★★★★☆
kin
家屬，同類 (kin)

0987 kingpin [ˈkɪŋˌpɪn]　　　　　　　首腦，核心人物
n. the main or essential person or thing

The person in the middle wearing a suit is the kingpin of the gang. I want all of you to remember his face.

站在中間身穿西裝的就是幫派首腦，大家要記住他的長相。

★★★★★
king, pin
保齡球中央瓶 (kingpin)

0988 kneel [nil]　　　　　　　　　　　跪下
v. bend or rest on a knee or the knees

The betrayer was caught by the other members of the gang and forced to kneel before his angry boss.

背叛者被幫派成員逮到，逼他跪在盛怒首腦面前。

★★★★★
knee
膝蓋 (knee)

0989 laboratory [`læbrə,tɔrɪ] ★★★★☆ 實驗室，研究室
n. a room or building for scientific experimentation or research
The explosion was created by the chemicals in the laboratory. All the scientists there were shell-shocked.
實驗室裡的化學藥品引發爆炸，嚇壞現場所有科學家。

labor
工作 (labor) 場所 (-tory)

0990 laborious [lə`bɔrɪəs] ★★★★☆ 吃力的，費力的
a. hard; arduous; strenuous; toilsome
After running nearly to the top of the mountain, his breathing had become loud and laborious, and he decided that it would be a good time to quit smoking.
跑到快接近山巔時，氣喘吁吁的他決定是時候該戒煙了。

labor
需要賣力工作 (labor) 的

0991 labor-saving [`lebə,sevɪŋ] ★★★☆☆ 省力的
a. eliminating or lessening physical labor
The computer, while being a great labor-saving device, has removed the personality and friendliness as well as the sloppiness and disorganization of paperwork.
電腦是極省力的裝置，雖抹煞了日常文書工作中的人性與親切，但也消除了混亂和無組織。

labor, save
節省力氣 (saving) 工作 (labor)

0992 laggard [`lægəd] ★★★☆☆ 動作緩慢者，遲鈍者，落後者，懶散者
n. slowpoke; sluggard; dawdler
When it comes to asking for a raise, my colleague James is no laggard. However, he is always tardy in the morning.
同事詹姆斯說到要求加薪從不落人後，但上班總是遲到。

lag
落後 (lag) 於後面的人 (-ard)

0993 largesse [`lɑrdʒɪs] ★☆☆☆☆ 慷慨贈與
n. generosity; philanthropy
The 100,000-dollar largesse from an anonymous benefactor made it possible for the charity organization to feed the homeless in the community.
匿名捐助者十萬元的慷慨贈禮讓慈善機構得以照顧社區流浪街友。

large
懷有寬大 (large) 心胸

0994 lassitude [`læsə,tjud] ★★☆☆☆ 疲勞，倦怠
n. fatigue; exhaustion; weariness
After working for ten hours, and then drinking for three more, he always felt an overwhelming lassitude when he finally arrived home.
工作十小時再喝了三小時酒後，他回到家總覺得極度疲倦。

lazy
懶洋洋 (lazy) 的

0995 lax [læks] ★★★☆☆ 馬虎的，散漫的
a. lazy; neglectful; negligent
We often hear James say that his wife is a lax housekeeper. But we do not think that he is so neat in his office work.
詹姆斯常說妻子持家馬虎，但自己的辦公室工作也做得差強人意。

relax
鬆懈 (relax) 的

0996 layer [`leə] ★★★★★ 層
n. thickness of material laid over a surface or forming a horizontal division
The explorer wore layer upon layer of winter clothes, but he was still cold in the bitter northern winter.
探險家穿了一件件冬衣，但在嚴寒刺骨的北國冬天仍覺得很冷。

lay
橫置 (lay) 之物 (-er)

0997 legislature [ˈlɛdʒɪsˌletʃɚ]　　　　　　　　　　立法機構　| legal
n. the lawmaking body of a state　　　　　　　　　　　　　　　| 訂立法律 (legal) 之處

The United States of America has a bicameral legislature, which has two chambers; the House and the Senate.
美國有參、眾兩院制的立法機構。

0998 legitimate [lɪˈdʒɪtəmɪt]　　　　　　　　　　合法的，正統的　| legal
a. legal; lawful　　　　　　　　　　　　　　　　　　　　　　| 合乎法律 (legal) 的

After Prohibition was abolished, many bootleggers who smuggled alcohol from Canada turned into legitimate businessmen.
禁酒令廢除後，從加拿大走私販賣私酒者都成了合法生意人。

0999 lessen [ˈlɛsn̩]　　　　　　　　　　變小，變少，減輕　| less
v. reduce; abate; alleviate　　　　　　　　　　　　　　　　| 變成 (-en) 較少的 (less)

The nurse applied some ointment on the athlete's wound and after a while it came to lessen the pain.
護士在運動員傷口上塗抹藥膏後，過一陣子痛楚就減輕了。

1000 liberate [ˈlɪbəˌret]　　　　　　　　　　使自由，解放，釋放　| liberty
v. free; discharge; emancipate; release; unshackle　　　　　| 給予自由 (liberty)

The animal lover conspired to liberate all the circus animals. But the animals were tied up with chains or held in cages.
愛護動物者想釋放馬戲團的表演動物，但牠們全被鏈子栓住或關在籠裡。

Tea Time... ☕

<From the name of a city>
Magnet
Magnet was originally discovered in Magnesia, ancient city in Asia Minor.

〈來自城市名〉磁石
磁石最早是在小亞細亞古城梅格尼西亞發現的。（註：西元前六世紀希臘科學家在梅格尼西亞發現一種具有吸力的礦石，從此 magnesia 這個地名便成了英文 magnet「磁」的字根。）

❖ **magnetic** [mægˈnɛtɪk] *a. actuated by magnetic attraction* | 有磁性的

To enter the research institute the researchers had to use magnetic cards. The security of the institute was almost perfect.
研究員進入研究大樓須使用磁卡，大樓安全幾乎滴水不漏。

1 Complete each word by filling in the blank with proper spelling so that it has the same meaning as suggested. Then please write the meaning of each word in Chinese.

1. 絕對可靠的 = i n _ _ _ _ i b l e
2. 罪大惡極的 = i n _ _ _ o u s
3. 地獄的 = _ _ _ _ _ n a l
4. 潛入 = i n _ _ _ _ _ a t e
5. 微小的 = _ _ _ _ _ _ _ _ s i m a l
6. 激動的 = i n _ _ _ _ m a t o r y
7. 可燃的 = _ _ f l a m m a b l e
8. 發起 = _ _ _ _ _ a t e
9. 極度的 = i n _ _ _ _ _ a t e
10. 沒有味道的 = i n _ _ _ i d

11. intimidate = _____
12. investigation = _____
13. irreparable = _____
14. jettison = _____
15. jocular = _____
16. judicial = _____
17. judicious = _____
18. juror = _____
19. kindred = _____
20. kneel = _____

2 Choose a word that best completes the sentence.

21. This math problem is beyond my _____. I cannot solve it.
   (A) ken   (B) core   (C) substance   (D) gist

22. After long hours of _____ work, the worker was exhausted.
   (A) combustible   (B) laborious   (C) infinitesimal   (D) ignitable

3 The highlighted word is closest in meaning to which of the following?

23. Hey, you laggard . Please hurry up.
   (A) jeopardy   (B) fatigue   (C) hazard   (D) slowpoke

24. I tried to lessen my workload by handing over some of my work to the new hand.
   (A) discharge   (B) emancipate (C) reduce   (D) liberate

25. Jack tried to intimidate his classmates by bluffing.
   (A) segregate   (B) scare   (C) commence   (D) inaugurate

Practice Test 02

1

The highlighted word is closest in meaning to which of the following?

1. It was reported that the `drought` **in Australia was unprecedented.**
(A) dryness
(B) duration
(C) dweller
(D) embodiment

2. I wonder whether this mushroom is `edible` **or not.**
(A) embarrassed
(B) equivalent
(C) eatable
(D) erroneous

3. The maintenance of his car is so `exorbitant` **that Mr. Baker has decided to sell it.**
(A) extramarital
(B) excessive
(C) fallible
(D) fanatic

4. His daughter is `finicky` **about food and eats like a bird.**
(A) fastidious
(B) foolhardy
(C) flammable
(D) glossy

5. Because of the `laborious` **work at the office, he gets back home exhausted.**
(A) jocular
(B) judicious
(C) arduous
(D) legitimate

2

Please answer the following questions.

> **(Comic Tale 1)**
>
> New Orleans was experiencing an `execrable` rainy period. It had rained for 4 consecutive days without any letup in sight and many low-lying areas were deluged. Almost all of the farm houses in Jack's village were inundated and the villagers were `dispirited`. At last the rain abated and several days later the villagers who had been `evacuated` to the nearest elementary school got back to their severely damaged homes. All the villagers, young and old, cooperated to restore their dilapidated abodes and to reorganize all the shattered stuff. Jack asked one of his neighbors how much damage the storm had caused him. The neighbor responded, "Darn it! Damn carp ate all the corn I planted in the backyard. I caught some of them in the attic!"

(Comic Tale 2)

I visualize a subway train as a microcosm of the world. Diverse characteristics of various people can be found there; greediness, talkativeness, curiosity, altruism and even fastidiousness.

I was riding the subway to work, when a lady dressed up in snow-white attire, got into the train and stood in front of a middle-aged man instead of taking the empty seat just next to him. She readily took out her snow-white handkerchief from her handbag and wrapped the strap. She must have hated touching the surface of the strap. I didn't know why, but my curiosity allowed me to guess that she was germ-conscious or the strap was terribly sticky with cosmetics or something. In the meanwhile, the man sitting in front of her was dozing. The train was pulling into a station and the engineer's maneuvering of the brake was not infallible . The train came to a tremulous stop. Because of this, the finicky lady dropped her hankie, which fell onto the lapel of his suit and finally perched on the fly of his pants. The shaky stop must have disturbed the man. In a semi-conscious state, the man found the white patch of cloth. He must have thought that the hankie was the tail of his shirt. He inserted it into his pants and fell fast asleep again.

6. The word exorbitant is closest in meaning to which of the following?

(A) infantile (B) terrible

(C) errable (D) exorbitant

7. The word dispirited is closest in meaning to which of the following?

(A) depressed (B) distraught

(C) diurnal (D) edible

8. The word evacuated is closest in meaning to which of the following?

(A) withdrawn (B) incapacitated

(C) impoverished (D) kindled

9. The word infallible is closest in meaning to which of the following?

(A) judicious (B) sensible

(C) laborious (D) flawless

10. The word finicky is closest in meaning to which of the following?

(A) infernal (B) infamous

(C) inert (D) fastidious

MP3
42

1001 libertine [`lɪbəˌtin]　　　　　★☆☆☆☆　　放蕩者，酒色之徒　　liberty

n. a man who leads an unrestrained, sexually immoral life; rake

貪圖解放和自由 (liberty) 的人

That libertine was expelled from the Catholic school. His behavior was thought to be inexcusable.

放蕩者被逐出天主教學校，因其行為不可饒恕。

1002 licentious [laɪ`sɛnʃəs]　　　★★☆☆☆　　放蕩的，放肆的　　license

a. profligate; reprobate

做什麼都好像都被允許 (license)

The prosecutor did not doubt that the licentious man had committed sexual harassment toward her. Therefore, he began to search for some evidence.

檢察官不懷疑登徒子對她性騷擾，於是開始收集相關證據。

1003 lineage [`lɪnɪdʒ]　　　　　★★★★★　　血統，家世　　line

n. ancestry; blood; descent; extraction; origin; pedigree

一個家族行列 (line)

In the past, during the Yi Dynasty, a man of humble lineage had little chance to become a high-ranking official.

在朝鮮李朝時代，出身卑微者少有機會成為朝廷高官。

1004 linguistics [lɪŋ`gwɪstɪks]　　★★★★★　　語言學　　language

n. the science of language, including phonology, morphology, syntax and semantics

學習語言 (language)

He had a great command of linguistics, but because he was so shy he could never find the right words to say to a pretty girl.

他的語言學造詣很高，但因為太害羞而不知道該跟漂亮女子說什麼。

1005 liquidate [`lɪkwɪˌdet]　　　★★★★☆　　根除，除去，清償　　liquid

v. clear; purge; eliminate; remove; uproot; eradicate

丟入液體 (liquid) 中消失

The soldier liquidated the enemy soldiers single-handedly. Later he was given a medal of honor for his heroic act.

士兵單憑一己之力就除掉敵軍，隨後因英勇行為獲頒勳章。

1006 livelihood [ˌlaɪvlɪˌhʊd]　　★★★★★　　生計　　live

n. living; subsistence; sustenance

為生活 (live) 而必須做的工作

The last few decades have seen many Korean women who have earned their own livelihood or have helped to earn the livelihood of their families.

近幾十年來有許多韓國婦女獨立養活自己或協助扛起家計。

1007 longevity [lɑn`dʒɛvətɪ]　　★★★★☆　　長壽，長命　　long

n. long life; great span of life

活得長 (long)

Many species of sea turtles enjoy such longevity that we don't know exactly how long they can live.

許多海龜壽命極長，不知道究竟會活多久。

1008 longitude [`lɑndʒəˌtud]　　★★★★★　　經度，經線　　long

n. distance east or west of the Greenwich meridian, measured in degrees

由上而下畫出的長 (long) 線

The longitude of a particular place is measured from the prime meridian, which lies across Greenwich, England.

一地的經度多寡是從經過英國格林威治的本初子午線開始測量的。

1009 lower [`loɚ] ★★★★★

降低，減少

low
使往低處 (low) 降

v. demean; degrade; reduce in height, amount, value, etc.

The alluvial deposits that have been accumulating over the years are now posing a problem In that the clay and gravel contents are lowering the quality of the soil.

經年累積的沖積物沉澱，如今造成問題，泥沙含量降低了土壤品質。

1010 luscious [`lʌʃəs] ★★★☆☆

美味的，香甜的

delicious
截取 delicious (美味的) 一字的後半段字母來造字

a. delectable; delicious; yummy; palatable

In the Garden of Eden, Eve could not resist the temptation of the luscious fruit and the sweet talk of the serpent.

伊甸園裡的夏娃禁不起甜美果實的誘惑和蛇的花言巧語。

1011 mammal [`mæml] ★★★★★

哺乳動物

mom
吃母 (mom) 奶的

n. animals that give birth to live offspring and feed their young on milk from the breast

The walrus is a gregarious aquatic mammal and is found in arctic waters. Like a whale it gives birth to a cub.

海象是住在北極海域的群居水棲哺乳動物，跟鯨一樣哺育幼獸。

1012 mandatory [`mændə,tɔrɪ] ★★★★☆

強制的，必須的，命令的

command
必須按照命令 (command) 去做的

a. compulsory; imperative; obligatory; required

I think I'll have to attend the meeting because attendance is mandatory. Anybody who does not come will be fined.

因為強制出席所以我必須參加會議，缺席者將處以罰金。

1013 marital [`mærətl] ★★☆☆☆

婚姻的，夫妻間的

marriage
和結婚 (marriage) 有關的

a. nuptial; matrimonial; conjugal

Their marital problems were never serious enough to overcome the bliss and harmony they felt when they got married.

他們的婚姻問題不大，不足以傷害婚姻生活的美滿快樂。

1014 masquerade [,mæskə`red] ★☆☆☆☆

化裝舞會

masque, mask
每人都戴面具 (masque)

n. a formal dance at which masks and other disguises are worn

Every Halloween his school throws a fantastic masquerade ball that is the social event of the year.

他就讀的學校每到萬聖節都會舉辦盛大的化裝舞會，作為年度聯誼盛事。

1015 masterful [`mæstəfəl] ★★☆☆☆

熟練的，出色的，精彩的

master
如大師 (master) 般的

a. proficient; adept; expert; masterly; skilled; skillful; adroit; deft; dexterous

With a masterful final stroke, the famous artist finally completed the smile on his version of the Mona Lisa's face, although people still preferred the original.

著名畫家以精彩的最後一筆完成蒙娜麗莎微笑作品，但大家還是較喜歡原作。

1016 maternal [mə`tɜnl] ★★★★☆

母親的，母系的

mother
媽媽 (mater-＝mother) 的

a. of or like a mother; related through the mother's side of the family

One of the animals which is famous for maternal affection is a monkey. A mother monkey will refuse to eat anything if her baby is dead.

猴子以母愛著稱，如果幼猴死掉，母猴會拒絕進食。

1017 maternity [mə`tɜnətɪ] ★★★☆☆ 母愛，產婦

n. motherhood

In order to reduce the maternity and infant mortality rates, more and more mother-child health clinics are being established in our country.

為了降低產婦和嬰兒死亡率，國內開辦許多母子健診中心。

mother
成為媽媽 (mater- =mother)

1018 memoir [`mɛmwɑr] ★★☆☆☆ 回憶錄

n. autobiography

A memoir of a great explorer which is thought to have been written in the early 16th century was found.

完成於十六世紀初的偉大探險家回憶錄已經找到了。

memory
寫下記憶 (memory) 中的事物

1019 mercantile [`mɜkən‚til] ★★☆☆☆ 商業的，商人的

a. of trade and commerce; of merchants

The people's strong mercantile tendencies have allowed them to succeed in the cutthroat world of international trade.

人民強烈的經商傾向讓他們在全球國際貿易割喉戰中勝出。

merchant
重視商人 (merchant) 的

1020 merchandise [`mɜtʃən‚daɪz] ★★★★★ 商品，貨品

n. commodities; goods

The merchandise they sold was inferior to that found in the large department stores, but since they undercut their competitor, they always seemed to make money.

他們賣的商品品質比大百貨公司的還要差，但因價格較便宜所以似乎有獲利。

merchant
商人 (merchant) 販售之物

1021 mercurial [mɜ`kjurɪəl] ★★☆☆☆ 多變的 / 善變的，輕浮的

a. mobile / capricious; changeable; volatile

His wife was impossible to please because of her mercurial nature, which was like the weather in London.

他妻子如倫敦天氣般的善變個性極難取悅。

mercury
如水銀 (mercury) 般滾動而形狀多變的

1022 mettle [`mɛtl] ★☆☆☆☆ 毅力，勇氣

n. courage; guts; pluck; spirit

Nancy is a lady of some mettle. Everybody is sure she will not be afraid when she delivers her speech.

南西很有毅力，大家確信她演講時不會害怕。

metal
如金屬 (metal) 般堅毅

1023 midst [mɪdst] ★★★☆☆ 當中，中間

n. middle

In the midst of all the excitement, she suddenly realized that she had forgotten her purse at home, and so she had no money.

她在一陣興奮中突然發現皮包忘在家裡，所以身上沒錢。

middle
中間 (middle)

1024 militia [mɪ`lɪʃə] ★☆☆☆☆ 民兵部隊，義勇軍，自衛隊

n. force of civilians who are trained as soldiers and reinforce the regular army in the internal defense of the country in an emergency

At last the governor and other officials decided to call in the militia to put down the disturbance at the City Hall.

最後州長和其他官員決定召集自衛隊鎮壓市政府暴動。

military
鎮壓示威的軍隊 (military)

1025 misappropriation [ˌmɪsəproprɪˈeʃən]　　　　　侵吞　★★☆☆☆

n. embezzlement; peculation

The corrupt government official who was convicted of misappropriation was divested of all authority.

獲判侵吞罪的腐敗政府官員被褫奪公權。

proper, appropriate

不 (mis-) 適當地 (proper) 取用

MP3 43

1026 miscellaneous [ˌmɪsḷˈenɪəs]　　　　林林總總的，各式各樣的　★★★☆☆

a. varied; various; heterogeneous; diverse; diversified

At the garage sale everybody was interested in miscellaneous goods which filled the small garage.

大家對塞滿小小車庫的各類跳蚤市場商品很感興趣。

miscellany

如散文雜集 (miscellany) 般多樣的

1027 mischance [mɪsˈtʃæns]　　　　　　　不幸，橫禍　★★★☆☆

n. accident; mishap; misfortune; disaster

When the driver fell asleep at the wheel and drove through the storefront, some shoppers in the store were hurt in the mischance.

駕駛人打瞌睡把車開進店面，導致部分顧客在這起不幸意外中受傷。

chance

不好的 (mis-) 運勢 (chance)

1028 misfit [ˈmɪsˌfɪt]　　　　　　　　　不適應環境者　★★☆☆☆

n. a person not well suited to his work or his surroundings

Greg turned out to be a real misfit. He lacked the ability to adjust in his office. He felt alienated.

葛瑞格變得極不適應環境，他在辦公室裡無法適應而感到孤立。

fit

不 (mis-) 適應 (fit) 的人

1029 mishap [ˈmɪsˌhæp]　　　　　　　　　事故，災禍　★★★★☆

n. accident; casualty; mischance; misfortune; disaster

The explorers were fortunate; they returned home without any mishap. Everybody else thought that they were missing.

探險者幸運地毫髮未傷平安返家，大家都以為他們失蹤了。

happen

發生 (hap-) 不好的 (mis-) 事

1030 mobility [moˈbɪlətɪ]　　　　　　　　　　流動性　★★☆☆☆

n. being mobile

People are more likely to change jobs in our country than they are in Japan. There can be several possible explanations for the greater job mobility in our country.

我國人民比日本人更容易換工作，對此較高的工作流動性有幾種可能性的解釋。

move

帶有變動 (mob-＝move) 性質

1031 monetary [ˈmʌnəˌtɛrɪ]　　　　　　　　　貨幣的　★★★★☆

a. numismatic; pecuniary; financial; fiscal

Korea's monetary unit is the won and the US's is the dollar.

韓國貨幣單位是韓圜，至於美國則是美元。

money

和錢 (money) 有關的

1032 nasal [ˈnezḷ]　　　　　　　　　　　鼻子的，鼻中的　★★★☆☆

a. of or in the nose

The sister replied to her little brother's question with a nasal voice. Actually, she did not know why a lamb does not shrink even after it gets drenched in a shower, while wool does.

姊姊用鼻音回答弟弟問題，事實上她不知道為什麼羊洗澡後不會縮水，但羊毛卻會。

nose

和鼻子 (nose) 有關的

1033 **nationality** [ˌnæʃənˈælətɪ] ★★★★★ 國籍

n. membership of a particular nation

Even though the man was of a different nationality, she loved him anyway, and they planned to marry as soon as possible.

即使男子國籍不同她還是愛他，兩人計畫盡快完婚。

nation
屬於某國 (nation) 的

1034 **navigate** [ˈnævəˌget] ★★★★★ 駕駛

v. steer a ship; pilot an aircraft

After the pilot suffered a heart attack, no one knew how to navigate the aircraft. However, one of the passengers was able to contact the air traffic control tower with a cell phone.

飛行員心臟病發作但無人知道如何駕駛飛機，其中有名旅客總算用手機聯絡上機場管制塔台。

navy
如海軍 (navy) 航行於海上

1035 **needy** [ˈnidɪ] ★★★★★ 貧窮的

a. poor; destitute; indigent; impoverished

Every Christmas the church gathers food and money to give to the needy, homeless and less fortunate members of the community.

每逢耶誕節教會就會募集食物和金錢救助社區窮人、流浪街友和不幸者。

need
處於需要或缺乏 (need) 狀態

1036 **negligence** [ˈnɛɡlədʒəns] ★★★★★ 粗心，疏忽

n. neglect; default; delinquency; indolence

It was due to extreme negligence that the heater had not been properly serviced in ten years, so it wasn't really surprising when it exploded.

由於十年來暖氣機沒有妥善維修的嚴重疏失，最後爆炸了並不十分意外。

negative
不積極的，否定的 (negative)

1037 **numerous** [ˈnjumərəs] ★★★★★ 許多的

a. many

Benjamin Franklin was versatile; he made outstanding contributions in numerous fields. He even invented various things, such as a lightning rod, a swimming flipper, and a stove.

多才多藝的富蘭克林在許多領域都有傑出貢獻，甚至還發明避雷針、蛙鞋和省柴火爐等各種物品。

number
大的數字 (number)

1038 **obese** [oˈbis] ★★★★☆ 極肥胖的

a. fat; corpulent

Nutritionists recommend that obese people should follow a low-fat diet.

營養學家建議肥胖者應採低脂飲食。

over, eat
過度 (ob-＝over) 進食 (es-＝eat) 的

1039 **observatory** [əbˈzɜvəˌtorɪ] ★★★★☆ 天文台，氣象台

n. building from which the stars, the weather, etc. can be observed by scientists

Samuel started to work in the observatory after he graduated from college with a degree in astronomy.

山繆爾自大學畢業拿到天文學學位後就在天文台工作。

observe
觀察 (observe) 天空

1040 **offend** [əˈfɛnd] ★★★★☆ 冒犯，觸怒，得罪

v. irritate; provoke; displease; hurt one's feelings; pique

Sue's boss was deeply offended when she didn't invite him to her house-warming party. In fact, she did not want to hear a sermon from him, especially at a party.

fence
越過他人圍牆 (fence) 進入

蘇沒有邀請老闆參加喬遷派對，讓他感到很不舒服。事實上她尤其不想在宴會上聽他長篇大論。

Chapter

1
2
3
4
5

1041 offense [ə`fɛns]　　　　　　　　　　　　★★★★★

攻擊 / 犯罪，罪行

n. attack; aggression; assault / crime; misdeed

The boy was caught shoplifting at a department store, but because this was his first offense he was released with a warning.

男孩在商店行竊被逮，警方念其初犯口頭告誡後就釋放他了。

fence
推倒法院的牆 (fence)

1042 offensive [ə`fɛnsɪv]　　　　　　　　　　★★★★★

冒犯的，無禮的

a. unpleasant; distasteful; disgusting; nasty; repugnant; repulsive; disagreeable; dreadful; horrible

Even though my speech might be a little offensive to some, many participants will surely support it.

即使我的演講可能對某些人造成些許冒犯，相信必能得到許多與會者的支持。

fence
越過圍牆 (fence) 的攻擊

1043 offering [`ɔfərɪŋ]　　　　　　　　　　　★★★☆☆

捐款，供奉

n. donation; alms

The little boy who came to church for the first time hesitantly put some coins in the basket as his offering.

第一次到教堂的小男孩遲疑地將一些硬幣放進捐獻箱裡作為捐款。

offer
帶來呈獻 (offer) 之物

1044 offing [`ɔfɪŋ]　　　　　　　　　　　　　★★☆☆☆

遠方可見之海面 / 近在眼前

n. the part of the sea visible from the shore / being imminent

Most people in the country didn't notice that a war was in the offing. There was no declaration of war from the rival country.

多數人民都沒有注意到戰爭已近在眼前，因為敵國並未宣戰。

off
在海岸或沿岸 (off the coast)

1045 ominous [`ɑmənəs]　　　　　　　　　　　★★☆☆☆

不祥的

a. indicative of future misfortune or calamity; portentous; sinister

My friend's kind advice served no better purpose than to fill my mind with more ominous forebodings.

朋友的忠告不但無濟於事，反而更讓我心中充滿不祥預感。

omen
感到不好的徵兆 (omen)

1046 opaque [o`pek]　　　　　　　　　　　　★★☆☆☆

不透明的

a. obscure; not transparent

Opal is an opaque gem. Opal is often of a milky white color.

蛋白石是乳白色的不透明寶石。

opal
如蛋白石 (opal) 般不透明的

1047 opportune [ˌɑpə`tjun]　　　　　　　　　★★★☆☆

及時的，適時的

a. timely; well-timed

Jack thought that it was a very opportune moment for him to leave the office, before his boss made him work late.

傑克認為最好趕在老闆要他加班前就先離開公司。

opportunity
時機 (opportunity) 恰當的

1048 ordinance [`ɔrdn̩əns]　　　　　　　　　★★☆☆☆

法令，命令

n. decree; regulation; rule; statute; law

The town in the suburban area enforced an ordinance against honking the horn after midnight.

郊區小鎮執行法令，入夜後禁鳴汽車喇叭。

order
法律的命令 (order)

1049 originate [əˈrɪdʒəˌnet]   產生，發生／發起，創始，起源   ★★★★★

v. generate; arise / introduce; inaugurate; initiate

This fossil seems to have originated during the Jurassic period.

這塊化石似乎起源於侏羅紀時代。

| origin |
| 起源、誕生 (origin) |

1050 ornate [ɔrˈnet]   裝飾華麗的／浮誇的，炫耀的   ★★★☆☆

a. elaborately and often pretentiously decorated or designed / flamboyant

The report that he submitted to his superior was fancy and very ornate, yet was lacking in substance and worth.

他提交給上司的報告文采華麗但缺乏內容。

| ornament |
| 極力裝飾 (ornament) |

Tea Time... ☕

<Aesop's Fable>	〈伊索寓言〉
A fox, after futile efforts to reach some grapes, scorns them as being sour.	搆不著葡萄的狐狸不屑地表示那是酸的。（註：「酸葡萄心理」是藉貶低自己得不到的東西來合理化個人失望的心情，也就是一種自我安慰心理。）

❖ **sour grape** [ˈsaurˌgrep] *n. a scorning or belittling of something only because it cannot be had or done* │ 酸葡萄心理

After Paul got his paycheck, he spent the rest of the day complaining to everyone about how he had been taken advantage of, but they knew it was just sour grapes and ignored him.

保羅拿到薪水後整天都在抱怨公司佔他便宜，但大家知道這是酸葡萄心理，所以不予理會。

1
2
3
4
5

Complete each word by filling in the blank with proper spelling so that it has the same meaning as suggested. Then please write the meaning of each word in Chinese.

1. 放蕩的	= _ _ _ _ _ t i o u s		11. mischance	= _____
2. 血統	= _ _ _ _ a g e		12. misfit	= _____
3. 語言學	= _ _ _ _ _ _ s t i c s		13. mobility	= _____
4. 長壽	= _ _ _ _ e v i t y		14. nationality	= _____
5. 降低	= _ _ _ e r		15. navigate	= _____
6. 哺乳動物	= _ _ _ m a l		16. obese	= _____
7. 熟練的	= _ _ _ _ _ _ f u l		17. observatory	= _____
8. 母親的	= _ _ _ _ _ n a l		18. offing	= _____
9. 商品	= _ _ _ _ _ _ _ _ i s e		19. ominous	= _____
10. 善變的	= _ _ _ _ _ _ i a l		20. originate	= _____

Choose a word that best completes the sentence.

21. The newly established government is trying to _____ the legacy of the past.

(A) lower   (B) navigate   (C) liquidate   (D) steer

22. Please calm down. I didn't mean to _____ you.

(A) offend   (B) generate   (C) initiate   (D) arise

23. Opal is _____. We cannot see through it.

(A) opportune   (B) opaque   (C) disgusting   (D) repulsive

The highlighted word is closest in meaning to which of the following?

24. When the obese lady stepped on the scale at the hospital, there was a sign saying, "Please consider this figure to be your IQ."

(A) ornate   (B) ominous   (C) fat   (D) opportune

25. The police could not decide who was responsible for the mishap .

(A) accident   (B) negligence   (C) indolence   (D) default

MP3
44

1051 oust [aʊst]   驅逐，逐出 ★★★☆☆

v. *banish; cast out; deport; displace; dispel; expel; ostracize*

There are many corrupt politicians and government officials who should be ousted from that country.

該國有許多應被驅逐出境的貪污政客和政府官員。

| out |
| 向外 (out) 驅趕 |

1052 overt [o`vɜt]   明顯的，公然的 ★★★★★

a. *observable; apparent; manifest*

My friend Jim made such an overt pass at the woman that everyone saw and heard, especially her husband, who was his new boss.

友人吉姆在眾目睽睽下公然和新老闆的妻子調情。

| over |
| 將蓋子 (cover) 掀開 |

1053 overwhelm [ˌovɚ`hwɛlm]   （情感、精神等）壓倒，使窘迫 ★★★★★

v. *be subject to the grip of something overpowering and usually distressing or damaging; overpower; smother*

Mrs. Rooney was totally overwhelmed by grief when she learned that her son had been killed in the war.

魯尼太太得知兒子戰死，感到不勝悲傷。

| over, helmet |
| 由上 (over) 覆蓋 (helm- = cover) |

1054 pal [pæl]   朋友，老兄，夥伴 ★★★☆☆

n. *buddy; chum; companion; comrade; crony*

I am sure that you are a real pal to stand by me at a difficult time like this. I am in financial difficulties.

我相信你這個真正的朋友會在艱困時候支持我，我現在有財務困難。

| pen pal |
| 筆友 (pen pal) |

1055 pallid [`pælɪd]   蒼白的，有病容的 ★★☆☆☆

a. *pale; ashen*

Christine must be pretty sick. She looks so pallid. I am afraid that she may fall down at any moment.

克莉絲汀一定病得很重，我擔心一臉病容的她隨時可能倒下。

| pale |
| 蒼白的 (pale) |

1056 partial [`pɑrʃəl]   部分的，不完全的 / 偏袒的，不公平的 ★★★★★

a. *partisan; fragmentary / biased; prejudiced; prepossessed*

Mr. Baker bore only partial responsibility for the accident; he was speeding, but the other driver drove through a red light.

貝克先生只需為這場意外負起部分責任，他雖超速但另一名駕駛卻闖紅燈。

| part |
| 傾向於某部分 (part) 的 |

1057 particle [`pɑrtɪkl]   微粒 ★★★★★

n. *bit; grain; iota; touch*

While a computer chip is being made, even the smallest dust particle should be avoided.

製造電腦晶片時就算是最小的浮塵微粒也應避免。

| part |
| 拆解成小部分 (part) |

1058 pastoral [`pæstərəl]   田園風光的，鄉村的 ★★★☆☆

a. *rural; bucolic*

A pastoral setting is often a painter's first choice because painting trees and wildlife is very soothing.

畫家創作的首要選擇常是田園風光，因為描繪林木和野生動物讓人心曠神怡。

| pastor |
| 像牧師 (pastor) 傳教般的詳和之地 |

1059 **perfunctory** [pə`fʌŋktərı]
★★☆☆☆

敷衍了事的，草率的，馬馬虎虎的

a. involuntary; uninterested

The employees did not ignore the importance of the motivational training. But their interest in it was faint and perfunctory.

員工沒忽略激勵訓練的重要性，但還是感到興趣缺缺，敷衍了事。

function
未能完全發揮作用 (function)

1060 **personnel** [ˌpɜsn̩`ɛl]
★★★★★

全體員工，人事部

n. persons employed in any work, enterprise, service, establishment, etc.

The personnel manager was responsible for taking care of all the employees' needs and problems, as well as hiring and replacing workers.

人事部經理負責處理員工需求和問題，同時也負責徵人。

person
對人 (person) 的管理

1061 **pestilence** [`pɛstl̩əns]
★★★★☆

急性傳染病，瘟疫

n. plague; scourge

Homosexuality has spread a pestilence called AIDS, or an acquired immuno-deficiency syndrome.

同性戀散播又稱後天免疫缺乏症候群的愛滋病。

pest
像鼠疫 (pest) 般的傳染病

1062 **petty** [`pɛtɪ]
★★★☆☆

心胸狹窄的，小器的 / 微不足道的，小的

a. narrow-minded / tiny; teeny-weeny; diminutive; minute

Jackson is so petty about money. I think that one of his favorite things to do is to count his money.

傑克遜很小器，我想他最愛做的事就是數鈔票。

pet
像寵物 (pet) 般小的

1063 **pinnacle** [`pɪnək̩l]
★★★★☆

頂峰，最高點

n. acme; culmination; peak; summit; apex

The pinnacle of her career was winning the Oscar, and ever since then, her career has been sliding downhill.

她的事業巔峰是贏得奧斯卡金像獎，但此後就每況愈下。

pin
像大頭針 (pin) 般的尖峰

1064 **placate** [`pleket]
★★★★★

安撫，平息

v. pacify; appease; assuage; mollify

In an effort to placate the opposition, the Prime Minister accepted some of the opponents' ideas, but he refused to accept all of them.

首相為了安撫反對黨而採納部分意見，但拒絕全部接受。

place
使坐在座位 (place) 上

1065 **placebo** [plə`sibo]
★★★★☆

安慰劑

n. harmless substance given as if it were medicine to calm a patient who mistakenly believes he is ill

The term 'placebo' is used to describe a pill that has no medical ingredients, but that often produces the same effect as genuine medication.

「安慰劑」是沒有醫藥成份的藥物，但往往能產生和真藥相同的治療效果。

place
使不安的人靜坐 (place) 下來的藥

1066 **placid** [`plæsɪd]
★★★★☆

安詳的，寧靜的

a. calm; peaceful; serene

The mother was holding her newborn child in her arms with a placid smile. The baby also wore a smile from time to time.

母親把新生嬰兒抱在懷裡露出安詳笑容，寶寶也不時微笑。

place
靜坐在位子 (place) 上的

1067 plateau [plæ`to]　　　　　　　　　　　　　　　高原，台地　　★★★★★
n. upland; tableland　　　　　　　　　　　　　　　　　　plate
The city was built on a wide plateau, nearly a kilometer up the side of the 　如盤子 (plate) 般的平坦之地
mountain, which offered a beautiful, panoramic view of the lush area.
那座城市建築在依山約一千公尺高的寬闊台地上，蒼翠繁茂的風光一覽無遺。

1068 plea [pli]　　　　　　　　　　　　　　　　　　答辯　　★★★☆☆
n. appeal; earnest request　　　　　　　　　　　　　　please
The judge gave a lenient verdict after listening to the defendant's plea. It 　拜託、請求 (please)
was clear that his misdeed was not intended.
法官聽完被告答辯後從輕量刑，因為很顯然不是預謀犯罪。

1069 poignant [`pɔɪnjənt]　　　　　　　　　尖刻的，犀利的 / 沉痛的　　★★★☆☆
a. pungent; piquant / agitating; perturbing　　　　　　poison
The death of her grandmother had a poignant effect on her for many 　像毒 (poison) 般辛辣的
weeks. She walked around as though she were in a daze.
祖母逝世讓她連續數周哀痛逾恆，茫然若失。

1070 precious [`prɛʃəs]　　　　　　　　　　　　貴重的，珍貴的　　★★★★★
a. costly; priceless; invaluable　　　　　　　　　　　price
A diamond is the most expensive among the precious stones. However, 　價格 (price) 昂貴的
even though not a gem, uranium is far more expensive.
寶石中最昂貴的是鑽石，鈾雖不是寶石，卻比鑽石更貴。

1071 prejudice [`prɛdʒədɪs]　　　　　　　　　　偏見，成見　　★★★★★
n. bias; prepossession　　　　　　　　　　　　　　judge
Science teaches us that we can take the future into our own hands if we 　預 (pre-) 作判斷 (judge)
rid ourselves of prejudice and superstition.
科學告訴我們若能摒棄成見和迷信，未來是掌握在我們手中的。

1072 premier [`primɪə]　　　　　　　　　第一的，首位的，首要的　　★★★★★
a. first; foremost; leading; principal　　　　　　　　prime
This company developed an amazing computer and has achieved a 　最頭等 (prime) 的
premier position in the electronics field.
這家公司開發令人驚豔的電腦產品，在電子產業中獨佔鰲頭。

1073 pretext [`pritɛkst]　　　　　　　　　　　　託辭，藉口　　★★★☆☆
n. excuse; a false reason or motive put forth to hide the real one　　pretend
I went over to her house to ask her out on a date, using the pretext of 　佯裝的 (pretend) 言詞
returning to her the book she had left in the library.
我用歸還她掉在圖書館的書作為藉口，去她家裡邀約她。

1074 primitive [`prɪmətɪv]　　　　　　　　　　　　原始的　　★★★★★
a. primeval　　　　　　　　　　　　　　　　　　prime, primary
The anthropology class studied the habits and hunting practices of 　時間上位居最前面的
primitive man.　　　　　　　　　　　　　　　　　　(primary)
人類學課程研究的是原始人的生活習慣和狩獵技巧。

1075 **privacy** [`praɪvəsɪ] 隱私，私生活

private
私人的 (private) 秘密

n. the quality or condition of being private; withdrawal from public view or company; seclusion

Pam didn't want her colleague to intrude on her privacy. So she tried not to tell her anything personal.

潘不願同事干涉私生活，因此絕口不提個人隱私。

MP3
45

1076 **probation** [pro`beʃən] 緩刑

prove
直到證明 (prove) 變好為止

n. keeping an official check on the behavior of people found guilty of crime as an alternative to sending them to prison

As it was his first offense, the offender was not sent to prison, but put on probation for six months.

念在是初犯，違法者未被送去坐牢而改判六個月緩刑。

1077 **prolong** [prə`lɔŋ] 延長

long
使又長又遠 (long)

v. extend; draw out; elongate; lengthen; protract; spin; stretch

Those who are seeking to prolong life usually turn to all kinds of drugs without knowing the effects.

追求長生不死的人往往求助於各種藥物卻不知其功效。

1078 **prosaic** [pro`zeɪk] 單調的，乏味的

prose
如乏味言論 (prose) 般無趣

a. dull; flat; drab

Some good painters are capable of bringing a sense of beauty to the most prosaic or flat landscapes.

有些好畫家能為最單調乏味的景色帶來美感。

1079 **punitive** [`pjunətɪv] 嚴苛的，苛刻的

punish
給予處罰 (punish)

a. inflicting a punishment

When Jane was a young child, her father was too punitive. He was so strict that she could hardly breathe in front of him.

珍小時候父親很嚴苛，太過嚴厲的他常壓得她喘不過氣來。

1080 **purblind** [`pɝ͵blaɪnd] 半盲的，視力模糊的 / 愚鈍的

blind
近乎看不見的 (blind)

a. almost blind; dim-sighted / lacking imagination

His mother-in-law was purblind. She could not see very well and she often mistook her son-in-law for her daughter.

他的丈母娘是半盲的，視力不好的她常把女婿誤認成女兒。

1081 **purview** [`pɝvju] 範圍，領域 / 視界

view
完整的 (pur-＝perfect) 看到 (view)

n. range; extent; orbit; reach; scope / ken

The purview of the professor's knowledge was so great that many students tried to take his class, but many failed to pass the entrance test.

教授知識淵博，許多學生想修他的課但入學考試卻不及格。

1082 **quartet** [kwɔr`tɛt] 四重唱，四重奏

quarter
分成四 (quart-) 部分的

n. a group consisting of four individuals

He has a deep voice and a good ear for music, so he was readily accepted as the bass singer in the Standfield Barbershop Quartet.

他的聲音低沉音感又好，因此立刻獲准出任史丹佛男聲四重唱的低音歌手。

1083 quell [kwɛl] ★★☆☆☆

消除，弭平   kill

v. overcome; suppress; put down

將欲望、害怕等予以根除 (kill)

Joanne tried to quell her fear and face the challenge head on, even though she knew that she would probably fail once again.

瓊安努力克服恐懼面對眼前挑戰，雖然知道可能會再度失敗。

1084 questionnaire [ˌkwɛstʃənˈɛr] ★★★★☆

問卷，調查表   question

n. written or printed list of questions to be answered by a number of people, especially to collect statistics or as part of a survey

針對不同主題試著提出問題 (question)

As a part of her statistics course, Susan had to pass out a questionnaire and then organize the results into a graph and write a report about her findings.

作為統計學課程的一環，蘇珊須發放問卷再將結果整理成圖表，最後撰寫一份調查結果報告。

1085 quiescent [kwaɪˈɛsn̩t] ★★★☆☆

靜止的，不動的   quiet

a. latent; dormant; inactive

安靜的 (quiet)、不活動的

The union has remained quiescent for over a year. The president of the company was happy, but the workers were full of complaints.

一年多來工會都不活躍，公司總裁感到高興但員工滿腹怨言。

1086 ramble [ˈræmbl̩] ★★★☆☆

漫步   amble

n. walk; stroll; promenade

四處走 (amble)

He persuaded her to be his companion in a ramble among the trees. But she said that she had a lot of Saturday chores.

他勸她一起到林中散步，但她表示要處理許多假日雜務。

1087 ransack [ˈrænsæk] ★★★★☆

徹底搜尋，尋遍   ranch, seek

v. rummage; search

到農場住屋 (ranch) 翻找 (seek)

Harris ransacked the entire house looking for his wife's wedding ring.

哈里斯尋遍全家想找妻子的婚戒。

1088 rapprochement [ˌræproʃˈmɑŋ] ★★☆☆☆

恢復邦交，重修舊好   approach

n. reconciliation; renewal of friendly relations, especially between countries

再次親密地接近 (approach)

The president tried to improve relations with the U.S. and contrived to effect some rapprochement with Red China.

總統試圖改善對美關係，並設法和中國修好。

1089 rebate [ˈribet] ★★★☆☆

折扣   base

n. discount; deduction

再次 (re-) 探底 (base)

The used car salesman offered a $500 rebate on any model to improve his sagging business. However, it was not effective.

中古車業務員提供不限車款一律五百美元的折扣來拉抬低迷買氣，但並不奏效。

1090 receipt [rɪˈsit] ★★★★★

收據   receive

n. written statement that something (especially money or goods) has been received

收到 (receive) 款項的證明

Mrs. Brown went to the clothing shop to ask for a refund, but was told that money could not be refunded without presenting a receipt.

伯朗太太到服飾店要求退費，但店家表示須出示收據。

1091 reckless [`rɛklɪs]　　　　　　　　　　　　★★★★☆

魯莽的

a. foolhardy; rash; thoughtless; impetuous

I have strongly believed that a reckless driver should be heavily fined. Therefore, I welcome the new stricter traffic law.

我深信魯莽駕駛應受重罰，所以欣然接受更嚴厲的交通法規。

reckon

沒有 (-less) 計算 (reckon) 就加總

1092 recrimination [rɪˌkrɪməˋneʃən]　　　　　★★☆☆☆

反責，反控

n. accusation in response to an accusation from somebody else

When he fired her after a single mistake, he received one recrimination after another from his employees.

他只因一個過失就開除她，於是受到員工不斷指責。

crime

再次 (re-) 揭發罪行 (crime)

1093 refine [rɪˋfaɪn]　　　　　　　　　　　　　★★★☆☆

使文雅，使優雅

v. smooth; cultivate

In an effort to refine his manners before the lady, he stopped swearing and spoke as politely as he could.

為了在女士面前表現得彬彬有禮，他說話客氣不罵髒話。

fine

再次 (re-) 把某事做得更好 (fine)

1094 reform [ˌriˋfɔrm]　　　　　　　　　　　　★★★★★

改革

n. change that removes or puts right faults, errors, etc.

The government showed signs of slowing democratic reforms by abrogating the right of free speech.

政府廢除言論自由權，顯示民主改革遲緩。

form

再次 (re-) 塑造形狀 (form)

1095 refund [`rɪˌfʌnd]　　　　　　　　　　　　★★★★★

退費

n. repayment; reimbursement

The customers demanded a full refund on the damaged goods which they had bought the previous week.

顧客上周購買到受損商品，所以要求全額退費。

fund

再次 (re-) 換成錢 (fund)

1096 refute [rɪˋfjut]　　　　　　　　　　　　　★★★★☆

反駁，駁斥

v. disprove; confute; rebut

I don't think we can refute Jane's argument in this matter, because her argument is well-founded.

我不認為在這件事上能反駁珍的論點，因為她有充分根據。

beat

反對 (re-) 並打倒 (fut-＝beat)

1097 reinforce [ˌriɪnˋfɔrs]　　　　　　　　　　★★★★★

加強，激勵

v. strengthen; energize; invigorate

The teacher advised Tommy's parents to punish him for bad behavior and reinforce any good actions.

老師建議父母對湯米要賞罰分明。

force

再次 (re-) 增加力量 (force)

1098 remedy [`rɛmədɪ]　　　　　　　　　　　　★★★★★

療法

n. cure; treatment

There is no known remedy for the common cold; there are only ways to temporarily mask the symptoms.

針對一般感冒沒有已知療法，目前的治療只能暫時掩蓋症狀。

medicine

對 (re-) 某疾病投藥 (medicine)

1099 remiss [rɪ`mɪs]   不小心的，疏忽的   ★★★★★

a. negligent; careless; lax; neglectful; indolent; delinquent; derelict

My friend John is too remiss; he always makes mistakes. I think that he does everything without any thought.

友人約翰很粗心老是犯錯，我認為他做每件事都不經考慮。

> mistake
> 反覆 (re-) 出錯 (mistake)

1100 remnant [`rɛmnənt]   殘餘，剩餘   ★★★★★

n. remainder; remains; leftover

In this country, people usually feed their dogs the remnants of their meal because people have difficulty finding special food products for pets.

在這個國家人們常拿剩菜餵狗，因為很難找到寵物專用食物。

> remain
> 殘留 (remain) 物

Tea Time... ☕

<Greek story> Ostracism
In ancient Greece, the temporary banishment of a citizen by popular vote; shells were used to write a name on in voting.

〈希臘故事〉貝殼流放制
古希臘人民可透過公投暫時流放某市民，投票時用貝殼書寫該人姓名。（註：貝殼流放制屬於祕密投票制，遭流放者多為威脅社會安定者，流放年限從五年到十年不等。故此字也可引申為「放逐、排斥、擯棄」等。）

❖ **ostracism** [`ɑstrəsɪzəm] *n. banishment; exile* | 放逐，排斥

The practice of political ostracism puts a significant amount of pressure on all politicians, for it would ruin their career if it happened to them.

實行政治放逐為所有從政者帶來莫大壓力，因為一旦遭到放逐將前途盡毀。

1 Complete each word by filling in the blank with proper spelling so that it has the same meaning as suggested. Then please write the meaning of each word in Chinese.

1. 使窘迫   = o v e r _ _ _ _ _
2. 有病容的   = _ _ _ _ i d
3. 微粒   = _ _ _ _ i c l e
4. 敷衍了事的   = p e r _ _ _ _ _ _ _ _
5. 人事部   = _ _ _ _ _ _ n e l
6. 瘟疫   = _ _ _ _ i l e n c e
7. 頂峰   = _ _ _ n a c l e
8. 痛切的   = _ _ _ _ _ b o
9. 安慰劑   = _ _ _ _ n a n t
10. 偏見   = p r e _ _ _ _ _ _

11. premier   = _____
12. primitive   = _____
13. probation   = _____
14. purview   = _____
15. quartet   = _____
16. questionnaire = _____
17. ransack   = _____
18. rebate   = _____
19. reckless   = _____
20. recrimination = _____

2 Choose a word that best completes the sentence.

21. I'd like a _____. I don't like the color of this dress.
   (A) reform   (B) remedy   (C) refund   (D) leftover

22. You need a _____ for the reimbursement of the expense.
   (A) prejudice   (B) rebate   (C) probation   (D) receipt

3 The highlighted word is closest in meaning to which of the following?

23. The people of the nation succeeded in ousting the despot.
   (A) extending   (B) dispelling   (C) protracting   (D) prolonging

24. Her kindness nearly overwhelmed me.
   (A) smothered   (B) expelled   (C) banished   (D) deported

25. We drove out of the city to take in the pastoral beauty.
   (A) partial   (B) fragmentary   (C) bucolic   (D) involuntary

MP3
46

1101 renegade [ˋrɛnɪˌged]　　　　　　　　　　叛徒，變節者
n. apostate; defector; deserter
★★★★☆
Some called him a traitor or a renegade as he turned his back on his country and supported the enemy.
有人說他是賣國賊或叛徒，因為他背叛祖國投效敵人。

negate
反覆 (re-) 否認 (negate)

1102 renew [rɪˋnju]　　　　　　　　　　　　恢復，更新
v. restore; rebuild; resume
★★★★★
Because I understand that Jack and Judy hope to renew their friendship, I am thinking about acting as a go-between.
我想做傑克和茱蒂的中間人，因為知道兩人想重修舊好。

new
再次 (re-) 變成新的 (new)

1103 renounce [rɪˋnauns]　　　　　聲明放棄，拋棄，與～斷絕關係
v. abdicate; resign; quit; forsake; abandon
★★★★★
The morning after a night of heavy drinking, many people say to others around them that they will renounce alcohol.
許多人宿醉清醒後都會表示再也不喝酒了。

announce
收回 (re-) 聲明 (announce)

1104 reparable [ˋrɛpərəbl̩]　　　　　　　　　　可修補的
a. that can be made good
★★★★★
Although it would be expensive, the damage to the chicken farm after the horrible storm was reparable.
暴風雨雖對雞舍造成重大損害但可修補。

repair
可重新修理 (repair) 的

1105 replace [rɪˋples]　　　　　　　　　　　替換，取代
v. alter; change
★★★★★
I want a wife who will take care of my needs and keep my house clean, who will pick up after my children, and after me. I want a wife who will keep my clothes clean, ironed, mended, replaced when necessary.
　　　　　　　　　　　　　　　Why I Want a Wife — Judy Syfers
我想要個妻子，能照顧我日常生活所需，保持居家整潔，並幫忙收拾孩子和我隨手亂丟的東西。我想要個妻子，能幫我洗燙縫補衣物，並定期汰舊換新。
　　　　　　　　　　　　　　　──《為何我想要個妻子》茱蒂·塞菲斯

place
將某人或某物放 (place) 得遠遠的

1106 reproach [rɪˋprotʃ]　　　　　　　　　　責備，指責
n. rebuke; blame; censure; discredit
★★★★★
The actions of the Pope of the Roman Catholic Church are thought by catholics to be beyond reproach.
天主教徒視羅馬天主教教宗的行為是無可非議的。

approach
靠近 (approach) 並對抗 (re-)

1107 requisite [ˋrɛkwəzɪt]　　　　　　　　　必要的 / 要素
a. essential / n. necessity
★★★★☆
All the requisite supplies were sent to the soldiers in the field, but they sorely missed all the luxury items back at home.
所有必要供應物資皆送交交戰地士兵，但他們更想念家鄉那些奢侈品。

require
變成亟需 (require) 之物

1108 **resources** [risɔrs] ★★★★★ 資源，豐饒

n. assets; wealth; riches

source
再次 (re-) 冒出的水源 (source)

The large open-pit copper mine in Utah reminds us that the United States is blessed with abundant resources.

猶他州露天開採的大片銅礦提醒我們上蒼賜予美國的豐饒資源。

1109 **retard** [rɪ`tɑrd] ★★★★☆ 使減緩，阻止

v. delay; decelerate; slow down

tardy
速度倒退 (re-) 減緩 (tardy)

The fire fighters soaked the neighboring buildings with the hope of retarding the spread of the fire.

消防隊員澆灌鄰近建物以期阻止火勢延燒。

1110 **reveal** [rɪ`vil] ★★★★★ 透露

v. make known; spill the beans; disclose; divulge; let on; unveil

veil
將面紗 (veil) 向後 (re-) 掀

It is a characteristic of a good detective story that one vital clue should reveal the solution to the mystery, but that the clue and its significance should be far from obvious.　　　　— Fred Hoyle

好偵探故事的特色在於具備揭露謎底的重要線索，但線索本身及其含意都不是顯而易見的。　　　　— 佛烈德‧霍伊爾

1111 **rotten** [`rɑtn̩] ★★★★☆ 行為惡劣的，無禮的

a. bad; spoiled; foul

rot
腐爛 (rot) 的

The teacher got fed up with the student's rotten behavior and sent the troublemaker to the dean's office.

老師受夠了學生的惡劣行為，於是將鬧事者送到訓導主任辦公室。

1112 **rummage** [`rʌmɪdʒ] ★★★★☆ 翻尋，到處找

v. search; ransack

room
在房 (room) 裡徹底找尋

Mr. White rummaged through the drawer for a pair of socks. At last, he found that his 5-year-old daughter was wearing his socks.

懷特先生翻遍抽屜想找雙襪子，最後發現五歲女兒穿在腳上。

1113 **semblance** [`sɛmbləns] ★★★★☆ 外貌，外觀 / 類似，相似，假裝

n. aspect; look / likeness; analogy; similarity

resemble
外表 (semble) 相像的 (resemble)

His sister, who got married last month, tried to keep up the semblance of happiness, yet she failed as soon as she began to cry.

他上月才新婚的姊姊努力佯裝很幸福，但做不到就哭了。

1114 **servitude** [`sɝvə‚tud] ★★★★☆ 奴役，束縛 / 勞役，苦役

n. bondage; slavery / drudgery

servant
像僕人 (servant) 般受奴役

Male dominance, or male chauvinism, in a culture leads to a female attitude of rebellion against the implied servitude.

父權文化的男性沙文主義導致女性反對奴役待遇。

1115 **shaky** [`ʃekɪ] ★★★★☆ 不堅定的，容易動搖的，靠不住的

a. insecure; wavering; rickety

shake
上下搖晃 (shake) 而不安定

His loyalty, always shaky, is now non-existent. He was a member who was searching for a chance to run away.

他始終搖擺不定的忠誠度業已蕩然無存，現在的他只想伺機逃跑。

1116 shatter [ˈʃætɚ]   毀損，使粉碎   ★★★☆☆

scatter
破碎而四散紛飛 (scatter)

v. break into small pieces; ruin; disintegrate; crush

Because of his shattered health, Shane couldn't continue his graduate work. He decided to take a good rest at home for several months.

夏恩因身體不好所以無法繼續研究所課程，並決定好好在家靜養數月。

1117 shoplifter [ˈʃɑpˌlɪftɚ]   商店扒手，順手牽羊者   ★★★★☆

shop, lift
在商店 (shop) 偷竊 (lift) 物品的人 (-er)

n. a person who steals displayed goods from a store

The store manager placed some closed circuit monitors in his store and posted a sign that said that shoplifters would be prosecuted.

經理在店內裝設閉路電視，並張貼標誌警告順手牽羊者將移送法辦。

1118 shortage [ˈʃɔrtɪdʒ]   不足，短缺   ★★★★★

short
短少的 (short)

n. insufficiency; lack

Since there was a gasoline shortage, everyone was forced to car pool and take public transportation.

人們因石油短缺被迫共乘或搭乘大眾運輸系統。

1119 simile [ˈsɪməˌlɪ]   直喻，明喻   ★★★★☆

similar
稱A和B相似 (similar)

n. a figure of speech in which one thing is likened to another, dissimilar thing by the use of like, as, etc.

'You are like a rose,' is a commonly used simile to impress a girl. The effect of the expression is quite reliable.

「妳像朵玫瑰」的直喻法能讓少女印象深刻，這種措辭相當有效。

1120 simulate [ˈsɪmjəˌlet]   模仿，偽裝   ★★★★★

similar
模仿得極相似 (similar)

v. imitate; mimic

In a radio program a sheet of tin was shaken to simulate the peal of thunder. And for the sound of raining a fan and some grains were used.

廣播節目以抖動鐵皮模仿雷鳴聲，至於風扇吹動穀粒就像雨聲。

1121 simultaneous [ˌsaɪmlˈtenɪəs]   同時的，同時發生的   ★★★★★

similar
在相似 (similar) 時間內發生的

a. contemporary; coexisting; concurrent

Audio-visual aid machines are very effective teaching tools in that they provide simultaneous audio and visual stimulus for the learner.

視聽器材是很有效的教學工具，因為能同時提供學習者聽覺和視覺刺激。

1122 skid [skɪd]   滑行   ★★★☆☆

ski
如滑雪 (ski) 般滑溜

n. sliding

The speeding car hit a patch of ice and went into an uncontrollable skid, eventually slamming into a telephone pole.

急駛的車輛追撞冰堆後失控打滑，最後撞上電線杆。

1123 slack [slæk]   市況蕭條的，生意清淡的   ★★★☆☆

slacks
生意像寬鬆褲子 (slacks) 般鬆垮

a. loose; lax; relaxed; inactive; leisurely

Spring is a slack time at skiing resorts in most regions of the world. The busy season is winter.

春天是全球各滑雪勝地的淡季，冬天才是旺季。

1124 slake [slek] 解（渴），充（饑） ★★★★☆

slacks

v. quench; allay or make thirst or desire less intense by satisfying

解渴或充飢後就不必再勒緊寬鬆的褲子 (slacks)

The beggar needed to slake his thirst so desperately that he was willing to steal a drink from the store.

乞丐需要解渴所以想到店裡偷飲料。

1125 sled [slɛd] 雪橇 ★★★☆☆

slide

n. any of several types of vehicles mounted on runners for use on snow, ice, etc.

滑雪 (slide) 用的雪橇

The injured skier who broke his leg while skiing down the steep slope had to be carried down the mountain on a sled.

滑下陡峭斜坡而跌斷腿的受傷滑雪者須靠雪橇運送下山。

1126 slipshod [`slɪp,ʃɑd] 散漫的，隨便的，草率的 ★★★★☆

sleeve, shoe

a. slovenly; disheveled; sloppy; messy

袖子 (sleeve) 長得快接近鞋子 (shoe)，一副邋遢狀

Vera has done a slipshod job on her report. She should not have written it in such a careless and untidy way.

薇拉的報告是草率寫完的，她不該用這麼隨便輕率的方式寫報告。

1127 sloppy [`slɑpɪ] 馬虎的，草率的 ★★★★☆

sleeve

a. slovenly; slipshod; messy

袖子 (sleeve) 太長，顯得散漫

Jim, one of my neighbors, always complains about his wife. He insists that she is a terrible cook and a sloppy housekeeper.

鄰居吉姆經常抱怨自己的妻子，說她做飯難吃持家馬虎。

1128 sloth [sloθ] 樹懶 ★★★☆☆

slow

n. any of several slow-moving, tree-dwelling mammals of tropical Central and South America that hang, back down, from branches and feed on fruits and vegetation

動作非常緩慢的 (slow) 動物

A sloth is an animal that is very slow and clumsy. It usually hangs down on a branch feeding on fruits and vegetation.

樹懶是動作緩慢又笨拙的動物，常倒掛在樹枝上吃蔬果。

1129 slovenly [`slʌvənlɪ] 隨便的，潦草的 ★★★★☆

sleeve

a. messy; slipshod

袖子 (sleeve) 太長，顯得隨便

The landlady at my boarding house is so slovenly in her housekeeping. She doesn't like to arrange things.

我的寄宿家庭女主人持家非常馬虎，不喜歡整理東西。

1130 sluggard [`slʌgəd] 懶人，遊手好閒者 ★★★★☆

slow

n. slowpoke; laggard

動作緩慢 (slow)

The office manager is such a sluggard that he spends most of his time at work reading the newspaper or just sleeping.

辦公室經理是個大懶人，上班時間大多在看報或睡覺。

1131 sluggish [`slʌgɪʃ] 性能不良的，功能不佳的 ★★★★★

slow

a. slow; slothful; dull; slow-moving

既慢 (slow) 又遲鈍

My brother's van, which has a diesel engine, has relatively good mileage, but its acceleration is so sluggish.

哥哥的柴油引擎貨車可跑較多哩數，但油門性能不佳。

MP3
47

1132 smog [smɑg] ★★★★☆

煙霧   smoke, fog

n. a noxious mixture of fog and smoke

煙 (smoke) 和霧 (fog)

The smog over the city was so thick that we couldn't even see the river from a half-mile away.

城市上空煙霧瀰漫，甚至看不清半哩外的河流。

1133 smother [`smʌðɚ] ★★★★☆

使窒息，使透不過氣   smoke

v. overwhelm; suffocate; choke

以煙 (smoke) 使之窒息

Some parents nowadays tend to smother their children with too much attention. Therefore, some children are sick of their parents' interference.

時下有些父母過度關心孩子使他們喘不過氣來，有些孩子因而厭惡父母干涉。

1134 snappy [`snæpɪ] ★★★☆☆

快速的，迅速的   snap

a. fast; rapid; quick; speedy; swift; hasty; expeditious

冷不防，猛然的 (snap)

A snappy solution to a complicated problem more often than not only makes the problem worse. Careful thought is important to avoid a mistake.

快速的解決辦法多半只會讓複雜的問題更加嚴重，仔細思考才能避免犯錯。

1135 sneak [snik] ★★★★☆

偷偷溜走   snake, snail

v. creep; glide; steal; move or go stealthily

像蛇 (snake) 般靜悄悄離開

Jack was required to help his father with the farm chores, but after breakfast he sneaked out of the house with a fishing rod.

父親要傑克協助農事，但早餐後他卻拿著釣竿偷溜出門。

1136 sovereignty [`sɑvrɪntɪ] ★★★★☆

主權   super, reign

n. the status, dominion, rule or power of a sovereign; supreme and independent political authority

坐在最高 (super) 位置上統治 (reign)

There were a lot of patriots who struggled for their nation's sovereignty during the French colonial rule.

法國殖民統治期間許多愛國者為國家主權奮鬥不懈。

1137 spacious [`speʃəs] ★★★★★

寬敞的，廣闊的，宏偉的   space

a. ample; capacious; commodious; roomy; wide

空間 (space) 很大的

After living in a small apartment for several years, the couple longed for a more spacious home.

在小公寓裡住了好幾年後，夫妻倆渴望擁有一個更寬敞的家。

1138 stagnant [`stægnənt] ★★★★☆

不景氣的，蕭條的   stay

a. static; immobile; stationary

停滯 (stay) 於某處

Mr. Kendall's business has been stagnant ever since the work stoppage. He is trying to find a good way to improve his business.

罷工使肯道爾先生的生意蕭條，他正設法拉抬生意。

1139 staid [sted] ★★★★☆

沈著的，穩重的，端莊的   stay

a. sedate; sober; solemn

停留在 (stay) 某處

Our new office manager is a middle-aged man of staid appearance. He seems to be very conservative.

辦公室新任經理是個外表穩重的中年男子，看起來似乎很保守。

1140 standoffish [ˌstænd`ɔfɪʃ]　　　　置身事外的，冷漠的，不親切的　　★★★★☆

a. unsociable; reserved: withdrawn; antisocial

I can hardly understand my co-worker Jane. Sometimes she is very friendly, and other times, she is so standoffish.

我搞不懂同事珍，她時而友善時而冷漠。

> stand, off
> 站 (stand) 得遠遠的 (off)

1141 subordinate [sə`bɔrdn̩ɪt]　　　　次要的　　★★★★★

a. collateral; dependent: secondary; subjective

　We cannot travel every path. Success must be won along one line. We must make our business the one life purpose to which every other must be subordinate.　　*Advice to a Young Man* —— Ernest Hemingway

人生道路不可能條條走一遭，成功來自心無旁騖。我們須專注於一個人生目標，其餘皆屬次要。

—— 《給年輕人的諍言》海明威

> order
> 下一階 (sub-) 的命令 (order)

1142 substantial [səb`stænʃəl]　　　　大量的，多的 / 本質上的，基本上的　　★★★★★

a. big; considerable; significant / essential

Even if he came in third in the contest, he knew that he would still win a substantial amount of money.

即使位居第三名，他知道仍能獲得大筆獎金。

> substance
> 具實體和本質 (substance) 的

1143 suburban [sə`bɝbən]　　　　市郊的，有郊區特點的，土氣的　　★★★★★

a. of, in, or residing in a suburb

His suburban lifestyle suited him perfectly, but it drove his lonely wife crazy. She insisted on moving to a big city.

郊區生活方式非常適合他，但寂寞的妻子快被逼瘋，堅持要搬到大都市定居。

> urban
> 位在於城市 (urban) 的次要 (sub-) 位置

1144 summit [`sʌmɪt]　　　　高峰會議 / 頂峰　　★★★★★

n. a conference at the summit / the highest point; top; apex

The Superpower summit between the two rival countries brought the era of detente to the globe.

敵對兩國的超級強權高峰會議標示著全球政治關係和緩時代的來臨。

> sum
> 加總 (sum) 後到達最高峰

1145 summon [`sʌmən]　　　　召喚　　★★★★★

v. convoke; convene; call together

The chairman summoned his staff members to his office to review the original draft for the proposed power plant.

董事長召喚部屬到他的辦公室審閱發電廠提案。

> sum
> 把全部的 (sum) 人叫到某處

1146 terminate [`tɝmə͵net]　　　　終止，結束　　★★★★★

v. halt; abolish; discontinue

The president vowed to terminate political surveillance, which was secretly conducted by the intelligence agency.

總統鄭重宣布終止情報局暗中執行的政治監視行動。

> terminal
> 火車或巴士行經路線的終點站 (terminal)

1147 thicket [`θɪkɪt]　　　　灌木叢　　★★★★☆

n. bush; underbrush; undergrowth

The thicket between Mr. Brown's and his neighbor's house was unattractive, but it stopped the neighbor's ugly dog from trespassing.

伯朗先生和鄰居家之間的灌木叢雖不美觀，卻能阻止鄰家惡犬擅闖。

> thick
> 濃密的 (thick) 草叢

1148 toilsome [ˈtɔɪlsəm]　　費力的，辛苦的，勞苦的　| toil
a. *hard; arduous; laborious; strenuous*

★★★☆☆

因感到勞累 (toil) 的

Studying English can sometimes be a very toilsome job since constant practice and diligence are required.

學英文有時是件很費力的事，因為需要不斷努力練習。

1149 tone-deaf [ˈtonˌdɛf]　　音盲的，不能分辨音調的　| tone

★★★★☆

a. *not able to distinguish accurately differences in musical pitch*

因耳朵被捂住而聽不到聲音 (tone)

Mr. Polley's friends eventually didn't want him to come with them to the karaoke because he was so tone-deaf that he would surely ruin every song he tried to sing.

友人不願讓波利先生一起去唱卡拉 OK，因為他這個大音癡肯定會搞砸每首歌。

1150 tornado [tɔrˈnedo]　　龍捲風　| turn

★★★★★

n. *cyclone; twister; a violently whirling column of air extending downward from a cloud, especially in Australia and the U.S.A.*

一直旋轉 (turn) 的漩渦狀風勢

The most lethal F-5 tornado ever recorded occurred in 1925. Its winds reached 300 miles an hour and swept through Missouri, Illinois, and Indiana, killing 695 people.

史上最具毀滅性的 F5 級龍捲風發生在一九二五年，每小時高達三百英里的風速橫掃美國密蘇里、伊利諾和印第安那等三州，造成六百九十五人喪生。

Tea Time... ☕

<From the name of an author>
Masochism
After Leopold von Sacher-Masoch (1835-95), Austrian writer, in whose stories masochism is described.

〈源自一作家名〉受虐
本字源自奧地利作家薩榭─馬索赫 (1835-95) 的姓氏，其作品描繪被虐待狂。（註：多次因性虐行為入獄的十八世紀法國作家 Marquis de Sade，其姓氏引申出 sadism 一字，指「虐待狂」。sadism 和 masochism 兩字並稱 sadomasochism，也就是 SM「性虐待」。）

❖ **masochism** [ˈmæzəˌkɪzəm] **n.** *a form of (esp. sexual) perversion characterized by gratification derived from one's own pain or humiliation* | 被虐待狂

His long bouts of drinking and self-misery were considered by all to be an overindulgence in masochism, and made him look pitiful to all his friends.

大家視他的長期酗酒和自怨自憐為被虐式的放縱，友人都覺得他值得同情。

1

Complete each word by filling in the blank with proper spelling so that it has the same meaning as suggested. Then please write the meaning of each word in Chinese.

1. 叛徒   = r e _ _ _ _ _ _
2. 恢復   = r e _ _ _
3. 無法挽回的   = _ _ _ _ _ a b l e
4. 責備   = r e _ _ _ _ _ _
5. 資源   = r e _ _ _ _ _ _ s
6. 阻止   = r e _ _ _ _
7. 行為惡劣的   = _ _ _ t e n
8. 相似   = _ _ _ _ _ _ n c e
9. 奴役   = _ _ _ _ _ _ u d e
10. 商店扒手   = _ _ _ _ l i f t e r

11. simultaneous – _____
12. slipshod   = _____
13. slovenly   = _____
14. sluggard   = _____
15. smother   = _____
16. snappy   = _____
17. sovereignty   = _____
18. stagnant   = _____
19. summit   = _____
20. summon   = _____

2

Choose a word that best completes the sentence.

21. People often _____ butter with margarine.
   (A) shatter   (B) renounce   (C) replace   (D) renew

22. Basically, our planet is a globe that contains a limited amount of _____.
   (A) resources   (B) requisite   (C) apostate   (D) renegade

23. The lady upstairs was singing Christmas carols in a frog-like voice. I noticed that she was really _____.
   (A) ample   (B) spacious   (C) roomy   (D) tone-deaf

3

The highlighted word is closest in meaning to which of the following?

24. The economy of my nation has been stagnant for a few years.
   (A) static   (B) commodious   (C) expeditious   (D) snappy

25. Refrigerating meat can retard the spread of bacteria.
   (A) unveil   (B) rummage   (C) decelerate   (D) divulge

★★★☆☆

1151 totalitarian [toˌtæləˈtɛrɪən]　　　極權主義的　　　total

a. dictatorial; autocratic; authoritarian

全部 (total) 由一個人來統治

We can rarely find free elections in a totalitarian country. The leader of the country is chosen by himself or a small group of people.

極權國家沒有自由選舉，極權領袖是由少數人或自己選出的。

★★★★★

1152 treatise [ˈtritɪs]　　　學術論文，專著　　　treat

n. dissertation; monograph; thesis

針對某主題加以論述 (treat) 的

Mr. Hendricks has been writing a long treatise on urban planning. He is interested in making a city free from traffic jams.

有志於杜絕塞車的漢屈克斯先生正在撰寫關於都市計畫的長篇論文。

★★★★☆

1153 trespass [ˈtrɛspəs]　　　擅闖，侵入　　　pass

v. encroach; infringe; invade; intrude; transgress; entrench

貫穿 (tres-) 或經過 (pass) 他人勢力範圍

Please be careful. If you trespass on Mr. Peterson's property, his ugly bulldog will run out and bite you in the leg.

請小心，若擅闖彼德森先生的住宅，惡犬會衝出來咬人。

★★★★☆

1154 trial [ˈtraɪəl]　　　試驗，考驗　　　try

n. agony; suffering; anguish; adversity; hardship; rigor; vicissitude

嘗試 (try)

A gem cannot be polished without friction, nor a man perfected without trials.
　　　　　　　　　　　　　　　　　— C. H. Spurgeon

寶石靠雕磨而光滑透亮，人因考驗而臻於完美。
　　　　　　　　　　　—十九世紀知名佈道家 C・H・司布真

★★★★☆

1155 turbulent [ˈtɜbjələnt]　　　動亂的，騷動的，狂暴的　　　turbine

a. boisterous; rowdy; clamorous; stormy

如渦輪引擎 (turbine) 般騷亂的

All the couple did was fight, cry, make up and then start the cycle again. It was a turbulent relationship, and they were only together for one week.

所有夫妻都是吵架、哭泣、和好，然後再重來一遍是個動亂的關係，而兩人甚至才在一起一周而已。

★★★★☆

1156 turnout [ˈtɜnˌaʊt]　　　集會 / 出席者，產量　　　turn, out

n. gathering / participant

出來 (turn out) 集合的人們

A: What is the notice about?

B: This is about the proposed motivational training. The boss is expecting a good turnout.

A：這是什麼通知？

B：有關激勵訓練的，老闆希望大家都參加。

★★★☆☆

1157 turnstile [ˈtɜnˌstaɪl]　　　旋轉門　　　turn

n. revolving door

旋轉 (turn) 的門

Please insert your ticket in this slot, and you can go through the turnstile.

請將票卡插入驗票機後即可進入旋轉門。

★★☆☆☆

1158 turtleneck [ˈtɜtlˌnɛk]　　　高領毛衣　　　turtle, neck

n. a sweater with a long neck

像烏龜 (turtle) 的脖子 (neck)

I decided to wear a turtleneck which my mother knitted for me because the weather was very cold.

天氣好冷於是我決定穿母親織的高領毛衣。

1159 twine [twaɪn]　　★★☆☆☆　　編織，纏繞
v. twist; plait; braid; wind

twist
搓捻 (twist) 後纏繞在一起

My sister likes to twine her hair into braids. But I personally dislike her hair style, because she looks too conservative.

姊姊喜歡將頭髮編成辮子，但我不喜歡她的髮型，因為看來很古板。

1160 twofold [`tufold]　　★★★★☆　　兩倍的，雙重的
a. ad. twice

two, fold
疊 (fold) 成兩 (two) 層的

After World War II there was a baby boom in this nation. Since then, the population of this nation has increased almost twofold.

第二次世界大戰後本國出現戰後嬰兒潮，從此人口幾乎翻漲兩倍。

1161 tycoon [taɪ`kun]　　★★★☆☆　　鉅子，大亨
n. magnate: entrepreneur

taikun
日本的大軍或將軍 (taikun)

Business tycoons like Andrew Carnegie and John Rockefeller have contributed to developing the United States.

安德魯‧卡內基和約翰‧洛克斐勒等企業鉅子都曾捐款協助創建美國。

1162 typhoid [`taɪfɔɪd]　　★★★☆☆　　傷寒
n. typhoid fever

typhus
斑疹傷寒 (typhus)

Typhoid is an infectious disease caused by bacillus and characterized by inflammation of the intestines.

傷寒是由傷寒桿菌引起的傳染病，症狀包括腸炎等。

1163 typhoon [taɪ`fun]　　★★★★☆　　颱風
n. tropical storm; hurricane; tropical cyclone

颱風
音同中文的颱風

Typhoons usually hit Korea along the coast of the South Sea, bringing heavy floods in late summer and early autumn.

夏末秋初之際，颱風常沿南海海岸而上侵襲韓國，並造成嚴重水患。

1164 typo [`taɪpo]　　★★★★★　　打字排印錯誤，誤植
n. typographical error

typing
打字 (typing) 出現的錯誤

Professor Smith found umpteen typos in Jane's thesis. So the professor told her to revise it carefully.

史密斯教授在珍的論文裡發現打字錯誤，於是要她仔細校正。

1165 tyrannical [tɪ`rænɪkl̩]　　★★★★★　　暴君的，殘暴的，專橫的
a. despotic

tyrant
和獨裁者 (tyrant) 有關的

The ruler was so tyrannical toward his subjects that no one respected him. Eventually, he was dethroned.

統治者對人民非常殘暴以致無人尊敬他，最後遭到罷黜。

1166 ultimatum [ˌʌltə`metəm]　　★★★★☆　　最後通牒
n. final notice

ultimate
最後 (ultimate) 通報的話

The United States sent the aggressor nation an ultimatum, in which the evacuation of the invader was called for.

美國對侵略國下達最後通牒，要求入侵者撤離。

1167 umbrageous [ʌmˈbredʒəs] ★★☆☆☆ 成蔭的，多蔭的

a. shady

Umbrageous trees are important for the survival of many kinds of animals in the forest.

對森林各種動物的生存而言綠樹成蔭是重要的。

umbrella
形成陰影的傘狀物 (umbrella)

1168 underbrush [ˈʌndəˌbrʌʃ] ★★★★★ 矮樹叢，林下灌木叢

n. undergrowth; bush; thicket

Because of the bush-fire, almost all the trees and underbrush in the forest were burnt.

林區大火幾乎燒燬所有森林樹木和矮樹叢。

under, brush
如樹木下方 (under) 的刷狀物 (brush)

1169 undergrowth [ˈʌndəˌɡroθ] ★★★★★ 樹叢，矮樹叢

n. underbrush; bush; thicket

The undergrowth was so thick that the hunters could not follow the beast as it fled deeper into the jungle.

濃密的矮樹叢使獵人無法追捕竄入的野獸。

under, grow
生長 (growth) 在樹木下方的 (under)

1170 under-the-table [ˈʌndəðəˈtebl] ★★★★☆ 祕密的，暗中的 / 非法交易的

a. covert; stealthy; clandestine / unlawful

The minister's reputation was tainted by the scandal that he had received a lot of under-the-table payments from aircraft importers.

部長因收受飛機進口商大筆非法款項而身敗名裂。

under, table
在桌子 (table) 底下 (under) 的

1171 upheaval [ʌpˈhivl] ★★★★★ 地殼隆起，鼓起 / 動亂 / 劇變，大變動

n. upturn / commotion: convulsion / change

The new government decided that a total upheaval was necessary, and as a result the entire parliamentary system changed dramatically.

新政府認為需全面改革，於是徹底改變整個議會制度。

heavy, heave
向上 (up) 舉起 (heave) 並翻轉過來

1172 upkeep [ˈʌpˌkip] ★★★★★ 保養，維修

n. maintenance

The upkeep of the great castle is too high even for a millionaire. It takes a week to clean it once, and it is a devil to keep warm in winter.

城堡維修費用高到連鉅富都覺得昂貴，裡外打掃一遍要花一周，寒冬很難保暖。

keep up
保持 (keep up)

1173 uprising [ˈʌpˌraɪzɪŋ] ★★★★☆ 起義

n. rebellion

The statue standing in the middle of the park was dedicated to commemorate the students' uprising.

公園中央豎立的雕像是為了紀念學生起義。

up, rise
向上 (up) 舉起 (rising)

1174 uproot [ʌpˈrut] ★★★★★ 連根拔除，根除，滅絕

v. eradicate; exterminate; root out; wipe out; annihilate

Our president is searching for effective ways to uproot widespread social evils.

總統正尋求有效方式杜絕普遍的社會罪惡。

root
將根 (root) 向上 (up) 拔出

1175 urbane [ɝ`ben] ★★★☆☆　　　彬彬有禮的，高雅的，有教養的　　urban
像都市 (urban) 人般洗練的

a. genteel; cultivated; refined; well-bred

George's urbane manner made him welcome at elegant social gatherings. Almost every other night he went to a party.

喬治的彬彬有禮使他在上流社交場合深受歡迎，幾乎每隔一晚就有邀約。

MP3 49

1176 usurp [ju`zɝp] ★★★★☆　　　篡奪，篡權　　use
占用 (use) 他人權力

v. seize illegally

The duke contrived to usurp the throne. However at the last moment his contrivance was revealed.

公爵密謀篡奪王位但最後計謀敗露。

1177 utilize [`jutḷˌaɪz] ★★★★★　　　利用，善用　　use
使用 (use)

v. make use of; use; employ

At the motor show we saw several compact cars which utilize solar energy. Many people were interested in them.

車展上有幾款利用太陽能發電的小型車吸引眾人目光。

1178 vaccination [ˌvæksn̩`eʃən] ★★★★★　　　預防接種　　vaccine
接種疫苗 (vaccine)

n. the act or practice of vaccinating

We were told that we needed complete physical exams and vaccinations before we could travel to Africa.

我們被告知前往非洲旅遊前須進行全身健檢和預防接種。

1179 vanish [`vænɪʃ] ★★★★★　　　消失不見　　vain
形成虛空 (vain) 狀態

v. disappear; evanesce; fade out; evaporate

The mother just saw her little child there, but now he's gone. How could he have vanished? She began looking for him.

媽媽剛才還看見自己的孩子，現在卻不見了。怎麼會消失無蹤呢？她開始到處尋找。

1180 vanity [`vænətɪ] ★★★★☆　　　自負，虛榮心　　vain
虛榮的 (vain) 心

n. vainglory; narcissism; conceit

As a college student, my uncle had one vanity, which was his hair. He spent lots of hours shampooing, brushing and styling it. Now he's bald.

舅舅念大學時的髮型讓他很自負，他花很多時間梳洗整理以致現在禿頭了。

1181 vehemently [`viəməntlɪ] ★★★★☆　　　激烈地　　vehicle
像車輛 (vehicle) 般有力

ad. intense; furious; fierce; violent; desperate

Mr. and Mrs. Chan argued vehemently for days before they realized that they could not live together.

陳先生和妻子大吵數日，最後發現兩人無法同處在一個屋簷下。

1182 vengeance [`vɛndʒəns] ★★★★☆　　　復仇，報復，報仇　　revenge
報仇 (revenge)

n. retaliation; avengement; counterblow; revenge; retribution

Hamlet felt a strong vengeance toward his uncle who had killed his father, but he could not do anything because he was indecisive.

哈姆雷特很想向舅舅報殺父之仇，但因優柔寡斷無法成事。

1183 vicarious [vaɪˈkɛrɪəs] ★★★☆☆

感同身受的，設身處地的，代人受罰的

vice-president
次的 (vice-) 總統 (president)

a. taking the place of another person

As a scapegoat, the priest received a vicarious punishment. Everybody else thought that he was strange.

神父甘願當代罪羔羊代人受罰，大家都覺得他太奇怪了。

1184 virulent [ˈvɪrʊlənt] ★★★★☆

致命的，劇毒的，充滿敵意的，惡毒的

virus
像濾過性病毒 (virus) 般的

a. malign; malignant

The virulent disease spread so quickly that the medical team was helpless to control the deaths of its victims.

致命疾病快速蔓延，醫療小組無法控制死亡人數。

1185 void [vɔɪd] ★★★★☆

空白，空虛 / 空的，沒有的

avoid
把位子空出來 (void)

n. vacuity; blankness; vacancy; emptiness / a. empty; hollow

When my best friend moved away I felt a strong void in my life that no one else could fill. I spent much time looking at his picture.

好友搬走後我感到無比空虛，沒有人可以填補，我花很長時間看著他的照片。

1186 volatile [ˈvɑlətl̩] ★★★★☆

揮發性的，揮發的

volleyball
像排球 (volleyball) 一樣在空中飛來飛去

a. evaporable; evaporating quickly

Volatile liquids, such as alcohol and gasoline, evaporate quickly when they are placed in an open space.

將酒精和汽油等揮發性液體放在戶外會快速揮發。

1187 web [wɛb] ★★★★★

蜘蛛網，網狀組織，圈套

weave
編織 (weave) 蛛網 (web)

n. spiderweb; cobweb

A spider uses a cobweb to catch insects, but it doesn't get stuck in its own web, even though it is very sticky.

蜘蛛利用蛛網捕捉昆蟲，蛛網雖黏卻困不住蜘蛛。

1188 whereabouts [ˌhwɛrəˈbaʊts] ★★★☆☆

行蹤，下落，所在

where
不知道到哪裡 (where) 去了

n. the place where a person or thing is

If anyone of you knows of his whereabouts, please contact me. He has been missing for days.

知道他行蹤的人請和我聯絡，他已失蹤數日。

1189 wilderness [ˈwɪldənɪs] ★★★★★

荒野，野外

wild
野生 (wild) 世界

n. hinterland; barren; wild land

Sam preferred to go camping and hiking deep in the wilderness among the lakes and trees. He even built a small hut beside a small lake.

山姆比較喜歡到湖畔林間的野外露營和健行，他甚至在小湖畔搭蓋一間簡陋小屋。

1190 wilful [ˈwɪlfəl] ★★★★☆

任性的，倔強的

will
堅持自己的意志 (will)

a. obstinate; headstrong; mulish; perverse; intractable

The wilful young girl decided to attend the party in spite of her father's warnings.

任性少女不顧父親警告執意要參加宴會。

★★★☆☆

1191 wistful [`wɪstfəl] 渴望的，沉思的 wish

a. showing or expressing vague yearnings; longing pensively

期待 (wish) 未來的心

Ronald and his wife often look wistfully at the interesting pictures which they took during their honeymoon.

羅南和妻子常若有所思地望著蜜月時拍攝的有趣照片。

★★★★☆

1192 wither [`wɪðə] 枯萎，凋謝 weather

v. dry up; shrivel; wilt; wane

經日曬雨淋 (weather) 而枯萎

The grapes withered on the vine because the owner of the orchard didn't pick them at the right time.

葡萄枯死在藤蔓上，因果園主人沒有及時採收。

★★★★☆

1193 workaholic [ˌwɝkə`hɔlɪk] 工作第一的人，工作至上者 work, alcoholic

n. a person having a compulsive need to work

對工作 (work) 上癮 (-holic)

Wolfgang Amadeus Mozart must have been a 'workaholic.' He wrote 789 compositions, including operas, symphonies, concertos, quartets and sonatas.

莫札特一定是工作至上者，因為他總共創作了七百八十九首樂曲，包括歌劇、交響曲、協奏曲、四重奏和奏鳴曲等。

★★★☆☆

1194 yardstick [`jɑrdˌstɪk] 碼尺，量尺 yard, stick

n. a graduated stick or rod one yard in length used in measuring; any test or standard used in measuring, judging, etc.

丈量尺碼 (yard) 的棍子 (stick)

Please pass me the yardstick so that I can measure this table. I wonder if it will fit in my study.

請給我量尺好測量這張桌子，不知道跟書房合不合。

★★☆☆☆

1195 yep [jɛp] 是，好（yes 的口語） yes

ad. yes

yes的強調說法

"Yep, I'm all ready for the rodeo," said the cowboy. But as soon as he finished his words, he fell down to the ground from the untamed bull.

牛仔說：「是的，我準備好要鬥牛了。」但一說完話就從難馴的牛背上摔到地上。

★☆☆☆☆

1196 yonder [`jɑndə] 在那邊 beyond

a. ad. beyond

越 (beyond) 至另一端

The ranch is over yonder by the forest. It will probably take you less than ten minutes to get there.

牧場在森林那邊，差不多要花十分鐘才能到達。

★★★★☆

1197 yummy [`jʌmɪ] 好吃的，美味的 Yum, yum!

a. delicious; luscious; palatable; tasty; savory; delectable

發出 yum, yum 聲，表示很美味

Children think cake and ice cream are yummy, but few like broccoli or carrots, which are good for their health.

孩子們都覺得蛋糕和冰淇淋好吃，只有少數人喜歡有益健康的花椰菜和紅蘿蔔。

★★☆☆☆

1198 zealot [`zɛlət] 狂熱份子 zeal

n. enthusiast; fanatic; maniac; bug

懷有熱誠 (zeal) 的人

The zealot was very excited about the upcoming celebration. He did everything during the process of preparation.

狂熱份子對即將來臨的慶典感到興奮無比，並盡全力做好準備。

1199 zodiac [ˈzodɪˌæk]

☆☆☆☆☆

黃道帶

ZOO
動物生肖名稱

n. *compass; twelve signs of constellations*

The signs of the zodiac are Aries, Taurus, Gemini, Cancer, Leo, Virgo, Libra, Scorpio, Sagittarius, Capricorn, Aquarius and Pisces.

黃道帶十二星座分別是牡羊、金牛、雙子、巨蟹、獅子、天秤、處女、天蠍、射手、摩羯、水瓶和雙魚座。

1200 zoolatry [zoˈɑlətrɪ]

★★☆☆☆

動物崇拜

ZOO
動物 (zo-) 崇拜 (-olatry) 的

n. *worship of animals*

Indians are known for their zoolatry. Cows are worshipped as sacred.

印第安人以動物崇拜聞名，將牛當成神明崇拜。

𝒯ea 𝒯ime... ☕

<Greek legend> Labyrinth

A structure containing an intricate network of winding passages hard to follow without losing one's way; a structure built by Daedalus for King Minos of Crete, to house the Minotaur.

〈希臘神話〉拉比林斯迷宮

狄德勒斯為克里特國王邁諾斯建造的迷宮，用來關住邁諾陶洛斯。迷宮裡有錯綜複雜的曲折道路，很容易迷路。（註：克里特國王邁諾斯請希臘最知名的工匠狄德勒斯建造巨大迷宮，為的是關住力大無窮、個性暴烈的人身牛頭怪物邁諾陶洛斯。Labyrinth 除了指「迷宮」外，也可用來比喻「錯綜複雜的事物」或「糾纏不清的關係」。）

❖ **labyrinthian** [ˌlæbəˈrɪnθɪən] **a.** *mazy; complex; intricate; complicated; tangled; enigmatic* | （像）迷宮的，曲折的，複雜的

Below the old castle was a labyrinthian cellar that stretched far down into the earth, and the villagers suspected that many mysteries and treasures were buried there.

古堡下方有迷宮般深入地底的地窖，村民懷疑裡面埋藏許多金銀珠寶和秘密。

1 Complete each word by filling in the blank with proper spelling so that it has the same meaning as suggested. Then please write the meaning of each word in Chinese.

1. 極權主義的 = t o t a l i _ _ _ _ _ _
2. 鉅子 = t y c _ _ _
3. 學術論文 = _ _ _ _ _ i s e
4. 擅闖 = t r e s _ _ _ _
5. 動亂的 = _ _ _ _ u l e n t
6. 考驗 = _ _ _ a l
7. 矮樹叢 = u n d e r _ _ _ _ t h
8. 大變動 = u p _ _ _ _ _ _
9. 起義 = _ _ r i s i n g
10. 連根拔除 = u p _ _ _ _

11. vaccination = _____
12. vehement = _____
13. vengeance = _____
14. virulent = _____
15. whereabouts = _____
16. wilderness = _____
17. workaholic = _____
18. yardstick = _____
19. wistful = _____
20. zealot = _____

2 Choose a word that best completes the sentence.

21. **They say that _____ and error is the source of our knowledge.**
    (A) trial   (B) typhoon   (C) treatise   (D) upheaval

22. **The corrupt official asked her for some _____ payments.**
    (A) under-the-table   (B) well-bred   (C) wilful   (D) barren

3 The highlighted word is closest in meaning to which of the following?

23. **After his friend passed away, the old man felt a sort of void in his life.**
    (A) conceit   (B) vanity   (C) vacuity   (D) vengeance

24. **The roses which Sam gave her withered because she forgot to put them in the vase.**
    (A) usurped   (B) eradicated   (C) exterminated   (D) wilted

25. **The upkeep of Mrs. Joyce's gas hog was exorbitant.**
    (A) vaccination   (B) commotion   (C) maintenance   (D) bush

Practice Test 03

1
The highlighted word is closest in meaning to which of the following?

1. The newly elected government was determined to `liquidate` the previous government's legacy.
   - (A) lower
   - (B) originate
   - (C) offend
   - (D) eradicate

2. She was a lady of some `mettle`. She was not afraid of walking in front of many men.
   - (A) courage
   - (B) mischance
   - (C) mobility
   - (D) negligence

3. You should know that you are becoming `obese` when it takes longer to dry yourself after a shower.
   - (A) needy
   - (B) numerous
   - (C) nasal
   - (D) fat

4. For a person who wants to take in `pastoral` beauty, this island is highly recommendable.
   - (A) partial
   - (B) bucolic
   - (C) overt
   - (D) ornate

5. We're going to have a surprise party for Mom. Please don't `reveal` the secret.
   - (A) vanish
   - (B) divulge
   - (C) slake
   - (D) utilize

2
Please answer the following questions.

(Comic Tale 1)

An old couple entered a fancy restaurant and took a seat in a dimly illuminated corner of the `spacious` restaurant. A waiter asked if they were ready to order. They were very picky about their choices. After a long discussion, they decided to order tender sirloin steaks. As soon as the food was delivered, the old man began to shovel it in, but the old woman didn't even touch her fork. All she did was `slake` her thirst by drinking some water. However, from the look of her, the waiter could tell that she was extremely hungry. Being worried, the waiter walked up to the lady and asked if anything was wrong. She said that everything was all right. Being afraid that he was too nosy, the waiter tried to stay away from the old couple's table. At last, the old man finished his meal, and he stealthily passed something to her across the table: HIS DENTURES!

(Comic Tale 2)

A newly wedded couple boarded the plane for their honeymoon. The bride was sitting in the window seat and the groom in the aisle seat. Neither of them had ever flown in an airplane, and there were numerous novel things which they had never seen. After the plane took off, their eyes were riveted to the scenes unfolding on the ground below. However, unfortunately, both of them were extremely near-sighted. After about an hour's flight, the bride exclaimed, "How amazing! Look down there, Jimmy! The immaculate white beach never ends even after an hour's flight! I've never imagined such a long beach could exist." "Really? Let me have a look at it," said the groom and leaned over towards the windows. He refuted the bride by saying, "Nonsense, it's not a beach but the runway. Oh, my Goodness, I've never imagined such a long runway could exist!" A stewardess, who was not able to placate her curiosity about what was going on, approached them and looked out through the window. It was the wing of the airplane.

6. **The word** spacious **is closest in meaning to which of the following?**
   (A) commodious
   (B) placid
   (C) poignant
   (D) petty

7. **The word** slake **is closest in meaning to which of the following?**
   (A) retard
   (B) originate
   (C) usurp
   (D) quench

8. **The word** numerous **is closest in meaning to which of the following?**
   (A) substantial
   (B) urbane
   (C) many
   (D) slipshod

9. **The word** refuted **is closest in meaning to which of the following?**
   (A) simulated
   (B) confuted
   (C) shattered
   (D) prolonged

10. **The word** placate **is closest in meaning to which of the following?**
    (A) offend
    (B) liquidate
    (C) allay
    (D) overwhelm

Passage 1

Black Holes

Many scientists insist that there are some regions of space that exert tremendous gravity. The gravity is so tremendous that it tugs at time, space and even at light. Because of this intense attractive force, time passes more slowly, space gets stretched out and light gets trapped. Since light cannot get out of the holes, the regions remain black and invisible.

John Wheeler, an American physicist, named these abysmal , sucking hollows "black holes." Even though the idea of black holes has not been averred by the conclusive discovery of an actual one, since 1915, when Albert Einstein proposed his theory of relativity, some scientists have studied the possibility of the existence of black holes and the cause of their formation. For instance, the German astronomer Karl Schwarzschild maintained that a star the size of the sun - 1,392,000 kilometers in diameter - would have to be compressed to less than 3 kilometers within a second for the gravity to be strong enough to harness light. In 1939 American physicists J. Robert Oppenheimer and Hartland S. Snyder contended that if a star is more than 3.2 times as massive as the sun and if its nuclear fuel is totally consumed, then it collapses under its own weight, becoming that small.

However, nowadays it is a general consensus that many stars including the sun emit energy through nucleic fusion and that if their nucleic fuels are consumed , stars dwindle in size. Stars, depending on their masses, enter three different phases. Stars which are less than 8 times as massive as the sun get cooler and cooler and become white dwarfs when their fuels are exhausted. Stars more than 8 times to dozens of times as massive as the sun collapse because of their own weight. This kind of collapse results in a core composed of neutrons, leading to a giant explosion, or a Big Bang, creating a Supernova. The explosion is responsible for a neutron star with a radius of less than 10 kilometers. This kind of star has extremely great density. However, on the other hand, larger stars which have enormous mass experience a collapse, but because of their great mass there is no explosion. Instead they keep on dwindling to a smaller size. As the contraction proceeds, the stars come to have greater density and correspondingly greater gravity. And therefore the contraction is accelerated accordingly, thereby forming black holes.

Nowadays it is estimated that the Milky Way has as many as 100 million black holes left behind by collapsed stars. In 1992 scientists using the Hubble Telescope found promising signs of a black hole approximately 3 million times as large as the mass of the sun, paving the way for the oncoming generation who will possibly cast light upon the mystery of black holes.

Scientists have turned their eyes also to white holes. Their insistence is that if there are black holes which suck in everything, there must be something which emits everything. This sort of idea stems from the theory of relativity. John Wheeler named the channel which is thought to link the two realms a "worm hole", insinuating that the channel "eats up" even time and space like a worm. Some scientists think that humans can travel at an excess of the speed of light through this worm hole.

1. **The highlighted word** abysmal **can be replaced by which of the following?**
   (A) bottomless
   (B) combative
   (C) commodious
   (D) reckless

2. **The highlighted word** averred **can be replaced by which of the following?**
   (A) ransacked
   (B) quelled
   (C) rambled
   (D) verified

3. **The highlighted word** collapses **can be replaced by which of the following?**
   (A) summons
   (B) smothers
   (C) disintegrates
   (D) replaces

4. **The highlighted word** consumed **can be replaced by which of the following?**
   (A) renewed
   (B) exhausted
   (C) reproached
   (D) ousted

5. **The highlighted word** emits **can be replaced by which of the following?**
   (A) is subject to
   (B) changes into vapor
   (C) withdraws from
   (D) gives off

Passage 2

Movies

Those who have seen the movie, *The Sound of Music*, the winner of the Academy Award for the best picture of 1965, might not easily forget the pleasing melodies of the "Do, Re, Mi" song, the comical dialogues among children, the romance and thrilling suspense. Julie Andrews plays the spunky Maria, a nun who does not fit in at the convent. When she is sent to live with a large family as their resident governess, she takes good care of the seven children, playing with and cheering up the children dejected due to their father's strict discipline. She teaches them lovely songs, so the children come to love Maria very much. Maria falls in love with and marries the children's father, the handsome Captain Von Trapp, whose role is played by the Canadian actor Christopher Plummer. However, Von Trapp and Maria decide to flee after the Nazi invasion of Austria. This 172-minute-long musical can be said to have it all; comedy, suspense, romance and much more.

Of course, besides *The Sound of Music*, we can hear about many others' reviews on various movies which have attracted many moviegoers as well. *Dr. Zhivago* enchants us with snowy scenery haunted by a beautiful musical score, "The Theme of Lara." *Star Wars*, a vintage pulp science fiction film written and directed by George Lucas, takes us to a fantastic galaxy far away. In *Cast Away*, Tom Hanks teaches us how it is possible for a person to use the blade of a skate to extract a decayed tooth and also allows us to imagine how talkative Robinson Crusoe might have become, if he had had a Wilson volleyball. And *The Lord of the Rings*, directed by Peter Jackson, shows us that a ring can be used to instigate unbridled imagination in addition to being used as an engagement ring like "my precious" in the film.

A movie is something that makes a movie buff jump up and down with joy. But even a spectator who goes to a theater only once in a blue moon, once inside a movie theater, tends to wait nervously for the movie to start. The dark inside of a theater encourages people to reveal their emotions more freely. Even though most modern spectators hesitate showing their emotions while watching a movie, some spectators in the past would often laugh their heads off, some would sob throughout ending up with swollen eyes, and some would tremble with fear, ending up hugging their date, whether unintentionally or intentionally. Others would yell until they lost their voices. It has happened that an overeager spectator has become totally engrossed in the love story or ongoing action of the movie and absent-mindedly put his hand into the popcorn bag of a neighboring spectator instead of his date's. Moviegoers are apt to identify themselves with the characters in the movies. We can tell the males who are coming out of a movie theater after seeing an Arnold Schwarzenegger or Bruce Lee movie by their stiff neck and shoulders.

Ever since Lumiere brothers experimented on their first motion-pictures in a basement of a cafe, the motion-picture industry has developed by leaps and bounds, weathering the competition of radio, theater and even television. Cary Grant, one of Hollywood's most respected actors, once said, "Filmmakers make a product at a factory and ship it out in cans." Anyway, it is certain that films attract moviegoers as strongly as cans of candies attract children.

6. **The highlighted word** `dejected` **can be replaced by which of the following?**
   (A) depressed
   (B) bulky
   (C) diurnal
   (D) discreet

7. **The highlighted word** `enchants` **can be replaced by which of the following?**
   (A) captivates
   (B) dogged
   (C) edible
   (D) evanescent

8. **The highlighted word** `extract` **can be replaced by which of the following?**
   (A) put down
   (B) make unable
   (C) cast out
   (D) pull out

9. **The highlighted word** `reveal` **can be replaced by which of the following?**
   (A) show
   (B) appeal
   (C) extend
   (D) reinforce

10. **The highlighted word** `attract` **can be replaced by which of the following?**
   (A) terminate
   (B) twine
   (C) allure
   (D) wither

Building Vocabulary for
iBT, SAT, GRE, TOEIC, GEPT

20天

01 | **02** |

CHAPTER

03

詞素家族記憶法

1201~2200

⁜ ac(r) = sour; sharp 酸的；尖銳的

★★★★☆

MP3 50

1201 acrid

[`ækrɪd]

a. bitterly pungent; irritating belong 辛辣的，刺鼻的

The gray air, acrid with sulfur dioxide, often sears our eyes. Air pollution is one of the greatest problems in my city.
刺鼻的二氧化硫髒污空氣常使雙眼乾澀，空氣污染是本城市最嚴重的問題之一。

★★★★★

1202 acid

[`æsɪd]

n. any of a class of substances that have a PH of less than 7; substance any sour 酸

DNA, a nucleic acid, which is known to determine the particular structure and function of every single cell, was discovered by Watson and Crick.
華生和克里克發現的去氧核糖核酸DNA能決定每個單一細胞的特殊結構和功能。

★★★★☆

1203 acrimonious

[ˌækrə`monɪəs]

a. bitter in manner or temper 苛刻的，毒辣的

Daniel made a few acrimonious comments at the party, and soon found that he had been left alone in the corner because no one wanted to listen to his sarcasm.
丹尼爾在宴會上提出一些苛刻評論，旋即發現自己被冷落，因為沒人想聽他的挖苦話。

★★★★☆

1204 acidulous

[ə`sɪdʒələs]

a. somewhat acid; tart 尖酸的，諷刺的

James had a very biting and bitter sense of humor, so many people described him as acidulous.
詹姆斯很喜歡嘲諷和挖苦他人，許多人都認為他為人尖酸刻薄。

★★★★☆

1205 acetic

[ə`sitɪk]

a. of or like vinegar 醋的

Acetic acid is a natural chemical that is used as a solvent in the manufacture of rubber and plastic.
製造橡膠和塑膠時作為溶劑使用的醋酸是天然化學物質。

★★★★☆

1206 acute

[ə`kjut]

a. sharp; acrimonious; intense 劇烈的，尖銳的

The new-born baby was so cute and lovely that its mother forgot about the horribly acute pain she had had while in labor.
漂亮、可愛的新生嬰兒使母親忘記分娩時的劇痛。

⁜ ad-= to, near 往，接近

★★★★★

1207 adjoin

[ə`dʒɔɪn]

v. be next to end; joined with 毗連，鄰近

Joe's forge adjoined our house, which was a wooden house, as many of

the dwellings in our country were - most of them, at that time.

Great Expectations —— Charles Dickens

喬伊的鐵工廠毗鄰我家的木造建築，當時住宅大多是木造的。

—— 《孤星血淚》狄更斯

★★★★★

1208 adjacent	***a.*** *neighboring; contiguous; abutting; bordering*	毗連的，鄰近的

[ə`dʒesn̩t]

The Korean Peninsula has both the advantage of easy access to adjacent cultures and the disadvantage of becoming the target of aggressive neighbors.

朝鮮半島的優勢在於容易親近鄰近文化，劣勢則是常成為鄰國侵略的目標。

★★★★★

1209 advent	***n.*** *the arrival of an important person or thing*	來臨，到來

[`ædvɛnt]

With the advent of the credit card, people can easily become addicted to spending too much money.

隨著信用卡的到來，人們容易變得揮霍。

★★★★★

1210 adjust	***v.*** *arrange; put in the correct order or position; make suitable*	調整，校準

[ə`dʒʌst]

If your car is making funny noises you may need to adjust your carburetor to fix the problem.

如果你的車發出奇怪噪音，最好校準化油器以解決問題。

★★★★☆

1211 adjunct	***n.*** *accessory; a subordinate thing*	附屬品，附加物

[`ædʒʌŋkt]

An appendix which was often thought to be an unnecessary adjunct is now thought to have its own characteristic function.

過去常認為附錄是多餘的附屬品，現在則被視為具獨特功能。

✛ (a)esthe = feel 感覺

★★★☆☆

1212 an(a)esthetic	***n.*** *a substance that produces insensibility to pain*	麻醉藥

[ænəs`θɛtɪk]

The traditional an(a)esthetic which is employed by dentists is novocaine, which mitigates the pain of drilling.

牙醫師施打的傳統麻醉藥奴佛卡因可減輕鑽牙痠痛。

★★★☆☆

1213 (a)esthetic	***a.*** *concerned with the appreciation of beauty*	藝術的，美學的

[ɛs`θɛtɪk]

His painting was an (a)esthetic success, beautiful and imaginative, but he knew that no one would ever understand it.

他的畫作是富有想像力的完美藝術成就，但他知道沒人懂他的畫。

★★☆☆☆

1214 **an(a)esthetize**	**v.** *administer an an(a)esthetic to; numb*	使麻醉
[əˈnɛsθəˌtaɪz]		

The doctor an(a)esthetized John's wound before stitching it. Otherwise he could never have withstood the pain.
醫師縫合約翰傷口前先將他麻醉，否則他將很難忍住這種痛。

★★★☆☆

1215 **(a)esthetics**	**n.** *the philosophy of the beautiful, especially in art*	美學
[ɛsˈθɛtɪks]		

As a professor of (a)esthetics, he was keenly aware of what was considered beautiful or tasteful in terms of art and life.
身為美學教授，他很清楚從藝術和人生的角度來看什麼才是完美或優雅的。

★★★☆☆

1216 **an(a)esthesia**	**n.** *the absence of sensation achieved by the administration of gases or the injection of drugs*	麻醉
[ˌænəsˈθiʒə]		

Once the an(a)esthesia wore off he would be in a lot of pain for at least a week. So he would need some pain killers.
麻醉消退後至少一周會相當疼痛，所以他需服用止痛藥。

✛ **ag, ig = act, do** 行動，做

★★☆☆☆

1217 **exigency**	**n.** *emergency; an urgent need or demand*	緊急狀態，緊要關頭
[ˈɛksədʒənsɪ]		

Fleeing the country in the event of a sudden war was an exigency for which he had not carefully planned.
他沒有緊急逃離突發戰事國家的周詳計畫。

★★★★★

1218 **agile**	**a.** *quick-moving; nimble; brisk; swift; active; lively; limber; sprightly*	敏捷的，靈活的
[ˈædʒəl]		

The polar bear, agile both in and out of water, is a supreme predator in the Arctic. Its movement can be unbelievably swift.
無論在海上或陸上動作都靈活的北極熊是北極最大的掠食者，牠的行動出乎意料地敏捷。

★★★★★

1219 **antagonize**	**v.** *evoke hostility or enmity in; counteract*	使敵對，使成敵人
[ænˈtægəˌnaɪz]		

When I was young, one of my brother's favorite pastimes was to antagonize me until we got in a fight.
小時候哥哥最大的消遣之一就是跟我作對，直到我們打起來。

★★★★★

1220 agitate

[`ædʒə‚tet]

v. arouse; excite; rouse 煽動，鼓動

The demagogue's inflammatory speech agitated people.
群眾煽動者激動的言論鼓動了民心。

✦ agri- = soil 土壤

★★★★☆

1221 agronomy

[ə`grɑnəmɪ]

n. the science of soil management and crop production 農藝學，農業經濟

John, in hopes of someday taking over his father's 1,000-acre farm, is studying agronomy so as to better understand the mass production of agriculture.
希望將來繼承父親千畝農場的約翰正在鑽研農藝學，以便更為熟悉農業量產。

★★★★★

1222 agriculture

[`ægrɪ‚kʌltʃə]

n. the science or practice of cultivating the soil and rearing animals 農業

This area is unsuitable for agriculture because its soil is too arid to grow plants. It rains only for a few days in a year.
此區不適合農業發展，因土壤太酸作物無法生長，年降雨天數也不足。

★★★★☆

1223 agrestic

[ə`grɛstɪk]

a. rustic; unpolished 鄉土味的，土氣的

The farmer had spent his entire life in a small village, and when he finally went to the city, he found that he could not overcome his agrestic behavior.
農夫終其一生都待在小鄉村，直到來到大都市才發現改不了鄉下習慣。

★★★☆☆

1224 agrarian

[ə`grɛrɪən]

a. of or relating to the land or its cultivation 耕地的，農業的

In matters of an agrarian nature, farmers are wiser than professors. They know everything about the soil.
農夫比教授更了解耕地的本質，他們熟悉土壤的一切。

✦ ali- = else, elsewhere 其他的，別處

★★★★☆

1225 alibi

[`ælə‚baɪ]

n. a claim, or the evidence supporting it, that when an alleged act took place one was elsewhere 不在場證明，藉口，託辭

Jimmy had a perfect alibi - he was not in the country when the murder took place. That's why he was found "not guilty."
吉米有充分的不在場證明，因為謀殺案發當時他不在國內，因此無罪開釋。

★★★★☆

1226 alias

[`elɪəs]

n. a false or assumed name; pseudonym   假名，化名

The fugitive went by an alias in order to hide his true identity. But the police finally captured him and put him in jail.

逃犯用化名隱藏真實身分，但終遭警方逮捕入獄服刑。

★★★★★

1227 alien

[`elɪən]

n. foreigner; extraterrestrial /   外國人，外僑，外星人 / 外國的，異國風情的
a. foreign; exotic; outlandish

She is an illegal alien living in the United States and must soon become a citizen in order to remain.

她是居留美國的非法外僑，如欲繼續居留就要盡速取得公民權。

★★★★★

1228 alienated

[`elɪənetɪd]

a. estranged; isolated; detached   感到孤獨的，不合群的，疏離的

I felt alienated among so many experts because I knew nothing about photography. Therefore, I just remained silent in the corner.

因為我對攝影一竅不通，置身眾多專家中使我感到疏離，於是站在一旁保持沉默。

✢ alt(o) = high 高的

★★★★☆

MP3
○
51

1229 altimeter

[æl`tɪmətə]

n. an instrument for showing height above sea or ground level,   高度表
a. especially one fitted to an aircraft

The altimeter indicated that we were flying at 8,000 feet above sea level. I was surprised to find that we were flying so high in the sky.

高度表顯示我們正飛行於海拔八千英尺的高度，我很驚訝我們飛得這麼高。

★★★★☆

1230 altar

[`ɔltə]

n. a table or flat-topped block, often of stone, for sacrifice or   聖壇
offering to a deity

Neil prayed at the altar that was positioned in the center of the cathedral. He really wished to get married to his classmate Jane.

尼爾在大教堂中央的聖壇禱告，希望能娶同學珍為妻。

★★★★★

1231 altitude

[`æltə‚tud]

n. the height of an object in relation to a given point;   海拔，標高
a high or exalted position

Planes fly at high altitudes in order to fly above the clouds. They often fly at thousands of feet above sea level.

飛機飛行於高海拔以便在雲層之上。它們通常飛行於幾千英尺高的海平面上。

★★★★☆

1232 exalt	**v.** *raise in rank or power; elevate; lift; uplift; upgrade / praise highly*	拔擢，提升 / 讚揚
[ɪgˋzɔlt]	The retiring mayor was exalted by the citizens. Every citizen wanted him to continue serving as mayor. 退休市長受到市民們的高度讚揚，大家都希望他繼續出任市長。	

❖ alter-, altr- = other, change 其他的，改變

★★★★☆

1233 altruist	**n.** *philanthropist*	利他主義者
[ˋæltruˌɪst]	Chris was known and respected as an altruist and was always in search of people to offer his help and aid. 總是樂於助人的克里斯是公認的利他主義者。	

★★★★★

1234 altercation	**n.** *debate; dispute; quarrel; controversy; wrangle; squabble; polemic*	爭執，爭吵
[ˌɔltɚˋkeʃən]	There was a violent altercation in the bar after two groups had too much to drink. The bartender was the only person who acted as a peacemaker. 雙方飲酒過量後在酒吧起了嚴重爭執，只有酒保扮演和事佬。	

★★★★★

1235 alternately	**ad.** *by turns; reciprocally; in rotation*	交互地，輪流地
[ˋɔltɚnɪtlɪ]	Jack alternately crouched and stood on tiptoe. The next day he couldn't walk because he had sore muscles in his legs. 傑克以腳尖交互蹲站，隔日即因腳痠而無法行走。	

★★★★★

1236 alternative	**n.** *choice; option*	選擇，二擇一
[ɔlˋtɝnətɪv]	The best thing for him to do was run away. There was no other alternative. His girlfriend was really upset. 他別無選擇只能逃跑，女友因此感到相當失望。	

❖ ambi-, amphi- = both; around 兩者；周圍

★★★★☆

1237 ambivalent	**a.** *having opposing feelings simultaneously*	曖昧的，有矛盾情結的
[æmˋbɪvələnt]	Because of Bill's ambivalent tone of voice, I could not understand which side he was on. Therefore, I was careful not to show my true intention. 比爾曖昧的聲調讓我無從得知他支持哪一方，於是我小心不表露我的真正意圖。	

★★☆☆☆

| 1238 **ambivert** | *n. a person who fluctuated between being an introvert and an extrovert* | 內外向個性兼具者 |

[ˋæmbɪvət]

He was considered as an ambivert because he was both shy and talkative. Sometimes he tries to avoid others and othertimes he talks a lot.

害羞而健談的他被視為是內外向兼具者，有時他渴望離群索居，有時卻很多話。

★★★★★

| 1239 **ambiguous** | *a. having an obscure or double meaning* | 模稜兩可的，有歧義的 |

[æmˋbɪgjʊəs]

Your sentence "Joan is not on good terms with Jane, because she is picky," is ambiguous; we could interpret it in two different ways.

你的句子「瓊和珍處不好，因為她很挑剔」是模稜兩可的，因為可以有兩種不同的解釋。

✛ ambl = walk 行走

★★★★☆

| 1240 **amble** | *v. move at an easy pace; stroll* | 漫步 |

[ˋæmbḷ]

The old man and his wife loved to amble through the park looking at the trees and birds and talking about old days.

這對老夫妻喜歡在公園漫步，一邊望著林間鳥群，一邊談著往日種種。

★★★★★

| 1241 **ambulance** | *n. a mobile hospital following an army / a vehicle specially equipped for conveying the sick or injured to and from a hospital* | 野戰醫院 / 救護車 |

[ˋæmbjələns]

The ambulance carrying the injured man to the hospital was stuck in traffic. The victim was slowly dying.

運送傷患前往醫院的救護車遇到塞車，傷者性命垂危。

★★★☆☆

| 1242 **preamble** | *n. a preliminary statement or introduction* | 先兆，前奏 |

[ˋpriæmbḷ]

With almost no preamble, the President began to address the problem of racial discrimination, which indicated that the conference was going to be very serious.

總統幾乎毫無預警地開始談論種族歧視問題，顯示那將是一場嚴肅的會議。

✛ ami, am(or) = love 喜愛

★★★☆☆

| 1243 **amiability** | *n. friendliness; cordiality* | 和藹，友善 |

[ˌemɪəˋbɪlətɪ]

I watched my boss's face pass from amiability to sternness. I could not venture to ask for a pay raise.

望著老闆的臉色從和善轉為嚴厲，使我不敢貿然提出加薪要求。

★★★★☆

1244 amicable

[ˈæmɪkəb!]

a. showing or done in a friendly spirit; friendly 友善的，和睦的

Our English professor was a kind and amicable person who was generally liked by everyone he met.
我們的英文教授非常親切友善，凡是認識的都喜歡他。

★★★★☆

1245 amorous

[ˈæmərəs]

a. showing, feeling, or inclined to sexual love; of or relating to sexual love 多情的，示愛的

His amorous glances and words were wasted on her because he was not her ideal type and she was not interested in him.
他示愛的眼神和言詞全都白費了，她對非理想對象的他毫無興趣。

★★★★☆

1246 enamored

[ɪnˈæməd]

a. captivated; charmed 迷戀的，愛慕的，傾心的

My sister has become more desperately enamored of the man day by day. She seems to think of him all day long.
我姊姊對那個男子日漸傾心，似乎整天都想著他。

✦ ampl = big 大的

★★★★★

1247 ample

[ˈæmp!]

a. plentiful; abundant; copious; lavish; sufficient / large 足夠的 / 廣大的

It would be a good idea for every family to prepare for natural disasters by stocking up on ample supplies of food and emergency equipment.
每戶人家都應儲備足夠糧食和緊急裝備以禦天災。

★★★★☆

1248 amplitude

[ˈæmplə,tud]

n. the maximum extent of a vibration or oscillation / abundance 振幅 / 廣大

An opera singer has a very large amplitude with his voice. It is said that some opera singers can break glasses by singing in a loud voice.
歌劇演唱家的聲音振幅很大，據說部分演唱家響亮的嗓音足以震碎玻璃。

★★★★★

1249 amplify

[ˈæmplə,faɪ]

v. increase the volume or strength of / augment 放大，增強 / 擴大

The sound was amplified many times with several loudspeakers so that everyone in the stadium could hear it.
聲音以幾個擴音器放大數倍，讓體育館內所有人都能聽到。

✛ anim = mind 精神中心

★★★★☆

| 1250 **animosity** | *n.* *hostility; antagonism; antipathy; ill will; malevolence; enmity; hatred; malice* | 仇視，敵意 |

[ˌænəˈmɑsətɪ]

Mr. Erickson showed animosity towards his employees and treated them very rudely. Eventually, most of them decided to quit.
艾瑞克遜先生憎恨並欺壓自己的員工，最後多數人決定離職。

★★★★☆

| 1251 **unanimity** | *n.* *oneness of mind* | 同意，全體一致 |

[ˌjunəˈnɪmɪtɪ]

The case was quickly resolved as there was total unanimity among the jurors as to the defendant's guilt.
訴訟案件迅速交付表決，因為陪審團一致同意被告有罪。

★★★☆☆

| 1252 **animadvert** | *v.* *criticize; censure* | 批評，責難 |

[ˌænəmædˈvɝt]

The student, after attending a lecture on the fall of communism in the Soviet Union, severely animadverted the unsubstantiated remarks that were made by the lecturer.
學生聽完一場有關前蘇聯共產主義滅亡的演講後，強烈批評演講者毫無事實根據的見解。

★★★★★

| 1253 **magnanimous** | *a.* *nobly generous; not petty in feelings or conduct* | 寬宏大量的 |

[mægˈnænəməs]

Our English instructor is a very magnanimous person. He is always generous towards us. Even my classmate Jim has received an A.
我們的英文講師非常寬宏大量，待學生慷慨大方，連同學吉姆也能拿 A 等。

★★★★☆

| 1254 **animus** | *n.* *ill feeling* | 敵意，惡意，反感 |

[ˈænɪməs]

Too often when parents get divorced, the animus shown toward their spouse carries over to the children and they also become the victims.
夫妻離婚時對原配的反感常延續到下一代身上，使孩子也成為受害者。

 *Tea Time...* ☕

> **<Greek alphabet> Iota**
> The ninth letter of the Greek alphabet, which is very small.
>
> 〈希臘語字母〉希臘語的第九個字母
> 希臘語的第九個字母，指極微小。（註：本字相當於英文字母的 i，用於否定句指「毫不～，一點也不～」。）

iota [aɪˈotə] *n.* *a very small quantity* | 極微小

Paul's wife did not care one iota for his feeble excuses because none of them could explain how he could forget their anniversary and go out drinking with his friends instead.
妻子完全不接受保羅的差勁藉口，因為他無法解釋為何會忘記結婚紀念日而跟友人出去喝酒。

1 Complete each word by filling in the blank with proper spelling so that it has the same meaning as suggested. Then please write the meaning of each word in Chinese.

1. 酸 = __ i d
2. 刻薄的 = ____ m o n i o u s
3. 醋的 = a c e ___
4. 毗連 = __ j o i n
5. 鄰近的 = __ j a c e n t
6. 來臨 = __ v e n t
7. 調整 = a d ____
8. 附屬品 = __ j u n c t
9. 美學的 = _____ e t i c
10. 靈活的 = __ i l e

11. antagonize = _____
12. agitate = _____
13. agronomy = _____
14. agriculture = _____
15. agrarian = _____
16. alias = _____
17. altimeter = _____
18. altitude = _____
19. alternative = _____
20. magnanimous = _____

2 Choose a word that best completes the sentence.

21. His _____ means enabled him to take a trip around the world.
    (A) ample (B) agrarian (C) amorous (D) ambiguous

22. My friend became _____ of one of his classmates. He was tongue-twisted when he was speaking in front of her.
    (A) abundant (B) enamored (C) alien (D) agrestic

3 The highlighted word is closest in meaning to which of the following?

23. A swallow is an agile flyer. It flies very swiftly.
    (A) a contiguous (B) an adjacent (C) an acidulous (D) a nimble

24. I had no other alternative but to go see the dentist. I tossed and turned all through the night because of the pain.
    (A) preamble (B) alibi (C) option (D) alter

25. His father exalted him to the skies. He got 70% on the vocabulary test.
    (A) agitated (B) praised (C) aroused (D) evoked

✦ ann, enni = year 年，年度

MP3
52

★★★★★

1255 annual

[`ænjʊəl]

a. occurring every year / living or lasting for one year / reckoned by the year　　每年的／一年一次的／一年生的

In our country precipitation is heavily concentrated in summer. Approximately 70% of the annual rainfall comes during June through September.

我國降雨量集中在夏季，大約百分之七十年降雨量都發生在六到九月。

★★★★★

1256 biennial

[baɪˋɛnɪəl]

a. lasting two years; occurring every two years　　兩年一度的

My school's athletic meet is held every other year. It is biennial. It was held last year, and therefore, we are going to have one next year.

本校運動會每兩年舉辦一次，去年才剛辦過所以明年會再辦一次。

★★★★☆

1257 annuity

[əˋnuətɪ]

n. a yearly grant or allowance　　年金，養老金

After he won the lottery, he received an annuity of $500,000 on the first day of January for the rest of his life.

他中樂透後在一月一日得到五十萬美元的年金安度餘生。

★★★★☆

1258 centennial

[sɛnˋtɛnɪəl]

a. occurring every 100 years / n. one hundredth　　百年一次的／一百周年紀念

Fortunately we've enjoyed 100 years of success in this business and I hope this centennial party will kick off the next 100 years of healthy growth.

我們很幸運能在這個行業創下百年成就，希望這場百年一次的盛會為我們帶來下個一百年的穩健成長。

★★★★★

1259 annals

[`ænḷz]

n. a narrative of events year by year; historical records　　年報，年鑑，編年史

Mike has spent several weeks going through the annals at the genealogical library trying to piece together his personal history.

邁克花了數周在宗譜藏書室裡查閱年鑑以拼湊其個人歷史。

✦ anthrop(o) = human beings 人類

★★★★★

1260 **anthropoid**	*n. a being that is human in form only, especially an anthropoid ape*	類人猿
[`ænθrə‚pɔɪd]		

Those who believe in the theory of evolution are convinced that modern man is a descendant of the anthropoid.
相信進化論的人認為現代人類是類人猿的後裔。

★★★★★

1261 **anthropology**	*n. the study of mankind*	人類學
[‚ænθrə`pɑlədʒɪ]		

By specializing in anthropology, Thomas has been able to fulfill his lifelong ambition to study the origins of human life.
湯瑪斯專攻人類學以實現鑽研人類生命起源的畢生抱負。

★★★☆☆

1262 **misanthropic**	*a. of or relating to a misanthrope*	討厭與人來往的
[‚mɪsən`θrɑpɪk]		

George is so antisocial that he almost seems misanthropic. He does not like to meet anybody at any time.
喬治不愛交際幾乎到討厭與人往來的地步，無論何時都不愛和人打交道。

★★★★☆

1263 **philanthropist**	*n. altruist*	慈善家，博愛主義者
[fə`lænθrəpɪst]		

A philanthropist is a person who shows love for mankind by doing good works for society. My counselor is an embodiment of altruism.
慈善家博愛世人並參與社會公益活動，我的指導教授就是利他主義的典範。

✦ anti- = against 反對

★★★☆☆

1264 **antiwar**	*a. against a war*	反戰的
[‚æntɪ`wɔr]		

Many Americans all across the country supported the U.S.'s activities in the Gulf War, but there were also many antiwar demonstrations that were held during the war.
全美各地有許多人支持美軍波灣戰爭，但戰爭期間也有不少反戰示威活動。

★★★★★

1265 **antibody**	*n. a substance which a person's or an animal's body produces in their blood in order to destroy substances which carry diseas*	抗體
[`æntɪ‚bɑdɪ]		

Those who are antibody-deficient must be very careful and remain healthy because of their body's inability to effectively fight disease.
抗體不足者平時應小心保持健康，因為他們的身體無法有效抵抗疾病。

★★★☆☆

1266 anticlimactic

[ˌæntɪklaɪˈmæktɪk]

a. disappointing you because the situation is not as exciting as you expected

虎頭蛇尾的

The beginning of the movie was very exciting. But the ending of it was pretty disappointing. It was anticlimactic.

電影開場白非常刺激，但結局卻叫人相當失望，真是虎頭蛇尾。

★★★★☆

1267 antithesis

[ænˈtɪθəsɪs]

n. the exact opposite of

顯著對比，正相反

Christine is the antithesis of what I believe a lady should be. I do not like the way she behaves and talks.

克莉絲汀與我認為的女士形象正好相反，我不喜歡她的言談舉止。

★★★★☆

1268 antidote

[ˈæntɪˌdot]

n. a medicine taken or given to counteract poison

解毒劑

The antidote helped the poisoning victim overcome the effect of the poison. Otherwise he could not have survived.

病患靠解毒劑治療中毒症狀，否則很難活命。

★★★★★

1269 antarctic

[ænˈtɑrktɪk]

a. of the south polar regions / the south polar region

南極的 / 南極地區的

Scientists have found that the antarctic is one of the best places on earth to study the hole in the ozone.

科學家發現南極是地球上最適合研究臭氧層破洞的地區之一。

✣ aqua- = water 水

★★★★★

1270 aquarium

[əˈkwɛrɪəm]

n. an artificial environment designed for keeping live fish or other water creatures for study or exhibition

水族館，魚缸

My niece has been begging me for months to buy her a dog, but I decided to buy her an aquarium instead so that she could have fish for pets.

姪女哀求我好幾個月買隻狗給她，但我決定改買魚缸好讓她養魚當寵物。

★★★☆☆

1271 aquaplane

[ˈækwəˌplen]

n. a board for riding on the water, pulled by a speedboat

滑水板

Nina prefers aquaplanes over water skis because the wide flat surface of the board provides more support and is therefore easier to use.

妮娜喜歡滑水板勝過滑水，因為寬平的板面提供更多支撐且更容易使用。

★★★★★

1272 aquatic

a. growing or living in or near water; (of a sport) played in or on water　　水上的，水中進行的

[ə`kwætɪk]

Francis lives in Southern California and spends most of his leisure time at the beach doing all kinds of aquatic sports.
住在南加州的法蘭西斯閒暇最常到海灘進行各種水上運動。

★★★☆☆

1273 Aqualung

n. a portable breathing apparatus for divers, consisting of cylinders of compressed air strapped on the back　水肺，潛水用氧氣筒

[`ækwə͵lʌŋ]

The inventor of the Aqualung probably had no idea that deep-sea diving would become so popular and informative.
潛水用氧氣筒發明者可能根本想不到深海浮潛會變得那麼受歡迎且具有教育意義。

✥ arch- = chief, first 最先 / - arch = ruler, leader 統治者

★★★★☆

1274 anarchy

n. disorder; lack of government　　　　無政府狀態，無秩序

[`ænəkɪ]

A society that rejects law and order is on the brink of anarchy. Then the society would degenerate into pandemonium.
不講法律和秩序的社會等於處在無政府狀態邊緣，接下來就會陷入大混亂。

★★★★★

1275 archetype

n. an original model; a prototype　　　　　　原型，典型

[`ɑrkə͵taɪp]

Inventor Hoffman is hoping that his new invention will become the archetype upon which all other inventions of this type will be based.
發明家霍夫曼希望新發明可作為其他發明的原型基礎。

★★★★★

1276 archaeologist

n. a scientist who studies human history and prehistory through the excavation of sites and the analysis of physical remains　考古學家

[͵ɑrkɪ`ɑlədʒɪst]

Archaeologists have discovered a new burial ground and are finding several new artifacts that are helping historians better understand the past.
考古學家發現一塊新墓地，其中部分新出土手工藝品有助於歷史學家了解過去。

★★☆☆☆

1277 archangel

[`ɑrk,endʒəl]

n. an angel of the highest rant　　　天使長，大天使

Such a charitable person as Philip is sure to be an archangel when he dies and goes to heaven. I think he is a personification of love and charity.

以菲利普如此慈悲為懷的個性，死後一定會上天堂成為天使長，我認為他是愛與慈悲的化身。

★★★☆☆

1278 archbishop

[`ɑrtʃ`bɪʃəp]

n. the chief bishop of a province　　　大主教

He has been a faithful member of the Catholic church for many years and has now reached the rank of archbishop in that church.

他多年來一直都是天主教會的忠誠成員，如今更晉升為大主教。

✦ ard-, ars- = burn 燃燒，發光

★★★★★

MP3 53

1279 ardor

[`ɑrdə]

n. zeal; burning enthusiasm; passion; fervency; fervor; eagerness　　　狂熱，熱情

The discovery of the New World gave a fresh impulse to the ardor of exploration and travel. Many explorers were looking forward to seeing the newly discovered continent.

新世界的發現為探險旅遊的狂熱帶來新刺激，許多探險家都期待看到新大陸。

★★★★★

1280 ardent

[`ɑrdənt]

a. eager; zealous; fervent; passionate; enthusiastic; fervid; avid　　　熱烈的，忠誠的

It has taken a long time to develop a lasting relationship, but now it is very obvious that their friendship has developed into a healthy, ardent relationship.

建立持久關係有賴長期培養，如今他們的友誼顯然發展成健全而熱切的關係。

★★★★☆

1281 arduous

[`ɑrdʒʊəs]

a. hard to achieve or overcome; laborious; tough; strenuous; onerous; burdensome; tiring; gruelling; backbreaking　　　艱鉅的，困難的

When I first started studying English I thought it would be very easy to learn, but on the contrary I have found that it is very arduous work.

初學英文時我以為很容易，但相反地，我發現它其實很困難。

★★★☆☆

1282 arson

[`ɑrsṇ]

n. the act of maliciously setting fire to property　　　縱火（罪）

There have been several fires in this area recently. The police suspect arson. They are looking for evidence.

本區近來發生多起火災，警方懷疑是縱火案，正深入調查中。

⁜ astro, aster = star 星

★★★★★

1283 astronaut	**n.** a person who is trained to travel in a spacecraft	太空人
[ˈæstrəˌnɔt]	Before becoming an astronaut one must train and study for many years, and then one may be allowed off the planet and into space. 成為太空人前需經多年訓練和學習，接著才有可能獲准離開地球登上太空。	

★★★★★

1284 astrologer	**n.** a pseudoscientist who foretells the future by studying the supposed influence of the relative positions of the sun, moon, and stars	占星家
[əˈstrɑlədʒə]	An astrologer believes that the movements and relative positions of celestial bodies influence human affairs. 占星家相信天體的運行及其相對位置會影響人類活動。	

★★★★★

1285 asteroid	**n.** any of the minor planets revolving round the sun, mainly between the orbits of Mars and Jupiter / a starfish	小行星 / 海星
[ˈæstəˌrɔɪd]	Comets are probably the most numerous astronomical bodies in the solar system except for small meteor fragments and the asteroids. 彗星可能是太陽系中除流星碎片和小行星外為數最多的星體。	

★★★★☆

1286 asterisk	**n.** a star-shaped mark	星號
[ˈæstəˌrɪsk]	The asterisk (*) is a star-shaped mark and it is found above the number '8' key on most typewriters or keyboards. 多數打字機或鍵盤的數字 8 按鍵上的星狀記號就是星號。	

⁜ audio- = hear 聽

★★★☆☆

1287 audit	**n.** an official examination of accounts / **v.** conduct an audit 審計 / 審核，查帳
[ˈɔdɪt]	The Internal Revenue Service audited his company's records because they suspected him of tax evasion. 國稅局懷疑他逃稅因此查核其公司帳目。

★★★★★

1288 auditorium	**n.** the part of a theater, etc. in which the audience sits	觀眾席，禮堂
[ˌɔdəˈtorɪəm]	The senior prom was held in the high school auditorium and the entire basketball court was filled with people. 畢業舞會在高中禮堂舉辦，整個籃球場擠滿了人。	

Chapter

1
2
3
4
5

★★★★☆

1289 audition

[ɔ`dɪʃən]

n. an interview for a role as a singer, actor, dancer, etc.　　　試鏡

I saw a television interview with a famous actor, and I was surprised when I heard him say that he was nervous when he auditioned for the main part in that movie.

我看了知名演員的電視專訪後感到驚訝，原來他為電影主角試鏡時會緊張。

★★★★★

1290 audible

[`ɔdəbl]

a. capable of being heard　　　可聽見的，聽得見的

I saw Pam yelling at me from across the store, but what she was saying was not audible. I motioned for her to come to me so we could talk.

潘在對街喊我，但我聽不到她說什麼，於是招呼她過來講話。

★★★★★

1291 audio-visual

[`ɔdɪo`vɪʒʊəl]

a. using both sight and sound　　　視聽（教學）的

A teacher frequently uses audio-visual aids while teaching his students because the aids stimulate more senses.

老師常利用視聽輔助教材授課，以刺激學生學習

✣ aut(o)- = self　自己，自動

★★★★★

1292 autocratic

[ˌɔtə`krætɪk]

a. of or relating to an absolute ruler; dictatorial　　　獨裁的，專制的

An administrator who makes decisions without seeking the opinions of others may be regarded as autocratic.

不聽取他人意見便逕自做出決定的行政官員可能會被視為專制、獨裁的。

★★★★☆

1293 autograph

[`ɔtə,græf]

n. signature of a celebrity　　　（名人的）親筆簽名

Jack was such a famous tennis player that I was very nervous while handing him the paper and pen for his autograph.

傑克是這麼有名的網球選手，我遞紙筆請他簽名時十分緊張。

★★★★☆

1294 autonomy

[ɔ`tɑnəmɪ]

n. self-government; independence　　　自治，主權國家

Many of the republics in the Soviet Union sought autonomy because they didn't think that the central government was doing a good job.

許多前蘇聯共和國認為中央政府無能而尋求自治。

★★★★★

1295 automation

[,ɔtə`meʃən]

n. the use of automatic equipment to save mental and manual labor

自動化

The automation of our factory has saved us space and money by allowing us to use fewer people with higher output.
工廠自動化使我們用較少人力創造較高產量，節省時間和空間。

★★★★☆

1296 automaton

[ɔ`tamə,tan]

n. robot

機器人

When automatons were first created, there were high expectations that they could some day replace humans in the workplace.
機器人首次問世時，外界曾高度預期將來會取代在職場工作的人類。

★★★★★

1297 authentic

[ɔ`θɛntɪk]

a. genuine; real; bona fide; sterling; factual

非假冒的，真實的

There are some people trying to sell imitation jewelry, so be sure that the jewelry is authentic when you buy it.
有些人企圖販售珠寶贗品，因此購買時需確保它是真貨。

✥ bel = fight 戰鬥

★★★★☆

1298 bellicose

[`bɛlə,kos]

a. eager to fight; warlike

好戰的，好鬥的

My roommate Frank is disliked by many people because of his argumentative disposition and bellicose character.
許多人都不喜歡我的室友法蘭克，因為他既好辯又愛鬥狠。

★★★★☆

1299 rebellion

[rɪ`bɛljən]

n. uprising; revolution; mutiny; insurrection; revolt; insurgency; defiance; resistance

叛亂，反抗

The most dangerous aftereffect of rebellion comes when the new government is worse than the one it replaced.
當新政府比被推翻的政府更腐敗時，將導致最危險的叛亂後果。

★★★★☆

1300 rebel

[rɪ`bɛl]

v. revolt; mutiny; rise up; defy; flout

反抗，反叛，反感

Edward wore an earring and grew his hair long in order to passively rebel against the strict attitudes of his father.
愛德華戴耳環留長髮以消極反抗父親嚴厲的態度。

★★★★☆

| 1301 **belligerent** | *a.* *jingoistic; bellicose; warring /* *aggressive; pugnacious* | 交戰中的 / 好戰的 |

[bə`lɪdʒərənt]

The Middle Eastern country has extremely belligerent feelings towards many western countries which are trying to help it in various ways.

中東國家對許多想提供各類協助的西方國家懷有極端好戰的情緒。

$\mathcal{T}$ea $\mathcal{T}$ime... ☕

<Character of a work> Don Quixote

1. a satirical romance by Cervantes, published in two parts. (1605, 1615)

2. the hero of this romance, who tries in a chivalrous but unrealistic way to rescue the oppressed and fight evil.

〈來自故事角色〉唐吉訶德

1. 作者塞凡提斯於一六〇五年和一六一五年分成兩部分出版的諷喻性中世紀騎士故事。

2. 此中世紀騎士故事裡的英雄以俠義卻不切實際的方式拯救弱勢者，並對抗邪惡勢力。（註：唐吉訶德勇於堅持自我，並挑戰當時社會種種不合理現象，他的不自量力帶有脫離現實的意味。後世便將其名引申為「不切實際的理想家」。）

quixotic [kwɪks`ɑtɪk] *a. extravagantly and romantically chivalrous; visionary; pursuing lofty but unattainable ideals* | 唐吉訶德式的，空想的，不切實際的

His quixotic ideas for the company endeared him with his friends, but no foreign investors took him seriously in the business world.

唐吉訶德式的經營之道使他受到友人們的喜愛，但沒有外資看好他在企業界的表現。

1 Complete each word by filling in the blank with proper spelling so that it has the same meaning as suggested. Then please write the meaning of each word in Chinese.

1. 兩年一度的   =   b i _ _ _ _ a l

2. 百年一次的   =   c e n t _ _ _ _ a l

3. 人類學   =   _ _ _ _ _ _ _ o l o g y

4. 討厭與人來往的   =   m i s _ _ _ _ _ _ _ i c

5. 反戰的   =   _ _ _ _ w a r

6. 顯著對比   =   a n t i _ _ _ _ _ _

7. 解毒劑   =   a n t i _ _ _ _

8. 水族館   =   _ _ _ _ r i u m

9. 潛水用氧氣筒   =   _ _ _ _ l u n g

10. 原型   =   _ _ _ _ e t y p e

11. archaeologist   =   _____

12. archbishop   =   _____

13. ardent   =   _____

14. astronaut   =   _____

15. asterisk   =   _____

16. auditorium   =   _____

17. audible   =   _____

18. autocratic   =   _____

19. autonomy   =   _____

20. rebellion   =   _____

2 Choose a word that best completes the sentence.

21. Jack, a 5-year-old child, was fishing in the _____. His cat was really excited.

(A) aquarium   (B) antibody   (C) annals   (D) anthropoid

22. The _____ found some fossils of cetaceans in Pakistan.

(A) archangel   (B) anarchy   (C) archetype   (D) archaeologist

3 The highlighted word is closest in meaning to which of the following?

23. Moving the sofa out of the house was really arduous work.

(A) gruelling   (B) ardent   (C) eager   (D) centennial

24. In this assembly line automatons are used for welding parts and painting.

(A) asteroids   (B) asterisks   (C) robots   (D) philanthropists

25. The nation was not on good terms with its belligerent neighbor country.

(A) authentic   (B) genuine   (C) aggressive   (D) audible

✥ ben(e)- = good 好的

MP3
54

★★★★★

1302 beneficiary

n. a person who receives benefits, especially under a person's will

受益人，受惠者

[ˌbɛnəˈfɪʃɪˌɛr]

The government's plan to lessen the tax burden was welcomed by most people, especially since the chief beneficiary are the workers in the lower income bracket.

政府的減稅計畫受到多數民眾歡迎，特別因為主要受惠者為中低收入工人。

★★★★★

1303 beneficial

a. advantageous; useful; profitable; valuable; salutary; favorable

有益處的，有幫助的

[ˌbɛnəˈfɪʃəl]

It has been a long known fact that eating right and exercising three times a week is very beneficial to maintaining good health.

眾所周知，適當飲食和每周三次運動對保持身體健康有極大幫助。

★★★★★

1304 benefactor

n. patron; supporter; sponsor; donor

捐助者，恩人

[ˈbɛnəˌfæktə]

Henry never knew his benefactor or why this mysterious person paid all his schooling and housing costs, but he would be eternally grateful.

亨利不認識捐助者，也不懂為什麼這位神祕者要幫忙繳清學費和住宿費，但他感激不盡。

★★★★★

1305 benefit

n. profit; gain; advantage

益處，好處

[ˈbɛnəfɪt]

I have read some sports magazines and I am becoming more convinced of the health benefits of jogging.

我讀了不少運動雜誌，也因此深信慢跑有益健康。

✥ cal-, cha-, chal- = heat 熱

★★★★★

1306 caloric

a. producing heat

熱量的，卡（路里）的

[kəˈlɔrɪk]

Nine out of ten people who are overweight don't exercise and eat very high caloric foods. They need to burn more calories or reduce their calorie intake.

十個超重者有九個都不運動並吃高熱量食物，他們必須燃燒多餘的熱量或降低熱量的攝取。

★★★☆☆

1307 chafe

v. rub; abrade / irritate; rage

磨擦／使惱怒

[tʃef]

Nothing chafes me more than when a student chews and pops his gum in class while I'm trying to teach.

最讓我惱怒的莫過於講課時有個學生嚼食口香糖並發出啵啵聲。

★★★★★

1308 calorie

[ˈkælərɪ]

n. a unit of heat 熱量，卡路里

Health-conscious people are very concerned about counting calories and making sure that their calorie intake is equal to or less than the number of calories they burn during exercise.

注重健康者非常在意熱量的計算，以確保攝取量不高於運動燃燒量。

★★★★☆

1309 nonchalance

[ˈnɑnʃələns]

n. indifference; apathy 無動於衷，漠不關心

The bedridden father was upset by his son's nonchalance about his health.

久病父親對兒子的漠不關心感到失望。

✣ calc, cal(x) = heel, kick, hard, lime 腳後跟，踢，硬的，石灰

★★★☆☆

1310 recalcitrant

[rɪˈkælsɪtrənt]

a. defiant; refractory; perverse; unruly; uncontrollable; insubordinate 頑強反抗的，固執的

Her recalcitrant attitude, more often than not, landed her in more trouble than she would have been in otherwise.

她的固執不屈態度，往往讓她陷入更多麻煩。

★★★☆☆

1311 callousness

[ˈkæləsnɪs]

n. indifference; insensitivity 無動於衷／冷淡

I am one who believes in self-help, so I have a lot of callousness when it comes to people who cry and complain because they don't get help from other people.

我相信自立自強，所以對他人哭著抱怨沒人幫忙無動於衷。

★★★☆☆

1312 callosity

[kæˈlɑsətɪ]

n. insensitivity / a hard thick area of skin usually occurring in parts of the body subject to pressure or friction 無情，冷漠／皮膚結繭

John was severely abused as a child and has become a very untrusting cold person. You can easily detect his callosity when you speak with him.

約翰幼時受過嚴重虐待，長大後變得十分冷酷不相信人，和他談話時能輕易察覺他的冷漠。

★★★★★

1313 calcium

[ˈkælsɪəm]

n. a soft grey metallic element of the alkaline earth group occurring naturally in limestone, marble, chalk, etc. 鈣

When I was young my mother would always force me to drink my milk because it is full of calcium which is an essential ingredient of strong healthy bones.

小時候媽媽總是逼我喝富含鈣質的牛奶，因為它是強健骨骼不可或缺的要素。

❖ cand, cend, cens, cin = fire, light 火，光

★★★★☆

1314 **candor**	*n. frankness*	坦誠
[`kændə]		

Norman is a very outspoken person, and I appreciate his candor very much. He always tells me the truth.
諾曼非常直言不諱，我很感激他的坦誠，他總是跟我說實話。

★★★★★

1315 **candid**	*a. frank; artless; forthright*	坦率的，直言的
[`kændɪd]		

Susan always tells it like it is, never tells a lie and is considered by many to be a very candid person.
蘇珊直言不諱從不撒謊，許多人都認為她非常坦率。

★★★★☆

1316 **incinerate**	*v. burn*	焚化，燒掉
[ɪn`sɪnə‚ret]		

The investigators conducted a week-long investigation into the arson case, but because the house was completely incinerated, there was no admissible evidence to be found.
調查員針對縱火案展開為期一周的調查，但因房屋全燬因此沒有發現有利證據。

❖ cant, chant = sing, call, shout 歌唱，呼叫，喊叫

★★★★☆

1317 **chant**	*v. recite; shout; repeat / sing; cantillate; intone*	反覆喊叫 / 詠唱
[tʃænt]		

The basketball game came down to the wire and the fans of the winning team all left the building, chanting "we're #1, were #1" in unison.
籃球比賽到了最後決勝關頭，獲勝隊伍支持者離開現場時一起喊著「我們是第一！第一！」

★★★★★

1318 **incentive**	*n. encouragement; incitement; inducement; stimulus; spur; provocation; impetus*	激勵，刺激
[ɪn`sɛntɪv]		

Nowadays a lot of department stores use discount coupons as incentives to attract more customers.
現在許多百貨公司利用折價券刺激買氣，以吸引顧客上門。

★★★★☆

| 1319 **enchant** | ***v.*** *charm; bewitch; fascinate; captivate; spellbind; attract; enrapture* | 使入迷，使陶醉 |

[ɪnˈtʃænt]

Jason used to tell his daughter the story of Pocahontas when he put her to bed, and it didn't take long before she became enchanted by that story.

傑森哄女兒睡前會講寶嘉康蒂（即風中奇緣）的故事給她聽，她立刻就著迷了。

★★★☆☆

| 1320 **cantata** | ***n.*** *a short narrative or descriptive composition with vocal solos* | 清唱劇 |

[kænˈtɑtə]

Mary has been singing with the choir for years now but this is by far the most difficult cantata that she has sung to date.

瑪麗多年來都在教堂唱詩班唱歌，但對她而言這是迄今最難唱的清唱劇。

★★★☆☆

| 1321 **recant** | ***v.*** *recall; revoke; retract; withdraw / renounce; abjure* | 取消／宣布放棄 |

[rɪˈkænt]

The citizens were forced to recant their beliefs before the communist officials right after the invasion.

國家遭到入侵後，人民被迫在共產黨官員面前宣布放棄個人信仰。

⊹ cap, cip = head 頭

★★★★☆

| 1322 **precipice** | ***n.*** *a vertical or steep face of a rock, cliff, mountain, etc.; cliff* | 懸崖，危機 |

[ˈprɛsəpɪs]

Mark stood atop the precipice, looking down at the village far below him. He was glad that he came to the mountains to go climbing on his vacation.

馬克站在懸崖頂下望遠處村莊，他很高興自己來登山度假。

★★★★★

| 1323 **precipitate** | ***v.*** *hasten; speed up; quicken; expedite; trigger; instigate* | 使陷於～，使突然發生 |

[prɪˈsɪpəˌtet]

In order not to precipitate any violence, Robert and his friends quickly left the bar and averted a fight that they would have lost.

羅伯特和友人為了不要引起暴力相向，速速離開酒吧避開可能會輸的打鬥。

★★★★☆

| 1324 **capitulate** | ***v.*** *surrender; yield; succumb; give way* | 投降，停止反抗 |

[kəˈpɪtʃəˌlet]

Only after several days of continued bombing by the U.N. forces did the invader decide to capitulate in accordance with the stipulations put across by the U.N.

入侵國受到聯合國軍隊連續轟炸數日後，決定根據聯合國規定投降。

1325 captain	**n.** *a Navy officer in command of a warship / a chief or leader*	艦長／隊長

[`kæptɪn]

The captain was in full command of the vessel when it ran aground spilling millions of gallons of crude oil into the ocean, and he is therefore held responsible for that disaster.

由艦長全權指揮的船隻觸礁導致數百萬加侖原油流入海中，艦長需為災難負起全部責任。

★★★★☆

1326 per capita	**a.** *for each person*	每人的，每人平均

[pə`kæpɪtə]

The per capita income of the country is a meager $700, which means on average a citizen earns only $700 a year.

該國平均國民所得是微薄的七百美元，換言之每個國民平均每年只賺七百美元。

★★★☆☆

1327 capitation	**n.** *a tax or fee at a set rate per person*	均攤，人頭稅

[͵kæpə`teʃən]

The capitation is a tax system which makes every person pay the same tax regardless of his income.

每人負擔相同稅額而不計個人收入的稅制稱為人頭稅。

✥ cap(t) = seize, catch, take 尺寸，抓，取

★★★★★

1328 capture	**v.** *seize; take captive; ensnare; entrap; snare; nab*	捕獲，俘虜，捕捉

[`kæptʃə]

Spiders, after capturing unsuspecting insects in their transparent webs of silk, rush to their victims, bind them, and suck their bodily juices for nourishment.

蜘蛛以透明蛛網捕捉不小心陷入的昆蟲，接著快速靠近獵物並吐絲捆綁，再吸食體液作為營養來源。

★★★★☆

1329 capacious	**a.** *roomy; spacious; commodious; sizeable; ample*	容量大的，廣闊的

[kə`peʃəs]

This apartment is expensive, but it is very comfortable and capacious. That is why it is a very popular location in this city.

公寓雖貴但非常寬敞舒適，難怪座落於都市熱門地段。

★★★★☆

1330 captive	**n.** *prisoner; hostage; detainee; internee*	俘虜，獵物

[`kæptɪv]

It is said that the use of wedding rings originally derived from the use of a rope to tie up captive brides.

據說婚戒的使用源於以繩索捆綁俘虜新娘。

★★★★☆

1331 recapitulate

v. *go briefly through again; summarize; sum up; reiterate*　　扼要重述

[ˌrikə`pɪtʃəˌlet]

The speaker recapitulated his speech for those who were late to the conference, and so they came to know what the purport of the speech was.

演講者扼要重述重點，使會議遲到者能掌握演講主旨。

★★★★☆

1332 precept

n. *a general or proverbial rule; maxim; proverb*　　訓誡，戒律

[`prisɛpt]

A social precept, such as virginity, should be a personal choice, not a directive from a collection of other people.

貞操等社會戒律應是個人選擇，而非來自眾人的集體指令。

★★★★★

1333 captivate

v. *charm; enamor; enchant; bewitch; enrapture; dazzle;*　　使著迷
infatuate; entrance

[`kæptəˌvet]

I couldn't take my eyes off her from the moment I saw her, and I have been captivated by her beauty ever since.

自相遇的那刻起我就無法將視線從她身上移開，她的美令我著迷。

❖ card, cord = heart　心

★★★★★

1334 cardinal

a. *chief; fundamental; key; leading*　　主要的，根本的

[`kardn̩əl]

The cardinal principle of the nation's education is the education of the whole person. Students are being taught to be more versatile.

國家教育的主要方針是全民教育，學生被教導成更多才多藝。

★★★★★

1335 accord

n. *agreement; treaty; pact; compact; contract / consent;*　　協議／一致
unanimity; concord; mutual understanding

[ə`kɔrd]

The two countries have signed an accord that will hopefully secure the peace of the world for many years to come.

兩國簽署協議以確保未來世界和平。

★★★☆☆

1336 electrocardiograph

n. *an instrument recording the electric currents*　　心電圖機
generated by a person's heartbeat

[ɪˈlɛktroˈkardɪəˌgræf]

After his daughter fainted he took her to the hospital. The doctors used an electrocardiograph to monitor her heart rate.

他將昏倒的女兒送進醫院，醫生使用心電圖機監測她的心跳速率。

★★★★★

1337 **discord**	*n.* disagreement; strife; dissension; conflict; disharmony	爭吵，喧鬧
[`dɪskɔrd]	It was no surprise to the people who knew Pam that she was accused of child abuse because her house seemed to be in complete discord at all times. 認識潘的人並不驚訝她被控虐待兒童，因為她家似乎總是充滿爭吵聲。	

★★★☆☆

1338 **cardiac**	*a.* of or relating to the heart / a person with heart disease	心臟（病）的 / 心臟病患
[`kɑrdɪ,æk]	The doctor warned Joe of potentially fatal cardiac problems if he continued to smoke and drink heavily. 醫生警告喬伊如果繼續抽煙酗酒恐將引發致命心臟病。	

★★★★★

1339 **concord**	*n.* agreement; harmony	一致，和睦，友好協定
[`kɑŋkɔrd]	At first the differences were great, but after much debate they were finally able to come up with a concord between themselves. 起初雙方歧見很深，但經過多方討論後終於達成友好協定。	

★★★★☆

1340 **cordial**	*a.* friendly	熱絡的，友好的
[`kɔrdʒəl]	The meeting began in a cordial and warm fashion. But at the last moment the participants were divided in their opinions and came to raise their voices. 會議在熱絡氣氛中展開，但最後與會者各持己見並提高音量講話。	

✢ carn(i) = body, flesh 身體，肉體，肉

★★★☆☆

1341 **carnage**	*n.* great slaughter; massacre; genocide; holocaust; butchery	大屠殺，殘殺
[`kɑrnɪdʒ]	The whole country is shocked and amazed at the enormous amount of destruction and carnage left behind by the invaders. 舉國上下都為入侵者造成的大量破壞和屠殺深感震驚。	

★★★★★

1342 **carnivore**	*n.* a flesh-eating animal	食肉動物
[`kɑrnə,vɔr]	A carnivore is a flesh-eating animal. It only eats meat. Tigers, leopards and lions are some animals that fall into this group. 食肉動物只吃肉，老虎、美洲豹、獅子等皆屬此類。	

★★★☆☆

1343 carnal

a. sensual; sexual; fleshly; erotic; voluptuous; lustful; lascivious; licentious; lewd　　肉體的，感官的，世俗的

[`kɑrnḷ]

Most religious leaders are concerned with the sharp increase of immoral and carnal sins that our young people are committing.

多數宗教領袖關切年輕人急遽增加的傷風敗俗罪惡。

★★★☆☆

1344 carnival

n. any festivities occurring at a regular date; revelry　　嘉年華會，狂歡

[`kɑrnəvḷ]

Jones's favorite time of the year is September when he goes to the rodeo and enjoys the rides at the carnival.

一年當中瓊斯最喜歡的就是九月牛仔秀，他喜歡在嘉年華會上展現馴牛絕技。

✢ cata- = down 向下

★★★★☆

1345 cataclysm

n. a great flood or deluge / disaster / upheaval　　大洪水 / 災難 / 劇變

[`kætə,klɪzəm]

The Bible says that God ordered Noah to build an Ark to save him from a cataclysm. It is said that it took Noah a hundred years to build the boat.

聖經說上帝指示諾亞建造方舟以躲避大洪水，據說造船花了一百年。

★★★☆☆

1346 catacomb

n. an underground cemetery　　地下墓穴

[`kætə,kom]

My uncle's favorite part of the trip to Egypt was his tour of the catacombs of the ancient King of Egypt.

埃及之旅最讓舅舅喜愛的就是參觀法老王地下墓穴。

★★★★★

1347 catastrophe

n. disaster; calamity; cataclysm; casualty; misfortune; fiasco 大災難，大慘敗

[kə`tæstrəfɪ]

Most scientists believe that a comet would cause a terrible catastrophe if it should collide with the planet earth.

多數科學家相信若彗星與地球相撞會引發嚴重大災難。

✢ cede, ceed, cess = go 行走

★★★★★

1348 excessive

a. immoderate; inordinate; exorbitant; excess; undue　　過度的，過分的

[ɪk`sɛsɪv]

If we don't correct the recent trend of excessive consumption, we'll never be able to overcome our current economic difficulties.

我們若不能導正目前過度消費的趨勢，將無法克服現在的經濟危機。

★★★★★

1349 accede	**v.** *agree; assent*	同意
[əkˋsid]	After many hours of negotiations both sides acceded to the terms of the treaty, thereby securing peace. 經過數小時協商後雙方同意協議條款並確保和平。	

★★★★★

1350 precedent	**n.** *a pervious case or legal decision*	先例，慣例，判例
[ˋprɛsədənt]	Sentencing the murderer to only five years in prison set a dangerous precedent for other trials involving armed robbery. 只判處殺人犯五年徒刑將為其他持槍搶劫審判立下危險判例。	

★★★★☆

1351 cede	**v.** *give up one's rights to / abdicate; forfeit*	割讓／讓與，交出
[sid]	During World War II, the Japanese fought long and hard, but it wasn't long after the atomic bomb was dropped that Japan ceded power to the allied forces. 第二次世界大戰期間日本頑強作戰，但原子彈投下不久便將權力移交給盟軍。	

Tea Time... ☕

<Egyptian legend> Crocodile tears From an old belief that crocodiles shed tears while eating their prey.	〈來自埃及神話〉鱷魚眼淚 本字源自鱷魚會邊流眼淚邊吃掉獵物的古老傳說。（註：後世將此詞引申為「假慈悲」或「偽善」。）

crocodile tears [ˋkrɑkəˏdaɪl tɪrs] **n.** *insincere grief* | 假慈悲

Her neighbors knew she had hated her husband intensely. When they saw her cry at the funeral, they knew she was shedding crocodile tears.

鄰居們知道她很討厭自己的先生，所以她在葬禮上哭泣時，大家都覺得是假慈悲。

1 Complete each word by filling in the blank with proper spelling so that it has the same meaning as suggested. Then please write the meaning of each word in Chinese.

1. 有益處的   = ____ficial
2. 捐助者   = ____factor
3. 益處   = ____fit
4. 熱量的   = cal____
5. 使惱怒   = cha__
6. 漠不關心   = non___lance
7. 固執的   = re___citrant
8. 冷淡   = ___losity
9. 坦率的   = cand__
10. 焚化   = in___erate

11. incentive   = _____
12. enchant   = _____
13. recant   = _____
14. precipice   = _____
15. precipitate = _____
16. capitulate   = _____
17. cardinal   = _____
18. concord   = _____
19. carnivore   = _____
20. catastrophe = _____

2 Choose a word that best completes the sentence.

21. To be _____ with you, I am not satisfied with your report.
    (A) capacious   (B) recalcitrant   (C) caloric   (D) candid

22. The two neighbors lived in _____. They helped each other with many things.
    (A) capitation   (B) precept   (C) concord   (D) cardiac

23. The blockbuster movie _____ many moviegoers.
    (A) capitulated   (B) captivated   (C) chanted   (D) recanted

3 The highlighted word is closest in meaning to which of the following?

24. Please do not incinerate this container.
    (A) burn   (B) recite   (C) recapitulate (D) ensnare

25. We had to accede to the terms which were suggested to us.
    (A) cede   (B) assent   (C) abdicate   (D) enrapture

⟐ chron- = time 時間

★★★★★

MP3 56

1352 chronic

[`krɑnɪk]

a. persisting for a long time; long-lasting; confirmed; hardened; inveterate; habitual

慢性的，長期的

It has been three years since the accident and his mother still suffers from chronic back pain.

意外發生後已過三年，他母親仍患有慢性背痛。

★★★★☆

1353 chronometer

[krə`nɑmətə]

n. a time-measuring instrument keeping accurate time

高度精準計時器

A chronometer is used when the astronauts go up in the space shuttle because it is extremely important to keep exact time while carrying out the missions.

太空人在太空梭內使用高度精準計時器，因為執行任務時須遵守準確時間。

★★★★★

1354 chronicle

[`krɑnɪkl]

n. history; annals

編年史，歷史記載

Many students use the chronicles in the library to do research and look up information for their history papers.

許多學生撰寫歷史報告時，會利用圖書館藏的編年史進行研究並查閱資料。

★★★★★

1355 chronological

[ˌkrɑnə`lɑdʒɪkl]

a. arranged in the order of their occurrence

按時間順序的

While the chain of events was still fresh in her mind, she sat down and listed as best as she could in chronological order the events that took place that night.

一連串事件令她記憶猶新，她坐下來按時間順序條列出當晚發生的事。

⟐ cid, cis = cut 切

★★★★★

1356 insecticide

[ɪn`sɛktəˌsaɪd]

n. a substance used for killing insects

殺蟲劑

One must always remember to wash fruit and vegetables before they are eaten, since many insecticides are harmful to humans as well as the insects they are intended for.

吃蔬果前須先清洗，因為能殺死昆蟲的殺蟲劑對人類一樣有害。

★★★★★

| **1357 pesticide** | *n. a substance used for destroying insects or other organisms harmful to cultivated plants or to animals* | 殺蟲劑 |

[`pɛstɪsaɪd]

If pesticide is sprayed on a fruit or vegetable in order to kill insects, what does it do to the people who eat it?

如果噴灑在蔬果上的殺蟲劑是為了殺死昆蟲，那麼對食用蔬果的人類又會產生什麼作用？

★★☆☆☆

| **1358 fratricidal** | *a. killing brothers or sisters* | 弒手足的 |

[ˌfrætrə`saɪdl]

Koreans fought a three-year fratricidal war. The suffering from the Korean Civil War was even worse because it was inflicted by people of the same race.

韓國人曾經歷三年的手足相殘之戰，同胞相殘使韓戰的苦難更甚。

★★★★★

| **1359 concise** | *a. brief; terse; laconic; compact; succinct; curtailed* | 簡潔的，簡明的 |

[kən`saɪs]

I enjoyed his lecture very much because of the concise way in which he presented the material.

我非常欣賞他的演講，因為他以簡單明瞭的方式呈現內容。

★★★★☆

| **1360 incise** | *v. engrave; carve* | 雕刻，刻入 |

[ɪn`saɪz]

Ancient Egyptians were able to incise very intricate designs on the walls of their kings' tombs, but we have yet to understand exactly what they mean.

古埃及人在法老王墓穴牆壁上雕刻繁複精細的圖案，世人迄今仍不知其意義。

★★★★★

| **1361 decisive** | *a. conclusive; ultimate / firm* | 決定性的 / 果決的 |

[dɪ`saɪsɪv]

Decisive action is necessary in a battle when there is no time to wait for approval or recommendations.

戰場上需行動果決，沒有時間等候批准或建議。

✦ cit = call 召喚，激起

★★★★★

| **1362 incite** | *v. arouse; rouse; ;instigate; stir; stimulate* | 激起，刺激 |

[ɪn`saɪt]

When the government decided to raise the price of alcohol by 50%, many people began to incite violent demonstrations to force the minimum wage up proportionately.

政府決定提高酒類產品百分之五十的價格時，刺激許多人展開暴力示威，要求最低工資也要比照調漲。

★★★☆☆

1363 cite

v. adduce as an instance; quote a passage in support of an argument

舉證，援引

[saɪt]

Ralph was able to cite, from memory, many examples of rude behavior on the part of tourists and travelers.

羅夫憑記憶舉出觀光客許多粗魯行為的例子。

★★★☆☆

1364 recitation

n. the act or an instance of reciting

朗誦，當眾吟誦

[ˌrɛsə`teʃən]

After the recitation of his poem, the poet closed his eyes for a while as if he were intending to hear the echo of his own voice.

詩人朗誦自己的詩後暫時闔眼，彷彿想聽聽自己的回音。

✥ claim, clam = shout; call 喊叫，呼叫

★★★★☆

1365 disclaim

v. deny

否認

[dɪs`klem]

Even though he was a major suspect in the murder of the woman, he disclaimed any and all of the allegations that were brought against him.

他雖然是女子謀殺案的主嫌，卻仍否認一切指控。

★★★★★

1366 proclaim

v. announce; declare; make known; herald; promulgate

宣告，宣布

[pro`klem]

Thomas wanted to proclaim his happiness to the whole world, but his bride-to-be would not approve of such an open display of affection.

湯瑪斯想向全世界宣布自己的快樂，但準新娘不願如此公開炫耀感情。

★★★★★

1367 exclaim

v. cry out; shout; bellow; blurt out; bawl; burst out; holler

喊叫，大叫

[ɪk`sklem]

"I won the lottery," was all he was able to exclaim before he died.

他死前只大叫了一聲：「我中樂透了。」

★★★★☆

1368 clamor

n. loud noise / vehement shouting; outcry

喧鬧／叫囂

[`klæmə]

The maintenance man began to pound the air conditioner and made a very large clamor that interrupted class.

維修人員開始猛搥冷氣機並發出極大噪音，打斷學生上課。

✥ clin, cliv = slope 傾斜

★★☆☆☆

1369 **acclivity**	*n. an upward slope*	上坡，向上傾斜

[ə`klɪvətɪ]

The walk up the hill to his home was an acclivity that always proved to him that he needed to exercise more often.

通往他家的上坡山路在在告訴他需要多運動。

★★☆☆☆

1370 **declivity**	*n. a downward slope*	下坡，向下傾斜

[dɪ`klɪvətɪ]

The truck was driving down a declivity when its brakes went out, but fortunately the driver was able to use the emergency escape ramp and bring the vehicle to a stop.

卡車下坡時煞車失靈，幸虧司機利用緊急出口閘道把車停住。

★★★★★

1371 **decline**	*v. decrease*	下降，下跌，衰退

[dɪ`klaɪn]

The employment rate is an accurate indicator of the strength of the economy, and this month that rate declined to its lowest level in five years.

作為經濟實力精確指標的就業率在本月下滑到五年來最低點。

★★★★☆

1372 **recline**	*v. lean back; repose*	斜躺，使後仰

[rɪ`klaɪn]

Eric loved to recline in his favorite rocking chair and watch a baseball game on TV on a Sunday afternoon.

周日下午艾瑞克喜歡躺在最愛的搖椅上收看電視棒球賽。

✥ clud, clude, clus = hold, boundary 包含，界限

★★★★★

1373 **include**	*v. contain*	包括

[ɪn`klud]

One of the biggest things I hated when I was a kid was that the manufacturers never included batteries with the toys.

小時候最讓我討厭的事情之一就是製造商從不把電池裝在玩具裡。

★★★★☆

1374 **recluse**	*n. hermit; lone wolf*	隱士，遁世者

[`rɛklus]

The old man who lives in that cottage must be a recluse; he avoids other people and never talks to anybody.

住在那棟農舍裡的老人一定是個隱居者，他躲開大家，不跟任何人說話。

★★★★★

1375 conclusion — *n. a final result* — 結論，結局

[kən`kluʒən]

The report was very well written, but I felt that the conclusion didn't completely wrap up all of the concepts that were used to support his argument.

報告寫得非常好，但我覺得結論沒有完整摘要他用來支持論點的全部概念。

★★★★★

1376 exclusive — *a. restrictive* — 排外的，限制他人加入的

[ɪk`sklusɪv]

The Rolling Hills Golf Club does not allow blacks to join and is considered one of the most exclusive country clubs in the United States.

不許黑人入會的滾坡高爾夫球俱樂部被視為全美最排外的鄉村俱樂部之一。

❖ co- = together 一起

★★★★★

MP3
57

1377 co-worker — *n. colleague* — 同事

[`ko,wɜkə]

His wife was his co-worker and they were together both at home and at the office. Other workers were envious of them.

妻子是他同事，兩人無論上下班都形影不離，羨煞其他同事。

★★★★★

1378 cooperate — *v. collaborate; work together; coordinate* — 合作

[ko`ɑpə,ret]

Doing something by yourself is admirable, but there are many times when it is necessary to cooperate in order to accomplish the prescribed goal.

獨力完成某事固然令人欽佩，但許多時候需要合作完成既定目標。

★★★★★

1379 coincidence — *n. co-occurrence; concurrence; simultaneity* — 巧合

[ko`ɪnsədəns]

"Where are you going, Jim?"
"I'm going to the post office."
"Oh, really? That's a coincidence. I'm going there too."

「你要去哪裡，吉姆？」
「我要去郵局。」
「噢，是嗎？那真巧，我也是。」

❖ **cogno, gno = know** 知道，了解

★★☆☆☆

1380 **incognito**	**a., ad.** *in disguise; in camouflage; under cover; under an assumed name*	隱姓埋名的，匿名地

[ɪnˋkɑgnɪˌto]

While the police were looking for him, he moved to a different city and tried to remain incognito by pretending he was a beggar.
他在警方搜索時搬到另一個都市，隱姓埋名偽裝成乞丐。

★★★☆☆

1381 **cognizant**	**a.** *aware*	知曉的，察知的

[ˋkɑgnɪzənt]

Since he had once been a lawyer, he was cognizant of his rights and duties after he was arrested.
由於他曾是律師，所以被捕後知道自己的權利義務何在。

★★★★☆

1382 **connoisseur**	**n.** *expert*	鑑賞家，行家

[ˌkɑnəˋsɝ]

Insadong, Seoul, which is famous for its numerous antique shops, attracts a lot of connoisseurs of handicrafts.
首爾仁寺洞以林立的古董店遠近馳名，也吸引許多手工藝品鑑賞家前往。

★★★☆☆

1383 **reconnaissance**	**n.** *patrol; investigation; survey; scrutiny*	偵察，勘察

[rɪˋkɑnəsəns]

The chief commander called on the reconnaissance team to find out about the enemy's weapons and supplies.
總司令要求偵察小隊查明敵軍武器和裝備情況。

★★★★★

1384 **precognition**	**n.** *foreknowledge*	預知

[ˌprikɑgˋnɪʃən]

In a flash of precognition, he knew that the plane was going to crash and that he wouldn't survive, so he took another flight.
他有預感會墜機身亡，因此改搭另一班飛機。

★★★★★

1385 **recognition**	**n.** *awareness; perception*	承認，察覺

[ˌrɛkəgˋnɪʃən]

It was the startling recognition of his ability as a singer that made Mr. Stocker quit his job as a salesman.
史塔克先生因令人驚豔的歌手天賦而辭掉業務員工作。

⚜ contra-, counter- = against 反對

★★★★★

| **1386 encounter** | **v.** face; meet with; bump into | 偶遇，碰到 |
| [ɪn`kaʊntə] | I can scarcely pick up a newspaper without encountering campus disturbances. There seem to be many demonstrations going on.
我翻開每份報紙都會看到校園暴動消息，似乎有許多示威活動正在進行。 | |

★★★★★

| **1387 contrast** | **v.** distinguish so as to reveal a difference / **n.** opposite | 使對照 / 對比 |
| [kən`træst] | Their six-year-old son pressed them into singing carols, and their frog-like voices contrasted with his musical gift of perfect pitch.
六歲兒子逼他們一起唱頌歌，青蛙般的歌喉跟兒子的天籟之音形成對比。 | |

★★★★★

| **1388 contrary** | **ad.** opposed | 對立的，相反地 |
| [`kɑntrɛrɪ] | Contrary to popular belief, birds are the most dangerous threat to aircraft. Even big aircraft can crash when they collide with a small bird.
與一般看法相反的是，飛機最危險的威脅來自鳥類，即使大型客機也會因為和小鳥相撞而墜毀。 | |

★★★★☆

| **1389 countervail** | **v.** resist; counterbalance | 對抗，抵銷，中和 |
| [`kaʊntə‚vel] | When hiking in the mountains it is important to carry some snake serum with you at all times to countervail the poison in case you get bit by a snake.
高山健行時隨身攜帶抗蛇毒血清是重要的，若被蛇咬可中和毒性。 | |

★★★★★

| **1390 contraband** | **a.** forbidden to be imported or exported / smuggled goods | 違禁的 / 違禁品 |
| [`kɑntrə‚bænd] | There are products that can legally be brought into the country and those which are contraband, so make sure that those products that you carry with you are allowed in.
有些產品可合法攜帶入境，有些則是違禁品，所以要確保攜帶的是獲准入境產品。 | |

★★★★★

| **1391 contradict** | **v.** be in opposition to or in conflict with / rebut | 與～相牴觸 / 反駁 |
| [‚kɑntrə`dɪkt] | The witness went over his version of the story time and time again so he wouldn't contradict himself when he got on the witness stand during the trial.
證人再三複習證詞，以免審判時站上證人席自相矛盾。 | |

★★★★★

1392 counterpart   *n. match; peer*   （地位、能力等）同等者，對應者

[ˋkaʊntɚˌpɑrt]

The Minister of Education from the South met with his counterpart from the North in a mini summit discussing the possibilities of cross educational ties.
南、北韓教育部長齊聚迷你高峰會討論跨教育合作的可行性。

★★★★★

1393 counter   *a. contrary*   相反的

[ˋkaʊntɚ]

Counter to her father's wishes, she married the man she loved. Her father decided not to attend the wedding.
她違背父親願望嫁給自己所愛的人，於是父親決定不去參加婚禮。

★★★★★

1394 counterclockwise   *ad. anticlockwise*   逆時針地

[ˌkaʊntɚˋklɑkˌwaɪz]

In the southern hemisphere, it is said that water drains counterclockwise, whereas in the northern hemisphere it drains clockwise.
據說南半球是逆時針排水，至於北半球則是順時針。

★★★★☆

1395 counterfeit   *a. forged; fake; fraudulent; imitation; phoney; sham*   偽造的，假冒的

[ˋkaʊntɚfɪt]

The bank teller knew that the money was counterfeit because the picture of the President was backwards.
銀行出納員知道鈔票是偽造的，因為上面的總統照是顛倒的。

★★★☆☆

1396 countermand   *v. revoke an order; cancel an order*   撤回，取消

[ˌkaʊntɚˋmænd]

The President was able to countermand the order to launch the missiles when he realized that there was no attack.
總統獲悉並無攻擊行動後便撤回發射飛彈的命令。

⁜ corp = body 身體

★★★★★

1397 incorporate   *v. unite; unify; integrate; merge; consolidate*   整合，結合

[ɪnˋkɔrpəˌret]

His recent book incorporates many useful ideas about adult education. Therefore many educators read the book to get some good ideas about education.
他近來的著作整合了許多成人教育觀點，因此許多教育家都從書中汲取好的教育觀念。

★★★☆☆

| 1398 **corps** | *n. a body of troops* | 團體，小組，部隊，兵團 |

[kɔr]（註：本字單複數同形，注意發音。單數為 [kɔr]，複數為 [kɔrz]。

The Peace Corps is an international group of volunteers who help rebuild nations destroyed by wars or natural disasters.
和平部隊是國際志工團體，專門協助重建遭受戰爭或天災破壞的國家。

★★★★☆

| 1399 **corpse** | *n. a dead body; carcass* | 屍體 |

[kɔrps]

Ancient Egyptians wrapped a corpse in a special kind of cloth and tried to preserve it. They believed that by doing so they could revive the dead.
古埃及人相信以特殊布料包裹死者屍體防腐保存，可讓死者復活。

★★★☆☆

| 1400 **corpulent** | *a. bulky in body; fat; obese; rotund; roly-poly; porky* | 肥胖的，肥大的 |

[`kɔrpjələnt]

That man never exercises and he consumes about 4,000 calories a day, and as a result is a very corpulent man.
那男子從不運動且每日攝取大約四千大卡熱量，因此非常肥胖。

Tea Time... ☕

<Greek myth> Laconia	〈來自希臘神話〉拉哥尼亞
Province on the coast of the Peloponnesos, Greece; 1,388sq. mi.; a region dominated by the city of Sparta; the people of Laconia were thought to be brief and terse in speech or expression.	總面積一千三百八十八平方英里的拉哥尼亞位於希臘伯羅奔尼撒半島沿岸，受斯巴達城統治，人民被教育成說話簡潔。（註：後世將本字的形容詞 laconic 引申為「要言不煩的，言簡意賅的」。）

laconic [lə`kanɪk] *a. brief or terse in speech; concise* | 簡潔的，簡明的，不多費唇舌的

The infamous swashbuckler responded to the prisoners' pleas with a laconic grunt that left no doubt in their mind as to their fate in his hands.
惡名昭彰的暴徒對被俘者的懇求只簡短地哼了一聲，眾人的命運顯然掌握在他手中。

1 Complete each word by filling in the blank with proper spelling so that it has the same meaning as suggested. Then please write the meaning of each word in Chinese.

1. 殺蟲劑	=	i n s e c t i _ _ _ e
2. 簡潔的	=	c o n _ _ _ e
3. 雕刻	=	i n _ _ _ e
4. 果斷的	=	d e _ _ _ i v e
5. 刺激	=	i n _ _ _ e
6. 朗誦	=	r e _ _ _ e
7. 否認	=	d i s _ _ _ _ _
8. 宣布	=	p r o _ _ _ _ _
9. 大叫	=	e x _ _ _ _ _
10. 喧鬧	=	_ _ _ _ o r

11. decline	=	_____
12. recluse	=	_____
13. conclusion	=	_____
14. exclusive	=	_____
15. cooperate	=	_____
16. coincidence	=	_____
17. recognition	=	_____
18. countervail	=	_____
19. counterpart	=	_____
20. counterfeit	=	_____

2 Choose a word that best completes the sentence.

21. The farmer sprayed some _____ to get rid of the pests on his crop plants.
(A) recitation (B) chronicle (C) insecticides (D) chronometer

22. What a _____. I'm going to the library, too.
(A) coincidence (B) conclusion (C) acclivity (D) clamor

3 The highlighted word is closest in meaning to which of the following?

23. The chronic ailment rendered the old man feeble.
(A) concise (B) long-lasting (C) succinct (D) decisive

24. The recluse lived in seclusion and avoided meeting other people.
(A) hermit (B) connoisseur (C) contrast (D) contraband

25. After she noticed that taxi drivers ignored her, the corpulent lady decided to go on a diet.
(A) cognizant (B) exclusive (C) fat (D) counter

Practice Test 01

1 The highlighted word is closest in meaning to which of the following?

1. With the advent of computers, modern people are able to find a large amount of
   information without going to the library.
   - (A) adjunct
   - (B) arrival
   - (C) unanimity
   - (D) preamble

2. Despite its seemingly ponderous movements, a polar bear is an agile predator.
   - (A) an adjacent
   - (B) a rustic
   - (C) a nimble
   - (D) an excessive

3. The altercation between her and her brother was started by her name-calling.
   - (A) altitude
   - (B) quarrel
   - (C) recitation
   - (D) catastrophe

4. The use of insecticides has had a malign effect on the ecosystem.
   - (A) pesticides
   - (B) chronicles
   - (C) chronometers
   - (D) clamors

5. Contrary to the popular belief, an airplane is one of the safest modes of transportation.
   - (A) accede
   - (B) opposed
   - (C) cordial
   - (D) cardinal

2 Please answer the following questions.

(Comic Tale 1)

The chief mate and the engineer of the Seagull, a giant tanker, were on bad terms with each other. Both of them had short tempers and all the crew on board thought that they were irreconcilable. They were probably more familiar with the shapes of each other's teeth than anyone else because they hardly passed by each other without showing their teeth. One day their animosity toward each other came to a head. They had a hectic argument about which of the two was more important to the tanker. Their argument lasted about half an hour until the captain succeeded in reconciling them. The captain told them that it would be a good idea for them to switch their roles to find out who was the more important person. The chief

mate went down to the engine room to work with the engines and his counterpart went up top to the deck to steer. Hardly had they switched their roles before the chief mate in the engine room radioed over the intercom, "Hey, up there, all the engines have abruptly stopped. I can't understand why!" The engineer responded, "She's aground!"

(Comic Tale 2)

Jimmy received a little Dalmatian dog from his intimate friend as a birthday gift. It was so cute that he decided to show it to his girl friend Nancy, and brought it to her house. Nancy really liked it, too. She gave it a kiss and a squeeze, causing Jimmy to be jealous. However, the dog must have had animus toward such a boisterous welcome. It groaned, whined, growled, moaned, barked, howled and even roared. Just then someone knocked at the door. She opened the door and there stood her grandmother with a big smile on her face. She hugged Nancy and exclaimed , "Congratulations, my pumpkin! At last you've got a proposal of marriage from Jimmy! Your grandfather did the same thing when he proposed to me."

6. The word animosity is closest in meaning to which of the following?
(A) advent
(B) anaesthetic
(C) argument
(D) enmity

7. The word captain is closest in meaning to which of the following?
(A) chief in command
(B) vertical face
(C) person who receives benefits
(D) height of an object

8. The word counterpart is closest in meaning to which of the following?
(A) peer
(B) corpse
(C) carnivore
(D) connoisseur

9. The word animus is closest in meaning to which of the following?
(A) ill feelings
(B) unanimity
(C) agronomy
(D) exigency

10. The word exclaimed is closest in meaning to which of the following?
(A) agitated
(B) ambled
(C) countermanded
(D) shouted

⟐ cred = trust 信任

★★★★★

MP3
58

1401 incredible

[ɪnˋkrɛdəbl]

a. unbelievable; inconceivable　　　　　　　　　　驚人的，難以置信的

Mary, a short lady, has an incredible appetite. She is such a voracious eater and that is why she is fat.

瑪麗身材矮小卻食量驚人，她食欲旺盛難怪會胖。

★★★★☆

1402 discredit

[dɪsˋkrɛdɪt]

v. distrust; mistrust　　　　　　　　　　　　　不相信，使不足信

The presidential candidate has made several comments about the incumbent that were specifically meant to discredit him as a trustworthy president.

總統候選人對現任元首提出諸多批評，主要用意在表示他不值得信賴。

★★★★★

1403 credit

[ˋkrɛdɪt]

n. trust　　　　　　　　　　　　　　　　　信用，信譽

Although a credit card is convenient in that you don't have to carry large amounts of cash, it can get you into many financial problems if spending is not controlled.

方便的信用卡雖然讓人不用隨身攜帶大量現金，但若不節制花費就會引發許多財務問題。

★★★★★

1404 credulous

[ˋkrɛdʒələs]

a. gullible　　　　　　　　　　　　　　　　輕信的，容易受騙的

James had a credulous nature and therefore he tended to believe everything that others told him. Therefore the con man easily took advantage of him and cheated him.

詹姆斯天生容易受騙上當，旁人說什麼都相信，所以會輕易被騙子欺騙利用。

★★★☆☆

1405 credo

[ˋkrido]

n. creed　　　　　　　　　　　　　　　　　信條

His personal credo was "Do to others as you would have them do to you," and he lived up to that until the day he died.

他一生奉行至死不渝的個人信條是「己之所欲亦施於人」。

⟐ cub, cum(b) = lay, lie 平放，位置

★★★★★

1406 incubate

[ˋɪŋkjəˌbet]

v. sit on or artificially heat (eggs) in order to bring forth young birds　　　　孵卵，孵化

The chicken's eggs were put under warm lights to incubate for three weeks before they hatched.

雞蛋被放在溫暖燈光下三周好孵化。

★★★☆☆

1407 encumber

[ɪnˋkʌmbɚ]

v. burden; weigh down; overburden; overload　　妨礙，困擾

Joy has always been a very bright and efficient employee, but ever since her divorce trial began she has become encumbered by the whole ordeal.

喬伊一向是開朗有效率的員工，但自從開始打離婚官司，痛苦折磨就困擾著她。

★★★★★

1408 accumulate

[əˋkjumjə‚let]

v. collect; gather; amass; mass; pile up;　　累積，堆積
heap up; assemble; stockpile

Nick, my American friend, has accumulated a lot of clothing while staying in the country because the prices are so inexpensive.

我的美國友人尼克待在國內時囤積了許多衣服，因為價格非常便宜。

★★★★★

1409 accumulation

[ə‚kjumjəˋleʃən]

n. collection; aggregation　　累積，積聚

A good writer is wise in his choice of subjects and exhaustive in his accumulation of materials.

—— Ernest Hemingway

好作家不但慎選寫作題材，同時鉅細靡遺地累積寫作素材。

——海明威

★★★☆☆

1410 incumbent

[ɪnˋkʌmbənt]

a. current / obligatory; mandatory　　現任的 / 負有義務的

The incumbent lawmaker is trying to clarify existing legislation and doing everything to make good laws for the underdogs of the nation.

現任立法委員試圖釐清現行法律，並盡全力制定有益於全國弱勢族群的法規。

★★★★☆

1411 cumulative

[ˋkjumjə‚letɪv]

a. formed by successive additions　　累積的，漸增的

Science is usually thought to be cumulative, because present knowledge is based on past knowledge.

科學常被視為是累積的知識，因為現有知識是建基在過去知識上的。

⁜ curs = run 跑

★★★☆☆

1412 cursive

[ˋkɝsɪv]

a. (of writing) done with jointed characters　　草寫的

It was pretty easy for me to learn to write Chinese characters, but it took a lot longer for me to learn to write cursive style.

學寫中文字很容易，但學草書卻花我了很多時間。

★★★★☆

1413 precursory

[priˋkɝsərɪ]

a. preliminary; introductory　　先驅的，預兆的

The opening scene gave a precursory glimpse of what was to follow, without giving away the ending of the film.

從電影開場白可一窺後續情節，但不會洩露結局。

1414 **recourse**	*n.* resort / *v.* turn to	求助，依賴 / 求助於～

[rɪ`kɔrs]

Since the righteous student who stood against the tyrannical government had no legal recourse, he had to abide by the decision of the jury and go to jail.

富有正義感的學生反抗專制政府，卻因為缺乏合法援助，只能等候司法判決入獄服刑。

★★★★★

1415 **cursory**	*a.* hasty; hurried; slapdash	粗略的，草率的

[`kɜsərɪ]

A cursory glance of the report seemed to indicate that it was well written, but a more careful reading was necessary before the teacher could give it a grade.

老師大略看一下報告似乎寫得不錯，但還需仔細閱讀才能評分。

✢ de-, deter- = down 向下

★★★☆☆

1416 **devalue**	*v.* reduce the value of	貶值

[di`vælju]

The massive strikes that have plagued the country have had a very negative effect on the economy, so much so that the nation's currency has been devalued overseas.

困擾國家的大罷工對經濟造成非常負面的影響，連貨幣都貶值。

★★★★★

1417 **detrimental**	*a.* harmful; deleterious; adverse; unfavorable; pernicious	有害的，不利的

[ˌdɛtrə`mɛnt!]

Although people know that smoking cigarettes is detrimental to their health, they keep on smoking, because it is very difficult to quit.

雖然人們知道抽煙有礙健康卻還是抽個不停，因為很難戒掉。

★★★★★

1418 **demote**	*v.* downgrade; reduce to a lower rank	降級，降等

[dɪ`mot]

The project that he was in charge of was a complete failure and cost the company several million dollars, which resulted in his being demoted from general manager to department manager.

他負責的專案完全失敗，還浪費公司數百萬元，使他從總經理降級為部門經理。

★★★★★

1419 **demerit**	*n.* fault / a mark given to an offender / drawbacks	過失 / 罪過 / 缺點

[dɪ`mɛrɪt]

His lying and cheating was a serious demerit and no one trusted him ever again. Therefore he could not find a real friend when he was in trouble.

他的撒謊和欺騙是極大缺點，教人再也無法相信，因此當他有難時找不到真正的朋友幫忙。

★★★★★

| 1420 **deteriorate** | **v.** *worsen; get worse; degenerate; degrade; spoil* | 使惡化，變壞 |

[dɪˋtɪrɪəˏret]

Nina's condition deteriorated rapidly and she went into acute kidney failure. At last she was admitted into the hospital.
妮娜的情況急遽惡化為急性腎衰竭，最後住進醫院。

★★★☆☆

| 1421 **defame** | **v.** *libel; slander* | 誹謗，中傷 |

[dɪˋfem]

The newspaper story about an alleged affair between the presidential candidate and a famous movie star defamed the candidate and ultimately caused him to lose the election.
報載與知名電影明星的疑似緋聞中傷總統候選人，最後使他落選。

❖ dexter- = right hand 右邊

★★★★★

| 1422 **dexterous** | **a.** *deft; nimble; ingenious; astute; keen; shrewd; canny; crafty* | 靈巧的，熟練的 |

[ˋdɛkstərəs]

David was driving the creaking station wagon with dexterous recklessness. The other passengers were very nervous.
大衛熟練而魯莽地開著嘎吱作響的休旅車，在座其他乘客都非常緊張。

★★★☆☆

| 1423 **ambidextrous** | **a.** *able to use both hands equally well* | 慣用兩手的 |

[ˏæmbəˋdɛkstrəs]

My nephew is an ambidextrous person, allowing him to easily use either hand with equal skill. I think he could be a good baseball player.
慣用雙手的姪子使用左右手都一樣熟練，我認為他能成為優秀棒球員。

★★★★☆

| 1424 **dexterity** | **n.** *adroitness; deftness; knack; proficiency; shrewdness* | 靈巧，熟練 |

[dɛksˋtɛrətɪ]

Nancy, a well-known pianist, has the dexterity to move her fingers effortlessly over the piano keys.
知名鋼琴家南西手指靈巧，能在琴鍵上移動自如。

❖ dia- = thorough, through 穿越

★★★★★

MP3
59

| 1425 **diagnosis** | **n.** *the identification of a disease by means of a patient's symptoms* | 診斷書，診斷結果 |

[ˏdaɪəgˋnosɪs]

Most doctors rely on test results to make a diagnosis. Based on this they write a prescription for their patient.
多數醫生憑檢驗結果做出醫療診斷，並為病患開立處方箋。

★★★★☆

1426 **diametrically**	**ad.** *completely; entirely*	正相反地，完全地
[ˌdaɪə`mɛtrɪkḷɪ]	Love and hate, at first sight diametrically opposite, share a trait—intensity. Love and hate also defy words. Can you define love and hate in a comprehensible and concrete way? No.	

Reader's Forum: War of the Sexes

乍看之下正相反的愛與恨其實有個共同特徵，那就是兩者都很強烈。愛與恨都難以用文字形容，你能用容易理解的具體方式來定義愛與恨嗎？答案是不能。
——《讀者論壇》兩性戰爭

★★★★☆

1427 **diagonal**	**a.** *oblique*	對角線的，斜的
[daɪ`ægənl]	The first instruction we received from our teacher was to draw a diagonal line from the top left-hand corner of the page to the bottom right-hand corner of the page. 老師給我們的第一個指示是從左上頁角畫一條對角線到右下方。	

★★★★★

1428 **diameter**	**n.** *width; thickness*	直徑
[daɪ`æmətɚ]	The city planners should have used a larger diameter of pipe when planning the sewage system for that area of the city because the population in that area has grown so fast that the amount of raw sewage now exceeds the capacity of the pipes. 都市計畫者規劃該區下水道系統時應使用較大直徑輸送管，由於該區人口成長快速，如今未經處理的污水已超出管線容納量。	

⁙ dic(t) = say, words 說，話語

★★★★★

1429 **abdicate**	**v.** *give up; renounce; surrender; disclaim; relinquish; waive*	放棄
[`æbdəˌket]	The King chose to abdicate the throne in favor of his son when his son reached a mature and responsible age. 王子長大成人並富有責任感時，國王選擇讓位給他。	

★★★★☆

1430 **dictate**	**v.** *ordain; decree; give orders*	命令
[`dɪktet]	I'm sick of listening to you and I won't stand your trying to dictate to me every little thing that you think I should do. 我受夠了唯命是從，無法忍受你命令我做每件你認為該做的小事。	

★★★★☆

1431 diction

[`dɪkʃən]

n. articulation; enunciation; elocution　　　　措辭，用語

Without correct diction, it is very difficult to become an effective politician, because the key to political success is having the ability to effectively communicate.

缺乏正確措辭將很難成為有效率的政治人物，因為政治成功關鍵在於具備有效溝通能力。

★★★☆☆

1432 dictum

[`dɪktəm]

n. a formal utterance / maxim　　　　正式發言 / 金玉良言

The candidate's campaign manager put forth a very powerful dictum predicting that the candidate would win the election by a landslide.

該候選人的競選總幹事發表強而有力的言論，預料將會以壓倒性票數贏得選戰。

⬦ dom = rule; home 統治；家

★★★★☆

1433 dominion

[də`mɪnjən]

n. rule; authority; control; jurisdiction　　　　統治，管轄

It is a man's responsibility to maintain dominion over his family, but that doesn't give him the right to abuse his wife or children.

男性職責在於掌理家庭，但並不因此有權虐待妻小。

★★★★★

1434 dominant

[`dɑmənənt]

a. primary; principal; prevailing; main; ruling; leading　　占優勢的，支配的

Left-handed people feel that they are special in some way. That is why Jane was very happy to see that her son's dominant hand was his left.

左撇子覺得自己在某方面很特別，所以珍發現兒子慣用左手時感到很高興。

★★★★★

1435 domicile

[`dɑməsḷ]

n. residence; quarters; habitation; abode　　　　住所，住處

One of the most important elements of a healthy society is trust among its citizens. I believe that trust begins in the domicile setting.

健全社會最重要的要素之一就是市民信任，我相信它是從住家四周環境開始培養起的。

★★★★☆

1436 domineering

[ˌdɑmə`nɪrɪŋ]

a. overbearing; imperious; autocratic; despotic; authoritarian; tyrannical　　　蠻橫的，跋扈的

Many domineering husbands tend to believe in male chauvinism. They believe in a wife's subordination to a husband.

許多跋扈丈夫信奉男性沙文主義，認為妻子應服從丈夫。

★★★★☆

1437 dominate

[`dɑmə,net]

v. rule; govern; control   支配，統治，控制

My friend Jim is very talkative, and he always tries to dominate the conversation. It's almost impossible for me to get a word in edgewise.

友人吉姆很愛講話，總想主導對話，害我幾乎插不上話。

★★★★☆

1438 domesticate

[də`mɛstə,ket]

v. tame   馴養，豢養

A dog is probably a kind of wolf that people have domesticated. A dog still has some traits of a wolf.

人類豢養的狗可能是某種狼，仍帶有狼的部分特徵。

★★★★★

1439 predominant

[prɪ`dɑmənənt]

a. dominant; ruling; preeminent   卓越的，占優勢的

The Brazilian soccer player is undoubtedly one of the most predominant players the World Cup Games have ever seen.

巴西足球員無疑是世界盃足球賽最優異的球員之一。

★★★★★

1440 domain

[do`men]

n. realm; dominion; territory; province   領域，範圍

The domain of the woman used to be the home, but it has expanded to the office these days.

過去女性的活動範圍是家庭，現在則擴展到辦公室。

★★★★★

1441 indomitable

[ɪn`dɑmətəbḷ]

a. unconquerable; unbeatable; invincible; unswerving; unwavering   不屈不撓的，不氣餒的

The doctors told him that he would never walk again, but with indomitable courage he battled pain and eventually regained the use of his legs.

醫生告訴他再也無法走路，但他憑著不屈不撓的勇氣克服痛楚，最後又能行走。

★★★★★

1442 domestic

[də`mɛstɪk]

a. household; home   家事的，國內的

The concept that domestic chores are for females only is outmoded foolishness. Males also should do their share of work.

認為女性應包辦大小家務是過時的愚昧觀念，男性也應分擔家事。

✣ don = give 給

★★★★★

1443 donate

[`donet]

v. contribute; subscribe   捐贈，贈與，捐獻

At Christmas time, many people donate to charity organizations. They must be moved by Christ's love for poor people.

許多人會在耶誕節捐助慈善機構。這些人必定有感於耶穌對窮人的關愛。

★★★★☆		
1444 condone	**v.** *forgive or overlook*	寬恕，赦免，原諒
[kən`don]	I regard honesty as one of the most important characteristics of a person and I cannot condone cheating of any kind on tests. 我認為誠實是做人最重要的美德之一，所以無法原諒考試作弊。	

★★★★★		
1445 donator	**n.** *contributor*	捐贈者
[`donetə]	I know a man who needs an organ transplant, and he is waiting for the hospital to find a donator. 我認識一個在醫院等待捐贈者進行器官移植的人。	

★★★★★		
1446 donor	**n.** *contributor*	捐贈者
[`donə]	When Bruce went to the police station to pick up his driver's license, the clerk asked him if he was interested in becoming an organ donor. 布魯斯到警局拿駕照時，書記員問他有沒有興趣成為器官捐贈者。	

❖ **duce, duct = lead, guide** 引導

★★★★☆		
1447 conduce	**v.** *lead or contribute to*	有助於～，導致
[kən`djus]	Rest conduces to health. We should replenish our energy when it is exhausted. Otherwise we might get sick. 休息有助於健康，精疲力竭時應補充體力，否則可能會生病。	

★★★★☆		
1448 sedition	**n.** *agitation; rabble-rousing; mutiny; insurrection; uprising; treason*	擾亂治安，鬧事
[sɪ`dɪʃən]	The students at the demonstration were arrested and charged with sedition and other anti-government acts. 被捕的示威學生被控擾亂治安和其他反政府行為。	

★★★★☆		
1449 seduce	**v.** *lure; entice; allure; tempt; decoy*	誘拐，引誘
[sɪ`djus]	Mr. Lantis tried many times to seduce the beautiful young woman, but she adamantly refused to even let him hold her hand. 藍提斯先生好幾次想引誘那位年輕貌美的女子，但她堅持拒絕，甚至不讓他牽手。	

★★★★☆

1450 induce

[ɪnˋdjus]

v. lead; cajole 引起,導致,勸誘

TV sometimes induces people to think that the world is more dangerous than it really is. They often feel extremely nervous while watching news on TV.

有時電視會讓人以為世界很危險,收看電視新聞時常感到非常不安。

★★★☆☆

1451 inductive

[ɪnˋdʌktɪv]

a. of or based on induction 歸納(性)的

People who study archaeology are usually very good at inductive reasoning. They make a conclusion based on various forms of evidence.

考古學研究者通常具有很好的歸納推理能力,並根據各類證據得出結論。

★★★★☆

1452 conduction

[kənˋdʌkʃən]

n. the transmission of heat or electricity through a substance 傳導,誘導

The conduction of electricity along a metal wire is improved if a higher grade of steel is used. Copper is a better conductor of electricity than just simple steel.

使用等級較高的鋼可提高電流通過金屬線的傳導力。比起純鋼,銅是更好的電導體。

★★★★☆

1453 inducement

[ɪnˋdjusmənt]

n. attraction; enticement; stimulus; encouragement 誘因,動機

As an inducement for Mike to study hard, his father promised to buy him a bike if he passed the exam.

父親為了鼓勵麥克用功念書,便答應如果考試及格會買腳踏車給他。

★★★★★

1454 addicted

[əˋdɪktɪd]

a. dependent on; hooked on; unable to do without 沈溺的,上癮的

These days more and more children are becoming addicted to junk food which has too many calories.

現在有愈來愈多孩童愛吃高熱量垃圾食物。

Tea Time... ☕

<English legend> Hobson's choice Thomas Hobson(1544-1631) of Cambridge, England, who owned livery stables and let horses in strict order according to their position near the door.	〈英國傳說故事〉霍布遜的選擇 十六世紀英國劍橋的湯瑪斯・霍布遜 (1544-1631) 以出租馬車為業,出租時有嚴格規定,只能挑靠近門邊的馬。 (註:霍布遜不讓顧客挑三揀四,凡是不服從規定者就別向他租馬車。後世便將此詞引申為「別無選擇餘地」。)

Hobson's choice [ˋhɑbsənz ˋtʃɔɪs] *a. choice of taking the thing offered or nothing* │ 別無選擇

The spy was asked how he preferred to be executed, by hanging or electrocution, which was a Hobson's Choice, since either way he would be dead so it didn't really matter to him.

間諜被問道想接受絞刑或電刑,對他而言反正都是死,別無其他選擇,因此哪種處決方式都無所謂。

1 Complete each word by filling in the blank with proper spelling so that it has the same meaning as suggested. Then please write the meaning of each word in Chinese.

1. 驚人的 = in ＿＿＿＿ible
2. 使不足信 = dis ＿＿＿＿it
3. 信用 = ＿＿＿＿it
4. 容易受騙的 = ＿＿＿＿ulous
5. 孵化 = in ＿＿＿ate
6. 累積 = ac ＿＿＿ulate
7. 累積的 = ＿＿＿ulative
8. 草寫的 = ＿＿＿＿ive
9. 先驅的 = pre ＿＿＿＿ory
10. 粗略的 = ＿＿＿＿ory

11. devalue = ＿＿＿＿＿＿
12. demote = ＿＿＿＿＿＿
13. deteriorate = ＿＿＿＿＿＿
14. defame = ＿＿＿＿＿＿
15. ambidextrous = ＿＿＿＿＿＿
16. diagnosis = ＿＿＿＿＿＿
17. diametrically = ＿＿＿＿＿＿
18. domesticate = ＿＿＿＿＿＿
19. conduce = ＿＿＿＿＿＿
20. inducement = ＿＿＿＿＿＿

2 Choose a word that best completes the sentence.

21. **The miser could ＿＿＿＿＿ a large fortune.**
(A) discredit (B) trust (C) accumulate (D) encumber

22. **Even a(n) ＿＿＿＿＿ glance will reveal that his report was well written.**
(A) cursory (B) detrimental (C) dexterous (D) astute

23. **The explorers had the ＿＿＿＿＿ belief that they could surmount all difficulties.**
(A) indomitable (B) diagonal (C) keen (D) ingenious

3 The highlighted word is closest in meaning to which of the following?

24. **The father tried to** induce **his daughter to study hard by promising that he would buy her a cell phone if she got a good score on the exam.**
(A) forgive (B) lead (C) donate (D) condone

25. **The clerk at the office asked him if he was interested in becoming an organ** donor **.**
(A) recourse (B) credo (C) donator (D) defame

✥ dys- = bad 壞的

★★☆☆☆

MP3 60

1455 dyslexia

[dɪs`lɛksɪə]

n. *an abnormal difficulty in reading and spelling*   失讀症，閱讀困難症

The sign "Kentucky Fried Chicken" might be read as "Kentucky Fried Kitchen" to someone who has dyslexia.

閱讀困難症患者可能會把「肯德基炸雞」讀成「肯德基廚房」。

★★★★☆

1456 dystrophy

[`dɪstrəfɪ]

n. *defective nutrition*   營養失調，營養不良

People with some forms of dystrophy must change their diet and eat more nutritious foods. Energy basically comes from the food they eat.

營養失調患者應改變飲食並多吃營養食物，基本上體力來自所攝取的食物。

★★★☆☆

1457 dyspepsia

[dɪs`pɛpʃə]

n. *indigestion*   消化不良

After eating at Mac's everyday for three weeks, he came down with a bad case of dyspepsia and had to go to the hospital.

他一連三周在麥克斯餐廳用餐後，得了嚴重消化不良必須就醫。

✥ empt = take out 取出，扣除

★★★★★

1458 exemption

[ɪg`zɛmpʃən]

n. *exception; immunity; impunity; exclusion*   免除

The night before his final exam, Paul dreamed that he had been granted an exemption because his marks and attendance during the semester had been perfect.

期末考前晚保羅夢見因為自己的學期成績和出席率都很高，所以獲准不用考試。

★★★★☆

1459 redemption

[rɪ`dɛmpʃən]

n. *the act or an instance of redeeming*   贖罪，彌補

There was no redemption for Adolf Hitler, who had ordered the deaths of six million innocent Jewish people.

下令處死六百萬無辜猶太人的希特勒難以贖罪。

★★★☆☆

1460 peremptory

[pə`rɛmptərɪ]

a. commanding; imperious; domineering   斷然的，不容置疑的

Our drill instructor has a very peremptory manner and he always expects us to obey his orders. We have never heard of a more strict drill instructor than him.

我們的步操教官非常專斷且令出必行，沒聽過有誰比他更嚴厲的。

❖ ethno- = race, people 種族，民族

★★★★★

1461 ethnic

[`ɛθnɪk]

a. racial   種族的，人種的

We can find many different ethnic groups in the United Sates, which is often called a melting pot.

號稱文化大熔爐的美國擁有許多不同種族。

★★★★☆

1462 ethnology

[ɛθ`nɑlədʒɪ]

n. the comparative scientific study of peoples   人種學

Ethnology is a branch of anthropology in which the organization and cultures of different races of people are studied.

人種學是人類學的旁支，專門研究不同種族的文化和組織。

★★☆☆☆

1463 ethnocentric

[ˌɛθnoˋsɛntrɪk]

a. evaluating other races and cultures by criteria specific to one's own   民族優越感的

Her father's ethnocentric attitudes would not allow her to marry the man she loved, simply because he was from another country.

父親的民族優越感不會讓她嫁給自己所愛的人，只因為他是外國人。

❖ eu- = good 好的

★★★★☆

1464 euphoria

[ju`fɔrɪə]

n. a feeling of well-being based on over-confidence   興奮，心情愉悅

Some of the nation's people were impatient and became engrossed in euphoria concerning national unification as soon as Germany became united.

德國統一使部分國民因國家一統顯得急切又興奮。

★★★★☆

1465 **euphemism**	*n.* a mild or vague expression substituted for one thought to be too harsh or direct	婉轉說法，委婉用語
[`jufəmɪzəm]	The expression "to pass away" is a nice euphemism for "to die." Sometimes we use a more roundabout way of speaking by using a milder expression. 「去世」是「死掉」的委婉說法，有時我們會以較溫和的措辭婉轉表達意見。	

★★★★☆

1466 **euthanasia**	*n.* the bringing about of a gentle and easy death in the case of incurable and painful disease	安樂死
[ˌjuθəˈneʒɪə]	There have been many arguments over the morality of performing euthanasia for terminally ill patients. 為臨終患者施行安樂死在道德上時有爭議。	

★★☆☆☆

1467 **eulogize**	*v.* praise in speech or writing	頌揚，稱讚
[`julə,dʒaɪz]	They described her as 'A FRIEND TO EVERYONE' and in my opinion they couldn't have chosen a better phrase to eulogize her. 大家形容她「知交滿天下」，在我看來這是最能頌揚她的。	

★★★★☆

1468 **eugenics**	*n.* the science of improving the population by controlled breeding for desirable inherited characteristics	優生學
[ju`dʒɛnɪks]	The study of eugenics will hopefully solve the problems of birth defects and hereditary diseases. 優生學研究可望解決先天缺陷和遺傳性疾病等問題。	

⁜ ex-, extra- = outside 外，出

★★★★☆

1469 **exodus**	*n.* a mass departure of people; flight	（人的）大批離開
[`ɛksədəs]	There were 65 thousand people packed into the stadium, and when the fire alarm sounded there was widespread hysteria as people made a mass exodus towards the exits. 球場擠滿了六萬五千人，火災警報鈴響時民眾陷入驚慌，大批人潮紛紛擠向出口。	

★★★★★

1470 extrinsic

a. irrelevant; extraneous; external; unrelated　　　附帶的，不相干的

[ɛk`strɪnsɪk]

One's appendix is often considered extrinsic since it serves no other purpose than to get infected.

闌尾常被視為是無用的，因為它除了易遭感染外一無是處。

★★★★★

1471 exotic

a. foreign; imported; outlandish　　　異國風情的，外來的，熱帶的

[ɛg`zɑtɪk]

This aquarium contains many exotic fish I have never seen before. It is said that they are from foreign countries.

水族館裡有許多我從未看過的熱帶魚，據說都是外來品種。

★★★★★

1472 extraneous

a. irrelevant; unrelated; impertinent; inappropriate /　　外來的 / 不相干的
unessential

[ɪk`strenɪəs]

I think you should stick to the important facts instead of wasting time talking about extraneous matters.

我認為你應專注在重要事實上，不要浪費時間談論不相干的事。

⟐ fac, feat, fec, feit, fic, fy = do, make　做，製做

★★★★★

1473 fiction

n. an invented idea or statement or narrative　　　小說，虛構，想像

[`fɪkʃən]

Some science fiction novels are concerned with extraterrestrial creatures that have invaded the Earth.

部分科幻小說是有關外星人入侵地球的。

★★★★★

1474 infectious

a. contagious; transmissible　　　傳染性的，傳染病的

[ɪn`fɛkʃəs]

Patients with infectious diseases must be kept away from others, since those kinds of diseases can be transmitted to others nearby.

傳染性疾病患者需與人隔離，因為會傳染給別人。

★★★★★

1475 fictitious

a. imaginary; unreal; fictional; made-up /　　杜撰的 / 偽造的
counterfeit; false; phoney

[fɪk`tɪʃəs]

When the teacher asked Tom why he was absent, he made up a fictitious story about how his grandmother got sick and he had to take care of her.

老師問湯姆為何缺席，於是他捏造要照顧生病祖母的謊言。

★★★★★

1476 **defective**	**a.** *imperfect; faulty; flawed; deficient; incomplete; marred; on the blink*	有缺陷的，不完美的

[dɪˋfɛktɪv]

Jane's grandfather has defective hearing and is unable to hear what is said to him in a normal voice. He needs to wear a hearing aid.

珍的祖父有聽力障礙聽不見正常音量，需戴助聽器。

★★★★☆

1477 **feasible**	**a.** *practicable; possible; attainable; achievable*	可行的，可能的

[ˋfizəbl]

My friend is trying to convince me to start a new business, but I'm still not sure if what he is proposing is feasible.

友人想勸我創業，但我不確定他的提議是否可行。

★★★★☆

1478 **factitious**	**a.** *fake; false; sham; counterfeit; falsified / artificial*	虛假的 / 人工的

[fækˋtɪʃəs]

Actors and actresses usually shed factitious tears, but when they are full of emotion, they shed real tears.

演員們常假裝流淚，只有真情流露時會流下真正眼淚。

★★★★★

1479 **feat**	**n.** *a noteworthy act or achievement; accomplishment; exploit*	豐功偉業，創舉

[fit]

Robert attempted his most daring feat to date when he tried to jump over a big truck on a motorcycle.

羅伯特騎摩托車飛越大卡車以挑戰迄今最膽大冒險的創舉。

★★★★☆

MP3 61

1480 **superficial**	**a.** *skin-deep; insubstantial / external*	膚淺的 / 外表的

[ˋsupɚˋfɪʃəl]

After all, beauty is skin deep only in the superficial sense.

Interpersonal Attraction —— Raymond S. Ross

美貌終究只是膚淺外表。

——《人際吸引》雷蒙‧S‧羅斯

★★★☆☆

1481 **efface**	**v.** *erase; rub or wipe out; obliterate*	抹滅，消除

[ɪˋfes]

If you do not constantly save information on a computer, a sudden power blackout may efface all your work.

使用電腦時應常經存檔，否則突然停電會消除所有資料。

★★★★★

1482 defy

[dɪˋfaɪ]

v. resist; disobey; flout; go against; thumb one's nose at 　使不能，使落空

Why do people in some countries drive on the left while those in others drive on the right? This is one of the questions that defy an easy answer.

為什麼有些國家靠左駕駛有些卻靠右？對此問題沒有簡單答案。

★★★★☆

1483 defector

[dɪˋfɛktə]

n. deserter; turncoat; traitor; renegade 　變節者，投奔自由者，投誠者

The defector, who ran away from the tyrannical nation, came to take shelter in another country and revealed some secret information about the despot.

投誠者逃離專制祖國到其他國家尋求庇護，並揭發暴君部分機密情資。

★★★★★

1484 deficit

[ˋdɛfəsɪt]

n. shortfall; shortage; deficiency 　不足（額），赤字

The biggest issue of the election this year is the national deficit, and what is going to be done in order to bring our nation out of debt.

今年選舉的最重要議題是國家赤字，以及如何避免舉債。

★★★★★

1485 sufficient

[səˋfɪʃənt]

a. adequate; enough; ample 　充分的，足夠的

The company wants to append a new addition onto their building, but there are not sufficient funds in the budget.

公司想進行大樓增建但預算不足。

★★★★★

1486 artificial

[ˌɑrtəˋfɪʃəl]

a. man-made; synthetic; fabricated; simulated 　人工的，人為的

Our soccer players usually play on artificial turf on rainy days because real grass is muddy and players get dirty.

下雨時我方足球員多在人工草皮球場練球，因為天然草皮泥濘不堪，會使球員全身髒污。

★★★★★

1487 defeat

[dɪˋfit]

n. reverse / v. conquer; be victorious over; get the better of; overpower; thrash 　敗北／戰勝，征服

The sail was patched with flour sacks and, furled, it looked like the flag of permanent defeat.

The Old Man and the Sea — Ernest Hemingway

船帆以麵粉袋縫補而成再收捲起來，看起來就像一面象徵永遠失敗的旗子。

——《老人與海》海明威

1488 officious	*a. intrusive; meddlesome / dictatorial; domineering*　多管閒事的 / 盛氣凌人的
[ə`fɪʃəs]	An officious person is apt to enlighten us about our faults. He often interferes with every small detail of our personal matters. 多管閒事者容易使我們發現個人缺點，因為他連小小的私事都要干涉。

★★★☆☆

1489 faction	*a. a small organized dissentient group within a larger one, especially in politics*　派系
[`fækʃən]	The gays and lesbians in America are now forming a new faction that is gaining political momentum. 美國同性戀者成立新派系以擴張政治勢力。

✢ fer, ver = carry, put　攜帶，運送，承受

★★★★★

1490 circumference	*n. perimeter*　圓周，周長，周圍
[sə`kʌmfərəns]	Even before a child is born, we are able to measure the circumference of its head by means of an ultrasonic scanning test. 我們可透過超音波掃瞄來估計未出生嬰兒的頭圍大小。

★★★★☆

1491 sever	*v. dissever; split*　終止，斷絕，切斷
[`sɛvə]	The United States had severed diplomatic relations with Iran even before Iran had started a nuclear project. They have not been on good terms with each other for many years. 美國在伊朗開始發展核子計畫前即已終止雙方外交往來，多年來關係交惡。

★★★★★

1492 deference	*n. obeisance; submission; acquiescence; obedience; compliance*　服從，遵從
[`dɛfərəns]	The knight pledged himself to act in deference to his king's wishes. Therefore, when the king ordered him to lead the army to war, he obeyed. 騎士誓言服從國王要求，於是當國王下令領軍作戰時他也從命。

★★★★★

1493 ferry	*n. ship; barge*　渡輪，渡口
[`fɛrɪ]	They preferred to take a ferry when they went on vacation to the island, rather than flying there directly, since the ferry ride was much more scenic. 他們寧願搭渡輪赴小島度假也不要搭機前往，因為海上沿途風光更明媚。

❖ ferver = boil 沸騰

Chapter

① ② ③ ④ ⑤

★★★☆☆

1494 **effervescent**	*a. bubbling; sparkling; fizzy; foaming*	冒泡的，起泡的
[ˌɛfɚˈvɛsn̩t]	Champagne is an effervescent wine because it releases tiny bubbles of gas when we open the bottle. 香檳是氣泡酒，開瓶時會釋放小氣泡。	

★★★★☆

1495 **fervor**	*n. vehemence; passion; zeal; ardor; eagerness; enthusiasm*	熱忱，熱情
[ˈfɝvɚ]	Mr. and Mrs. Stewart have been married for fifty years, and despite all of the hard times they have been through, they still maintain a certain fervor in their relationship. 結褵五十年的史都華夫婦儘管有過艱難時期，現在仍維持某種程度的熱情關係。	

★★★★☆

1496 **fervent**	*a. ardent; eager; earnest; animated; passionate; intense*	熱烈的，熱情的
[ˈfɝvənt]	The actress was always greeted with fervent applause since her movies were so popular and exciting. 女演員一向受到熱烈喝采，因為她主演的電影不但大受歡迎又好看。	

★★★★☆

1497 **ferment**	*v. leaven; brew; stir up; simmer; seethe*	使發酵
[fɚˈmɛnt]	I had some apple juice that sat untouched in my fridge for three weeks, and when I went to serve it to some guests, I realized that it had fermented. 蘋果汁放在冰箱三周原封不動，等我倒給客人喝時才發現發酵了。	

❖ fid = trust 信任

★★★★★

1498 **self-confident**	*a. self-assured*	自信的
[ˌsɛlfˈkɑnfədənt]	Brian was self-confident to the point of being arrogant, and many people were sure of his demise. 布萊恩自信到傲慢自大的程度，許多人相信他驕者必敗。	

★★★★☆

| 1499 **confidential** | *a. secret; private; hush-hush* | 機密的 |

[ˌkɑnfə`dɛnʃəl]

Please take this folder to the manager, and please don't show it to anyone else because the contents are extremely confidential.

請將這份文件夾交給經理，裡頭文件十分機密，不要讓別人看見

★★★★★

| 1500 **fidelity** | *n. faithfulness; loyalty* | 忠實，忠貞，忠誠 |

[faɪ`dɛlətɪ]

It is said that in the States one out of the three marriages ends up in divorce. I think one of the biggest reasons for divorce is the lack of fidelity between husband and wife.

據說美國每三對夫妻就有一對離婚，我認為最大原因之一是因為彼此缺乏忠誠。

★★★★☆

| 1501 **confide** | *v. tell a secret in confidence; talk confidentially to* | 吐露，傾訴 |

[kən`faɪd]

I have several friends in whom I confide my secrets. That is why they know every detail of my secrets.

我有幾個可傾訴祕密的朋友，這正是為什麼他們知道所有祕密。

Tea Time... ☕

<Roman story> Caesarean section
From the ancient story that Caesar had been born in this manner.

〈來自羅馬故事〉凱撒切開術
本詞來自古代故事，傳說凱撒是以這種方式誕生的。
（註：相傳凱撒誕生時母親因難產而施行剖腹生產，後世即以此詞為「剖腹生產」的代稱。）

Caesarean section [sɪˌzɛrɪən `sɛkʃən] *n. a surgical operation for delivering a baby by cutting through the mother's abdominal and uterine walls* | 剖腹生產

Caesarian section is usually performed when a woman has difficulty giving birth in the usual way.

產婦無法自然生產時，通常施以剖腹產。

Review Test 06

1

Complete each word by filling in the blank with proper spelling so that it has the same meaning as suggested. Then please write the meaning of each word in Chinese.

1. 失讀症   = ___lexia
2. 營養失調   = ___trophy
3. 免除   = ex____ion
4. 贖罪   = re____tion
5. 種族的   = ____ic
6. 民族優越感的   = _____centric
7. 婉轉說法   = __phemism
8. 頌揚   = __logize
9. 大批離開   = ex____
10. 異國風情的   = ex____

11. fiction   = _____
12. infectious   = _____
13. superficial   = _____
14. defy   = _____
15. sufficient   = _____
16. circumference = _____
17. sever   = _____
18. effervescent = _____
19. ferment   = _____
20. fidelity   = _____

2

Choose a word that best completes the sentence.

21. **Actors and actresses often shed _____ tears.**
   (A) ethnic   (B) factitious   (C) extrinsic   (D) racial

22. **There have been many arguments about _____, or mercy death.**
   (A) dystrophy   (B) redemption   (C) eugenics   (D) euthanasia

3

The highlighted word is closest in meaning to which of the following?

23. **I wonder if this is a feasible plan, because of the exorbitant cost.**
   (A) infectious   (B) contagious   (C) practicable   (D) superficial

24. **The nation has decided to sever diplomatic relations with the neighboring country.**
   (A) stir up   (B) cut off   (C) go against   (D) wipe out

25. **In the aquarium were many exotic fish which were bought from a foreign country.**
   (A) foreign   (B) artificial   (C) effervescent   (D) officious

⁘ fin = end, boundary 最終，限制

MP3 62

★★★★★

1502 finis	**n.** *the end*	（用於書末、電影終了等）終，完
[`faɪnɪs]		

"Finis!" John cried as he wrote the final word of his dissertation that had taken him ten years to finish.

約翰在花十年撰寫的博士論文上寫下最後一字「終！」後就哭了。

★★★★★

1503 infinite	**a.** *boundless; endless; unlimited; never-ending*	無限的，無窮的
[`ɪnfənɪt]		

Some people wastefully go through gasoline as if they thought this world had an infinite supply of oil.

有些人彷彿以為全球石油能無限供應似的浪費汽油。

★★★★★

1504 finale	**n.** *conclusion; the last movement of an instrumental composition; the close of a drama*	最後樂章，最後一幕
[fɪ`nælɪ]		

The finale of his musical composition was the best part because everything in the piece led up to that dynamic ending.

他的最終樂章是精華所在，因為逐漸帶入高潮迭起的結尾。

★★★★★

1505 fine	**a.** *slender; thin; filamentous / fine-grained*	苗條的 / 精細的
[faɪn]		

The spinster that showed up with the matchmaker had such a fine body that he wanted to marry her immediately.

由媒人陪同出席的未婚女子身材苗條，讓他想立刻迎娶。

⁘ flect, flex = bend 彎曲

★★★★★

1506 reflect	**v.** *show; reveal; uncover; evidence / think about; ponder on*	反映 / 思考
[rɪ`flɛkt]		

Most of William Faulkner's novels, including *Light in August* and *The Sound and the Fury*, reflect his Mississippi childhood experiences.

包括《八月之光》和《聲音與憤怒》在內的威廉‧福克納多數作品，都反映出他在美國密西西比州的童年生活經驗。

★★★★★

1507 flexible	**a.** *adaptable; variable / pliable; pliant*	有彈性的 / 易彎曲的
[`flɛksəbl]		

My schedule is very flexible, and I am available most of the time. So call me or stop at my office anytime.

我的行程很有彈性，大部分時間都有空，請隨時打給我或到辦公室來。

★★★☆☆

1508 **flection**	*n.* the act of bending or the condition of being bent of a limb or joint	彎曲（部分），彎，屈曲
[`flɛkʃən]	In a show of unbelievable flection, the gymnast put her ankles behind her head and rocked back and forth on her stomach. 在一場驚人的柔軟操表演中，體操選手將腳踝彎曲到後腦杓，再以腹部著地前後搖晃。	

★★★★★

1509 **reflection**	*a.* a reflected image / meditation; consideration; cerebration; discredit	映像 / 反省 / 非議
[rɪ`flɛkʃən]	Sue grew as pale as marble, and stood as a statue before the mirror, staring at her own reflection. 蘇長得像大理石般蒼白，站在鏡前如雕像般凝視自己的身影。	

★★★☆☆

1510 **deflect**	*v.* bend or turn aside from a straight course or intended purpose; avert; divert	使偏斜，使偏離
[dɪ`flɛkt]	The player would have caught the winning touchdown, but the ball was deflected off his fingertips. 運動員本來能接到冠軍達陣球，但球卻從指尖偏離。	

✢ flor = flower 花

★★★★☆

1511 **floral**	*a.* of flowers	花的，如花的
[`flɔrəl]	Tim tried to send flowers to his wife while she was traveling overseas, but he didn't know the name of a floral shop in the town where she was staying. 提姆想在妻子海外旅行時送花給她，卻不知道她落腳地的花店店名。	

★★★★☆

1512 **florid**	*a.* ruddy / elaborately ornate / flowery	氣色紅潤的 / 文體華麗的 / 如花的
[`flɔrɪd]	The contemporary poet's florid style of poetry was extremely beautiful to read, but difficult to understand. 當代詩人華麗的詞藻讀起來極美，卻難以理解。	

★★★★★

1513 **floriculture**	*n.* the cultivation of flowers	花卉栽培業，花卉園藝學
[`florɪ,kʌltʃə]	Floriculture, or flower farming, has emerged as a promising business in our country. More and more people are becoming interested in the lucrative business. 又稱花卉園藝的花卉栽培業在我國是前景看好的行業，愈來愈多人對此有利可圖的生意感興趣。	

1514 florescent

a. adorned; elaborate 開花的，繁榮昌盛的

[flo`rɛsn̩t]

At first the advertisement was done in regular blues and greens, but the president felt that it would get more people's attention if the ad were done in florescent colors.

廣告本來是以標準藍、綠色構成，但總裁覺得改成彩色能吸引更多人注意。

⚜ flu, flux = flow 流動

★★★★★

1515 fluid

n. liquid; solution / a. flowing 液體／流動的，流暢的

[`fluɪd]

The ballerina was dancing with grace and fluid motion. Everybody in the audience was attracted by her beautiful and smooth movements.

芭蕾舞者以優雅流暢的動作跳著舞，在場所有人都被她曼妙的舞姿吸引。

★★★★☆

1516 flux

n. continuous change; fluctuation; instability; wavering; mutation 變遷，不斷變化

[flʌks]

The government was always in a state of flux as the revolutionaries and counter-revolutionaries vied for power.

革命與反革命者相互奪權，導致政權不斷更替。

★★★★★

1517 affluence

n. wealth; opulence 豐富，富裕

[`æfluəns]

My uncle has lived in affluence since his business became a success. In the past he was living in poverty.

舅舅過去生活貧困，現在因事業有成而生活富裕。

★★★★★

1518 fluent

a. having command of a foreign language 流利的，流暢的

[`fluənt]

It is very difficult for you to become really fluent in a foreign language unless you spend several years living in a country where that language is spoken.

除非住在當地幾年否則很難有相當流利的外語能力。

★★★★★

1519 influx

n. a flowing in ; a continual stream of people or things （人、物的）湧入

[`ɪn‚flʌks]

Due to the political instability of China, the United Stated is now experiencing a serious influx of refugees from China, and U.S. policy makers are now trying to figure out what should be done.

中國政權不穩導致大批難民湧入美國，決策者正設法尋求因應之道。

✤ for- = away, off, extremely 遠離，完全的

★★★☆☆

1520 **forswear**	*v. abjure; renounce on oath; forgo / swear falsely*	戒除 / 做偽證
[fɔr`swɛr]	She decided to forswear drinking after she had prayed to the porcelain God the night before. She finally realized that alcohol is a toxic substance to her. 她前晚向上帝瓷像禱告後決定戒酒，因為終於明白酒精是有毒物質。	

★★★★★

1521 **forbid**	*v. prohibit; ban; interdict*	禁止，不許
[fə`bɪd]	Jack's mother forbade him to go fishing in the river unless someone older than he went with him. 除非有年長者陪同，否則母親不許傑克去河邊釣魚。	

★★★★☆

1522 **forgo**	*v. abstain from; relinquish*	放棄，對～斷念
[fɔr`go]	In the afternoon grandmother was tired, but she decided to forgo her nap so that she could answer the phone in case her granddaughter should call. 祖母下午很累但決定不要小睡片刻，以便接聽孫女可能打來的電話。	

★★★★★

1523 **forsake**	*v. give up; renounce; yield; waive*	放棄，拋棄
[fə`sek]	For financial reasons, Frank was forced to forsake his plan to take a trip to Hawaii. He had to save some more money. 法蘭克因財務問題而被迫放棄夏威夷旅遊計畫，他必須多存點錢。	

✤ fort = force, strength 強力

★★★★★

1524 **afford**	*v. have the means; meet the expense of*	力足以～，～得起
[ə`fɔrd]	I can't afford the fancy car, and therefore I must save money for one more year. But I don't think I can wait until I save up that much money. 我買不起昂貴的車而必須再存一年的錢，但我覺得等不了那麼久。	

★★★★★

1525 **forte**	*n. strong point; specialty; merit*	強項，優點，長處
[fɔrt]	Mr. Robbins is a very successful businessman and I think his forte is communicating with people and building trust with them. 羅賓斯先生是非常成功的商人，我認為他擅長與人溝通並建立互信。	

1526 fort	**n.** *a fortified position*	堡壘，要塞
[fɔrt]		

Some of the most popular tourist sights in America are the remains of old forts throughout the country that were built by the people who settled the West.

部分美國最熱門的觀光景點是百年前西部殖民者建造的古要塞遺跡。

★★★★☆

1527 fortress	**n.** *a military stronghold; fort*	軍事要塞，堡壘
[`fɔrtrɪs]		

In the days when the West was wild, one of the best methods of protection was to build a fortress surrounded by very high walls.

西部蠻荒時期最好的防衛之道就是建造高牆堡壘。

★★★★☆

1528 fortification	**n.** *the act or an instance of fortifying*	防禦工事
[ˌfɔrtəfə`keʃən]		

During the Cold War, both the United States and the Soviet Union began preparing their fortifications by manufacturing nuclear warheads.

冷戰時期美蘇雙方建造核子彈頭作為防禦工事。

❖ fra, frac, frag, frang, fric = break 打碎

MP3 63

★★★★★

1529 frail	**a.** *fragile; delicate; feeble; infirm*	體弱多病的，不結實的
[frel]		

Their son was born with a somewhat frail constitution. At the age of 5, he contracted a lung disease that lingered on even after he began his schooling at the age of 9.

他們的兒子生來體弱多病，五歲得了肺病，直到九歲入學都未能痊癒。

★★★★☆

1530 fragmentary	**a.** *piecemeal; incomplete; bitty; scrappy; patchy; skimpy* 零碎的，殘破不全的
[`frægmənˌtɛrɪ]	

A balanced view is difficult to obtain from isolated or fragmentary statements about reality.

從孤立或殘破不全的事實中很難得出全面觀點。

★★★★★

1531 fragile	**a.** *breakable; brittle; rickety; frangible; frail; flimsy; infirm* 易碎的，脆弱的
[`frædʒəl]	

Because these wine glasses are fragile, you should carry them very gingerly. Otherwise you may break them.

酒杯易碎所以要小心搬運，否則可能打破。

★★★★☆
1532 infringement | *n. violation; breach; contravention; infraction* | 侵權，違反

[ɪnˋfrɪndʒmənt]

One of the most famous cases concerning the infringement of someone's rights is the Rodney King case.
最有名的侵權案例之一就是羅德尼·金一案。

★★★★☆
1533 fracture | *v. break; crack* | 骨折，斷裂，裂縫

[ˋfræktʃə]

Our art teacher tripped and fell down the stairs and fractured her arm and now she has to wear a cast for the next six weeks until it heals.
我們的美術老師絆倒而跌下樓梯導致手臂骨折，現在要打上石膏六周直到癒合。

★★★★☆
1534 infraction | *n. infringement* | 違法，違背

[ɪnˋfrækʃən]

Even though in his mind everything he did was completely justified, the fact still remains that he committed an infraction of the law.
雖然他自認一切行為完全合理，但事實上已違法。

★★★★★
1535 fragment | *n. a part broken off; chip; shard* | 碎片，片斷，斷簡殘篇

[ˋfrægmənt]

The mirror hanging on the wall off his room fell of itself and broke into fragments. James thought that it was a sign of bad luck.
掛在詹姆斯房內牆上的鏡子掉落成碎片，使他認為是惡兆。

✣ frig = cold 冷的

★★★★★
1536 refrigerator | *n. a cabinet in which food is kept cold* | 冰箱

[rɪˋfrɪdʒəˌretə]

Jason bought a new refrigerator for his wife, which she liked, because it was equipped with an automatic defroster.
傑森買了一台妻子喜歡的冰箱給她，因為配有自動除霜功能。

★★★★★
1537 freeze | *v. turn into ice / n. immobilization* | 結冰 /（薪資、物價等的）凍結

[friz]

Due to the difficult economic conditions in our country, many companies have decided to put a freeze on hiring because they can't afford to expand their payrolls right now.
國內經濟困境使許多公司決定凍結人事，因為現階段無力增加薪資成本。

★★★★★

1538 freezing | *a.* cold | 冰凍的，極冷的

[`frizɪŋ]

Brrr! I'm freezing! The temperature must be lower than 10°C below zero. And furthermore the wind is like a knife.

呃，好冷啊！氣溫一定低於攝氏零下十度，外加寒風刺骨。

★★★★☆

1539 frigidity | *n.* apathy; callousness | 冷淡

[frɪ`dʒɪdətɪ]

She was well-known in the world of big business for the frigidity of her manner and the ruthless way she dealt with her opponents.

她在大企業界中向以態度冷酷著稱，面對敵手毫不留情。

❖ fug = run away 逃

★★★★☆

1540 fugitive | *n.* escapee; deserter; runaway | 逃犯，逃亡者

[`fjudʒətɪv]

The movie *The Fugitive* is about a doctor who is escaping the police and tries to prove his innocence.

電影《絕命追殺令》是有關一名醫生逃過警方追捕，想證明自己的清白。

★★★☆☆

1541 fugacious | *a.* evanescent; hard to capture or keep | 早謝的，短暫易逝的

[fju`geʃəs]

Certain trees have fugacious leaves that leave the tree bare at the end of summer, while others have leaves that stay all through autumn and even into winter.

某些樹木枝葉早謝，夏末就光禿一片；其他樹木在整個秋天、甚至冬天仍然枝葉茂盛。

★★★★★

1542 refugee | *n.* a person taking refuge, especially in a foreign country from war or persecution or natural disaster | 難民，流亡者

[ˌrɛfju`dʒi]

As a political refugee from the Communist country, the scientist was welcomed and given asylum in the United States..

來自共產國家的政治流亡科學家受到美國歡迎並提供政治庇護。

★★☆☆☆

1543 centrifuge | *n.* a machine with a rapidly rotating device designed to separate liquids from solids | 離心機

[`sɛntrəˌfjudʒ]

Washing machines are centrifuge machines that use centrifugal force in the spin cycle to wring the water out of the clothes.

洗衣機是一種離心機，利用脫水循環的離心力絞乾衣服上的水。

✥ gen, genit = birth, class, kind 產生，種，族

★★★★★

| 1544 **genesis** | *n. origin* | 起源，創始，發生 |

[`dʒɛnəsɪs]

The birth of the first test tube baby was the genesis of a new form of procreation that left many women feeling uncertain about their future as mothers.

首名試管嬰兒的誕生標示著新式生產的開始，許多為人母者因此對未來感到茫然。

★★★★☆

| 1545 **heterogeneous** | *a. diverse in character; varied in content* | 異質的，由不同成分構成的 |

[ˌhɛtərəˈdʒinɪəs]

Unlike the United States in which heterogeneous nationalities make up the population, Korea's population is quite homogeneous.

韓國人口的同質性甚高，不同於由各類人種組成的美國。

★★★★☆

| 1546 **congenital** | *a. existing from birth; inborn; inherent* | 與生俱來的，天生的 |

[kənˈdʒɛnətl]

Judy is one of the most talented dancers I know, and her parents tell me that she has been a congenital music lover from birth.

茱蒂是我見過最有才華的舞者之一，她的父母告訴我她天生熱愛音樂。

★★★★★

| 1547 **indigenous** | *a. originating naturally in a region; endemic; aboriginal* 當地特有的，土產的 |

[ɪnˈdɪdʒənəs]

Certain animals indigenous to South America are dying in great numbers due to the vast amount of rain forests being indiscriminately cut down and cleared.

由於大片雨林遭到任意砍伐殆盡，導致某些南美特有動物大量瀕臨死亡。

★★★★★

| 1548 **ingenuous** | *a. innocent; artless; naive; unsophisticated; guileless* | 坦率的，無邪的 |

[ɪnˈdʒɛnjʊəs]

All his employees liked him because of his open, honest and ingenuous way of dealing with them and their problems.

所有員工都喜歡他開朗率直的待人處事與解決問題之道。

★★★★★

| 1549 **congenial** | *a. pleasant because akin to oneself in temperament; agreeable* | 意氣相投的，友善的 |

[kənˈdʒinjəl]

When I first met my roommate he was an angry and unhappy individual, but now he has made a complete change and has become a very likable, congenial person.

初次見到室友時他易怒又不快樂，但現在卻大大改變，為人親切又友善。

★★☆☆☆

1550 androgen   *n.* a male sex hormone   男性荷爾蒙

[`ændrədʒən]

The male body has plenty of androgen that makes a man look and act like a man. It seems like many of today's males are lacking in this hormone.

男性體內有大量男性荷爾蒙，因此無論外觀或舉止都像男性。今日許多男性似乎都缺乏這類荷爾蒙。

★★★★★

1551 gene   *n.* a unit of heredity composed of DNA or RNA   基因，遺傳因子

[dʒin]

It had been a mystery why a child should have traits of both parents before the mystery of genes was unraveled.

在解開基因之謎前，子女為何會有雙親特徵一直是個謎。

★★★★★

1552 engender   *v.* give rise to; bring about; create   使產生，引起

[ɪn`dʒɛndə]

John has been credited with being the one who created the idea, but in fact it was Mike who engendered the project.

一般認為點子是約翰提出的，但事實上邁克才是計畫催生者。

★★★☆☆

1553 genealogy   *n.* lineage / the study of lines of descent   系譜，家系 / 系譜學

[ˌdʒinɪ`ælədʒɪ]

A study of one's genealogy usually turns up some interesting gossip about one's ancestors. Through the study we can learn about who was who and who was famous for what.

研究系譜學常會意外發現祖先的有趣傳說，並可得知祖先身分和出名原因。

★★★★★

1554 generate   *v.* create; originate; produce; bring about   造成，引發，帶來

[`dʒɛnəˌret]

It took Sam almost one year to perfect his invention and make it marketable. He is selling it now and it is beginning to generate a satisfactory income.

山姆花了幾乎一年精進發明並開發市場，現在開始販售並帶來可觀獲利。

Tea Time... ☕

\<From the name of a French city\> **Denim** This word is shortened and changed from the French term for the cloth, serge de Nimes (serge of Nimes), after Nimes, the French city where it was made.	〈來自法國城市名〉丹寧 本字是從法國小鎮尼姆製造的「尼姆的斜紋布料」一名簡縮而成的。（註：serge de Nimes 是法文，意指「以尼姆當地斜紋織布機織成的厚棉斜紋布料」，適合用來製作耐磨耐洗的工作服，也是現今牛仔褲最主要的布料。據說當初將這種布料引進英國的商人覺得此詞不好發音，於是才將它縮稱為 denim。）

denim [`dɛnəm] *n.* a heavy cotton cloth used for work clothes | 丹寧布

My father complained when I wore a denim shirt to the church on Sunday. He insisted that I should be dressed up.

父親抱怨我周日穿丹寧布襯衫上教堂做禮拜，他認為應盛裝出席。

1 Complete each word by filling in the blank with proper spelling so that it has the same meaning as suggested. Then please write the meaning of each word in Chinese.

1. 無限的 = in___ite
2. 有彈性的 = ____ible
3. 映像 = re_____ion
4. 花卉栽培業 = ____iculture
5. 富裕 = af___ence
6. 流利的 = ___ent
7. 戒除 = ___swear
8. 放棄 = ___sake
9. 力足以 = af____
10. 防禦工事 = ____ification

11. fragmentary = _____
12. infringement = _____
13. fracture = _____
14. refrigerator = _____
15. frigidity = _____
16. fugitive = _____
17. genesis = _____
18. heterogeneous = _____
19. indigenous = _____
20. generate = _____

2 Choose a word that best completes the sentence.

21. Before you sign a contract you should read it carefully, including the _____ print.
   (A) fine   (B) floral   (C) frail   (D) ruddy

22. Please stand still. There are some _____ of the vase on the floor.
   (A) fugitives   (B) fragments   (C) forts   (D) fortresses

23. She could be a world-famous musician despite her _____ defects.
   (A) congenital   (B) heterogeneous   (C) fluid   (D) fragmentary

3 The highlighted word is closest in meaning to which of the following?

24. In the medieval age people believed that four different body fluids determined a person's disposition and health.
   (A) flux   (B) fracture   (C) liquids   (D) infraction

25. A mother went to a post office to send her son the Bible. The clerk asked her if there was anything fragile . The mother said, "Ten Commandments."
   (A) brittle   (B) congenial   (C) ingenuous   (D) indigenous

✦ **grab, grap, grasp, grip = hold** 握住

★★★★★

MP3 64

1555 grab   *v. seize; capture; grip; grasp*   抓住，攫取

[græb]

The best way to fight a woman is with your hat - grab it and run.
— Barrymore

跟女人打架最好的方式就是用你的帽子——抓住它然後快跑。
—— 巴瑞摩爾

★★★★★

1556 grasp   *v. clutch at; seize; grab; grip; snatch / comprehend;*   抓住 / 領悟 / 理解力
follow; make head or tail of; get the point of / comprehension

[græsp]

Susan took piano lessons for three years when she was young but she never did like it because she just couldn't seem to get the grasp of how to do it well.

蘇珊小時候學了三年鋼琴但不是真的喜歡，因為她不知道怎樣才能彈好鋼琴。

★★★☆☆

1557 grapple   *v. grip; hold; clasp; clutch / struggle with;*   扭打 / 設法處理
contend with; tackle

[`græpl]

I have a problem that I have been grappling with for a month. I think I finally figured out how to solve it.

有個問題我已經花了一個月設法處理，現在終於想到解決辦法。

★★★★★

1558 grasping   *a. avaricious; greedy; rapacious*   貪婪的

[`græspɪŋ]

The entire appetizer plate was taken by a grasping woman. She was an extremely voracious woman.

整盤開胃菜都被一個貪心女子拿光了，她真是個非常貪婪的女人。

★★★★★

1559 grip   *n. handgrip / grasp; clutch*   把手 / 緊握，抓牢

[grɪp]

A long cold spell has gripped our nation since the latter part of November. It looks like the cold weather will last for a long time.

自十一月底起寒冷天氣便籠罩我國，看來應該還會再持續一段時間。

❖ graf, graph, grav = write, draw 寫

★★★★☆

| 1560 **graffiti** | *n. pieces of writing or drawing scribbled, scratched, or sprayed on a surface* | 塗鴉 |

[græ`fitɪ]

Unlike other big cities around the world, one of the most impressive things about this city is the lack of graffiti on the subway walls.
不同於其他國際大都市，這座城市最讓人印象深刻之處是地鐵牆上沒有塗鴉。

★★★☆☆

| 1561 **graft** | *n. implantation / implant; transplant; splice; insert* | 接枝 / 外科移植 |

[græft]

Eva was in a terrible accident and suffered third degree burns on parts of her body, but thanks to some expert skin grafting by her doctors she was able to recover quite well.
伊娃出了嚴重意外，全身遭三度灼傷，幸虧醫生進行表皮移植才能迅速恢復健康。

★★★★☆

| 1562 **graphic** | *a. vivid; picturesque; lifelike; photographic* | 生動的，寫實的 |

[`græfɪk]

When we took drivers' education they showed us a film about the importance of not drinking and of wearing our seat belts, and some of the scenes in that film were quite graphic.
參加駕訓時播放的宣導影片告訴我們不酒駕和繫好安全帶的重要性，其中有些場景十分寫實。

★★★☆☆

| 1563 **graphite** | *n. black lead* | 石墨 |

[`græfaɪt]

Lead pencils actually do not contain lead. The material that makes the mark is graphite. Otherwise too many elementary school kids would have lead poisoning.
鉛筆其實不含鉛而是石墨，否則許多小學學童會鉛中毒。

★★★☆☆

| 1564 **monograph** | *n. treatise; paper* | 專題論文，專題著作 |

[`mɑnəˌgræf]

The archeologist wrote a world-famous monograph on the treasures of Egypt. He gained his reputation thanks to his exhaustive research and original thesis.
考古學家撰寫了一篇舉世聞名的埃及寶藏專題論文，詳盡研究和獨到觀點使他聲名大噪。

| 1565 **bibliography** | *n. a list of the books referred to in a scholarly work* | 參考書目 |

[ˌbɪblɪˈɑgrəfɪ]

Bibliographies are very useful in that by referring to them, the reader can easily find the original sources.

參考書目非常實用，讀者只要參考它便可輕易找到原始出處。

★★★★☆

| 1566 **engrave** | *v. inscribe; carve; incise* | 雕刻，刻上 |

[ɪnˈgrev]

The jeweler was able to engrave all the names of the members of the International Darts Team on their Championship Cup.

工匠將國際飛鏢代表隊的所有隊員姓名刻在冠軍盃上。

★★★☆☆

| 1567 **calligraphy** | *n. handwriting / the art of handwriting* | 筆跡 / 書法 |

[kəˈlɪgrəfɪ]

Korean calligraphy has been affected by the respective contemporary Chinese writing styles.

韓國書法受當代中國個別書法風格所影響。

✛ grat = free of charge, delight, gratitude　免費的，令人高興或感激的

★★★★☆

| 1568 **ingratitude** | *n. unthankfulness; ungratefulness* | 忘恩負義，不知感恩圖報 |

[ɪnˈgrætəˌtjud]

A person is very apt to complain of the ingratitude of those who have risen far above him. This kind of complaint usually stems from jealousy.

愛抱怨升官發達者不知感恩圖報的人其實是出於妒忌。

★★★★★

| 1569 **gratitude** | *n. thankfulness; appreciation; gratefulness; acknowledgement* | 謝意，感恩 |

[ˈgrætəˌtjud]

I have done a lot of things for Bernard and I don't expect anything in return, but it would be nice if he would show a little gratitude instead of being so indifferent about everything.

我為伯納德做那麼多事並不求任何回報，如果他能表達一絲謝意而不是凡事冷淡就好了。

★★★★★

| 1570 **gratify** | *v. delight; cheer; please* | 使高興，使滿意，使喜悅 |

[ˈgrætəˌfaɪ]

It took Mary five years to get through school because she had a lot of family problems, so it was especially gratifying when she finally got her degree.

瑪麗因許多家庭問題花了五年才畢業，等終於拿到學位時感到特別高興。

★★★★★

1571 congratulate

v. express pleasure at the happiness or good fortune　　　　向～道賀

[kənˈɡrætʃəˌlet]

Even though we were political opponents during the election, the first thing he did when the election results were out was congratulate me on my successful victory.

即使互為選戰對手，選舉結果一揭曉他便在第一時間祝賀我獲勝。

★★★☆☆

1572 gratis

ad. without charge; free　　　　免費地

[ˈɡretɪs]

Our brochure has been designed to show the structure and function of our organization. It is sent gratis upon application.

小冊子的設計在於說明本組織架構和功能，如需索取即免費寄達。

★★★★☆

1573 gratuitous

a. uncalled-for; unwarranted; unfounded; ungrounded　　無端的，不必要的

[ɡrəˈtjuətəs]

People are tired of the gratuitous violence so often seen in Hollywood movies. They worry about the malignant effect exerted upon young people.

好萊塢電影裡不必要的暴力鏡頭令人厭煩，大家擔心會對年輕人造成不良影響。

★★☆☆☆

1574 ingratiate

v. flatter; adulate; curry favor with; shine up to　　逢迎，巴結，奉承

[ɪnˈgreʃɪˌet]

Since Jack was desperate for a promotion, he worked hard and did many favors in a vain attempt to ingratiate himself to his boss.

傑克很想升官，於是努力工作並奉承上司，但徒勞無功。

★★★★★

1575 grateful

a. thankful; showing gratitude　　　　感激的，感謝的

[ˈɡretfəl]

My friend John always helps me whenever I need his help and I am grateful for his friendship.

友人約翰總在我需要幫忙時伸出援手，他的友誼令我感激。

✣ grav = heavy　重的

★★★★★

1576 grave

a. serious; critical; sober　　　　嚴重的，重大的

[grev]

The air pollution problem is becoming a matter of grave concern. Some day we might have to buy fresh air-contained bags.

空氣污染已成為重大問題，或許有朝一日人類得購買新鮮空氣袋。

★★★★★

| 1577 **grief** | *n. deep sorrow; intense mourning; sadness* | 痛心，憂傷 |

[grif]

Despite the great expectations Mrs. Reed had of her son, he gives her a lot of grief because he is now a drug addict and can't get a job.

瑞德太太對兒子期望很高，但他犯有毒癮又失業，讓她很傷心。

★★★★★

| 1578 **gravity** | *n. gravitation; weight* | 重力，地心引力 |

[`grævətɪ]

Gravity is a very important thing in our lives that we all take for granted. Just imagine how things would be if we didn't have it.

地心引力在日常生活中極重要卻常被視為理所當然，只要想想若少了它事物會變成什麼樣子。

★★★★★

| 1579 **gravitational** | *a. of or relating to gravitation* | 引力的，重力的 |

[`grævə`teʃənḷ]

Due to the powerful gravitational pull of the earth, it takes hundreds of thousands of pounds of thrust to get the space shuttle into orbit.

由於地心引力很強，所以需要數千萬磅驅動力才能將太空梭送上運行軌道。

★★★★☆

| 1580 **grieve** | *v. moan; lament* | 使悲傷，哀悼 |

[griv]

Only after the funeral Judy was able to grieve for her grandfather since beforehand she had been too busy making the funeral arrangements.

茱蒂一直忙於喪葬事宜，直到葬禮結束才總算能哀悼祖父。

❖ gred, gress = go 行走

★★★☆☆

| 1581 **transgression** | *n. offense; violation; misdeed; crime; wrongdoing; infraction* | 違反，罪過 |

[træns`grɛʃən]

We were surprised at the transgressions that were committed against innocent people during the riots in Los Angeles.

我們對洛城暴動傷及無辜百姓的罪行感到震驚。

★★★☆☆

| 1582 **regress** | *v. return to a former state* | 退步，倒退 |

[rɪ`grɛs]

The psychiatrists had been confident about the patient's recovery, but soon after he was released he began to regress.

精神科醫師有信心病患能痊癒，但他一出院卻再度發病。

★★☆☆☆

1583 nonaggression

[ˌnɑnəˈɡrɛʃən]

n. restraint from aggression 不侵略

The two factions agreed to a nonaggression pact that stopped the fighting for a while, leaving the city in peace.

雙方同意簽署互不侵犯條約暫時停戰，好讓城市恢復平靜。

★★★★★

1584 progress

[ˈprɑɡrɛs]

n. advancement; improvement; betterment; growth; development 進展，發展

No progress has been made by the company since our last meeting. The company is still dawdling on the new project.

公司新專案自上次會後便毫無進展，還在原地踏步。

★★★★★

1585 ingredient

[ɪnˈɡridɪənt]

n. constituent; element; factor; component 成分，原料

The culinary expert let me know the recipe of the dish I enjoyed. She listed the ingredients one by one.

烹飪大師提供我愛吃的料理食譜，並將原料一一列出。

✣ greg = gather 聚集

★★★★★

1586 aggregate

[ˈæɡrɪˌɡet]

v. amount to / a. collected in to one mass / n. collection 合計 / 總計的 / 集合

The charity organization held an event to raise the necessary funds. The money collected aggregated to ten thousand dollars.

慈善機構舉辦募款活動，總計募得一萬美元。

★★★☆☆

1587 egregious

[ɪˈɡridʒəs]

a. outstandingly bad; terrible 極差的

Raymond's acting was so egregious that the audience laughed at him and he felt humiliated. Afterwards he decided to quit his acting.

雷蒙表演得很差被觀眾嘲笑，使他無地自容，後來便決定停止演出。

★★★★★

1588 congregation

[ˌkɑŋɡrɪˈɡeʃən]

n. assembly; crowd 聚集，人群

I was scheduled to give a speech, and I wasn't expecting many people to be in the congregation, but when I arrived there were hundreds in attendance.

我預定發表演說，原以為不會有太多人參加，但抵達現場才發現有數百名觀眾。

★★★★★

1589 segregation

n. segmentation; seclusion; partition 隔離，分離

[ˌsɛgrɪ`gɛʃən]

A formal end to segregation was announced in the 1960's in America, yet the reality of separating blacks and whites continues to this day, albeit in a much more subtle way.

美國在六十年代正式宣布廢止種族隔離政策，但黑白分裂的事實卻以更隱晦的方式延續至今。

★★★☆☆

1590 gregarious

a. fond of company; living in flocks 群居的，喜群居的

[grɪ`gɛrɪəs]

The gregarious nature of sheep makes it easy for a sheep dog to keep them grouped in a herd and control them.

羊的群居天性使牧羊犬可從容將羊集合成群，方便放牧。

✛ habit = live, house 居住，房屋

★★★★★

1591 inhabit

v. reside in; live in; occupy; populate 居住，棲息於～

[ɪn`hæbɪt]

Wolves used to inhabit the western part of the mountain range, but the farmers had so many problems keeping their livestock from getting eaten that they trapped and killed all of the wolves.

狼群原本棲息在西邊山脈，但因農夫無力阻止家畜遭噬，於是誘殺所有狼隻。

★★★★☆

1592 habitation

n. home; habitat 住處，住所，棲息地

[ˌhæbə`teʃən]

The hunter thought he could successfully hunt animals without first knowing their habitation. However, he soon realized that animals are very nimble and difficult to hunt.

獵人以為不熟悉動物棲息地也能滿載而歸，但他馬上明白牠們極敏捷且難以獵捕。

★★★★★

1593 habitat

n. habitation; dwelling; abode; natural home 棲息地，產地

[`hæbəˌtæt]

Even though hunters kill animals, anyone who is considered a real hunter is also a conservationist and is very actively involved in trying to preserve the habitat of the animals they hunt.

獵人雖獵殺動物，但真正的獵人同時也是自然生態保育者，會非常積極保護動物棲息地。

★★★★★

| 1594 **inhabitant** | **n.** *resident; occupant* | 居民，居住者 |

[ɪn`hæbətənt]

The rock cliffs in the southern end of colorado are full of rock dwellings that were created by the indians many years ago, and now anthropologists are trying to learn more about the inhabitants who built them.

科羅拉多州南端岩壁上有許多早年印第安人建造的石屋，人類學家正設法深入了解其居民。

❖ here, hes = stick to 黏；固守

★★★★★

| 1595 **adherent** | **n.** *supporter; follower* | 支持者，追隨者，擁護者 |

[əd`hɪrənt]

The leader of the mob had several adherents who supported him. They pledged themselves to follow him to the last moment to fulfill their purpose.

暴民首腦有許多擁護者，誓言追隨他直到達成最後目標。

★★★★★

| 1596 **hesitate** | **v.** *stammer; stutter; falter* | 遲疑，猶豫，躊躇 |

[`hɛzə,tet]

If you need any further information concerning the applicant, please do not hesitate to write to us.

若您需要任何有關申請者的進一步資料，請不要客氣來信詢問。

★★★★★

| 1597 **coherent** | **a.** *consistent; logical; logically-connected* | 連貫的，有條理的，一致的 |

[ko`hɪrənt]

As soon as the police arrived on the scene, they began questioning the witness, but nothing the man said was coherent because he was in shock.

警方一到現場便開始詢問目擊證人，但他因驚慌而說話顛三倒四。

★★★★★

| 1598 **adhere** | **v.** *stick to* | 遵守，緊黏，信奉 |

[əd`hɪr]

The workers at the company were forced to adhere to the new director's rules even though they disagreed with them.

公司員工雖不同意但被迫遵守新總監下達的規定。

✦ hetero- = different 不同 / homo- = the same 相同

★★★★☆

1599 **heterogeneous**	*a. diverse; varied*	異質的，由不同成分構成的

[ˌhɛtərə`dʒɪnɪəs]

The United States is made up of people from many heterogeneous ethnic groups. We can have many opportunities to meet people of different races.

美國由各類人種組成，所以有許多機會認識不同種族的人。

★★★☆☆

1600 **homogenize**	*v. make homogeneous*	使單一化，使類同

[hə`mɑdʒə͵naɪz]

The landlord decided to homogenize his new apartment complex, making every room identical and uniform.

房東決定將新的複合式公寓單一化，也就是讓每個房間都一模一樣。

★★★☆☆

1601 **heterodox**	*a. not orthodox; heretical*	非正統的，異端的

[`hɛtərə͵dɑks]

Doctor Smith's research has been widely criticized by many of the other doctors in his field because his heterodox point of view is not in line with other professionals'.

史密斯醫師的研究受到同領域許多醫生諸多批評，因其非正統觀點和其他專家格格不入。

Tea Time... ☕

<Greek myth> Nemesis **The goddess of retributive justice, or vengeance.**	〈來自希臘神話〉納米希斯 希臘神話中專司因果報應和復仇的女神。（註：本字源自希臘文νέμειν，意為「to give what is due（給予其應得的）」，引申為「報應，天譴」或「復仇者，報復者」。）

nemesis [`nɛməsɪs] *n. retributive justice; a downfall caused by this / an agent of such a downfall* | 報應 / 復仇者，報復者

He considered his ex-wife to be his personal nemesis since no matter where he went, or what he did, she was always there first and made his life miserable.

他認為前妻是復仇者，無論走到哪裡，她總是第一個出現破壞他的生活。

Complete each word by filling in the blank with proper spelling so that it has the same meaning as suggested. Then please write the meaning of each word in Chinese.

1. 設法處理 = grap___
2. 寫實的 = grap___
3. 專題論文 = mono____h
4. 參考書目 = biblio____hy
5. 書法 = calli____hy
6. 忘恩負義 = in____itude
7. 向~道賀 = con____ulate
8. 逢迎 = in____iate
9. 重力 = ____ity
10. 哀悼 = ____ve

11. transgression = _____
12. progress = _____
13. aggregate = _____
14. congregation = _____
15. gregarious = _____
16. habitation = _____
17. inhabitant = _____
18. adherent = _____
19. hesitate = _____
20. heterogeneous = _____

Choose a word that best completes the sentence.

21. There was a lot of _____ on the wall of the school.
(A) ingredients   (B) grafts   (C) constituents   (D) graffiti

22. Wild geese are _____ birds. They generally live in a large flock.
(A) gregarious   (B) gravitational   (C) gratis   (D) grateful

The highlighted word is closest in meaning to which of the following?

23. Most children do not want gratuitous interference from their parents.
(A) thankful   (B) graphic   (C) unfounded   (D) vivid

24. If there were no gravity , students wouldn't have to spend much money on bus fares.
(A) grief   (B) gravitation   (C) transgression   (D) progress

25. Many animals are in danger of extinction because natural habitats are being destroyed.
(A) abodes   (B) congregations   (C) monographs   (D) adherents

Practice Test 02

1

The highlighted word is closest in meaning to which of the following?

1. Even a cursory glance reveals that his report leaves much to be desired.
   (A) detrimental
   (B) fragile
   (C) frail
   (D) hurried

2. She could not stand her husband's domineering attitude any more.
   (A) fervent
   (B) artificial
   (C) overbearing
   (D) sufficient

3. There are many scenes of gratuitous violence on TV. Children's overexposure to violence will surely have a bad influence on them.
   (A) unwarranted
   (B) grateful
   (C) egregious
   (D) fragmentary

4. The art student could not grasp what the economics professor explained. When the professor asked what would happen at the point where a red demand curve and a blue supply curve meet, the student answered, "It would become purple."
   (A) generate
   (B) hibernate
   (C) comprehend
   (D) ingratiate

5. When Jimmy went hiking alone, he was in a lot of hot water. He fractured his leg on top of the mountain.
   (A) defied
   (B) afforded
   (C) broke
   (D) defeated

2

Please answer the following questions.

Koalas

Koalas, originally indigenous to Australia, feed strictly on the leaves of eucalyptus trees. Full-sized adults eat up to a pound a day. A special appendix helps the koala digest the tough leaves, which are usually detrimental to other creatures. Young koalas are weaned at seven months when they begin to eat leaves on their own. Koalas never leave the trees, and as such are well adapted to their arboreal habitat . Like humans, they too have a sort of opposable finger, the index finger, which acts to oppose the other fingers. Therefore they are

able to grab things. In the safety of the trees, koalas spend three quarters of the day sleeping.

A female koala, a marsupial, will keep its young, no bigger than a grapefruit, in its pouch. When the cub outgrows the pouch, it crawls outside and clings to its mother's back. A female koala carries its baby until the baby is about a year old. When the baby is two years old, it will become fully independent, allowing the mother to conceive once more. A baby koala is oftentimes found sitting on a branch with its arms raised above its head just like a human child being punished by its mother. Maybe the baby koala is being punished by its mother because it is a sleepyhead. Anyway, its dominant activity is sleep.

6. The word indigenous is closest in meaning to which of the following?

(A) egregious   (B) aboriginal

(C) heterogeneous   (D) graphic

7. The word detrimental is closest in meaning to which of the following?

(A) harmful   (B) exclusive

(C) cursory   (D) cumulative

8. The word habitat is closest in meaning to which of the following?

(A) congregation   (B) abode

(C) genealogy   (D) fragment

9. The word grab is closest in meaning to which of the following?

(A) afford   (B) forgo

(C) grasp   (D) grieve

10. The word dominant is closest in meaning to which of the following?

(A) indomitable   (B) primary

(C) credulous   (D) ethnic

✣ hum = soil, earth 土壤，地面

★★★★☆

MP3 66

1602 posthumous

['pɑstʃuməs]

a. occurring after death / published after the author's death　死後的 / 死後出版的

The author's book was not published by the time he died. It was published two years after his death, so it was a posthumous book.

作者著作在他死時尚未問世，而是死後兩年才推出，所以是部遺作。

★★★★★

1603 humble

['hʌmbl]

a. modest; unassuming / inferior; ignoble　謙虛的 / 出身卑微的

Whenever learning a foreign language, it is important to learn the culturally correct behavior of the country whose language you are learning, because what is considered humble behavior in one country may be considered very rude in another.

學習外語一定要了解符合該國文化的適當行為，一國視為謙虛的舉動在他國也許是失禮表現。

★★★☆☆

1604 humus

['hjuməs]

n. soil; the organic constituent of soil　腐植質，腐植土

This is a good place to collect a good sample of humus because the forest is so dense that there is always a lot of decay to be found in the top soil.

這是收集腐植土標本的好地點，因為森林樹木林立，表土中常含有大量腐化物質。

★★★★☆

1605 humiliate

[hju'mɪlɪˌet]

v. disgrace; shame; abas　使蒙羞，使丟臉

The politician was sitting in a nice restaurant having an enjoyable meal when a woman suddenly came up to him, threw her wine in his face, and stormed out of the restaurant. The politician was obviously humiliated by the incident.

政治人物在高級餐廳享用佳餚時，一女子突然走上前把酒灑在他臉上隨即揚長而去，讓他感到非常丟臉。

✣ hydro = water 水

★★★★☆

1606 hydroplane

['haɪdrəˌplen]

v. skim over the surface of water　水上滑行

It was raining and the roads were wet when I was driving home. All of a sudden another car pulled out in front of me so I slammed on the brakes. My car began hydroplaning and slid sideways into a telephone pole.

我開車回家時天雨路滑，一輛車突然衝到面前，害我只好緊急煞車，接著向一旁打滑撞上電線桿。

★★★★☆

1607 dehydrate

[di'haɪdret]

v. remove water from; make the body deficient in water　使脫水

I have run in several marathons, and the first thing I learned when beginning my training was to drink lots of water so as not to get dehydrated.

我跑過許多場馬拉松賽，開訓時學到的第一件事就是飲用大量水份以免脫水。

★★★★★

1608 hydrogen

[`haɪdrədʒən]

n. a colorless gaseous element, without taste or odor 氫

Water is formed when two hydrogen atoms are combined with one oxygen atom.
水是由兩個氫原子和一個氧原子組成的。

★★☆☆☆

1609 hydrophobia

[ˌhaɪdrəˈfobɪə]

n. a morbid aversion to water 恐水症 / 狂犬病

Paul's near death experience while swimming when he was ten years old is thought to be the main cause for his hydrophobia that still plagues him today.
保羅十歲時游泳的瀕死經驗是他迄今仍受恐水症所苦的主因。

When the wild dog bit him, Mr. Baker had to go to the doctor to get medicine to prevent hydrophobia, commonly called 'rabies.'
貝克先生被野狗咬傷後前往醫院注射疫苗，以免感染俗稱「狂犬病」的恐水症。

★★★★☆

1610 hydrant

[`haɪdrənt]

n. a pipe with a nozzle to which a hose can be attached for drawing water from the main; fire plug 消防栓

The house I grew up in had a fire hydrant on the corner which was nice in case there was a fire.
我從小住到大的房子街角有個消防栓，以防發生火災。

❖ hyper- = over, beyond 超過，越過

★★★☆☆

1611 hypersensitive

[ˌhaɪpəˈsɛnsətɪv]

a. excessively sensitive 過度敏感的

I do not think that the short story writer can be a good writer unless he stops being hypersensitive to criticism.
我不認為短篇小說家能成為好作家，除非不對書評過度敏感。

★★★★★

1612 hypertension

[ˌhaɪpəˈtɛnʃən]

n. abnormally high blood pressure 高血壓，過度情緒緊張

Although symptoms for hypertension are sometimes obvious, many times people have no symptoms at all and are surprised to learn that they actually have high blood pressure.
高血壓症狀有時雖明顯，但也常有毫無症狀的人赫然發現原來自己有高血壓。

★★★★☆

1613 hyperbole

[haɪˈpɝbəˌlɪ]

n. exaggeration 誇張用語

When the traveler said that he was "so hungry he could eat a horse," the waiter, who didn't understand the hyperbole, politely told him that they didn't serve horse meat in their restaurant.
旅客表示「餓得能吃下一匹馬」，聽不懂誇張用語的服務生客氣表示，店裡不供應馬肉料理。

★★★☆☆

1614 **hyperacidity**	*n. excessive acidity, as of the gastric juice*	胃酸過多症
[ˌhaɪpərəˈsɪdətɪ]	As a teenager, I had a bad acne problem and tried everything to get rid of it. It wasn't until I learned that I had a condition of hyperacidity in my stomach that I was able to take measures to reduce the acid in my body and get rid of my zits. 我在青春期有粉刺問題，試過各種方式都無效，直到發現有胃酸過多症，治好後粉刺也消了。	

⁘ hypo- = under, low 在～之下，低的

★★★★★

1615 **hypocrite**	*n. pretender; double-dealer*	偽善者，偽君子
[ˈhɪˌpəkrɪt]	"Mom, Jack must be a hypocrite, because he goes to school with a smile on his face every morning." 「媽，傑克一定是偽君子，他每天早上都笑著上學。」	

★★★★★

1616 **hypocrisy**	*n. deceit; pretence; double-dealing; duplicity*	虛偽，矯情
[hɪˈpɑkrəsɪ]	I tried several times to tell Sam that his hypocrisy was going to be the end of him. In the end, he found that people couldn't trust him and he forfeited his reputation. 我多次想告訴山姆虛偽會害了他，最後他發現大家不再相信他，而他也失去信譽。	

★★★★☆

1617 **hypochondria**	*n. morbid depression*	憂鬱症
[ˌhaɪpəˈkɑndrɪə]	Every time I talked to my aunt, she told me that she had a different type of illness. At last I found that the only sickness she really had was a severe case of hypochondria. 每次跟姑姑講話她總說得了另一種病，最後我發現她只得了一種嚴重疾病，那就是憂鬱症。	

⁘ it = go 走動

★★★★☆

1618 **obituary**	*n. death notice; necrology*	訃聞
[əˈbɪtʃuˌɛrɪ]	The old man happened to read the 'Obituary' column in the newspaper to find that his friend Mr. White had passed away. 老人碰巧讀到報載訃聞才知道友人懷特先生去世了。	

★★★★★

1619 **transient**	*a. transitory; temporary; passing*	短暫的，瞬間的，易變的

[`trænʃənt]

Working at the personnel department for over twenty years, Mr. Baker really needed at least a transient novelty, so he asked to be transferred.

貝克先生在人事部工作超過二十年，很想要有些新鮮改變，於是要求輪調。

★★★★☆

1620 **transition**	*n. change; alteration; change-over*	轉變，轉換

[træn`zɪʃən]

The transition from farm life to city life is not easy. A person who has moved to a city often has difficulty adapting to city life.

從農家生活轉變成都市生活並不容易，搬到都市居住的人常難以適應都市生活。

⁂ idio- = peculiar, personal 奇特的，個人的

★★★☆☆

1621 **idiosyncrasy**	*n. eccentricity; a mode of behavior, peculiar to a person*	特有氣質，癖性

[ˌɪdɪə`sɪnkrəsɪ]

That man is a little strange and has a lot of idiosyncrasies that really bother me, like biting his nails and picking his nose.

那個人有點怪，還有許多困擾我的怪癖，例如咬指甲和挖鼻孔等。

★★★★★

1622 **idiom**	*n. a group of words established by usage /* *a characteristic mode of expression in music, art, etc.*	慣用語 / 表現風格

[`ɪdɪəm]

Although idioms are an important part of learning a foreign language, there are far more important things that should be mastered before spending too much time studying them.

慣用語固然是學習外語的重要一環，但花大量時間學習前還有更重要的有待掌握。

★★★★☆

1623 **idiot**	*n. a stupid person; an utter fool*	傻瓜，笨蛋

[`ɪdɪət]

Many people thought Pip was an idiot because he often did silly things without first thinking about the consequences.

許多人認為皮普是笨蛋，因為他經常沒有先把後果考慮清楚就去做蠢事。

★★★★★

1624 **idiomatic**	*a. relating to or conforming to an idiom*	慣用語法的

[ˌɪdɪə`mætɪk]

She is a very good English speaker and she knows a lot of idiomatic expressions which help her find the right words for the right moment.

她能說一口道地英文，還知道許多能用在適當場合的慣用語法。

✦ igni = fire 火

★★★☆☆

1625 igneous   *a. produced by volcanic or magmatic action*   火的，火成的

[`ɪgnɪəs]

A famous tourist site in the state of Idaho is the igneous volcanic rock formations that were formed hundreds of thousands of years ago when volcanos in that area were active.
愛達華州有個著名觀光景點是由數十萬年前該區活火山形成的火成岩岩層。

★★★★★

1626 ignition   *n. a mechanism for starting the combustion*   點火裝置

[ɪg`nɪʃən]

My friend was complaining to me because I had broken his key off in the ignition, and it cost him fifty dollars to replace the ignition in his car.
友人抱怨我將他的車鑰匙卡斷在點火裝置內，害他花了五十美元換新的。

★★★★★

1627 ignite   *v. cause to burn; kindle*   使著火

[ɪg`naɪt]

One day while hiking in the mountains, I fell into a lake and got everything in my pack wet, but the worse thing about it was that I couldn't ignite a fire to dry everything out with my wet matches.
某天我在山裡健行失足掉進湖裡，把整個背包都弄濕了，更糟的是濕火柴點不著，無法弄乾衣物。

★★★★★

1628 indignation   *n. annoyance; exasperation; resentment; fury; rage*   憤怒，憤慨

[ˌɪndɪg`neʃən]

Douglas felt very strongly that he had been dealt with in a very unjust way and the indignation in his voice was very obvious to everyone in the room.
道格拉斯強烈覺得自己受到不公平待遇，在場所有人都聽得出他聲音中的憤慨。

✦ itiner- = journey, walk 旅行，走

★★★☆☆

1629 itinerant   *a. traveling from place to place*   巡迴的，旅行的

[aɪ`tɪnərənt]

As an itinerant salesman, Mr. Frazer had to go from neighborhood to neighborhood in order to sell his products and he was always very tired at the end of the day.
外務員佛雷澤先生必須挨家挨戶推銷產品，一整天下來總是很累。

★★★★★

1630 itinerary   *n. a record of travel; a detailed route*   旅行計畫，行程表

[aɪ`tɪnəˌrɛrɪ]

They received their itinerary from the travel agent, and they knew that their holiday in Hawaii had been very well organized and that they would have a great time.
他們收到旅行社代辦給的行程表，並知夏威夷之旅已妥善規劃，屆時將盡興而歸。

★★★☆☆

¹⁶³¹ **itinerating**	*a. traveling from place to place*	巡迴的，巡行的
[ɪˈtɪnəˌretɪŋ]	The King's itinerating judge left the palace and traveled from village to village trying to solve the often misunderstood legal problems of the peasants. 國王的巡迴法官離開皇宮巡行於大小村落，解決常遭農民誤解的法律問題。	

⊹ -itis = inflammation 發炎

★★★★★

¹⁶³² **arthritis**	*n. inflammation of a joint*	關節炎
[arˈθraɪtɪs]	Antibiotics are often used in the treatment of pneumonia, tonsillitis and arthritis. Once they were thought to be a cure-all. 常用來治療肺炎、扁桃腺炎和關節炎的抗生素一度被視為萬靈丹。	

★★★★☆

¹⁶³³ **dermatitis**	*n. inflammation of the skin*	皮膚炎
[ˌdɝməˈtaɪtɪs]	The sore on Mr. Cooper's leg started out very small and continued to grow larger. He went to the doctor and learned that it was dermatitis. 古柏先生的腿瘡起先很小接著愈長愈大，他去看醫生後才知道是皮膚炎。	

★★★★☆

¹⁶³⁴ **gastritis**	*n. inflammation of the lining of the stomach*	胃炎
[gæsˈtraɪtɪs]	Oliver's aunt had many problems with her stomach and the doctors tried for a long time to determine exactly what caused the problems. They were finally able to determine that the source of the problems was gastritis. 奧利佛的姑姑胃不好，醫生診斷多時要確認病因，最後總算查出是胃炎。	

★★★★☆

¹⁶³⁵ **hepatitis**	*n. inflammation of the liver*	肝炎
[ˌhepəˈtaɪtɪs]	If any member of the family gets hepatitis B, it is wise to check with a physician about getting vaccinated. 家中如果有人得了 B 型肝炎，最好請教醫師有關疫苗接種問題。	

⊹ ject, jet = shoot, throw 射，投

★★★★★

¹⁶³⁶ **injection**	*n. shot; inoculation; vaccination*	注射，打針
[ɪnˈdʒɛkʃən]	Even if Nancy is terribly ill in bed, she avoids consulting a doctor, because she abhors injections. 南西即使重病在床也不願意看醫生，因為她討厭打針。	

★★★★☆

1637 **dejected**	*a. downcast; downhearted; depressed; dispirited; discouraged; despondent; gloomy*	沮喪的，情緒低落的
[dɪ`dʒɛktɪd]	When my grandmother failed the driving-test again, she felt really dejected. She had thought she would make it this time. 祖母考駕照再度失敗後情緒低落，她還以為這次能過關。	

★★★★★

1638 **projector**	*n. an apparatus for projecting rays of light*	投影機，幻燈機
[prə`dʒɛktɚ]	The pictures which the explorers took during the expedition were projected onto the screen by a slide projector. 探險者將遠征考察中拍攝的照片以幻燈機投影在螢幕上。	

✥ journ = day 天，白天

★★★★☆

1639 **sojourn**	*n. a temporary stay; stopover*	逗留，短暫停留
[`sodʒɚn]	After a 3-day sojourn in Seoul, the American president is going to visit Tokyo this week. While he is staying in Seoul, he will have a brief talk with his Korean counterpart. 美國總統在首爾短暫停留三天後，本周將訪問東京。首爾停留期間將與韓國總統展開簡短會談。	

★★★★☆

1640 **adjourn**	*v. put off; postpone; delay / break off a meeting*	使延期／休會，延會
[ə`dʒɚn]	We decided to adjourn the meeting because it was so late. We were supposed to have another meeting the next week. 由於時間太晚於是我們決定休會，等到下周再開會。	

★★☆☆☆

1641 **journeyman**	*n. a qualified mechanic or artisan / a mere hireling*	熟練工匠／短期雇用人員
[`dʒɚnɪmən]	Richard has studied as an apprentice carpenter for many years and now he is a qualified journeyman carpenter who is looking for a job in a company. 理查多年來學作木匠學徒，現在已是熟練工匠的他正在求職。	

★★★★★

1642 **journal**	*n. a daily record of events; magazine*	日誌，期刊
[`dʒɚnl̩]	The archeologist kept a valuable journal of his findings and discoveries as he traveled through the jungles of Africa. He intended to publish it when he returned to his home. 考古學家遊歷非洲叢林時，將個人考察和發現記載在日誌上，回到家鄉後打算出版成書。	

★★★★★

1643 **journalist**	*n. reporter; newspaperman; columnist*	新聞記者

[`dʒɜnlɪst]

A journalist tries to uncover all the facts and the truth about the news story he is investigating.

新聞記者努力找出有關正在調查的新聞報導的所有事實真相。

✦ junc = join 連結

★★★☆☆

1644 **junction**	*n. intersection; crossing; conjunction; juncture*	交會處，交叉點

[`dʒʌŋkʃən]

In the Old West of the United States, at the junction of two railroad lines, a small town always seemed to develop.

舊時美國西部鐵路交會點常發展成小鎮。

★★★☆☆

1645 **juncture**	*n. junction; a critical point of time*	連接點，時機

[`dʒʌŋktʃə]

George Bush was famous for saying, "That wouldn't be prudent at this juncture," which only meant that he didn't want to deal with that particular issue at that time.

美國總統布希因說出「此刻不需審慎」一語而聲名大噪，這句話只代表他當時不想處理該特殊議題。

★★★★★

1646 **conjunction**	*n. the action of joining*	連同，結合

[kən`dʒʌŋkʃən]

The FBI came to work in conjunction with the CIA to catch the international jewel thieves, because they needed some cooperation.

由於需要通力合作，美國聯邦調查局會同中央情報局共同組捕國際珠寶大盜。

✦ jur = swear; law 宣誓；法律

★★★☆☆

1647 **abjure**	*v. renounce; swear perpetual absence from*	棄絕，公開放棄

[əb`dʒʊr]

The government promised to abjure illegitimate surveillance. However, many people did not believe that the government would renounce its illegal action.

政府公開承諾揚棄非法監控行動，但許多人並不相信政府能做到。

★★★☆☆

1648 **perjury**	*n. a breach of an oath; mendacity*	偽證（罪）

[`pɜdʒərɪ]

The union head was found guilty of having lied when giving evidence in court and was sentenced to one-year imprisonment for perjury.

工會領袖在法庭上作偽證獲判偽證罪名成立，並處以一年徒刑。

★★★★★

1649 **jury**	*n.* *a body of usually twelve persons sworn to render a verdict on the basis of evidence submitted to them in a court of justice*	陪審團

[ˋdʒʊrɪ]

The judge was glad that the decision of the court was in the hands of the jury and not him because he was not sure how he felt about the defendant's plea of innocence.

法官很高興將由陪審團做出裁決而非由他做主，因為他不確定自己怎麼看被告的無罪抗辯。

✣ juven = young 年輕

★★★★☆

1650 **juvenescence**	*n.* *youth*	年輕，青春

[͵dʒuvəˋnɛsn̩s]

A king in ancient China tried to get the elixir of life to regain his juvenescence. He sent many people to get the medicine for youth, but to no avail.

中國古代皇帝想得到返老還童的長生不老藥，於是派遣許多人四處尋找，但卻徒勞無功。

★★★☆☆

1651 **juvenility**	*n.* *youth / immaturity*	少年 / 幼稚行為

[͵dʒuvəˋnɪlətɪ]

His outrageous behavior is probably due to his juvenility. We had better try to understand him in that he is still immature.

他無法無天的行為或許是出於年少無知，我們應試著了解他還不夠成熟。

★★★★★

1652 **juvenile**	*a.* *young; youthful*	少年的，年輕的

[ˋdʒuvən̩l]

After leaving the orphanage, the boy became a juvenile delinquent and was always on the wrong side of the law.

男孩離開孤兒院後就變成少年累犯。

Tea Time... ☕

<Medieval myth> Disposition
In medieval times people believed that four fluids were responsible for one's health and disposition: blood, phlegm, choler and black bile.

〈來自中古世紀神話〉個性
中古世紀人們相信人的健康狀況和個性是由四種液體來決定的，分別是血液、痰、黃膽汁和黑膽汁。（註：中古世紀延續古希臘思想，認為四液調合才能改善體質，變化氣質。）

disposition [͵dɪspəˋzɪʃən] *n.* *disposal; arrangement / character; temper; personality; humor* | 安排 / 脾氣，個性

I don't know my neighbor very well, but we see each other coming and going and he seems to have a good disposition.

我並不十分了解鄰居，但大家平常進進出出，我看他個性似乎不錯。

1
Complete each word by filling in the blank with proper spelling so that it has the same meaning as suggested. Then please write the meaning of each word in Chinese.

1. 冬眠 = _ _ _ _ _ n a t e
11. transition = _____

2. 死後的 = p o s t _ _ _ o u s
12. idiosyncrasy = _____

3. 使丟臉 = _ _ _ i l i a t e
13. idiot = _____

4. 使脫水 = d e _ _ _ _ a t e
14. igneous = _____

5. 消防栓 = _ _ _ _ a n t
15. ignition = _____

6. 過度敏感的 = _ _ _ _ _ s e n s i t i v e
16. indignation = _____

7. 高血壓 = _ _ _ _ _ t e n s i o n
17. arthritis = _____

8. 胃酸過多症 = _ _ _ _ _ a c i d i t y
18. injection = _____

9. 偽君子 = _ _ _ _ c r i t e
19. projector = _____

10. 憂鬱症 = _ _ _ _ c h o n d r i a
20. juvenile = _____

2
Choose a word that best completes the sentence.

21. **Mr. White received an _____ which notified him that his friend Mr. Brown had passed away.**

(A) idiom   (B) obituary   (C) itinerary   (D) injection

22. **A television set is often referred to as an _____ box.**

(A) idiot   (B) ignition   (C) arthritis   (D) inflammation

23. **The secretary's _____ was caused by male chauvinism among the male workers.**

(A) indignation   (B) deceit   (C) alteration   (D) duplicity

3
The highlighted word is closest in meaning to which of the following?

24. **The chairman of the board decided to adjourn the meeting.**

(A) grief   (B) gravitation   (C) postpone   (D) progress

25. **Almost all children really hate an injection .**

(A) a projector   (B) a shot   (C) a hypocrite   (D) a hydrant

⚬ leag, leg, lig = bind 束縛，捆綁

MP3
68

★★★★★

1653 allegiance

[ə`lidʒəns]

n. loyalty 忠誠，忠貞，效忠

Before he became a British citizen he had to swear allegiance to the Queen and the British flag.

他成為英國人前須先向女王和英國國旗宣示效忠。

★★★★★

1654 obliged

[ə`blaɪdʒd]

a. thankful 感激的

Martha is much obliged for all the benefits you gave her. Without your help she might have too much difficulty adapting to the new job.

瑪莎對你的照顧感激不盡，若非你伸出援手，她可能很難適應新工作。

★★★★★

1655 colleague

[`kɑlig]

n. team-mate; fellow worker; co-worker; associate 同事，同僚

I'd like to express my heartfelt thanks to all of my colleagues who have stood by me and given me support throughout my career.

我想向幫助並支持我擴展職涯的所有同事致上由衷謝意。

★★★★★

1656 legacy

[`lɛgəsɪ]

n. something handed down by a predecessor 留傳後世之物，遺產

The new president is trying to liquidate the past legacies which have been handed down from the previous tyrannical government.

新總統正努力根除前任專制政府遺留的歪風。

★★★★★

1657 league

[lig]

n. confederation; federation; union; association; guild; fraternity 聯盟，同盟

Jim has shown aptitude for baseball ever since he was 4 years old, and is now one of the best players in the league.

吉姆自四歲起便展現打棒球的天分，現在更是聯賽最佳球員之一。

⚬ lect, lig = choose 選擇

★★★★★

1658 collection

[kə`lɛkʃən]

n. accumulation; aggregation 聚集，收集

A collection of facts is no more science than a dictionary is poetry.

事實的總和不等於科學，正好比字典不等於詩集一樣。

★★★★★

1659 election

[ɪˈlɛkʃən]

n. choice; nomination; vote　　　　　　　　　　　　　選舉

The president announced that he intended to run for one more term in the presidential elections.

總統宣布將角逐下一任總統大選。

★★★★★

1660 select

[səˈlɛkt]

v. choose; pick　　　　　　　　　　　　　　　選擇，挑選，選拔

Since the class was full, many students were forced to select another course to complete their semester.

由於人數已滿，許多學生被迫改選另一門課以湊足學分。

★★★★★

1661 eligible

[ˈɛlɪdʒəbḷ]

a. fit or entitled to be chosen; qualified; suitable　　　合格的，有資格的

Your computer literacy and excellent typing skill will make you eligible for the position. Furthermore, you have significant job experience.

你的電腦能力和出色的打字技巧有資格擔任此職務，此外你也具備絕佳工作經驗。

⁜ len(t) = bend 彎曲

★★★★★

1662 lens

[lɛnz]

n. a piece of a transparent substance with one or both sides curved for concentrating or dispersing light-rays in optical instruments　　鏡頭

These pictures are unclear because of the dirty lens on your camera. To get a sharp picture, you should try to keep the lens clean.

照相機鏡頭太髒以致這些照片模糊不清，為使照片清晰應保持鏡頭乾淨。

★★★★☆

1663 relentlessly

[rɪˈlɛntlɪslɪ]

ad. doggedly; rigidly　　　　　　　　　　毫不留情地，不間斷地

For the past few years, summers were hot and humid, and winters were relentlessly cold. We have had extreme weather.

過去幾年來夏季既炎熱又潮濕，冬季卻非常寒冷，是極端的氣候形態。

★★★★★

1664 lenient

[ˈlinɪənt]

a. merciful; tolerant; forgiving; magnanimous　寬大的，仁慈的，慈悲為懷的

When Jane was a child, her father was so strict that she thought it was impossible for him to be lenient.

珍小時候父親很嚴厲，她以為他不可能寬大仁慈。

❖ lev = light 輕的

★★★★★

1665 **lever**	*n. a bar resting on a pivot, used to help lift a heavy or firmly fixed object / v. move something with a lever*	槓桿 / 以槓桿撬開

[ˋlɛvɚ]

A very long wooden stick was used to lever that giant rock. Without the stick we could not have been able to move it.
我們把長木棍當作槓桿撬起巨石，若沒有它就無法移動石頭。

★★★★★

1666 **alleviate**	*v. ease; lessen; make less severe*	使減輕，使緩和

[əˋlivɪ͵et]

Donovan took aspirin to alleviate his migraine and felt better in about 30 minutes. He was amazed at its efficacy.
唐納文服用阿斯匹靈減輕偏頭痛，不到半小時就覺得好多了，讓他感到藥效驚人。

★★★★★

1667 **elevation**	*n. height; altitude*	高度，海拔，標高

[͵ɛləˋveʃən]

The plateau has an average elevation of approximately 4,000m above sea level. At this height, people have difficulty with breathing.
高原平均高度約海拔四千公尺，人們處在這樣的高度會呼吸困難。

❖ liter = letter 字母

★★★★☆

1668 **alliteration**	*a. the occurrence of the same letter or sound at the beginning of adjacent or closely connected words*	頭韻（法）

[ə͵lɪtəˋreʃən]

Note the alliteration in the following sentence; Peter Piper picked a pack of pickled peppers, so how many peppers did Peter Piper pick?
注意下列文句的頭韻：彼德・派柏挑了一包醃辣椒，彼德・派柏挑了多少辣椒？

★★★★★

1669 **literal**	*a. word for word*	字面上的，逐字的

[ˋlɪtərəl]

The literal translation of this book could confuse many readers. Therefore we should read between the lines.
這本書的直譯會讓許多讀者混淆，所以應領會言外之意。

★★★★★

1670 literary | *a. of literature* | 文學的

[`lɪtəˌrɛrɪ]

The author in his later days started writing literary criticism on novels. His criticism was thought to be very incisive among writers.

作者晚年開始撰寫小說文學評論，文藝界普遍認為其評論非常尖銳。

★★★★★

1671 literate | *a. able to read and write; learned* | 識字的，能讀寫的

[`lɪtərɪt]

Only a quarter of the children in Mrs. Nichols's class are literate. Most of her students cannot read or write.

妮可斯太太班上只有四分之一學童識字，多數學生都不會讀或寫。

⁂ lith = stone 石頭

★★★★★

1672 neolithic | *a. of or relating to the later Stone Age, when ground or polished stone weapons and implements prevailed* | 新石器時代的

[ˌniə`lɪθɪk]

Judging from its shape and texture, this tool must be from the neolithic age. The tool from the Old Stone Age is quite different.

此器具從外形和構造判斷必定來自新石器時代，舊石器時代器具與此大不相同。

★★★★★

1673 paleolithic | *a. of the early Stone Age* | 舊石器時代的

[ˌpelɪo`lɪθɪk]

The Stone Age is often divided into the paleolithic period, or the Old Stone Age and the neolithic period, or the New Stone Age.

石器時代通常畫分為舊石器和新石器時代等兩個時期。

★★★☆☆

1674 monolithic | *a. massive; huge; enormous; colossal; gigantic; giant* | 巨石的

[ˌmɑnl`ɪθɪk]

Easter Island, Chile, is famous for its monolithic stone statues. Scientists have wondered how people could erect the gigantic stone statues.

智利復活島以巨人石雕聞名，科學家們納悶古人如何將這些巨大石像豎立起來。

⁂ loc = place 地點，放置

★★★★★

1675 local | *a. regional; endemic; district* | 本地的，當地的

[`lokl]

Jim asked the secretary if he could make a local telephone call. She just nodded her head without so much as looking at him.

吉姆問祕書能否撥打本地電話，她只是點點頭，甚至沒正眼瞧他。

★★★☆☆

| 1676 **dislocate** | **v.** *disjoint* | 使脫臼 |

[`dıslo͵ket]

He couldn't walk any more. His hip felt as if he had dislocated it. There was no other alternative. He asked his wife to carry him on her back.

他覺得髖關節似乎脫臼了無法行走，在別無選擇的情況下只好要求妻子背他。

★★★★☆

| 1677 **localize** | **v.** *restrict to a particular place* | 使局部化，使限於一區 |

[`lokḷ͵aız]

The health authority wanted to localize the epidemic. People were forbidden to take a trip unless they got the vaccine.

衛生當局想縮小疫情範圍，因此凡是未接種疫苗的居民禁止出外旅遊。

★★★★★

| 1678 **locate** | **v.** *situate; place / discover; detect* | 位於～ / 找出 |

[`loket]

Mom thought that she left her cell phone somewhere in the kitchen, but she couldn't locate it. The next day she found it in the refrigerator.

母親認為自己的手機掉在廚房某處但遍尋不著，隔天在冰箱裡發現了。

★★★★☆

| 1679 **allocation** | **n.** *assignment; allotment* | 分配，配置 |

[͵ælə`keʃən]

The youngest daughter got upset when she found out that she didn't get as much money as the others. She complained to her parents about the unfair allocation of funds.

小女兒發現自己得到的零用錢比大家少而感到心煩，便向雙親抱怨分配不公。

✥ log, loq = words, say 説，言

MP3
69

★★★★☆

| 1680 **loquacious** | **a.** *talkative* | 多話的，非常健談的 |

[lo`kweʃəs]

The atmosphere made all of the picnickers so loquacious. Nobody could stop talking. All of them were able to relieve their stress which had been caused by their boss.

由於氣氛良好，野餐者話匣子一開就停不下來，大家總算能減輕老闆帶來的壓力。

★★★★☆

| 1681 **epilogue** | **n.** *a speech or short poem addressed to the audience by an actor at the end of a play* | 結束語，跋，尾聲 |

[`ɛpə͵lɔg]

Even though she is a very big star, she still gets very nervous when she is asked to give an epilogue after a performance.

她雖已是大明星，但應邀在表演最後朗誦尾聲仍感到相當緊張。

★★★★★

1682 **prologue**	*n.* a preliminary speech; foreword	序言,序幕,開場白

[`prolɔg]

In the prologue of *"Romeo and Juliet,"* the entire tale is told in a few short lines of poetry.

《羅密歐與茱麗葉》的序幕,以短短幾行詩句訴說整個故事。

★★★★★

1683 **colloquialism**	*n.* a colloquial word or phrase	口語用法

[kə`lokwɪəl͵ɪzəm]

It is one thing to know grammatical English, but another to know and understand colloquialism.

懂得英文文法未必理解口語用法。

★★★☆☆

1684 **colloquy**	*n.* conversation	正式談話,討論

[`kɑləkwɪ]

I am very nervous because my boss has asked me to prepare a new report for our colloquy that is scheduled for next week.

老闆要我提交一份新報告以備下周討論時使用,讓我很緊張。

✦ lut, lu(v) = water 水

★★☆☆☆

1685 **ablution**	*n.* the ceremonial washing of parts of the body or sacred vessels	沐浴儀式

[əb`luʃən]

Before the shaman could begin the ritual, the devotees had to perform a complete ablution in the river and cleanse their bodies and spirits.

僧侶舉行儀式前信徒須在河中潔身沐浴,以洗滌身體、淨化靈魂。

★★★★★

1686 **deluge**	*n.* a great flood; inundation / a great outpouring	大洪水 / 大批湧至

[`dɛljudʒ]

Every year during the Christmas season post offices all over the country receive a deluge of Christmas cards and letters to Santa Claus that they don't know what to do with.

每年耶誕全國郵局都會收到大批湧至的耶誕卡和寄給耶誕老人的無法投遞信件。

★★★★★

1687 **dilute**	*v.* reduce the strength of a fluid by adding water or another solvent	稀釋

[dɪ`lut]

Use this cleaner to clean the floors and if you think that it is too strong you can add water to dilute it.

請用這個清潔劑清理地板,如果覺得太濃就加水稀釋。

✛ luc, lum, lus = light 光，明亮的

★★★★★

1688 lucid

[`lusɪd]

a. *clear; easy to understand*   清晰易懂的

Ernest Hemingway's novels are written in such a lucid style that most readers can easily understand them.
海明威的小說是以清晰易懂的筆調寫成的，多數讀者都能輕鬆理解。

★★★★★

1689 luminary

[`lumə,nɛrɪ]

n. *a natural light-giving body / a person as a source of intellectual light or moral inspiration*   發光體 / 心靈導師

As the greatest luminary body known to man, the sun has been the focus of many primitive religions.
作為人類所知最大的發光體，太陽一直是許多原始宗教的膜拜焦點。

★★★★★

1690 luminous

[`lumənəs]

a. *shiny; radiant; lustrous; shimmering; gleaming*   發光的，明亮的

As the moon came up full, the lake was luminous and tranquil. At last the man got the courage to pop the question.
月圓時湖畔明亮而寧靜，最後男子鼓起勇氣求婚。

★★★★★

1691 illuminate

[ɪ`lumə,net]

v. *lighten; cast light upon*   照亮

We watched the news broadcasts of the war and saw how the explosions from the bombs illuminated the whole sky during the night raids.
我們收看戰爭新聞報導，看見夜襲炸彈爆炸並照亮整個夜空。

★★★☆☆

1692 pellucid

[pə`lusɪd]

a. *transparent; clear / mentally clear*   清澈的 / 清晰的

His pellucid style of writing was an indication of how clear, clean and logical his thinking was.
他清晰的文體顯示其敏銳精確且深具邏輯的思考模式。

★★★☆☆

1693 lackluster

[`læ,lʌstə]

a. *drab; dull; colorless; dismal; vapid*   死氣沉沉的，無生氣的

Jane gave her future husband a rather lackluster smile when he said that they would have to live with his parents after they got married.
當未來的丈夫告訴珍婚後要跟公婆同住，她給他一個苦笑。

★★★☆☆

1694 luster

[`lʌstə]

n. *gloss; brilliance; sheen; gleam; luminosity*   光澤，光輝

My grandfather's silver watch has lost its luster after many years of neglect. The surface has tarnished.
祖父的銀錶因久未保養而失去光澤，表面都有了鏽污。

★★★☆☆

| **1695 luminant** | *a. emitting light* | 發光的 |

[`lumɪnənt]

The boy started to shiver as the luminant object started to approach him. He then saw that it was a firefly.

男孩因發光物體靠近而開始發抖,接著才發現是螢火蟲。

★★★★☆

| **1696 translucent** | *a. semi-transparent* | 半透明的 |

[træns`lusn̩t]

Quartz is often a translucent, or semitransparent mineral, whereas opal is opaque and glass is transparent.

石英通常是半透明礦物,而蛋白石是不透明的,至於玻璃則是透明的。

★★★★★

| **1697 elucidate** | *v. explain; explicate; expound; unravel* | 闡明,闡述 |

[ɪ`lusə‚det]

Mrs. Collins elucidated the point which was not clear to me. After she explained it to me, I could clearly understand what it was.

我不懂柯林斯太太闡述的要點,等她說明後才終於明白。

★★★★★

| **1698 lustrous** | *a. glossy; shiny; burnished* | 有光澤的,發亮的 |

[`lʌstrəs]

Silver is a most lustrous metal. When it is cleanly polished, silver shines brightly. Therefore, it has often been used for decorations.

銀是最有光澤的金屬,完全拋光後閃閃發亮,因此經常用來裝飾。

❖ lud, lus = play 遊戲

★★★★☆

| **1699 ludicrous** | *a. laughable; farcical; funny; facetious; jocose* | 滑稽的,可笑的 |

[`ludɪkrəs]

The comedian was so ludicrous in his speech as well as in his dress that we couldn't help laughing.

喜劇演員滑稽的談吐和裝扮逗得我們哄堂大笑。

★★★★☆

| **1700 collusion** | *n. intrigue; conspiracy* | 共謀,串通 |

[kə`luʒən]

Members of the organization have entered into a collusion swearing that they will die rather than reveal the secrets.

組織成員共同發誓寧死也不會洩露祕密。

1701 **illusion**	*n. misjudgment; misbelief / fantasy; hallucination*	錯覺／幻覺，假象
[ɪ`luʒən]		

After having too many drinks, the farmer had the illusion of invulnerability and got into a fight with a giant figure. Unfortunately it turned out to be a bull.

酒醉農夫幻想自己刀槍不入而和彪形大漢打了起來，結果犯下愚蠢大錯。

★★★★☆

1702 **elusive**	*a. difficult to find or catch; evasive; delusory*	難以捉摸的，狡黠的
[ɪ`lusɪv]		

Ted Bundy was one of the most elusive serial killers known in America, but the police finally caught up with him and put him to death.

泰德‧邦迪是美國最狡黠的連續殺人犯之一，但警方終於將他逮捕到案並處以死刑。

Tea Time... ☕

<From the name of an Athenian statesman and lawgiver> Draconian After Draco, Athenian statesman and lawgiver. (7th century B.C.)	〈來自古雅典政治家暨立法者之名〉德拉寇的 本字源自西元前七世紀古雅典政治家暨立法者德拉寇之名。（註：拉丁文的 Draco 指「龍」，德拉寇根據習慣法編製古雅典第一部立法嚴苛的成文法，無論犯什麼罪幾乎都是一律處死，後世以其名的形容詞 draconian 為「嚴苛的，殘酷的」之意。）

draconian [drə`konɪən] *a. very harsh; severe* | 嚴苛的，殘酷的

The government will take draconian measures to inhibit drunk driving. There will be a massive crackdown on driving while intoxicated (DWI).

政府將採取嚴格措施禁止酒醉駕車，並將展開大規模取締行動。

Review Test 10

1 Complete each word by filling in the blank with proper spelling so that it has the same meaning as suggested. Then please write the meaning of each word in Chinese.

1. 聯盟	= _ _ _ _ u e		11. neolithic	=	_____
2. 遺產	= _ _ _ a c y		12. monolithic	=	_____
3. 效忠	= a l _ _ _ i a n c e		13. dislocate	=	_____
4. 同事	= c o l _ _ _ _ u e		14. allocation	=	_____
5. 聚集	= c o l _ _ _ _ i o n		15. loquacious	=	_____
6. 有資格的	= e _ _ _ i b l e		16. colloquy	=	_____
7. 毫不留情地	= r e _ _ _ _ l e s s l y		17. luminous	=	_____
8. 使減輕	= a l _ _ _ i a t e		18. translucent	=	_____
9. 字面上的	= _ _ _ _ _ a l		19. ludicrous	=	_____
10. 文學的	= _ _ _ _ _ a r y		20. illusion	=	_____

2 Choose a word that best completes the sentence.

21. Mrs. Smith never thought that her son would be a _____ delinquent.
(A) lucid   (B) lustrous   (C) pellucid   (D) juvenile

22. The solution to air pollution problems has always been _____.
(A) loquacious   (B) neolithic   (C) elusive   (D) literary

3 The highlighted word is closest in meaning to which of the following?

23. I am sure that the applicant is eligible for the position.
(A) lenient   (B) qualified   (C) local   (D) literate

24. After the deluge one of the flood victims caught a carp in his attic.
(A) epilogue   (B) ablution   (C) inundation   (D) allocation

25. I could easily locate my colleague among people because of his great stature.
(A) discover   (B) select   (C) lever   (D) dislocate

✤ mag-, maj- = big 大

★★★★★

1703 magnitude

n. significance; importance; consequence / largeness; greatness

重要／巨大

[`mægnə,tjud]

I think every one of our members should realize the magnitude of this problem. We need to fight for a pay raise.

我想大家應該了解問題的重要性，我們必須爭取加薪。

★★★★★

1704 majestic

a. stately and dignified; grand; imperial; magnificent

有威嚴的

[mə`dʒɛstɪk]

The lion carries himself with a majestic and royal attitude, when in actual fact it is one of the laziest animals in the jungle.

獅子外表威武尊貴但其實是最懶惰的叢林動物之一。

★★★★★

1705 majority

n. bulk; mass; lion's share / greater number

過半數／大多數

[mə`dʒɔrətɪ]

The majority of the voters did not vote for the Democratic candidate, and consequently he was defeated in the election.

絕大多數選民未投給民主黨候選人，因此他在選戰中敗北。

✤ mal- = bad, wrong 不好的，錯誤的

★★★★☆

1706 malediction

n. curse

詛咒，誹謗

[,mælə`dɪkʃən]

With her dying breath, the witch cast such a malediction on her attackers that many feared for the safety of their families for many years to come.

女巫臨死前詛咒攻擊者，使許多人擔心未來自家安全。

★★★★☆

1707 malevolent

a. evil; hostile

不懷好意的，壞心腸的

[mə`lɛvələnt]

A belief in goblins and the malevolent power of Friday the 13th can be a sort of superstition. It cannot be explained through science.

對惡靈和十三號星期五邪惡力量的信仰是某種無法以科學解釋的迷信行為。

★★★☆☆

1708 malinger

[mə`lɪŋɡə]

v. exaggerate or feign illness in order to escape duty　　裝病逃避

His head hurt so much from drinking the night before that Gilbert had no choice but to malinger to escape another day's work at the office.

吉伯特前晚飲酒後頭痛欲裂，隔天沒辦法只好裝病不上班。

★★★★★

1709 malfunction

[mæl`fʌŋkʃən]

n. a failure to function / v. fail to function normally　　故障，失調 / 機能失常

Old aircraft are regularly checked for abrasions because wear and tear can often lead to a serious malfunction.

老舊飛機定期檢查磨損情況，以免造成嚴重故障。

★★★★☆

1710 malcontent

[`mælkən,tɛnt]

a. discontented; rebellious / n. a discontented person; rebel　　不滿現狀的 / 不滿現狀者

Jim is a malcontent. He is always unhappy about the situation in our company. All he does at work is complain.

不滿現狀的吉姆總是對公司現況感到不快，每天上班都在抱怨。

★★★★★

1711 malign

[mə`laɪn]

a. injurious; malignant; malevolent; evil / v. slander　　惡意的 / 誹謗，中傷

The president was maligned because of his controversial policies. Most of his adversaries slandered him behind his back.

總統因爭議性政策受到多數對手暗中誹謗。

★★★☆☆

1712 maladroit

[,mælə`drɔɪt]

a. clumsy; bungling　　笨拙的，不熟練的

The boss is displeased because you handled the situation in a very maladroit way. I think that you have made a mess.

老闆對你以極不熟練的方式處理此事感到生氣，我想你搞砸了。

★★★★☆

1713 malefactor

[`mælə,fæktə]

n. criminal; evil-doer; offender　　罪犯，做壞事者，違法者

People who litter in public places are malefactors. It is natural that they should be heavily fined.

在公共場合亂丟垃圾的違法者應受重罰。

★★★★☆

1714 malady

[`mælədɪ]

n. disease; ailment; a morbid condition　　疾病，弊端

Romeo's malady of the heart could only be cured by the unconditional love of the beautiful Juliet.

羅密歐的心病只能靠貌美茱麗葉無條件的愛才能痊癒。

1715 **maladjusted**	*a.* not correctly adjusted; unable to adapt to or cope with the demands of a social environment	不適應環境的
[ˌmælə`dʒʌstɪd]	It was found that Harold's daughter had psychological problems. He decided to send her to a school for maladjusted children. 哈洛的女兒有精神問題，他決定送她到適應困難兒童特殊學校就讀。	

★★★★★

1716 **malnutrition**	*n.* undernourishment; insufficient nutrition	營養失調
[ˌmælnju`trɪʃən]	Protein malnutrition usually occurs when a person doesn't eat a balanced diet or he doesn't eat enough food. 蛋白質營養不良症通常發生在飲食不均衡或不充足的人身上。	

★★★☆☆

1717 **malice**	*n.* hostility; the intention to do evil	惡意，敵意，怨恨
[`mælɪs]	The boss looked at him with such malice as he was profusely apologizing for sleeping late that he found himself unable to utter another word. 老闆懷恨地看著再三道歉睡過頭的他，使他說不出話來。	

❖ mani, manu = hand　手

★★★★★

1718 **manual**	*a.* hand-operated / *n.* handbook	手的，體力的 / 手冊
[`mænjʊəl]	His doctor told him that his leg would continue to hurt as long as he did heavy manual labor. But he had no choice but to work to support his family. 醫生表示若繼續從事大量體力勞動將傷及腿部，但他別無選擇必須幹活養家。	

★★★★★

1719 **manuscript**	*n.* a book, document, etc. written by hand	原稿，手稿
[`mænjə,skrɪpt]	When he had completed his best manuscript to date, the exhausted author promised himself a long and well-deserved vacation. 疲憊作者完成迄今最棒的作品原稿後，決定給自己放個應得的長假。	

★★★★★

1720 **manipulate**	*v.* handle; operate; maneuver	操縱，操作
[mə`nɪpjə,let]	Do you know how to manipulate this sophisticated gadget? It is so complicated that I don't know where to begin. 你知道怎麼操作這個精密機械嗎？它太複雜了使我不知從何著手。	

★★★★★

1721 manifest

a. apparent; evident; obvious; patent; conspicuous; explicit /
v. show

顯然的 / 顯示

[ˈmænəˌfɛst]

The truth of Mike's statement was manifest since everyone could plainly see that he was not lying.

邁克的聲明顯然屬實，因為大家能明顯看出他不是在說謊。

★★★☆☆

1722 manacles

n. shackles; handcuffs; fetters

手銬

[ˈmænək!z]

The criminal was led off to the state prison in manacles. Everyone knew that if he had been left with his hands free, he would attack the policemen.

罪犯戴上手銬押往州立監獄，大家都知道如果他沒上手銬一定會攻擊警方。

★★★★★

1723 manufacture

n. making; production; fabrication / v. make;
fabricate; assemble

製造 / 加工

[ˌmænjəˈfæktʃə]

Many companies have begun to manufacture their products in Asia because of the low labor costs.

許多企業因人工成本低廉開始在亞洲加工製造產品。

❖ mania = insanity, madness 瘋狂，錯亂的

★★★★★

1724 mania

n. craze; passion; fad; preoccupation; yearning; craving

瘋狂，～迷

[ˈmenɪə]

Mrs. Manning seems to have a mania for watching baseball on TV. She often watches it with her telephone unplugged.

曼尼太太似乎是個電視棒球迷，經常拔掉電話線好專心看電視。

★★☆☆☆

1725 pyromania

n. an obsessive desire to set fire

縱火癖，縱火狂

[ˌpaɪrəˈmenɪə]

No doctors or psychiatrists could cure his pyromania. The fires Mark Holmes set caused at least ten deaths and thousands of dollars in damage.

沒有醫師或精神病學家能治癒馬克·福爾摩斯的縱火癖，他至少造成十死和數千美元財物損失。

★★☆☆☆

1726 monomania

n. obsession of the mind by one idea or interest

偏執狂，狂熱

[ˌmɑnəˈmenɪə]

The whole country's struggle for economic freedom has paralyzed the citizens with money-making monomania; gaining riches at the cost of their morals and values.

全國爭取經濟自主使人民陷入賺錢狂熱中，就算犧牲道德與價值觀也要致富。

★☆☆☆☆

1727 kleptomania	*n. a recurrent urge to steal*	竊盜癖

[ˌklɛptə`menɪə]

The girl was diagnosed as having kleptomania. She has a strong and uncontrollable desire to steal things.
女孩經診斷患有竊盜癖，有無法控制的強烈欲望想偷東西。

★☆☆☆☆

1728 kleptomaniac	*n. thief*	竊盜狂

[ˌklɛptə`menɪæk]

Being a kleptomaniac means that you will always have new and interesting things around your house that you don't remember buying.
竊盜狂家中常有不記得買過的有趣新東西。

★★★☆☆

1729 maniacal	*a. insane; lunatic; mad; demented; deranged; crazy; loony*	瘋狂的

[mə`naɪəkl]

His eyes had taken on a maniacal gleam when he saw the gold ring lying on the ground before him, and his companions knew that they would be unable to stop him from trying to get it.
他看到地上的金戒指後眼裡閃現一抹瘋狂，同伴知道無法阻止他去撿。

⁑ mass = heap, pile 堆積，大量

★★★★★

MP3
71

1730 mass	*n. pile; heap; load; stack; mound; bunch; bundle; hoard; accumulation; aggregation; conglomeration; agglomeration; hunk*	眾多，大量

[mæs]

The office manager stuffed a mass of papers into his briefcase and walked out of his office. The papers were related with the M&A.
經理將一大堆有關併購的文件塞入公事包後離開辦公室。

★★★★★

1731 amass	*v. accumulate; rack up; pile up; muster; stock up; stockpile; hoard; set aside*	積聚，累積

[ə`mæs]

The carpenter has amassed large sums of money by working very hard for many years. He has decided to donate his money to a charity organization.
木匠多年來努力工作累積了不少財富，並決定捐給慈善機構。

★★★★★

1732 massive

a. bulky; immense; mammoth; colossal; titanic; prodigious; gargantuan; mighty; jumbo; humongous　　大規模的，強大的

[ˋmæsɪv]

There is a massive crackdown on illegal parking. Please park your car at the parking lot; otherwise they might tow away your car.

目前正大規模取締違法停車，所以請將車輛停放在停車場，否則會被拖吊。

⁜ med-, mid- = middle　中間

★★★★★

1733 medium

a. average; middle; standard / n. means; mechanism; method　中等的 / 媒介

[ˋmidɪəm]

The burglar was of medium height and build; neither remarkably tall nor uncommonly short; neither fat nor skinny.

搶匪中等身材，既不特別高也不非常矮，不胖也不瘦。

★★★★★

1734 intermediate

a. middle; medial; intermediary　　中間的，中級的

[ˌɪntəˋmidɪət]

Mr. Baker should have stayed on the intermediate level ski slopes instead of trying to ski on the expert ones. He fell and seriously injured himself which put a quick end to his long skiing vacation.

貝克先生應待在中級滑雪道而不是高級。結果他摔成重傷，滑雪長假也旋即結束。

★★★★☆

1735 mediate

v. arbitrate; intercede　　調停，斡旋，使和解

[ˋmidɪˌet]

The previous president was able to mediate the negotiations between the two war-torn countries. Afterwards, he was honored as a great peace-maker.

前總統居中調停戰亂國間的談判，隨後獲表揚為偉大的和平締造者。

★★★★☆

1736 meddle

v. interfere; intrude; butt in; thrust one's nose in; intervene; interlope snoop; tamper　　干涉，管閒事

[ˋmɛdḷ]

Don't meddle in my affairs. Please mind your own business. I do not want anybody to interfere with me.

別干涉我的事，請管好你自己就行了，我不想要任何人干預。

★★★★☆

1737 meddlesome

a. interfering; nosy; inquisitive　　愛管閒事的

[ˋmɛdḷsəm]

Gilbert was such a meddlesome person that no one bothered trying to keep anything secret from him.

吉伯特很愛管閒事，大家在他面前也懶得保密。

★★★★★

1738 intermediary | *n.* go-between; mediator; peacemaker; arbitrator | 仲裁者，調停者

[ˌɪntəˈmidɪˌɛrɪ]

His job as an intermediary between the union and the management of the company meant that he was always sought after by everyone in the company, but he had few real friends.

他的職責是作為工會和企業管理階層間的調停者，雖然大家總是爭相找他，但他沒幾個知交。

✥ mel, mil, mol = soft, sweet, powder 柔軟，甜，粉末

★★★★★

1739 melody | *n.* tune | 旋律，美妙音樂

[ˈmɛlədɪ]

The songs which the famous composer wrote were known for having both a good melody and a serious message.

該知名作曲家所作的歌曲以旋律優美和意境深遠聞名。

★★★★★

1740 watermelon | *n.* a large smooth green melon with red pulp and watery juice | 西瓜

[ˈwɔtəˌmɛlən]

Our grandfather told us that a watermelon is ripe if we get a hollow sound when we knock on it.

祖父說敲打西瓜聽到中空聲音就是熟了。

★★★★☆

1741 mill | *n.* a building fitted with a mechanical apparatus for grinding corn | 磨坊

[mɪl]

The adventurous peasant decided to open a mill where grain was crushed. There was no place nearby where farmers could grind their corn.

大膽冒險的農夫決定要開一家碾穀物的磨坊，因為附近沒有可以供農夫碾磨穀物的地方。

★★★☆☆

1742 mellow | *a.* soft; musical; melodious; mellifluous | 柔美的，圓潤的

[ˈmɛlo]

I really like Jane's voice. What girl has ever spoken in such mellow tones? Her sonorous voice always makes me happy.

我很喜歡珍的聲音，哪個女孩誰能像她這樣說話輕柔？她圓潤的聲音總讓我開心。

❖ men, min, mne, mni = mind, remember 精神，記得

★★★☆☆

| 1743 **amnesty** | *n. a general pardon* | 大赦，特赦 |

[ˋæmˌnɛstɪ]

After the Civil War, the American president gave special amnesty to the Southern leaders to make the Restoration process less bitter.
南北戰爭結束後，美國總統大赦南方領袖以減輕重建過程的痛苦。

★★★☆☆

| 1744 **amnesia** | *n. a partial or total loss of memory; forgetfulness* | 健忘症 |

[æmˋniʒɪə]

When the old man suffering from amnesia went to see a doctor, he could not remember the purpose of his visit to the doctor's office.
患有健忘症的老人去看醫生，卻不記得來醫院的目的。

★★★☆☆

| 1745 **reminiscence** | *n. recollection; memory; remembrance* | 回憶，話舊，追憶 |

[rɛməˋnɪsn̩s]

At the college reunion, many of the alumni broke into a long reminiscence that covered both the good times and the bad.
許多校友在大學同學會上突然追憶起過去的點點滴滴。

❖ merg, mers = plunge 投入，跳入

★★★★★

| 1746 **emerge** | *v. appear; come out; come forth; come into view* | 浮現，脫穎而出 |

[ɪˋmɝdʒ]

James was not expected to win the tournament, but he slowly emerged as the most steady player of the day. He came out ahead in the end.
詹姆斯本來不期望獲勝，卻漸漸脫穎而出成為比賽中最穩健的選手，最後一馬當先贏得勝利。

★★★★★

| 1747 **immerse** | *v. absorb; involve; engross; engage; occupy; plunge* | 使埋首於～ |

[ɪˋmɝs]

At last Mr. Newman totally immersed himself in his dissertation. Because of his concentration he was able to finish it in a single year.
最後諾曼先生全神貫注在博士論文上，只花一年時間就完成了。

★★★★★

| 1748 **submerge** | *v. dive; sink; plummet* | 潛入水中，潛航 |

[səbˋmɝdʒ]

The submarine captain gave the order to submerge and they prepared for an underwater attack.
潛艇指揮官下令潛航預備進行水中攻擊。

★★★★★

| 1749 **merge** | *v. join; blend* | 會合，使融合，使合併 |

[mɜdʒ]

It is very dangerous not to accelerate quickly enough when merging onto a freeway. A car which is going too slow can cause a danger on a freeway.

在高速公路上會車若不立即加速是很危險的，慢速會車會影響行車安全。

★★★☆☆

| 1750 **emergent** | *a. newly formed or made independent* | 出現的，開始引人注目的 |

[ɪˋmɜdʒənt]

The leaders of the emergent nation had so many things to do. First, they had to elect a president and set up a legislature.

有許多事尚待新興國家領袖完成，首先要選出總統並成立立法機關。

Tea Time... ☕

| <Greek myth> Hypnos
The god of sleep, identified by the Romans with Somnus. | 〈來自希臘神話〉修普諾斯
希臘神話裡主掌睡眠的天神，相當於羅馬神話的睡眠之神索姆納斯。（註：Hypnos 和 Somnus 兩字皆是後世許多關於睡眠醫學名詞的字源。） |

hypnosis [hɪpˋnosɪs] *n. a sleep-like state in which the subject acts only on external suggestion; artificially produced sleep* | 催眠，催眠狀態

Recently some dentists use hypnosis instead of novocain to kill pain, and this method is growing quickly in popularity.

近來部分牙醫師以日漸普及的催眠為病患止痛，而不是使用傳統麻醉藥奴佛卡因。

hypnotize [ˋhɪpnəˏtaɪz] *v. produce hypnosis in; fascinate; bewitch* | 對～施以催眠

Some psychiatrists hypnotize their patients to bring out their hidden memory. Some patients say that they have had a former life.

有些精神科醫師會將病患催眠以發掘隱藏記憶，部分病患表示自己有前世。

1 Complete each word by filling in the blank with proper spelling so that it has the same meaning as suggested. Then please write the meaning of each word in Chinese.

1. 重要 = ___ n i t u d e
2. 詛咒 = ____ d i c t i o n
3. 不懷好意的 = ____ v o l e n t
4. 不滿現狀者 = ___ c o n t e n t
5. 違法者 = ____ f a c t o r
6. 營養失調 = ___ n u t r i t i o n
7. 體力的 = ____ a l
8. 操作 = ____ p u l a t e
9. 製造 = ____ f a c t u r e
10. 縱火癖 = p y r o _____

11. monomania = _____
12. kleptomaniac = _____
13. massive = _____
14. medium = _____
15. mediate = _____
16. meddlesome = _____
17. melody = _____
18. mellow = _____
19. amnesty = _____
20. submerge = _____

2 Choose a word that best completes the sentence.

21. The _____ of the people were against building a factory in their neighborhood.
    (A) malediction   (B) majority   (C) malady   (D) mania

22. My computer _____ and prints out the wrong data.
    (A) manipulates   (B) emerges   (C) malfunctions   (D) manufactures

23. My uncle started a computer-related business and was able to _____ a large fortune.
    (A) amass   (B) meddle   (C) intercede   (D) interfere

3 The highlighted word is closest in meaning to which of the following?

24. One patient suffering from amnesia went to a doctor. But when the doctor asked him what caused him trouble, the patient could not remember. So the doctor told him, "Please go back home and forget it."
    (A) reminiscence   (B) forgetfulness   (C) intermediary   (D) manacles

25. The owners of the two companies signed a contract to merge the two companies into one.
    (A) manifest   (B) submerge   (C) malinger   (D) join

⁜ -minent = jut out 突出

★★★★★

MP3
72

1751 prominent

a. protruding; protrusive; bulging; jutting / conspicuous; noticeable; discernible; striking; outstanding   凸出的 / 顯著的

[`prɑmənənt]

His protruding chin is his most prominent feature, of which he was very conscious. Therefore, we avoided talking about it.
下巴凸出是他最明顯的特徵，由於他很在意，所以我們避免談論。

★★★★★

1752 imminent

a. impending; looming; menacing; near at hand; in the wind; in the offing; on the horizon   逼近的

[`ɪmənənt]

They went hiking in the cliffs of Mt. Bald, and the trail they were on was very dangerous. However, they didn't know that they were in imminent danger.
他們到博德山的峭壁健行，然而登山小徑十分危險，他們並不知道身處迫切危險中。

★★★★★

1753 eminent

a. distinguished; esteemed; exalted; prominent; revered; honored; noteworthy; renowned; celebrated   崇高的，卓越的

[`ɛmənənt]

Albert Einstein was one of the world's most eminent scientists. He proposed the Theory of Relativity, which was too difficult for laymen to understand.
愛因斯坦是世上最卓越的科學家之一，他提出的相對論是一般人難以理解的。

★★★★★

1754 preeminent

a. peerless; excellent; matchless; eminent; superb   超群的，卓越的

[pri`ɛmənənt]

Regardless of people's opinion of him, I am certain that the lawmaker is a preeminent figure in his own party.
不管別人怎麼看，我相信那名立法委員在法政界是出類拔萃的。

⁜ mini-, minu- = small 小

★★★★★

1755 minute

a. tiny; minuscule; miniature; infinitesimal; microscopic; diminutive   微小的，細微的

[mə`njut]

Of course there are also single-celled organisms, but most organisms are composed of many minute cells.
除單細胞生物外，絕大多數生物都是由許多微小細胞組成的。

★★★★★

1756 **minimum**	*a. the smallest possible amount / minimal*	最少的 / 最低限度
[`mɪnəməm]	The minimum you are allowed to withdraw from this ATM is twenty dollars. If you want to withdraw less than that, you should go to the bank teller. 自動提款機最低提領限額是二十美元,如果想領更少,請至櫃台辦理。	

★★★☆☆

1757 **minimize**	*v. reduce; diminish; prune*	使減至最低限度,低估
[`mɪnə,maɪz]	It is reported that a telecommuting system can minimize tardiness and absenteeism by eliminating commutes. 不用通勤的電子通勤系統據稱可將拖延和曠職情況降到最低。	

★★★☆☆

1758 **miniature**	*a. diminutive; minute; midget; dwarf; pygmy; Lilliputian*	迷你的,小型的
[`mɪnɪətʃə]	Her brother was an amazing general, but only in matters that concerned his miniature toy soldiers. 只要遇到跟迷你玩具士兵有關的事,她弟弟就變成厲害的將軍。	

✣ mis, mit, mit = send 送

★★★★★

1759 **emit**	*v. discharge; eject; emanate; give off; radiate; exude; ooze; vent*	排放,釋放
[ɪ`mɪt]	The government is taking various measures to control those factories which emit toxic gases into the air. 政府採取多種措施控管排放有毒氣體的工廠。	

★★★★★

1760 **dismiss**	*v. discharge; oust; release; lay off*	打發走,開除,打消
[dɪs`mɪs]	Mr. Hoffman couldn't dismiss his dead wife's memory. He often tossed and turned all through the night. 霍夫曼先生無法忘記亡妻,常因此徹夜難眠。	

★★★☆☆

1761 **missionary**	*n. evangelist; preacher; a person doing missionary work*	傳教士
[`mɪʃən,ɛrɪ]	She came to know about Christianity through a missionary who taught her English. Later she also decided to become an evangelist herself. 她從教英文的傳教士那裡認識到基督教教義,隨後也決定成為傳道者。	

★★★☆☆

1762 **remit**	*v. send money in payment*	匯錢,匯寄
[rɪ`mɪt]	Since John was not allowed to remit payment by mail, he had to go to the police station in person to pay the fine. 由於不許匯錢,所以約翰必須親自到警察局繳交罰金。	

★★★★★		
1763 commit	**v.** sentence; confine; shut up; imprison; incarcerate; lock up	犯罪，判處，押送
[kə`mɪt]	From the time of his arrest the man maintained his innocence, but he was committed to prison anyway. 男子自被捕後便堅稱清白，但仍被關進監獄。	

✣ moni = show, tell 顯示，告訴

★★★★★		
1764 monitor	**n.** a television receiver / **v.** watch; observe; supervise	螢幕 / 監控，監測
[`mɑnətə]	After staring at the computer monitor for too long, Robert felt as though his eyes were burning. 羅伯特久盯電腦螢幕後感到雙眼刺痛。	

★★★★☆		
1765 admonish	**v.** give advice to; advise / reprimand	告誡 / 訓誡
[əd`mɑnɪʃ]	When I was young, my father would admonish me to live an honest life. I have tried to live up to his advice. 小時候父親總是告誡我要誠實做人，我也努力遵循教誨。	

★★★☆☆		
1766 premonition	**n.** foreboding; presentiment; hunch; funny feeling	預感
[,primə`nɪʃən]	Awaking from a strange dream, she had a premonition that her husband would be promoted. In the afternoon she received a call from her husband. 她從奇怪的夢裡醒來預感丈夫會升職，下午就接到他的來電。	

★★★★★		
1767 demonstrate	**n.** show; make evident; evince; evidence; exhibit; manifest; display	示範
[`dɛmən,stret]	Whenever you are intending to teach a new skill to someone, whatever that skill may be, it is extremely important that you demonstrate the skill several times so the learner can pick it up correctly. 如果要傳授新技能，無論是哪一種，最重要的是再三示範，好讓學習者確實掌握。	

★★★☆☆		
1768 remonstrate	**v.** make a protest; argue forcibly	抗議，諫勸
[rɪ`mɑnstret]	Laura remonstrated the taxi driver for his rudeness. She had never been confronted with a taxi driver worse than him before. 蘿拉抗議計程車駕駛的無禮，她從未遇過比他更差勁的駕駛。	

✥ mono- = one 單一

★★★☆☆

1769 **monotheism**	*n.* the doctrine that there is only one God	一神論，一神教
[ˋmɑnəθiˌɪzəm]	Christianity is one of the few religions that practice monotheism. Christians believe that there is only one God. 基督教是少數幾個一神論宗教之一，基督徒只信仰一個上帝。	

★★☆☆☆

1770 **monocle**	*n.* a single eyeglass	單片眼鏡
[ˋmɑnək!]	The owner of the store wore a monocle all the time because he thought it looked fashionable, but everyone else thought he looked funny. 商店老闆趕流行配戴單片眼鏡，但大家都覺得看來滑稽。	

★★★★★

1771 **monopolistic**	*a.* of or relating to monopoly	壟斷的，獨占性的
[məˌnɑpəˋlɪstɪk]	The oil market was cornered by a monopolistic company. The company solely controlled the market price of oil. 石油市場由一家單獨操控油價的獨占企業壟斷。	

★★★☆☆

1772 **monotony**	*n.* lack of variety	單調，千篇一律
[məˋnɑtn̩ɪ]	Lewis, who is an overly energetic child, is nearly crushed by the monotony of everyday school life. 過動兒路易斯快被千篇一律的學校生活搞瘋了。	

✥ mut = change 改變

★★★★☆

1773 **mutable**	*a.* liable to change; changeable	易變的，反覆無常的
[ˋmjutəb!]	*"The Prince and the Pauper"* is a story about the mutable nature of fortune. Even a man of a high status can degenerate to a lower status. 《乞丐王子》的故事是有關命運的無常本質，即使是地位崇高者也會淪為卑下者。	

★★★★★

1774 **commuter**	*n.* a person who travels some distance to work	通勤者
[kəˋmjutɚ]	In the mornings and evenings there are so many commuters going to and from work. Naturally there are terrible traffic jams during the rush hour. 從早到晚都有許多上下班通勤者，尖峰時間自然會有可怕的塞車。	

1775 mutual	**a.** *reciprocal; interactive; complementary*	相互的
[`mjutʃʊəl]	It is urgent that people from different provinces understand each other and develop mutual trust. 不同領域者亟需相互瞭解並建立互信。	

★★★★☆

1776 mutation	**n.** *a genetic change; metamorphosis; transformation*	突變，變種
[mju`teʃən]	The toxic waste from the nuclear power plant caused strange mutations to take place in the wildlife nearby. 核能發電廠的有毒廢棄物使附近野生生物產生怪異突變。	

❖ nat = birth 出生，誕生

★★★★☆

1777 prenatal	**a.** *of the period before birth*	產前的，出生前的
[pri`netl]	His mother suffered greatly during the prenatal exercises that the doctors suggested she perform in order to increase her strength during the delivery. 醫生建議他的母親做產前運動以增強分娩體力，讓她吃了很多苦頭。	

★★★★★

1778 natural	**a.** *inherent; inborn / normal*	天然的，與生俱來的 / 正常的
[`nætʃərəl]	Conservationists insist that we should not change the setting from its natural state. They insist that humans try to leave nature as it is. 自然生態保育者堅持人們不應改變自然環境而應任其自然發展。	

★★★★★

1779 native	**a.** *national; domestic; indigenous; inherent; inborn / **n.** aborigine*	祖國的，天生的 / 土著
[`netɪv]	Miss Steiner's native language is German. But she speaks French fluently as well, even though it is not her mother language. 史坦納小姐的母語是德語，但非母語的法語也說得非常流利。	

★★★★☆

1780 prenatally	**ad.** *before birth*	產前地，出生前地
[pri`netlɪ]	She took medicine prenatally, which might have been harmful to the development of her unborn child. 她產前曾服用可能危害腹中胎兒成長的藥物。	

MP3
73

❖ neg = deny, negative 否定

★★★☆☆

| 1781 **negate** | *v. assert the non-existence of* | 否定，使無效 |
| [nɪˋget] | How can we negate God?
我們怎能否定上帝？ | |

★★★★★

| 1782 **neglect** | *v. disregard; ignore; slight; pay no attention to;*
be remiss about; pay no heed to | 忽視，疏忽 |
| [nɪˋglɛkt] | My sister is a very careless driver. She often neglects to pay attention to road signs and she has got several tickets for this month.
我姊姊開車很粗心，經常沒注意看交通標誌，這個月就被開了好幾張罰單。 | |

★★★★★

| 1783 **negative** | *a. pessimistic / opposing; gainsaying* | 負面的 / 否定的 |
| [ˋnɛgətɪv] | Proceeding with the previous plan would only bring negative effects. I think we had better set up a new plan.
繼續執行原先的計畫只會帶來負面影響，我認為最好擬定新計畫。 | |

❖ nihil, nul = zero 沒有

★★★☆☆

| 1784 **nihilist** | *n. skeptic; doubter; cynic* | 虛無主義者，無政府主義者 |
| [ˋnaɪəlɪst] | Adolf Hitler was a power-mad nihilist. He rejected all political or religious authority.
反對所有政治或宗教權威的希特勒是個有權力欲的無政府主義者。 | |

★★☆☆☆

| 1785 **nil** | *n. nothing; zero; naught* | 無，零分 |
| [nɪl] | The Brazilian soccer players were very skillful. The possibilities of our winning seemed to be practically nil.
巴西足球員球技精湛，我方獲勝可能性幾乎為零。 | |

★★★★☆

| 1786 **nullify** | *v. make null; invalidate; cancel* | 使無效，取消 |
| [ˋnʌləˌfaɪ] | Because we could not reach an agreement on that issue, we nullified the entire contract. So the entire issue was cancelled.
我們因未能就該議題達成共識而取消整個合約，因此整起件事也一筆勾銷。 | |

★★★☆☆		
1787 null	*a. invalid; not binding*	無效的，無價值的
[nʌl]	The contract was considered null and void because he accepted employment at a different company. 由於他接受另一家公司的聘雇，因此合約視同無效。	

★★★★☆		
1788 annul	*v. declare invalid; cancel*	取消，宣告～無效
[əˋnʌl]	Since the shipment was delayed without notice, the chairman annulled the contract and he found another distributor. 董事長因無預警的交貨延遲而宣告合約無效，並另行尋找經銷商。	

⁂ noc, nox = poison 毒

★★★★☆		
1789 noxious	*a. harmful; unwholesome*	有害的，有毒的
[ˋnɑkʃəs]	The noxious fumes of the tire burning on the campfire were overpowering and in moments everyone felt sick. 營火晚會上燃燒廢輪胎產生的有毒煙霧令人無法忍受，大家立刻感到不適。	

★★★☆☆		
1790 innocuous	*a. not injurious; harmless; inoffensive*	無毒的，無害的
[ɪˋnɑkjʊəs]	Don't be afraid of this insect. It's innocuous. Even though you are bitten by it, you'll not die. 別怕這隻無毒昆蟲，就算被咬也不會死。	

★★★★★		
1791 innocent	*a. not guilty; guiltless; honest; faultless / unsuspecting; ingenuous; trustful; gullible; credulous; guileless; artless; unsophisticated; naive; childlike*	無辜的，清白的 / 純真無邪的
[ˋɪnəsn̩t]	Sometimes I itch to tell his wife everything I know, but then I think of all the innocent people who would be hurt, and I back off. 有時我很想向他妻子坦白一切，但一想到所有因此受到傷害的無辜者，我就退縮了。	

★★★★☆		
1792 obnoxious	*a. disgusting; offensive; sickening; loathsome; obscene; nasty*	討厭的，可憎的
[əbˋnɑkʃəs]	She wished she could shower horrible curses on this person, who was the most obnoxious person she had ever met. 她真希望能詛咒這個自己見過最討厭的人。	

✛ noct-, nox- = night 夜晚

★★★★★

1793 **equinox**	**n.** *the time or date at which the sun crosses the celestial equator, when day and night are of equal length*	晝夜平分時點，春（秋）分
[`ikwəˌnɑks]	It is interesting to note that the equinox happens twice each year, once in March and once in September. 有趣的是每年有兩次晝夜平分時點，分別是三月的春分和九月的秋分。	

★★★★☆

1794 **nocturnal**	**a.** *active by night / nightly*	夜間活動的 / 夜間的
[nɑk`tɜnəl]	Owls and bats are nocturnal animals since they sleep during the day and stay awake during the night. 貓頭鷹和蝙蝠都是日間休息晚間活動的夜行動物。	

★★☆☆☆

1795 **nocturne**	**n.** *a picture of a night scene / a short composition of a romantic nature*	夜景畫 / 夜曲
[`nɑktɜn]	The artist's nocturne was a black canvas, called simply "Night with No Light." People thought that it made no sense. 藝術家的夜景畫是一幅名為「無光之夜」的漆黑油畫，大家都覺得沒道理。	

✛ nov = new 新

★★★★★

1796 **novel**	**a.** *new; unusual; unfamiliar; unconventional; fresh*	新的，新奇的
[`nɑvl]	To create an automatic page-turner would be a novel idea. 創造自動翻頁器會是個新奇點子。	

★★★★★

1797 **novice**	**n.** *beginner; neophyte; newcomer; proselyte; tyro; amateur; apprentice; greenhorn; fledgling; rookie*	初學者，新手
[`nɑvɪs]	I'm just a novice as far as fencing is concerned. I have just started to take lessons, and teaching some other person is out of the question. 我只是個剛開始學習擊劍的新手，不可能教別人。	

★☆☆☆☆

1798 **novitiate**	**n.** *the period of being a novice*	見習，見習期
[no`vɪʃət]	He knew that he would someday be a full-fledged monk in the Order of Saint Francis, but he would have to survive the rigors of his novitiate years first. 他知道自己有朝一日將成為訓練有素的聖方濟會修道士，但必須先捱過嚴苛的見習生活。	

★★★★★

1799 **innovative**	*a. bringing in new methods*	創新的
[`ɪnə͵vetɪv]	My neighbor Charles was not a successful inventor because he was unable to come up with an original thought himself. He had to be satisfied with innovative improvements of things that already existed. 缺乏原創想法的鄰居查爾斯不是成功發明者，只能安於現有發明的創新改良。	

★★★☆☆

1800 **novelty**	*n. a new or unusual thing*	新穎事物，新奇經驗
[`navḷtɪ]	Most young people are interested in novelty; they usually search for new things: new cars, new games and new places. 多數年輕人對新穎事物感興趣，常會尋找新車、新遊戲和新地點等新鮮事物。	

Tea Time... ☕

<Medieval story> Sanguine **From sanguis (blood), one of the four imaginary humors of the body which was believed in medieval times to cause cheerfulness.**	〈來自中古世紀神話〉血紅的 本字源自中古世紀相信能產生愉悅感的人體四種體液之一的血液。（註：中古世紀相信人體由血液、痰、黃膽汁和黑膽汁等四種體液比例決定其體質和性格，四大性格分別是熱情、遲鈍、暴躁和憂鬱。）

sanguine [`sæŋgwɪn] *a. optimistic; confident/ florid; ruddy* │ 樂天的，樂觀的 / 氣色紅潤的，血紅色的

Her father was an optimistic kind of person; He had a sanguine outlook on everything. He firmly believes that his spinster daughter will find a handsome man to marry.

她的樂天父親樂觀看待一切，堅信待字閨中良久的女兒會嫁給俊男。

sanguinary [`sæŋgwɪn͵ɛrɪ] *a. bloody; bloodthirsty* │ 血腥的，殺戮的，血淋淋的

The sanguinary actions of the Crusaders of the 12th century in Jerusalem have been characterized with the statement that the "streets ran ankle deep with blood."

十二世紀十字軍在耶路撒冷展開的殺戮行動據稱血流成河。

1

Complete each word by filling in the blank with proper spelling so that it has the same meaning as suggested. Then please write the meaning of each word in Chinese.

1. 凸出的 = p r o _ _ _ _ _ _
2. 迫近的 = i m _ _ _ _ _ _
3. 最低限度 = _ _ _ _ m u m
4. 打消 = d i s _ _ _ _
5. 傳教士 = _ _ _ s i o n a r y
6. 押送 = c o m _ _ _
7. 告誡 = a d _ _ _ _ s h
8. 示範 = d e _ _ _ s t r a t e
9. 獨占性的 = _ _ _ _ p o l i s t i c
10. 無常的 = _ _ _ a b l e

11. mutation = _____
12. prenatal = _____
13. negate = _____
14. negative = _____
15. nihilist = _____
16. noxious = _____
17. innocent = _____
18. nocturnal = _____
19. novice = _____
20. innovative = _____

2

Choose a word that best completes the sentence.

21. Myth has it that a crow's cry bodes a(n) _____ rain.

    (A) minute   (B) prominent   (C) monopolistic   (D) imminent

22. My nephew's hobby is collecting _____ model cars.

    (A) impending   (B) miniature   (C) natural   (D) inborn

3

The highlighted word is closest in meaning to which of the following?

23. Young people are interested in novel things.

    (A) guileless   (B) new   (C) negative   (D) innocent

24. Daughter: Wonderful Daddy. You'll surely know What I Want. Why don't you remit me some soon?

    (A) send   (B) commit   (C) demonstrate   (D) admonish

25. The volcano is now emitting lava and ash.

    (A) discharging   (B) negating   (C) remonstrating   (D) dismissing

Practice Test 03

1 The highlighted word is closest in meaning to which of the following?

1. My little nephew really abhors an injection . Even a doctor's mention of it makes him rant and rave.

    (A) a hydrant

    (B) an idiot

    (C) a lever

    (D) a shot

2. Mosquitoes were humming relentlessly all through the night. So the campers had no choice but to come out of their tents and plunge into the water.

    (A) doggedly

    (B) locally

    (C) literally

    (D) loquaciously

3. Sue's malnutrition has been caused by her insufficient intake of food and an unbalanced diet.

    (A) mania

    (B) undernourishment

    (C) majority

    (D) luster

4. The IRS has noticed that the rich man amassed most of his fortune through land speculation.

    (A) minimized

    (B) emitted

    (C) accumulated

    (D) malingered

5. A passenger was determined to admonish the bus driver to drive more carefully and began to walk up to the driver, when the driver stepped on the gas abruptly.

    (A) commit

    (B) advise

    (C) remit

    (D) submerge

2 Please answer the following questions.

Sharing

In recent years in a small village in India, many people, the majority of whom were children, were reportedly killed by an elusive serial killer. For several months the villagers trembled with fear, believing that they were cursed by a malevolent spirit. They took various measures to avert the disaster, but to no avail. At last, when almost all of the children of the village were sacrificed, scientists were brought in and a relentless search for clues started. The mystery of the serial murders began to be unveiled when a child bore witness to a wolf's attack on his cousin. He saw his cousin being attacked and dragged by a wolf. He rushed to the wolf and wrestled with it in a desperate attempt to rescue his cousin. Luckily, both of the children survived the fight. Finally, the villagers and scientists knew that the serial killer was a wolf. It was also found that some farmers of the village had set fire to that wolf's burrow and killed the cubs because the wolf caused some damage to their crops. Of course, this must be a very exceptional case, but we can get an important lesson from what happened: we humans should not try to monopolize the natural setting provided for all living things.

6. **The word majority is closest in meaning to which of the following?**
   (A) malady
   (B) bulk
   (C) mutation
   (D) commuter

7. **The word elusive is closest in meaning to which of the following?**
   (A) eminent
   (B) juvenile
   (C) evasive
   (D) lustrous

8. **The word malevolent is closest in meaning to which of the following?**
   (A) minute
   (B) nocturnal
   (C) innocent
   (D) evil

9. **The word relentless is closest in meaning to which of the following?**
   (A) rigid
   (B) lenient
   (C) eligible
   (D) local

10. **The word monopolize is closest in meaning to which of the following?**
    (A) have the largest share
    (B) make a protest
    (C) assert the nonexistence of
    (D) come forth

❖ nom, nym, onomato = name; call 名字；稱呼

★★★☆☆

MP3 74

1801 ignominiously

[ˌɪɡnəˈmɪnɪəslɪ]

ad. shamefully

不光彩地，不名譽地

The incumbent president had expected a landslide triumph, but he was ignominiously defeated in the election.
現任總統原本預料將獲得壓倒性勝利，但卻在選戰中不光彩地落選。

★★★★★

1802 nominate

[ˈnɑməˌnet]

v. name; appoint; designate; recommend

提名

Mr. Baker was nominated for the 'Best Citizen' award. I'm sure he will receive the award. He has dedicated his time and efforts to the development of the city.
貝克先生獲提名角逐「最佳市民獎」，我相信必能得獎，因為他為了都市發展奉獻時間和精力。

★★★★☆

1803 pseudonym

[ˈsudṇˌɪm]

n. alias; pen-name; an assumed name

假名，化名

His writing was so erotic and controversial that he was forced to use a pseudonym in order to hide his identity.
他的作品既煽情又有爭議性，因此被迫使用假名隱藏身分。

★★★☆☆

1804 heteronym

[ˈhɛtərəˌnɪm]

n. a word with the same spelling as another but with a different meaning and pronunciation

拼法相同但異音異義的字

Heteronyms, such as "bow" (a weapon that fires arrows) and "bow" (a gesture of respect) can be very confusing to someone learning English because they are spelled the same, but have very different meanings and pronunciations.
拼法相同但發音和意義各異的字會讓學習英文者感到很困擾，例如「弓箭」的 bow 和「鞠躬」的 bow。

★★★★☆

1805 synonym

[ˈsɪnəˌnɪm]

n. a word that means exactly the same as another

同義字

'Detest' is a synonym for 'hate.' They have the same meaning.
Detest（憎惡）是 hate（憎恨）的同義字，兩者意義相同。

★★★☆☆

1806 onomatopoeia

[ˌɑnəˌmætəˈpiə]

n. the formation of a word from a sound associated with what is named

擬聲字

'Bang-bang,' 'buzz,' and 'thud' are examples of onomatopoeia. They are words coined in association with sounds.
「砰砰」、「嗡嗡」和「轟隆」等造字都是和聲音相關的擬聲字。

★★★☆☆

1807 anonymous

a. nameless　　　　　　　　　　　　　　　　　　　　　匿名的，不具名的

[ə`nɑnəməs]

Reporters announced that there was an eyewitness to the murder, but they didn't reveal the name because the person requested to remain anonymous.

記者聲稱該起兇案有一名目擊者但未透露姓名，因其要求匿名。

✥ ob- = against 反對

★★★☆☆

1808 object

v. protest; raise objection; argue; refuse　　　　　　　　　　反對

[`ɑbdʒɪkt]

What gives you the right to object to our proposition when you cannot even suggest a new one? You should follow our suggestion.

提不出新建議的你憑什麼反對我方提議？你應聽取我方建議。

★★★★★

1809 obstruct

v. block; check; hamper; slow; impede; retard;　　　　　　堵塞，妨礙
hinder; thwart; interrupt

[əb`strʌkt]

After the accident, his car was stuck in the middle of the road and left to obstruct traffic until it was towed.

意外發生後他的車被困在路當中妨礙了交通，直到被拖離現場。

★★★★★

1810 objective

n. target; goal; aim; purpose / a. impartial; dispassionate　目標／客觀的

[əb`dʒɛktɪv]

Our main objective is to export sixty percent of our products. Presently we are selling about half of our products overseas.

我們的主要目標是外銷六成產品，現階段我們約有五成商品賣到海外。

★★★☆☆

1811 obscene

a. dirty / offensive; outrageous; repulsive;　　　　　　　　下流的／可憎的
repugnant; obnoxious

[əb`sin]

These days there are many obscene commercials on television, and so we often have to turn the channel.

近來有許多不入流的電視廣告使我們得經常轉台。

★★★★★

1812 obstacle

n. impediment; hindrance; obstruction; hurdle;　　　　　　障礙
stumbling block; barrier

[`ɑbstəkl]

The fact that he had no job or a foreseeable bright future had always been an obstacle in his path to getting married.

他既失業又看不見美好未來的事實常成為婚姻路上障礙。

✛ opt(t) = eye, see　眼睛，看

★★★☆☆

| 1813 **myopic** | *a. short-sighted; nearsighted* | 眼光短淺的，狹隘的 |

[maɪˋɑpɪk]

Myopic quests serving partisan and selfish interests should be avoided. Representatives should give priority to matters related to the life of the general public.

為政黨和自身利益服務的狹隘追求都應避免，民代們應優先謀求社會大眾福祉。

★★★★★

| 1814 **optical** | *a. of sight; visual / of or relating to optics* | 視力的／光學的 |

[ˋɑptɪkl]

Because his glasses were not well fitted, the old man decided to go to the optical store to get them adjusted. Instead, he wound up in a public bath.

老人因眼鏡不合適而決定拿到眼鏡行調整，結果卻跑到了公共澡堂。

★★☆☆☆

| 1815 **autopsy** | *n. postmortem; necropsy* | 驗屍，屍體解剖 |

[ˋɔtɑpsɪ]

The autopsy done on the murder victim confirmed investigator's suspicions that the woman had died of arsenic poisoning.

兇案被害者的驗屍報告證實調查人員的懷疑，該名女子是死於砷中毒。

★★★★★

| 1816 **optics** | *n. the scientific study of sight and the behavior of light* | 光學 |

[ˋɑptɪks]

He studied optics at university, and after graduation he decided to open an optical store. He was happy to help people see things clearly with the glasses he designed for them.

他在大學念光學，畢業後決定開眼鏡行。能藉由自己設計的眼鏡幫助別人看清東西，讓他感到高興。

✛ or = speak　說

★☆☆☆☆

| 1817 **orator** | *n. a person making a speech; an eloquent public speaker* | 演說者，雄辯家 |

[ˋɔrətə]

It is said that New York's 42nd street is inhabited by all kinds of street people, from homeless kids, to street corner orators, and to junkies.

據說紐約四十二街住著流浪兒、街頭演說者和吸毒者等各種遊民。

★☆☆☆☆

1818 oration   *n. a formal speech*   正式演說，演講

[ɔ`reʃən]

The speaker's oration outlasted last year's entire conference. Eventually, many of the members started to yawn.

演講者的演說比去年整場會議時間還要長，最後許多人開始呵欠連連。

★★★★☆

1819 inexorable   *a. relentless; obstinate*   無動於衷的，不為所動的

[ɪn`ɛksərəbl]

Her father was inexorable regarding her curfew, and no amount of persuasion would change his mind.

父親對她的門禁規定不為所動，任何勸說都無法改變他的心意。

❖ ortho = correct 正確

★★★★★

1820 orthodox   *a. accepted; authoritative; official; standard; established; conventional; conservative*   傳統的

[`ɔrθə͵dɑks]

My school follows a very orthodox methodology, whereas Daniel's school is considered liberal and free, which is why his school usually has more students enrolled.

我就讀的學校採取傳統教學方式，丹尼爾的學校則公認開明自由，因此常有較多學生入學。

★★★☆☆

1821 orthodontics   *n. the treatment of irregularities in the teeth and jaws*   齒顎矯正

[ɔrθə`dɑntɪks]

After finishing his degree in dentistry, my nephew went back to school to specialize in orthodontics.

姪子拿到牙醫學位後回學校專攻齒顎矯正。

★★★☆☆

1822 orthopedics   *n. the branch of medicine dealing with the correction of deformities of bones or muscles*   整形外科

[͵ɔrθə`pidɪks]

Orthopedics is the branch of surgery dealing with the treatment of deformities and injuries of the bones and muscles.

整形外科是外科手術分支之一，負責整治骨骼和肌肉的畸形與傷殘。

★★★★☆

1823 unorthodox   *a. unconventional; heretical; offbeat; way-out*   非正統的，異端的

[ʌn`ɔrθədɑks]

Nancy behaved and dressed in a very unorthodox manner, which displeased her traditional parents.

南西的奇裝異服和怪異舉止觸怒保守雙親。

✣ out- = surpass, out 勝過，外，出

MP3
75

★★★☆☆

1824 outstrip

[aut`strip]

***v.** surpass in competition; outdo; outdistance*

超過，勝過

If we do not work with all of our might, others will outstrip us in the race. Therefore, we should not be lazy.
若不全力以赴將會被他人超越，因此我們不可怠惰。

★★★★☆

1825 outgrow

[aut`gro]

***v.** grow too big for; leave behind a childish habit as one matures*

長大而不再～

I hope my nephew will outgrow his bed-wetting habit when he begins school. I don't need peculiar abstract works of art anymore.
希望姪子開始上學後能改掉尿床習慣，我不需要古怪抽象的藝術品。（註：指床單上的尿漬）

★★★☆☆

1826 outdistance

[aut`distəns]

***v.** leave a competitor behind*

領先，遠超過

Mr. Brown hopes that his novel *The Bear* will outdistance *The Good Earth* in its circulation. He has spent almost ten years completing the novel.
伯朗先生希望以近十年時間寫成的小說《熊》的銷量能遠超過《美好大地》。

★★★☆☆

1827 outweigh

[aut`we]

***v.** exceed in weight, value, importance or influence; preponderate over; outbalance*

勝過

Computers seem to outweigh human intellect. They are employed even for extremely complicated calculations.
能處理極複雜計算的電腦似乎比人類聰明。

★★★★★

1828 outlive

[aut`liv]

***v.** live longer than*

比～長命

Mrs. Swanson outlived her husband by 20 years, living up to 102. For the past twenty years she has always carried a picture of her husband.
活到一百零二歲的史旺森太太比先生多活了二十年，她一直以來都隨身攜帶亡夫的照片。

❖ pan-, panto- = all 全部

★★★★★

1829 **pantomime**	*n.* the use of gestures and facial expression to convey meaning, especially in drama and dance	以手勢示意
[`pæntə‚maɪm]	A pantomime is often the only way to make oneself understood when one person, who doesn't speak the local language, asks directions from a local person. 不懂當地語言者問路時，唯一能讓他理解的方式常是以手勢指出方向。	

★★★★★

1830 **panorama**	*n.* an unbroken view of a surrounding region	全景，全貌
[‚pænə`ræmə]	He paid a lot of money for a room from which he could see the panorama of the Rocky Mountains and the surrounding lakes. 他支付大筆的錢訂房以觀看洛磯山全貌和鄰近湖泊。	

★★★☆☆

1831 **panacea**	*n.* a universal remedy	萬靈丹
[‚pænə`sɪə]	There is no panacea that cures all diseases. If a universal remedy existed, there would be no one dead except for a person who dies while struggling to get the remedy. 世上沒有能治所有疾病的萬靈丹，如果真的有，除了努力想得到藥的人之外無人會死。	

❖ para- = side by side, pair 並肩，一起

★★★★★

1832 **comparison**	*n.* the act or an instance of comparing	比較，對照
[kəm`pærəsṇ]	The younger brother did not appreciate the comparison made by his parent between him and his brother. 弟弟不喜歡雙親拿他跟哥哥做比較。	

★★★★☆

1833 **paraphrase**	*v.* express the meaning of a passage in other words	釋義，改寫
[`pærə‚frez]	Many people try to paraphrase Shakespeare, but they always use more words than Shakespeare wrote. 許多人試圖改寫莎士比亞作品，卻無法比原著更精鍊。	

★★★★★

[1834] **parallel**	*a.* side by side and having the same distance continuously between them / similar; corresponding; congruent; analogous	平行的／相似的
[ˋpærəˌlɛl]	He drove east along a road that was parallel to the one he wanted to be on. He was going in the right direction, but was too far north. 他向東平行行駛於想前往的路上，方向雖正確但太偏北。	

★★★★★

[1835] **parasite**	*n.* an organism living in or on another and benefiting at the expense of the other	寄生蟲，食客
[ˋpærəˌsaɪt]	Pseudo-journalists are often considered social parasites. They are always trying to find someone whom they can take advantage of. 總在伺機利用他人的假記者常被視為社會寄生蟲。	

✢ pass, path = feel, emotion 感覺，情緒

★★☆☆☆

[1836] **pathos**	*n.* a quality in speech, writing, events, etc. that excites pity or sadness	悲愴性
[ˋpeθɑs]	Her play was filled with pathos. It dealt with the homeless and poor people and the troubles they have in life. 她的戲劇充滿悲愴性，該劇描繪遊民和窮人的艱苦生活。	

★★☆☆☆

[1837] **apathetic**	*a.* having or showing no emotion or interest; indifferent	無動於衷的
[ˌæpəˋθɛtɪk]	I was very excited about the new concept, but when I told my boss about it, his apathetic reaction gave me the impression that he didn't think it was all that good of an idea. 我對於新點子感到興奮，但告訴老闆後，他的無動於衷讓我覺得他不認為這是個好點子。	

★★★★☆

[1838] **passion**	*n.* ardor; eagerness; intensity; fervor; zeal; zest; enthusiasm; fanaticism; mania; craze; predilection	熱愛，熱情
[ˋpæʃən]	Mr. Bullis had a passion for teaching, which is why he was in school for forty years, earning a small sum of money that was hardly enough to support his family. 布利斯先生熱愛教書，所以能執教四十年但微薄薪水卻不足以養家糊口。	

★★★★★

1839 sympathetic

a. compassionate; solicitous; warm-hearted; tender-hearted; well-meaning; good-natured; empathetic　　同情的

[ˌsɪmpəˈθɛtɪk]

Shane was sympathetic to his neighbor who had great misfortune. His neighbor's house was destroyed by a tornado.

夏恩對鄰居的重大不幸深表同情，鄰居的住家毀於龍捲風。

★★★☆☆

1840 impassive

a. deficient in or incapable of feeling emotion; serene; unemotional; callous; stony　　無感覺的，無表情的

[ɪmˈpæsɪv]

A successful poker player must learn to be impassive during the game and give away no clues about the cards in his hand to the other players.

成功的撲克牌玩家須學會泰然自若，不露出任何線索讓對手得知自己手中的牌。

❖ pater-, patr- = father; fatherland 父親，祖國

★★★★★

1841 patriotic

a. devoted to and ready to support his or her country　　愛國的

[ˌpetrɪˈɑtɪk]

Jacob was very patriotic, and when the war broke out, he was the first in line to join the army and defend his home.

雅各非常愛國，戰爭爆發後便率先從軍保家衛國。

★★☆☆☆

1842 repatriate

v. restore a person to his or her native land　　遣返

[riˈpetrɪˌet]

The newcomer had to be repatriated since he did not have a proper visa. He did not know that it was already expired.

新到移民因無有效簽證而須遭遣返，他不知道已經過期了。

★★★★★

1843 patron

n. benefactor; supporter; advocate; champion; sponsor; booster　　贊助者，資助者

[ˈpetrən]

Since he invested so much money in the new theater, he was given the title, "Patron of the Arts."

埃及之旅最讓舅舅喜愛的就是參觀法老王地下墓穴。

★★★☆☆

1844 patrician

n. aristocrat　　貴族，顯貴

[pəˈtrɪʃən]

Julius Caesar had a patrician background, and therefore, it would have been easy for him to be elected to the Roman Senate, but instead he chose to become Emperor.

出身貴族的凱撒可輕易加入羅馬元老院，但他卻選擇成為大帝。

| 1845 **paternal** | *a. fatherly; patrimonial* | 父親的，由父親遺傳的 |

[pə`tɜnl]

Color blindness is not a paternal defect; it is a maternal one. The defect is handed down from a mother, not from a father.

色盲不是遺傳自父親的缺陷而是得自母親。這種缺陷是由母親而非父親傳給下一代的。

Tea Time... ☕

<Roman legend> Colossus
A gigantic statue of Apollo set at the entrance to the harbor of Rhodes and included among the seven wonders of the ancient world.

〈來自羅馬神話〉太陽神阿波羅巨像
羅德斯島港口矗立的太陽神阿波羅巨大雕像，名列世界七大奇觀之一。（註：此巨大青銅雕像據稱高達三十六公尺，後因地震倒塌，殘骸遭變賣或搬運一空。Colossus 的形容詞 colossal 便帶有「巨像的，巨像似的，龐大的」之意，引申為「少有的，異常的」。）

---

colossal [kə`lɑsl] *a. enormous; gigantic; huge; like a colossus in size* │ 巨大的，驚人的，可觀的

One of the mysteries concerning the Egyptian Pyramids is that 2,300,000 15-ton colossal blocks of stones, which were carried from approximately 800km away, were fitted together so precisely that even the point of a knife can not be inserted between them.

埃及金字塔的謎團之一是將兩百三十萬個十五噸重的大石塊搬運到約八十萬公尺高度，並極精確地疊放在一起，即使是刀尖也無法插入縫隙。

1 Complete each word by filling in the blank with proper spelling so that it has the same meaning as suggested. Then please write the meaning of each word in Chinese.

1. 同義字 = s y n o _ _ _
2. 擬聲字 = o _ _ _ a t o p o e i a
3. 反對 = _ _ j e c t
4. 妨礙 = _ _ s t r u c t
5. 眼光短淺的 = m y _ _ i c
6. 光學 = _ _ _ i c s
7. 正式演說 = _ _ a t i o n
8. 不為所動的 = i n e x _ _ a b l e
9. 傳統的 = _ _ _ _ _ d o x
10. 齒顎矯正 = _ _ _ _ _ d o n t i c s

11. outstrip = _____
12. outlive = _____
13. pantomime = _____
14. panacea = _____
15. comparison = _____
16. parallel = _____
17. apathetic = _____
18. patriotic = _____
19. impassive = _____
20. paternal = _____

2 Choose a word that best completes the sentence.

21. **He got an _____ letter, and so he did not know who sent it.**
    (A) orthodox   (B) optical   (C) anonymous   (D) objective

22. **My little brother has _____ his jacket. He is now interested in mine.**
    (A) outgrown   (B) outlived   (C) repatriated   (D) paraphrased

23. **An emperor penguin is famous for its _____ affection.**
    (A) impassive   (B) paternal   (C) apathetic   (D) patriotic

3 The highlighted word is closest in meaning to which of the following?

24. **The inexorable heat of a desert forces many animals to sleep below the surface of the earth during the day.**
    (A) unorthodox   (B) unconventional   (C) impartial   (D) relentless

25. **Tortoise: You know, they say that one of my ancestors outstripped a rabbit.**
    Rabbit: You know, every rabbit does not sleep in the middle of a race.
    (A) protested   (B) blocked   (C) outdistanced   (D) outgrew

❖ pec, pic, piq, punc, pung = prick; point 刺，點

MP3
76

★★★★★

1846 punctuate

[`pʌŋktʃuˌet]

v. insert punctuation marks in　　　　　　　不時打斷，加標點

His campus life was punctuated by frequent rallies. He and some other righteous students were convicted of treason.

他的校園生活被頻繁的集會遊行打斷，和其他幾位富有正義感的學生一起被判謀反。

★★★☆☆

1847 piquant

[`pikənt]

a. pungent; keen; acute　　　　　　　　　辛辣的，夠刺激的

Many women like to gossip, but enjoying piquant gossip is not restricted to just women. My neighbor Jack is an example.

許多女性喜歡聊八卦，但熱衷刺激八卦的可不限女性，鄰居傑克就是一例。

★★★★☆

1848 puncture

[`pʌŋktʃə]

v. pierce; penetrate; perforate　　　　　　　刺穿，戳破

I had hardly finished blowing up a balloon for my nephew when he punctured it with a ball-point pen. The average lifespan of a balloon was about twenty seconds.

我還沒吹好氣球給姪子，他就用原子筆把它戳破了，氣球平均壽命約二十秒。

★★★★☆

1849 picayune

[ˌpɪkəˈjun]

a. petty; insignificant　　　　　　　　琐碎的，無足輕重的

I think it's folly to lay any emphasis on these picayune details. They are not important enough to be talked about at the moment.

我認為強調這些琐碎細節是愚蠢的，現階段它們無足輕重，因此毋需討論。

★★★★☆

1850 pungent

[`pʌndʒənt]

a. astringent; caustic; stinging; sharp; acrid; acrimonious; sarcastic　尖銳的

The senator was very upset by a pungent remark from a reporter, who asked the senator if he had been involved in smuggling.

參議員因記者詢問是否涉嫌走私的尖銳言詞而深感心煩。

★★★★★

1851 prick

[prɪk]

n. the act of pricking / v. puncture; pierce; punch; perforate　刺／戳破

It only takes one sharp prick of a needle to burst a balloon, no matter how thick the plastic is.

無論氣球塑膠有多厚，只要用針一刺便可戳破。

★★★★★

1852 punctual

[`pʌŋktʃuəl]

a. observant of the appointed time; on time; prompt　　準時的，守時的

A notice at a faculty lounge; "Your baby whopping cranes" are waiting for you with a long neck, with their stomachs growling. Please be punctual in feeding 'em.

教職員休息室有張公告：「你的長脖子寶寶」肚子咕嚕咕嚕地引頸盼望著你，敬請準時餵食。

★★★☆☆

1853 acupuncture | *n. a method of treating various conditions by pricking the skin with needles* | 針灸治療

[`ækjʊ͵pʌŋktʃə]

To kill pain, some dentists use acupuncture, but this method requires years of training and some trust from their patients.
部分牙醫利用針灸止痛，但此法需要多年訓練和醫病互信。

★★★★☆

1854 punch | *v. puncture; perforate; pierce* | 剪（票），打（洞）

[pʌntʃ]

The train conductor came up to me to punch my ticket. But I could not find it. I even took off my shoes.
列車車掌前來剪票，但我連鞋都脫了也找不到車票。

★★★★★

1855 woodpecker | *n. any bird of the family Picidae that taps tree trunks in search of insects* | 啄木鳥

[`wʊd͵pɛkə]

When we hear woodpeckers tap their beaks on the tree, we often worry that their beaks might break.
我們聽到啄木鳥敲擊樹木時，常擔心牠們可能會因此折斷鳥嘴。

✣ ped, pod = foot 足

★★★★★

1856 pedestal | *n. base; foundation; platform; stand* | 基座，臺座

[`pɛdɪstl̩]

The Statue of Liberty is standing on a pedestal on which a famous poem *"The New Colossus"* is inscribed.
自由女神像站在刻有名詩〈新巨像〉的基座上。

★★★★★

1857 pedal | *n. foot-operated levers* | 踏板

[`pɛdl̩]

I replaced the pedals on my 10-speed bicycle with a special kind which racers use. With the new pedals, I could ride my bike much faster.
我將十速腳踏車踏板換成賽車專用的，有了新踏板就能騎快點。

★★★☆☆

1858 peddle | *v. sell goods as a pedlar; sell (drugs) illegally* | 沿街叫賣

[`pɛdl̩]

Floyd was peddling little trinkets from door to door. Many village women would gather around him whenever he came.
每當沿街叫賣小飾品的佛洛伊德出現，就會有許多村婦聚集在他身邊。

★★★★☆

1859 pedigree

['pɛdə,gri]

n. descent; ancestry; genealogy; blood line; extraction; lineage; stock; heritage; family

家世,血統

Before the lady bought the very expensive dog, she had a private investigator check its pedigree to see if it really was descended from the dog that the King of Morocco once owned.

該名貴婦在以高價購買名犬前,先請私家偵探調查其血統是否的確是摩洛哥國王愛犬的後代。

★★★★☆

1860 tripod

['traɪpɑd]

n. a three-legged stand for supporting a camera

三腳架

My hobby is taking pictures, and my brother bought me a good tripod for my birthday. It was stable enough to support my medium-format camera.

我的興趣是攝影,哥哥送我一個很好的三腳架作為生日禮物,它足以牢牢撐托我的中幅相機。

★★★★☆

1861 expeditiously

[ˌɛkspɪ'dɪʃəslɪ]

ad. quickly; rapidly; swiftly

迅速地

Todd let a real good opportunity slip right through his fingers when he didn't act expeditiously enough to obtain the exclusive contract.

陶德未能迅速拿下獨家經營合約,平白讓大好機會從指縫間溜走。

★★★☆☆

1862 peddler

['pɛdlə]

n. pedlar; dealer

小販

When the old peddler came around trying to sell his wares, the people of the small village came out to see if he brought something new.

年邁小販前來兜售商品時,小村的村民跑出來看看它有沒有帶來新鮮貨。

★★★★★

1863 impede

[ɪm'pid]

v. retard; hinder; obstruct; bar; block; thwart; check; baulk; inhibit; hamper; foil

妨礙,阻撓

The company is trying to put together a very important business deal, but its rival companies are doing everything to impede its efforts and ruin its chances of succeeding in business.

該公司正努力談成一筆極重要的交易,但對手卻全力阻撓並破壞生意談成的機會。

★★★★★

1864 pedestrian

[pə'dɛstrɪən]

n. walker; stroller; rambler / *a.* boring; dull; banal; mundane; commonplace; tedious; monotonous; hackneyed; trite; spiritless

行人 / 沉悶的,平凡的

Being a pedestrian means that you don't have to pay for car insurance, or gasoline, but you have to buy new walking shoes frequently.

當行人,可以不必付車險或油費,但得經常購買新的步行鞋。

✤ pend, pens = hang 懸掛

Chapter

1
2
3
4
5

★★★★☆

1865 **pendant**	*n. a hanging jewel attached to a necklace*	垂飾

[`pɛndənt]

The pendant which was hung from a gold chain glimmered with a clear, red luster. It looked like a real ruby.

金鍊垂飾上閃耀著紅色光澤，看來像是真正的紅寶石。

★★★★☆

1866 **pending**	*a. unsettled; undetermined; undecided; on ice; in the air* 懸而未決的，迫近的

[`pɛndɪŋ]

There still remain a lot of complex issues pending between the two neighboring countries. Both of them are trying to resolve their problems.

兩鄰國間仍存有不少複雜議題懸而未決，雙方都試圖要解決問題。

★★★★☆

1867 **pendulum**	*n. a weight suspended so as to swing freely*	鐘擺

[`pɛndʒələm]

Before mechanical watches were invented, people used a pendulum to regulate the speed of a clock mechanism.

機械錶發明前，人們用鐘擺來調節時鐘機械裝置的速度。

★★★★★

1868 **independent**	*a. not depending on another person; self-reliant*	獨立自主的

[ˌɪndɪ`pɛndənt]

Many American parents teach their children from birth to be independent by making them sleep in separate rooms from their parents, and by teaching their kids how to solve their own problems.

許多美國父母從小教育子女獨立自主，不但不和父母同睡一室，也教導孩子們如何解決問題。

✤ per- = through, thorough 穿過，橫越

★★★★★

1869 **perforate**	*v. make a hole; pierce; drill; bore; penetrate*	穿孔，貫穿

[`pɝfəˌret]

After the captain emptied the gun, he examined the target he had been shooting at, and was proud to see his ability to perforate it.

隊長清槍後檢查自己射擊的槍靶，對貫穿目標感到自豪。

★★★★★

1870 **persistent**	*a. tenacious; persisting; continuous; interminable; incessant; unswerving*	固執的

[pə`sɪstənt]

Small kids are persistent questioners. They usually keep on asking questions. One day my niece asked me how come a lamb doesn't shrink in size even after it gets wet in the rain.

小孩是固執的發問者，他們總是不斷提問。某日姪女問我為什麼羊淋了雨不會縮小。

★★★★☆

| 1871 **perplex** | *v. confuse; bewilder; puzzle; baffle; disconcert; stun; dumbfound* | 使困惑，使混亂 |

[pə`plɛks]

It perplexed and annoyed the boy not to be able to solve the math homework problem. At last he asked his father to help him. But his father was also confused.

男童無法解開數學家庭作業題目而感到困惑煩惱，最後只好拿去問父親，但父親也不懂。

★★★★☆

| 1872 **perverse** | *a. stubborn; wayward; intractable; wilful; cantankerous; bad-tempered* | 倔強任性的 / 反常的 |

[pə`vɜs]

The flippant child seemed to be in a perverse mood. It seemed to be impossible to control him. He insisted on doing things in his own way.

這個沒有禮貌的孩童似乎任性而難以管教，他堅持要順他的意去做。

✛ peri- = around 圍繞

★★★☆☆

MP3 77

| 1873 **periscope** | *n. an apparatus with a tube and mirrors or prisms, by which an observer in a trench or a submerged submarine can see things* | 潛望鏡 |

[`pɛrə,skop]

The submarine captain looked through the periscope and found out that a giant warship was approaching.

潛艇指揮官透過潛望鏡發現大型軍艦逼近。

★★☆☆☆

| 1874 **periphery** | *n. the boundary of an area; an outer or surrounding region; outskirts; edge; perimeter* | 周圍 |

[pə`rɪfərɪ]

Victor saw something on the periphery of his vision which he was convinced was the ghost of his dead grandmother.

維克多相信自己眼角餘光瞥見的是死去祖母的鬼魂。

★★★★★

| 1875 **perimeter** | *n. boundary; border; margin; periphery; verge* | 周邊 |

[pə`rɪmətə]

The army set guards around the perimeter of the captain's tent so that no one would disturb the secret meeting.

軍隊戍守在指揮官營帳四周，因此無人能打擾機密會議。

✢ pet = strive; rush at 怒力；衝向

★★★★★

1876 **competence**	*n. ability; capacity*	能力，勝任，稱職
[ˋkɑmpətəns]	No one doubts Louis's competence in solving all kinds of math problems. His classmates usually turn to him whenever they have difficulty with mathematical equations. 無人懷疑路易斯的數學解題能力，同學遇到不懂的數學方程式常向他求助。	

★★★★☆

1877 **petition**	*n. a formal written request / plea; solicitation*	請願書／陳情
[pəˋtɪʃən]	Mr. Joyce had to get five hundred signatures on a petition before the board of directors of his company considered any of his proposals. 喬伊斯先生須獲得五百人共同簽署請願，公司董事會才會考慮其提案。	

★★★★★

1878 **appetite**	*n. a natural desire to satisfy bodily needs especially for food*	食慾，胃口
[ˋæpə,taɪt]	Judy has a very large appetite, which is the direct cause of her weight problem. I think she is unable to curtail her desire to eat. 茱蒂胃口很大，直接引發她的體重問題，我認為她無法克制食慾。	

★★★★☆

1879 **impetuous**	*a. reckless; rash; impulsive*	衝動的，性急的
[ɪmˋpɛtʃuəs]	It was impetuous of the man to try to hug the lady during the blackout. He wound up in the aquarium. 男子在停電時衝動的要去抱住這名女士，結果摔入水箱。	

✢ phon- = sound 聲音

★★★☆☆

1880 **phony**	*a. fake; factitious; false; fictitious; fraudulent; imitation; mock; pseudo; sham; spurious*	假的
[ˋfonɪ]	One time Tommy put a fake frog in Cindy's desk at school. When she took out her notebook, there it was. But she didn't know it was phony right away. 某次湯米在課堂上把假青蛙放在辛蒂抽屜，她一拿出筆記本就看到它，但沒有馬上認出是假的。	

★★★★☆

1881 **phonograph**	*n. gramophone*	留聲機
[ˋfonə,græf]	The invention of the phonograph by Thomas Edison marked the end of the oral traditions of music. 愛迪生發明的留聲機代表口傳音樂的結束。	

★★★★☆

1882 **phonetics**	*n. the study of vocal sounds and their classification*	語音學

[fə`nɛtɪks]

Tanaka studied phonetics for many years, but it never helped his pronunciation, and no one ever really knew what he was saying when he spoke English.

田中研究語音學多年但對其發音毫無幫助，他講英文時沒人聽得懂。

❖ plai, plex, plic, ploi, ply = fold 摺疊，重疊

★★★☆☆

1883 **replica**	*n. reproduction; duplicate*	複製品，模型

[`rɛplɪkə]

This museum displays a replica of a Turtle Ship. The model has been built almost exactly the same as the original.

這家博物館陳列一艘幾乎原寸大小的龜甲船複製品。

★★★★☆

1884 **implication**	*n. incrimination; inculpation; involvement; entanglement / connotation; denotation*	共犯 / 含蓄，暗示

[ˌɪmplɪ`keʃən]

The defendant was judged guilty by implication. He was not the prime culprit, but he was found to be deeply involved in the crime.

被告以共犯罪名獲判有罪，他雖非主嫌但在此起犯罪中涉案甚深。

★★★☆☆

1885 **duplicity**	*n. double-dealing; deceitfulness / doubleness*	口是心非，欺騙 / 兩倍

[du`plɪsətɪ]

Her duplicity of character was the key factor that allowed her to commit the perfect crime. She was a master of deception.

口是心非的性格是她得以犯下完美罪行的關鍵因素。她是個詐騙大師。

★★★★★

1886 **duplicate**	*n. copy; reproduction; replica; photocopy*	複製品，副本

[`dupləkɪt]

The art collector paid $100,000 for a painting that he later found out was not an original but an exact duplicate.

藝術品收藏家花了十萬美元收購畫作，後來才發現不是原作而是複製品。

★★☆☆☆

1887 **plait**	*v. braid; form hair into a plait / n. braid; pigtail*	編辮子 / 髮辮

[plet]

A woman who wears her hair in a plait often seems to be strict or stern and unapproachable. That's why I have advised my sister to change her hair style.

綁辮子的女性常看來嚴肅而難以親近，因此我建議妹妹改變髮型。

★★★★★

1888 exploit

v. make use of a resource / utilize; take advantage of　　　開墾，開採 / 利用

[ɪk`splɔɪt]

People are trying to exploit all kinds of natural resources. At this rate, the earth might be depleted before the end of this century.

人類試圖要開採所有的自然資源。依此速度，也許在本世紀結束前，地球就已經枯竭了。

★★★★☆

1889 plight

n. difficulty; predicament; quandary; trouble　　　困境，不幸遭遇

[plaɪt]

Carrie was in a dreadful plight. She found herself broke in the streets of New York. She had no one to turn to.

凱莉陷入可怕的困境，身無分文流落紐約街頭，無依無靠。

★★★★★

1890 complex

a. complicated / n. a building made up of related parts　　　複雜的 / 複合式建物

[kəm`plɛks]

It wasn't until I realized exactly how complex the problem really was that I began to try to understand what the causes were.

我直到發現問題有多複雜後才開始試著了解起因。

⟐ ple = fill 充滿

★★★★★

1891 implement

v. execute; carry out; accomplish　　　履行，實施，執行

[`ɪmpləmənt]

New laws are sometimes difficult to implement. Usually it takes some time to put them into effect.

新法有時難以執行，通常要花點時間才能生效。

★★★★★

1892 plentiful

a. ample; abundant; profuse; copious; lavish; bountiful　　　充裕的，豐富的，多的

[`plɛntɪfəl]

The bachelor was glad to have met such a woman of plentiful charm. She was the ideal type he had been dreaming of.

該名單身漢很高興能遇到如此迷人的女子，她正是他夢寐以求的理想對象。

★★★★★

1893 complement

n. something that completes; finishing touch　　　補充物，相輔相成

[`kɑmpləmənt]

The actress's new hair style was a complement to her already beautiful face. She looked even more beautiful.

女明星的新髮型和姣好容貌相輔相成，使她看起來愈發美麗。

★★★★☆

1894 plenteous	***a.*** *plentiful*	豐富的，豐產的
[`plɛntɪəs]	After an especially plenteous harvest, the farmers celebrated their bounty, singing and dancing together for many days. 農民們在大豐收後連日唱歌跳舞慶祝收成。	

★★★★☆

1895 replenish	***v.*** *fill up again; refill; replace; renew*	補充，再補足
[rɪ`plɛnɪʃ]	My nation used to import millions of tons of rice to replenish our reserves. Now, we are producing enough food to support all of our people. 過去我國進口數百萬噸稻米以補足存糧，現在我們已能自給自足。	

★★★☆☆

1896 plenary	***a.*** *entire; full / absolute*	完全的 / 絕對的
[`plinərɪ]	A king holds plenary authority over all the people who live in his kingdom, and can therefore decree death, imprisonment, or freedom for criminals as he sees fit. 國王擁有國境全體人民的絕對管轄權，可視情況判處死刑、下令監禁或釋放囚犯。	

★★★★★

1897 completely	***ad.*** *entirely; fully; totally; from the word go; lock, stock and barrel*	完全地，徹底地
[kəm`plitlɪ]	Some supporters of antismoking campaigns try to prohibit cigarette smoking completely in public places. 部分禁煙運動支持者試圖推動公共場所全面禁煙。	

Tea Time...

<From the name of a king>
Mausoleu
From King Mausolus of Caria, whose large tomb, created in Asia Minor about 350 B.C., was one of the Seven Wonders of the world.

〈來自國王名〉莫索洛斯大陵寢
卡里亞王國統治者莫索洛斯於西元前三五零年建於小亞細亞的巨大陵墓，為世界七大奇觀之一。（註：莫索洛斯大陵寢現址位於土耳其，陵寢奠基在長三十八公尺、寬三十二公尺的基座上，氣勢雄偉有如神廟，世人譽為陵寢建築典範。後世亦直接以此字作為「陵墓，陵寢」之意。）

mausoleum [ˌmɔsə`liəm] ***n.*** *a large, stately tomb* | 陵寢，陵墓
We visited many mausoleums during our trip to the historic city, and we couldn't believe such structures were used as tombs.
遊覽歷史古都時我們參觀許多陵寢，如此的陵墓建築實在令人難以置信。

1

Complete each word by filling in the blank with proper spelling so that it has the same meaning as suggested. Then please write the meaning of each word in Chinese.

1. 不時打斷 = _ _ _ _ t u a t e
2. 戳破 = _ _ _ _ t u r e
3. 尖銳的 = _ _ _ _ e n t
4. 針灸治療 = a c u _ _ _ _ t u r e
5. 基座 = _ _ _ e s t a l
6. 血統 = _ _ _ i g r e e
7. 行人 = _ _ _ e s t r i a n
8. 鐘擺 = _ _ _ _ u l u m
9. 獨立自主的 = i n d e _ _ _ _ e n t
10. 貫穿 = _ _ _ f o r a t e

11. perplex = _____
12. perimeter = _____
13. competence = _____
14. appetite = _____
15. phonograph = _____
16. phonetics = _____
17. replica = _____
18. exploit = _____
19. implement = _____
20. plenteous = _____

2

Choose a word that best completes the sentence.

21. The child _____ the balloon with a pin.

(A) punctuated   (B) peddled   (C) punctured   (D) impeded

22. The photographer mounted his camera on a(n) _____.

(A) tripod   (B) acupuncture   (C) pedigree   (D) pendulum

3

The highlighted word is closest in meaning to which of the following?

23. The matter is still pending .

(A) independent   (B) unsettled   (C) persistent   (D) perlexed

24. The perverse youngster did not listen to his parents' advice.

(A) plenary   (B) plentiful   (C) wayward   (D) impetuous

25. I would like to make a duplicate of this key.

(A) plait   (B) copy   (C) phonetics   (D) plight

⁎ pond = weigh, weight 稱重，重量

★★★★☆

MP3 78

1898 preponderance
[prɪˈpɑndərəns]

n. dominance; predominance　　　　　　　優勢，優越，勝過

That nation is enjoying a preponderance of military power over its neighboring countries, and it has control over many issues.
該國享有優於鄰近諸國的軍事力量，因此對許多議題具有主導權。

★★★★★

1899 ponder
[ˈpɑndə]

v. brood over; mull over; deliberate over; meditate on;　　認真思考
ruminate over; chew over; reflect on; muse over; contemplate; consider

Before taking an important step, Alfred always ponders over the best thing to do. Sometimes he spends several days making an important decision.
艾佛列德採取重要行動前總是認真思考最佳對策，有時要花好幾天才做成一個重大決定。

★★★☆☆

1900 ponderous
[ˈpɑndərəs]

a. heavy; unwieldy; cumbersome　　　　　　　沈重的，笨重的

The porter's legs nearly buckled under the ponderous weight. To carry a bale of rice was too burdensome for him.
沈重重量幾乎使搬運工人的腿直不起來，搬運一大包米對他來說太重了。

⁎ pos(it) = put 放置

★★★☆☆

1901 repository
[rɪˈpɑzəˌtɔrɪ]

n. a place where things are stored or may be found;　　儲藏室，陳列處
storehouse

This rack is a repository for my growing collection of miniature model cars. I think I have collected about three hundred different models.
這個架子是我存放迷你模型車收藏品之處，我收集了大約三百種款式各異的模型。

★★☆☆☆

1902 juxtaposed
[ˌdʒʌkstəˈpozd]

a. placed side by side　　　　　　　　　　　並列的，並排的

The original and the reproduction were juxtaposed for a more thorough examination. It was not easy to tell the difference.
原件和複製品並列放置以供仔細檢查，但不容易分辨差異。

★★★★☆

1903 superimpose
[ˌsupərɪmˈpoz]

v. lay a thing on something else　　　　　　　重疊在～之上

About 10 inches of fresh snow were superimposed on top of the overhanging snow. The climbers thought that there might be an avalanche.
大約十吋新積雪積在懸垂的冰雪上，登山者認為可能會有雪崩。

★★★★★

1904 **impose**	*v. exact a tax; levy tax / burden a person with*	課（稅）／打擾
[ɪmˋpoz]		

I hate to impose on my friends, but there are times when I have no choice but to bother them in order to get the help needed to solve my problems.

我討厭打擾友人，但有時為了解決問題不得不麻煩他們幫忙。

❖ post- = after 後，向後

★★★★☆

1905 **posterity**	*n. descendants; heirs; offspring; progeny*	後世，子孫
[pasˋtɛrətɪ]		

We should try not to deplete the natural resources for the good of our posterity. We had better think that the earth was temporarily borrowed from our descendants.

為了後世福祉我們不該耗損自然資源。我們最好把地球看作是向後代子孫暫借的。

★★★★★

1906 **postscript**	*n. an additional remark at the end of a letter*	信末附筆，書籍附錄
[ˋpostˏskrɪpt]		

As a postscript, Mr. McKenzie decided to write "I love you" at the bottom of the letter, hoping in his heart that she felt the same way.

麥肯錫先生決定在信件末尾寫上「我愛妳」的附筆，希望她也有同感。

★★★☆☆

1907 **postwar**	*a. occurring or existing after a war*	戰後的
[ˏpostˋwɔr]		

The postwar situation was not much better than the prewar one, which meant that fighting the war had been effectively pointless.

戰後情況沒比戰前改善多少，代表戰爭其實是毫無意義的。

★★★★★

1908 **postpone**	*v. delay; adjourn; defer; suspend; keep in abeyance*	使延期，延遲
[postˋpon]		

Procrastinators always postpone today's work until tomorrow. They often do the same thing the next day.

拖延的人總是把今天的工作拖到明天再做，隔天又再故技重施。

❖ potent = power 能力

★★★★☆

1909 **omnipotent**	*a. having great or absolute power*	萬能的，擁有無上權力的
[amˋnɪpətənt]		

The despot thought of himself as an omnipotent ruler, but the truth was that he was only a 'big fish in a little pond.'

暴君認為自己是萬能領袖，其實他只不過是個「井底之蛙」。

1910 **potentate**	*n. monarch; ruler*	君主，統治者，有權勢者
[`potn̩ˌtet]	His dream of becoming a supreme leader, the "Potentate of All Asia," crumbled when he lost all his money, influence, and power in the revolution that swept his country. 席捲全國的革命勢力使他失去所有財富、影響力和權力，也粉碎他成為至高無上「亞洲之王」的夢想。	

★★★★☆

1911 **impotent**	*a. powerless; lacking all strength; enfeebled; debilitated / sterile; barren*	虛弱的，無力的 / 不起作用的
[`ɪmpətənt]	His rage was impotent, because the mistake had been his own, and there was no one else to blame. 他的憤怒起不了任何作用，因為錯誤是他自己造成的，無法怪罪別人。	

★★★★☆

1912 **potent**	*a. powerful; mighty; vigorous; influential; compelling*	有效的，有影響力的
[`potn̩t]	The poison was so potent that only a single drop would be enough to kill a strong and healthy elephant. 這毒藥的毒性極強，只要一小滴就足以毒死一頭健壯大象。	

⁜ prehend, prehens = catch, take 抓，取

★★★★★

1913 **apprehensive**	*a. fearful*	不安的，恐懼的，擔心的
[ˌæprɪ`hɛnsɪv]	The boy is so shy that he's apprehensive about talking. His teacher is trying to teach him not to be afraid of talking. 害羞男童害怕發言，老師設法教他別怕開口。	

★★★★★

1914 **comprehensive**	*a. extensive; sweeping; all-embracing; exhaustive*	廣泛的，全面的
[ˌkɑmprɪ`hɛnsɪv]	The CEO said that the business plan was not detailed enough, and suggested that we come up with a more comprehensive plan. 執行長表示營運計畫不夠詳細，建議我們提出更全面的計畫。	

★★★★★

1915 **pregnancy**	*n. the condition or an instance of being pregnant*	懷孕
[`prɛgnənsɪ]	Scientists have proven that children of mothers who are addicted to drugs during pregnancy many times become addicted to drugs, as well. 科學家證實有毒癮的孕婦往往會產下同樣有毒癮的後代。	

★★★★★

1916 **apprentice**	*n. trainee; novice; learner; beginner; tender-foot*	初學者，學徒
[ə`prɛntɪs]	My friend Peter wanted to become a plumber, and he needed to get some on-the-job training. He started working at a plumbing company as	

an apprentice so that he could learn the trade from more experienced plumbers.

想當水管工人的友人彼德需要在職訓練。他開始在修水管公司當學徒，以便向有經驗者學習。

★★★★☆

1917 reprehensible

a. blameworthy 該受責備的

[ˌrɛprɪˈhɛnsəbl]

The teacher did not know what to do about the reprehensible behavior of the unruly student. He finally sent him to the dean.

老師不知道如何處理任性學童該受責備的行為，最後將他送到訓導主任面前。

★★★★☆

1918 impregnable

a. unassailable; invincible; unconquerable; unbeatable 堅不可摧的

[ɪmˈprɛgnəbl]

The king's castle had always been considered impregnable, which is until the invading force of barbarians attacked and conquered it.

國王的城堡在遭受異族入侵襲擊並攻陷前，一向被視為堅不可摧。

✧ press = press 擠，壓

★★★★★

1919 pressure

n. stress; demand / compression 壓力，壓迫／壓制

[ˈprɛʃɚ]

His parents put great pressure on him, first to get married, then to produce a son, and then to divorce his wife who could not have a baby.

父母給他極大壓力，先是叫他結婚，然後要抱孫，最後又要他跟不孕妻子離婚。

★★★★★

1920 repress

v. check; restrain; quell; suppress; curbs 壓抑

[rɪˈprɛs]

This morning a bicyclist hit me, but he pedaled away without so much as apologizing to me. I had difficulty repressing my anger.

今早有個人騎腳踏車撞到我，但連句道歉都沒說就騎走了，讓我很難嚥下怒氣。

★★★★★

1921 impression

n. an effect produced especially on the mind or feelings 印象

[ɪmˈprɛʃən]

My father always taught me the importance of first impressions. I didn't really understand how important they were until I had been in business for a few years.

父親常教導我第一印象的重要性，但直到就業幾年後我才真正了解它有多重要。

★★★★☆

1922 pressing

a. urgent; pivotal; momentous; crucial 迫切的，緊急的

[ˈprɛsɪŋ]

Frank has some pressing matters to attend to before he goes out with her this evening. The most important thing is to camouflage his baldness.

法蘭克傍晚與她外出前需先處理一些緊急事務，其中最重要的就是遮掩自己的禿頭。

✢ prim = first 最初

★★★★★

1923 primeval

[praɪˈmivl̩]

a. of or relating to the first age of the world; primitive   初期的，原始的

Many people called the Amazon area primeval because much of the area was wild, untamed and generally unexplored.

許多人認為亞馬遜河流域是原始地帶，因為大部分區域都是野生而未開發的。

★★★★★

1924 primary

[ˈpraɪˌmɛrɪ]

a. prime; leading; predominant; cardinal; preeminent / earliest; first   首要的 / 最初的

Primary education is vital to young children because it instills certain traits that are necessary for survival in any society, namely; honesty, sharing and hard work.

國小教育對孩童非常重要，因為它逐步灌輸誠信、分享與努力等社會生存必備特質。

★★★★★

1925 prime

[praɪm]

a. main   主要的，最初的，原始的

The newspaper carrier was the prime suspect in the robbery, and he was arrested by the police. He went on to be convicted for his crime.

搶案主嫌是一名派報生，他遭警方逮捕後接著被定罪。

★★★☆☆

1926 primordial

[praɪˈmɔrdɪəl]

a. existing at or from the beginning; primeval   原始的

The primordial customs of many African tribes are considered to be barbaric by our modern standards.

從現代標準來看，許多非洲部落的原始習俗都是野蠻的。

✢ priv = separate 使分開

★★★★★

1927 deprive

[dɪˈpraɪv]

v. strip; dispossess   奪走，剝奪，使喪失

Children who live in third world countries rarely can have the opportunity to go to university, and are deprived of many other luxuries found in advanced countries.

第三世界孩童少有就讀大學的機會，連先進國家享有的許多奢侈也被剝奪。

★★★★★

1928 private

[ˈpraɪvɪt]

a. personal; individual / secret; confidential   私人的 / 非公開的，機密的

His den was a private room in his house that neither his wife nor children ever entered, and this is where he did most of his work.

他在家中的私人專用小房間連妻兒都不能進入，那是他完成大半工作之處。

★★★★☆

| 1929 **privilege** | *n. a right, advantage or immunity belonging to a person, class or office* | 特權，特別待遇 |

['prɪvl̩ɪdʒ]

One of the privileges of belonging to our golf club is that you are allowed to use the golf course at any time.
加入我們高爾夫球俱樂部的特別待遇之一是可自由使用球場。

★★★☆☆

| 1930 **privation** | *n. destitution; pauperism; penury; indigence* | 窮困，貧苦 |

[praɪ'veʃən]

The old widow's life of privation started to affect her health. She was leading a lonely life without any help from others.
年邁寡婦的窮困生活開始影響健康，她過著無人援助的孤獨生活。

⚜ proto- = first 最初

★★★★★

| 1931 **prototype** | *n. model; archetype; pattern* | 原型 |

['protə‚taɪp]

The prototype of the computer, 'the Whirlwind,' was a large calculator that was the size of a room and very slow.
名為「旋風」的電腦原型是一部跟房間一樣大、運算極慢的大型計算機。

★★★★★

| 1932 **protagonist** | *n. hero; heroine; leading role / supporter* | 主人翁 / 倡導者 |

[pro'tægənɪst]

At the age of 14, Hans Christian Anderson arrived in Copenhagen, like many of his fictional protagonists.
安徒生十四歲來到哥本哈根，如同他筆下許多主人翁一樣。

★★★★☆

| 1933 **protocol** | *n. the original draft of a diplomatic document / diplomatic etiquette* | 草約 / 外交禮節 |

['protə‚kɔl]

To be a successful diplomat or ambassador, one must study and understand protocol and foreign customs.
要成為成功外交官或大使，就必須學習並熟諳外交禮節和外國習俗。

★★★★★

| 1934 **proton** | *n. a stable elementary particle with a positive electric charge* | 質子 |

['protɑn]

A proton is a positively charged atomic particle, much larger than an electron, which is negatively charged.
質子是帶正電荷的原子粒子，比帶負電荷的電子大得多。

❖ psychi- = mind 精神，心靈

★★★☆☆

1935 **psyche**	*n. soul; spirit*	靈魂，精神，心理，心理學
[`saɪkɪ]		

The murderer's tortured psyche was a fascinating object of study for a team of expert psychologists, who never really understood why he killed so many people.

對不明白兇手為何謀殺這麼多人的心理學家團隊而言，其扭曲心理是極吸引人的研究對象。

★★★☆☆

1936 **psychic**	*n. fortune-teller; spiritualist; seer; prophet*	靈媒
[`saɪkɪk]		

In the Orient, one may visit a fortune-teller for information about the future, whereas in the West, people visit a psychic.

東方人找算命師卜問未來，西方人則找靈媒。

★★★★☆

1937 **psychiatrist**	*n. a doctor of medicine specializing in psychiatry*	精神病醫師，精神病學家
[saɪ`kaɪətrɪst]		

In order to treat severe depression, the psychiatrist recommended weekly group therapy sessions for his patients.

精神病醫師為治療重度憂鬱患者，建議每周進行一次團體治療。

❖ puls = drive 迫使，驅動

★★★★★

1938 **compulsory**	*a. mandatory*	必須做的，義務的，強制的
[kəm`pʌlsərɪ]		

Everyone has the right to education. Education shall be free, at least in the elementary and fundamental stages. Elementary education shall be compulsory.

人人都有受教育的權利，至少在初級和基礎階段教育應該免費。初級教育應屬義務性質。

★★★☆☆

1939 **pulsation**	*n. pulse*	脈搏，跳動
[pʌl`seʃən]		

The doctor placed his hand upon her heart. There was no pulsation. She was stone dead. The doctor decided to apply an electric shock.

醫生將手按在她的心臟上卻感覺不出跳動和任何生命跡象，醫生決定施以電擊。

★★★★★

1940 **impulsive**	*a. instinctive*	衝動的，受一時情緒驅使的
[ɪm`pʌlsɪv]		

His impulsive behavior is a point of real concern for his teachers and parents, because they are afraid that those tendencies will lead to problems in the future.

他衝動的行為是父母師長十分關切的問題，他們擔心這些傾向會在未來變成問題。

★★★★☆

1941 **propulsion**	*n. thrust; pushing forward*	推進，推進力
[prə`pʌlʃən]	Over the last one hundred years there have been remarkable developments in the field of propulsion, resulting in manned space flight. 過去百年來推進力領域有長足的發展，結果開啓了由人駕駛的太空飛行。	

✛ rad = root 根

★★★★★

1942 **eradicate**	*v. root out; destroy; get rid of; remove*	連根拔除，消滅
[ɪ`rædɪˌket]	It was sickening to watch the evening news and witness the Bosnians selectively eradicate Muslims in the campaign of ethnic cleansing. 透過晚間新聞目睹波士尼亞人在種族淨化運動中選擇性地消滅回教徒，讓人感到不舒服。	

★★★★★

1943 **radish**	*n. a cruciferous plant with a fleshy pungent root*	蘿蔔
[`rædɪʃ]	Farmer Brown once grew a radish so big that he needed two other people to help him carry it to the agricultural fair. 農夫伯朗曾種出很大的蘿蔔，需要三人合力抬到農產品市場。	

★★★★☆

1944 **radical**	*a. fundamental; essential*	根本的，基本的，徹底的
[`rædɪkl̩]	Two radical advances in education have taken place since this minister took office; one was the abolition of the entrance exam, and the other was the adoption of compulsory education to the level of high school. 自部長上任以來已推動兩大基本教育發展，一是廢除入學考試，二是推行高中義務教育。	

✛ rap(t) = seize 奪取

★★★☆☆

1945 **enrapture**	*v. charm; bewitch; spellbind; fascinate; enchant*	使著迷，使狂喜
[ɪn`ræptʃə]	Helen was so beautiful that he was enraptured the first time he saw her, and he followed her around like a puppy-dog for months. 他第一眼看見海倫的美貌就著迷了，於是一連好幾個月像隻小狗般跟在她身邊。	

★★★☆☆

| 1946 **rapacious** | *a. greedy; covetous; grasping; ravenous* | 貪婪的，貪得無厭的 |

[rə`peʃəs]

The rapacious nature of a victorious army often spells disaster for the citizens of the vanquished nation.

勝利軍隊貪得無厭的本性往往為戰敗國人民帶來災禍。

★★★☆☆

| 1947 **rapture** | *n. ecstasy; delight; exultation* | 癡狂，滿心歡喜 |

[`ræptʃə]

The girl always evoked such a feeling of rapture whenever Steven saw her walk into his classroom, that eventually he asked her out on a date.

史帝芬每當看到女孩走進教室總是感到滿心歡喜，最後他終於約她出去。

✛ rect = right　正確

★★★★☆

| 1948 **rectify** | *v. adjust; make right; correct; amend* | 矯正，改正，導正 |

[ˌrɛktə`faɪ]

The blunder on your part has caused terrible problems. Therefore, please rectify the situation and let us know as soon as possible.

你犯下的大錯帶來嚴重問題，請於改正後盡快告知我們。

★★★★★

| 1949 **rectangular** | *a. shaped like a rectangle* | 矩形的，長方形的 |

[rɛk`tæŋgjələ]

City blocks are often more rectangular than square. In reality, it is difficult to make the four sides all equal in length.

都市街廓常是長方形而非正方形，因為事實上很難讓四邊等長。

★★★★☆

| 1950 **rectitude** | *n. righteousness; honesty* | 正直，誠實，清廉 |

[`rɛktəˌtud]

The businessman had a certain rectitude about how business was supposed to be handled. It was out of the question for him to think about tax evasion.

這名誠實的商人知道該如何經營事業，所以他不可能逃漏稅。

Tea Time... ☕

| <Greek myth> Iris | 〈來自希臘神話〉彩虹女神 |
| **The Greek goddess of the rainbow and the messenger of the gods.** | 希臘神話中的彩虹女神和諸神信使。（註：由於彩虹女神負責以彩虹聯絡天和地，所以也是諸神信使。） |

iris [`aɪrɪs] *n. rainbow / the opaque colored portion of the eye / iris plant* | 彩虹 / 虹膜 / 鳶尾花

James was suffering from inflammation of the irises. The doctor told him that irises are the round, colored parts of the eyes.

詹姆斯得了虹膜炎，醫生告訴他虹膜是雙眼中帶有顏色的圓形部分。

1

Complete each word by filling in the blank with proper spelling so that it has the same meaning as suggested. Then please write the meaning of each word in Chinese.

1. 認真思考 = _ _ _ _ e r
2. 儲藏室 = r e _ _ _ i t o r y
3. 重疊在上 = s u p e r i m _ _ _ e
4. 後世 = _ _ _ _ e r i t y
5. 延遲 = _ _ _ _ p o n e
6. 萬能的 = o m n i _ _ _ _ _ _
7. 統治者 = _ _ _ _ _ _ a t e
8. 懷孕 = _ _ _ _ n a n c y
9. 全面的 = c o m _ _ _ _ _ _ _ i v e
10. 學徒 = a p _ _ _ _ t i c e

11. impregnable = _____
12. pressure = _____
13. impression = _____
14. primeval = _____
15. private = _____
16. protagonist = _____
17. compulsory = _____
18. eradicate = _____
19. enrapture = _____
20. rapture = _____

Chapter
① ② ③ ④ ⑤

2

Choose a word that best completes the sentence.

21. The country is enjoying its _____ in military power over its neighboring country.

(A) repository   (B) preponderance   (C) postwar   (D) potentate

22. His father wrote in his _____, "Stay single, please, my son."

(A) postscript   (B) pressure   (C) impression   (D) privation

23. The man had no alternative but to succumb to his wife's _____.

(A) pressure   (B) apprentice   (C) protagonist   (D) protocol

3

The highlighted word is closest in meaning to which of the following?

24. We should preserve natural resources for the good of our posterity .

(A) trainee   (B) monarch   (C) descendants   (D) storehouse

25. Despite their seemingly ponderous movements, polar bears are very agile.

(A) juxtaposed   (B) cumbersome   (C) omnipotent   (D) impotent

❖ robo = firm 穩固

★★★★☆

MP3 80

| 1951 **corroborate** | *v. confirm; give support to; substantiate* | 證實 |

[kə`rɑbə,ret]

That was one case the lawyer didn't want to lose. He did extensive research and found several people to get on the witness stand and corroborate his side of the story.

律師不想輸掉官司，於是展開大規模調查並找到幾名證人證實其說詞。

★★★★☆

| 1952 **robust** | *a. sound; sturdy; stout; strong; muscular; vigorous* | 強健的，強壯的 |

[ro`bʌst]

I'm in robust health now. I've never been healthier. I do not feel exhausted, even after work at the office.

我現在身體強壯，從來沒有這麼強健過，就算下班後也不會累。

★★★★☆

| 1953 **robot** | *n. automaton* | 機器人 |

[`robət]

The invention of the robot has revolutionized factory work, and increased unemployment at an alarming rate.

機器人發明徹底改變工廠作業，並使失業人數以驚人速度增加。

❖ rog = ask 詢問

★★★★☆

| 1954 **interrogative** | *a. of a question* | 疑問的，表示疑問的 |

[,ɪntə`rɑɡətɪv]

A question is another word for an interrogative statement or sentence, which is used when we are seeking information.

問題是疑問敘述或疑問句的另一種用詞，多用於尋找資訊時。

★★★☆☆

| 1955 **interrogation** | *n. the act or an instance of interrogating; questioning* | 審訊，質問 |

[ɪn,tɛrə`ɡeʃən]

The suspect seemed shaken after his interrogation by the police officers, who were suspicious of him.

嫌犯遭疑其涉案的警方審訊後似乎嚇壞了。

★★★★☆

1956 abrogate

[`æbrə,get]

v. repeal; annul; abolish 取消，廢除

The government abrogated that law last year, because it was no longer necessary for the maintenance of law and order.
政府去年廢除該法，因為已無戒嚴必要。

★★★☆☆

1957 rogue

[rog]

n. scoundrel; villain; wretch; charlatan; scamp; rat; bastard 流氓，無賴

He was always a rogue, and many of the people who worked with him didn't trust him at all.
他的無賴行徑使許多一起工作的人都不信任他。

★★★★☆

1958 arrogant

[`ærəgənt]

a. presumptuous; assuming; conceited; pompous; haughty; overbearing; assertive 自大傲慢的，自負的

The manager is an arrogant person and thinks he is the best at everything he does. Naturally his subordinates do not like him very much.
自負的經理認為自己最厲害，屬下們自然非常討厭他。

✥ sag = know 知道，理解

★★☆☆☆

1959 sage

[sedʒ]

n. wise man; guru; pundit; oracle 聖賢，哲人，德高望重者

Confucius, who had lived from 551 to 479 B.C., is thought to be one of the greatest Chinese sages.
生於西元前五五一年、卒於西元前四七九年的孔子被視為中國最偉大的聖賢之一。

★★☆☆☆

1960 presage

[prɪ`sedʒ]

v. portend; foreshadow / *n.* omen; portent 預示／預兆

Such hostilities between the two countries may presage war. It seems that a war will break out at any moment.
兩國間的敵意可能預示著戰爭的發生，戰事似乎一觸即發。

★★☆☆☆

1961 sagacious

[sə`geʃəs]

a. astute; shrewd; acute-minded 睿智的，有遠見的

When they were faced with any kind of problem, the villagers gathered around the sagacious old man to hear his wise words.
每當村民遇到問題時，都會聚集在睿智老人身邊聆聽他的教誨。

⁂ sal, sault, sult = jump 跳躍

★★★★☆

1962 **desultory**	*a. shifting; unsteady; wavering; fitful; spasmodic*	隨便的，散漫的

[`dɛsəl,tɔrɪ]

I personally had a difficult time sitting through his meetings, because of his lack of direction and the overall desultory way in which he carried out his meetings.

我和他開會很痛苦，因為他主持會議既無方向又散漫。

★★★★☆

1963 **salient**	*a. conspicuous; outstanding; noticeable; striking; distinctive* 顯著的，醒目的

[`selɪənt]

One of the most salient traits of Japanese ladies was the subordination to men. However, these days more and more women believe that they are an equal gender.

日本女性的顯著特色之一是服從男性，但現在愈來愈多女性相信兩性平等。

★★★☆☆

1964 **sally**	*n. outburst; charge*	突圍，出擊，突然發作

[`sælɪ]

The coach let out a sally of anger as his team lost. The players were trembling with fear, saying nothing.

教練因輸球而勃然大怒，嚇得球員們不敢出聲。

★★★★★

1965 **result**	*n. consequence; effect*	結果，成果，效果

[rɪ`zʌlt]

Anxiously, the family awaited the result of the test that would determine which university their daughter would go to.

家人焦急等待著決定女兒上哪所大學的考試結果。

★★★★★

1966 **assault**	*n. attack; raid; incursion; invasion; blitz*	襲擊，譴責，抨擊

[ə`sɔlt]

The military assault on the city was bloody and many lives were lost. Many nations laid blame on the invader.

軍隊血腥襲擊該城導致多人喪生，許多國家紛紛譴責入侵者。

❖ salus- = health; good 健康，美好

★★★☆☆

| 1967 **salute** | *v. greet; make a salute to* | 向～行禮，向～致意 |

[sə`lut]

Junior officers are usually required to salute officers whenever eye contact is made. A salute is given to show respect toward superiors.

資淺軍官見到資深者需行禮致意，以示尊敬。

★★★☆☆

| 1968 **salubrious** | *a. health-giving; wholesome* | 有益健康的 |

[sə`lubrɪəs]

There are many types of food that are considered salubrious, or good for the health, even though most of them are not delicious.

許多食物被認為有益身體健康，儘管它們大部分都不美味。

★★★★☆

| 1969 **salvage** | *v. save; rescue; retrieve* | 打撈，搶救，營救 |

[`sælvɪdʒ]

After the Titanic was discovered, there were many attempts to salvage the gold and riches that were rumored to remain at the bottom of the sea with the wreck.

發現鐵達尼號後，許多人企圖打撈據稱與失事殘骸一同沉入海底的金銀珠寶。

★★★★☆

| 1970 **salutary** | *a. producing good effects; beneficial* | 有益健康的，有益的 |

[`sæljə,tɛrɪ]

Many people ignore the salutary advice of their doctors, such as to stop smoking and to do more exercise.

許多人忽略醫生有益健康的建議，例如戒煙和多運動等。

★★☆☆☆

| 1971 **salutatory** | *a. of salutation* | 致上敬意的，歡迎的 |

[sə`lutə,torɪ]

When the company president gave his salutatory address, which lasted for more than an hour, everyone knew that the seminar would run overtime.

公司總裁花了超過一小時致歡迎詞，於是大家知道研討會將超時。

❖ san = health 健康

★★★★★

| 1972 **sane** | *a. of sound mind; right in the head; all there; right-minded* | 神智清楚的 |

[sen]

The actual difference between being sane and insane is still a mystery, as far as the workings of the brain are concerned.

就大腦運作而言，神智清楚和精神錯亂之間的真正差別仍是個謎。

| **1973 insanity** | *n. madness; lunacy; mental disorder; mania; neurosis; craziness* | 瘋狂，精神錯亂 |

[ɪn`sænətɪ]

There is a fine line between genius and insanity. One can lead to the other without a noticeable change of mannerisms.
天才和瘋子間只有一線之隔，兩者的轉變在言行態度上沒有顯著變化。

★★★★★

| **1974 sanitation** | *n. sanitary conditions* | 公共衛生，環境衛生 |

[ˌsænə`teʃən]

One of the greatest concerns of an organic farm is sanitation. In this method of farming, farmers don't use chemical fertilizers or pesticides.
有機農場的最大考量點之一是公共衛生，因為有機農業不用化學肥料或殺蟲劑。

★★★★★

| **1975 unsanitary** | *a. not sanitary; sordid* | 不衛生的，有礙健康的 |

[ʌn`sænəˌtɛrɪ]

I don't want to eat at this restaurant, because it is unsanitary, and its food and service leave much to be desired.
我不想在那家不衛生的餐廳用餐，那裡的食物和服務都有待改進。

❖ sanct = sacred 神聖的

★★★☆☆

| **1976 sanctuary** | *n. sacred place* | 聖殿，教堂，寺院 |

[`sæŋktʃuˌɛrɪ]

Even the mild-featured maidens seemed to dread contamination; and many a stern old man arose, and turned his repulsive and unheavenly countenance upon the gentle boy, as if the sanctuary were polluted by his presence.

The Gentle Boy — Nathaniel Hawthorne

即使是溫柔少女也似乎害怕受到污染，許多老人變得嚴厲，以厭惡和兇惡的表情面對溫文少年，彷彿他的存在污染了教堂。

——《溫文少年》霍桑

★★☆☆☆

| **1977 sanctimonious** | *a. hypocritical; self-righteous; canting* | 偽善的 |

[ˌsæŋktə`monɪəs]

The sanctimonious behavior of those people is only a mask to cover the real corruption and devilry.
那些人的偽善行為只是掩飾其真正貪污惡行的面具。

★★★★☆

| 1978 **sanctify** | *v. consecrate; hallow; make sacred* | 使神聖化 |

[`sæŋktə,faɪ]

After the death of Elvis, many people began to sanctify his belongings and treat him as though he had been a god.

貓王死後許多人開始神化他的所有物，並把他看作神明。

★★★☆☆

| 1979 **sanctity** | *n. holiness of life; saintliness; piety / sacredness* | 聖潔，虔誠 / 神聖 |

[`sæŋktətɪ]

He recognized a score of the church members of Salem village famous for their special sanctity.

Young Goodman Brown — Nathaniel Hawthorne

他認出其中有許多以特別虔誠著稱的賽倫村教會成員。

── 《小伙子布朗》霍桑

⋯ sat = water 滿足

★★★★☆

| 1980 **saturate** | *v. fill to capacity* | 使飽和 |

[`sætʃə,ret]

The decline in coronary heart disease in America in the past twenty-five years may result from a reduction in the consumption of saturated fats.

過去二十五年來美國冠狀動脈心臟病罹患率下降的原因或許在於飽和脂肪攝取量的減少。

★★★★★

| 1981 **satisfaction** | *n. contentment* | 滿意，滿足 |

[,sætɪs`fækʃən]

Personal satisfaction is a quality that one should consider strongly before accepting a job and making it a career.

求職創業前應認真考慮個人滿足感問題。

★★★★☆

| 1982 **insatiable** | *a. never satisfied* | 永不滿足的，貪得無厭的 |

[ɪn`seʃəbl]

His insatiable greed for power has left him with no supporters. He did not even hesitate to use violent means to achieve his ends.

他的貪權使他失去支持者，他為達目的甚至毫不猶豫地使用暴力。

★★★☆☆

| 1983 **satiate** | *v. satisfy* | 使飽足，使充分滿足 |

[`seʃɪ,et]

It took three full bottles of cold water to satiate his thirst after spending three weeks in the desert.

他待在沙漠三周後足足喝了三瓶冰水才解渴。

✣ scrib, script = write, draw a line 寫，畫線

★★★★★

1984 script	*n. manuscript*	劇本，腳本，底稿
[skrɪpt]		

Unlike a novel or a poem, a play is written to be performed. In some respects a script is to a stage production what a musical score is to a concert, or what an architectural blue print is to a building.

Introduction to Theater — Oscar G. Brockett

戲劇和小說或詩不同之處在於它是演出的。從某種角度來看，劇本對戲劇製作的重要性就好比配樂對音樂會或建築藍圖對建物的重要性。

──《戲劇導讀》（美國印第安那大學戲劇系教授）奧斯卡‧G‧布羅凱特

★★★★★

1985 description	*n. account; narrative; representation*	描寫，敘述，形容
[dɪ`skrɪpʃən]		

It took the police only two days to locate the suspect in the crime due to the very accurate description that the eyewitness gave them.

由於目擊者提供非常精確的描述，警方只花了兩天就找到嫌犯。

✣ se- = separate 分開，分散

★★★★★

1986 seclude	*v. isolate*	使隔離，使孤立，使隱居
[sɪ`klud]		

The monk moved into the mountains to seclude himself from the world and the evil that he saw everywhere.

僧侶遷到山中與世隔絕，同時也隔離隨處可見的罪惡。

★★★★★

1987 security	*n. a secure condition or feeling*	安全，防護，保障
[sɪ`kjurətɪ]		

Doctors say that the latency period of AIDS gives a false sense of security. Some people do not know that the AIDS virus has invaded their bodies.

醫師表示愛滋病潛伏期會製造安全假象，有些人並不知道病毒已侵入體內。

★★★★★

1988 secede	*v. withdraw; resign; break away; defect; break away from; turn one's back on; wash one's hands of; leave*	退出，脫離
[sɪ`sid]		

George's wife wanted him to secede from the party. At last, he decided to defer to his wife's wishes and left the party.

妻子希望喬治退黨，最後他決定聽從她的要求離開。

❖ sec , seq = follow 緊跟

★★★★★

| 1989 **subsequently** | *ad. later on; afterwards* | 其後,隨後,接著 |

[`sʌbsəkwəntlɪ]

The engineer complained loudly about how he was treated at work, and subsequently he got a pink slip.
工程師大聲抱怨自己受到的工作待遇,他隨後遭到解雇。

★★★☆☆

| 1990 **obsequious** | *a. servilely obedient; cringing; toadying; sycophantic; ingratiating; menial; flattering; bootlicking* | 阿諛奉承的 |

[əb`sikwɪəs]

Even though he's a capable man, I will not hire him because I dislike his obsequious manner. I do not like his flattery.
他雖能幹但我不會雇用他,因為我討厭他的阿諛奉承態度和他的恭維。

★★★★☆

| 1991 **sequence** | *n. succession; order* | 次序,順序,連續 |

[`sikwəns]

This library has a list of books in alphabetical sequence. So it will be convenient for you to find any book that you are looking for.
這間圖書館的書目是按照字母順序排列的,所以方便尋找你任何想找的書。

★★★☆☆

| 1992 **sequel** | *n. a novel, film, etc. that continues the story of an earlier one / consequence; supplement* | 續集 / 結局 |

[`sikwəl]

The popular *The Lord of the Rings* consists of a first novel, followed by two sequels. These three books together comprise a trilogy.
大受歡迎的《魔戒》包括首集小說和兩集續集,三本書合起來構成三部曲。

❖ sect = cut 切,割

★★★★★

| 1993 **intersection** | *n. a place where two roads intersect* | 交叉口,十字路口 |

[ˌɪntə`sɛkʃən]

The intersection of Main Street and King Street was always busy, and many people tried to avoid that area while driving through downtown.
緬因街和金恩街交叉口一向塞車,許多駕駛人進城時都會設法避開該路段。

★★★★☆

1994 **sect**	*n.* religious group; denomination; cult / faction	宗派，黨派 / 派別

[sɛkt]

When the old Patriarch died, one Buddhist sect rose above the others and became the ruling group.

當年邁創教者病逝後，一支佛教宗派崛起成為統治核心。

★★★☆☆

1995 **sectarian**	*a.* partisan; factional; cliquish / prejudiced; partial	派系的 / 有偏見的

[sɛk`tɛrɪən]

The sectarian thinking of the office manager was what caused his department to fall behind the others.

辦公室經理的派系之見導致他的部門落後於其他部門。

Tea Time... ☕

<Medieval story> Phlegmatic From phlegm, one of the four imaginary humors of the body which was believed in medieval times to cause sluggishness or dullness.	〈來自中古世紀神話〉多痰的 本字源自中古世紀相信能產生遲鈍或呆滯的人體四種體液之一的痰。（註：中古世紀的血液、痰、黃膽汁和黑膽汁等四種體液分別類比於中國的空氣、水、火和土等四種元素，控制人體健康和情緒。）

phlegmatic [flɛg`mætɪk] *a.* unemotional; apathetic | 冷淡的，漠然的，遲鈍的

comedian just could not cheer up the phlegmatic crowd. He did everything, but there was no response whatsoever.

喜劇演員無法讓冷漠觀眾開心起來，無論他做什麼，觀眾都沒反應。

1 Complete each word by filling in the blank with proper spelling so that it has the same meaning as suggested. Then please write the meaning of each word in Chinese.

1. 嘲笑	= d e _ _ _ _		11. salutatory	= _____	
2. 可笑的	= _ _ _ i c u l o u s		12. sanitation	= _____	
3. 證實	= c o r _ _ _ _ r a t e		13. unsanitary	= _____	
4. 疑問的	= i n t e r _ _ _ a t i v e		14. sanctuary	= _____	
5. 廢除	= a b _ _ _ a t e		15. sanctimonious	= _____	
6. 自負的	= a r _ _ _ a n t		16. saturate	= _____	
7. 睿智的	= _ _ _ a c i o u s		17. description	= _____	
8. 散漫的	= d e _ _ _ _ o r y		18. seclude	= _____	
9. 顯著的	= _ _ _ i e n t		19. subsequently	= _____	
10. 有益健康的	= _ _ _ _ b r i o u s		20. intersection	= _____	

2 Choose a word that best completes the sentence.

21. Many of his contemporaries thought that Edison's experiment on an incandescent light bulb was _____.

(A) deride   (B) ridiculous   (C) ridicule   (D) sanctimonious

22. Please heed his _____ advice.

(A) interrogative   (B) arrogant   (C) salutary   (D) robust

3 The highlighted word is closest in meaning to which of the following?

23. This restaurant seems to be unsanitary . Let's not eat here.

(A) sordid   (B) sane   (C) vigorous   (D) sectarian

24. The chairman disliked the general manager's obsequious manner.

(A) partisan   (B) servile   (C) hypocritical   (D) beneficial

25. Some American authors rebuked the Puritans' sanctimonious attitude.

(A) absurd   (B) insatiate   (C) self-righteous   (D) laughable

1 The highlighted word is closest in meaning to which of the following?

1. **To be a knowledgeable and versatile person, comprehensive reading is very important.**
   (A) extensive
   (B) omnipotent
   (C) juxtaposed
   (D) complex

2. **The Flyer which was made by the Wright brothers was the prototype of the modern plane.**
   (A) privilege
   (B) archetype
   (C) plight
   (D) repository

3. **The jet propulsion of an airplane is not powerful enough to make the plane continuously rise up into the sky like a rocket.**
   (A) pedestrian
   (B) assault
   (C) thrust
   (D) rectitude

4. **The crossbill has a very robust mandible which is used to crack open a cone.**
   (A) stout
   (B) ridiculous
   (C) phony
   (D) ponderous

5. **The spoiled child perforated his little sister's balloons with a pencil.**
   (A) impeded
   (B) pierced
   (C) repatriated
   (D) outweighed

2 Please answer the following questions.

Wyoming

The least populated state in the United States is Wyoming. Even its prime city of Cheyenne has a small number of residents. In this scarcely populated wilderness, one may wander for weeks without seeing another person.

To attract enough settlers for statehood, romantic names were assigned such as Yellowstone and Wind River. The territorial legislature in 1869 even took the then radical step of promising women the franchise, or the right to vote. Yet despite such efforts, settlers were failed to be impressed by Wyoming and its wide expanse of wasteland. Daniel Webster called it a place fit only for savages, wild beasts, whirlwinds of dust, and cactuses.

But nowadays, Wyoming is considered to be one of the most beautiful states, containing as it does plentiful natural wonders. Wyoming's mountain range, which rises above 10,000 feet, consists of a barren icy realm and rocks eroded by wind and time.

6. **The word prime is closest in meaning to which of the following?**
   (A) main
   (B) private
   (C) phony
   (D) compulsory

7. **The word radical is closest in meaning to which of the following?**
   (A) rapacious
   (B) essential
   (C) impulsive
   (D) rectangular

8. **The word impressed is closest in meaning to which of the following?**
   (A) everlasting
   (B) make sacred
   (C) greatly affected
   (D) make right

9. **The word plentiful is closest in meaning to which of the following?**
   (A) ponderous
   (B) apprehensive
   (C) copious
   (D) complex

10. **The word eroded is closest in meaning to which of the following?**
    (A) renegaded
    (B) sculptured
    (C) placated
    (D) ousted

⁘ **sed, ses, sid = set, sit** 坐落，坐

MP3 82

★★★★★

1996 session

[`sɛʃən]

n. *assembly; conference; meeting; hearing*　　　　會議，集會，開庭

It is reported that there will be an emergency session of the United Nations Security Council next week.
據報聯合國安理會將於下周召開緊急會議。

★★★★☆

1997 supersede

[ˌsupə`sid]

v. *replace; take the place of; oust*　　　　代替，取代

The board of directors decided to supersede the unsuccessful old program with the new one. The old one caused a great loss to the company.
董事會決定以新方案取代導致公司大量虧損的舊有失敗計畫。

★★★★☆

1998 obsession

[əb`sɛʃən]

n. *fixed idea; fixation; preoccupation; prepossession; hang-up*　　　　著迷，癡迷

Paul thought he loved her, but everyone else knew that it was not simple love or adoration, but a fanatical obsession.
保羅以為自己愛她，但所有人都明白這不是單純的愛或傾慕，而是狂熱的癡迷。

★★★☆☆

1999 sedative

[`sɛdətɪv]

n. *tranquilizer*　　　　鎮靜劑

The doctor prescribed a strong sedative for the woman, since she had become hysterical. After she took the medicine, she was able to calm down.
醫生開立強效鎮靜劑給情緒激動的女子，她服藥後總算鎮定下來。

★★★★☆

2000 residence

[`rɛzədəns]

n. *abode; home; domicile; place; house; habitation; dwelling*　　住宅，住所

Welcome to my humble residence.
歡迎光臨寒舍。

★★★☆☆

2001 sedentary

[`sɛdn̩ˌtɛrɪ]

a. *stationary; immobile; housebound; unmoving*　　　　久坐的，不遷移的

The professor seldom does exercise or takes a walk; He is living a very sedentary life. All he does is read books in his study.
教授很少運動或散步，他過著固定不動的生活，就只是坐在書房閱讀。

★★★★★

2002 subsidy

[`sʌbsədɪ]

n. *money granted by the government; funding; bounty; grant*　　津貼，補助金

This country is actively promoting a mechanization drive, providing farmers with subsidies and loans.
這個國家積極推動農業機械化，並提供農民津貼和貸款。

★★★★☆

2003 sedate   *v. put under sedation*   使鎮靜

[sɪ`det]

In order to overcome insomnia, millions of people turn to drugs, but they are not experiencing real sleep. They are merely sedated.

無數人靠藥物治療失眠，但他們不是真正入睡，只是鎮靜下來。

★★★☆☆

2004 residual   *a. remaining; leftover*   殘留的，剩餘的

[rɪ`zɪdʒʊəl]

The police spent three hours looking for residual traces of the robber's presence in the house. At last, they found a fingerprint on the door knob.

警方花了三個鐘頭尋找搶匪在屋內留下的現場跡證，最後終於在門把上採到一枚指紋。

★★★★★

2005 sedimentary   *a. settled to the bottom of a liquid*   沉積的，沖積的

[ˌsɛdə`mɛntərɪ]

The sedimentary type of rock beneath the city made it impossible for the urban planners to build a subway system.

都市下方的沉積岩使都市計畫者無法興建地下鐵。

✤ **sen = old** 老的

★★★★☆

2006 senile   *a. having the weaknesses or diseases of old age; dotty; in one's dotage; decrepit; suffering from Alzheimer's disease*   衰老的，年邁的

[`sinaɪl]

The senile old woman claims that she was actually abducted by an alien from outer space when she was young.

年邁婦人堅稱年輕時曾遭外星人綁架。

★★★★★

2007 senior   *a. older / elder*   年長的 / 資深的

[`sinjə]

Since Mr. Kim was the senior employee at the company party, he felt it was his duty to pay for the meal and drinks.

金先生在公司聚會裡是資深員工，所以覺得自己應該請客。

★★★★★

2008 senator   *n. a member of a senate*   參議員

[`sɛnətə]

The senator knew the political world from the inside; he had a keen insight into the risks of political combat.

參議員通曉政界內幕，他對政治惡鬥的危險性有獨到見解。

❖ **sens, sent = feel** 感覺

★★★★★

2009 **sense**	*n. the ability to perceive or feel or to be conscious of the presence or properties of things*	感覺，意識，觀念

[sɛns]

It is easy to get lost in a city if you do not have a good sense of direction. We are especially likely to come out of the wrong exit of the subway.
方向感不好的人很容易在都市迷路，特別是很有可能走錯地下鐵出口。

★★★★★

2010 **sentimental**	*a. maudlin; over-emotional*	感情用事的，多愁善感的

[ˌsɛntə`mɛntl̩]

Judy's sentimental behavior was fitting at the end of the school years, but it still annoyed the more cynical students. She sobbed, cried and wailed all through the class.
茱蒂的多愁善感符合學年結束心情，但仍滿不在乎的同學感到惱怒，因為她整堂課都在嗚咽啜泣。

★★★★☆

2011 **presentiment**	*n. a vague expectation; foreboding*	不祥預感

[prɪ`zɛntəmənt]

When Anita lost the necklace which Ken had given to her, she had a presentiment that she wouldn't be able to get married to him.
當艾妮塔弄丟肯恩送的項鍊時，她有種無法嫁給他的不祥預感。

★★★★★

2012 **resent**	*v. show or feel indignation at; have hard feelings about*	憎恨，厭惡

[rɪ`zɛnt]

Jane's Asian boss resented her smoking in front of him. She was confused as to why her boss got so angry.
珍的亞洲籍老闆討厭她在他面前抽煙，但她不懂老闆為何如此生氣。

★★★☆☆

2013 **insensate**	*a. without physical sensation; unconscious; senseless*	無感覺的，無情的

[ɪn`sɛnset]

Some drugs are known to create an insensate bodily condition for those who use them.
已知部分藥物會使服用者失去身體感覺。

★★★★☆

2014 **consensus**	*n. general agreement / collective opinion*	意見一致／輿論

[kən`sɛnsəs]

There has been the general consensus in my nation that land speculation is too extreme, and it should be deterred.
國內輿論一致認為土地投機買賣過熱，應加以遏止。

★★★★★

2015 **consent**	*v. comply; concur; accede; acquiesce*	同意，贊成，答應

[kən`sɛnt]

Mr. Brown consented to take his family to the amusement park this coming Sunday. His wife, not to speak of his children, jumped up and down with joy.
伯朗先生答應周日帶家人去主題樂園玩，妻兒無不雀躍萬分。

★★★★★

| 2016 **sensitive** | *a. delicate; tender; touchy; susceptible; thin-skinned; vulnerable; hypersensitive* | 敏感的 |

[`sɛnsətɪv]

Don't mention her eyes. She's very sensitive about her prominent eyes. If you do, her eyes will suddenly get even wider.
別提她的雙眼，因為她對自己的凸眼非常敏感。如果你提了，她的雙眼會突然瞪得更大。

✥ sepia = black; rot 黑；腐壞

★★★☆☆

| 2017 **antiseptic** | *n. disinfectant* | 消毒劑 |

[ˌæntə`sɛptɪk]

A tincture of iodine has long been considered by doctors to be a good antiseptic because of its healing properties.
長期以來碘酒因其療效而被醫師視為極佳的消毒劑。

★★☆☆☆

| 2018 **sepia** | *n. the fluid secreted by cuttlefish / a dark red-dish-brown color* | 烏賊墨汁 / 深褐色 |

[`sipɪə]

I took some photographs with black-and-white film, and I took the film to the print shop to have it developed and printed. I asked them to print the pictures on color paper so that I can have sepia pictures.
我用黑白軟片拍了些照片再拿到照相館沖洗。我請他們洗彩色的，這樣我才能有深褐色照片。

★★★★☆

| 2019 **septic** | *a. putrefying* | 腐敗的，敗血的 |

[`sɛptɪk]

A septic tank is one in which the organic matter in sewage is disintegrated through bacterial activity.
腐敗蓄水池的污水中含有透過細菌分解的有機物質。

✥ sert, sort- = join, the same kind 參與，同類

★★★★★

MP3
83

| 2020 **insert** | *v. put in* | 插入，嵌入 |

[ɪn`sɜt]

The nurse inserted a needle into my arm. I have never seen a more giant syringe in my entire life.
護士將針筒插入我的手臂，我這輩子從來沒看過這麼粗的針筒。

★★★★★

| 2021 **desert** | *v. forsake; abandon; leave high and dry; leave in the lurch; turn one's back on* | 拋棄，遺棄，離棄 |

[dɛ`zɜt]

Nick deserted Sue when she needed him. He just left her high and dry. She was so disappointed with him.
尼克在蘇需要時離開她，使她陷入困境，她對他非常失望。

		★★★★☆	
2022	**sort**	**v.** *assort; classify* / **n.** *category; kind*	分類整理 / 種類，品種
	[sɔrt]	The old man's relatives brought all of their children to his birthday party, so he had a hard time sorting out who belonged to whom. 親戚帶所有子女來參加老人的生日會，他很難區別誰是誰的孩子。	

		★★★★☆	
2023	**assort**	**v.** *categorize; classify* / *arrange in groups*	分類，分級 / 使相配
	[ə`sɔrt]	At the blind date, the oddly assorted pairs had their first chance to talk to each other. They began their conversation with such cliché questions. 一對配對奇怪的男女在盲目約會上終於等到聊天機會，兩人從一些陳腔濫調問題開始聊起。	

		★★★★☆	
2024	**consort**	**v.** *associate with; keep company with*	結交，往交
	[kən`sɔrt]	David was forced to consort with all types of criminals while he was working as an undercover detective. 大衛在臥底期間被迫和各種罪犯往來。	

		★★★★★	
2025	**resort**	**n.** *a place frequented for holidays or for a specified purpose* / **v.** *turn to*	度假勝地 / 求助
	[rɪ`zɔrt]	Hawaii is known for its fun and relaxing vacation resorts. Most Americans hope to enjoy their vacation there. 夏威夷是既有趣又能令人放鬆的著名度假勝地，許多美國人都希望在當地度假。	

❖ sic, suc = juice, water 多汁的，水

		★★★★☆	
2026	**succulent**	**a.** *juicy* / *luscious; yummy; palatable*	多汁的，水分多的 / 美味的
	[`sʌkjələnt]	The tangerine was so succulent that he could actually feel his mouth watering. It was full of juice and delicious. 橘子水分多到讓他感到滿嘴都是水，真是汁多味美。	

		★★★☆☆	
2027	**sucker**	**n.** *a gullible or easily deceived person* / *a pipe through which liquid is drawn by suction* / *a person or thing that sucks*	笨蛋 / 吸管 / 吸吮者
	[`sʌkə]	The used car salesman's motto was that there was "a sucker born every minute." He is always optimistic about making a sale. 該名二手車銷售員的座右銘是「每分鐘都有笨蛋誕生」。他對成交總是充滿樂觀。	

★★★☆☆

2028 desiccant | *n. a substance used as a drying agent* | 乾燥劑

[`dɛsəkənt]

A desiccant is a substance that absorbs a great deal of water, and is used as a drying agent. It is helpful in reducing the humidity in air.
乾燥劑可吸收大量水分，它被當成乾燥的媒介幫助減少空氣中的濕氣。

★★★★★

2029 suck | *v. draw (a fluid) into the mouth by making a partial vacuum* | 吸吮，吸食

[sʌk]

Myth has it that Count Dracula had an uncontrollable desire to suck the blood from a young virgin's neck.
相傳德古拉公爵有難以克制的欲望，想從年輕處女頸部吸血。

★★★★☆

2030 suction | *n. the act or an instance of sucking* | 吸力，吸入

[`sʌkʃən]

The vacuum that the woman bought at a department store was very expensive, but its suction power was rather weak.
女子在百貨公司買到的吸塵器非常貴，但吸力很弱。

✦ sol = only, one 單獨

★★★★☆

2031 solitude | *n. seclusion; loneliness* | 孤獨

[`sɑlə,tud]

There are times when we want a person's company, and there are times when we prefer solitude.
有時我們想要他人作伴，有時卻寧願獨處。

★★★☆☆

2032 solo | *a. unaccompanied; solitary; unaided / n. a vocal or instrumental piece or passage, or a dance, performed by one person* | 單獨表演的 / 單獨表演

[`solo]

Ellen was especially nervous before the concert, since it was to be her first solo performance.
艾倫在音樂會開演前特別緊張，因為這是她第一次單獨表演。

★★★★★

2033 solitary | *a. alone; unattended; lonesome; lonely / secluded; individual* | 單獨的 / 孤獨的

[`sɑlə,tɛrɪ]

The prisoner was sentenced to solitary confinement after he beat up four prison guards during an attempted breakout.
囚犯企圖越獄並在毆打四名獄卒後被判處單獨監禁。

★★★★★

2034 desolate | *a. ruined; deserted; uninhabited; barren; bleak; dreary* | 荒涼的，杳無人煙的

[`dɛsḷɪt]

That town, before the flood, was a nice and friendly place to visit, but now nobody lives there, and it has become a desolate, empty place.
水災發生前該小鎮是個值得一遊的好地方，如今卻變得杳無人煙，一片荒涼。

❖ solu, solv = melt; solve 溶化；解決

★★★★★

2035 **resolution**	*n. determination / solution; unraveling*	決心，決定 / 解決，解答
[ˌrɛzəˈluʃən]		

Each year he made **resolutions** on New Year's Eve, but he never kept one of them. Therefore, he decided to make a different one. It was 'not to make any resolutions.'

每到新年前夕他都會許下新年新希望，但從未實現。於是他決定來點不同的：「不再許任何新希望」。

★★★★☆

2036 **solvent**	*n. a solvent liquid / a. having enough money to meet one's liabilities*	溶劑 / 有償付能力的
[ˈsɑlvənt]		

When using oil-based paints, it is always advisable to have some **solvent** nearby. Otherwise, you might not be able to use the paints because they dry quickly.

使用油性塗料時最好準備一些溶劑，否則油漆會乾得很快而無法使用。

★★★★☆

2037 **soluble**	*a. that can be dissolved / that can be solved*	可溶解的 / 可解決的
[ˈsɑljəbl]		

Instant coffee, since it is **soluble** in hot water, is a quick alternative to brewing or percolating coffee beans.

可溶解於熱水的即溶咖啡是濾煮咖啡豆之外的另一個省時選擇。

★★★★★

2038 **resolve**	*v. make up one's mind; determine / solve; figure out/ n. determination*	下決心 / 解決 / 決心
[rɪˈzɑlv]		

Christy gathered her **resolve** to finally break up with her boyfriend, even though she knew that it would be hard.

雖然覺得很難辦到，但克莉絲蒂終於下定決心要跟男友分手。

★★★★★

2039 **solution**	*n. resolution*	解答，解決（辦法）
[səˈluʃən]		

Neither the students, nor the teacher, could find a **solution** for that ambiguous problem. At last, they decided to skip the problem and move onto the next.

無論是學生或老師都無法為模稜兩可的問題提出解答，最後他們決定跳過先看下一題。

❖ somn = sleep 睡眠

★★★☆☆

2040 **somnolent**	*a. inducing drowsiness*	催眠的
[ˈsɑmnələnt]		

My English instructor's voice has a **somnolent** effect. Whenever he begins to talk, I feel so sleepy.

英語講師的聲音有催眠作用，每當他開始講話，我就覺得好想睡。

★★☆☆☆

| 2041 **somnambulism** | *n.* *sleepwalking* | 夢遊症 |

[sɑm`næmbjə,lɪzəm]

His somnambulism had become so serious that one morning, his wife found him outside the house, in the car, trying to drive to work in his pajamas while still asleep.

他的夢遊症日益嚴重，某日妻子發現他在睡夢中身穿睡衣坐在車內，打算出發上班。

★★★★☆

| 2042 **insomnia** | *n.* *habitual sleeplessness; inability to sleep* | 失眠症 |

[ɪn`sɑmnɪə]

Sam suffers from insomnia. He can't get a good night's sleep without drugs. One day, he took twice as many pills as the doctor had instructed, and he slept well. Next morning, when he went to work, his boss asked him where he had been on the previous day.

山姆受失眠之苦，不吃藥就睡不好。某日他服用兩倍的醫生建議劑量結果睡得香甜。隔日上班時老闆卻問他昨天到哪去了。

⁘ son = sound 聲音

★★★☆☆

| 2043 **sonorous** | *a.* *resonant* | 響亮的，宏亮的，鏗鏘有力的 |

[sə`nɔrəs]

The opera singer is well-known for his sonorous baritone voice. He especially has a multitude of female admirers.

這名歌劇男低音以其低沉宏亮的嗓音聞名，特別受到許多女性仰慕者的青睞。

★★★★☆

| 2044 **sonar** | *n.* *a system for the underwater detection of objects by reflected or emitted sound* | 聲納 |

[`sonɑr]

An American submersible named Alvin located the sunken ship "the Titanic" by means of sonar. It was lying at the depth of 12,000 feet.

美國深海探測潛艇艾文號靠聲納找到位於海平面以下一萬兩千英呎的鐵達尼號沉船位置。

★★★☆☆

| 2045 **resonant** | *a.* *echoing; resounding; vibrating* | 共鳴的，回音的 |

[`rɛzn̩ənt]

There is a certain resonant frequency that will shatter crystal, and it is said that some opera singers can reach it during a song.

據說有些歌劇演唱者在歌唱時可達到足以震碎水晶的某種共鳴頻率。

★★★★★

| 2046 **consonant** | *n.* *a speech sound in which the breath is at least partly obstructed and which to form a syllable must be combined with a vowel* | 子音 |

[`kɑnsənənt]

Students of English must concentrate on and master the pronunciation of consonants. Many Oriental students especially have difficulty telling the difference between 'f' and 'p.'

學英文的學生必須學好子音發言。許多東方學生特別無法分辨子音 [f] 和 [p]。

✥ spect, spic = see 看

★★★★★

2047 **prospect**	*n. expectations; outlook; vista*	展望，希望，前途

[`prɑspɛk]

The prospect of untold riches drove the early European explorers in search of the mythical "eastern route" to China.
早期歐洲探險家受到大筆財富驅使，開始尋找神秘的「東方貿易路線」，最後來到中國。

★★★★★

2048 **inspect**	*v. look closely into; scrutinize; probe; investigate*	仔細檢查，審查

[ɪn`spɛkt]

The boss will inspect the work of all of his employees, because the productivity of the workers has been going down for six months in a row.
老闆將仔細檢查所有員工的工作成果，因為員工生產力已連續六個月下滑。

★★★☆☆

2049 **espionage**	*n. the practice of spying; spying*	間諜活動

[`ɛspɪənɑdʒ]

Mr. Carpenter was convicted of industrial espionage. Several of his spies had infiltrated a rival firm.
卡本特先生因從事商業間諜活動被叛有罪。他的一些間諜已滲透到一間對手公司。

★★★★☆

2050 **spectacle**	*n. sight*	景象

[`spɛktəkl]

Another spectacle that depresses the male and makes him fear women, and therefore hate them, is that of a woman looking another woman up and down to see what she is wearing.
The Case Against Women — James Thurber
另一個使男人沮喪、害怕並進而討厭女人的景象是女人會互相上下打量，看看對方穿什麼。　　　　　　——《對女人提告》（美國當代作家）詹姆斯·桑伯

★★★☆☆

2051 **speculative**	*a. of, based on, engaged in, or inclined to speculation / involving the risk of loss*	思索的／投機的

[`spɛkjə‚letɪv]

Don't put everything you have in that speculative stock. You are going for stone-broke. You know they say, "Never put all your eggs in one basket."
別把所有財產押在那支投機股上，否則會賠個精光。俗話說：「雞蛋不要放在同一個籃子裡。」

Tea Time... ☕

<Roman story> Salary **In ancient Rome salt was often given as a salary for a soldier.**	〈來自羅馬傳說〉鹽餉，薪俸 古羅馬時代以鹽作為士兵糧餉。（註：本字源自拉丁文 salarium，意指古羅馬時代發給士兵的「鹽餉」，在當時鹽是非常珍貴的物品，後世便將本字引申成「薪資，薪俸」。）

salinity [sə`lɪnətɪ] *n. the degree of being salty* | 鹽分，鹽度，鹽性

The salinity of the ocean water is not constant. The waters near a coast are less salty because of the input of fresh water, while those in the tropical area are saltier because of the evaporation of water.
海水鹽度不一，沿岸海水因淡水匯入故鹽度較低，熱帶地區則因水分蒸發導致鹽度較高。

1 Complete each word by filling in the blank with proper spelling so that it has the same meaning as suggested. Then please write the meaning of each word in Chinese.

1. 取代   = super___e
2. 癡迷   = ob___sion
3. 久坐的   = ___entary
4. 沉積的   = ___imentary
5. 資深的   = ___ior
6. 參議員   = ___ator
7. 多愁善感的 = ____imental
8. 不祥預感 = pre____iment
9. 無感覺的 = in____ate
10. 敏感的 = ____itive

11. antiseptic   = _____
12. desert   = _____
13. assort   = _____
14. resort   = _____
15. succulent   = _____
16. desiccant   = _____
17. solitude   = _____
18. resolution   = _____
19. somnambulism = _____
20. insomnia   = _____

2 Choose a word that best completes the sentence.

21. The zookeepers decided to _____ the lion before moving it to another place.
    (A) sedate   (B) resent   (C) consent   (D) comply

22. Do you happen to have some _____ for this cut?
    (A) desert   (B) antiseptic   (C) senator   (D) sense

23. This orange is not _____ enough.
    (A) septic   (B) insensate   (C) succulent   (D) sensitive

3 The highlighted word is closest in meaning to which of the following?

24. It has been the general consensus that taxes are too high.
    (A) agreement   (B) residence   (C) abode   (D) subsidy

25. Jane is so sentimental that she sheds tears even when she sees a leaf falling.
    (A) soluble   (B) maudlin   (C) somnolent   (D) solitary

❖ spire = breathe 呼吸

★★★★★

MP3 84

2052 inspiration

[ˌɪnspəˈreʃən]

n. a supposed creative force or influence on poets, artists, musicians, etc., stimulating the production of works of art   靈感

Thomas Edison said that an idea was ninety-nine percent perspiration and one percent inspiration.

愛迪生曾說發明構想來自百分之九十九的努力和百分之一的靈感。

★★★★★

2053 respiration

[ˌrɛspəˈreʃən]

n. the act or an instance of breathing   呼吸

Artificial respiration was needed to save the drowning victim. Fortunately, there was a man who knew how to do it. He began to blow air through the victim's mouth and nose and succeeded in helping her start breathing.

溺水者需施以人工呼吸，幸好在場有個男子會。他開始將空氣吹進她的口鼻裡，成功將她救回。

★★★★★

2054 expiry

[ɪkˈspaɪrɪ]

n. the end of the validity or duration of something   期滿，終止

The expiry date on his driver's license had come and gone, so he was forced to take his driver's test again, but he failed.

他的駕照過期了，他被迫重考，但沒考過。

★★★★☆

2055 aspirant

[əˈspaɪrənt]

n. a person who aspires   追求者，胸懷大志者

Dr. Turner was the only aspirant that had applied for the small, but highly respected faculty at the university.

透納博士是唯一一位爭取在規模雖小卻頗負盛名的大學出任教授的人。

★★★★★

2056 perspire

[pəˈspaɪr]

v. sweat   出汗，流汗

When my employer started to blame me for the incident, I started to heavily perspire.

上司因該事指責我時，我開始汗流浹背。

★★★★☆

2057 transpiration

[ˌtrænspəˈreʃən]

n. perspiration / emission   蒸發／散發

The transpiration of sweat through the skin is necessary to keep the body cool. Evaporation is extremely effective for cooling the body.

汗水透過皮膚蒸發以保持身體涼爽是必要的。蒸發對身體降溫非常有效。

✣ spr+vowel（母音）, sp+vowel（母音）+r = scatter 分散，散播

★★★★☆

| 2058 **sparsely** | **ad.** *thinly* | 稀少地 |

[`spɑrslɪ]

The capital of my country is densely populated. So I sometimes wish that I could live in a more sparsely populated area.

我國家的首都人口稠密，所以有時我希望我能住在人口稀少的地區。

★★★★★

| 2059 **spray** | **v.** *sprinkle* | 噴灑，噴塗 |

[spre]

As soon as Mary heard her date slam the car door, she ran into the bathroom to spray on a little more perfume.

當瑪麗一聽到約會對象砰地關上車門，便衝進浴室再多噴點香水。

★★★★★

| 2060 **sporadic** | **a.** *intermittent; fitful; periodic; spasmodic; occasional* | 時有時無的，零星的 |

[spə`rædɪk]

Although the thunder was long and loud, the lightning was sporadic. We could see the light only from time to time.

雖然雷聲又久又隆隆作響，但閃電卻時有時無，我們只能零星看見閃光。

★★★★★

| 2061 **sprinkler** | **n.** *a device for sprinkling water on a lawn or to extinguish fires* 自動灑水裝置 |

[`sprɪŋklə]

During the water shortage, no one was allowed to use their lawn sprinkler systems. Firefighters had to carry the water which people needed so desperately.

缺水期間不可使用草坪自動灑水裝置，消防隊員須扛水給亟需用水民眾。

★★★★★

| 2062 **prosper** | **v.** *flourish; thrive* | 使繁榮，使昌盛，使成功 |

[`prɑspə]

His business began to prosper once the war between the two countries ended and trade resumed.

兩國戰爭結束、重啟貿易交流後，他的生意也開始好轉。

✣ str+vowel（母音）= tight 緊的，繃緊的

★★★★☆

| 2063 **strenuous** | **a.** *grueling; exhausting; demanding; tough; arduous; laborious; toil-some; burdensome* | 費力的，奮發的 |

[`strɛnjʊəs]

Running is more strenuous exercise than walking. Therefore, I prefer walking. Running is more exhausting.

跑步比步行費力，所以我寧願步行，跑步太累了。

★★★★★

2064 restrict

[rɪ`strɪkt]

v. limit; confine; bound 限制，限定

Because the hall was not spacious enough, we restricted the number of attendants to 100, and people who wanted to participate had to make reservations in advance.

由於大廳空間不足，我們將與會者名額限制在一百名，且有意參加者需事先預約。

★★★★★

2065 strict

[strɪkt]

a. rigorous; severe; austere; stern; harsh 嚴格的，嚴厲的

Strict discipline is necessary for an unruly child. There is a famous proverb: spare the rod, spoil the child.

任性孩童需嚴加管教，俗話說：「不打不成器。」

★★★★☆

2066 strand

[strænd]

v. put into a difficult, helpless position / n. string 使陷於困境／繩，線

After the war, many POW's were stranded in that country. They were detained in several concentration camps.

戰後許多戰俘在該國陷於困境，被拘留在幾個集中營裡。

★★★★★

2067 restrain

[rɪ`stren]

v. hold back from action; check; suppress; curb 抑制，遏制

When the news came that he had won the lottery, Lewis could hardly restrain himself from singing and shouting like a madman.

消息顯示路易斯中了樂透時，他忍不住像瘋子般又叫又唱起來。

★★★★★

2068 constrain

[kən`stren]

v. restrict severely / confine; imprison / compel; urge 壓制／限制／迫使

I don't like Jim very much. No matter how hard I try, I can't constrain myself whenever he is around, and I end up saying something that causes us to get into a fight.

我很不喜歡吉姆，無論多努力都無法自我克制，最後總是一言不和跟他吵起來。

★★★★★

2069 strait

[stret]

n. a narrow passage of water connecting two seas or large bodies of water / a. narrow 海峽／狹窄的

The Bering Strait lies between Asia and North America. It is believed that Asian people moved to America by crossing the land bridge.

白令海峽位於亞洲和北美洲之間，一般相信亞洲人穿越陸橋遷移到美洲。

⁜ **super = above, on top of** 超過，在～頂端

★★★☆☆

²⁰⁷⁰ **superable**	*a. able to be overcome*	可勝過的，可征服的，可超越的

[`supərəbl]

Every problem related with human beings, except death, is superable if one tries hard enough to find the solution.

除了死亡之外，人類遭遇的所有問題都是可以超越的，只要努力就能找出解決的辦法。

★★★★☆

²⁰⁷¹ **supernatural**	*a. preternatural; inexplicable; uncanny / ghostly; spectral*	超自然的，神奇的 / 神怪的，鬼怪的

[ˌsupə`nætʃərəl]

Maggie became a true believer in supernatural beings when she awoke from a deep sleep to see an apparition at the foot of her bed.

自從瑪姬從熟睡中醒來看見幽靈站在床尾後，就變得相信超自然生物。

★★★★☆

²⁰⁷² **superb**	*a. supreme; splendid*	極好的，上乘的，一流的

[su`pɝb]

Bob was a superb cook, and he thought it would help him find a good wife. However, instead he became a good cook for his wife who could not cook at all.

鮑伯是一流廚師，他覺得這有助於找到好老婆。然而他卻變成無廚藝妻子的好大廚。

★★★★☆

²⁰⁷³ **superlative**	*a. paramount; supreme; consummate; superior; best; matchless; peerless; superb; ace*	最好的，無與倫比的

[su`pɝlətɪv]

She was a superlative skater, and eventually won a gold medal in speed skating at the Winter Olympics.

她是最強的溜冰選手，最後在冬季奧運會競速溜冰項目中贏得金牌。

★★★☆☆

²⁰⁷⁴ **insuperable**	*a. impossible to overcome*	不能克服的

[ɪn`supərəbl]

There has always been an insuperable gulf between him and me. There has always been a certain kind of conflict between us.

我和他之間存有難以克服的鴻溝，成為我們一定形式的衝突。

★★★★★

²⁰⁷⁵ **supreme**	*a. outstanding; pre-eminent; leading; superlative; sublime*	至高無上的

[sə`prim]

Many atheists, because they don't believe in a supreme creator, accept the theory of evolution as a possible explanation for the origin of life as we know it today.

許多無神論者因為不相信至高無上的創造者，因此以進化論作為生命起源的可能性解釋。

★★★☆☆

2076 **supremacy**	*n.* the state of being supreme; pre-eminence; superiority 　至高無上，絕對優勢
[sə`prɛməsɪ]	The feeling of supremacy over another race is the basis of all forms of racism. We should know that all human beings are created equal. 認為自己凌駕於其他種族之上的想法是種族主義的基礎，我們應了解所有人類都是生而平等的。

✤ sur- = up　在～之上，向上

★★★★★

2077 **surplus**	*a.* excess; leftover; extra; spare / *n.* excess; glut 　過剩的 / 剩餘
[`sɝpləs]	Till the seventeenth century, the wealthier sections in England, landlords and businessmen who had any surplus money, were in difficulties where to keep it. Some hid their wealth in their gardens. 　　　　　　　　　　　　　　*The Origin of Modern Banks* — Victor Cohen 直到十七世紀英國的富裕階級、地主和商人都不知該把閒錢存放在哪裡，有些人只好藏在花園裡。 　　　　　　　　　　　　　── 《現代銀行的起源》維克多‧柯恩

★★★★★

2078 **surrender**	*v.* relinquish; forgo; forsake; give up; yield; abandon / capitulate; raise the white flag; throw up one's hands; succumb; submit 　放棄 / 投降
[sə`rɛndə]	The General vowed never to surrender, but when push came to shove, he was forced to retreat. 將軍發誓絕不投降，但面臨最後關頭時還是被迫撤退。

★★★★★

2079 **surface**	*n.* the outside of a material body 　表面
[`sɝfɪs]	The diver came up to the surface of the water to breathe. All the other people were worried when the diver remained in the water for nearly three minutes. 潛水者浮出水面呼吸，當他持續待在水中將近三分鐘，所有人都擔心起來。

★★★★☆

2080 **surveillance**	*n.* scrutiny; reconnaissance 　監視，看守，監督
[sə`veləns]	The surveillance cameras at a bank are hardly ever turned off, night or day. They help prevent burglaries. 銀行監視攝影機無論日夜很少關掉，以防搶劫。

★★★★★

2081 **surpass**	*v.* outdo; outperform; outstrip; outdistance / exceed; go beyond 　超過，凌駕 / 非～能勝任
[sə`pæs]	He studied for hours, yet he was never able to surpass his G.P.A. of 2.50. At last he decided to quit school. 他念了好久的書，卻無法超過學業總平均點數 G.P.A. 2.50 分，最後決定休學。

✦ tac, tic = silent 沈默的

★★★★☆

| 2082 **reticent** | *a. taciturn; unresponsive; reserved; tight-lipped* | 無言的,沈默的 |

[`rɛtəsn̩t]

Never be reticent. You can speak openly to anyone here. Please feel free to speak out if you have a good idea.

請暢所欲言千萬不要保持沉默,如果有好點子請大方說出來。

★★★★☆

| 2083 **taciturn** | *a. reticent; uncommunicative; mute* | 沈默寡言的,無言的 |

[`tæsə,tɜn]

Nancy seemed to be so shy and taciturn that I couldn't talk to her. However I ventured to approach her and began to talk to her.

南西似乎很害羞又沈默寡言,無法和她交談。但我大膽靠近她開始聊天。

★★★★☆

| 2084 **tacit** | *a. understood or implied without being stated* | 默許的,心照不宣的 |

[`tæsɪt]

Father nodded his head without saying anything. He gave me his tacit consent. And then he wore a warm smile.

父親點頭不發一語,並帶著和藹笑容默許我去做。

✦ tach, tack, tact, tang, ting, tag, tig = touch 接觸

★★★★☆

| 2085 **contingent** | *a. dependent on* | 視~情況而定的,以~為條件的 |

[kən`tɪndʒənt]

Whether or not they win the game is contingent upon whether or not Larry Bird is able to play.

他們能否贏球要看大鳥柏德能不能下場打球。

★★★★★

| 2086 **tag** | *v. follow closely; trail behind / n. label* | 緊緊跟隨 / 標籤,牌子 |

[tæg]

Wherever I go, my kids want to tag along with me. Sometimes I like their company because I don't feel lonely with them.

不管走到哪裡孩子們都黏著我,有時我喜歡他們作伴因為這樣不會感到孤單。

★★★★★

| 2087 **contiguous** | *a. touching; in contact* | 接觸的,鄰近的,相鄰的 |

[kən`tɪgjuəs]

My house is located in a good residential area, contiguous to shops, schools and other local amenities.

我家位於緊鄰商圈、學校和其他文教設施的優良住宅區。

2088 contagious

[kən`tedʒəs]

a. likely to transmit disease by contact; infectious — 接觸傳染的

The chicken pox is a very contagious disease. When children have it they are encouraged to stay home from school because they could give the disease to the other children.

水痘是非常容易接觸傳染的疾病。孩童長水痘時應待在家中不要上學，以免傳染給其他學童。

★★★★★

2089 tackle

[`tækl]

v. grapple with; cope with; face up to; face; confront; address — 捉住，面對，處理

I think you should tackle the challenge head on at the earliest possible moment. If you keep avoiding the challenge, you will never overcome your fear.

我認為你應盡速面對挑戰，如果一再逃避將永遠無法克服恐懼。

★★★★★

2090 tangible

[`tændʒəbl]

a. perceptible by touch; touchable; palpable — 可觸知的，有形的

As she faced her attacker, the sense of fear in the air was almost tangible. But she took out the whistle she was carrying and blew it loudly.

當她面對攻擊者，幾乎連空氣中都可以嗅出她的恐懼，但隨即拿出攜帶的哨子大聲吹響。

★★★★☆

2091 tactile

[`tæktl]

a. of the sense of touch; perceived by touch — 觸覺的，能觸知的

The doctor's tactile search of the injured area produced nothing except pain. At last the patient began to call him names.

醫師觸診受傷部位弄得病患很痛，病人最後開始罵人。

★★★★☆

2092 contaminate

[kən`tæmə,net]

v. pollute / defile; poison; foul; spoil; taint — 污染 / 毒害，弄髒

Though their horses were thirsty and tired, they couldn't let them drink out of the pond because it was contaminated.

儘管馬匹又累又渴，卻不能喝池水，因為已遭到污染。

✥ tail = cut 切，減

★★★★★

2093 detail

[dɪ`tel]

n. small items or particulars; fine points; specifics — 細節，詳情，細目

FEMALE ROOMMATE WANTED
One room near campus. Available July 1. Rent $100 per month until August 31. $110 thereafter. Call Tom for details, 817-7453.

＊ 誠徵女性室友 ＊
近校園，七月一日起入住，八月底前月租一百美元，九月起一百一十美元。欲知更多詳情請電洽湯姆 817-7453。

★★★★★

2094 curtail

[kɜ`tel]

v. reduce; cut down; shorten　　　　　　　　　　縮減，縮短，省略

My teacher received an emergency phone call during class and asked if we could curtail class so that he could go home to take care of the emergency.

老師在課堂上接到了緊急電話，便詢問我們能不能提早下課，好讓他回家處理緊急狀況。

★★★★★

2095 retailer

[`ritelə]

n. a small merchant　　　　　　　　　　　　　　　零售店

In the 1930s in America, there were many retailers, which were frequently called "Five-and-dimes." Kress was one of the most successful.

美國三〇年代有許多稱為 Five-and-dimes 的廉價零售商店，其中最成功的是克里斯商店。

✦ tain, ten, tin = hold 握，持

★★★☆☆

2096 continence

[`kɑntənəns]

n. self-restraint in sexual activity; total abstinence　　　禁慾，自制

The minister advised sexual continence. As soon as the minister ended his sermon, all the people in the congregation were silent.

牧師建議禁慾的長篇大論結束後，集會場上一片啞然。

★★★☆☆

2097 pertinent

[`pɜtnənt]

a. relevant; germane; apposite; appropriate; suitable; fitting　　有關的

Charles knew that the meeting was pertinent to his current project, but he felt that lunch with his girlfriend was more important.

查爾斯知道會議和目前進行中的案子有關，但他覺得跟女友共進午餐更重要。

★★★☆☆

2098 abstinence

[`æbstənəns]

n. the act of abstaining from food or alcohol;　　　　節制，戒酒
self-denial; temperance

When he awoke the next morning, he swore he would never drink again, but he knew that abstinence would be very difficult.

他隔日清醒後發誓絕不再喝酒，但他知道很難戒酒。

★★★★★

2099 tenacious

[tɪ`neʃəs]

a. firm; sturdy; rigid; fast; tight / dogged;　　　緊握的 / 堅持的，頑強的
pertinacious; unswerving; determined;
stalwart; steadfast; unwavering; adamant; inflexible; unyielding

I noticed her fear because of her tenacious grip on my arm all through the movie. When I came back home I noticed I had received a bruise on my arm.

她因為害怕，整場電影都緊抓著我的手臂不放，回家後我手臂都瘀青了。

★★★★☆

| 2100 **pertinacious** | *a. stubborn; persistent / tenacious* | 不屈不撓的 / 頑強的 |

[ˌpɜtn̩ˋeʃəs]

The Champion once again proved to the world just how pertinacious he was by winning the competition for the fifteenth year in a row.
冠軍選手連續十五年獲勝，再次向全世界證明他的不屈不撓。

★★★★★

| 2101 **maintenance** | *n. the process of maintaining; upkeep* | 維修，保養，維持 |

[ˋmentənəns]

His career as the building maintenance engineer had always seemed good enough to him, but his wife had become tired of the humdrum life.
大樓維修工程師的工作對他來說夠好了，但妻子卻厭倦平凡生活。

Tea Time... ☕

<From the name of an American feminist> Bloomers	〈來自美國女權運動者之名〉燈籠褲
Bloomers were named after Mrs. Amelia Jenks Bloomer(1818-94), an American champion of women's rights.	燈籠褲是以美國女權運動健將愛米莉亞·珍肯斯·布倫姆女士之名命名的。（註：布倫姆女士 (1818-94) 發明一種能穿在裙子內的寬鬆燈籠褲，方便婦女活動自如。）

bloomers [ˋblumɚ] *n. women's loose, baggy trousers drawn close at the ankles and worn under a short skirt* │ 女用燈籠褲

The mother advised her daughter not to wear her bloomers while riding her bicycle because they may get stuck in the chain.
母親建議女兒騎腳踏車時不要穿可能會卡住鏈條的燈籠褲。

1

Complete each word by filling in the blank with proper spelling so that it has the same meaning as suggested. Then please write the meaning of each word in Chinese.

1. 靈感   = i n _ _ _ _ a t i o n
2. 追求者   = _ _ _ _ _ a n t
3. 期滿   = _ _ p i r y
4. 觸覺的   = _ _ _ _ i l e
5. 投機的   = _ _ _ _ u l a t i v e
6. 呼吸   = r e _ _ _ _ _ t i o n
7. 蒸發   = t r a n _ _ _ _ _ t i o n
8. 稀少地   = _ _ _ _ s e l y
9. 自動灑水裝置 = _ _ _ _ n k l e r
10. 使繁榮   = p r o _ _ _ _

11. strenuous   = _____
12. restrict   = _____
13. restrain   = _____
14. superable   = _____
15. superlative = _____
16. surpass   = _____
17. taciturn   = _____
18. contiguous   = _____
19. contagious   = _____
20. tangible   = _____

2

Choose a word that best completes the sentence.

21. **The _____ of his business is very bright.**
    (A) sprinkler   (B) transpiration   (C) prospect   (D) spray

22. **The _____ says 60 dollars plus tax.**
    (A) price-tag   (B) contact   (C) strait   (D) respiration

3

The highlighted word is closest in meaning to which of the following?

23. **The general had no alternative but to surrender to the enemy troops.**
    (A) strand   (B) tackle   (C) yield   (D) expiry

24. **One of Jim's colleagues tends to perspire in front of the boss.**
    (A) tackle   (B) surpass   (C) sweat   (D) contaminate

25. **I do not like strenuous exercise. I think walking would be enough.**
    (A) exhausting   (B) intermittent   (C) supreme   (D) superb

❖ ten, tend, tens = pull, thin 拉，拖，稀少

★★★☆☆

2102 attenuate

[ə`tɛnjuˌet]

v. *make thin / reduce in force*   使變薄 / 使變弱，衰減

After a thorough investigation, it was determined that the machine malfunctioned because an important part attenuated and broke.

經過仔細檢查後，判定機器是因一重要零件壞掉而故障的。

★★★☆☆

2103 extenuate

[ɪk`stɛnjuˌet]

v. *lessen the seeming seriousness of guilt or an offense by reference to some mitigating factor*   減輕，掩飾

The circumstances of the murder provided little room to extenuate the guilt of the suspect, who had been caught holding the knife.

兇案現場狀況使持刀兇嫌難以脫罪。

★★★★★

2104 tension

[`tɛnʃən]

n. *stress; pressure; tenseness*   緊張氣氛，精神緊張

As they waited for the announcement of the Academy Award winner, the tension in the air was so thick you could cut it with a knife.

等待宣布奧斯卡金像獎得主時，全場氣氛緊張，叫人透不過氣來。

★★★☆☆

2105 tenuous

[`tɛnjuəs]

a. *flimsy; slight; slender; insubstantial; feeble*   薄弱的，貧乏的

I couldn't agree with his tenuous argument, which wasn't cogent enough. Furthermore, his argument wasn't based on reality.

我不同意他說服力不足的薄弱論證，何況他的論證也不是根據事實。

★★★★☆

2106 contentious

[kən`tɛnʃəs]

a. *argumentative; quarrelsome; controversial*   有異議的，足以引起爭論的，好爭辯的

There are a lot of problems to overcome in our turbulent and contentious society. We must be alarmed at the number of actions at law.

在動盪且爭議不斷的社會中，有許多問題尚待克服，我們必須對許多法律訴訟有所警覺。

★★★★☆

2107 distend

[dɪ`stɛnd]

v. *swell; inflate*   使膨脹，使擴張

David ate so much that his stomach began to distend, and he could not sit comfortably in his jeans.

大衛吃太飽肚子很撐，穿牛仔褲坐著很不舒服。

★★★★★

2108 extent

[ɪk`stɛnt]

n. *the space over which a thing extends; scope*   程度，限度，範圍

I didn't know to what extent I could push the project. I did not even know if the project was feasible.

我不知道我可以將此專案推到什麼程度，甚至不知道是否可行。

❖ terr = earth; soil 地；土壤

★★★★★

²¹⁰⁹ **territory**	*n. domain*	國家領土，版圖
[ˋtɛrə͵tɔrɪ]	Korea is characterized by abundant hills and mountains, which occupy almost 70 percent of its territory. 韓國特色為山陵茂密，幾乎占國土面積的百分之七十。	

★★★★☆

²¹¹⁰ **terrain**	*n. topography; ground; territory*	地形，地勢，地域
[tɛˋren]	Knowing the terrain is always a good thing before going on a hike. Otherwise we might get lost in the deep forest. 健行前先熟悉地形永遠是好事，否則可能會在茂密森林中迷路。	

★★★☆☆

²¹¹¹ **inter**	*v. bury*	埋葬
[ɪnˋtɝ]	The princess decided to inter the dead king's sword with him in the tomb. He loved the sword which he had carried everywhere when he had conquered the surrounding nations. 王子決定將死去國王的劍一同埋入墓中。國王生前甚愛這把劍，征戰鄰國時也隨身攜帶。	

★★★★☆

²¹¹² **subterranean**	*a. underground*	地下的，隱蔽的
[͵sʌbtəˋrenɪən]	The hostages began to dig a subterranean passage to escape from the concentration camp. It took them almost a couple of months to make a 10-meter-long tunnel. 人質開始挖掘地下通道以逃離集中營，花了好幾個月才完成十公尺長的地道。	

❖ term, tern = end 結束

★★★★☆

²¹¹³ **terminus**	*n. a station at the end of a railway or bus route; terminal*	終點站，終點
[ˋtɝmənəs]	This subway station is a terminus; it is the end of the line. All the passengers should get off the train when the train arrives at this station. 本地下鐵車站是此線終點站，到站後所有乘客都應下車。	

★★★★★

2114 terminal

n. a terminus for trains or long-distance buses / a. deadly; mortal

終點的／末期的

[`tɜmənḷ]

One of the most difficult tasks for a medical doctor is that he sometimes has to tell his patient that he is terminally ill.

醫生最困難的工作之一就是有時需告訴病患他已病入膏肓。

★★★★★

2115 eternal

a. everlasting; timeless; endless; immortal; infinite

永久的，永恆的

[ɪ`tɜnḷ]

When they first met they hated each other, but it wasn't long before they overcame their differences and became eternal friends.

他們剛認識時互相討厭對方，不久便克服歧異成為終生摯友。

★★★☆☆

2116 conterminous

a. having a common boundary

毗連的，相接的

[kən`tɜmɪnəs]

The conterminous border between the United States and Canada makes it convenient for the two countries to transport goods back and forth.

美加國界相連方便兩國往返運輸貨物。

★★★★☆

2117 termination

n. end; cessation; windup; close; dissolution; finish; conclusion

終了，結束

[ˌtɜmə`neʃən]

He was facing termination because of his bad attitude and irresponsibility at work. He was given a pink slip.

他因態度不佳又缺乏責任感而面臨失去工作。他收到了解雇通知單。

✦ the(o) = god 神，上帝

★★★☆☆

2118 theocracy

n. a form of government by God or a god directly or through a priestly order

神權國家

[θɪ`ɑkrəsɪ]

In ancient Egypt, theocracy was practiced as the Pharaohs were considered as gods. They wielded absolute authority.

古埃及實行專制神權統治而視法老王為神明，法老具有絕對的權力。

★★★★★

2119 theology

n. the study of theistic religion; the rational analysis of a religious faith

神學

[θɪ`ɑlədʒɪ]

If more people were to study theology, then understanding of others' cultures and ways of life would be easier, since they are so closely tied to religion.

如果更多人學習神學，就會更容易了解他人的文化和生活方式，因為這些是和宗教息息相關的。

★★★☆☆

2120 atheist | *n.* non-believer | 無神論者

[`eθɪɪst]

He is an atheist. He firmly believes that there is no God. But he has realized that he needs a certain being whom he can turn to.
他是堅決不信上帝的無神論者，但後來發現自己需要某個可以依靠的存在。

❖ therm- = heat 熱

★★★★★

2121 thermometer | *n.* an instrument for measuring temperature | 溫度計

[θə`mɑmətə]

During the heat wave, the thermometer reached nearly 120°F, the highest on record. I had never experienced such hot weather.
熱浪來襲時，溫度計顯示將近華氏一百二十度的最高記錄，我從來沒有遇過這麼熱的天氣。

★★★★★

2122 thermostat | *n.* a device that automatically regulates temperature | 自動控溫裝置

[`θɜmə,stæt]

One must constantly adjust the thermostat in order to regulate the temperature of the house during the year.
人們須經常校準自動控溫裝置以調節全年的室內溫度。

★★★☆☆

2123 thermal | *a.* of or producing heat | 熱的，溫度的

[`θɜml̩]

Evaporated seawater condenses into rain, converting thermal energy into wind power in tremendously awesome amounts.
海水蒸發冷凝成雨水，並將熱能轉化成強大的風力。

❖ tic, tit = tickle 使癢

★★★★☆

2124 entice | *v.* lure; tempt; wile away; allure; decoy; seduce; coax; induce; beguile; sweet talk; soft-soap | 誘使，慫恿

[ɪn`taɪs]

A desire for gold enticed many people to California. Many prospective gold miners rushed there.
淘金熱誘使許多人前往加州，許多滿懷希望的挖金礦者都湧入當地。

★★★★☆

2125 tickle

*v. titillate / **n.** an act of tickling*　　　　　　使發癢／搔癢

[`tɪkl]

Don't tickle me. I can't stand it any more. I can't even breathe.
別搔我癢，我受不了，無法呼吸了。

★★★☆☆

2126 titillate

v. tickle / excite　　　　　　　　　　　　　　使癢／使高興

[`tɪtl͵et]

In an effort to titillate his audience, Samson wore silly clothes and a stupid grin on his face, but it didn't work. They were too serious.
山姆森穿著愚蠢戲服咧著嘴想逗觀眾笑，但沒用，大家還是一臉嚴肅。

⁘ tom = cut　切割

★★☆☆☆

MP3 87

2127 dichotomy

n. a division into two / a difference between two things, especially things that are opposite to each other　　分裂／二分法

[daɪ`kɑtəmɪ]

Sometimes there is a great dichotomy between what Jeff says and what he does. I think that he sometimes tries to hide his real intentions.
傑夫有時言行非常不一，我認為他有時想隱藏他真正的意圖。

★★☆☆☆

2128 anatomize

v. examine in detail; analyze; dissect　　　　　仔細分析，分解

[ə`nætə͵maɪz]

Engineers must have the ability to anatomize the machinery they work on so that they can examine each individual piece when something goes wrong.
工程師需具備拆解機械的能力，以便在機器出問題時能逐一檢查每一各別的部分。

★★★☆☆

2129 appendectomy

n. the surgical removal of the appendix　　　　闌尾切除手術

[͵æpən`dɛktəmɪ]

His appendix ruptured, and he was rushed to the hospital, where the doctor was called in to perform an emergency appendectomy on him.
他的闌尾破裂，他趕往醫院，醫生被請來進行緊急切除手術。

⁘ tort = twist　扭

★★★★☆

2130 tortuous

a. twisted; winding; serpentine; meandering; crooked; crooked sinuous; bent; curved　　迂迴曲折的，繞圈子的

[`tɔrtʃuəs]

The process of negotiation between the two countries is bound to be tortuous and time-consuming.
兩國談判過程註定要迂迴耗時。

★★★★☆

2131 **contort**	*v.* twist or force out of normal shape; twist	使扭曲，曲解
[kən`tɔrt]	When our teacher's face contorted with anger, we kept silent. From time to time we watched his twisted face through our fingers. 老師的臉因憤怒而扭曲時，我們保持沉默，不時從指縫中偷看他扭曲的臉。	

★★★★☆

2132 **tortoise**	*n.* turtle	烏龜
[`tɔrtəs]	The hare laughed hysterically when the tortoise told him that he could win the race, since he was such a slow animal. 烏龜表示能贏得比賽時，引來野兔一陣狂笑，因為牠實在太慢了。	

★★★★★

2133 **torture**	*v.* torment; persecute	折磨，使為難
[`tɔrtʃə]	"Please don't torture us any longer with your terrible singing. It's painful to our ears," we said to him. 我們對他說：「請不要再用你恐怖的歌聲折磨我們了，耳朵好痛啊。」	

★★★★☆

2134 **torsion**	*n.* twisting	扭轉，扭曲，扭力
[`tɔrʃən]	The torsion increased as we twisted and turned the wire, causing it to coil up. At last the wire broke. 我們在扭絞電線時扭力增加，使它捲成一團，最後就斷了。	

✛ tract, treat = draw 拉

★★★☆☆

2135 **entreat**	*v.* ask earnestly for	懇求，乞求，請求
[ɪn`trit]	Jack entreated her to tell him how things had been going. He was so curious about his sister's first date. 傑克懇求妹妹說出第一次約會的經過，因為他非常好奇。	

★★★★★

2136 **attractive**	*a.* captivating; appealing; luring; catching; seductive; enchanting; alluring; fetching; comely	有吸引力的，嫵媚動人的
[ə`træktɪv]	Pam wasn't especially attractive as a young girl, but she has certainly grown to be a very beautiful woman. 潘小時候並不特別吸引人，但長大後成為十分漂亮的女人。	

★★★★☆		
2137 subtract	**v.** *deduct; take away*	減去，去掉
[səb`trækt]	Nick never went to school and never learned to add or subtract, not to speak of learning to multiply or divide numbers. 尼克沒上過學，也沒學過加減法，更別說乘除法。	

⁘ trans- = pass, across 通過，穿過

★★★★★		
2138 transparent	**a.** *clear; pellucid; diaphanous; limpid*	透明的，一目了然的
[træn`spɛrənt]	Maggie's father wouldn't let her leave the house in her thin, transparent skirt, even though she told him it was in fashion to wear see-through clothes. 父親不讓瑪姬穿著可一目了然的薄襯衫外出，即使她告訴父親這樣的透明打扮是一種流行。	

★★★★☆		
2139 transcribe	**v.** *make a copy of, especially in writing*	抄寫，謄寫
[træn`skraɪb]	Before a teacher teaches this "TV soaps" course, he or she must transcribe the television show and write out each and every word. 老師講授「電視連續劇」課程前須先抄寫電視節目裡的每一個字。	

★★★★☆		
2140 transmission	**n.** *the act or an instance of transmitting; the mechanism by which power is transmitted*	傳送，傳播
[træns`mɪʃən]	The spy was able to complete his secret transmission before being caught by the secret police. 間諜可以在遭祕密警察逮捕前完成機密傳送。	

★★★★☆		
2141 transplant	**v.** *relocate; plant in another place*	移植，移種
[træns`plænt]	Korean farmers willingly participate in cooperative work to transplant and harvest rice, and they give their cooperation after their harvest. 韓國農民樂意參與稻米移植與收割的合作工作，收成後便投入協力合作。	

★★★★☆		
2142 transform	**v.** *change; modify; transfigure; metamorphose*	使變化，使改變
[træns`fɔrm]	The beauty consultant told the spinsters that the new skin cream would transform them into princesses. 美容顧問告訴未婚婦女，新面霜能將她們變成公主。	

★★★★★

2143 **transfer**	*v. change from one station, route, etc. to another on a journey; switch*	轉車

[træn`sfɝ]

Nearly every morning Anthony's grandmother explains to him where he should transfer from one subway line to another, as if he were a little child.

安東尼的祖母幾乎每天早上都要跟他解釋到哪裡去轉搭地下鐵,好像他還是個孩子一樣。

✥ trench, trunc = cut 截斷,切除

★★★☆☆

2144 **entrench**	*v. embed; establish firmly*	使確立,使深留

[ɪn`trɛntʃ]

The Oriental idea that a wife should be obedient to her husband is deeply entrenched in his mind. However, his wife has hardly complained about that.

妻子應順從丈夫的東方觀念深植在他腦海裡,但他的妻子幾乎不曾就此有所抱怨。

★★★☆☆

2145 **trenchant**	*a. keen; acute; sharp; poignant; penetrating; incisive; biting; mordant; sarcastic; bitter; acerbic; tart; acrid; acrimonious; acidulous; caustic*	尖酸刻薄的

[`trɛntʃənt]

After a rather trenchant argument, the husband and wife didn't speak to each other for several weeks.

經過激烈爭執後,丈夫與妻子好幾周都不跟對方講話。

★★★☆☆

2146 **trench**	*n. a long, narrow ditch; a ditch dug by troops to stand in and be sheltered from enemy fire*	戰壕,溝渠

[trɛntʃ]

"Get back down in the trench before you get shot in the head," yelled the sergeant to the private who was standing absentmindedly.

陸軍中士對著茫然呆立的小兵大吼:「在頭部中彈前快進戰壕來。」

✥ trit = rub 磨擦

★★★★☆

2147 **trite**	*a. hackneyed; banal*	平庸的,陳腐的

[traɪt]

He answered the judge with such a trite tone of voice that the judge soon lost his temper and charged him with contempt of court.

他以一副都是老套的語調回答法官詢問,法官一氣之下便控告他蔑視法庭。

★★☆☆☆

2148 trituration	**n.** *a triturated preparation*	粉末

[ˌtrɪtʃəˈreʃən]

The trituration of deer-horn and other ingredients of Oriental medicine is a secret that has been handed down for centuries.

鹿茸粉末和其他東方藥材是祖傳的祕方。

★★☆☆☆

2149 contrite	**a.** *completely penitent; remorseful; affected by guilt*	懺悔的，痛悔的

[ˈkɑntraɪt]

The malefactor decided to change his ways of living, and went to the church with a broken heart and contrite spirit seeking repentance for his sins.

罪犯決定洗心革面，並懷著傷心和懺悔來到教堂為其罪行尋求救贖。

★★☆☆☆

2150 attrition	**n.** *erosion*	損耗，磨損，消耗

[əˈtrɪʃən]

This alloy does away with the attrition problem in that it does not wear down with normal usage.

合金不會因日常使用而磨損，因此沒有損耗問題。

Tea Time... ☕

<Greek myth> Hygeia **The goddess of health.**	〈來自希臘神話〉海吉亞 希臘神話中主宰健康的女神。（註：除健康外，海吉亞也主宰衛生、保健、醫療等，她教導大家透過自然方式保持健康，而不是等到生病再來治療。因此英文的 hygiene「衛生」和 health「健康」等字皆來自其名。）

hygiene [ˈhaɪdʒin] **n.** *a study of maintaining health; conditions or practices conducive to aintaining health* | 衛生，衛生學

Many dentists have become concerned with preventive dentistry, and have trained patients to become responsible for their own oral hygiene.

許多牙醫日益關切口腔預防醫學，並訓練病患負起責任照顧個人口腔衛生。

1 Complete each word by filling in the blank with proper spelling so that it has the same meaning as suggested. Then please write the meaning of each word in Chinese.

1. 使膨脹 = ___tend
2. 程度 = __tent
3. 烏龜 = ____oise
4. 損耗 = __trition
5. 減輕 = ex___uate
6. 緊張氣氛 = ____ion
7. 薄弱的 = ___uous
8. 有異議的 = con___tious
9. 領土 = ___ritory
10. 地形 = ___rain

11. subterranean = _____
12. conterminous = _____
13. terminal = _____
14. theology = _____
15. thermometer = _____
16. dichotomy = _____
17. contort = _____
18. entreat = _____
19. attractive = _____
20. transplant = _____

2 Choose a word that best completes the sentence.

21. The science student had some difficulty adjusting to the _____ class. One day he submitted a report in which he made a typo, "Atom and Eve."
(A) theology   (B) dichotomy   (C) terminal   (D) terminus

22. The high _____ of the mountain was covered with glaciers.
(A) theocracy   (B) terrain   (C) termination   (D) terminus

23. The doctor was hesitant to tell his patient that he had a _____ disease.
(A) terminal   (B) timeless   (C) thermal   (D) attractive

3 The highlighted word is closest in meaning to which of the following?

24. The philosopher's ideas were deeply entrenched into his followers' mind.
(A) transformed   (B) entreated   (C) embedded   (D) transcribed

25. Most of the time preparing for an exam is sheer torture for me.
(A) torsion   (B) torment   (C) transmission   (D) territory

⁜ verb = words 言詞

★★★★☆

MP3
88

2151 verbalize

[`vɝbḷ͵aɪz]

***v.** express in words*　　　用言語表達

The teacher was constantly encouraging us to verbalize our ideas. He wanted us to speak out as often as possible.
老師經常鼓勵我們表達自己的想法，並要我們盡量大方說出來。

★★★☆☆

2152 verbose

[vɚ`bos]

***a.** wordy*　　　冗長的，囉嗦的

Not only was the speaker very inconsistent, but he was verbose, so the listeners soon lost interest in his wordy speech.
演講者不但前後矛盾而且囉嗦，聽眾馬上對冗長演講失去興趣。

★★★☆☆

2153 reverberate

[rɪ`vɝbə͵ret]

***v.** be returned or echoed repeatedly*　　　使迴響

The sounds of the gunshot were still reverberating off the hotel walls. There was a fight in the city where the tourist was staying.
槍聲迴盪在飯店牆上。觀光客停留的都市發生了槍戰。

⁜ vad, vas = go 走

★★★★★

2154 pervade

[pɚ`ved]

***v.** permeate; spread throughout*　　　瀰漫，滲透

The fragrance of these lilies has pervaded the room. I hear that the smell of lilies can be dangerous. So let's open the window.
百合花香瀰漫整個房間，聽說百合香味有害人體，我們快開窗吧。

★★★★★

2155 evasive

[ɪ`vesɪv]

***a.** seeking to evade something*　　　避而不答的，推托的

Last week I asked Mary, one of my classmates, to go to the movies, but she didn't say yes or no. She seemed to be very evasive.
上周我邀請同學瑪麗去看電影，但她沒說好或不好，似乎很推托。

★★★★★

2156 invade

[ɪn`ved]

***v.** enter a country under arms to subdue it*　　　入侵，侵略

When the King finally realized that the enemy soldiers had gathered along the border, it was already too late, because they had already begun to invade his lands.
國王終於發現敵軍集結在邊界，但為時已晚，敵軍已開始入侵國土。

⁙ vene, vent = come 來

★★★★★

2157 intervene	**n.** interfere; meddle; intrude; strike in; poke one's nose in; barge in; butt in; horn in; intercede	打擾，干預
[ˌɪntə`vin]	May I just intervene for one moment? I know that it's rude of me to intrude with my opinion, but I don't think that the project will work. 我可以打擾一下嗎？我知道現在加入個人意見有點無禮，但我不認為此案可行。	

★★★★★

2158 revenue	**n.** a state's annual income from which public expenses are met / income	稅收 / 收入
[`rɛvəˌnu]	Most tax returns are audited by the Internal Revenue Service. Therefore, tax evasion is almost sure to be revealed. 絕大多數的報稅表是由國稅局稽查，所以逃漏稅幾乎都會被發現。	

★★★★★

2159 convene	**v.** assemble	聚集
[kən`vin]	We watched a show on penguins, and it was interesting to learn how they convene in large groups during the mating season. 我們收看企鵝節目時有趣地學到，牠們在交配期會大量聚集成群。	

★★★☆☆

2160 misadventure	**n.** accident; misfortune	災禍，意外，不幸
[`mɪsədˌvɛntʃə]	Their walk through the park became quite a misadventure when they realized that they were hopelessly lost. 當他們發現迷路時，一場公園散步演變成不幸。	

★★★★★

2161 conventional	**a.** traditional; orthodox; established / conservative	傳統的 / 保守的
[kən`vɛnʃənl]	Mr. Peterson sure has a conventional way of doing business, and he has been very successful with the projects that he has undertaken. 彼德森先生經營事業的確保守，但承接的案子都非常成功。	

⁙ ver = truth 真實

★★★★☆

2162 verity	**n.** truth; fact	真相，事實
[`vɛrətɪ]	That heavy smoking can cause respiratory problems is a scientifically established verity, a fact even smokers know. But quitting smoking is still difficult. 吸煙過量會引發呼吸道問題是經科學證實、連吸煙者也知道的事實，然而戒煙還是很難。	

★★★★★

2163 verify

[ˋvɛrəˌfaɪ]

v. affirm; confirm; authenticate　　査證，核對，證實

The journalist was told to verify all his facts before publishing his article. So he went out to search for a witness.
記者被告知發表報刊文章前須先查證所有事實，於是他外出尋找證人。

★★★★☆

2164 veritable

[ˋvɛrətəbl]

a. real; true; genuine; authentic　　真正的，名副其實的

It is a veritable friend that is always there when you need him. They say that a friend in need is a friend indeed.
真正的朋友會在需要時伸出援手，俗話說患難見真情。

★★★☆☆

2165 verisimilitude

[ˌvɛrəsəˋmɪləˌtud]

n. the appearance or semblance of being true or real　　逼真

Verisimilitude is the quality of appearing to be true. A movie which has great verisimilitude makes us believe that the movie is based on fact.
逼真看起來像是真的，逼真的電影會讓人相信是根據事實拍攝的。

★★★☆☆

2166 veracity

[vəˋræsətɪ]

n. truthfulness; truth　　誠實，正直，真實性

People appreciate veracity, loyalty and trust in both a spouse and a friend. Therefore, many people want to have a friend who is reliable.
人們欣賞配偶和朋友的誠實、忠誠和信任，所以許多人想要值得信賴的朋友。

★★★★☆

2167 verdict

[ˋvɝdɪkt]

n. decision; judgment　　判決，裁決，裁定

The defendant sat in the courtroom, nervously waiting for the judge to read the verdict. When he was found innocent, he shed tears of joy.
被告緊張地坐在法庭上等候法官宣讀判決，聽到獲判無罪時流下欣慰之淚。

✢ verg, vers, vert = turn　轉

★★★★★

2168 versatile

[ˋvɝsətɪl]

a. resourceful; all-round; many- sided; dexterous; handy; all-around / variable　　多功能的 / 易變的

The fashion designer's winter collection was versatile. Most of the clothing could be worn to the office as well as to the theater.
服裝設計師發表的冬裝適合各種場合，大部分無論上班或看表演都適合穿著。

★★★★☆

2169 averse

a. opposed; disinclined; unwilling; reluctant; 反對的，不願意的，嫌惡的
loath; against

[ə`vɝs]

His weight problem stems from his unwillingness to eat the right foods and his averse feelings towards exercising.

他的體重問題是因不正確的飲食和不運動所造成的。

★★★★☆

2170 inverted

a. reversed 上下顛倒的

[ɪn`vɝtɪd]

The U.S. is shaped like an inverted triangle. It roughly looks like a reversed form of a triangle.

美國國土形狀像個上下顛倒的三角形，大致是個倒三角形。

★★★★☆

2171 adversary

n. enemy; opponent; antagonist / competitor; rival 敵手，敵人 / 對手

[`ædvə,sɛrɪ]

When the fight was over, the champion had to admit that his opponent had been a worthy adversary.

比賽結束後，冠軍選手承認對手是個可敬的敵手。

★★★★☆

2172 diverge

v. deviate; turn away; digress; stray; drift 離題，偏離，背離

[daɪ`vɝdʒ]

The argument began to diverge when the ambassadors started to argue religious beliefs instead of international politics.

當大使開始爭辯宗教信仰而非國際政治時，整場爭論就離了題。

★★★★★

2173 convertible

a. a car with a folding or detachable roof / that can 敞篷的 / 可轉換的
be converted

[kən`vɝtəbl]

James's car is really terrific and convenient. It has a convertible top. However, a terrible thing happens when it rains overnight and the top is open.

詹姆斯的敞篷車既棒又方便，但車頂大開又遇到整夜大雨時就釀成可怕災禍。

★★★★☆

2174 diversify

v. make diverse 使多樣化

[də`vɝsə,faɪ]

The lack of energy resources in our country makes it essential to diversify the sources of energy and to develop nuclear power.

我國缺乏能源因此必須使能源多樣化，並發展核能發電。

★★★☆☆		
2175 extrovert	**n.** *an outgoing or sociable person*	個性外向者
[`ɛkstro,vɜt]	Paul has been an extrovert, which has not always been good for him. He has gotten into many fights because of his aggressive character. 個性外向對保羅而言並非總是好事，他常因好鬥跟人打架。	

★★★☆☆		
2176 conversant	**a.** *well acquainted with a subject, person, etc.*	熟悉的，精通的
[kən`vɜsn̩t]	Dr. Bell has been studying insect life for over 35 years and is considered by most to be the most conversant on the subject. 貝爾博士研究昆蟲生命超過三十五年，是公認最精通這個主題的人。	

★★★★★		
2177 avert	**v.** *turn away one's eyes / prevent; ward off*	移開視線 / 防止，避免
[ə`vɜt]	Jane could hardly stand the violent scenes in the movie. She couldn't help averting her eyes. 珍幾乎無法忍受電影暴力鏡頭，忍不住移開視線。	

★★★★☆		
2178 adversity	**n.** *the condition of adverse fortune; misfortune*	逆境，厄運，災難
[əd`vɜsətɪ]	Of all the virtues, cheerfulness and enthusiasm are the most profitable. Enthusiasm flourishes more often in adversity than it does in prosperity. — Ernest Hemingway 愉快和熱情是最有益的美德，逆境比順境更容易使熱情洋溢。 ——海明威	

✣ via = way 道路

MP3
89

★★★★☆		
2179 obviate	**v.** *get round or do away with a need; preclude*	排除，消除
[`ɑbvɪ,et]	This instrument obviates the necessity of doing it manually. It is convenient and efficient to use this instrument because it is automatic. 這部機器不必用手操作，因為是自動的所以不但方便效率也高。	

★★★★★		
2180 via	**prep.** *by way of*	經由，取道，憑藉
[`vaɪə]	The water of the river will be pumped via an open aqueduct to his land. Then he will not have to haul water any more. 河水經由開放導水管抽取到他的田地上，他再也不必拖著水了。	

★★★☆☆

2181 pervious

[`pɝvɪəs]

a. accessible; receptive 能接納的，可穿透的

The governor's mind was pervious to the arguments of the members of the opposition, but he refused to change his policies.

州長能接納反對黨的論點，但拒絕改變政策。

✥ vid, vis = see 看

★★★★☆

2182 vista

[`vɪstə]

n. view 展望，遠景

The president's visit to his bordering nation helped to open up new vistas of cooperative relations. The two nations have not been on good terms.

總統訪問鄰國有助於開啓合作關係的新展望，過去兩國關係並不友好。

★★★★☆

2183 revise

[rɪ`vaɪz]

v. consider and alter / amend; modify 改觀 / 修正

The students decided to revise their opinion of the new teacher when he gave them all passing grades on a difficult exam.

學生決定對新老師改觀，就在他讓大家在很難的考試中全部過關時。

★★★★☆

2184 improvise

[`ɪmprə‚vaɪz]

v. compose or perform extempore; an lib; extemporize; play (it) by ear 臨時做～，即席表演

We had planned to hold the picnic outside next to the river, but because it rained, we were forced to improvise and move the party to a nearby restaurant.

我們本來計畫在河畔野餐，但因雨被迫臨時改到附近餐廳。

★★★★☆

2185 visibility

[‚vɪzə`bɪlətɪ]

n. the range of vision as determined by the conditions of light and atmosphere 能見度

During the snowstorm, driving was quite dangerous as visibility was low. Furthermore, the roads were very slippery.

暴風雪期間駕車非常危險，因為能見度低，路面也很濕滑。

★★★★★

2186 invisible

[ɪn`vɪzəbl]

a. not visible to the eye 看不見的，無形的

The partners don't talk to each other. They usually pass each other as if they are mutually invisible. They are totally estranged.

這對搭擋互不交談，經過對方身邊也視若無睹，完全疏遠彼此。

★★★☆☆

2187 provident

a. having or showing foresight; far-sighted; shrewd;   有先見之明的 / 節儉的
sagacious; judicious / frugal; economical; thrifty

[`prɑvədənt]

It was a provident and prudent gesture to set aside half of his lottery winnings for his children and grandchildren.

他將半數樂透獎金留給子孫是有先見之明的審慎行為。

★★★★★

2188 supervise

v. superintend; oversee; keep an eye on   監督，照看，看顧

[ˌsupɚ`vaɪz]

Babies need a baby-sitter if a parent cannot supervise them. They need constant care and should be protected from all kinds of danger.

如果父母無法看顧嬰兒，則需要褓姆照顧。嬰兒需要不斷照料以免遇到危險。

✥ viv, val = life; live 活

★★★★★

2189 vivid

a. clear; lifelike; lively   歷歷在目的，栩栩如生的

[`vɪvɪd]

The memories of her ex-husband are still very vivid in her mind. She often regrets having divorced him.

她對前夫的回憶仍歷歷在目，常後悔跟他離婚。

★★★★★

2190 vigorous

a. strong and active; robust; energetic; vivacious;   精力充沛的，健壯的
dynamic; forceful

[`vɪgərəs]

They have an extremely vigorous son; he is always running, jumping and shouting. So they have made it a rule to keep all fragile things out of his reach.

他們有個精力非常充沛的兒子，總是又叫又跳，因此經常得把易碎品放在他搆不到的地方。

★★★★☆

2191 vivify

v. enliven; animate; make lively   使有生氣，使生動

[`vɪvəˌfaɪ]

Our art teacher constantly reminded us to vivify our dull paintings with bright colors. He preferred a bright painting.

美術老師經常提醒我們要用鮮艷色彩使單調畫作富有生氣，他偏好鮮艷畫作。

★★★★☆

2192 valiant

a. brave; courageous   勇敢的，英勇的

[`væljənt]

Although our soccer team made a valiant effort, we could not defeat the British team, which was more than a match for us.

雖然我方足球隊表現英勇，卻無法擊敗比我們更強的英國隊。

★★★☆☆

2193 **vivacity**	*n.* vitality	活力，朝氣，活潑

[vaɪˋvæsətɪ]

When Pip was talking about his girl friend, his eyes were full of vivacity. Nothing could stop him from talking about her.

皮普提到女友時雙眼總是充滿活力，沒有什麼能阻止他談論她。

★★★★☆

2194 **invalid**	*a.* a person enfeebled or disabled by illness or injury / not valid; null and void; ineffective	體弱多病的 / 無效的

[ɪnˋvælɪd]

He was an only child. When he was born his father was fifty years old, and his mother had been an invalid for almost twenty years.

Light in August — William Faulkner

身為獨子的他出生時父親已五十歲，母親則臥病在床將近二十年。

—— 《八月之光》（美國小說家暨諾貝爾文學獎得主）威廉‧福克納

✦ voc, vok = call 呼叫

★★★★★

2195 **advocate**	*n.* supporter; champion; upholder; proponent; patron; protagonist	提倡者，擁護者

[ˋædvəkɪt]

Those who are working so as to protect the rights of consumers are known as consumer advocates.

為保護消費者權益奔走的人稱為消費者保護團體。

★★★★★

2196 **provoke**	*v.* irritate; annoy; pique; enrage; madden; incense; infuriate; exasperate; get on one's nerves; upset; offend	激怒，使惱怒

[prəˋvok]

Anne was provoked by her landlady's name-calling, and at last they got into a hair-pulling fight.

女房東的謾罵激怒了安，最後兩人大打出手。

★★★★★

2197 **evoke**	*v.* arouse; rouse; raise; call forth	喚起，引起

[ɪˋvok]

Joy's sad and touching story evoked the sympathy of all the people who were listening. Some of them began to sob.

喬伊悲傷而動人的故事引發所有聽眾的同情心，有些人開始啜泣。

【註：下面是本書三千單字中三個開頭的 w 不發音的單字，雖然與詞素無關，但並列於此供讀者學習。】

★★★★★

| 2198 **whimsical** | *a.* *capricious; erratic; eccentric; wavering; flighty; fickle; unpredictable; volatile* | 古怪的，奇怪的 |

[ˋhwɪmzɪkl̩]

"It's difficult to keep track of all the whimsical purchases of my spoiled daughter," complained the rich man.

富翁抱怨：「真難了解我那驕縱女兒購買的所有奇怪東西。」

★★★★☆

| 2199 **wreck** | *n.* *destruction; wreckage; shipwreck* | 殘骸，失事 |

[rɛk]

The car accident was very serious, as it left three people dead and four injured. The car was a total wreck.

車禍意外非常嚴重，共有三人喪生四人受傷，失事車輛全毀。

★★★★★

| 2200 **wrinkle** | *n.* *crease; furrow* | 皺摺，皺紋 |

[ˋrɪŋkl̩]

There were lots of wrinkles on one sleeve of his shirt, while the other side was sharply ironed. Asked why, he answered: "My mom wants me to find a lady who can iron both of them."

他一邊衣袖很皺，另一邊卻熨得很平，問他為什麼，他回答：「母親要我找個能熨兩邊衣袖的女子。」

Tea Time... ☕

<Medieval story> Bilious
From bile, one of the four imaginary humors of the body which was believed in medieval times to cause crankiness.

〈來自中古世紀神話〉膽汁的
本字源自中古世紀相信能產生暴躁情緒的人體四種體液之一的膽汁。（註：造成易怒和暴躁的是黃膽汁，引發憂鬱和沮喪的則是黑膽汁。）

bilious [ˋbɪljəs] *a.* *peevish; ill-natured; ill-tempered; cranky* | 易怒的，乖戾的

Ellen, one of my colleagues, is so bilious that I feel nervous when I am with her. It seems like she is cranky by nature.

同事艾倫非常易怒，和她共處讓我感到緊張，她似乎天生暴躁。

1

Complete each word by filling in the blank with proper spelling so that it has the same meaning as suggested. Then please write the meaning of each word in Chinese.

1. 冗長的   = _ _ _ _ o s e
2. 用言語表達   = _ _ _ _ a l i z e
3. 使迴響   = _ _ v e r b e r a t e
4. 推托的   = _ _ _ _ i v e
5. 入侵   = _ _ v a d e
6. 真正的   = _ _ _ _ t a b l e
7. 殘骸   = w r _ _ _
8. 皺摺   = _ _ _ n k l e
9. 擁護者   = _ _ v o c a t e
10. 英勇的   = _ _ _ _ a n t

11. evoke = _____
12. whimsical = _____
13. vigorous = _____
14. pervade = _____
15. vivid = _____
16. invalid = _____
17. intervene = _____
18. misadventure = _____
19. conventional = _____
20. verify = _____

2

Choose a word that best completes the sentence.

21. **We cannot avoid death or the Internal _____ Service.**
    (A) Revenue   (B) Adversity   (C) Vivacity   (D) Invalid

22. **The teacher's comic story _____ much laughter among her students. They laughed their heads off.**
    (A) evoked   (B) obviated   (C) averted   (D) diversified

3

The highlighted word is closest in meaning to which of the following?

23. **The members of the union convened to discuss their working conditions.**
    (A) assembled   (B) averted   (C) diverged   (D) intervened

24. **The nation took astute measures to avert a war.**
    (A) evade   (B) prevent   (C) pervade   (D) supervise

25. **Most of the students were against conventional methods of testing.**
    (A) pervious   (B) invalid   (C) vigorous   (D) traditional

Practice Test 05

1

The highlighted word is closest in meaning to which of the following?

1. The old man is leading a very sedentary life. He stays home all throughout the year.
   - (A) sentimental
   - (B) immobile
   - (C) residual
   - (D) senile

2. I had a hard time preventing the small child from eating the desiccant in the candy can.
   - (A) solvent liquid
   - (B) small items
   - (C) drying agent
   - (D) narrow ditch

3. The author of the book was upset when he received a trenchant criticism from a reader.
   - (A) sharp
   - (B) contrite
   - (C) abstruse
   - (D) trite

4. Tom is a veritable friend whom I can fall back on whenever I have trouble.
   - (A) conventional
   - (B) true
   - (C) conversant
   - (D) vigorous

5. Many sages have said that it is important for us to be provident . We may have rainy days.
   - (A) invalid
   - (B) voluntary
   - (C) invisible
   - (D) thrifty

2

Please answer the following questions.

Astrology

Astrologers study heavenly bodies to learn what influence they may have on human affairs. Even though many people think of astrology as nothing but a sort of superstition, it is also true that some people who are faced with important decisions resort to astrologers. Others even think that they are able to prevent misfortune or to be more provident . One of the most publicized examples is the case of Ronald Reagan's wife. It is said that frightened by an assassination attempt on March 30, 1981, Nancy Reagan had consulted a California astrologer about the most favorable times and dates for important events in the president's life; what time Air Force One should take off or land; whether or not the president should sign a treaty; whether or not the president should undergo a surgery; and

whether or not the president should have a press conference.

Astrological advice and forecasts can be found in many daily newspapers and magazines. An individual's astrological horoscope is believed to be determined by the position of all the planets at the time of his birth. Astrologers divide the year into 12 equal sections which are called the zodiac. The divisions of the zodiac are called signs, the 12 of which are Aquarius, Pisces, Aries, Taurus, Gemini, Cancer, Leo, Virgo, Libra, Scorpio, Sagittarius and Capricorn. Even though horoscopes are based on pseudoscience, many people still like to check their daily horoscope, some for fun, some for advice on important matters, and others for wisdom.

6. The word sort is closest in meaning to which of the following?
(A) verity
(B) avenue
(C) suction
(D) kind

7. The word resort is closest in meaning to which of the following?
(A) turn
(B) transfer
(C) transform
(D) attract

8. The word prevent is closest in meaning to which of the following?
(A) avert
(B) subtract
(C) tickle
(D) transcribe

9. The word provident is closest in meaning to which of the following?
(A) contiguous
(B) transparent
(C) sagacious
(D) attractive

10. The word determined is closest in meaning to which of the following?
(A) diverged
(B) obviated
(C) invaded
(D) decided

Passage 1

The Bermuda Triangle

It is said that one of the most mysterious locations in the world is the Bermuda Triangle, the three points of which are Miami, Florida and the islands of Bermuda and Puerto Rico. The Triangle is thought to be treacherous because many vessels and aircraft have disappeared there in a mysterious manner. This is the location that even Shakespeare chose for the setting of his work "*The Tempest*."

Rumor has it that many ships and aircraft have disappeared in this area but nobody knows whereto. No remains of the wreckage have ever been found. In December 1945, five American fighter planes, Flight 19, which had launched from a Florida training base, disappeared after sending a radio message in which the leader of the aviators said that his compass malfunctioned. One of the other planes which went searching for them disappeared too. One of the pilots who returned to the base was horror-stricken and said that he had been kidnapped by green-skinned creatures and that he narrowly escaped. Also back in 1492, Christopher Columbus allegedly saw a mysterious flame of fire and then found his compass wasn't working properly. Even a gigantic marine liner, such as the Queen Elizabeth, lost its electrical power while sailing in this area in 1974.

Nowadays some people hold that there might be a powerful magnetic force, whereas others insist that there might be a gate to a 4th-dimensional world in the Triangle through which the missing ships and airplanes might have passed, immersing into another world. However, one of the clearest facts is that nobody has unraveled the mystery so far and that many aviators and navigators do not like to venture there.

It seems likely that even an eel, with its scaleless and slippery skin, cannot escape the influence of the mysterious Bermuda Triangle. It is said that American and European eels, after living in freshwater bodies of water for most of their lives, gather together, breed and expire in the Triangle. How come they congregate and die there? Another interesting fact is that the lifespan of European eels is one year longer than that of American counterparts. Scientists suspect that it is because it takes the former one more year to complete their journey to the Triangle. The eels which are hatched in the abyss of the Triangle find their way back to the waters from which their parents came without having been there themselves. Some scientists assert that magnetism is responsible for their returning to their parents' habitats, while others argue that olfactory functions might let them directly follow their nose to the rivers, lakes and even ponds where their predecessors resided. Still others contend that the young take advantage of the position of stars and constellations.

There are many mysteries which surround the Bermuda Triangle and the eels which head for the destination to end their lives. Even though many efforts are being made to solve the riddles, it seems unlikely that they can be easily unraveled. Wherever the mystery of the Triangle may stem from, it seems as difficult to solve as that of the eternal love triangle.

1. **The highlighted word** location **can be replaced by which of the following?**
   (A) place
   (B) termination
   (C) terminus
   (D) terrain

2. **The highlighted word** malfunctioned **can be replaced by which of the following?**
   (A) leave high and dry
   (B) was out of order
   (C) make sport of
   (D) reduced in force

3. **The highlighted word** immersing into **can be replaced by which of the following?**
   (A) entering
   (B) depriving
   (C) pondering
   (D) objecting

4. **The highlighted word** expire **can be replaced by which of the following?**
   (A) deride
   (B) corroborate
   (C) resolve
   (D) die

5. **The highlighted word** congregate **can be replaced by which of the following?**
   (A) cut down
   (B) hold back from action
   (C) gather together
   (D) figure out

6. **The highlighted word** complete **can be replaced by which of the following?**
   (A) adjust
   (B) finish
   (C) adjoin
   (D) rebut

7. **The highlighted word** habitats **can be replaced by which of the following?**
   (A) pedals
   (B) continuous changes
   (C) tripods
   (D) living places

8. **The highlighted word** predecessors **can be replaced by which of the following?**
   (A) orthopedists
   (B) descendants
   (C) prototypes
   (D) ancestors

9. **The highlighted word** resided **can be replaced by which of the following?**
   (A) abrogated
   (B) lived
   (C) saturated
   (D) sedated

10. **The highlighted word** eternal **can be replaced by which of the following?**
    (A) superlative
    (B) succulent
    (C) supernatural
    (D) everlasting

The Redwood

The earth's tallest living thing is the redwood. During a lifetime of approximately 2,000 years, it may grow up to about 400 feet. Its close relative, the big tree, or the giant sequoia, may live for 3,000 years and it may reach heights of more than 250 feet. Beginning as a seed no larger than the head of a pin, the redwood eventually matures to staggering heights. Some 400 years later, the redwood may possess a trunk of 20 feet wide. But in comparison to the giant sequoia with its 35-foot diameter, the redwood appears trim.

The most massive tree in the world is believed to be the General Sherman Tree in California's Sequoia National Park. It is estimated to be about 2,700 years old and to have a diameter of over 35 feet at the bottom. One of its branches is more than 7 feet in diameter, allowing a person to lie on it crosswise. It is postulated that the General Sherman Tree weighs about 6,167 tons. If cut down, it would take more than 300 gigantic trucks which have loading capacity of 20 tons to carry the felled tree at once.

For a long time people have wondered how a redwood tree with amazing heights pumps water up to the top. It has long been a mystery among botanists. Air pressure is known to support a column of water up to as high as 10 meters, but for a redwood tree, it is a different story. Some have insisted that it is root pressure that pushes up water to the top of a tree, while others have maintained that living cells act as water pumps. However, a confined to which a redwood belongs is found to have relatively low root pressure and even a dead tree which pushes some amounts of water to an appreciable height is suggested as rebutting evidence. Recently, however, it has been revealed that surface-tension is responsible. Water evaporating through surfaces of leaves creates a negative pressure in the column inside the plant. It is amazing that the tension of the column of solution in a tube of small bore is almost as strong as that of a string of wire of the same diameter.

Both the redwood tree and the sequoia are needle-leaved trees which bear fruiting cones, and their spongy bark is usually about 12 inches thick. In the past, fallen redwoods were utilized by Yurok Indians to build canoes and homes. The Yuroks revered the trees, believing that Wah-Pek-oo-May, an Indian spirit, sprayed a magic concoction on the trees to make them resistant to fire. Anyway, redwoods resist forest fires as well as attack by insects and blights. Even fallen redwoods do not decay for hundreds of years. Today redwood timber is usually employed not only for making furniture, shingles, and panels but also in carpentry and general construction, mainly because it is light, fine grained and easily worked with.

Today the redwood is found in the coastal belt from California to Southern Oregon, while the sequoia is conifer to a relatively small area on the western slopes of the Sierra Nevada. Nowadays most of the 70 distinctive big-tree groves are under the protection of state or national parks. The giants which are soaring up to the sky are admired, caressed and hugged by a multitude of admiring visitors.

11. **The highlighted word massive can be replaced by which of the following?**
(A) maniacal　　　　　　　　　　　　(B) gigantic
(C) annual　　　　　　　　　　　　　(D) transient

12. **The highlighted word diameter can be replaced by which of the following?**
(A) potentate　　　　　　　　　　　　(B) duplicity
(C) width　　　　　　　　　　　　　　(D) pendulum

13. **The highlighted word maintained can be replaced by which of the following?**
(A) held　　　　　　　　　　　　　　(B) resented
(C) perspired　　　　　　　　　　　　(D) tortured

14. **The highlighted word conifer can be replaced by which of the following?**
(A) perennial plant　　　　　　　　　　(B) broad-leaved tree
(C) deciduous tree　　　　　　　　　　(D) needle-leaved tree

15. **The highlighted word rebutting can be replaced by which of the following?**
(A) verbal　　　　　　　　　　　　　(B) hypothetical
(C) confuting　　　　　　　　　　　　(D) vacuous

16. **The highlighted word solution can be replaced by which of the following?**
(A) novices　　　　　　　　　　　　　(B) fluids
(C) genes　　　　　　　　　　　　　　(D) solids

17. **The highlighted word sprayed can be replaced by which of the following?**
(A) saturated　　　　　　　　　　　　(B) incinerated
(C) acceded　　　　　　　　　　　　　(D) sprinkled

18. **The highlighted word insects can be replaced by which of the following?**
(A) recluses　　　　　　　　　　　　　(B) worms
(C) clamors　　　　　　　　　　　　　(D) precedents

19. **The highlighted word confined can be replaced by which of the following?**
(A) included　　　　　　　　　　　　　(B) declined
(C) demoted　　　　　　　　　　　　　(D) restricted

20. **The highlighted word multitude can be replaced by which of the following?**
(A) feat　　　　　　　　　　　　　　(B) crowd
(C) gravity　　　　　　　　　　　　　(D) recourse

Building Vocabulary for
iBT, SAT, GRE, TOEIC, GEPT

01 | 02 | 03

CHAPTER

04

05

Answers

主題式記憶法1：校園學術篇

2201~2700

MP3
90

2201 academy [ə`kædəmɪ] ★★★★☆

Jack has decided to enter West Point, the nation's premier military academy. He wants to become an officer.

傑克決定進入美國高等軍事學院西點軍校就讀，他想成為軍官。

學校，學院
n. *a school usually above the elementary level; a high school or college in which special subjects or skills are taught*

2202 accredit [ə`krɛdɪt] ★★★★☆

The Ministry of Education accredited the college in 1980.

教育部於一九八〇年認可該學院。

認可，承認合格
v. *give official authorization to or approval of*

2203 administration [əd,mɪnə`streʃən] ★★★★★

A: Where is the administration building? I think I'll have to find out about my registration.

B: That brown building over there.

A：行政大樓在哪裡？我得查查註冊情況。

B：那邊那棟棕色大樓就是了。

行政，管理
n. *the execution of public affairs as distinguished from policy-making*

2204 alma mater [`ɑlmə `mɑtə] ★★★★☆

That school over there is my alma mater, which I graduated from last year.

那邊那所學校就是我去年畢業的母校。

母校
n. *a school, college, or university which one has attended or from which one has graduated*

2205 alumnus [ə`lʌmnəs] ★★★☆☆

Paul is an alumnus of the class of 2000.

保羅是二〇〇〇年的該班畢業校友。

cf. pl. alumni（註：alumnus 通常僅指男校友，複數 alumni 可兼指男女同校的男女校友，用法不同。）

男校友
n. *a person who has attended or has graduated from a particular school, college, or university*

2206 annotate [`ænə,tet] ★★★☆☆

Most of the students preferred an annotated book, because the original work is too difficult to understand.

大多數學生偏愛附有註解的書，因為原著太難懂了。

為～作註解
v. *make or furnish critical or explanatory notes or comment*

2207 anthology [æn`θɑlədʒɪ] ★★★☆☆

Jane has decided to buy Jim an anthology of love poetry as his birthday gift. She hopes that he will like it.

珍決定買情詩選集給吉姆作為生日禮物，希望他會喜歡。

選集，詩集，文選
n. *a collection of selected literary pieces or passages or works of art or music*

2208 anthropologist [,ænθrə`pɑlədʒɪst] ★★★★☆

The anthropologist will go to the archaeological site to learn about the location of prehistoric peoples' residences.

人類學家將前往考古遺址以了解史前人類居住地。

人類學家
n. *a scholar engaged in the science of human beings*

2209 applicant [`æpləkənt］ ★★★★★

There are too many applicants for the position, so we haven't decided whom to choose.

該職位有太多申請者，因此我們尚未決定錄取哪一位。

申請者，應徵者
n. one who applies

2210 assessment [ə`sɛsmənt] ★★★★★

After each student's presentation, Professor Erickson filled out the assessment form. He graded each student on several areas.

每位學生都上台報告後，艾瑞克遜教授便填寫評分表，針對數個項目給每位學生打分數。

評分，評價，評估
n. the action or an instance of assessing; appraisal

2211 apply [ə`plaɪ] ★★★★★

Many people who want to study at this university visit the campus before they apply.

許多想就讀這所大學的人在提出申請前參觀校園。

(特別是以書面提出) 申請
v. make an appeal or request especially in the form of a written application

2212 appointment [ə`pɔɪntmənt] ★★★★★

I would like to see Professor Jackson, but I did not make an appointment with him. What should I do?

我想見傑克遜教授但沒有事先約好，請問該怎麼做？

會面約定，正式約會
n. an arrangement for a meeting; engagement

2213 archaeologist [ˌɑrkɪ`ɑlədʒɪst] ★★★★★

The archaeologist succeeded in excavating some valuable artifacts from an ancient tomb.

考古學家從古墓中成功挖掘出部分貴重手工藝品。

考古學家
n. a scholar who is engaged in the scientific study of material remains

References...

- artifact n. 手工藝品	- imprint n. 痕跡
- Bronze Age n. 青銅器時代	- intact a. 完好如初的
- carbon-14 analysis n. 碳十四放射性同位素定年分析法	- matrix n. 母岩，基岩
- diggings n. 挖掘地	- mound n. 土墩，塚
- excavate v. 挖掘	- relics n. 廢墟
- exhume v. 掘出	- remains n. 遺跡
- extinct a. 絕種的	- remnant n. 遺物，遺跡
- extract v. 採掘，提煉	- ruins n. 廢墟
- fossil n. 化石	- specimen n. 標本
- hieroglyphic n. 象形文字	- stratum n. 地層 *pl.* strata
- Ice Age n. 冰河時代	- unearth v. 挖出
- impression n. 印記，壓痕	- weathering n. 風化作用

2214 assignment [ə`saɪnmənt] ★★★★★

A: What is the assignment?

B: We're supposed to write a paper on urban migration by tomorrow.

A：課外作業是什麼？

B：明天前要交一篇都市遷移報告。

課外作業，分派任務
n. a usually assigned piece of work often to be finished within a certain time

2215 **attend** [ə`tɛnd] ★★★★★

To pass this course, every one of you should attend more than 80 percent of the class sessions.

這門課的上課出席率須超過八成才會及格。

出席，參加
v. be present at

2216 **audio-visual aids** [`ɔdɪo`vɪʒʊəl edz] ★★★★★

Audio-visual aids are crucial for students' motivation. So many teachers frequently use them.

視聽教學輔助教材對學生學習動機至關重要，所以許多老師經常使用。

視聽教學輔助教材
n. udio-visual teaching materials

2217 **audition** [ɔ`dɪʃən] ★★★★★

A: I've come to audition for your Chamber Orchestra. My name is Jim Smith and I play the violin.
B: All right. But I guess you need some time to warm up?

A：我來參加室內管弦樂團試音，我叫吉姆·史密斯，拉小提琴。
B：沒問題，但我想你需要時間暖暖身吧？

參加試鏡／試鏡，試音
v. give a trial performance / n. a trial performance to appraise an entertainer's merits

2218 **award** [ə`wɔrd] ★★★★★

A: Have you ever received an award?
B: Actually, last year I was given the Student of the Year award.

A：你得過獎嗎？
B：事實上我去年拿到傑出學生獎。

頒獎，授與／獎，獎品
v. confer or bestow as being deserved or merited or needed / n. something that is conferred or bestowed especially on the basis of merit or need

2219 **B.A.** [ˌbi`e] ★★★★★

Jack is not doing his best, so it may be impossible for him to get his B.A. in four years.

傑克並未盡全力，所以他可能無法在四年內取得文學士學位。

文學士
n. bachelor of arts

2220 **background** [`bæk͵graʊnd] ★★★★★

The papers which you submit will be evaluated by graduate school students with a strong background in writing.

你繳交的報告將由具有優異寫作背景的研究生評分。

（教育、出身等）背景
n. the circumstances or events antecedent to a phenomenon or development

2221 **backpack** [`bæk͵pæk] ★★★★☆

Henry is always carrying a bulky backpack. He says that he carries almost all of his books with him.

亨利總是背著大背包，他表示他幾乎將所有書帶在身上。

背包
n. a piece of equipment designed for use while being carried on the back

2222 **bibliography** [ˌbɪblɪ`ɑgrəfɪ] ★★★★★

The graduate student thought that he had finally finished his thesis. But he forgot to put a bibliography at the end of it.

研究生以為終於寫完論文了，但其實他忘記在最後附上參考書目。

參考書目，目錄學
n. a list often with descriptive or critical notes of writings relating to a particular subject, period, or author

2223 **bike rack** [baɪk ræk]

★★★★☆

脚踏車停放架
n. a rack where a bike is kept

Because every shuttle bus at our university has a bike rack, students who ride a bike to come to school can take a bus to go back home, and vice versa.

大學接駁公車都有腳踏車停放架，騎腳踏車上學的學生可搭公車回家，反之亦然。

2224 **biography** [baɪˋɑgrəfɪ]

★★★★★

傳記
n. a usually written history of a person's life

Most parents want their children to read a biography of a famous person. But children usually prefer reading detective stories or science fiction novels.

大多數父母希望子女閱讀名人傳記，但子女寧願看偵探故事或科幻小說。

2225 **bite** [baɪt]

★★★★★

咬，一口之量／咬，啃
n. a small amount of food /
v. seize especially with teeth or jaws so as to enter, grip, or wound

While studying in the library, I felt very tired. I kept on yawning and my stomach made a weird noise. So I decided to go grab a bite.

我在圖書館念書時覺得很累，一直打呵欠，肚子還發出怪聲，所以決定隨便去吃點東西。

2226 **bomb** [bɑm]

★★★★☆

炸彈／轟炸，慘敗
n. an explosive device fused to detonate under specified conditions / ***v.*** *goof up*

Sam had been doing well until last semester, but this semester he bombed the mid-term exam and ended up getting a C.

山姆上學期表現很好，但這學期期中考考得很差，只得到 C。

2227 **brochure** [broˋʃur]

★★★★★

小冊子
n. pamphlet; booklet

We are going to hand out brochures informing the students of the upcoming performance.

我們將發送小冊子通知同學有關接下來表演的事。

2228 **bulletin** [ˋbulətɪn]

★★★★★

公告，公報
n. a brief public notice issuing usually from an authoritative source

A: How did you know about the job vacancy?
B: I saw the ad on the bulletin board.

A：你怎麼會知道有職位空缺？
B：我看到公布欄上的廣告。

2229 **campus post office** [ˋkæmpəs post ˋɔfɪs]

★★★☆☆

校園郵局
n. a post office at the campus

The campus post office of our university is open from 9:00 a.m. until 6:00 p.m., and they have P.O. boxes too.

大學校園郵局的營業時間從上午九點起到晚上六點為止，同時也提供郵政信箱服務。

2230 **campus tour guide** [ˋkæmpəs tur gaɪd]

★★☆☆☆

校園參觀導遊
n. a tour guide for a visitor to a campus

Joe will work as a campus tour guide. He is now determined to help visitors learn about the university and have a good impression.

即將擔任校園參觀導遊的喬伊決定幫助參觀者了解校園，並產生好印象。

2231 certificate [sə`tɪfəkɪt]

★★★★★

Sam did a very good job in the speech contest. He was chosen as the grand prize winner and received a certificate of merit as well as a plaque.

山姆在演講比賽中表現優異，獲選為首獎得主，並獲頒獎狀和獎牌。

證書
n. *a document containing a certified statement especially as to the truth of something*

2232 check out [`tʃɛk ˌaʊt]

★★★★★

A: What should I do to check out this book?
B: You need to show your student ID.

A：請問要如何借書？
B：須出示學生證。

借書，結帳離開
v. *satisfy all requirements in taking away*

2233 class trip [`klæs trɪp]

★★★★☆

All the students of Prof. Brown's class were excited about the class trip scheduled for the next week.

伯朗教授班上所有學生都為將於下周舉辦的班級旅遊感到興奮。

班級旅遊
n. *a class outing*

2234 commencement [kə`mɛnsmənt]

★★★★★

Because of the anticipated bad weather, this year's commencement is scheduled to be held in the gymnasium.

由於預測天候不佳，今年的畢業典禮預定在體育館內舉行。

畢業典禮
n. *the ceremony or the day for conferring degrees or diplomas*

2235 competence [`kɑmpətəns]

★★★★★

The purpose of this test is to give students the chance to demonstrate their competence in English.

本測驗目的在於讓學生有機會展現英語能力。

能力，勝任，稱職
n. *ability; knowledge*

2236 computer lab [kəm`pjutə læb]

★★★★☆

The computer lab at our college is so fully packed with students that we have to wait in a long line to get on a computer.

大學電腦研究室裡擠滿了學生，我們要排隊排很久才能用到電腦。

電腦研究室
n. *a computer laboratory*

2237 consultant [kən`sʌltənt]

★★★★★

I think I should have a consultant at my side. I don't know what kind of subjects I should take.

我想我該找課程諮詢顧問幫忙，因為我不知道該選哪門課。

顧問，諮詢者
n. *one who gives professional advice or services*

2238 copyright [`kɑpɪˌraɪt]

★★★★★

According to this contract, the author, not the publishing company, holds the copyright on this book.

根據這份合約，本書版權在作者手上，並不屬於出版商。

版權，著作權
n. *the exclusive legal right to reproduce, publish, sell, or distribute something*

2239 counselor [`kaʊnslə] ★★★★★

指導老師，顧問
n. a person who gives advice

I've come to make an appointment to see a counselor some time next week.

我想預約下周和指導老師會面。

2240 course requirement [kors rɪ`kwaɪrmənt] ★★★★★

修課規定
n. a requirement for a course

Satto, a student from Japan, is determined to fulfill his course requirements as soon as possible.

來自日本的學生佐藤下定決心要盡快修完規定的學分。

2241 court [kɔrt] ★★★★★

（網球等）場地，法庭
n. a quadrangular space walled or marked off for playing one of various games with a ball; an official assembly for the transaction of judicial business

First of all, we need to reserve the tennis court for the upcoming competition. Let's go to the gym office.

首先要預約接下來的網球比賽場地。我們到體育館辦公室吧。

2242 cram [kræm] ★★★★☆

（為應考）倉促用功
v. prepare hastily for an examination

Please do not cram for the exam. I think it would be better for you to spread your study out over many days before the exam.

請不要臨時抱佛腳，我想你最好能將溫書時間分散在考前幾天。

2243 credit [`krɛdɪt] ★★★★★

學分／歸功於～
n. recognition by a school or college that a student has fulfilled a requirement leading to a degree / v. bring credit or honor upon

At most colleges and graduate schools, students need a certain number of credits so as to be awarded a degree.

多數大學和研究所學生須修滿一定學分才能拿到學位。

2244 credit-by-exam system [`krɛdɪt baɪ ɪg`zæm `sɪstəm] ★★☆☆☆

學分考制度
n. a system in which a school gives credits to the student who has passed an exam

Since this university has a credit-by-exam system, students who pass the related exam are given credits, even though they are not registered in the course.

這所大學實施學分考制度，學生即使未選修課程，只要通過相關考試就能拿到學分。

2245 crib [krɪb] ★★★☆☆

抄襲，剽竊
n. plagiarism

The university has decided to nullify the contract with the professor, whose thesis was found to be a crib of another person's thesis.

該大學決定解聘被發現抄襲他人論文的教授。

2246 deadline [`dɛd,laɪn] ★★★★★

截止日
n. a date or time before which something must be done

If you really want to study Spanish, you should remember that you should register before the registration deadline.

如果你真的想修西班牙文，要記得在選課截止日前辦理登記。

2247 defense [dɪˋfɛns]

★★★★☆

答辯
n. *an argument in support or justification*

Nick's defense is due next week, and so he's doing his best to be better prepared. He has collected a stack of materials and has tried to organize his ideas.

尼克的論文答辯預定在下周舉行,因此他盡全力做好準備。他收集了大量資料並試著整理自己的想法。

2248 department office [dɪˋpɑrtmənt ˋɔfɪs]

★★★★★

系辦公室
n. *an office of a department*

I think I'll have to go to the department office to ask about my term paper. They are still holding mine.

我必須到系辦查查我的期末報告,因為到現在還被扣著沒有發還。

2249 department head [dɪˋpɑrtmənt hɛd]

★★★★★

系主任
n. *head of a department*

Jack has had financial difficulties, and he has decided to appeal to explain his difficult situation with the department head.

傑克有經濟困難,於是決定求助於系主任,向他解釋自己的困境。

2250 dining hall [ˋdaɪnɪŋ hɔl]

★★★★★

餐廳
n. *restaurant; cafeteria*

At this university, every student has to show his ID card when they eat at the dining hall.

在這所大學餐廳用餐的學生,每位都必須出示學生證。

2251 dorm [dɔrm]

★★★★★

宿舍
n. *dormitory*

Please always conform to the regulations of our dorm. One of the most important things is that we have a 12 o'clock curfew.

請遵守宿舍規定,其中最重要的是十二點的門禁。

Tea Time... ☕

<Roman myth> Luna
In ancient times people believed that a person can become insane, affected by the moon (luna).

〈來自羅馬神話〉露娜
古時候人們相信受月亮影響的人會變得瘋狂。(註:羅馬神話中主掌月亮的女神為露娜,luna 即為 moon 的代稱。後世有關「月亮」或「瘋狂」的字詞,多以 luna- 為首。)

❋ **lunatic** [ˋlunəˏtɪk] **n.** *an insane person; madman; maniac* | 瘋子,精神錯亂者

Only a lunatic would have made a senseless decision like that. No sane person would ever have spent all his money on lottery tickets.

只有瘋子才會做出那麼愚蠢的決定,正常人絕不會把所有財產都拿去買樂透彩券。

1

Complete each word by filling in the blank with proper spelling so that it has the same meaning as suggested. Then please write the meaning of each word in Chinese.

1. 男校友   = a l u m _ _ _
2. 選集   = a n t h o _ _ _ _
3. 申請者   = a p p l i _ _ _ _
4. 評分   = _ _ _ _ s s m e n t
5. 出席   = _ _ t e n d
6. 獎   = a _ _ _ _
7. 背景   = _ _ _ _ g r o u n d
8. 會面約定   = _ _ p o i n t m e n t
9. 小冊子   = b r o c h _ _ _
10. 公告   = b u l l e _ _ _

11. certificate   = _____
12. commencement = _____
13. competence   = _____
14. counselor   = _____
15. credit   = _____
16. dorm   = _____
17. cram   = _____
18. alma mater   = _____
19. archaeologist = _____
20. audition   = _____

2

Choose a word that best completes the sentence.

21. I'm so hungry. Let's go grab a _____.
    (A) bite   (B) copyright   (C) assignment   (D) anthology

22. I have your book in my _____.
    (A) background   (B) backpack   (C) competence   (D) credit

23. I am reading the _____ of Benjamin Franklin.
    (A) alumnus   (B) assessment   (C) autobiography (D) defense

3

The highlighted word is closest in meaning to which of the following?

24. The commencement will be on April 15.
    (A) crib   (B) court   (C) consultant   (D) graduation

25. The purpose of this English test is to evaluate students' competence to communicate in English.
    (A) ability   (B) administration (C) annotate   (D) defense

★★★★★

2252 due [du]

I have an English composition assignment due at 2:00 tomorrow. So I'm terribly busy working on it.

明天下午兩點我得交出一篇英文作文報告，所以現在很忙。

預定的
a. having reached the date at which payment is required

★★★★★

2253 elective [ɪˋlɛktɪv]

In addition to requirements which students should take, universities offer many classes as electives.

大學除了必修課程外，還提供許多選修課程。

選修課程
n. an elective course or subject

★★★★☆

2254 eligibility [ˌɛlədʒəˋbɪlɪtɪ]

The graduate school of this university has such strict eligibility criteria that I might not be admitted.

這所大學研究所的招生資格符合標準很嚴，我可能無法獲准入學。

合格，適任
n. being qualified to participate or be chosen

★★★★★

2255 enroll [ɪnˋrol]

Before you enroll in Professor Brown's class, you should take the prerequisite Biology 100.

你修伯朗教授的課前，應該先修生物學 100 這門必修。

入學，註冊
v. enroll oneself or cause oneself to be enrolled

★★★★☆

2256 epitome [ɪˋpɪtəmɪ]

The professor's lecture captured the epitome of his theory.

教授的授課內容涵蓋其學說大綱。

梗概，摘要，大綱
n. a brief presentation or statement of something

★★★★★

2257 evaluate [ɪˋvæljʊˌet]

At the end of the semester, the students will have a chance to evaluate their classes.

學生在學期結束時將有機會進行教學評量。

評量，評價
v. determine or fix the value of; estimate

★★★★☆

2258 excerpt [ˋɛksɝpt]

"To be or not to be, that is the question," is an excerpt from Shakespeare's *Hamlet*.

「生存或死亡，這就是問題所在」是莎士比亞名著《哈姆雷特》中的摘錄。

摘錄，引述
n. a passage (as from a book or musical composition) selected, performed, or copied; extract

★★★★★

2259 exchange student [ɪksˋtʃendʒ ˋstudn̩t]

A: Welcome aboard. Where are you from?
B: I'm an exchange student from Singapore.

A：歡迎搭乘本班機。請問你是從哪裡來的？
B：我是來自新加坡的交換學生。

交換學生
n. a student who goes to a foreign country to study, usually as a part of a programme

2260 expulsion [ɪk`spʌlʃən] ★★★☆☆

Jack had hardly considered the possibility of his expulsion from the school. But everyone else thought that he had been too negligent in his studies and school life.

傑克沒想過會被退學，但大家都認為他在學業和學校生活上都太散漫了。

退學，開除
n. the act of expelling

2261 extracurricular activity [ˌɛkstrə`rɪkjələ æk`tɪvətɪ] ★★★★★

I have been thinking about joining the baseball club for an extracurricular activity. But I am afraid I am a little too short.

我考慮過參加棒球社課外活動，但是擔心自己有點太矮。

課外活動
n. a student's activity out of a curriculum

2262 faculty [`fækltɪ] ★★★★★

A: Did you happen to see Prof. Brown?
B: Maybe he is in the faculty lounge right now.

A：你有看到伯朗教授嗎？
B：他現在也許在教職員休息室。

（大學全體）教職員
n. the teaching and administrative staff and those members of the administration having academic rank in an educational institution

---

2263 failure [`feljə] ★★★★★

Bill's negligence resulted in his failure in Professor Smith's class.
比爾上課懶散，結果被史密斯教授當掉。

不及格
n. a state of inability to perform a normal function

2264 fair [fɛr] ★★★★★

Our university has so many things to do for fun on campus. We have plays, ethnic exhibits and art fairs.

我們大學校園裡有戲劇表演、民俗展和藝術博覽會等許多有趣活動。

市集，博覽會，展覽會
n. an exhibition designed to acquaint prospective buyers or the general public with a product

---

2265 fee [fi] ★★★★★

I had wanted to sign up for a baseball team, but I found out that I had to pay the fee. It was 40 dollars per season.

我想加入棒球隊，但發現每季要繳交四十美元的會費。

學費，會費
n. tuition

2266 feedback [`fid,bæk] ★★★★☆

If you have some time, could you please fill out this form? It is a type of feedback survey.

你如果有空，可以請你填寫這份意見調查表嗎？

意見回饋，回應，迴響
n. the transmission of evaluative or corrective information about an action, event

---

2267 festival [`fɛstəvl̩] ★★★★★

Many of the students at the college were looking forward to this year's film festival. Last year the students enjoyed many interesting films shown there.

許多大學生都期待今年的電影節，去年大家欣賞了許多有趣電影。

節慶活動
n. an often periodic celebration or program of events or entertainment having a specified focus

2268 fill up [fɪl `ʌp]

額滿
v. be filled

It's quite important for you to sign up for Professor Russel's history class far in advance, because his class usually fills up quickly.

你提早選修羅素老師的歷史課是很重要的，因為他的課通常很快額滿。

2269 final [`faɪnl̩]

期末考
n. the last examination in a course

The final is near at hand, so I think I'll have to study pretty hard. But I'm not sure if there will be vacant seats in the library.

期末考就要到了，我得加緊用功念書，不過不確定圖書館有沒有空位。

2270 first aid [ˌfɝst `ed]

急救
n. emergency care or treatment given to an ill or injured person before regular medical aid can be obtained

Tom took the first aid certification course. He learned all aspects of first aid, including cardio-pulmonary resuscitation and mouth-to-mouth resuscitation.

湯姆選修急救檢定課程，學會心肺復甦術和口對口人工呼吸等所有急救常識。

2271 flip [flɪp]

翻閱，翻頁
v. cause to turn and especially to turn over

Jack was in the library, flipping through the pages. But he could not concentrate on his studies.

傑克在圖書館裡翻閱書頁，可是無法專心念書。

2272 fraternity [frə`tɝnətɪ]

兄弟會
n. a student organization for scholastic, professional, or extracurricular activities

This university has a dry campus policy. Therefore, students are not allowed to drink alcohol anywhere on the campus, even at the fraternity house.

這所大學禁止學生在校內任何地方飲酒，即使是兄弟會館也不例外。

2273 freshman [`frɛʃmən]

大一新生
n. a first-year student

Jane has decided to sign up for volunteer work, which involves helping freshman students to adapt to school life. Just one hour per week is not a big obligation.

珍決定加入志工行列，協助大一新生適應校園生活，每周只花一小時不算太大責任。

2274 full-timer [`ful`taɪmə]

全職工作者，專任者
n. a person who works full-time

It's impossible for me to be a full-timer, because I have too much work to do this semester.

我不可能做全職工作，因為這學期課業很重。

2275 gathering [`gæðərɪŋ]

集會，聚會
n. meeting

Whenever we have a gathering at the campus, James helps us in many ways. He is willing to go on food runs and does everything to be helpful.

每次校園集會詹姆斯都大力幫忙，不但樂於跑腿買食物，也盡力提供協助。

2276 GPA ★★★★★

Because my GPA is below 3.0, I don't think it'll be possible for me to apply for one of the graduate schools.
我的學業總平均點數低於 3.0，所以無法申請任何研究所。

學業總平均點數
n. grade point average

2277 grade [gred] ★★★★★

Mary is such a good student that it may be possible for her to skip a grade.
瑪麗表現如此優異也許能跳級。

年級，成績／評分
*n. a class organized for the work of a particular year of a school course / **v.** evaluate*

2278 graduate school [`grædʒʊɪt ˌskul] ★★★★★

The difference between undergraduates and graduate school students: When the professor says, "Good morning," the former respond by saying, "Good morning." But the latter immediately write it down.
大學生和研究生的差別在：於教授道早安時，前者會回答「早」，但後者會立刻抄下這句話。

研究所
n. a school for a holder of an academic degree or diploma

2279 glossary [`glɑsərɪ] ★★★☆☆

While reading *King Lear*, I encountered several archaic words, so I had to consult Shakespeare's glossary.
我讀《李爾王》時遇到許多古字，必須查閱莎士比亞辭典。

詞彙表，專業辭典，術語彙編
n. a collection of textual glosses or of specialized terms with their meanings

---

2280 guidance professor [`gaɪdn̩s prə`fɛsɚ] ★★★★★

I have a 10 o'clock appointment with the guidance professor. I think I will have to get some advice about my job preparation.
我和輔導老師約好上午十點會面，我想詢問有關工作準備上的建議。

輔導老師
n. a professor who gives advice on vocational or educational problems to students

---

2281 gym [dʒɪm] ★★★★★

Jim and Judy usually go to the gym in the afternoon. Strangely enough, Jim is doing some aerobics and Judy is lifting weights.
吉姆和茱蒂經常下午一起到體育館，奇怪的是，吉姆跳有氧舞蹈而茱蒂練舉重。

體育館
n. gymnasium

2282 ID [`aɪ di] ★★★★★

James lost his student ID card, so he had to get a new one issued at the registration office.
詹姆斯遺失了學生證，必須到註冊組補辦一張新證。

身分證，身分證明
n. identification card

2283 inscribe [ɪn`skraɪb] ★★★☆☆

James is graduating summa cum laude, and his name will be inscribed on the wall of the administration building.
詹姆斯以最優等成績畢業，他的名字將被刻在行政大樓牆上。

刻，雕，題寫
v. write, engrave, or print as a lasting record

2284 intramural [ˌɪntrəˈmjurəl]

★★★☆☆

The students of the English Department are going to have an intramural athletic meet after the midterm exam.

期中考後外文系學生將舉辦校內運動大會。

校內的，校際的
a. competed only within the student body

2285 invalid [ˈɪnvælɪd]

★★★☆☆

I think there is something amiss. I am sure I remember my password, but I'm having problems logging in to this site. It alleges my password is invalid.

我想這有點問題，我確定記得密碼，但進不去這個網站，上面說密碼無效。

無效的
a. not valid; without foundation or force in fact, truth, or law

---

2286 jump-start [ˌdʒʌmpˈstɑrt]

★★☆☆☆

A: Oh, my! My car won't start. It seems like the battery is out of juice.
B: We'll have to jump-start the car.

A：天啊！我的車發不動，電瓶似乎沒電了。
B：我們得向人接電啟動車子。

接電啟動（車輛等）
v. start (an engine or vehicle) by temporary connection to an external power source

---

2287 language course [ˈlæŋgwɪdʒ kors]

★★★★★

I'm afraid you'll have to take one more semester of the language course. I think that your speaking ability needs to be improved.

恐怕你得再修一學期語言課程，以提高你的口語能力。

語言課程
n. a course for language learning

2288 language partner [ˈlæŋgwɪdʒ ˈpɑrtnə]

★★☆☆☆

The language partner is spending two or three hours a week with foreign students, helping them improve their English.

語言學伴每周花兩到三小時協助外籍學生提高英語能力。

語言學伴
n. a partner who helps a student, especially a foreign student to improve a language

---

2289 leave of absence [liv əv ˈæbsn̩s]

★★☆☆☆

Rose went to the administration to apply for a leave of absence for one semester. Her health condition has been not so good.

羅絲到行政大樓申請請假一學期，她的身體狀況不太好。

請假
n. permission to be absent from a course or employment

2290 lecture [ˈlɛktʃə]

★★★★★

Professor White, I enjoyed your lecture. It was very impressive.

懷特教授，我很喜歡你的授課，令人印象深刻。

授課
n. a discourse given before an audience or class especially for instruction

---

2291 libel [ˈlaɪbl̩]

★★☆☆☆

The English professor's previous student kept on writing bad words about him on the school website. So the professor decided to bring an action of libel against him.

英語教授以前的學生一直在學校網站上寫他的壞話，於是教授決定告他誹謗。

誹謗，中傷
n. a written or oral defamatory statement or representation that conveys an unjustly unfavorable impression

---

2292 **literacy** [ˋlɪtərəsɪ]

★★★★★

能力，知識
n. *the quality or state of being literate*

Computer literacy is an absolute must to apply for this position. Not knowing how to operate a computer is not different from being blind.

申請這份工作者一定要具備電腦能力，不會操作電腦的人和瞎子無異。

2293 **literature** [ˋlɪtərə‚tʃur]

★★★★★

文學，文學作品
n. *the production of literary work especially as an occupation*

Bob is interested in 19th century American literature, especially novels.

鮑伯對十九世紀美國文學感興趣，特別是小說。

- annals n. 編年史	- flowery a. 詞藻華麗的	- pseudonym n. 筆名，假名
- autobiography n. 自傳	- journal n. 日誌	- rhyme n. 押韻
- allegory n. 寓言	- lyric n. 抒情詩	- satire n. 諷刺文學
- bestiary n. 動物寓言集	- metaphor n. 隱喻	- simile n. 明喻
- brochure n. 小冊子	- miscellany n. 文集，雜集	- stanza n. 詩的一節
- chronicle n. 編年史，年代記	- novelette n. 短篇（中篇）小說	- symbolism n. 象徵主義
- denouement n. 結局	- novella n. 短篇故事	- synopsis n. 梗概
- encyclopedia n. 百科全書	- ode n. 頌歌	- thesaurus n. 辭典
- epic n. 史詩	- prose n. 散文	- thesis n. 命題
- fable n. 寓言	- protagonist n. 主角	- tract n. 短文

2294 **lodging house** [ˋlɑdʒɪŋ haʊs]

★★☆☆☆

宿舍，公寓
n. *rooming house*

A: What's the landlady like at your lodging house?
B: Oh, she's very nice. She is just like my mom.

A：你的公寓女房東人怎麼樣？
B：她人非常好，就像我媽一樣。

2295 **lottery** [ˋlɑtərɪ]

★★★☆☆

樂透彩券，抽籤
n. *a drawing of lots used to decide something*

Our college has limited parking space, and so parking permits are usually issued through a lottery.

我們大學的停車位有限，所以停車許可證通常是經過抽籤核發的。

2296 **M.A.** [‚ɛmˋe]

★★★★★

文學碩士
n. *master of arts*

A: How long will it take for me to get an M.A. degree?
B: It depends on how hard you study.

A：我多久可以拿到文學碩士文憑？
B：那要看你有多用功。

2297 **magna cum laude** [‚mægnə kʊm ˋlɔdɪ]

★★★★☆

以優異成績地
ad. *with great distinction*

This resume shows that the applicant graduated from his university magna cum laude.

從履歷中可以看出應徵者是以優異成績自大學畢業的。

2298 major [`medʒɚ]

★★★★★

主修科目 / 主修
n. an academic subject chosen as a field of specialization / *v.* pursue an academic major

A: What's your major?
B: I'm majoring in English.

A：你的主修是什麼？
B：我主修外文。

- anthropology n. 人類學
- astrology n. 占星學
- biology n. 生物學
- cardiology n. 心臟病學
- cosmology n. 宇宙論
- cytology n. 細胞學
- dermatology n. 皮膚病學

- ecology n. 生態學
- endocrinology n. 內分泌學
- entomology n. 昆蟲學
- etymology n. 詞源學
- histology n. 組織學
- meteorology n. 氣象學
- ornithology n. 鳥類學

- pathology n. 病理學
- petrology n. 岩石學
- pharmacology n. 藥理學
- physics n. 物理學
- physiology n. 生理學
- seismology n. 地震學

2299 matriculant [mə`trɪkjələnt]

★★★☆☆

大學考生
n. a person who enrolls as a member of a body and especially of a college or university

The professors and the other school authorities decided to grant admission to the matriculant whose GPA was high enough.

教授和學校當局決定同意學業總平均點數夠高的大學考生入學。

2300 matriculation [mə`trɪkjə`leʃən]

★★★☆☆

大學入學許可
n. enrolling as a member of a body and especially of a college or university

The matriculation ceremony was held in the auditorium, which was filled with the freshmen and their parents.

開學典禮在擠滿大一新生和家長的禮堂舉行。

2301 membership [`mɛmbɚʃɪp]

★★★★★

會員，會員資格
n. the state or status of being a member

A: Do I have to pay to use this sports center?
B: If you are a full-time student, you don't need to. Membership is included in your tuition.

A：請問使用體育館要付費嗎？
B：如果你是全職學生就不用，因為會員資格已包含在學費中。

Tea Time... ☕

<Greek story> Spartan	〈來自希臘故事〉斯巴達人
Spartans were believed to be warlike, brave, stoic, frugal, etc.	一般相信斯巴達人好戰、剛勇、禁慾、簡樸。（註：斯巴達人流傳已久的強悍勇敢、生活刻苦形象，使後世以此字為「剛勇的、踏實的、簡樸的」等字的同義詞。）

✱ **Spartan** [`spɑrtn̩] *a. austere; frugal; plain* | 斯巴達人的，簡樸的，苦行的

He was a very stern man and approved of the Spartan quality of his military quarters, which consisted of a bed, a lamp, a small table and nothing else.

他是個非常嚴厲的人，就連軍營也充分展現斯巴達精神，裡頭除了睡床、燈、小桌外一無所有。

Review Test 02

Chapter

1
2
3
4
5

1

Complete each word by filling in the blank with proper spelling so that it has the same meaning as suggested. Then please write the meaning of each word in Chinese.

1. 選修課程 = e l e c _ _ _ _
2. 合格 = _ _ _ g i b i l i t y
3. 入學 = _ _ r o l l
4. 評量 = e _ _ _ u a t e
5. 摘錄 = _ _ c e r p t
6. 退學 = e x p u l _ _ _ _
7. 大學全體教職員 = _ _ _ u l t y
8. 不及格 = f a i l _ _ _ _
9. 意見回饋 = f e e d _ _ _ _
10. 期末考 = _ _ _ a l

11. flip = _____
12. fraternity = _____
13. freshman = _____
14. glossary = _____
15. gym = _____
16. intramural = _____
17. lecture = _____
18. literature = _____
19. lottery = _____
20. matriculation = _____

2

Choose a word that best completes the sentence.

21. **Students' English speaking ability will be _____ by the professor.**
(A) enrolled   (B) evaluated   (C) jump-started   (D) excerpted

22. **The tuition _____ is beyond my means. It is too high.**
(A) fraternity   (B) epitome   (C) expulsion   (D) fee

3

The highlighted word is closest in meaning to which of the following?

23. **This ID card is invalid . You should have a new one issued.**
(A) void   (B) final   (C) major   (D) due

24. **The student union is going to have a gathering this coming Saturday.**
(A) meeting   (B) libel   (C) literacy   (D) grade

25. **I really enjoyed Professor Donaldson's lecture .**
(A) eligibility   (B) glossary   (C) class   (D) feedback

MP3
94

2302 midterm exam [`mɪdˌtɜm ɪg`zæm]

★★★★☆

期中考
n. an exam in the middle of a semester

Because the midterm exam draws near, the library is fully packed with students. All of the students seem to be absorbed in studies.

因為期中考快到了，所以圖書館裡擠滿專心念書的學生。

2303 musicology [ˌmjuzɪ`kɑlədʒɪ]

★★★★☆

音樂學，音樂理論
n. the study of music as a branch of knowledge or field of research as distinct from composition or performance

A: Listen to this music. The tone is so melodious, isn't it?
B: Yes, it is. By the way, it seems you have an excellent ear for music. You should have majored in musicology.

A：聽聽這段音樂，旋律很優美，不是嗎？
B：是啊。順便一提，你的音樂鑑賞力似乎很好，應該主修音樂學才對。

Reference...

- adagio ad. 慢板地	- dynamic mark n. 力度記號
- ad lib n. 即興演奏	- ensemble n. 合奏，合唱
- allegretto ad. 稍快板地	- etude n. 練習曲
- allegro ad. 快板地	- execution n. 演奏技巧
- amoroso ad. 戀曲地	- fantasia n. 幻想曲
- andante ad. 行板地	- fiddle n. 小提琴
- appreciation n. 鑑賞，欣賞	- fingering n. 指法
- aria n. 詠嘆調	- flat n. 降半音記號
- arpeggio n. 琶音	- forte ad. 強音地
- arrange v. 改編	- fugue n. 賦格曲
- art rock n. 藝術搖滾	- half note n. 二分音符
- ballad n. 民謠，流行抒情歌曲	- improvisation n. 即興曲
- bass n. 男低音	- juxtaposition n. 並列
- cacophony n. 不和諧音	- kettledrum n. 定音鼓
- cantata n. 清唱劇	- largo ad. 最緩板地
- chamber music n. 室內樂	- major scale n. 長音階
- choir n. 唱詩班	- melody n. 旋律，主調
- chord n. 和弦，和音	- minim n. 二分音符
- chromatic a. 半音階的	- minor scale n. 小音階
- clef n. 譜號	- motif n. 主題
- composer n. 作曲家	- movement n. 拍子
- concertgoer n. 常聽音樂會者，樂迷	- musical notation n. 樂譜記號
- concerto n. 協奏曲	- note n. 音符
- concord n. 和聲	- nocturne n. 夜曲
- concours n. 比賽	- octave n. 八度音階
- conductor n. 指揮	- opus n. 編號作品
- conservatory n. 音樂學校	- orchestra n. 管弦樂團
- counterpoint n. 對位法，對位旋律	- overture n. 前奏曲，序曲
- crescendo ad. 漸強地	- piano ad. 弱拍地
- crotchet n. 四分音符	- percussion n. 敲打樂器
- decrescendo ad. 漸弱地	- performance n. 演奏
- duet n. 二重唱，二重奏	- phonograph record n. 唱片

- prelude n. 前奏曲	- symphony n. 交響曲
- quaver n. 顫音	- tempo n. 拍子
- recital n. 獨奏會	- timbre n. 音色，音質
- refrain n. 覆唱句，副歌	- time signature n. 拍子記號
- rehearsal time n. 排演時間	- tone n. 全音
- requiem n. 安魂曲	- tone-deaf a. 音盲的
- rhythm n. 節拍，節奏	- tune n. 和音，旋律
- rhythm and blues n. 節奏藍調	- tutti ad. 合奏地
- rondo n. 輪旋曲	- undertone n. 低音
- rest n. 休止符	- vigoroso ad. 強音地
- scale n. 音階	- vivace ad. 活潑地
- score n. 樂譜	- vocalization n. 聲樂練習曲
- semiquaver n. 十六分音符	- whole note n. 全音符
- sharp n. 升半音記號	- wind instrument n. 管樂器
- staccato n. 斷音	- woodwind n. 木管樂器
- strings n. 弦	- xylophone n. 木琴

2304 nose dive [`noz ,daɪv]

★★★★☆

Jack's grades have taken a nose dive ever since he bought his car. His grades had previously been above average.

傑克的成績在買車後一落千丈，他以前的成績高於一般水準。

暴跌
n. a sudden extreme drop

2305 note [not]

★★★★★

Most of Professor White's Philosophy class students take notes, but they do not understand his lecture.

大多數上懷特教授哲學課的學生都會做筆記，但沒人聽得懂。

筆記，記錄
n. memorandum

2306 off [ɔf]

★★★★★

Tomorrow is July 4th. As you know, we are off tomorrow. I hope that you will think of the patriots who dedicated themselves to the nation's independence.

明天是七月四日，大家都知道停課一天，希望各位想想為國家獨立犧牲奉獻的愛國志士。

休息，不工作，停止
a. in absence from or suspension of regular work or service

2307 orientation [ˌɔrɪɛn`teʃən]

★★★★★

All of the freshmen are supposed to attend the orientation, which will be scheduled next Monday.

所有大一新生都應出席下周一舉辦的校園導覽活動。

校園導覽
n. the act or process of orienting or of being oriented

2308 pajama party [pəˈdʒæməz ˈpɑrtɪ]

★★★☆☆

The girl students will throw a pajama party at Jane's house. They are already excited about it.

女學生將在珍的家裡舉辦睡衣派對，大家都感到非常興奮。

睡衣派對
n. a party in which teen-aged girls spend the night together in pajamas

---

2309 parking-space [ˈpɑrkɪŋ spes]

★★★★★

The parking-spaces at the campus are so limited that the school authorities are having a hard time trying to solve the problem.

校園停車位相當有限，學校當局很難解決問題。

停車位
n. space for parking

2310 participation [pɑrˌtɪsəˈpeʃən]

★★★★★

For the evaluation of this class, the final and mid-term exams are essential, but the students' attendance and participation will also be important.

關於這門課的評分，期中和期末考固然重要，但學生出席率和上課參與也同樣重要。

參與，分享
n. the act of participating

2311 pastime [ˈpæsˌtaɪm]

★★★★★

Professor Pollock is taking pictures of flowers at the campus, which is his pastime. He is going to have an exhibit next month.

波拉克教授的消遣是拍攝校園花卉，下個月將推出作品展。

消遣，娛樂
n. something that amuses and serves to make time pass agreeably; diversion

---

2312 permit [pəˈmɪt]

★★★★★

If you really want to drive your car, you will have to buy a parking permit, which is 150 dollars a year.

如果你想駕車，須購買每年一百五十美元的停車許可證。

許可證，執照
n. a written warrant or license granted by one having authority

---

2313 physical education [ˌfɪzɪkḷ ɛdʒəˈkeʃən]

★★★★★

I wish we would have more physical education. P.E. classes seem to give me more energy.

真希望能多上點體育課，體育課似乎能帶給我更多活力。

體育課，體育教育
n. instruction in the development and care of the body

2314 piracy [ˈpaɪrəsɪ]

★★★☆☆

We should be very careful about literary piracy when writing a thesis or a book.

撰寫論文或書籍時應特別注意著作權侵害問題。

剽竊，著作權侵害，盜印
n. the unauthorized use of another's production, invention, or conception especially in infringement of a copyright

2315 **pre-lab report** [prɪ læb rɪ`port] ★★☆☆☆

When doing the pre-lab report, the students wrote down the purpose and procedure of their experiment.

撰寫實驗準備報告時,學生要寫出實驗目的和步驟。

實驗準備報告
n. a report for a lab

2316 **pre-med** [prɪ`mɛd] ★★★☆☆

One of my friends is majoring in biology, but he usually says that he is majoring in pre-med, because he hopes to be a medical student.

我有個友人主修生物學,但他常說自己主修醫學院預科,因為他想成為醫學院學生。

醫學院預科,醫預科學生
n. a premedical student or course of study

2317 **prerequisite** [ˌpri`rɛkwəzɪt] ★★★★★

James wanted to take Chemistry 223, but he did not know that he should have taken the prerequisite, Chemistry 100.

詹姆斯想修化學 223,但他不知道須先修過化學 100 必修課。

必修,必要條件
n. something that is necessary to an end or to the carrying out of a function

---

2318 **presentation** [ˌprɛzn̩`teʃən] ★★★★★

You did a good job on your presentation. The students, as well as the professor, were really impressed.

你的上台報告做得很好,讓全班同學和教授都印象深刻。

上台報告
n. the act of presenting

2319 **proctor** [`prɑktə] ★★★☆☆

We took the exam without a proctor. Of course, no students cheated on the exam. The students felt so proud of themselves.

我們在無人監考的情況下考試,當然沒有人作弊,學生們都以自己為榮。

監考老師,監考者
n. supervisor; monitor

2320 **professor emeritus** [prə`fɛsə ɪ`mɛrətəs] ★★★☆☆

Professor Phillips is a professor emeritus. He has been teaching students at this university for over 30 years.

菲利普斯教授是在本大學授課超過三十年的名譽教授。

cf. professor extraordinary 客座教授 / exchange professor 交換教授

名譽教授
n. a professor retired from professional life but permitted to retain as an honorary title the rank of the last office held

---

2321 **prom** [prɑm] ★★★★☆

While his friends are busy preparing for the upcoming prom, David hasn't yet found a partner.

當朋友們忙著準備即將來臨的班級舞會時,大衛卻連舞伴都還沒找。

班級舞會
n. a formal dance given by a high school or college class

2322 **proofs** [prufs]

★★★★☆

The author read the proofs with extreme care. He thought that there should not be even a single typo.

作者仔細閱讀校稿，他認為連一個打字錯誤都不該出現。

校稿，校對稿
n. a copy (as of typeset text) made for examination or correction

2323 **pull off** [pʊl ɔf]

★★★★☆

One of the reasons James always pulls off his grades in math is that he is trying to teach his little brother the same subject that he is learning.

詹姆斯數學成績一向很好的原因之一是他同時教弟弟自己正在學的東西。

得勝，成功
v. accomplish successfully

2324 **quarter** [ˈkwɔrtə]

★★★★★

The school year is split into quarters, so we have four terms a year.

一學年分成四學期，所以一年共有四個學期。

（四學期制學校的）一學期
n. one of four equal parts into which something is divisible

2325 **quit** [kwɪt]

★★★★★

A: Please do not quit. Keep on going.
B: I have already failed too many classes.

A：請不要休學，要繼續下去。
B：我有太多門課不及格。

離開，放棄，停止
v. depart; give up

2326 **recruit** [rɪˈkrut]

★★★★★

The company I am working at is planning to recruit more employees. If you are interested in applying for a position at the company, I'll give you some information.

我服務的公司正打算雇用更多員工，如果你有興趣應徵的話，我可以提供一些資訊。

雇用，聘用
v. seek to enroll

2327 **reevaluate** [riˈvæljʊˌet]

★★★☆☆

Joe received such a low grade on his paper that he asked the professor to reevaluate his grade.

喬伊的報告分數很低，他請求教授重新評分。

重新評分，再評量
v. evaluate again

2328 **reference** [ˈrɛfərəns]

★★★★★

One student who has been negligent in his studies came over to Professor Joyce and asked him to write a reference. But the professor did not know who he was.

某個不用功的學生請喬伊斯教授寫推薦信，但教授完全不認得他。

推薦信
n. a statement of the qualifications of a person

2329 **register** [`rɛdʒɪstə]
★★★★★

A: Where do I have to register for this semester?
B: Please go to the registration office upstairs.

A：請問本學期註冊要到哪裡辦理？
B：請到樓上註冊組。

註冊
v. *enroll formally especially as a voter or student*

2330 **registration** [ˌrɛdʒɪ`streʃən]
★★★★★

Is there any way for me to postpone my registration? My parents haven't sent me the money yet.

請問有沒有任何辦法可以延期註冊？因為我父母還沒有寄錢來。

入學，註冊
n. *enrollment*

2331 **rejection** [rɪ`dʒɛkʃən]
★★★★☆

James has been feeling rejection from Prof. Smith. It must be because he hasn't submitted his paper.

詹姆斯一直覺得被史密斯教授排斥，一定是因為自己還沒交報告的緣故。

拒絕，排斥
n. *failure an unwillingness to grant something asked for*

2332 **rent** [rɛnt]
★★★★★

A: I want to know if it is possible for me to rent a PO box.
B: Sure, it is possible. It's 4 bucks per month.

A：我想知道可以租用郵政信箱嗎？
B：當然可以，月租四美元。

租用
v. *take and hold under an agreement to pay rent*

2333 **required course** [rɪ`kwaɪrd kors]
★★★★★

Even though I did not like the subject or the professor, I had to take Biology 221, because it was a required course.

我雖然不喜歡這門課或任課老師，但還是得修生物學 221，因為它是必修。

必修課程
n. *a compulsory course*

2334 **research** [`risɜtʃ]
★★★★★

Most professors are pretty busy doing research, preparing for classes, and teaching students.

大部分教授都忙著做學術研究、備課和教書。

學術研究
n. *studious inquiry or examination*

2335 **researcher** [rɪ`sɜtʃə]
★★★★★

To be a good researcher, one should be able to analyze a variety of phenomena.

想成為優秀研究員，就要能分析種種現象。

研究員
n. *one who does research*

2336 resumé [ˌrɛzuˈme]

★★★★★

履歷
n. *curriculum vitae*

To apply for this position, you should send us your resumé, which describes your educational background and job experience.

想申請這份工作的人需寄交詳述教育背景和工作經驗的個人履歷。

2337 retake [riˈtek]

★★★★☆

重修
v. *take or receive again*

Judy took Physics 224 last semester, but she failed. She has no choice but to retake the class, because it is a required course.

茱蒂上學期修過物理學 224 但是被當，她別無選擇只能重修這門課，因為它是必修。

2338 room change [ˈrum tʃendʒ]

★★☆☆☆

換房
n. *a change of a room*

Even though you apply for a room change, your request will be approved only under special circumstances.

即使申請換房，也只有在特殊情況下才能得到批准。

2339 scholarship [ˈskɑləˌʃɪp]

★★★★★

獎學金
n. *a grant-in-aid*

Jim has applied for a scholarship, but unfortunately his grades have not been good enough.

吉姆申請獎學金，不幸的是他的分數不夠高。

2340 score [skɔr]

★★★★★

成績，分數
n. *mark*

To apply to this college, you should send us your transcript, TOEFL score, and two references.

想申請這所大學的人需寄交學校成績單、托福成績單，以及兩封推薦信。

2341 security [sɪˈkjurətɪ]

★★★★☆

保全，保安
n. *measures taken to guard*

Our university set up security cameras to prevent campus crime last year. Fortunately, the crime rate has decreased.

我們大學去年裝設保全攝影機以防止校園犯罪，所幸犯罪率已經下降。

2342 session [ˈsɛʃən]

★★★★★

上課時間，學期，集會
n. *the period during the year or day in which a school conducts classes; class; meeting*

To begin with, let us make this simple. The more sessions you attend, the higher grade you will receive.

首先簡單來說，有來上愈多課的同學分數就愈高。

2343 shuttle bus [ˈʃʌtl̩ bʌs] ★★★★★

Our school's shuttle bus runs from 7:00 a.m. until 11:00 p.m., and it arrives every 20 minutes.

我們學校的接駁公車行駛時間從早上七點到晚上十一點，每二十分鐘發一班車。

接駁公車
n. a vehicle used in a shuttle

2344 skate [sket] ★★★☆☆

Jim had been skating through all of his classes, getting all A's, until he got a D in Spanish.

吉姆上課都用混的還都拿到 A 等，直到修西班牙文才拿到 D 等。

草率行事，遊手好閒
v. proceed in a superficial or blithe manner

2345 skip [skɪp] ★★★★★

Joe had to skip class yesterday because he was aching all over. He developed a fever after the class trip.

喬伊昨天渾身痠痛所以翹課，他在班級旅遊後就發燒了。

翹課，未出席
v. fail to attend or participate in

2346 smoke-free [ˌsmokˈfri] ★★★★☆

All the buildings are smoke-free. So if you want to smoke, please go outside and enjoy your smoking just next to the ashtray provided.

所有大樓全面禁煙，想吞雲吐霧的人請到外面煙灰缸旁。

禁煙的
a. not allowed to smoke

2347 sorority [səˈrɔrətɪ] ★★★★☆

Nancy is going to take Jane to the sorority house after class today. Jane has made few friends because she is extremely shy.

南西今天下課要帶珍到姊妹會館，珍很害羞所以朋友不多。

姊妹會
n. a club of women

2348 sport [spɔrt] ★★★★★

A: What's your favorite sport?
B: Well, I am crazy about watching soccer. But I am not good at playing it.

A：你最喜歡的運動是什麼？
B：嗯，我很喜歡看足球賽，但踢得不好。

運動
n. physical activity engaged in for pleasure

Reference...

- bobsled n. 連橇賽	- pentathlon n. 五項運動
- canoeing n. 駕獨木舟	- rowing n. 划船
- croquet n. 槌球賽	- sledding n. 滑雪橇
- decathlon n. 十項運動	- snorkeling n. 浮潛
- ice skating n. 滑冰	- snowmobiling n. 騎雪上摩托車
- kayaking n. 單人皮艇運動	- windsurfing n. 風帆衝浪運動

2349 student advisor [`studn̩t əd`vaɪzɚ] ★★★☆☆

學生顧問，導師
n. an advisor for students

Mrs. Brown is a student advisor who tries to help students by giving them advice on various matters. She chooses subjects, and leads a good campus life.

導師伯朗太太在各種事務上提供學生建議。她協助選課，並引導一個優質的校園生活。

2350 student lounge [`studn̩t laʊndʒ] ★★★★★

學生交誼廳
n. a room for students' leisure activities

The student lounge is so spacious and comfortable that it is one of my favorite places on the campus.

寬敞又舒適的學生交誼廳是我最愛的校園一角之一。

2351 student union [`studn̩t `junjən] ★★★★★

學生會
n. a union of students

Paul decided to register for a student union class, which will help him to get a part-time job.

保羅決定修學生會課程，以便得到兼職工作。

Tea Time... ☕

<From the name of a Scottish theologian> Dunce Used by Renaissance humanists to ridicule followers of John Duns Scotus, a Scottish theologian.	〈來自一蘇格蘭神學家之名〉鄧斯 文藝復興人文主義者以此字嘲笑蘇格蘭神學家鄧斯哥德的信徒。（註：成績差或不乖的學生受罰時所戴的圓錐形紙帽稱為 dunce cap 或 dunce's cap。dunce 通常被引申為「蠢材，笨蛋」之意。）

✱ **dunce** [dʌns] *n. dull-witted person* | 笨蛋，傻瓜，劣等生

Jeff was such a dunce at school. He was really stupid. He had never gotten more than 60% on any of his exams.

傑夫在學校是個傻瓜，他真的很笨，每次考試不曾排在百分之六十之內。

1

Complete each word by filling in the blank with proper spelling so that it has the same meaning as suggested. Then please write the meaning of each word in Chinese.

1. 參與	= _ _ _ _ i c i p a t i o n		11. quit	= _____
2. 消遣	= _ _ _ t i m e		12. off	= _____
3. 許可證	= p e r _ _ _		13. proof	= _____
4. 著作權侵害	= _ _ _ a c y		14. rent	= _____
5. 上台報告	= _ _ _ s e n t a t i o n		15. scholarship	= _____
6. 監考者	= _ _ _ c t o r		16. security	= _____
7. 重新評分	= _ _ e v a l u a t e		17. session	= _____
8. 註冊	= _ _ _ _ s t r a t i o n		18. skip	= _____
9. 必修	= _ _ _ r e q u i s i t e		19. sorority	= _____
10. 雇用，聘用	= _ _ c r u i t		20. prom	= _____

2

Choose a word that best completes the sentence.

21. **To apply for the job opening, Jack sent the company a _____.**
    (A) resumé   (B) score   (C) note   (D) sorority

22. **The _____ was sure not to be negligent so that the students could not cheat during the exam.**
    (A) session   (B) proctor   (C) proofs   (D) orientation

23. **Some students insist that _____ should be granted to poor students.**
    (A) piracy   (B) pastime   (C) permit   (D) scholarships

3

The highlighted word is closest in meaning to which of the following?

24. **The students are doing some field research .**
    (A) retake   (B) studies   (C) security   (D) score

25. **A good score on the test is important to apply for a scholarship.**
    (A) mark   (B) reference   (C) skip   (D) rejection

MP3 96

2352 stuff [stʌf]   ★★★★★

A: I am so bored. Haven't you got any cool stuff to do?
B: Why don't we go to the concert? The college band will have a concert in the evening.

A：我好無聊，有沒有好玩的事可以做？
B：何不去聽演唱會？大學樂團傍晚有表演。

物品，東西
n. thing

2353 summa cum laude [`sʌmə ˌkʌm `lɔdɪ]   ★★★★☆

Even though Sam graduated from the university summa cum laude, he is still having a hard time finding a job.

即使山姆以最優等成績畢業，還是很難找到工作。

最優等地
ad. with highest distinction

2354 summer time [`sʌmə ˌtaɪm]   ★★★★★

Summer time is the period during which the clocks are put forward, so that we can have extra daylight in the evening.

在夏令時間期間，時鐘被往前撥快，因此到了傍晚還能看到陽光。

夏令時間，日光節約時間
n. daylight saving time

2355 surf [sɝf]   ★★★★★

I have been surfing the Internet for some information on 19th century American painters.

我上網搜尋十九世紀美國畫家的資訊。

上網搜尋，上網瀏覽
v. scan a wide range of offerings for something of interest

2356 syllabus [`sɪləbəs]   ★★★★★

During the first class, the professor will give you the syllabus. You'll then know the purpose of the class and which textbooks to use.

教授會在第一堂課發放課程大綱，各位就會知道課程目的和使用哪些教科書。

教學（課程、授課）大綱
n. a summary outline of a discourse, treatise, or course of study or of examination requirements

---

2357 talent [`tælənt]   ★★★★★

I'm sure Ellen has a talent for music. She is able to play almost every kind of musical instrument, and furthermore she is a born singer.

我肯定艾倫有音樂天份，她幾乎能彈奏所有樂器，外加有副天生好嗓子。

天份，天資
n. ability; gift

2358 term paper [`tɝm ˌpepə]   ★★★★★

Mike's computer malfunctioned and shut down all of a sudden. Unfortunately he lost almost all of the term paper he was working on.

麥克的電腦故障、突然關機，幾乎所有正在進行的學期報告都不幸沒了。

學期報告
n. a major written assignment in a school or college course

2359 thesis [`θisɪs]   ★★★★★

Professor Donne's English students are supposed to submit a thesis on American transcendentalism by the end of this month.

唐恩教授的外文系學生須在本月底前繳交美國超越主義論文報告。

論文
n. a dissertation embodying results of original research and especially substantiating a specific view

2360 track [træk]   ★★★★☆

The counselor gave me some good ideas which could get me back on track.

指導老師提供一些好建議好讓我步上軌道。

軌道，軌跡
n. the course along which something moves or progresses

2361 transcript [ˈtrænˌskrɪpt]   ★★★★★

Please send us your resume and transcript to the address attached. The due date is July 14.

請將履歷和學校成績單寄到所附地址，七月十四日截止。

學校成績單
n. an official copy of a student's educational record

2362 transfer [trænˈsfɝ]   ★★★★★

John is interested in transferring to the University of Toronto. He is going to send in his transcript.

約翰想轉到多倫多大學，正準備寄出學校成績單。

轉學，轉校
v. move to a different school

2363 Trojan Horse [ˈtrodʒən hɔrs]   ★★★☆☆

You should be careful of a Trojan Horse. It may get into your computer while you are downloading seemingly useful files, such as music files.

你要小心木馬程式，它可能會隨著下載音樂檔等似乎有用的檔案時入侵電腦。

木馬程式
n. a seemingly useful computer program that contains concealed instructions which when activated perform an illicit or malicious action; virus

---

2364 tuition [tuˈɪʃən]   ★★★★★

Every student seems to be working to help pay their tuition. It has been the general consensus that the tuition is too high.

每個學生似乎都得打工幫忙付學費，輿論一致認為學費太貴了。

學費
n. fee

2365 tutoring [ˈtutərɪŋ]   ★★★★★

To use our online tutoring service, you should enroll first. And then to be tutored you can log on between 9:00 a.m. and 6:00 p.m.

要使用線上家教服務者請先註冊，家教開放時間自上午九時到下午六時。

家教
n. private teaching

2366 typo [ˈtaɪpo]   ★★★★☆

It is important for you to read your report carefully before you submit it to the teacher. If there are umpteen typos, you will not get a good grade.

交報告給老師前要先仔細閱讀，如果有很多打字錯誤，就很難拿到高分。

打字排印錯誤，誤植
n. typographical error

2367 undergraduate [ˌʌndəˈgrædʒuɪt]   ★★★★★

At a university, each undergraduate is allowed to make his or her own curriculum. But to graduate, each student needs a certain number of credit hours in requirements and electives.

在大學裡，每個大學生都可選擇自己想上的課程，但要畢業則需一定的必修和選修學分。

大學生
n. a student at a college or university who has not received a bachelor's degree

2368 user name [`juzɚ nem]

Because he forgot his user name and password, he used his secret question. The question was "What is your first girlfriend's / boyfriend's name?"

他因為忘記使用者名稱和密碼，於是使用安全問題進入，題目是：「你的初戀情人叫什麼名字？」

★★★★★
使用者名稱
n. the name of a user

2369 valid [`vælɪd]

The TOEFL score that the applicant had was from last year. So he wondered if it was still valid.

申請者的托福成績是去年的，他納悶是否還有效。

★★★★☆
有效的
a. having legal efficacy or force

2370 waiting list [`wetɪŋ lɪst]

John wanted to enroll in American History 100, but found that the class was full. So he had to put his name on a waiting list.

約翰想修美國史 100，但發現已額滿，所以得將姓名填在候補名單上。

★★★★★
等待名單，候補名單
n. a list of those waiting

2371 weapon possession [`wɛpən pə`zɛʃən]

A: Criminal cases of weapon possession are rare at universities.
B: Right. But it is true that there were some cases.

A：校園持有槍械犯罪很少見。
B：是的，但還是有些實例。

★★★☆☆
槍械持有
n. possession of a weapon

2372 web site [wɛb saɪt]

Please visit the university web site. You will be able to find out about some interesting events for the citizens which are prepared by the students.

請瀏覽大學網站，你將看到學生為市民準備的一些有趣活動。

★★★★★
網站
n. a group of World Wide Web pages

2373 winter-break [`wɪntɚbrek]

James is going to participate in an Oregon expedition during the winter-break. He is preparing for it by improving his health.

詹姆斯將在寒假參加奧勒岡探險隊，現在正在改善健康狀況以做好準備。

★★★★★
寒假
n. winter vacation

✧ Architecture 建築

2374 aisle [aɪl]

Most of the audience were rolling in the aisles because the drama was so funny.

許多觀眾湧進走道，因為那齣戲太有趣了。

★★★★★
席間走道，通道
n. a passage (as in a theater or railroad passenger car) separating sections of seats

---

2375 arch [artʃ]

When we visited the mansion, one of the most impressive aspects was a rose arch.

我們參觀宅邸時，最令人印象深刻的景觀之一就是玫瑰拱門。

★★★★★
拱門
n. something resembling an arch in form

2376 bay window [be `wɪndo] ★★★☆☆

凸窗

n. a window or series of windows forming a bay in a room and projecting outward from the wall

Many buildings in San Francisco have bay windows, which are often appreciated by people who love sunshine.
許多舊金山建築物都有熱愛陽光的民眾最喜歡的凸窗。

2377 beam [bim] ★★★☆☆

橫樑

n. a long piece of heavy often squared timber suitable for use in construction

Many gold prospectors during the Gold Rush built some sod huts by putting up some posts and beams.
在淘金熱期間許多淘金者搭建有柱子和橫樑的簡陋茅舍。

2378 block [blɑk] ★★★☆☆

塊

n. a compact usually solid piece of substantial material

The Inuit build igloos made out of blocks of packed snow.
伊紐特人用冰雪壓製而成的雪塊建造圓頂小屋。

2379 blueprint [`blu͵prɪnt] ★★★★★

藍圖，詳細方案

n. a detailed plan or program

A great architect drafted a blueprint for a building which would be used as a student union hall.
偉大建築師草擬作為學生會大樓的建物藍圖。

2380 brick [brɪk] ★★★☆☆

磚，磚塊

n. a handy-sized unit of building or paving material typically being rectangular

The Native-Americans who resided in the Southwest region of the United States often used adobe bricks to build houses.
居住在美國西南部的美洲原住民常以泥磚建造屋舍。

2381 building code [`bɪldɪŋ kod] ★★★★☆

建築法規

n. a system of principles or rules for buildings

The subsidy from the government was granted only when the building met the building code.
只有在建物符合建築法規的前提下，才會發放政府津貼。

2382 building material [`bɪldɪŋ mə`tɪrɪəl] ★★★★☆

建材

n. materials for buildings

Marble is one of the most expensive building materials.
大理石是最昂貴的建材之一。

2383 cabin [`kæbɪn] ★★★★★

小屋

n. a small one-story dwelling usually of simple construction

It is said that as a child Abraham Lincoln lived in a log cabin.
據說林肯幼時住在小木屋。

2384 cellar [`sɛlə] ★★★★★

地下室，地窖

n. basement

A cellar is one of the safest places at which we can escape a tornado.
地下室是躲避龍捲風最安全的地方之一。

2385 condominium complex [`kɑndə͵mɪnɪəm `kɑmplɛks] ★★★★☆

複合式公寓

n. a multiunit structure

A condominium complex uses land space economically, and it can accommodate many families.
複合式公寓有效利用土地空間，並可容納許多家庭。

2386 corridor [ˈkɔrədə] ★★★★☆

The floor of the corridor the old building was made out of wood.
老舊建築物的走廊地板是以木材建造而成的。

走廊，迴廊，通道
n. passageway

2387 courtyard [ˈkɔrtˌjɑrd] ★★★☆☆

A courtyard is an enclosed area of a house.
住宅的天井是圍起來的中庭。

中庭，天井
n. a court or enclosure adjacent to a building

2388 dome [dom] ★★★☆☆

The domed stadium, which was built to host the World Cup Games, is capable of accommodating 70,000 people.
為主辦世界盃足球賽而建造的巨蛋球場共可容納七萬名觀眾。

圓頂 / 使成圓頂
n. a large hemispherical roof or ceiling / v. make something domy

---

2389 eaves [ivz] ★★★☆☆

In Florida, natives often built houses with long eaves because of frequent rain.
美國佛羅里達州的原住民因經常下雨而建造長簷屋舍。

屋簷
n. the lower border of a roof that overhangs the wall

2390 edifice [ˈɛdəfɪs] ★★★☆☆

The city has decided to demolish the dilapidated edifice, which had been used as the mayor's residence, and to build a new modern building.
都市決定拆除原作為市長官邸的老舊大廈，並建造一棟現代化新建物。

大廈，雄偉建築物
n. building; pile

2391 facade [fəˈsɑd] ★★★☆☆

The facade of the building has been finished with shiny glass.
建物正面以閃閃發亮的玻璃加工。

建物正面，外觀
n. the front of a building

2392 ferroconcrete [ˈfɛroˈkɑnkrit] ★★☆☆☆

The owner of the old traditional house has decided to replace it with a modern building built with ferroconcrete.
屋主決定以鋼筋混凝土建造的現代化建築取代傳統老舊建物。

鋼筋混凝土
n. reinforced concrete

2393 fireplace [ˈfairˌples] ★★★★★

To keep the inside warm for the whole night, the family put some backlogs in the fireplace.
為保持室內整晚溫暖，那戶人家添加一些木頭到壁爐內。

壁爐
n. hearth

2394 fire-resistant [fair riˈzistənt] ★★★★☆

The famous hotel burnt down. They should have used fire-resistant building materials.
知名建物遭到焚燬，應該要使用防火建材才對。

防火的
a. resistant to fire

2395 foundation [faunˈdeʃən] ★★★★★

It is essential to pour deep foundations to build a high-rise building.
地基要灌得夠深才能打造高聳建物。

地基
n. basis

1
2
3
4
5

2396 garage [gəˋrɑʒ] ★★★★★

The Browns are having a garage sale, where they are selling old magazines, clothing, and household appliances.
伯朗家正在舉行舊貨出清，其中包括過期雜誌、衣物和家電用品等。

車庫
n. *a structure for a car; a shelter or repair shop for automotive vehicles*

2397 grating [ˋgretɪŋ] ★★★☆☆

Yesterday a burglar broke into Jack's house, so he is going to have grating installed for security.
昨天竊賊闖入傑克家中，所以他打算安裝鐵窗防盜。

鐵窗，格板
n. *a wooden or metal lattice used to close or floor an opening*

2398 insulation [ˌɪnsəˋleʃən] ★★★★☆

Styrofoam is often used as an insulation material.
聚苯乙烯常被用來作為絕緣材料。

絕緣，絕緣體
n. *material used in insulating*

2399 keystone [ˋki͵ston] ★★★☆☆

The granite keystones supporting the arch were so impressive that the mansion looked like a palace.
撐托拱門的花崗岩拱心石令人印象深刻，宅邸看起來就像一座皇宮。

拱心石，楔石
n. *the wedge-shaped piece at the crown of an arch that locks the other pieces in place*

2400 lodge [lɑdʒ] ★★★★☆

Along the riverside were some lodges built by the aborigines. They were built out of adobe bricks and were thatched with grass.
土著沿著河畔建造一些泥磚茅舍。

小屋
n. *a house set apart for residence in a particular season*

2401 patio [ˋpɑtɪ͵o] ★★★☆☆

Around the patio of the Spanish house were some shrubs and small flowers.
西班牙式建築的陽台四周有矮樹叢和小花。

天井，中庭，陽台
n. *courtyard*

2402 pillar [ˋpɪlɚ] ★★★☆☆

The towering wooden pillars supporting the roof of the palace were about 30 inches thick.
撐托皇宮屋頂的高聳木柱約有三十英吋粗。

柱子
n. *post*

2403 porch [portʃ] ★★★★★

Nancy cannot erase the memory of her grandmother, who was standing in front of the porch, waving her hand.
南西無法忘記常站在門口揮手的祖母。

門廊，門口，陽臺
n. *a covered area adjoining an entrance to a building and usually having a separate roof*

2404 residence [ˋrɛzədəns] ★★★★★

The White House, the official residence of the President of the United States, was burnt down during the War of 1812.
美國總統官邸白宮曾於一八一二年燬於戰火。

住所，住宅，官邸
n. *house; habitation*

2405 railing [ˋrelɪŋ] ★★★★☆

There is an iron railing around the Statue of Liberty.
自由女神像四周圍著鐵欄杆。

欄杆，扶手，柵欄，圍欄
n. *a barrier consisting of a rail and supports*

2406 seismic technology [`saɪzmɪk tɛk`nɑlədʒɪ]

★★★☆☆

地震科技

n. technology relating to an earth vibration

Intermittent earthquakes in the nation have made people pay more attention to seismic technology.

國內陸續發生的地震使民眾更加關心地震科技。

2407 skyscraper [`skaɪ,skrepɚ]

★★★★★

摩天大樓

n. a very tall building

The Sears Tower in Chicago is one of the world's tallest skyscrapers.

位於芝加哥的希爾斯摩天大樓是全球最高的摩天大樓之一。

2408 sod hut [sɑd hʌt]

★★☆☆☆

茅屋，茅舍

n. a small cottage made by covering the roof with turf

Early settlers in the Old West often built sod huts.

早期舊西部移民常建造茅舍。

2409 soundproof facility [`saʊnd,pruf fə`sɪlətɪ]

★★☆☆☆

隔音設備

n. a facility to insulate the passage of sound

The residents of the apartment complex have decided to set up soundproof facilities to block noise from the highway.

複合式公寓的住戶決定安裝隔音設備以阻絕高速公路上的噪音。

2410 steeple [`stip!]

★★☆☆☆

尖塔，尖頂

n. a tall structure usually having a small spire at the top and surmounting a church tower

I can easily find this church because of the steeple.

尖塔讓我能夠輕易找到教堂。

2411 tepee [`tipi]

★★★☆☆

帳篷

n. tipi

Bison hides were often utilized for the covering of Native-American tepees.

野牛皮常被用來作為美洲原住民帳篷的外蓋。

Tea Time... ☕

<Aesop's Fable> Lionize **In folklore and fable the lion is often considered king of beasts.**	〈來自伊索寓言〉視～為名人 在民間傳說和寓言中獅子常被視為萬獸之王。（註：《伊索寓言》裡有關獅子的故事多達八十六則，其中獅子多以威猛強勢的領袖姿態出現，例如 the lion's share 指的就是「最好或最大的一塊」。）

✻ **lionize** [`laɪən,aɪz] *v. treat as a celebrity* | 捧～為名人，視～為名人

The con man was able to lionize the rich widow so well that she believed him when he asked her for a loan of a million dollars, but she never saw the money, or him, again.

騙子將富有寡婦捧著上天，接著向她借一百萬元，她也深信不疑，但從此錢和人都不知去向。

1 Complete each word by filling in the blank with proper spelling so that it has the same meaning as suggested. Then please write the meaning of each word in Chinese.

1. 學校成績單 = _ _ _ _ s c r i p t
2. 轉校 = _ _ _ _ _ f e r
3. 大學生 = _ _ _ _ _ g r a d u a t e
4. 人類學家 = _ _ _ _ _ _ _ o l o g i s t
5. 走廊 = _ _ _ r i d o r
6. 中庭 = c o u r t _ _ _ _
7. 壁爐 = _ _ _ _ p l a c e
8. 絕緣 = _ _ _ _ _ a t i o n
9. 建物正面 = _ _ _ a d e
10. 小屋 = _ _ _ g e

11. grating = _ _ _ _ _ _ _ _
12. tutoring = _ _ _ _ _ _ _ _
13. brick = _ _ _ _ _ _ _ _
14. cabin = _ _ _ _ _ _ _ _
15. beam = _ _ _ _ _ _ _ _
16. aisle = _ _ _ _ _ _ _ _
17. eaves = _ _ _ _ _ _ _ _
18. cellar = _ _ _ _ _ _ _ _
19. typo = _ _ _ _ _ _ _ _
20. syllabus = _ _ _ _ _ _ _ _

2 Choose a word that best completes the sentence.

21. He spent morning hours _____ the Internet.
   (A) surfing   (B) tutoring   (C) grating   (D) beaming

22. John had to read his report carefully before submitting it. It was full of _____.
   (A) syllabus   (B) blocks   (C) typos   (D) corridors

3 The highlighted word is closest in meaning to which of the following?

23. I hear that you're going to move. Did you pack your stuff ?
   (A) transfer   (B) things   (C) arch   (D) dome

24. I am sure that Jane has a talent for music.
   (A) cabin   (B) gift   (C) block   (D) brick

25. The original blueprint for this building was drawn up by the owner of the building.
   (A) draft   (B) keystone   (C) clan   (D) descendant

✦✦ **Arts** 藝術

MP3 98

2412 abstract [`æbstrækt]
★★★★★

Most laymen have difficulty understanding abstract art.

多數門外漢很難了解抽象藝術。

抽象的
a. *having only intrinsic form with little or no attempt at pictorial representation or narrative content*

2413 brushwork [`brʌʃ,wɜk]
★★★★☆

Van Gogh's peculiar brushwork often made people think that his paintings were incomplete.

梵谷奇特的畫風常使人誤以為他還沒畫完。

繪畫，畫風
n. *work done with a brush*

2414 canvas [`kænvəs]
★★★★★

During the picnic, the artist drew an oil painting on the canvas, while his family members were yawning under a shady tree.

野餐時，畫家在油畫布上作畫，家人則在樹蔭下伸懶腰。

油畫布，油畫
n. *a piece of cloth backed or framed as a surface for a painting*

2415 collage [kə`lɑʒ]
★★★☆☆

James's nephews were creating a collage by applying small pieces of paper cut out from all of the magazines.

詹姆斯的外甥用雜誌上剪下的小碎紙製作拼貼作品。

拼貼作品
n. *an artistic composition made of various materials (as paper, cloth, or wood) glued on a surface*

2416 composition [,kɑmpə`zıʃən]
★★★★★

I think that the composition of this painting is excellent, but it seems to be a little bit too simple.

我認為這幅畫的構圖很出色，但似乎有點過於單調。

構圖，構成
n. *arrangement into specific proportion or relation and especially into artistic form*

2417 contour line [`kɑntur laın]
★★★☆☆

To show your students the image, you should stress the contour lines of the subject.

展現圖像給學生看時，應強調其輪廓線。

輪廓線，等高線，地形線
n. *an outline especially of a curving or irregular figure*

2418 exhibit [ɪg`zɪbɪt]
★★★★★

At the exhibition, a guard had to be assigned to dissuade children from touching the exhibits.

在展覽會上須指派警衛勸導孩童不要觸摸展覽品。

展示會，展覽會／展示，陳列
n. *exhibition* / **v.** *show*

2419 hue [hju]
★★★★☆

The blackish hue makes the painting a little bit dismal.

黑色使畫作略顯陰鬱。

顏色，色彩，色澤
n. *color*

2420 manner [ˋmænə]   ★★★★★

This is a picture in the manner of Picasso. It shows a nice combination of two faces.

這幅畫有畢卡索的風格，巧妙結合了兩個臉龐。

風格
n. method of artistic execution or mode of presentation

2421 movement [ˋmuvmənt]   ★★★★★

Realism was a movement of art which evolved out of romanticism.

寫實主義是從浪漫主義發展出來的藝術趨勢。

運動，活動，趨勢
n. trend; tendency

Reference...

- art Deco n. 裝飾藝術	- Fauvism n. 野獸主義	- Post-impressionism n. 後印象派
- Barbizon school n. 巴比松學派	- Futurism n. 未來主義	- Pre-Raphaelitism n. 前拉斐爾派
- Baroque n. 巴洛克主義	- Impressionism n. 印象派	
- Constructivism n. 建構主義	- Mannerism n. 矯飾主義	- Realism n. 寫實主義
- Cubism n. 立體主義	- Neo-classicism n. 新古典主義	- Romanticism n. 浪漫主義
- Dada n. 達達主義	- Op Art n. 歐普藝術	- Surrealism n. 超現實主義
- Expressionism n. 抽象主義	- Pop Art n. 普普藝術	- Vorticism n. 漩渦主義

2422 palette [ˋpælɪt]   ★★★☆☆

The painter used a palette knife to scoop some of the paint.

畫家用調色刀舀出一些顏料。

調色盤
n. a thin oval or rectangular board or tablet that a painter holds and mixes pigments on

2423 perspective [pəˋspɛktɪv]   ★★★★☆

This picture seems to be out of perspective. The objects in the background appear too large.

這幅畫作似乎不成比例，背景物顯得太大。

遠近畫法，透視畫
n. the technique or process of representing on a plane or curved surface the spatial relation of objects as they might appear to the eye

2424 rendering [ˋrɛndərɪŋ]   ★★★★☆

The rendering by this artist is so realistic that people often think that the objects in his paintings are from a photograph.

畫家的表現手法很寫實，人們常以為畫中物是照相照出來的。

表現
n. representation

Reference...

- etching n. 蝕刻畫	- Pointillism n. 點描派	- tempera n. 蛋彩畫
- formative arts n. 造型藝術	- plaster cast n. 石膏像	- terra-cotta n. 赤土陶器
- fresco n. 壁畫	- portrait n. 半身雕塑像	- torso n. 未完成作品
- illustration n. 插畫	- relief n. 浮雕	- washes n. 淡水彩畫
- intaglio n. 陰刻，凹刻	- sculpture n. 雕像	- watercolor n. 水彩畫
- lithograph n. 平版印刷	- sketch n. 素描	- wood carving n. 木雕
- mural n. 壁畫	- still life n. 靜物畫	
- oil painting n. 油畫	- still picture n. 靜畫	

2425 retrospective [ˌrɛtrəˈspɛktɪv]

★★★☆☆

The gallery is planning on having a retrospective of a dead painter.
美術館計畫推出已故畫家的回顧展。

回顧的，懷舊的 / 回顧展
a. pertaining to retrospection /
n. a retrospective exhibition

⁂ Astronomy 天文學

2426 aggregate [ˈægrɪgɪt]

★★★★☆

A constellation is an aggregate of stars.
星座是群星集合體。

集合體，聚集
n. congregation

2427 big bang [bɪg bæŋ]

★★★★★

It is estimated that the big bang resulted from a supernova.
大爆炸估計起因於超級新星。

大爆炸
n. big explosion

2428 black hole [ˌblæk ˈhol]

★★★★★

A black hole is said to suck everything into it, including time and space.
據說黑洞會吸噬包括時間和空間在內的一切。

黑洞
n. a celestial object that has
a gravitational field so
strong that light cannot
escape it

2429 celestial body [səˈlɛstʃəl ˈbɑdɪ]

★★★★★

We do not know how many celestial bodies there are in space.
我們不知道太空中有多少天體。

天體，星體
n. heavenly body

2430 chunk [tʃʌŋk]

★★★★☆

It is insisted that a giant chunk of iron and nickel flew into the atmosphere
of the earth, causing an ice age.
有人堅決主張大量鐵和鎳飛入地球大氣層，導致冰河時代來臨。

大塊
n. a short thick piece or lump

2431 collide [kəˈlaɪd]

★★★★☆

Twenty-odd chunks of asteroids collided with Jupiter.
二十多顆小行星和木星相撞。

碰撞，相撞
v. come together with solid
objects

2432 comet [ˈkɑmɪt]

★★★★★

Halley's Comet comes near the earth every 76 years.
哈雷彗星每隔七十六年接近地球一次。

彗星
n. a celestial body that
appears as a fuzzy head

2433 constellation [ˌkɑnstəˈleʃən]

★★★★★

We could observe many constellations of stars through a telescope at
the observatory.
我們可透過天文臺望遠鏡觀測許多星座。

星座，星群
n. a group of stars

MP3 99

2435 Copernican [ko`pɜnɪkən] ★★☆☆☆

Nicolaus Copernicus proposed the Copernican theory of the universe.
哥白尼提出有關宇宙的哥白尼學說。

哥白尼的，哥白尼學說的
a. of or relating to Copernicus or the belief that the earth rotates daily on its axis and the planets revolve in orbits around the sun

2436 corona [kə`ronə] ★★★☆☆

The corona is the outermost layer of the sun.
日暈是位於太陽最外層的光環。

日暈，月暈
n. a usually colored circle often seen around and close to a luminous body

2437 cosmology [kɑz`mɑlədʒɪ] ★★★☆☆

One of my friends is majoring in cosmology. He is learning about stars and their formation.
我有位朋友主修宇宙論，他正在學習星星及其構造。

宇宙論
n. a branch of metaphysics that deals with the nature of the universe

2438 debris [də`bri] ★★★★★

Many scientists insist that the debris from the Big Bang became stars.
許多科學家堅稱大爆炸碎片形成了星星。

碎片
n. the remains of something broken down or destroyed

2439 depression [dɪ`prɛʃən] ★★★★★

The probe revealed that there are some depressions on the surface of Mars.
太空探測器顯示火星表面有凹洞。

窪地，凹地
n. hollow

2440 ecliptic [ɪ`klɪptɪk] ★★★☆☆

The Sun's course is referred to as the ecliptic.
太陽運行的軌道稱為黃道。

黃道
n. the great circle of the celestial sphere that is the apparent path of the sun

2441 elliptical [ɪ`lɪptɪkl] ★★★☆☆

Galaxies are thought to be comprised of various forms. An elliptical galaxy is one of them.
一般認為銀河系包括各種不同類型，橢圓星系是其中一種。

橢圓的
a. of, relating to, or shaped like an ellipse

2442 equinox [`ikwə,nɑks] ★★★★☆

The length of the day and the night are the same at the autumnal and the vernal equinoxes.
春分和秋分的晝夜長度相等。

晝夜平分時，春分，秋分
n. either of the two times each year (as about March 21 and September 23) when the sun crosses the equator and day and night are everywhere on earth of approximately equal length

2443 explosion [ɪk`sploʒən] ★★★★★

The explosion of a star creates a sudden burst of light, creating a nova.
星體爆炸時會突然爆發光亮並形成新星。

爆炸
n. the act or an instance of exploding

2444 heavenly body [ˌhɛvənlɪ ˈbɑdɪ] ★★★★★

Tides of the sea are caused by the attractive force between heavenly bodies.
海洋潮汐受天體引力影響。

天體
n. celestial body

2445 horoscope [ˈhɔrəˌskop] ★★★★☆

The astrologer depends on the horoscope for his fortune-telling.
占星家靠占星術算命。

占星術，星象
n. an astrological forecast

- Aquarius n. 水瓶座
- Aries n. 牡羊座
- Cancer n. 巨蟹座
- Capricorn n. 摩羯座
- Gemini n. 雙子座
- Leo n. 獅子座
- Libra n. 天秤座
- Pisces n. 雙魚座
- Sagittarius n. 射手座
- Scorpio n. 天蠍座
- Taurus n. 金牛座
- Virgo n. 處女座

2446 meteorite [ˈmitɪərˌaɪt] ★★★★★

Many small meteorites enter the atmosphere of the earth, but most of them are burnt up in flames.
許多小流星會進入地球大氣層，但絕大多數都燃燒成火光。

流星
n. a meteor that reaches the surface of the earth without being completely vaporized

2447 monitor [ˈmɑnətə] ★★★★★

Many scientists are monitoring the movement of the comets and asteroids.
許多科學家正在監測彗星和小行星的運行。

監控，監測
v. observe; investigate

2448 nebula [ˈnɛbjələ] ★★★★☆

A nebula is a cloud of dust or gas within the galactic system.
星雲是銀河系中的雲塵或雲氣。

星雲
n. any of numerous clouds of gas or dust in interstellar space

2449 orbit [ˈɔrbɪt] ★★★★★

The probe launched by the United States is orbiting the planet Venus.
美國發射的太空探測器正環繞金星運行。

天體運行軌道／環繞軌道運行
n. circle / *v.* revolve in an orbit around

2450 perigee [ˈpɛrɪˌdʒi] ★★★☆☆

The perigee is the point in a planet's orbit at which it is nearest to Earth.
行星軌道最接近地球的點稱為近地點。

近地點
n. the point in the orbit of an object (as a satellite) orbiting the earth that is nearest to the center of the earth

2451 perihelion [ˌpɛrɪˈhilɪən] ★★☆☆☆

The perihelion is the point in a planet's orbit at which it is nearest to the sun.
行星軌道最接近太陽的點稱為近日點。

近日點
n. the point in the path of a celestial body (as a planet) that is nearest to the sun

2452 planet [`plænɪt] ★★★★★

Scientists excluded Pluto from the list of the planets of the sun.
科學家將冥王星排除在太陽系行星之外。

行星
n. any of the large bodies that revolve around the sun in the solar system

2453 Ptolemaic [ˌtɑləˈmeɪk] ★★☆☆☆

Greek astronomer Claudius Ptolemaeus proposed the Ptolemaic theory.
希臘天文學家托勒密提出托勒密理論。

托勒密的
a. of or relating to the second century geographer and astronomer Ptolemy of Alexandria and especially to his belief that the earth is at the center of the universe with the sun, moon, and planets revolving around it

2454 pulsar [`pʌlsɑr] ★★★★☆

A pulsar is a cosmic source of rapidly pulsating radio signals.
脈衝星是發出快速無線電波動的星體。

脈衝星，波霎
n. a celestial source of pulsating electromagnetic radiation characterized by a short relatively constant interval between pulses that is held to be a rotating neutron star

2455 quasar [`kwezɑr] ★★★★☆

A quasar is a very small star-like cosmic source of light and radio waves.
類星體是似星而發出光亮和無線電波的小星體。

類星體
n. any of a class of celestial objects that resemble stars but whose large redshift and apparent brightness imply extreme distance and huge energy output

2456 revolve [rɪˈvɑlv] ★★★★★

It took many centuries to prove that the Earth revolves around the sun.
地球繞著太陽轉的事實花了好幾個世紀才得到證實。

運轉
v. circle

2457 rotation [roˈteʃən] ★★★★★

The turning of the Earth on its axis is referred to as the rotation of the Earth.
地球繞地軸旋轉稱為自轉。

自轉，旋轉
n. the action or process of rotating on or as if on an axis or center

2458 satellite [`sætḷˌaɪt] ★★★☆☆

The moon, which is the sole satellite of the Earth, exerts the greatest influence on the tides of the sea.
地球唯一的衛星月球對海洋潮汐發揮巨大影響力。

衛星，人造衛星
n. a celestial body orbiting another of larger size

- Mercury n. 水星   - Jupiter n. 木星
- Venus n. 金星   - Saturn n. 土星
- Earth n. 地球   - Uranius n. 天王星
- Mars n. 火星   - Neptune n. 海王星

（註：太陽系八大行星距離太陽由近至遠排列如上，舊稱冥王星的 Pluto 已在 2006 年被降級成矮行星，現稱為「小行星 134340 號」，故不再有「太陽系九大行星」之稱。）

2459 solstice [ˈsɑlstɪs]

The summer solstice is the longest day of the year.

夏至是一年當中白晝最長的一天。

★★★★☆

至

n. the time of the sun's passing a solstice which occurs about June 22 to begin summer in the northern hemisphere and about December 22 to begin winter in the northern hemisphere

2460 supernova [ˌsupəˈnovə]

A supernova is a nova of immense brightness or intensity.

超級新星是具有巨大亮度和強度的新星。

★★★★★

超新星

n. the explosion of a star in which the star may reach a maximum intrinsic luminosity one billion times that of the sun; superstar

2461 velocity [vəˈlɑsətɪ]

Light travels at a velocity of approximately 186,000 miles a second.

光以大約每秒十八萬六千英里的速度行進。

★★★★★

速度，速率

n. speed; rate

2462 zodiac [ˈzodɪˌæk]

In the horoscope there are twelve zodiac signs.

在占星術中黃道帶共有十二宮。

★★★★☆

黃道帶

n. an imaginary band in the heavens centered on the ecliptic that encompasses the apparent paths of all the planets except Pluto and is divided into 12 constellations or signs each taken for astrological purposes to extend 30 degrees of longitude

2463 zenith [ˈzinɪθ]

The zenith is the point of the sky directly overhead.

天頂是位在頭頂正上方的天空頂點。

★★★★☆

天頂

n. the point of the celestial sphere that is directly opposite the nadir and vertically above the observer

---

Tea Time... ☕

<Greek myth> Narcissus A beautiful youth who, after Echo's death, is made to pine away for love of his own reflection in a spring and thus changed into the Narcissus.	〈來自希臘神話〉納西賽斯 回音女神愛柯死後，美少年愛上自己的水中倒影而日益消瘦，死後化成水仙。（註：本字帶有「自戀」之意，「自戀者」為 narcissist，「自我陶醉的」即為 narcissistic。）

✻ **narcissism** [nɑrˈsɪsɪzəm] *n.* excessive or erotic interest in oneself, one's physical features, etc. | 自戀，自我陶醉

The king's compliments on her beauty seem to be the source of her narcissism. She believes that she is the most beautiful in the whole world.

國王對她美貌的讚揚似乎是她自戀的來源，她相信自己是全世界最美的人。

1

Complete each word by filling in the blank with proper spelling so that it has the same meaning as suggested. Then please write the meaning of each word in Chinese.

1. 柱子	= _ _ _ l a r	11. exhibit	–	_____
2. 摩天大樓	= _ _ _ s c r a p e r	12. comet	=	_____
3. 尖塔	= _ _ _ e p l e	13. corona	=	_____
4. 抽象的	= _ _ _ t r a c t	14. debris	=	_____
5. 構圖	= _ _ _ p o s i t i o n	15. equinox	=	_____
6. 帳篷	= t e _ _ _	16. horoscope	=	_____
7. 活動	= _ _ _ _ m e n t	17. meteorite	=	_____
8. 遠近畫法	= _ _ _ s p e c t i v e	18. orbit	=	_____
9. 集合體	= a g _ _ _ _ a t e	19. depression	=	_____
10. 相撞	= c o l _ _ _ _	20. explosion	=	_____

2

Choose a word that best completes the sentence.

21. The outermost layer of the sun is called the _____.
    (A) canvas   (B) brushwork   (C) corona   (D) rendering

22. The satellite _____ the moon.
    (A) aggregated   (B) orbited   (C) collided   (D) rendered

23. Most laymen have difficulty understanding _____ paintings.
    (A) abstract   (B) manner   (C) railing   (D) ecliptic

3

The highlighted word is closest in meaning to which of the following?

24. The overall hue of this painting is dismal.
    (A) color   (B) depression   (C) nebula   (D) monitor

25. The residence of the natives was built with mud.
    (A) patio   (B) pillar   (C) railing   (D) house

Practice Test 01

1

The highlighted word is closest in meaning to which of the following?

1. The assessment form will be filled out by the professor after all the students make a speech.
   (A) evaluation
   (B) administration
   (C) tuition
   (D) syllabus

2. The score on this test will be held valid for two years.
   (A) intramural
   (B) primeval
   (C) good
   (D) patriarchal

3. The graduate student is writing a thesis on the effect of global warming.
   (A) edifice
   (B) corridor
   (C) paper
   (D) tutoring

4. To pass this course you should attend at least 80 percent of the class sessions, submit a term paper and take two tests.
   (A) retake
   (B) rent
   (C) participate in
   (D) enroll in

5. I didn't attend Professor Brown's class today. Do we have any assignments ?
   (A) scholarship
   (B) score
   (C) homework
   (D) prom

2 Please answer the following questions.

It was the beginning of a new (1)_____ at the university, and Prof. Brown was excited and (2)_____, as always. Like many teachers who take pride in their (3)_____, Prof. Brown always makes a point of memorizing all of his students' names. So at the beginning of every semester, he always asks each of his students to (4)_____ a passport-sized picture with their names. This semester, however, there was one picture of a young man whose picture was terrible; not only was it in black and white, but it was extremely blurry, and the picture's (5)_____ was very poor. So the professor found the student and asked him why his picture was so terrible. The student smiled sheepishly and replied, "I didn't have time to have my picture taken." Prof. Brown asked, "So how did you get this one?" The student answered as he looked down, "I put my face on the Xerox machine."

6. What would be the most appropriate word in blank (1)?
(A) semester
(B) depression
(C) pillar
(D) composition

7. What would be the most appropriate word in blank (2)?
(A) primeval
(B) intramural
(C) enthusiastic
(D) abstract

8. What would be the most appropriate word in blank (3)?
(A) profession
(B) explosion
(C) movement
(D) perspective

9. What would be the most appropriate word in blank (4)?
(A) collide
(B) submit
(C) rent
(D) retake

10. What would be the most appropriate word in blank (5)?
(A) rendering
(B) definition
(C) steeple
(D) relief

✦ **Animals & Plants** 動植物

2464 amphibian [æmˋfɪbɪən]

★★★★★

Amphibians, such as frogs and toads, live both on land and in the water.

青蛙和蟾蜍等都是水陸兩棲動物。

兩棲動物
*n. an amphibious organism;
especially : any of a class of
cold-blooded vertebrates
intermediate in many
characters between fishes
and reptiles*

2465 artery [ˋɑrtərɪ]

★★★★☆

Arteriosclerosis refers to the hardening of the arteries.

動脈硬化症指的是動脈的硬化。

動脈
*n. any of the tubular branching
muscular- and elastic-walled
vessels that carry blood from
the heart through the body*

2466 arthropod [ˋɑrθrəˏpɑd]

★★★★

Trilobites, which lived during the Paleozoic period, fall into the arthropod group.

存活於古生代的三葉蟲屬於節肢動物。

節肢動物
*n. any of a phylum
(Arthropoda) of invertebrate
animals*

2467 biome [ˋbaɪˏom]

★★★★☆

A biome is a biotic community of plants and animals.

生物群落是動植物生物群聚。

生物群落，生物群聚
*n. a major ecological
community type*

2468 botany [ˋbɑtn̩ɪ]

★★★★☆

Biology can be divided into botany and zoology.

生物學可分為植物學和動物學。

植物學
*n. a branch of biology
dealing with plant life*

2469 capillary [ˋkæpl̩ˏɛrɪ]

★★★★☆

Capillary vessels are small blood vessels which spread into all areas of the body.

毛血管是遍布全身的細小血管。

毛血管
*n. any of the smallest blood
vessels*

2470 carbohydrate [ˏkɑrboˋhaɪdret]

★★★★★

Humans should intake carbohydrates, fats and protein as foods.

人類應攝取碳水化合物、脂肪和蛋白質作為食物來源。

碳水化合物，醣
*n. any of various neutral
compounds of carbon,
hydrogen, and oxygen*

2471 cell [sɛl]

★★★★★

Cells are surrounded by thin, mucous membranes.

細胞外包裹著一層薄薄的黏膜。

細胞
*n. a small usually microscopic
mass of protoplasm bounded
externally by a semipermeable
membrane*

2472 chromosome [ˋkroməˏsom]

★★★★★

Chromosomes are involved in the process of cellular replication and division.

染色體和細胞複製與分裂過程有關。

染色體
*n. any of the rod-shaped or
threadlike DNA-containing
structures of cellular
organisms*

2473 clone [klon] ★★★☆☆

At last, human beings succeeded in cloning a lamb.
最後，人類成功複製了一頭羊。

無性繁殖／複製，使無性繁殖
n. the aggregate of genetically identical cells or organisms asexually produced /
v. produce a clone

2474 coelenterate [sɪ`lɛntə,ret] ★★★☆☆

A hydra is classified as a coelenterate, which has a hollow body.
身體中空的水螅屬於腔腸動物。

腔腸動物
n. any of radially symmetrical invertebrate animals including the corals, sea anemones, jellyfishes, and hydroids

---

2475 coelacanth [`silə,kænθ] ★★☆☆☆

A coelacanth, once considered to be extinct, was found in the waters of Australia.
曾被視為絕種的空棘魚在澳洲外海被發現。

空棘魚
n. any of lobe-finned fishes known chiefly from Paleozoic and Mesozoic fossils

---

2476 courtship [`kɔrtʃɪp] ★★★★★

An ostrich's courtship dance is a boisterous procedure.
駝鳥求偶的舞姿誇張喧鬧。

動物求偶
n. the act, process, or period of courting

2477 cuticle [`kjutɪkl̩] ★★★★☆

The cuticles of some plants are often covered with trichome.
部分植物的角質層常覆蓋毛狀體。

角質層，上皮，表皮
n. an outer covering layer

2478 cytoplasm [`saɪtə,plæzəm] ★★★★☆

Cytoplasm in a cell is the protoplasm of a cell, external to the nuclear membrane.
細胞內的細胞質是原生質，位在核膜外。

細胞質
n. the organized complex of inorganic and organic substances external to the nuclear membrane of a cell

---

2479 endosperm [`ɛndə,spɜm] ★★★☆☆

The gymnosperm, as opposed to the endosperm, has its seeds exposed to the outside.
相對於胚乳的裸子植物，其種子是裸露在外的。

胚乳
n. a plant which forms seeds within the embryo sac

2480 endangered [ɪn`dendʒəd] ★★★★★

The manatee of Florida are now listed as an endangered species, and efforts to preserve them are ongoing.
美國佛羅里達州的海牛現在被列為瀕臨絕種動物，保育行動正在進行中。

瀕臨絕種的
a. being or relating to an endangered species

2481 fauna [`fɔnə] ★★★★☆

The fauna and flora of a tropical rain forest are extremely varied.
熱帶雨林的動植物群相當多樣化。

動物群
n. the animals characteristic of a region, period, or special environment

2482 fern [fɜn] ★★★★☆

The royal fern, a member of the fern species, is often thought of as an indicator species.

西洋薇屬蕨類植物,常被視為指標物種。

蕨類植物,羊齒植物
n. *any of flowerless spore-producing vascular plants*

2483 filament [`fɪləmənt] ★★★★☆

The filament in a flower is a stem, at the top end of which is an anther.

花絲是柱狀構造,最頂端就是花藥。

花絲
n. *the anther-bearing stalk of a stamen*

- anther n. 花藥
- canopy n. 株冠
- corolla n. 花冠
- epidermis n. 表皮
- nectary n. 蜜腺
- ovary n. 子房
- ovule n. 胚珠
- petal n. 花瓣

- pistil n. 雌蕊
- receptacle n. 花托
- sepal n. 萼片
- stalk n. 莖
- stamen n. 雄蕊
- stigma n. 柱頭
- style n. 花柱

MP3 101

2484 gastropod [`gæstrə,pɑd] ★★★★☆

Mollusks, such as snails, fall into the gastropod family.

蝸牛等軟體動物屬腹足動物科。

腹足動物
n. *any of mollusks (as snails and slugs) usually with a univalve shell or none*

2485 habitat [`hæbə,tæt] ★★★★★

Many natural habitats of animal species are being destroyed by human activity.

許多動物的自然棲息地都遭到人類活動的破壞。

動物棲息地,植物產地
n. *the place or environment where a plant or animal naturally or normally lives and grows*

2486 kingdom [`kɪŋdəm] ★★★★★

The kingdom is one of the three primary divisions into which natural objects are classified. These three are the animal kingdom, mineral kingdom, and plant kingdom.

生物可分類為三界,分別是動物界、礦物界,以及植物界。

界
n. *a major category in biological taxonomy that ranks above the phylum and below the domain*

- kingdom n. 界
- phylum n. 門
- class n. 綱
- order n. 目

- family n. 科
- genus n. 屬
- species n. 種
- variety n. 多樣性

2487 lichen [ˋlaɪkən] ★★★★☆

The disappearance of lichen from the surface of rock indicates that its surrounding forest is being polluted.
岩石表面地衣的消失顯示鄰近森林已受到污染。

地衣
n. any of numerous complex plantlike organisms made up of an alga and a fungus

2488 lipid [ˋlaɪpɪd] ★★★★★

Mrs. Smith underwent liposuction for the removal of lipid from her bodily tissue.
史密斯太太接受抽脂手術以去除身體組織內的脂質。

脂質，油脂
n. any of various substances that are soluble in nonpolar organic solvents

2489 microorganism [͵maɪkroˋɔrgən͵ɪzəm] ★★★★★

Microorganisms are so small that they are invisible to the naked eye.
微生物極為細小，是肉眼看不見的。

微生物
n. an organism of microscopic or ultramicroscopic size

2490 mollusk [ˋmɑləsk] ★★★★★

A mollusk, such as a cuttlefish, has a soft body.
烏賊等軟體動物擁有柔軟軀幹。

軟體動物
n. any of invertebrate animals (as snails, clams, or squids) with a soft unsegmented body

2491 nomenclature [ˋnomən͵kletʃə] ★★☆☆☆

Homo sapiens is the nomenclature for a human being.
智人是現代人的學名。

命名法，學名
n. an international system of standardized New Latin names used in biology for kinds and groups of kinds of animals and plants

2492 parasite [ˋpærə͵saɪt] ★★★★★

The varroa mite is a formidable parasite of wild honeybees. It destroys more than 95 percent of wild honeybees.
蜂蟎是野蜂難以對付的寄生蟲，能殺死百分之九十五的野蜂。

寄生蟲
n. an organism living in, with, or on another organism

2493 pore [por] ★★★☆☆

This plant has many pores, or small holes, on the surface of its leaves.
這株植物的葉片表面有許多氣孔小洞。

氣孔，細孔，毛孔
n. a minute opening especially in an animal or plant

2494 reptile [ˋrɛptl] ★★★★★

Snakes, turtles and lizards are reptiles, which all require a source of warmth, like the sun, to warm their bodies.
蛇、龜和蜥蜴都是爬蟲類動物，需要太陽等熱源來維持體溫。

爬蟲類動物
n. any of a class (Reptilia) of air-breathing vertebrates that include the alligators and crocodiles, lizards, snakes, and turtles

2495 symbiosis [͵sɪmbaɪˋosɪs] ★★★★★

Symbiosis refers to commensalism between two different species.
共生指的是兩個不同物種間的相依互利關係。

共生
n. the living together in more or less intimate association or close union of two dissimilar organisms

2496 trichome [ˋtrɪˌkom]

The trichome on the stem of a plant is often a good deterrent against parasites.

植物莖上的毛狀體可以嚇阻寄生蟲。

藻絲，毛狀體
n. an epidermal hair structure on a plant

𝒯ea 𝒯ime... ☕

<Architecture> Dovetail **Dovetail is a part or thing shaped like a dove's tail. A projecting, wedge-shaped part fits into a corresponding cut-out space to form an interlocking joint.**	〈來自建築學〉鴿尾榫頭，楔形榫頭 鴿尾榫頭是形似鴿尾的楔形建材，可與相應缺口互相接合以形成緊扣的接頭。（註：由於楔形榫頭可牢牢接合，因此本字當動詞用時可引申為「密合，吻合」。）

✖ **dovetail** [ˋdʌvˌtel] **v.** *combine; fit* / **n.** *a joint formed by a mortise with a tenon shaped like a dove's spread tail or a reversed wedge* │ 用榫頭接合，使吻合 / 楔形榫頭

What a coincidence! Jane's plan exactly dovetails with mine. I thought that it would be a good idea to go to the movies.

真巧，珍的計畫跟我的完全吻合，我正想去看電影。

*1*Complete each word by filling in the blank with proper spelling so that it has the same meaning as suggested. Then please write the meaning of each word in Chinese.

1. 近地點 = _ _ _ _ g e e

2. 行星 = _ _ _ n e t

3. 波霎 = _ _ _ _ a r

4. 類星體 = _ _ _ s a r

5. 自轉 = _ _ _ _ t i o n

6. 衛星 = _ _ _ _ l l i t e

7. 至 = _ _ _ s t i c e

8. 節肢動物 = a r t h r o _ _ _

9. 生物群落 = _ _ _ m e

10. 毛血管 = _ _ _ _ l l a r y

11. zenith = _____

12. cell = _____

13. clone = _____

14. cytoplasm = _____

15. gastropod = _____

16. nomenclature = _____

17. symbiosis = _____

18. catalyst = _____

19. enzyme = _____

20. fauna = _____

*2*Choose a word that best completes the sentence.

21. The _____ earth is revolving around the sun.

(A) planet   (B) pulsar   (C) quasar   (D) perigee

22. The _____ is created when there is a huge explosion of a giant star.

(A) zenith   (B) solstice   (C) supernova   (D) fauna

*3*The highlighted word is closest in meaning to which of the following?

23. It is insisted that humans can travel at an excess of the velocity **of light through a worm hole.**

(A) rotation   (B) speed   (C) perihelion   (D) Ptolemaic

24. An obese person really hates lipid **.**

(A) fat   (B) lichen   (C) fern   (D) reptile

25. The surface of this leaf has many pores **.**

(A) kingdoms   (B) trichomes   (C) bores   (D) parasites

∴ **Chemistry** 化學

2497 catalyst [`kætḷɪst] ★★★★☆

A catalyst is an agent which increases the speed of a chemical reaction.
催化劑是加速化學反應的媒介。

催化劑
n. *an agent that provokes or speeds significant change or action*

2498 electron [ɪ`lɛktrɑn] ★★★★★

If a balanced element gets a free electron from outside, it becomes a negative ion.
安定元素若向外得到自由電子，就會變成負離子。

電子
n. *an elementary particle consisting of a charge of negative electricity*

2499 enzyme [`ɛnzaɪm] ★★★★★

The enzyme detergent is popular among housewives, because it is thought to cause less water pollution.
酵素清潔劑廣受家庭主婦愛用，因為能減少水污染。

酵素
n. *any of numerous complex proteins that are produced by living cells and catalyze specific biochemical reactions at body temperatures*

2500 inorganic [ˌɪnɔr`gænɪk] ★★★★★

Inorganic matter cannot be dated by means of C-14 analysis.
無機物無法透過碳十四放射性同位素分析法確定年代。

無機的
n. *being or composed of matter other than plant or animal*

2501 ion [`aɪən] ★★★★★

A positive ion is an element which has lost an electron.
正離子是少帶一個電子的元素。

離子
n. *an atom or group of atoms that carries a positive or negative electric charge*

2502 litmus paper [`lɪtməs ˌpepə] ★★★★☆

We tested the solution with litmus paper to see if it is acidic or alkaline.
我們以石蕊試紙檢驗溶液酸鹼性。

石蕊試紙
n. *paper colored with litmus and used as an indicator*

2503 molecular [mə`lɛkjələ] ★★★★★

The molecular structure of water is quite simple; two atoms of hydrogen and one atom of oxygen.
水分子構造非常簡單，它包含兩個氫原子和一個氧原子。

分子的，由分子組成的
a. *of, relating to, consisting of, or produced by molecules*

2504 organic [ɔr`gænɪk] ★★★★★

Organic matter which is less than 50,000 years old can be dated by using radiocarbon dating method.
五萬年以下的有機物可透過放射性碳同位素定年法確定年代。

有機的
a. *of, relating to, or containing carbon compounds*

2505 oxidation [ˌɑksəˈdeʃən] ★★★★★

Oxidation is the combination of a substance with oxygen.

氧化作用是指物質和氧氣結合的過程。

氧化，氧化作用
n. *the act or process of oxidizing*

2506 periodic table [ˌpɪrɪɑdɪk ˈtæbl̩] ★★★★☆

The first element on the periodic table is hydrogen.

化學元素周期表上的第一個元素是氫。

化學元素周期表
n. *an arrangement of chemical elements based on the periodic law*

2507 proton [ˈprotɑn] ★★★★★

Protons are positively charged, while electrons are negatively charged.

質子帶正電，電子則帶負電。

質子
n. *an elementary particle that is identical with the nucleus of the hydrogen atom*

✦ Environment 環境

2508 conservation [ˌkɑnsəˈveʃən] ★★★★★

Energy conservation is quite essential, because natural resources are not boundless.

節約能源相當重要，因為自然資源是有限的。

保存，保護，維護
n. *a careful preservation and protection of something*

2509 damage [ˈdæmɪdʒ] ★★★★★

The hail caused too much damage to the crops.

冰雹對農作物造成極大損失。

損害，損失
n. *loss or harm resulting from injury to person, property, or reputation*

2510 desertification [ˌdɛzətɪfɪˈkeʃən] ★★★★★

The rate of desertification is unprecedented.

土地沙漠化的速度是前所未有的。

荒漠化，沙漠化
n. *the process of becoming a desert*

2511 ecosystem [ˈikoˌsɪstəm] ★★★★★

The destruction of the ecosystem will cause the disintegration of the food chain from the bottom up.

生態系統的破壞將導致食物鏈從下到上全面瓦解。

生態系統
n. *the complex of a community of organisms and its environment functioning as an ecological unit*

2512 exhaustion gas [ɪgˈzɔstʃən gæs] ★★★★★

These days, most big cities are shrouded in smog, which has been caused by the exhaustion gas of the residents' vehicles.

近來居民車輛排放出來的廢氣使多數大都市一片煙霧瀰漫。

廢氣
n. *gas which is exhausted*

2513 environmental [ɪn,vaɪrən`mɛntl̩]

★★★★★

We should stop environmental disruption if we wish to continue our existence on Earth.

如果我們想繼續生存在地球上，就應阻止環境破壞。

環境的，有關環境保護的

a. pertaining to the circumstances, objects, or conditions by which one is surrounded

2514 environmentally-friendly product
[ɪn,vaɪrən`mɛntl̩ı `frɛndlı `prɑdʌkt]

★★★★☆

We are trying to produce environmentally-friendly products.

我們正設法製造環保商品。

環保商品

n. a product that is environmentally friendly

2515 global warming [,globl̩ `wɔrmɪŋ]

★★★★★

Global warming has raised the Earth's temperature.

全球暖化已導致地球溫度上升。

全球暖化

n. an increase in the earth's atmospheric and oceanic temperatures

2516 algae [`ældʒi]

★★★★★

Because of green algae, this lake appears green.

湖水因綠藻而顯得青綠。

水藻，海藻

n. plants or plantlike organisms of any of several phyla, divisions, or classes of chiefly aquatic

2517 greenhouse effect [`grinhaʊs ə,fɛkt]

★★★★★

The greenhouse effect is one of the main culprits of global warming.

溫室效應是導致全球暖化的主因之一。

溫室效應

n. warming of the surface and lower atmosphere of a planet

2518 ground water [graʊnd `wɔtɚ]

★★★★★

The dumping of untreated sewage water leads to the pollution of ground water.

傾倒未處理污水導致地下水污染。

地下水

n. water within the earth especially that supplies wells and springs

2519 impact [`ɪmpækt]

★★★★★

According to the environmental impact evaluation, this area is not suitable for building a dam.

根據環境影響評估，此區不適合建水壩。

影響，作用

n. influence

2520 indicator species [`ɪndə,ketɚ `spiʃiz]

★★★☆☆

The spotted owl is often considered an indicator species.

斑鴞常被視為指標物種。

指標物種

n. an organism or ecological community so strictly associated with particular environmental conditions that its presence is indicative of the existence of these conditions

2521 ozone layer [`ozon ˌleə] ★★★★★

Air pollution has lead to a hole in the ozone layer.
空氣污染導致臭氧層破洞。

臭氧層
n. an atmospheric layer at heights of about 20 to 30 miles that is normally characterized by high ozone content

2522 preservation [ˌprɛzəˋveʃən] ★★★★★

This forest is in good preservation.
這座森林受到良好保育。

保護，維護，保存，保育
n. protection

2523 recyclable [riˋsaɪkləbl] ★★★★★

Please put recyclables in this bin.
請將可回收資源放在這個箱子裡。

可回收資源 / 可回收利用的
n. a substance available for reuse

2524 sulfur dioxide [ˌsʌlfə daɪˋɑksaɪd] ★★★★☆

Air filled with sulfur dioxide sears our eyes.
空氣中滿布的二氧化硫使雙眼乾澀。

二氧化硫
n. a pungent toxic gas SO2

MP3 103

✣ Economy 經濟

2525 appropriation [əˌpropriˋeʃən] ★★★☆☆

The government has decided to make an appropriation of 10,000 dollars for the special project.
政府決定為該專案提撥一萬元經費。

提撥，撥用，撥款
n. an act or instance of appropriating

2526 assess [əˋsɛs] ★★★★★

The IRS assessed a heavy tax on the man who has been suspected of land speculation.
疑似進行土地投機買賣的男子遭國稅局課以重稅。

徵稅，罰款
v. determine the rate or amount of (as a tax)

2527 auction [ˋɔkʃən] ★★★★★

The owner of the diamond ring decided to sell it at auction.
物主決定在拍賣會拍賣鑽石。

拍賣
n. a sale of property to the highest bidder

2528 ATM [ˌe ti`ɛm] ★★★★★

Nancy withdrew some money at the ATM, and her daughter became startled at the money that the ATM spat out.
南西到自動提款機領錢，女兒對機器吐出的錢感到驚訝。

自動提款機，自動櫃員機
n. automated teller machine

2529 avocation [ˌævəˈkeʃən]　　★★★★☆

My uncle is growing many different kinds of orchids as an avocation.
我舅舅的興趣是種植不同品種的蘭花。

副業，興趣，愛好
n. hobby

2530 bargain [ˈbɑrgɪn]　　★★★★★

They are going to build a giant shopping mall in my neighborhood. I think I'll be able to get a good bargain there.
我家附近要蓋一座大型購物中心，我想那裡可以買到便宜貨。

特價品，便宜貨，交易
n. an advantageous purchase

2531 barter [ˈbɑrtə]　　★★★★★

Before the advent of currency, people traded through a barter system.
在貨幣問世前，人們透過以物易物方式進行交易。

以物易物／進行以物易物交易
n. the act or practice of carrying on trade by bartering /
v. trade or exchange

2532 bidding [ˈbɪdɪŋ]　　★★★★☆

The bidding was very competitive. Almost twenty companies entered the bidding.
競標十分激烈，約有二十家企業參與投標。

投標，出價
n. making a bid

2533 bill [bɪl]　　★★★★☆

We received a bill of debt instead of cash as payment.
我們收到欠款支票而非現金付款。

帳單，支票
n. an individual or commercial note

2534 balance [ˈbæləns]　　★★★★★

The Smiths are having a hard time with their bank balance.
史密斯一家人的銀行存款入不敷出。

餘額，結存
n. an amount in excess especially on the credit side of an account

---

2535 bond [bɑnd]　　★★★★☆

Stocks and bonds are traded on the stock exchange.
股票和債券都在證券交易所進行交易。

債券
n. an interest-bearing certificate of public or private indebtedness

---

2536 boom [bum]　　★★★★★

The cycles of boom and bust seem to be about 10 years in this nation.
這個國家的景氣興衰似乎大約是每十年循環一次。

繁榮
n. a rapid widespread expansion of economic activity

2537 budget [ˈbʌdʒɪt]　　★★★★★

We are on a tight budget.
我們的預算很吃緊。

預算
n. the amount of money that is available for, required for, or assigned to a particular purpose

2538 **buoyant** [`bɔɪənt] ★★★★☆

Stocks have shown buoyant trends for three weeks in a row.
股票已連續三周呈現上漲趨勢。

（股票）上漲的
a. *capable of maintaining a satisfactorily high level*

2539 **check** [tʃɛk] ★★★★★

Checks and balances are essential in the economic cycle.
制衡對經濟循環而言是必要的。

制約
n. *a sudden stoppage of a forward course or progress*

2540 **commodity** [kə`mɑdətɪ] ★★★★★

These days, prices of commodities are extremely high.
近來物價非常高。

商品，日用品
n. *goods*

2541 **consolidation** [kən͵sɑlə`deʃən] ★★★★☆

The representatives from the two companies agreed on a consolidation.
兩家公司代表同意合併。

合併
n. *merger*

2542 **covenant** [`kʌvənənt] ★★★★☆

All the member nations are to conform to the covenant of the League of Nations.
所有會員國應遵守國際聯盟盟約。

盟約，契約
n. *agreement; compact*

2543 **deflation** [dɪ`fleʃən] ★★★★★

During deflation, prices of commodities tend to go down.
通貨緊縮期間物價會走低。

通貨緊縮
n. *a contraction in the volume of available money or credit*

2544 **demand** [dɪ`mænd] ★★★★★

The price is where the demand and supply curves meet.
價格是供需曲線的相會點。

需求 / 要求
n. *the quantity of a commodity or service wanted at a specified price and time* / **v.** *request*

2545 **depreciation** [dɪ͵priʃɪ`eʃən] ★★★★☆

With the anticipated depreciation of the currency, the profits from trade with foreign countries are expected to increase.
隨著貨幣預期貶值，對外貿易獲利可望提高。

貶值
n. *lowering in estimation or esteem*

2546 **due** [du] ★★★★★

This bill is due tomorrow.
這張支票明天到期。

到期的
a. *required or expected*

2547 endorse [ɪnˋdɔrs]

★★★★☆

背書
v. inscribe one's signature on a check

Please endorse this check.
這張支票請背書。

2548 equilibrium [ˌikwəˋlɪbrɪəm]

★★★★☆

均衡，均勢
n. balance

The crude oil market has been in a state of equilibrium for over 6 months.
原油市場已維持超過六個月的均勢。

2549 exploitation [ˌɛksplɔɪˋteʃən]

★★★★☆

剝削
n. an act or instance of exploiting

The owner of this company has been accused of the exploitation of labor.
企業主被控剝削勞工。

MP3
104

2550 fiasco [fɪˋæsko]

★★☆☆☆

完全失敗
n. a complete failure

The project ended in a fiasco.
計畫以失敗收場。

2551 fiscal [ˋfɪskl]

★★★★★

財政的，會計，國庫的
a. financial

The nation's fiscal policy has been constant.
國家財政政策向來不變。

2552 forgery [ˋfɔrdʒərɪ]

★★★☆☆

偽造
n. the crime of falsely and fraudulently making or altering a document

He was prosecuted for forgery of official documents.
他因偽造文書遭到起訴。

2553 glut [glʌt]

★★★★★

供應過剩
n. surplus

There was a glut of vegetables in the market.
市場蔬菜供過於求。

2554 installment [ɪnˋstɔlmənt]

★★★★☆

分期付款
n. one of the parts into which a debt is divided when payment is made at intervals

Pam is thinking about buying a piece of furniture on a 6-month installment plan.
潘考慮以六個月分期付款方式購買一件家具。

2555 interest [ˋɪntərɪst]

★★★★★

利息
n. a charge for borrowed money generally a percentage of the amount borrowed

Mr. Erickson defaulted on the payment, and he has to pay interest for delinquency.
艾瑞克遜先生拖欠款項，必須支付利息作為滯納金。

2556 intangible [ɪnˋtændʒəbl]

★★★★☆

無形的
a. impalpable

The traditional dance has been designated as an intangible asset of the nation.
傳統舞蹈被指定為國家的無形資產。

2557 laissez-faire [ˌlɛse ˈfɛr] ★★★☆☆

According to the doctrine of laissez-faire, the government should not interfere in economic affairs beyond the minimum necessary for the maintenance of peace and property rights.

根據放任主義原理，政府不應在維持和平與財產權的最低需求以外干涉經濟事務。

放任主義
n. a doctrine opposing governmental interference in economic affairs

---

2558 letter of credit [ˈlɛtɚ ɔv ˈkrɛdɪt] ★★★★☆

The businessman needed to have a letter of credit issued.

商人需開立信用狀。

信用狀
n. a letter addressed by a banker to a correspondent certifying that a person named therein is entitled to draw on the writer's credit up to a certain sum

---

2559 lending [ˈlɛndɪŋ] ★★★☆☆

Recently, banks' lending rates are on the rise.

近來銀行放款利率節節上升。

借貸
n. letting out (money) for temporary use on condition of repayment with interest

---

2560 merger [ˈmɝdʒɚ] ★★★★★

There is going to be hostile M&A, or merger & acquisition, between the two companies.

兩家公司之間將出現惡意併購。

合併
n. consolidation

2561 money order [ˈmʌnɪ ˌɔrdɚ] ★★★★☆

Please send us a check or money order.

請寄支票或匯票給我們。

匯票
n. an order issued by a post office, bank, or telegraph office for payment of a specified sum of money

---

2562 monthly statement [ˈmʌnθlɪ ˈstetmənt] ★★★★☆

I've begun to have a monthly statement issued.

我準備要發布月報表。

月報表，月結單
n. a summary of activity in a financial account over a month

2563 note [not] ★★★★☆

The company to which we shipped our products gave us a promissory note instead of cash.

公司以期票支付我們運送過去的產品而不是付現。

票據，期票
n. a written promise to pay a debt

2564 panic [ˈpænɪk] ★★★★★

The financial panic in the 1930's, or the Great Depression, began in the United States.

又稱經濟大蕭條的三○年代經濟大恐慌源於美國。

經濟大恐慌
n. a sudden widespread fright concerning financial affairs

2565 par [pɑr] ★★★☆☆

The price of this stock went down far below the par value.

這支股票的股價遠低於面值。

票面價值，面值
n. the face amount of an instrument of value

2566 **stagflation** [stæg`fleʃən]

During the stagflation, prices still remained too high despite the ongoing deflation.

停滯性通貨膨脹期間儘管通貨緊縮，物價卻持續攀升。

★★★☆☆

停滯性通貨膨脹
n. *persistent inflation combined with stagnant consumer demand and relatively high unemployment*

2567 **teller** [`tɛlə]

The man went to a bank teller to ask about the exchange rate.

男子詢問銀行出納員有關匯率問題。

★★★★★

出納員
n. *a member of a bank's staff concerned with the direct handling of money received or paid out*

2568 **traveler's check** [`trævləz ˌtʃɛk]

It's safer to carry traveler's checks than cash when travelling overseas.

出國旅遊時攜帶旅行支票比現金安全。

★★★★★

旅行支票
n. *a draft purchased from a bank, signed by the purchaser at the time of purchase and again at the time of cashing as a precaution against forgery*

2569 **vault** [vɔlt]

Most of the gold which is kept in the vault of the New York Federal Reserve belongs to other nations, not to the United States.

大部分存放在紐約聯邦準備銀行金庫裡的黃金都是屬於其他國家而非美國的。

★★★☆☆

金庫，保險庫，保險箱
n. *safe*

2570 **welfare** [`wɛlˌfɛr]

More and more nations are paying attention to child welfare.

愈來愈多國家關切兒童福利。

★★★★★

福利，社會救濟
n. *the state of doing well especially in respect to good fortune, happiness, well-being, or prosperity*

2571 **withdrawal** [wɪð`drɔəl]

Do I have to fill out this withdrawal slip to withdraw some money?

請問是否必須填寫提款單才能提款？

★★★★★

提款
n. *the act of taking back or away something that has been granted or possessed*

Tea Time...

<From a character of a work>
Malapropism
In Richard Sheridan's play *The Rivals*, a character, Mrs. Malaprop, is character-ized by the slip of making humorous results by misapplying words, like 'the pineapple of politeness' instead of 'the pinnacle of politeness.'

〈來自文學作品角色名〉錯誤發音相近字
在理查‧薛里頓的劇作《情敵》中，馬拉普羅普太太這個角色常因不小心誤用文字而引發可笑的結果，例如把「禮貌的最高點」念成「禮貌的鳳梨」等。（註：後世從此姓引申出 malapropism 一字，表示「因錯用發音相近字詞而帶來滑稽結果」。）

❋ **malapropism** [`mæləprɑpˌɪzəm] **n.** *a usually humorous application of a word* | 文字的滑稽誤用

My landlady, who was a little pedantic, liked to use difficult words while talking to me. One day, we were talking about TV's influence on kids. She said that there is too much 'violins' on TV, which was a clear malapropism.

有點愛賣弄學問的女房東跟我說話時喜歡使用生難字。某天我們談到電視對孩童的影響，她表示電視節目裡的「小提琴」太多了。這顯然是文字的滑稽誤用。（註：將「暴力 violence」誤用成發音相近的「小提琴 violins」。）

1
Complete each word by filling in the blank with proper spelling so that it has the same meaning as suggested. Then please write the meaning of each word in Chinese.

1. 無機的	= _ _ o r g a n i c	
2. 分子的	= _ _ _ _ c u l a r	
3. 氧化作用	= _ _ _ d a t i o n	
4. 維護	= c o n _ _ _ _ a t i o n	
5. 質子	= _ _ _ t o n	
6. 生態系統	= _ _ _ s y s t e m	
7. 徵稅	= a s _ _ _ _	
8. 拍賣	= _ _ _ t i o n	
9. 以物易物	= _ _ _ t e r	
10. 投標	= _ _ _ d i n g	

11. desertification	=	_____
12. recyclable	=	_____
13. bill	=	_____
14. balance	=	_____
15. bond	=	_____
16. commodity	=	_____
17. consolidation	=	_____
18. demand	=	_____
19. depreciation	=	_____
20. welfare	=	_____

2
Choose a word that best completes the sentence.

21. This plastic container is _____.
(A) bargain   (B) covenant   (C) recyclable   (D) buoyant

22. I had to _____ my check when I paid for the thing I chose.
(A) assess   (B) endorse   (C) bond   (D) boom

23. When is this book _____?
(A) due   (B) organic   (C) budget   (D) demand

3
The highlighted word is closest in meaning to which of the following?

24. Fortunately, the damage caused by the accident was slight.
(A) deflation   (B) harm   (C) algae   (D) auction

25. The impact on the environment will be evaluated by some experts.
(A) consolidation   (B) depredation   (C) influence   (D) equilibrium

MP3 105

⁜ **Geography & Geology** 地理與地質

2572 archipelago [ˌɑrkə`pɛləˌgo] ★★☆☆☆

An archipelago is made up of many islets.
群島由許多小島構成。

群島，列島
n. a group of islands

2573 arid [`ærɪd] ★★★★★

Deserts are mostly arid, but they are not always useless.
沙漠大多是不毛之地，但並不是毫無價值的。

乾旱的，乾燥的，不毛的
a. excessively dry

2574 ashes [`æʃɪz] ★★★★★

The volcano which had been dormant for ages began to spew lava and ashes.
蟄伏已久的休火山開始噴出岩漿和火山灰。

火山灰
n. fine particles of mineral matter from a volcanic vent

2575 asthenosphere [æs`θinəˌsfɪr] ★★★★☆

Asthenosphere, or the lower part of the mantle, is somewhat plastic and fluid.
地函下部的軟流圈是可塑性較高的流動固體。

軟流圈
n. a zone which lies beneath the lithosphere and within which the material is believed to yield readily to persistent stresses

---

2576 atoll [`ætɑl] ★★★☆☆

The atoll off our coast consists of coral reefs, and it is often dangerous to sailing boats there.
海岸外的環礁由珊瑚礁構成，航行到該處相當危險。

環礁，環狀珊瑚島
n. a coral island consisting of a reef surrounding a lagoon

2577 bay [be] ★★★★☆

There is often a race near this promontory dividing two bays.
分隔兩海灣的海岬常有急流。

海灣
n. an inlet of the sea or other bodies of water usually smaller than a gulf

---

2578 butte [bjut] ★★☆☆☆

A desert butte in Arizona is often employed as a backdrop for cowboy movies.
亞利桑那州的沙漠孤峰常被用來當作西部片的背景。

孤山，孤峰
n. an isolated hill or mountain with steep or precipitous sides usually having a smaller summit area than a mesa

---

2579 caldera [kæl`dɛrə] ★★★☆☆

Yellowstone National Park is located in the caldera region.
黃石國家公園位在塌陷火山口地帶。

塌陷火山口
n. a volcanic crater

2580 crater [`kretə] ★★★★★

The crater caused by the eruption of the volcano is about a mile in diameter.
火山爆發形成的火山口直徑約有一英里寬。

火山口
n. the bowl-shaped depression around the orifice of a volcano

2581 crust [krʌst] ★★★★★

The crust is the outermost layer of the earth.
地殼位於地球最外層。

地殼
n. the hardened exterior or surface part

2582 earthquake [ˈɝθˌkwek] ★★★★★

A massive earthquake of Richter magnitude 8.6 struck the region.
芮氏地震規模八・六的大地震侵襲該區。

地震
n. a shaking or trembling of the earth

2583 erode [ɪˈrod] ★★★★★

After the forest was cleared, the land was easily eroded.
森林被砍伐殆盡後，土地會很容易遭到侵蝕。

侵蝕
v. wear away by the action of water

2584 eruption [ɪˈrʌpʃən] ★★★★★

The eruption cycle of Yellowstone is about 600,000 years. But the previous eruption took place 620,000 years ago.
黃石國家公園的火山爆發周期約為六十萬年，但上次火山爆發是六十二萬年前。

爆發，噴出
n. an act, process, or instance of erupting

2585 fossil [ˈfɑsl̩] ★★★★★

Fossil records are very important for scientists to date the layers of the earth.
化石記錄對科學家確定地層年代而言非常重要。

化石
n. a remnant, impression, or trace of an organism of past geologic ages that has been preserved in the earth's crust

2586 geometric [dʒiəˈmɛtrɪk] ★★★★★

We can find many different geometric shapes around us.
在我們四周可發現許多幾何圖形。

幾何的
a. of, relating to, or according to the methods or principles of geometry

Reference...

- acute angle n. 銳角
- apex n. 頂點
- circle n. 圓形
- concentric circles n. 同心圓
- cone n. 圓錐體
- cube n. 立方體
- cylinder n. 圓柱體
- diameter n. 直徑
- diagonal a. 對角線的
- edge n. 邊
- ellipse n. 橢圓
- ellipsoid n. 橢球
- equilateral triangle n. 等邊三角形
- heptagon n. 七角形
- hexagon n. 六角形
- hypotenuse n. 直角三角形斜邊
- isosceles triangle n. 等腰三角形

- obtuse angle n. 鈍角
- oval a. 橢圓形的
- pentagon n. 五邊形
- perpendicular a. 垂直的
- polygon n. 多邊形
- quadrilateral n. 四邊形
- radius n. 半徑
- rectangle n. 矩形
- rhombus n. 菱形
- right angle n. 直角
- semicircle n. 半圓形
- sphere n. 球形
- spiral a. 螺旋形的
- square n. 正方形
- triangle n. 三角形
- triangular prism n. 三稜柱
- vertex n. 頂點

2587 geyser [ˈgaɪzə]
★★★★★

Intermittent springs are also called geysers.
斷續噴出的噴泉又稱間歇泉。

間歇泉
n. a spring that throws forth intermittent jets of heated water and steam

2588 guyot [ˈgaɪət]
★★☆☆☆

A guyot refers to an underwater mountain with a truncated top.
海底平頂山指的是自海底矗立、頂峰截平的山脈。

海底平頂山
n. a flat-topped seamount

2589 landmass [ˈlænd͵mæs]
★★★★★

It is now known that there are seven large landmasses on Earth.
目前已知地球有七大陸塊。

大陸塊
n. a large area of land

2590 lithosphere [ˈlɪθə͵sfɪr]
★★★★☆

The lithosphere is thought to be composed of the crust and the upper part of the mantle of the earth.
一般認為岩石圈由地殼和上部地函構成。

岩石圈
n. the outer part of the solid earth composed of rock

2591 magma [ˈmægmə]
★★★★★

It is estimated that there is a massive magma chamber below the surface of Yellowstone National Park.
黃石國家公園地表底下估計有巨大岩漿庫。

岩漿
n. molten rock material within the earth from which igneous rock results by cooling

2592 makeup [ˈmek͵ʌp]
★★★★★

The makeup of the soil was analyzed by using a sieve.
透過篩網分析土壤構造。

構造
n. physical, mental, and moral constitution

2593 mesa [ˈmesə]
★★☆☆☆

The Anasazi Indians made staircases to reach the high mesa.
安納薩吉印第安人建造階梯以到達高地。

台地
n. an isolated relatively flat-topped natural elevation

2594 mineral [ˈmɪnərəl]
★★★★★

We can find various sorts of minerals, even in a handful of soil.
即使在一把泥土裡也能發現多種礦物。

礦物
n. an inorganic substance

Reference...

- basalt **n.** 玄武岩
- calcite **n.** 方解石
- dolomite **n.** 白雲石
- galena **n.** 方鉛礦
- granite **n.** 花崗岩
- gypsum **n.** 石膏

- lime **n.** 石灰
- lodestone **n.** 天然磁石
- marble **n.** 大理石
- obsidian **n.** 黑曜石
- pumice **n.** 浮石
- quartz **n.** 石英

- sandstone **n.** 沙岩
- sedimentary rock
  n. 沈積岩
- shale **n.** 頁岩
- schist **n.** 片岩
- talc **n.** 滑石

2595 Pangaea [`pændʒɪə] ★★★★★

The original super-continent was called Pangaea, and it was broken into two parts, Gondwanaland and Laurasia.
原始超級陸塊稱為盤古大陸，後來分裂成岡瓦納古陸和勞亞古陸。

盤古大陸，原始大陸
n. a hypothetical land area believed to have once connected the landmasses

---

2596 plate tectonics [ˌplet tɛk`tɑnɪks] ★★★★★

The theory of plate tectonics was proposed in the 1960's.
板塊構造論在六〇年代提出。

板塊構造論
n. a theory in geology: the lithosphere of the earth is divided into a small number of plates

---

2597 prairie [`prɛrɪ] ★★★★★

The prairie along the Mississippi is often flooded during the summer.
密西西比河沿岸大草原常在夏季氾濫成災。

大草原
n. land in or predominantly in grass

2598 promontory [`prɑmən‚tɔrɪ] ★★★☆☆

People often made a lighthouse on a promontory protruding into the sea.
人們常在突出於海中的海角上建造燈塔。

海岬，海角
n. a high point of land or rock projecting into a body of water

---

2599 pyroclastic [ˌpaɪrok`læstɪk] ★★☆☆☆

One of the most dangerous factors in a volcanic eruption is the pyroclastic flow.
火山爆發的最危險因素之一是火山塵暴。

火山塵，火山碎屑
a. formed by or involving fragmentation as a result of volcanic or igneous action

---

2600 reef [rif] ★★★★★

Coral reefs are very fragile. Even the touch of a diver may kill them.
珊瑚礁非常易碎，即使被潛水者碰觸也可能造成死亡。

礁，沙洲
n. a ridge of rocks or sand, often of coral debris, at or near the surface of the water

---

2601 Ring of Fire [rɪŋ əv faɪr] ★★★★☆

Many earthquakes occur along the Pacific Ring of Fire.
許多地震都發生在環太平洋火山帶上。

火環
n. belt of volcanoes &frequent seismic activity nearly encircling the Pacific

---

2602 salinity [sə`lɪnətɪ] ★★★★☆

The salinity of the sea is not constant. The sea in tropical areas is saltier than the sea into which rivers flow.
海水鹽度不一，熱帶地區比河川流入區域的鹽度更高。

鹽度
n. the degree of being salty

2603 sand dune [`sænd dun] ★★★★☆

Sand dunes are named differently by their forms: a linear sand dune, parabolic sand dune, and crescent dune.
沙丘依不同形狀可命名為線形沙丘、拋物線沙丘和新月形沙丘。

沙丘
n. a hill or ridge of sand piled up by the wind

2604 sierra [sɪˋɛrə]

★★★☆☆

The Sierra Nevada has 12 peaks which rise more than 4,270 meters above sea level.

內華達山脈有十二座超過海拔四千兩百七十公尺的山峰。

鋸齒狀山脊
n. a range of mountains especially with a serrated or irregular outline

2605 taiga [ˋtaɪgə]

★★★★☆

There are many needle-leaved trees in the taiga region, which is below the tundra.

位在凍原以下的針葉林帶有許多針葉林。

針葉林帶
n. a moist subarctic forest dominated by conifers (as spruce and fir) that begins where the tundra ends

2606 trace [tres]

★★★★☆

The archaeologists could find some traces of an ancient civilization at the site.

考古學家在遺址中發現部分古文明遺跡。

遺跡，痕跡
n. a minute and often barely detectable amount or indication

2607 tropic [ˋtrɑpɪk]

★★★★★

The Tropic of Cancer is the northernmost latitude reached by the overhead sun, and its opposite is the Tropic of Capricorn.

北回歸線相對於南回歸線，是太陽所能直射的極北緯度。

回歸線
n. either of the two parallels of terrestrial latitude

2608 tropical [ˋtrɑpɪk!]

★★★★★

The tropical rain forest is being destroyed at the rapid rate of one acre per second.

熱帶雨林以每秒一英畝的快速速度遭到破壞。

熱帶的，位於熱帶的
a. of, relating to, occurring in, or suitable for use in the tropics

2609 tundra [ˋtʌndrə]

★★★★★

The soil below the surface of the tundra region is permafrost.

凍原地表土壤是永凍層。

凍原
n. a level or rolling treeless plain that is characteristic of arctic and subarctic regions

2610 vent [vɛnt]

★★★☆☆

The channel through which lava is spewed is called a vent.

岩漿噴出的通道稱為火山口。

火山口
n. an opening for the escape of a gas or liquid or for the relief of pressure

---

Tea Time... ☕

<Colloquialism> Shanghai	〈口語用法〉強迫當水手
Originally said of sailors kidnapped for crew duty on the China run.	原指在中國航程中劫持水手從事船務。（註：也就是逼人「上海」工作的意思。）

✽ **shanghai** [ˋʃæŋˋhaɪ] *v. force a person to be a sailor on a ship by using drugs or other trickery* | 強迫當水手

Some of the new crew members were shanghaied from the port at which they last stopped. They never wanted to become sailors.

部分新進人員在最後停留的港口被強迫上船，他們從不想當水手。

1

Complete each word by filling in the blank with proper spelling so that it has the same meaning as suggested. Then please write the meaning of each word in Chinese.

1. 財政的   = ___ c a l
2. 偽造   = ____ e r y
3. 利息   = ____ r e s t
4. 無形的   = i n ____ i b l e
5. 借貸   = ____ i n g
6. 合併   = ____ e r
7. 出納員   = ____ e r
8. 金庫   = ___ l t
9. 提款   = ____ d r a w a l
10. 福利   = ___ f a r e

11. par   = _____
12. bay   = _____
13. mineral   = _____
14. geometric   = _____
15. erg   = _____
16. prairie   = _____
17. fiasco   = _____
18. archipelago = _____
19. glut   = _____
20. ashes   = _____

2

Choose a word that best completes the sentence.

21. The combustion of _____ fuels has caused serious air pollution problems.
    (A) caldera   (B) guyot   (C) pyroclastic   (D) fossil

22. The _____ of Mount St. Helens in the Cascade Range in Washington State was in 1980.
    (A) eruption   (B) geyser   (C) promontory   (D) crater

3

The highlighted word is closest in meaning to which of the following?

23. This land is so arid that it is not suitable for agriculture.
    (A) dry   (B) mineral   (C) oval   (D) polygon

24. The makeup of the soil was analyzed by the geologist.
    (A) constitution   (B) pumice   (C) quartz   (D) sandstone

25. The prairie along the Mississippi is often flooded during the summer.
    (A) lime   (B) granite   (C) shale   (D) grassland

MP3
107

✛ **Language** 語言

2611 accent [ˈæksɛnt]

One of my colleagues speaks with a Texas accent.
我有位同事操德州口音。

★★★★★

口音，腔調
n. *rhythmically significant stress on the syllables*

2612 cognate [ˈkɑgnet]

Languages of the same cognate usually have some similarities.
同源語言通常具有某種相似性。

★★★☆☆

同源的／同源詞，同系語言
a. *related by descent from the same ancestral language /*
n. *the languages of the same ancestor*

2613 conjugation [ˌkɑndʒəˈgeʃən]

Students who are studying English have a hard time memorizing many irregular conjugations.
學英文的學生很難記住不規則詞形變化。

★★★☆☆

詞形變化
n. *a schematic arrangement of the inflectional forms of a verb*

2614 contraction [kənˈtrækʃən]

'Ne'er' is a contraction of 'never.'
never（從未）的縮寫是 ne'er。

★★★☆☆

縮寫形
n. *a shortening of a word, syllable, or word group*

2615 dialect [ˈdaɪəˌlɛkt]

His Scottish dialect was too difficult for me to understand.
我很難聽懂他的蘇格蘭方言。

★★★★★

方言
n. *a regional variety of language*

2616 jargon [ˈdʒɑrgən]

The medical student's book is full of medical jargon.
醫學系學生用書充滿醫學術語。

★★★★☆

術語，行話
n. *confused unintelligible language; the technical terminology*

2617 lexicon [ˈlɛksɪkɑn]

The word 'Internet' entered the American lexicon at the end of the 20th century.
美語辭典在二十世紀末新增 internet（網際網路）一字。

★★★★☆

辭典，語彙
n. *a book containing an alphabetical arrangement of the words in a language and their definitions*

2618 morphology [mɔrˈfɑlədʒɪ]

Morphology is a branch of linguistics.
語言形態學是語言學的一支。

★★★☆☆

語形學，語言形態學
n. *the system of word-forming elements and processes in a language*

2619 nonverbal [ˌnɑnˈvɜbl]

We had to resort to every kind of nonverbal communication, such as gestures, smiles, bows, etc.
我們須仰賴手勢、笑容、鞠躬等各種非語言溝通。

★★★★☆

非語言的
a. *being other than verbal*

2620 oral [`ɔrəl] ★★★★★

Children should be taught to be responsible for their own oral hygiene.

應教育孩童注重個人口腔衛生。

口頭的，口腔的，口服的
a. *of, given through, or involving the mouth; uttered by the mouth or in words*

2621 phonetic [fə`nɛtɪk] ★★★★★

For the child, some of the phonetic alphabet appeared so strange that he did not know how to pronounce it.

孩童對部分語音字母感到陌生而不會發音。

語音的，語音學的
a. *of or relating to spoken language or speech sounds*

2622 prefix [`pri,fɪks] ★★★★★

To learn about prefixes and suffixes is useful for increasing your word power.

學習字首和字尾對增加字彙能力很有幫助。

字首
n. *an affix attached to the beginning of a word*

2623 syllable [`sɪləbl̩] ★★★★★

The word 'happy' consists of two syllables.

happy（快樂）一字由兩個音節構成。

音節
n. *a unit of spoken language*

2624 diphthong [`dɪfθɔŋ] ★★★☆☆

/au/ and /aɪ/ are diphthongs.

[au] 和 [aɪ] 都是雙母音。

雙母音
n. *a gliding monosyllabic speech sound*

2625 vernacular [və`nækjələ] ★★★★☆

Most students from the same nation usually communicate with each other in their own vernacular.

大部分來自相同國家的學生會以方言溝通。

方言
n. *a vernacular language, expression, or mode of expression*

✥ Medicine 醫學

2626 abrasion [ə`breʒən] ★★★★★

We need to apply some tincture of iodine to this abrasion.

我們必須在擦傷的皮膚上塗些碘酒。

擦傷
n. *a wearing, grinding, or rubbing away by friction*

2627 bandage [`bændɪdʒ] ★★★★★

The nurse applied an adhesive bandage to his wound.

護士將黏性繃帶敷在他的傷口上。

繃帶
n. *a strip of fabric used especially to cover, dress, and bind up wounds*

2628 administer [əd`mɪnəstə] ★★★★★

The doctor has decided to administer some medicine to the patient.
醫生決定開藥給病人服用。

配藥，開藥
v. give medicine

2629 afflict [ə`flɪkt] ★★★★★

He is afflicted with a serious disease.
他被重病折磨。

使痛苦，折磨
v. distress so severely as to cause persistent suffering or anguish

2630 ailment [`elmənt] ★★★★★

Even a doctor was unable to prescribe the exact medicine for his ailment.
即使是醫生也無法為他的病痛開立明確藥方。

病痛，小病
n. a bodily disorder or chronic disease

2631 analgesic [͵ænæl`dʒizɪk] ★★★★☆

After the surgery, the doctor had to administer some analgesic to kill the pain.
手術過後醫生須開立止痛藥為病人止痛。

止痛藥
n. an agent for producing analgesia

2632 antacid [ænt`æsid] ★★★★☆

You can buy this antacid at a shopping mall.
你可以在購物中心買到制酸劑。

制酸劑
n. an agent that counteracts or neutralizes acidity

2633 blood pressure [`blʌd ͵prɛʃə] ★★★★★

The medical student learned how to use a blood pressure gauge.
醫學系學生學習使用血壓計。

血壓
n. pressure that is exerted by the blood

2634 braces [bres] ★★★★☆

Old Man: I do not want to wear dentures.
Dentist: Then, would you wear braces?
老人：我不想戴假牙。
牙醫：那你願意戴牙套嗎？

齒顎矯正器，牙套
n. something that connects or fastens

2635 canker [`kæŋkə] ★★★★☆

I have a terrible canker sore. I cannot eat anything.
我長了嚴重口瘡，沒辦法吃任何東西。

口腔潰瘍，口瘡
n. an erosive or spreading sore

2636 constipation [͵kɑnstə`peʃən] ★★★★☆

Nine out of ten people who occupy the bathroom for a long time suffer from constipation.
十個長時間占用廁所的人有九個患有便秘。

便秘
n. abnormally delayed or infrequent passage of usually dry hardened feces

2637 cut [kʌt]   ★★★★★

傷口
***n.** a wound made by something sharp*

This is only a minor cut. I'll apply some antiseptic.
這只是個小傷口，我會塗點消毒藥水。

2638 deficiency [dɪˋfɪʃənsɪ]   ★★★★★

不足，缺乏
***n.** a shortage of substances necessary to health*

Vitamin C deficiency may cause scurvy.
缺乏維他命C可能導致壞血症。

2639 delivery [dɪˋlɪvərɪ]   ★★★★★

分娩
***n.** giving birth*

His wife is in the delivery room. She has been in labor for more than 10 hours.
他的妻子已經在產房內分娩超過十個鐘頭。

2640 disorder [dɪsˋɔrdə]   ★★★★★

失調，不適，（小）病
***n.** an abnormal physical or mental condition*

These days, more and more people are suffering from various kinds of skin disorders.
近來有愈來愈多人罹患各種皮膚過敏。

- AIDS (=acquired immuno-deficiency syndrome) n. 愛滋病
- Alzheimer's disease n. 阿滋海默症
- amnesia n. 健忘症
- anaemia n. 貧血
- anorexia nervosa n. 厭食症
- atrophy n. 萎縮症
- autism n. 自閉症
- avian influenza n. 禽流感
- beriberi n. 腳氣病
- cystic fibrosis n. 纖維囊腫
- dengue fever n. 登革熱
- depilation n. 脫毛
- dermatitis n. 皮膚炎
- diabetes n. 糖尿病
- diphtheria n. 白喉
- Down's syndrome n. 唐氏症
- dystrophy n. 營養不良症
- encephalitis n. 腦炎
- fibrositis n. 纖維組織炎
- hepatitis n. 肝炎
- hypertension n. 高血壓
- hypotension n. 低血壓
- leukaemia n. 白血病
- Parkinson's disease n. 帕金森氏症
- pneumonia n. 肺炎
- rabies n. 狂犬病
- rickets n. 軟骨症，佝僂症
- rubella n. 德國麻疹
- scurvy n. 壞血症
- tachycardia n. 心跳過快
- tuberculosis n. 肺結核
- typhoid n. 傷寒

2641 discharge [dɪsˋtʃɑrdʒ]   ★★★★★

釋放／出院，准許離開
***n.** the act of discharging /* ***v.** release from confinement, custody, or care*

He recovered from his illness and was discharged from the hospital.
他康復後已出院。

2642 dose [dos]   ★★★★★

一劑藥量／按劑量服藥
***n.** an amount of something likened to a prescribed or measured quantity of medicine /* ***v.** give medicine to*

The doctor prescribed a daily dose of aspirin.
醫生開立阿斯匹靈每日服用劑量。

2643 endoscopy [ɛnˋdɑskəpɪ]

For most people, it is a horrible experience to undergo endoscopy.
對大多數人來說做內視鏡檢查是很恐怖的經驗。

★★★★☆

內視鏡檢查
n. an examination using an illuminated usually fiber-optic flexible or rigid tubular instrument

---

2644 exacerbate [ɪgˋzæsəˌbet]

His cough was exacerbated by smoking.
吸煙使他的咳嗽惡化。

★★★☆☆

使惡化，使加重
v. aggravate; worsen

2645 fatal [ˋfetl]

Even though medicine has developed by leaps and bounds, there are still many fatal diseases.
儘管醫學發展非常迅速，仍有許多致命的疾病。

★★★★★

致命的
a. terminal

2646 feeble [ˋfibl]

Pneumonia has rendered him feeble.
肺炎使他變得虛弱。

★★★★☆

虛弱的，衰弱的，無力的
a. week

2647 fever [ˋfivə]

My baby has developed a fever.
我寶寶發燒了。

★★★★★

發燒
n. a rise of body temperature above the normal

2648 floss [flɔs]

Dentist: What's your hobby?
Little Kid: Dental flossing.
牙醫：你的嗜好是什麼？
小孩：用牙線潔牙。

★★★★★

牙線 / 用牙線潔牙
n. soft thread of silk or mercerized cotton for embroidery / v. use dental floss on

---

2649 gauze [gɔz]

Please pass me some sterilized gauze.
請給我一些消毒紗布。

★★★★★

紗布
n. a loosely woven cotton surgical dressing

2650 hallucination [həˌlusnˋeʃən]

The patient who is addicted to drugs often suffers from hallucinations.
毒癮患者常有幻覺。

★★★★☆

幻覺
n. perception of objects with no reality usually arising from disorder of the nervous system or in response to drugs

---

2651 incision [ɪnˋsɪʒən]

Some people avoid receiving an operation involving an incision during spring tides.
有些人避免在初一、十五的滿潮期間進行開刀手術。

★★★★★

手術切口，開刀
n. a wound made especially in surgery

2652 malocclusion [ˌmælə`kluʒən] ★★★★☆

Orthodontists try to correct malocclusion.
齒顎矯正醫師設法矯正牙齒咬合不正。

牙齒咬合不正
n. abnormality in the coming together of teeth

2653 medic [`mɛdɪk] ★★★★☆

Medics on the battlefield have to make desperate efforts to help wounded soldiers in defiance of flying bullets.
戰地軍醫須在槍林彈雨中奮不顧身地救助傷兵。

軍醫，醫務兵
n. one engaged in medical work or study

2654 mitigate [`mɪtəˌget] ★★★★★

This pill will mitigate your migraine.
這顆藥丸能減輕你的偏頭痛。

使緩和，減輕
v. alleviate; soften

2655 operation [ˌɑpə`reʃən] ★★★★★

The doctors have decided to perform an operation on the patient.
醫生決定為病人進行手術。

手術
n. a procedure performed on a living body

2656 stethoscope [`stɛθəˌskop] ★★★★★

When the doctor put the stethoscope on his chest, it tickled him.
醫生把聽診器放在他胸上，讓他覺得癢。

聽診器
n. a medical instrument for detecting sounds produced in the body

2657 stretcher [`strɛtʃɚ] ★★★★☆

The medics carried the victim on a stretcher.
軍醫用擔架運送傷者。

擔架
n. a device for carrying a sick, injured, or dead person

2658 susceptible [sə`sɛptəbl] ★★★★★

Most elderly people are susceptible to colds.
多數老年人容易罹患感冒。

易患～的
a. vulnerable; subject; liable

2659 symptom [`sɪmptəm] ★★★★★

The child who had a fever showed symptoms of influenza.
發燒孩童出現流行性感冒症狀。

症狀，徵候
n. something that indicates the presence of bodily disorder

2660 therapy [`θɛrəpɪ] ★★★★★

Even after he was discharged from the hospital, he had to undergo physical therapy for several weeks.
他即使出院後仍須進行數周物理治療。

治療，療法
n. treatment especially of bodily, mental, or behavioral disorder

2661 toxic [`tɑksɪk]

★★★★★

When the building was on fire, many people died because of toxic gases.
建築物著火時，許多人因吸入有毒氣體而死亡。

有毒的
a. poisonous

2662 trauma [`trɔmə]

★★★★☆

The victim of the accident was borne to the trauma center of the city.
在意外事故中受傷的患者被送往市立創傷中心。

外傷，傷口，創傷
n. an injury (as a wound) to living tissue caused by an extrinsic agent

2663 vaccinate [`væksn̩ˌet]

★★★★★

The children in the under-developed country needed to get vaccinated against typhus.
未開發國家的孩童須施打預防針，以免感染斑疹傷寒。

打預防針，接種疫苗，種牛痘
v. administer a vaccine

2664 ward [wɔrd]

★★★★★

The patient with the communicable disease was housed in an isolation ward.
罹患傳染性疾病的患者住在隔離病房。

病房 / 防止
n. a large room in a hospital where a number of patients often requiring similar treatment are accommodated / v. prevent

---

𝒯ea 𝒯ime... ☕

<Greek philosophy> Sophist
In ancient Greece, any of a group of teachers of rhetoric, politics, philosophy, etc., some of whom were notorious for their clever, specious arguments.

〈來自希臘哲學〉詭辯家
在古希臘，部分修辭學、政治學、哲學等教師以狡黠詭辯、似是而非的論辯博得惡名。（註：本字源於「sophoi」，指「哲人，智者」。）

❖ **sophisticated** [sə`fɪstɪˌketɪd] *a. highly developed and complex; complicated; intricate* | 精密的，高性能的，極複雜的

Because semi-skilled workers are being replaced by sophisticated machines, the problems of unemployment will only be increased.
由於精密機器取代半專業工人，失業人數只會更高。

1 Complete each word by filling in the blank with proper spelling so that it has the same meaning as suggested. Then please write the meaning of each word in Chinese.

1. 針葉林帶   = ___ g a
2. 熱帶的   = ____ i c a l
3. 遺跡   = ___ c e
4. 口音   = __ c e n t
5. 非語言的   = ___ v e r b a l
6. 語音的   = ____ e t i c
7. 擦傷   = ___ a s i o n
8. 繃帶   = ____ a g e
9. 開藥   = ____ n i s t e r
10. 制酸劑   = ___ a c i d

11. syllablc   – _____
12. afflict   = _____
13. braces   = _____
14. deficiency   = _____
15. delivery   = _____
16. floss   = _____
17. fever   = _____
18. diphthong   = _____
19. lexicon   = _____
20. prefix   = _____

2 Choose a word that best completes the sentence.

21. **The subarctic area, or the _____, has many needle-leaved trees.**
    (A) tundra   (B) taiga   (C) salina   (D) sierra

22. **A person who does not speak the language of the country he visits has to resort to _____ communication.**
    (A) lexicon   (B) oral   (C) prefix   (D) nonverbal

23. **He is suffering from a _____ whose name is not known.**
    (A) endoscopy   (B) disorder   (C) gauze   (D) hallucination

3 The highlighted word is closest in meaning to which of the following?

24. **The ailment that gave him too much pain was at last subdued because of the newly invented medicine.**
    (A) dose   (B) bandage   (C) disease   (D) cut

25. **His condition was exacerbated as he did not quit smoking.**
    (A) afflicted   (B) administered   (C) discharged   (D) worsened

Day 10

MP3
109

✢ Physics 物理

2665 absolute zero [`æbsəlut zɪro`]

★★☆☆☆

絕對零度

It is actually impossible to reach absolute zero.
事實上不可能達到絕對零度。

n. a theoretical temperature characterized by complete absence of heat and motion and equivalent to exactly -273.15℃

2666 centrifugal [sɛn`trɪfjʊgl̩]

★★★☆☆

離心的

Centrifugal force is the opposite of centripetal force.
離心力相對於向心力。

a. proceeding or acting in a direction away from a center or axis

---

2667 half life [`hæf laɪf]

★★★☆☆

半衰期

The 6,175-year half life of carbon is used to date organic matter.
碳的六千一百七十五年半衰期可用來確定有機物年代。

n. the time required for half the amount of a substance

2668 inertia [ɪ`nɝʃə]

★★★★☆

慣性

A moving object tends to keep on moving because of the force of inertia.
動者恆動是基於慣性作用。

n. indisposition to motion, exertion, or change

2669 measure [`mɛʒɚ]

★★★★★

度量單位 / 測量

A measure is a unit in which we express size, speed, weight, etc.
表示尺寸、速度、重量等可使用度量單位。

n. the act of measuring /
v. estimate or appraise by a criterion

- ampere **n.** 安培，電流強度單位
- angstrom **n.** 埃，光波波長單位
- calorie **n.** 卡路里，熱量單位
- candela **n.** 燭光，發光強度單位
- coulomb **n.** 庫侖，電量實用單位
- decibel **n.** 分貝，聲音強度單位
- fathom **n.** 噚，水深單位（一噚為六英尺）
  (= 6 feet)
- hertz **n.** 赫茲，頻率單位

- joule **n.** 焦耳，功或能單位
- kelvin **n.** 克氏溫標，絕對溫標單位
- knot **n.** 海浬，航速和流速單位
- lumen **n.** 流明，光束能量單位
- maxwell **n.** 馬克士威，磁通量單位
- ohm **n.** 歐姆，電阻單位
- pascal **n.** 帕斯卡，壓力單位
- tesla **n.** 特斯拉，磁通密度單位
- volt **n.** 伏特，電壓單位

2670 quantum [`kwɑntəm]

★★★★☆

量子

Quantum theory is related to the properties and behavior of small particles.
量子理論與粒子的性質和作用有關。

n. any of the very small increments or parcels into which many forms of energy are subdivided

2671 torque [tɔrk] ★★★☆☆

Even if there is no initial torque imposed on it, a cat is capable of twisting itself in midair and landing on its feet, even when it is dropped upside down.

即使起初沒有施以扭轉力,以頭朝下腳在上姿勢落下的貓也能在半空中自我翻轉,再以四腳著地。

扭矩,轉矩,扭轉力
n. a turning or twisting force

✤ Politics

2672 aristocracy [ˌærəˈstɑkrəsɪ] ★★★☆☆

Aristocracy is a form of government ruled by aristocrats.
貴族政治是由貴族領導的政治體制。

貴族政治,菁英政治
n. government by the best individuals or by a small privileged class

- autocracy n. 獨裁政治
- democracy n. 民主政治
- despotism n. 專制政治
- hierocracy n. 教士政治

- matriarchy n. 母權制
- oligarchy n. 寡頭政治
- patriarchy n. 父權統治,父權制

- plutocracy n. 財閥政治
- technocracy n. 技術官僚政治
- theocracy n. 神權政治
- totalitarianism n. 極權主義

2673 ballot [ˈbælət] ★★★★★

A ballot is stronger than a bullet.
選票強過子彈。(註:美國總統林肯名言,他認為暴力或槍桿無法控制人民。)

選票
n. a sheet of paper used to cast a secret vote

2674 cabinet [ˈkæbənɪt] ★★★★★

When a new government is established, almost all of the cabinet members are changed.
當新政府成立,幾乎全體內閣閣員都遭到替換。

內閣,全體閣員
n. a body of advisers of a head of state

2675 capitalism [ˈkæpətḷˌɪzəm] ★★★★★

The superiority of capitalism was proven by the disintegration of communism.
共產主義的瓦解證實了資本主義的優越。

資本主義,資本主義制度
n. an economic system characterized by private or corporate ownership of capital goods

2676 consul [ˈkɑnsḷ] ★★★★☆

Mr. Kim is going to meet the consul because of his visa problem.
金先生因簽證問題將與領事會面。

領事
n. an official appointed by a government to reside in a foreign country to represent the commercial interests of citizens of the appointing country

2677 delegate [ˈdɛlɪgət] ★★★★☆

The leader will delegate his deputy to preside at the convention.
領導者將委派副手主持會議。

代表 / 委派出任代表,授權
n. a person acting for another /
v. appoint as one's representative

2678 deputy [`dɛpjətɪ]

★★★★★

The deputy governor will be attending the opening ceremony in place of the governor.

副州長將代替州長出席開幕典禮。

副手，代理人
n. *a person appointed as a substitute with power to act*

2679 hegemony [hɪ`dʒɛmənɪ]

★★★★☆

Many politicians are known to struggle for hegemony.

眾所周知許多政治人物會爭奪領導權。

領導權，支配權
n. *preponderant influence or authority over others*

2680 inaugurate [ɪn`ɔgjəˌret]

★★★★★

J. F. Kennedy was inaugurated as the president in 1961.

甘迺迪於一九六一年正式就任總統。

使正式就任
v. *induct into an office with suitable ceremonies*

2681 independent [ˌɪndɪ`pɛndənt]

★★★★★

The lawmaker withdrew from the party and became an independent.

該立法委員退黨後，成為無黨籍人士。

無黨籍人士
n. *one that is not bound by or definitively committed to a political party*

2682 official [ə`fɪʃəl]

★★★★★

It is the general consensus that government officials should be more responsive to the peoples' needs.

輿論一致認為政府官員對民眾需求應有更多回應。

官員，公務員
n. *one who holds or is invested with an office*

2683 overthrow [ˌovɚ`θro]

★★★★☆

The military clique contrived to overthrow the government.

軍閥密謀推翻政府。

打倒，推翻，廢除
v. *subvert; overturn; upset*

2684 parliament [`pɑrləmənt]

★★★★★

As a member of parliament, Mr. Johnson is trying to live an exemplary life for the people of the nation.

身為國會議員的一份子，強森先生努力以身作則，為民表率。

議會，國會
n. *legislature*

2685 poll [pol]

MP3
110

★★★★★

Polls showed less than 50% of the people support the president.

民調顯示不到五成民眾支持總統。

民調，民意調查
n. *vote*

2686 ratify [`rætəˌfaɪ]

★★★★☆

The revision of the constitution was drafted, and the national assembly ratified it.

修憲案起草後獲國民大會正式批准。

正式批准，認可
v. *approve; sanction*

2687 riot [ˈraɪət] ★★★★☆

The conflict was initiated by the police endeavor to put down a riot by force.

衝突起自警方動用武力全力鎮壓暴動。

暴動，暴亂
n. uprising; insurrection

2688 secession [sɪˈsɛʃən] ★★★★☆

The exact cause of the Civil War is still not known, but South Carolina's secession from the Union initiated the conflict between the North and the South.

南北戰爭的真正起因迄今未明，但雙方衝突肇始於南卡羅萊納州脫離聯邦。

脫離聯邦，脫黨
n. withdrawal; formal withdrawal from an organization

2689 status quo [ˌstetəs ˈkwo] ★★★★☆

If the government does not improve the status quo, the economy may become worse.

政府若不改善現狀，經濟情況可能惡化。

現狀
n. the existing state of affairs

2690 stopgap [ˈstɑpˌgæp] ★★★☆☆

The prime minister is going to make a stopgap cabinet.

首相將組成臨時內閣。

臨時替代 / 臨時的，暫時的
n. something that serves as a temporary expedient /
a. makeshift

2691 suffrage [ˈsʌfrɪdʒ] ★★★★★

The Wyoming Territory granted suffrage to women in order to attract more immigrants.

懷俄明領地同意給予婦女選舉權以吸引更多移民。

選舉權，投票權
n. franchise

2692 turmoil [ˈtɜmɔɪl] ★★★★☆

The mob was causing turmoil, and the police used water guns to dispel it.

暴民引發混亂，並遭警方動用水柱驅離。

騷動，混亂
n. commotion; uproar

⁘ Psychology 心理學

2693 amentia [əˈmɛnʃɪə] ★★☆☆☆

Amentia and dementia are both mental disabilities.

精神錯亂和失智症都屬於精神失能。

精神錯亂
n. mental retardation; a condition of lack of development of intellectual capacity

2694 Oedipus complex [ˈɛdəpəs ˌkɑmplɛks] ★★★★☆

An Oedipus complex is a positive feeling that a child develops toward the parent of the opposite sex.

戀父或戀母情結是指子女對性別相反的父母一方懷有的直接情感。

戀父情結，戀母情結
n. the positive libidinal feelings of a child toward the parent of the opposite sex

2695 id [ɪd]

★★★☆☆

本我

The id is often considered to be the source of instinct.

本我常被視為是本能的來源。

n. the one of the three divisions of the psyche in psychoanalytic theory that is completely unconscious and is the source of psychic energy derived from instinctual needs and drives

2696 identity [aɪˈdɛntətɪ]

★★★★★

自我認同

Young people who worship many idols could end up having an identity crisis.

崇拜偶像的年輕人常會產生自我認同危機。

n. the distinguishing character or personality of an individual

2697 libido [lɪˈbido]

★★★☆☆

性衝動，本能衝動

According to Freud, libido is considered as being a sexual desire.

根據佛洛伊德理論，本能衝動被視為是一種性需求。

n. sexual drive

2698 Rorschach test [ˈrɔrʃɑk tɛst]

★★☆☆☆

羅夏克墨漬測驗

There are no right or wrong answers in a Rorschach test.

羅夏克墨漬測驗的答案沒有對錯可言。

n. a personality and intelligence test in which a subject interprets inkblot designs in terms that reveal intellectual and emotional factors

2699 schizophrenia [ˌskɪzəˈfrinɪə]

★★★☆☆

精神分裂症

The patient suffering from schizophrenia is usually separated from other people.

罹患精神分裂症的病患通常與其他人隔離。

n. a psychotic disorder characterized by loss of contact with the environment

2700 stimulus [ˈstɪmjələs]

★★★★★

刺激

In education, the principle of the stimulus and response is often employed.

教學上常運用刺激與反應原理。

n. something that rouses or incites to activity

Tea Time... ☕

<Roman story> Decimate
In ancient Rome, Soldiers could be lined up and every tenth(10th) man killed as a method of control.

〈來自羅馬故事〉每十人抽殺一人
在古羅馬時代常命令士兵列隊，每十人抽殺一人，以作為控制手段。（註：這是古羅馬懲治士兵的方式。本字多以被動式「be decimated by」表示。）

＊ **decimate** [ˈdɛsəˌmet] *v.* select by lot and kill every tenth man; destroy ｜ 每十人抽殺一人，大批殺死，殺戮

The enemy soldiers were decimated by the artillery fire.
敵軍遭砲火重擊。

1 Complete each word by filling in the blank with proper spelling so that it has the same meaning as suggested. Then please write the meaning of each word in Chinese.

1. 牙齒咬合不正	=	_ _ _ o c c l u s i o n
2. 減輕	=	_ _ _ _ g a t e
3. 手術	=	_ _ _ _ a t i o n
4. 聽診器	=	s t e t h o _ _ _ _ _
5. 慣性	=	_ _ e r t i a
6. 度量單位	=	m e a _ _ _ _
7. 量子	=	_ _ _ _ t u m
8. 貴族政治	=	_ _ _ _ _ o c r a c y
9. 副手	=	_ _ _ u t y
10. 領事	=	_ _ _ s u l

11. trauma	=	_____
12. ward	=	_____
13. vaccinate	=	_____
14. centrifugal	=	_____
15. torque	=	_____
16. cabinet	=	_____
17. hegemony	=	_____
18. parliament	=	_____
19. status quo	=	_____
20. schizophrenia	=	_____

2 Choose a word that best completes the sentence.

21. The development of medicine has made it possible for doctors to perform an operation without an _____.

(A) independent   (B) id   (C) identity   (D) incision

22. The president was _____ on the first day of this year.

(A) warded   (B) mitigated   (C) inaugurated   (D) measured

3 The highlighted word is closest in meaning to which of the following?

23. James's secession from the labor union was imitated by many other members and led to the disintegration of the union.

(A) libido   (B) withdrawal   (C) stimulus   (D) capitalism

24. The rioters tried to overthrow the government.

(A) overturn   (B) ratify   (C) stopgap   (D) suffrage

25. The toxic gas from the factory exerted a malign effect on its surrounding environment.

(A) stretcher   (B) official   (C) amentia   (D) poisonous

Practice Test 02

1 The highlighted word is closest in meaning to which of the following?

1. **The island nation is taking various measures to preserve** corals **off its coast.**
   (A) reefs
   (B) front
   (C) taiga
   (D) trace

2. **The skin** disorder **was found to be caused by the toxic gases from the neighboring factory.**
   (A) dust
   (B) cyclone
   (C) disease
   (D) emission

3. **An old and infirm person is** susceptible **even to a common cold.**
   (A) fatal
   (B) feeble
   (C) subject
   (D) nautical

4. **The** turmoil **outside the city hall was caused by the mob who was trying to meet the mayor in person.**
   (A) commotion
   (B) horn
   (C) suit
   (D) penalty

5. **Little children are often confused between their** mother language **and a foreign language they are learning.**
   (A) hegemony
   (B) vernacular
   (C) feature
   (D) congestion

2 Please answer the following questions.

> **Comic Tale**
>
> At a Sunday school of a church, a preacher was teaching (1)_____ school kids. He insisted that they get rid of bad habits, especially swearing. He told the children that if they swore, God would punish them and that Santa Claus would never bring them any nice presents at Christmas. While he (2)_____ his sermon, an insect was buzzing around him, finally landing on his nose. He drove it away several times by (3)_____ his face, but the insect returned every time and whirled around his face, bugging him. At last he swatted his nose with his palm, but the agile creature escaped the (4)_____ blow. The preacher (5)_____, "Pray, go away, nice and cute fly! Oops, this is not a fly. My lord, it's a bee! Damn it!"

6. What would be the most appropriate word in blank (1)?

   (A) toxic   (B) feeble

   (C) fatal   (D) elementary

7. What would be the most appropriate word in blank (2)?

   (A) inaugurated   (B) delivered

   (C) measured   (D) mitigated

8. What would be the most appropriate word in blank (3)?

   (A) mitigating   (B) contorting

   (C) afflicting   (D) inaugurating

9. What would be the most appropriate word in blank (4)?

   (A) lethal   (B) susceptible

   (C) subject   (D) nautical

10. What would be the most appropriate word in blank (5)?

   (A) ratified   (B) warded

   (C) delegated   (D) mumbled

Biomimetics

We humans often boast that our bodily functions are peerless amongst all animals on earth. However, this boasting makes sense only within the boundary of efficiency, for there are many different sorts of animal functions surpassing those of human beings.

An ant is capable of returning to its colony even when it is placed as far away as 200m. A fly does not need even a 1mm-long runway to take off or land. We can generally not find a child who cries when a mosquito inserts its blood-sucking needles into the skin, nor can we find a child who does not wail when a nurse inserts a hypodermic syringe into the skin. A bat's hearing is known to be by far more sensitive than radar or sonar. A bat is able to send out 48,000Hz ultrasonic waves and locate its prey and avoid obstacles by using echoes. In a survey, a bat's echolocating ability was tested. In a dark room, 28 fine lines of wire were suspended disorganizingly, and ultrasonic waves similar to a bat's were amplified with 70 loudspeakers. The bat did not hit any of the lines while flying amongst the tangles of them. A cat, even when dropped upside down, is known to be able to right itself in midair. Even though there is no torque imposed on it, a cat, which is remarkably flexible, can twist the front and the rear part of its body in the opposite direction, getting its feet on the ground safe and sound. A dog is said to be able to distinguish and memorize about 500,000 different kinds of smells. Compared to humans, most dogs have an uncomparably keener sense of smell. A dog's nose is efficiently built to allow for greater perceptions of smells. It is shaped so as to allow air to circulate inside towards the sensory areas. The dog's nose is also normally damp to allow for scent particles to dissolve in its nasal secretions. Because of the accuracy of a dog's sense of smell, domestic breeds have been employed to sniff out drugs, firearms, bombs and even edible truffles.

There is also a substance made by an animal and yet regarded as remarkable. A spider's cobweb, if properly synthesized, is believed to be approximately 5 times as strong as steel wire of the same diameter in tensile strength. It is more elastic than nylon, creating for an ideal material, if it can be readily produced in bulk. There have been many scientists who endeavor to unravel the mystery of a spider's silk-making gene. Spider silk could replace materials which are currently used in the manufacture of such items as car bumpers, ligaments, sutures, and even landing cables on aircraft carriers.

As more and more remarkable things surrounding animals are revealed, humans have desired to learn more about animals and their amazing functions and substances. A new branch of science known as biomimetics, aiming at analyzing animals' mysterious substances and behaviors and applying them to the development of science, is getting its momentum. It sure is time for us to learn through nature.

1. **The highlighted word** peerless **can be replaced by which of the following?**
   (A) prominent   (B) matchless
   (C) famous   (D) luxurious

2. **The highlighted word** surpassing **can be replaced by which of the following?**
   (A) patriotic   (B) apathetic
   (C) outdoing   (D) negative

3. **The highlighted word** locate **can be replaced by which of the following?**
   (A) salvage   (B) sedate
   (C) attend   (D) find

4. **The highlighted word** suspended **can be replaced by which of the following?**
   (A) hung   (B) released
   (C) resumed   (D) inhabited

5. **The highlighted word** amplified **can be replaced by which of the following?**
   (A) located   (B) magnified
   (C) adhered   (D) hibernated

6. **The highlighted word** efficiently **can be replaced by which of the following?**
   (A) relentlessly   (B) wisely
   (C) effectively   (D) massively

7. **The highlighted word** dissolve **can be replaced by which of the following?**
   (A) paraphrase   (B) amass
   (C) melt   (D) alleviate

8. **The highlighted word** edible **can be replaced by which of the following?**
   (A) complex   (B) eatable
   (C) nocturnal   (D) plenteous

9. **The highlighted word** synthesized **can be replaced by which of the following?**
   (A) replenished   (B) made
   (C) defied   (D) adhered

10. **The highlighted word** manufacture **can be replaced by which of the following?**
    (A) making   (B) restoration
    (C) innovation   (D) demolition

Passage 2

Superstition

Many Americans do not like to walk under a ladder. Is it because the ladder is so rickety that they fear that it might collapse all of a sudden? Maybe not. It is mainly because of a superstitious belief. Superstitious people think that walking under a ladder will bring bad luck. Superstitions cannot be defined clearly, nor can they be verified through science. Superstitions are often of religious or cultural origin.

There are so many examples of superstitious beliefs around the world that it seems like humans have a genius for creating them. Americans say that if their left hands itch, they will receive a gift. On May Day, some American ladies let their ring pass through a cake and keep the ring under their pillow. They believe by that doing so they can see their future husbands in their dreams. The fear of the number 13 stems from the Bible, which tells us that at the Last Supper there were 13 participants, including Judas. Many tall buildings omit numbered the 13th floor, skipping from 12 to 14. Many superstitious westerners believe that if a black cat crosses the street just in front of them, they will be unlucky. During the medieval period, it was thought that wicked witches could change themselves into black cats. Breaking a mirror is thought to bring seven years of bad luck. A comedian said that an old man aged 90 came to break a mirror while beautifying himself in the morning and jumped up and down with joy. The ancient Romans believed that a mirror reflects a person's soul, and that it takes seven years to renew a person's soul if it is destroyed with the mirror. There is a superstition in Italy that a person should not kill a snake unless the moon is full. Some Italians believe that snakes get drunk on the grapes in the vineyards when the moon is full, and that if they kill them when snakes are sober , bad luck will befall them. Some oriental adults threateningly tell children that if they whistle at night, snakes will come. Or they tell their daughter that if she sits at the corner of a table, she will be a spinster. In China, people never give a clock as a gift, because the word for a clock sounds like the word for a corpse .

There are also superstitious ways and methods through which people believe that they can "more positively" protect themselves from misfortune . Spilling salt while cooking has been thought to bring bad luck, and if the believer of this superstition spills salt, he will take a small amount of salt and throw it over his left shoulder to dispel the evil spirit which is supposedly standing there. Those who have dreamed a bad dream knock on wood to prevent bad things from taking place. The custom of carrying the bride over the threshold and tying cans to the car of the newlyweds probably originated in the hope that those practices would prevent a bad omen or frighten away evil spirits. Amulets and good-luck charms have also been used to ward off evil spirits. In America, a rabbit's foot or a horseshoe have been carried as good-luck charms. In Korea, the patches of cloth cut from a baby's first clothes, rice cakes and even forks have been used to wish examinees good luck. In Japan, folding 1,000 paper cranes has been believed to help fulfill the aspirant's wishes.

11. **The highlighted word** collapse **can be replaced by which of the following?**
    (A) adjust   (B) condone
    (C) conduce   (D) disintegrate

12. **The highlighted word** defined **can be replaced by which of the following?**
    (A) implied   (B) explicated
    (C) defamed   (D) induced

13. **The highlighted word** verified **can be replaced by which of the following?**
    (A) diminished   (B) devalued
    (C) averred   (D) demoted

14. **The highlighted word** genius **can be replaced by which of the following?**
    (A) mettle   (B) guts
    (C) dilettante   (D) gift

15. **The highlighted word** wicked **can be replaced by which of the following?**
    (A) sanctimonious   (B) melancholy
    (C) malevolent   (D) benevolent

16. **The highlighted word** sober **can be replaced by which of the following?**
    (A) serious   (B) not drunk
    (C) grave   (D) not gingerly

17. **The highlighted word** corpse **can be replaced by which of the following?**
    (A) desecration   (B) dead body
    (C) defense   (D) connoisseur

18. **The highlighted word** misfortune **can be replaced by which of the following?**
    (A) cuisine   (B) deadlock
    (C) crusade   (D) catastrophe

19. **The highlighted word** dispel **can be replaced by which of the following?**
    (A) repel   (B) crouch
    (C) crystallize   (D) batter

20. **The highlighted phrase** ward off **can be replaced by which of the following?**
    (A) prevent   (B) protect
    (C) appraise   (D) animate

Building Vocabulary for
iBT, SAT, GRE, TOEIC, GEPT

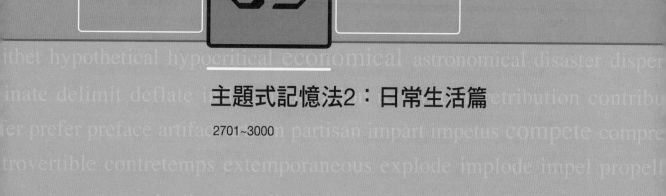

CHAPTER

04

05

Answers

主題式記憶法2：日常生活篇

2701~3000

✦ Airport 機場

【註：本章的錄音方式為先念例句中套色的關鍵單字，接著再念例句。在念完一個主題的實用句後，接著會列出出相關單字的音標和中英文解釋供讀者參閱。】

2701 Is my seat an aisle seat or a window seat?	我的座位是靠走道還是靠窗？
2702 I think I'll have to pick up my baggage at the baggage claim area.	我必須到行李提領區領行李。
2703 Please show me your boarding pass.	請讓我看看你的登機證。
2704 The business class is almost twice as expensive as the economy class.	商務艙幾乎比經濟艙貴兩倍。
2705 A stewardess does her best to serve all passengers in the cabin.	女空服員盡心服務機艙所有旅客。
2706 I need to pick up my bag at the carousel.	我必須到行李轉盤提領行李。
2707 How many carry-on bags can I carry?	我可以攜帶幾件隨身行李？
2708 You need to insert a coin to use this cart.	你要投幣才能使用手推車。
2709 Passengers are not allowed in the cockpit.	旅客不許進入駕駛艙。
2710 Air traffic controllers in a control tower control air traffic.	塔台管制員進行飛航管制。
2711 A customs officer at the airport asked me if anybody had asked me to carry his luggage.	機場海關人員問我是否有人請我代提行李。
2712 Flight 707 from San Francisco is delayed.	從舊金山起飛的七〇七號班機延誤。
2713 We can see many people shedding tears at the departure gate.	我們可以看見許多人在出境大門流淚話別。
2714 I found the prices at the duty-free shop were so low.	我發現免稅店商品售價很低廉。
2715 In the case of an emergency, you should exit the plane according to the emergency protocol.	發生緊急情況時，應根據緊急應變計畫從飛機撤離。
2716 It is difficult to become a flight attendant because qualifications are pretty high.	由於資格要求很高，要成為空服員很難。
2717 All the passengers for Chicago, please go to gate No. 5.	前往芝加哥的旅客請至五號登機門。
2718 Did you get over your jet lag?	你的時差調過來了嗎？
2719 The landing of my plane was so smooth. All the passengers felt comfortable.	我的班機順利降落，所有旅客都感到安心。
2720 Does this airport limousine go to the Hilton Hotel?	請問這輛機場接駁巴士有到希爾頓飯店嗎？
2721 He could not put his bag in the overhead compartment because the bag was too big.	他的行李太大，無法放進頭頂上方置物櫃。
2722 The passport that the gangster was carrying was found to be a forgery.	歹徒所持護照經發現是偽造的。
2723 I think I had better have a porter carry my bags.	我想我最好請行李搬運員幫忙提行李。
2724 The runway is cleared. Now we are going to take off.	機場跑道已清除，現在我們即將起飛。
2725 The old lady was afraid of passing through the security check point.	老太太怕通過安檢站。
2726 It would be more convenient for me to take the shuttle bus to the air terminal.	搭乘接駁車前往機場航廈會比較方便。
2727 It takes less time to go to the States because of the tailwind.	搭機赴美所需時間較短，因為是順風飛行。
2728 You should fasten your seat belts during the takeoff and landing.	班機起降時應繫好安全帶。

²⁷²⁹ The plane was taxiing on the taxiway to approach the runway.	飛機在滑行道上滑行並接近跑道。
²⁷³⁰ This air terminal has more than 100 gates.	機場航廈有超過一百個登機門。
²⁷³¹ Could you please help me pull out the tray table?	請你幫我把折疊餐桌拉出來好嗎？
²⁷³² Please put me on the waiting list.	請將我放入後補名單中。

★★★★★

²⁷⁰¹ **aisle seat** [`aɪl sit]　　走道座位
n. a seat next to a passageway or walkway

★★★★★

²⁷⁰² **baggage claim area** [`bægɪdʒ klem `ɛrɪə]　　行李提領區
n. an area where people claim their baggage

★★★★★

²⁷⁰³ **boarding pass** [`bordɪŋ pæs]　　登機證
n. a pass for boarding a plane

★★★★★

²⁷⁰⁴ **business class** [`bɪznɪs klæs]　　商務艙
n. business class

★★★★★

²⁷⁰⁵ **cabin** [`kæbɪn]　　機艙
n. the passenger or cargo compartment

★★★★★

²⁷⁰⁶ **carousel** [ˌkæru`zɛl]　　行李轉盤，行李輸送帶
n. a circular conveyor

★★★★★

²⁷⁰⁷ **carry-on bag** [`kærɪˌɑn bæg]　　隨身行李
n. a piece of luggage suitable for being carried aboard an airplane by a passenger

★★★★★

²⁷⁰⁸ **cart** [kɑrt]　　手推車
n. a small wheeled vehicle

★★★☆☆

²⁷⁰⁹ **cockpit** [`kɑkˌpɪt]　　駕駛艙，座艙
n. a space or compartment in a usually small vehicle (as a boat, airplane, or automobile) from which it is steered, piloted, or driven

★★★★☆

2710 control tower [kən`trol `tauə]

n. a tower where air traffic controllers control traffic

管制塔台

★★★★★

2711 customs officer [`kʌstəmz `ɔfəsə]

n. customs official

海關人員

★★★★★

2712 delay [dɪ`le]

v. stop, detain, or hinder for a time

延誤

★★★★★

2713 departure [dɪ`partʃə]

n. departing

出境

★★★★★

2714 duty-free shop [`djutɪ`fri ʃap]

n. a shop selling duty-free goods

免稅店

★★★☆☆

2715 emergency protocol [ɪ`mɝdʒənsɪ `protə,kɑl]

n. a detailed plan of a scientific or medical experiment, treatment, or procedure

緊急應變計畫

★★★★★

2716 flight attendant [flaɪt ə`tɛndənt]

n. a person who attends passengers on an airplane

空服員

★★★★★

2717 gate [get]

n. a means of entrance or exit

登機門

★★★★★

2718 jet lag [dʒɛt læg]

n. a condition that occurs following long flight through several time zones, and probably results from disruption of circadian rhythms in the human body

時差

★★★★★

2719 landing [`lændɪŋ]

n. going or bringing to a surface (as land or shore) after a voyage or flight

降落

★★★★★

2720 airport limousine [`ɛr,port `lɪmə,zin]

n. a large vehicle for transporting passengers to and from an airport

機場接駁巴士

★★★★

²⁷²¹ **overhead compartment** [`ovə`hɛd kəm`partmənt]　頭頂上方置物櫃
n. overhead bin

★★★★★

²⁷²² **passport** [`pæs‚pɔrt]　護照
n. a permission or authorization to go somewhere

★★★★★

²⁷²³ **porter** [`pɔrtə]　行李搬運員
n. a person who carries burdens

★★★★★

²⁷²⁴ **runway** [`rʌn‚we]　跑道
n. a paved strip of ground on a landing field for the landing and takeoff of aircraft

★★★☆☆

²⁷²⁵ **security check** [sɪ`kjurətɪ tʃɛk]　安全檢查
n. measures taken to guard against espionage or sabotage, crime, attack, or escape

★★★★★

²⁷²⁶ **shuttle** [`ʃʌtl̩]　接駁車
n. a vehicle used to shuttle

★★☆☆☆

²⁷²⁷ **tailwind** [`tel‚wɪnd]　順風
n. a wind having the same general direction as a course of movement

★★★★★

²⁷²⁸ **takeoff** [`tekɔf]　起飛
n. a rise or leap from a surface in making a jump or flight

★★★★★

²⁷²⁹ **taxiway** [`tæksɪ‚we]　飛機滑行道
n. a usually paved strip for taxiing, as from the terminal to a runway at an airport

★★★★★

²⁷³⁰ **terminal** [`tɜmənl̩]　機場航廈
n. airport

★★★☆☆

²⁷³¹ **tray table** [tre `tebl̩]　折疊餐桌
n. a table on which to place a tray

2732 waiting list [ˋwetɪŋ lɪst]

n. a list or roster of those waiting, as for admission

後補名單

✤ **Animals** 動物

2733	He was grinning like an ape.	他像隻猿猴般露齒而笑。
2734	Do not make an ass of him.	別出他洋相。
2735	Many animals in a desert spend the day in a burrow.	許多沙漠動物白天都待在地洞裡。
2736	A chameleon camouflages itself by changing its body color.	變色龍靠改變身體顏色來偽裝自己。
2737	Unlike most species of bats, this bat is diurnal.	這隻蝙蝠是晝行性的，和絕大多數品種不同。
2738	A grizzly bear lies dormant during the winter.	大灰熊在冬季冬眠。
2739	There is a lake at which many different kinds of fowl gather together.	湖畔聚集了許多不同種類的飛禽。
2740	A hare can easily run up the slope of a mountain because it has long hind legs.	野兔後腳長，能輕易跳上山坡。
2741	Animals that hibernate in a burrow should get enough nutrition during the autumn.	在洞穴冬眠的動物須在秋天攝取足夠食物。
2742	The skin of a leopard has often been used as a luxurioush rug.	美洲豹皮常被用來當作豪華地毯。
2743	A mole is blind, but it is able to tell the difference between light and darkness.	鼴鼠雖然看不見，卻能分辨明暗。
2744	The child was hard to control. Actually, he was as obstinate as a mule.	這孩子很難管教，事實上他固執得像頭驢子。
2745	An otter is a largely aquatic carnivorous mammal of the weasel family.	水獺基本上是鼬科水棲肉食哺乳動物。
2746	Judging from its flabby body posture, this monkey seems to be pretty sick.	從鬆軟無力的體態研判，這隻猴子似乎病得不輕。
2747	The rate of the propagation of wolves in this area has decreased.	此區狼的繁殖率已下降。
2748	The rate of reproduction of alligators in Florida has been recovered.	佛羅里達州短吻鱷的繁殖率已有所提升。
2749	The preservation of wildlife is vital for maintaining the ecological balance.	為維持生態平衡，野生動物保育是極為重要的。

2733 ape [ep]

n. a large monkey

猿猴

2734 ass [æs]

n. an African mammal that is the ancestor of the donkey

驢子

★★★★☆

2735 burrow [ˋbɝo]
n. hole; cave

洞穴，地洞

★★★★☆

2736 camouflage [ˋkæməˌflɑʒ]
v. conceal or disguise by camouflage

偽裝，掩飾

★★★☆☆

2737 diurnal [daɪˋɝn̩]
a. active chiefly in the daytime

晝行性的，日間活動的

★★★★★

2738 dormant [ˋdɔrmənt]
a. inactive; latent

冬眠的，睡著的

★★★★☆

2739 fowl [faʊl]
n. birds

飛禽

Reference...

- coot n. 大鷸	- magpie n. 喜鵲
- crow n. 烏鴉	- nightingale n. 夜鶯
- dove n. 鴿	- owl n. 貓頭鷹
- falcon n. 隼	- pigeon n. 鴿子
- grouse n. 松雞	- sparrow n. 麻雀
- hawk n. 鷹	- turkey n. 火雞
- lark n. 雲雀	

★★☆☆☆

2740 hare [hɛr]
n. any of various swift long-eared lagomorph mammals

野兔

★★★★☆

2741 hibernate [ˋhaɪbɚˌnet]
v. lie dormant

冬眠

★★★★☆

2742 leopard [ˋlɛpɚd]
n. panther

美洲豹

★★★★☆

2743 mole [mol]
n. any of numerous burrowing insectivores with tiny eyes, concealed ears, and soft fur

鼴鼠，田鼠

★★★☆☆

2744 mule [mjul]
n. a hybrid between a horse and a donkey

騾子

★★★☆☆

2745 otter [ˋɑtɚ]
v. an aquatic carnivorous mammal that falls into the weasel family

水獺

★★★☆☆

2746 posture [ˋpɑstʃɚ]
n. the position or bearing of the body, whether characteristic or assumed, for a special purpose

姿勢，姿態

★★★☆☆

2747 propagation [ˌprɑpəˋgeʃən]
n. increase (as of a kind of organism) in numbers

繁殖

★★★★☆

2748 reproduction [ˌriprəˋdʌkʃən]
n. propagation

繁殖

★★★★★

2749 wildlife [ˋwaɪldˌlaɪf]
n. life forms in the wild

野生動物

✦ **Body** 身體

2750 The vermiform appendix is a blind tube that extends from the cecum in the lower right-hand part of the abdomen, and it was often thought of as a useless relic.	闌尾是一條不通的細管，從右下腹部盲腸延伸出來，常被視為無用的殘存器官。
2751 An artery is a vessel which carries blood from the heart through the body.	動脈是從心臟運送血液到全身的血管。
2752 The atrium receives blood from the veins, and forces it into the ventricle.	靜脈的血液回流到心房後，再壓縮到心室內。
2753 Marilyn Monroe was often called a "blonde bombshell."	瑪麗蓮·夢露常被稱為「金髮美人」。
2754 My calf muscles are sore. Yesterday I walked more than 10 miles.	我昨天步行超過十英里，所以小腿肌肉痠痛。
2755 He has plenty of cheek. He is asking for more money.	他厚著臉皮要求更多錢。
2756 Chin up! You have another chance to try.	振作起來！還有機會可以一試。
2757 Many ladies wish to have long ciliation.	許多女士希望有長長的睫毛。
2758 The inflammation of the conjunctiva is often caused by polluted air.	結膜炎通常是由髒污空氣引起的。
2759 A cornea covers the iris and pupil, and admits light to the interior.	眼角膜覆蓋虹膜和瞳孔，並使光線進入眼裡。

2760 An esophagus is the part of the body that carries foods from the throat to the stomach.
食道是身體的一部分,將食物從咽喉傳送到胃中。

2761 His wife had an operation in which she had her gall bladder removed.
他的妻子接受膽囊切除手術。

2762 Worker bees build cells as their wax-producing glands become functional.
工蜂的蠟腺發育成熟後,就開始築蜂巢房。

2763 The excessive secretion of gastric juices in the gut causes ulcers.
腸內過多的胃液分泌物導致潰瘍。

2764 An intestine is the tubular part of the alimentary canal extending from the stomach to the anus.
腸是消化道內的管狀構造,從胃延伸到肛門。

2765 An iris is the opaque contractile diaphragm perforated by the pupil, and it forms the colored portion of the eye.
能收縮的虹膜是不透明隔膜,中心的圓形開口是瞳孔,並構成眼睛的顏色。

2766 Most of the female students in my class envy Jane's long eye lashes.
班上許多女學生都羨慕珍的長睫毛。

2767 Lids are the movable folds of skin which can be closed over the eyeball.
眼瞼是覆蓋在眼球上的皮膚皺褶,可自動開合。

2768 Kidneys are bean-shaped organs that excrete waste products of metabolism.
腎臟是狀似扁豆的器官,負責排出人體新陳代謝後的廢物。

2769 A liver secretes bile and causes important changes in many of the substances which are contained in the blood.
肝臟分泌膽汁,能對血液內所含物質產生重要變化。

2770 At the top of the mountain we shouted at the top of our lungs.
我們在山巔上放聲大叫。

2771 Unlike incisors, molars with rounded or flattened surfaces are used for grinding foods.
臼齒和門牙不同,其或圓或平的表面可用來咀嚼磨碎食物。

2772 I think my dog is in bad shape, seeing that it has some eye mucus.
我覺得我的狗生病了,因為它有一些眼睛分泌物。

2773 Nerves connect parts of the nervous system with the other organs.
神經纖維將神經系統與其他器官連結起來。

2774 We need to ingest enough food for good nutrition.
我們需攝取足夠食物以獲得完整營養。

2775 The pupils of our eyes contract when exposed to light.
眼睛瞳孔接觸到光線就會收縮。

2776 A rectum is the terminal part of the intestine from the sigmoid colon to the anus.
直腸位於乙狀結腸到肛門之間的消化道最末端。

2777 The retina is the light-sensitive layer of tissue at the back of the inner eye, and it acts like film in a camera.
視網膜是位於眼球後方的感光層組織,作用如同相機底片。

2778 The sclera is the white outer wall of the eye.
鞏膜是眼球壁最外層的白色纖維膜。

2779 I think I'll have to go see the doctor. I have a sore throat.
我喉嚨痛必須去看醫生。

2780 His problems with the respiratory tract were probably caused by his heavy smoking.
他的呼吸道毛病可能是來自煙癮太大。

2781 A ventricle receives blood from an atrium and forces it into the arteries.
心房的血液流到心室後,再壓縮到動脈裡。

★★★★☆

2750 **appendix** [əˋpɛndɪks]
　　n. a narrow blind tube at the end of the cecum
闌尾,盲腸

★★★★☆

2751 artery [`ɑrtərɪ]   動脈

n. a vessel that carries blood from the heart through the body

★★☆☆☆

2752 atrium [`etrɪəm]   心房

n. the chamber of the heart that receives blood from the veins

★★★★★

2753 blonde [blɑnd]   金髮

n. pale yellowish-brown color; blonde hair

★★☆☆☆

2754 calf [kæf]   小腿

n. the anterior part of the leg below the knee

★★★★★

2755 cheek [tʃik]   臉頰

n. the fleshy side of the face

★★★★★

2756 chin [tʃɪn]   下巴

n. the lower portion of the face

★★☆☆☆

2757 ciliation [sɪlɪ`eʃən]   睫毛

n. cilia

★★☆☆☆

2758 conjunctiva [ˌkɑndʒʌŋk`taɪvə]   結膜

n. the mucous membrane that lines the inner surface of the eyelids

★★★☆☆

2759 cornea [`kɔrnɪə]   眼角膜

n. the transparent part of the coat of the eyeball

★★☆☆☆

2760 esophagus [ɪ`sɑfəgəs]   食道

n. a muscular tube that carries food to the stomach

★★☆☆☆

2761 gall [gɔl]   膽汁

n. bile

★★★★☆

²⁷⁶² **gland** [glænd]　　　　　　　　　　　　　　　　腺

n. *any of various secreting organs*

> - endocrine gland **n.** 內分泌腺
> - exocrine gland **n.** 外分泌腺
> - lymph gland **n.** 淋巴腺
> - mammary gland **n.** 乳腺
> - pancreas **n.** 胰腺
> - pituitary gland **n.** 腦下垂體
>
> - suprarenal gland **n.** 腎上腺
> - sweat gland **n.** 汗腺
> - adrenal gland **n.** 副腎腺
> - thymus **n.** 胸腺
> - thyroid gland **n.** 甲狀腺

★★★★☆

²⁷⁶³ **gut** [gʌt]　　　　　　　　　　　　　　　　腸，消化道

n. *the tube through which food passes from your stomach*

★★★★★

²⁷⁶⁴ **intestine** [ɪnˋtɛstɪn]　　　　　　　　　　　　腸

n. *the long tube in your body through which food passes after it leaves your stomach*

★★★★☆

²⁷⁶⁵ **iris** [ˋaɪrɪs]　　　　　　　　　　　　　　　　虹膜

n. *the colored portion of the eye*

★★★★☆

²⁷⁶⁶ **lash** [læʃ]　　　　　　　　　　　　　　　　眼睫毛

n. *eye lash*

★★★★☆

²⁷⁶⁷ **lid** [lɪd]　　　　　　　　　　　　　　　　眼瞼

n. *eye lid*

★★★★★

²⁷⁶⁸ **kidney** [ˋkɪdnɪ]　　　　　　　　　　　　　腎臟

n. *an organ in the body cavity near the spinal column that excretes waste products of metabolism*

★★★★★

²⁷⁶⁹ **liver** [ˋlɪvɚ]　　　　　　　　　　　　　　　肝臟

n. *a large very vascular glandular organ*

★★★★★

²⁷⁷⁰ **lungs** [lʌŋz]　　　　　　　　　　　　　肺臟（註：通常作複數形）

n. *one of the usually paired compound saccular thoracic organs which constitute the basic respiratory organs of air-breathing vertebrates*

★★☆☆☆

2771 molar [`molɚ]

n. a tooth with a rounded or flattened surface adapted for grinding

臼齒

- canine n. 犬齒
- denture n. 假牙
- incisor n. 門牙

- milk tooth n. 乳齒 (= deciduous tooth)
- wisdom tooth n. 智齒

★★☆☆☆

2772 mucus [`mjukəs]

n. a viscid slippery secretion in the eye

眼睛分泌物，黏液

★★★★★

2773 nerve [nɝv]

n. any of the filamentous bands of nervous tissues

神經，神經纖維

★★★★★

2774 nutrition [nju`trɪʃən]

n. the act or process of nourishing

營養

Fare（菜色類）
- appetizer n. 開胃菜
- apple pie n. 蘋果派
- baked potato n. 烤洋芋
- caviar n. 魚子醬
- cooked rice n. 米飯
- escargot n. 法式田螺
- fried clam n. 油煎蛤蜊
- french fries n. 炸薯條
- fruit cocktail n. 什錦水果沙拉
- hero sandwich n. 巨無霸三明治
- jello n. 果凍
- meatball n. 肉丸
- noodle n. 麵條
- onion rings n. 洋蔥圈
- pickle n. 酸黃瓜
- pork chop n. 豬排
- pretzel n. 蝴蝶餅，扭結餅
- relish n. 開胃菜，佐料
- roast beef sandwich n. 煙燻牛肉三明治
- shrimp cocktail n. 雞尾酒蝦
- spaghetti n. 義大利麵
- submarine sandwich n. 潛艇堡
- tossed salad n. 生菜沙拉

Fruits and Vegetables（蔬果類）
- artichoke n. 朝鮮薊
- avocado n. 酪梨
- breadfruit n. 麵包果
- broccoli n. 綠色花椰菜
- cabbage n. 甘藍菜
- cantaloupe n. 香瓜
- cauliflower n. 白色花椰菜
- celery n. 芹菜
- chicory n. 菊苣
- cucumber n. 黃瓜
- eggplant n. 茄子
- garlic n. 大蒜
- ginger n. 薑
- grapefruit n. 葡萄柚
- kale n. 甘藍菜
- leek n. 韭菜
- lettuce n. 萵苣
- manioc n. 樹薯
- mustard n. 芥菜
- pea n. 豌豆
- pimiento n. 紅椒
- plum n. 李子，梅子
- pumpkin n. 南瓜

- radish n. 蘿蔔
- spinach n. 菠菜
- squash n. 節瓜
- sweet potato n. 蕃薯，地瓜

- taro n. 芋頭
- turnip n. 蕪菁
- yam n. 山藥

★★★★☆

2775 pupil [ˋpjupl̩]　　　　　　　　　　　瞳孔
n. the contractile aperture in the iris of the eye

★★★★☆

2776 rectum [ˋrɛktəm]　　　　　　　　　直腸
n. straight intestine

★★★★☆

2777 retina [ˋrɛtn̩ə]　　　　　　　　　　視網膜
n. the sensory membrane that lines the eye

★★☆☆☆

2778 sclera [ˋsklɪrə]　　　　　　　　　　鞏膜
n. the dense fibrous opaque white outer coat enclosing the
eyeball except the part covered by the cornea

★★★★★

2779 throat [θrot]　　　　　　　　　　　咽喉，喉嚨
n. the part of the neck in front of the spinal column

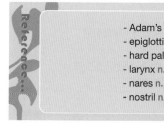

- Adam's apple n. 喉結
- epiglottis n. 會厭軟骨
- hard palate n. 硬顎
- larynx n. 喉頭
- nares n. 鼻孔（註：單數為 naris）
- nostril n. 鼻孔

- olfaction n. 嗅覺
- soft palate n. 軟顎
- velum n. 軟顎
- vestibule n. 前庭
- vocal cord n. 聲帶

★★★★★

2780 tract [trækt]　　　　　　　　　　　道
n. a system of body parts or organs that act together to
perform some function

★★☆☆☆

2781 ventricle [ˋvɛntrɪkl̩]　　　　　　　心室
n. a chamber of the heart which receives blood from a
corresponding atrium

✧ Films 電影

2782 A father buying tickets at the boxoffice said, "Three beauties and one beast, please."	一位父親在戲院售票口買票,並說:「請給我三張美女票,一張野獸票。」
2783 During the previous government, many people complained about strict censorship.	在前政府主政時期,許多民眾抱怨嚴格的電影審查制度。
2784 The invention of a cinematograph drastically changed the way people spent their leisure time.	電影技術的發明大大改變人們的休閒方式。
2785 A documentary film about the war was shown to the visitors at the war memorial hall.	戰爭紀念館放映戰爭紀錄片供遊客觀賞。
2786 A double feature is a movie program with two main films.	兩場連映是指一次放映兩部影片。
2787 What time is the first run?	何時放映首輪片?
2788 The full shot of the spectacular landscape in the movie was impressive.	電影中的壯麗全景令人印象深刻。
2789 Because of the hype for the movie, many spectators rushed to the theater.	許多觀眾因造勢宣傳而湧進戲院看電影。
2790 The fuzzy image made it difficult for me to tell which was which.	模糊的影像讓我很難分辨哪個是哪個。
2791 The kinetoscope, invented by Edison, allowed only one person at a time to see a sequence of pictures.	愛迪生發明的西洋鏡觀影機一次只能容許一個人觀看連續影片。
2792 A montage is a technique of film editing in which a series of short stories is edited to make a sequence of narratives.	蒙太奇是將一系列短片剪輯成連續性故事的電影剪接技術。
2793 The movie producer needed to buy some suits of armor as props for the movie.	電影製片需為電影添購幾副盔甲道具。
2794 The movie shown at the film festival got a good puff.	影展上放映的電影獲得好評。
2795 The spectacular scene needed a shot at a long range.	壯麗的景色需透過遠距拍攝。
2796 The synchronous recording was very difficult. Unnecessary noises were also included.	同步錄音很難做到,因為連不必要的雜音也會被收錄進去。
2797 The newly released film was a great success at the box office.	最新上映的電影創下極高票房。
2798 The running time of *The Sound of Music* is 172 minutes.	《真善美》片長一百七十二分鐘。
2799 The writer of the scenario sets up each individual camera shot.	編劇為每個拍攝鏡頭進行分鏡。
2800 Most of the first movies in movie history were short subjects lasting less than 30 minutes	電影史上多數早期電影都是不到三十分鐘長的短片。
2801 Until 1927, movies were all silent.	在一九二七年前電影都是默片。
2802 Tom Hanks was a famous personality who starred in *Forrest Gump*.	湯姆・漢克是主演《阿甘正傳》的知名演員。
2803 My grandmother had difficulty understanding the foreign movie because there were no subtitles.	我的祖母看不懂外語片,因為沒有字幕。

★★★★★

2782 boxoffice [ˋbɑksˏɔfɪs]
n. an office where tickets of admission are sold

售票口,票房收入

★★★★★

²⁷⁸³ **censorship** [ˈsɛnsəˌʃɪp]　　　　　　　　　　　　　　檢查制度，審查制度
　　　n. the practice or system of censoring something

★★☆☆☆

²⁷⁸⁴ **cinematograph** [ˌsɪnəˈmætəˌgræf]　　　　　　　　電影放映機，電影技術
　　　n. a motion-picture camera and projector

★★★★★

²⁷⁸⁵ **documentary** [ˌdɑkjəˈmɛntərɪ]　　　　　　　　　電影記錄的，記實的 / 紀錄片
　　　a. a factual film / *n.* a documentary presentation

★★★★★

²⁷⁸⁶ **feature** [ˈfitʃɚ]　　　　　　　　　　　　　　　　影片
　　　n. a movie program

★★★☆☆

²⁷⁸⁷ **first run** [fɜst rʌn]　　　　　　　　　　　　　　首輪放映，首輪戲院
　　　n. exhibiting first-run movies

★★☆☆☆

²⁷⁸⁸ **full shot** [ful ʃɑt]　　　　　　　　　　　　　　全景
　　　n. a full photographic exposure

★★☆☆☆

²⁷⁸⁹ **hype** [haɪp]　　　　　　　　　　　　　　　　　公開宣傳
　　　n. promotional publicity of an extravagant or contrived
　　　kind

★★★★★

²⁷⁹⁰ **image** [ˈɪmɪdʒ]　　　　　　　　　　　　　　　　影像
　　　n. visible representation

★★★☆☆

²⁷⁹¹ **kinetoscope** [kɪˈnitəˌskop]　　　　　　　　　　西洋鏡觀影機
　　　n. a device for viewing through a magnifying lens a
　　　sequence of pictures

★★☆☆☆

²⁷⁹² **montage** [mɑnˈtɑʒ]　　　　　　　　　　　　　　蒙太奇
　　　n. a composite picture made by combining several
　　　separate pictures

★★★☆☆

²⁷⁹³ **props** [prɑps]　　　　　　　　　　　　　　　　道具（註：通常作複數形）
　　　n. something used in creating or enhancing a desired
　　　effect

★☆☆☆☆

2794 puff [pʌf]
n. a commendatory or promotional notice or review

吹捧，誇讚

★★★★☆

2795 range [rendʒ]
n. scope; extent / *v.* extend

距離 / 延伸

★★★★★

2796 recording [rɪˋkɔrdɪŋ]
n. the electrical or mechanical inscription of sound waves

錄音

★★★★★

2797 release [rɪˋlis]
n. the act of permitting performance or publication /
v. perform

放映 / 上映

★★★★☆

2798 running time [ˋrʌnɪŋ taɪm]
n. the duration of a motion picture, a theatrical
performance, or a recording

片長

★★★★★

2799 scenario [sɪˋnɛrɪˏo]
n. shooting script; screenplay

情節，劇本

★★☆☆☆

2800 short subject [ʃɔrt ˋsʌbdʒɪkt]
n. short film

短片

★★★☆☆

2801 silent film [ˋsaɪlənt fɪlm]
n. a movie with no sounds

默片

★★★★★

2802 star [stɑr]
n. a fellow star in a film, play, etc.

明星

★★★★★

2803 subtitle [ˋsʌbˏtaɪtl]
n. a printed translation of the dialogue of foreign film that
appears bit by bit at the bottom of the frame

字幕

MP3
115

✣ **Fish & Fishing** 魚與釣魚

2804 In this nation, only the angler with a permit is allowed to angle.	在這個國家，只有領有執照的釣客可以釣魚。
2805 In this nation, using an earthworm as a bait is illegal.	在這個國家，以蚯蚓為魚餌為非法的。
2806 A fish's bladder contains air in it.	魚鰾裡含有空氣。
2807 The angler put the fish he caught in the coop.	釣客將釣到的魚放進籠裡。
2808 A shark's fin is people's favorite food at a Chinese restaurant.	魚翅是中國餐館裡最受歡迎的一道菜。
2809 We decided to use a hackle fly.	我們決定使用簑毛鉤。
2810 A fish breathes through the gills.	魚以鰓呼吸。
2811 An anglerfish has its own hook and line.	釣琵琶魚有專屬釣鉤和釣線。
2812 The lateral line of a fish is connected to sense organs which are sensitive to low vibrations.	魚的體側線和感覺器官相連，能感應低淺的振動。
2813 A lure which is often designed to resemble fish prey is attached to the end of the fishing line.	釣線的尾端繫著用來作為類似魚類食物的魚餌。
2814 A shark's maxillary is known to be powerful enough to break a skull.	眾所周知鯊魚的上頜骨相當有力，足以咬碎頭蓋骨。

★★★★★

2804 angler [ˋæŋglə]　　　　　　　　　　　　　　垂釣客，釣者
　　n. one that angles

★★★★★

2805 bait [bet]　　　　　　　　　　　　　　　　餌，誘餌
　　n. something (as food) used in luring, especially to a hook or trap

★★★☆☆

2806 bladder [ˋblædə]　　　　　　　　　　　　　膀胱
　　n. a membranous sac in animals that serves as the receptacle of a liquid or contains gas

★★☆☆☆

2807 coop [kup]　　　　　　　　　　　　　　　　籠子
　　a. a cage or small enclosure

★★★★☆

2808 fin [fɪn]　　　　　　　　　　　　　　　　　鰭
　　n. an external membranous appendage of an aquatic animal

★★★☆☆

2809 fly [flaɪ]　　　　　　　　　　　　　　　　蟲形魚鉤
　　n. a fishhook dressed (as with feathers or tinsel) to suggest an insect

★★★☆☆

2810 gill [gɪl]

鰓

n. an organ (as of a fish) for obtaining oxygen from water

★★★★★

2811 hook [hʊk]

釣魚鉤

n. a curved or bent device for catching, holding, or pulling

★★★☆☆

2812 lateral line [ˋlætərəl laɪn]

側線

n. a canal along the side of a fish

★★★★★

2813 lure [lʊr]

誘餌，魚餌

n. bait

★★☆☆☆

2814 maxillary [ˋmæksəˌlɛrɪ]

上頜骨

n. jaw

Tea Time... ☕

\<From the name of a minister\> **Spoonerism** **After Rev, William A. Spooner (1844-1930), of New College, Oxford, who was noted for such slips.**	〈來自一牧師之名〉兩字以上的頭音互換 本字源自以常犯這種錯誤聞名的牛津大學新學院牧師威廉・A・史本納（1844-1930）。（註：這類錯置不是出於故意，但顛倒後常產生意想不到的「笑」果。）

✱ **spoonerism** [ˋspunərɪzəm] *n. an unintentional interchange of sounds, usually initial sounds, in two or more words ex.)* '*well-oiled bicycle*' → '*well-boiled icicle*' │ 兩字以上的頭音互換

A spoonerism is a slip made by a speaker in which the first sounds of two words are changed over, often with a humorous result. An example; "our dear old queen" for "our queer old dean."

頭音互換錯誤指的是說話者誤將兩字的頭音互相顛倒，因而產生滑稽結果。例如把「我們親愛的老女王」講成「我們古怪的老院長」。

1

Complete each word by filling in the blank with proper spelling so that it has the same meaning as suggested. Then please write the meaning of each word in Chinese.

1. 行李轉盤   = ___ o u s e l   11. mole   = _____
2. 手推車   = c a __   12. mule   = _____
3. 駕駛艙   = ____ p i t   13. propagation = _____
4. 出境   = d e ____ u r e   14. camouflage = _____
5. 降落   = ____ i n g   15. diurnal   = _____
6. 行李搬運員   = ____ e r   16. fowl   = _____
7. 順風   = t a i l ____   17. otter   = _____
8. 洞穴   = ___ r o w   18. posture   = _____
9. 冬眠的   = ____ a n t   19. reproduction = _____
10. 冬眠   = _____ a t e   20. wildlife   = _____

2

Choose a word that best completes the sentence.

21. When did you come back? Did you get over your _____?
   (A) passport   (B) jet lag   (C) landing   (D) takeoff

22. Could you please help me to put this bag in the _____?
   (A) overhead compartment   (B) emergency protocol
   (C) tailwind   (D) reproduction

23. A mammal breathes through lungs, while a fish through _____.
   (A) maxillary   (B) gills   (C) fins   (D) retinas

24. A(n) _____ is a tooth for grinding foods.
   (A) incisor   (B) pupil   (C) iris   (D) molar

25. His heavy smoking has caused some problems to his respiratory _____.
   (A) nutrition   (B) gland   (C) tract   (D) gall

Practice Test 01

1 The highlighted word is closest in meaning to which of the following?

1. We should ingest enough food to get sufficient nutrition .
   - (A) nourishment
   - (B) kidney
   - (C) appetizer
   - (D) retina

2. An animal that hibernates should eat enough food during the autumn.
   - (A) increases in number
   - (B) lies dormant
   - (C) ordains
   - (D) orbits

3. The scenario of the movie was written by a world-famous novelist.
   - (A) prop
   - (B) subtitle
   - (C) screenplay
   - (D) image

4. Many young people in the country are strongly against the strict censorship on films.
   - (A) documentary
   - (B) feature
   - (C) montage
   - (D) gag

5. A lure is attached to the end of the fishing line.
   - (A) coop
   - (B) bladder
   - (C) bait
   - (D) angler

2 Please answer the following questions.

Comic Tale

Bad habits die hard.

Once upon a time, there lived three young farmers in a small village in Wyoming. They were close friends and liked to help one another in doing many things. They used to sow seeds and harvest the fields together. By the way, strangely enough, each of them had a peculiar habit. John, the oldest of the three, had a habit of scratching his head. No one could (1)_____ him from scratching his head for a single minute. Nick had another peculiar habit. He continuously wiped his nose with his sleeve because of his runny nose. The

youngest of the three was Henry. He was in the habit of scratching his back and shoulders.

One summer day, while they were taking a rest under a shady tree, they decided to make a bet. Whoever could stay still the longest without (2)_____ to his habit was supposed to win the bet. They were staring at one another, trying to (3)_____ their itches.

Five minutes had hardly passed when John broke the silence. "Last week I saw a (4)_____ deer around here. It had nice antlers here and here." Saying this, John continued (5)_____ his head "here" and there with his thumb.

At that moment Nick lost no time to say, "Really? If I had seen the deer, I could have shot it with a bow and arrow like this." Saying this, he wiped his nose with his sleeve.

Taking advantage of the chance, Henry blurted, "If I had been there, I could have carried the dead deer on my shoulder." Saying this, he scratched his shoulder.

6. What would be the most appropriate word in blank (1)?
(A) allure
(B) prevent
(C) release
(D) persuade

7. What would be the most appropriate word in blank (2)?
(A) adapting
(B) adjusting
(C) reporting
(D) resorting

8. What would be the most appropriate word in blank (3)?
(A) erode
(B) excavate
(C) suppress
(D) subvert

9. What would be the most appropriate word in blank (4)?
(A) toxic
(B) giant
(C) terminal
(D) carnivorous

10. What would be the most appropriate word in blank (5)?
(A) replacing
(B) aborting
(C) scratching
(D) outdoing

✣ Journalism 新聞

2815 We hope that our magazine will outdistance the circulation of our competitor.	希望我們的雜誌發行量能遠超過競爭對手。
2816 My uncle is a columnist for a daily newspaper.	我舅舅是日報專欄作家。
2817 I cannot stand obscene TV commercials.	我不能忍受猥褻的電視廣告。
2818 A correspondent is an on-the-scene reporter who contributes reports to a newspaper, radio or television news.	特派員是提供新聞報導給報社、電台或電視的現場記者。
2819 The reporter was assigned to cover the war.	記者負責報導戰事。
2820 The editor-in-chief decided to quit because of strict censorship.	總編因嚴格的審查制度而決定辭職。
2821 A newspaper or magazine editorial gives the opinions of an editor.	報章社論反映主筆見解。
2822 This newspaper is famous for carrying an exclusive.	此報以報導獨家新聞聞名。
2823 The newspaper announced the tsunami disaster in an extra.	該報以特刊方式發布海嘯災情。
2824 The newspaper gave a false report.	報紙提供假新聞。
2825 A feature is a featured article in a newspaper or magazine.	專題報導是報章雜誌的特別報導。
2826 A gag is an official check or restraint on debate or free speech.	言論箝制是官方對論辯或自由言論的審查或管制。
2827 This syndicate is one of the world's largest distributors of text features for newspapers.	這個報業聯盟是全球最大的文字報紙發行商之一。
2828 A follow-up is a news story providing additional information on a story or article previously published.	針對已刊載的新聞提供更多額外資訊稱為後續報導。
2829 The newspaper has received a foreign dispatch from a reporter.	報社接獲記者的外電新聞稿。
2830 Journalism is the collecting, writing, editing, and presenting of news or news articles in newspapers, television, radio and magazines.	新聞工作是指在報紙、電視、電台和雜誌上採訪、撰稿、編輯和發布新聞。
2831 In a democratic nation freedom of the press should be guaranteed.	民主國家應保障新聞自由。
2832 This newspaper is trying to get a scoop on other papers.	報社設法取得關於其他報紙的獨家新聞。

★★★★★

2815 circulation [ˌsɝkjəˈleʃən]
n. the distribution of a newspaper or magazine

發行量，銷售量

★★★★★

2816 columnist [ˈkɑləmɪst]
n. one who writes a newspaper or magazine column

專欄作家

★★★★★

2817 commercial [kəˈmɝʃəl]
n. advertisement / a. occupied with or engaged in business

商業廣告 / 商業的，商務的

★★★★★

²⁸¹⁸ **correspondent** [ˌkɔrəˈspɑndənt]　特派員，通訊記者
n. on-the-scene reporter

★★★★☆

²⁸¹⁹ **cover** [ˈkʌvə]　採訪，報導
v. report news about

★★★★★

²⁸²⁰ **editor** [ˈɛdɪtə]　編輯，報章專欄主筆
n. someone who edits, especially as an occupation

★★★★★

²⁸²¹ **editorial** [ˌɛdəˈtɔrɪəl]　報章社論
n. a newspaper or magazine article

★★★★★

²⁸²² **exclusive** [ɪkˈsklusɪv]　獨家新聞
n. a news story at first released to or reported by only one source

★★★★★

²⁸²³ **extra** [ˈɛkstrə]　特刊，號外
n. a special edition of a newspaper

★★☆☆☆

²⁸²⁴ **false report** [fɔls rɪˈport]　假新聞
n. inaccurate report

★★★★☆

²⁸²⁵ **feature** [ˈfitʃə]　專題報導，特別報導
n. a featured article in a newspaper or magazine

★★★☆☆

²⁸²⁶ **gag** [gæg]　言論箝制
n. censorship

★★☆☆☆

²⁸²⁷ **syndicate** [ˈsɪnsɪkɪt]　報業聯盟
n. a group of newspapers under one management

★★☆☆☆

²⁸²⁸ **follow-up** [ˈfɑlo ʌp]　後續報導
n. a news story presenting new information on a story published earlier

★★★☆☆

2829 dispatch [dɪsˋpætʃ]
n. *a special report that is sent to a newspaper or broadcasting organization by a journalist who is in a different town or country*

新聞稿，快電

★★☆☆☆

2830 journalism [ˋdʒɝnḷˌɪzəm]
n. *the occupation of reporting, writing, editing, photographing, or broadcasting news*

新聞工作

★★★★★

2831 press [prɛs]
n. *the gathering and publishing or broadcasting of news /* *v.* *compress*

新聞，新聞界／擠壓

★★★★☆

2832 scoop [skup]
n. *information especially of immediate interest /* *v.* *take out or up with or as if with a scoop*

獨家新聞，最新內幕消息／舀起，搶先報導

✦ Ocean & Sailing　海洋與航行

2833	Bring the ship about.	掉頭。
2834	Heave anchor.	起錨。
2835	The ship was going at half speed astern.	船正以半速後退。
2836	They began to fill the ballast tank with water after unloading the ship.	卸貨後他們開始在壓載艙中注滿水。
2837	A high bore rushed to the shore.	一波高潮湧向海岸。
2838	The bow is the forward part of a ship.	船頭是船隻的前端。
2839	A watchman on the bridge found an iceberg ahead.	船橋上的守望員發現前方有冰山。
2840	A cathead is a projection near the bow of a ship to which the anchor is hung.	繫錨架是位於船頭附近的突出物，用來懸吊船錨。
2841	The clipper was used to ship tea from China.	過去常以快帆將茶運出中國。
2842	The rapid currents of the Colorado River created the Grand Canyon.	科羅拉多河的急流打造出大峽谷。
2843	The passenger was walking on the deck, looking at the sunset.	旅客走上甲板觀看日落景色。
2844	The ship was overloaded. The draft line was below the surface of the water.	船已超載，導致吃水線低於海平面。
2845	"The Gulf" is often used to refer to the Persian Gulf.	「波灣」常用來指波斯灣。
2746	The old hulk has been at the bottom of the sea for a century.	老舊廢船沉在海底一世紀。
2747	The Titanic was sailing at 22.5 knots.	鐵達尼號以時速二十二．五海里的速度航行。
2748	We fly the flag at half-mast on Memorial Day.	我們在陣亡將士紀念日降半旗致哀。
2849	He walked along the wooden pier and boarded the ship.	他沿著木造碼頭走，接著登船。

2850 A figurehead is the figure on a ship's bow, and in the past it was often the image of a female figure.

船頭雕像指的是位於船頭的塑像，過去常是女性塑像。

2851 The attraction from the moon and sun is the main cause of the flow and ebb.

日月引力是造成漲退潮的主因。

2852 There is a lagoon along the coast which is separated from the sea by a sandbank.

沿海潟湖以沙洲與外海相隔。

2853 At the launching ceremony some skeptics insisted that the Clermont, built by Robert Fulton, would never move.

在富爾敦建造的克萊蒙特號下水典禮上，部分懷疑論者堅稱這艘船不可能發動。

2854 With the development of navigation, more and more lighthouses are stopping their operation.

隨著導航技術的發展，愈來愈多燈塔也停止運作。

2855 Great Britain was a maritime nation.

大不列顛是沿海國家。

2856 One nautical mile is equivalent to 1,852 miles.

一海里等於一千八百五十二英里。

2857 The admiral took advantage of a rapid race to repel the invaders.

艦隊司令利用急流擊退入侵者。

2858 The captain of the drifting ship radioed to the coast guard.

漂流船隻的船長發送無線電給海岸巡防隊。

2859 It is said that the sea level has risen more than 400 feet since the peak of the last ice age about 18,000 years ago.

據說自一萬八千年前最後一個冰河期的高峰起，海平面已上升超過四百英尺。

2860 Hoist the main sail.

升起主帆。

2861 The ship was ripped open on the starboard side because of a collision with an iceberg.

船隻因撞擊冰山導致右舷裂開。

2862 The first mate turned the steering wheel to the left.

大副將舵輪向左轉。

2863 The stern is the rear part of a ship.

船尾是船隻的後端。

2864 The highest tide of the month is called the spring tide.

一個月當中最高的潮汐稱為滿潮。

2865 Fishermen's Wharf is a famous attraction in San Francisco.

舊金山漁人碼頭是一個熱門景點。

★★★★★

2833 about [ə`baut]
ad. backward / prep. concerning

朝相反方向 / 關於

★★★★☆

2834 anchor [`æŋkə]
n. a device, usually of metal, attached to a ship or boat by a cable which is used to hold a vessel stationary

錨

★★☆☆☆

2835 astern [ə`stɜn]
ad. backwards

向後地

★★★☆☆

2836 ballast [`bæləst]
n. a heavy substance placed in such a way as to improve stability and control

壓載物，壓艙物

★★☆☆☆

2837 bore [bɔr]
n. a tidal flood with a high abrupt front

高潮，怒潮

★★★★☆

2838 bow [bo]
n. the forward part of a ship / **v.** bend the head, body, or knee in reverence

船頭／鞠躬，低頭

★★☆☆☆

2839 bridge [brɪdʒ]
n. the forward part of a ship's superstructure from which the ship is navigated

船橋，艦橋

★☆☆☆☆

2840 cathead [`kæt,hɛd]
n. a projecting piece of timber or iron near the bow of a ship to which the anchor is hoisted and secured

繫錨架

★★★★☆

2841 clipper ship [`klɪpə ʃɪp]
n. a fast sailing ship

快速帆船，快帆

★★★★★

2842 current [`kɝənt]
n. a tidal or nontidal movement

水流

★★★★★

2843 deck [dɛk]
n. a platform in a ship

甲板

★★★★☆

2844 draft [dræft]
n. the depth of water a ship draws, especially when loaded

吃水

★★★★★

2845 gulf [gʌlf]
n. a part of an ocean or sea extending into the land

海灣

★★★★★

2846 hulk [hʌlk]
n. the body of an old ship unfit for service

廢船

★★★★★

2847 knot [nɑt]
n. one nautical mile per hour

海里

★★★★★

²⁸⁴⁸ **mast** [mæst]
n. any upright wooden or metal supporting pole, especially one carrying the sails of a ship

桅杆，旗杆

★★★★★

²⁸⁴⁹ **pier** [pɪr]
n. a structure (as a breakwater) extending into navigable water, for use as a landing place or promenade, or to protect or form a harbor

碼頭，防波堤

★★★☆☆

²⁸⁵⁰ **figurehead** [`fɪgjə,hɛd]
n. the figure on a ship's bow

船頭雕飾，船首像，船頭雕像

★★★★★

²⁸⁵¹ **flow** [flo]
n. flood / v. movement of a liquid

漲潮 / 流動

★★★☆☆

²⁸⁵² **lagoon** [lə`gun]
n. a body of shallow saltwater separated from the deeper sea

潟湖

★★★★☆

²⁸⁵³ **launch** [lɔntʃ]
v. set a boat or ship afloat

使船下水

★★★★★

²⁸⁵⁴ **lighthouse** [`laɪt,haʊs]
n. a structure with a powerful light that gives a continuous or intermittent signal to navigators

燈塔

★★★★☆

²⁸⁵⁵ **maritime** [`mærə,taɪm]
n. of or pertaining to sailing on a sea or ocean

海的，海事的，沿海的

★★★☆☆

²⁸⁵⁶ **nautical** [`nɔtɪkl]
a. of, relating to, or associated with seamen, navigation, or ship

航海的，海上的

★★☆☆☆

²⁸⁵⁷ **race** [res]
n. a strong or rapid current of water flowing through a narrow channel / v. have a race

急流 / 競賽

★★★★☆

2858 radio [`redɪ,o]
發送無線電
v. send a radio message to

★★★★★

2859 sea level [`si lɛvl]
海平面
n. the level of the surface of the sea

★★★★★

2860 sail [sel]
帆，篷
n. an extent of fabric (as canvas) by means of which wind is used to propel a ship through water

★★★☆☆

2861 starboard [`stɑr,bɔrd]
右舷（相反詞：larboard「左舷」）
n. the right side of a ship or aircraft looking forward

★★★★☆

2862 steering [`stɪrɪŋ]
掌舵
n. directing the course

★★★★★

2863 stern [stɜn]
船尾
n. back of the ship

★★★★★

2864 tide [taɪd]
潮汐，潮水，浪潮
n. the alternate rising and falling of the surface of the ocean

★★★★★

2865 wharf [hwɔrf]
碼頭，停泊處
n. a structure built along or at an angle from the shore of navigable waters so that ships may lie alongside to receive and discharge cargo and passengers

MP3
118

❖ **Society** 社會

2866 The United States takes a census every 10 years. 美國每十年進行一次人口普查。

2867 The organization is carrying out a charity drive for the homeless in the city. 該組織為街友舉辦慈善活動。

2868 Some citizens are carrying out a civic movement to prohibit alcohol. 部分市民展開禁煙運動。

2869 History has seen the disintegration of communism. 歷史見證了共產主義的覆亡。

2870 Choosing an occupation is a matter of grave concern. 選擇職業是一件重大的事。

2871 The police are trying to arrest the principal offender of the burglary.

警方企圖逮捕搶案主嫌。

2872 The United States has a very strict penal code.

美國刑法甚嚴。

2873 The penalty for violating the law was strict.

違法將受到嚴厲處罰。

2874 The leader of the party filed a suit against the malicious prosecution.

政黨領袖提出誣告訴訟。

2875 The police had a search-warrant issued.

警方申請搜索票。

2876 The authorities confiscated all the smuggled goods from the smuggler.

當局從走私者手上查扣所有走私品。

2877 The man filed a suit for damages against the perpetrator.

男子控告犯罪者，並要求賠償損失。

★★★★★

2866 **census** [`sɛnsəs]

n. a usually complete enumeration of a population

人口普查，人口調查

★★★★★

2867 **charity** [`tʃærətɪ]

n. relief of the poor; an institution engaged in relief of the poor

慈善，慈善團體

★★★★★

2868 **civic movement** [`sɪvɪk `muvmənt]

n. a movement of the citizenry

民權運動

★★★★★

2869 **communism** [`kɑmju͵nɪzəm]

n. a doctrine based on revolutionary Marxian socialism

共產主義

★★★★★

2870 **occupation** [͵ɑkjə`peʃən]

n. job

工作，職業

- accountant n. 會計師	- curator n. 館長
- architect n. 建築師	- dean n. 院長
- athlete n. 運動員	- dental hygienist n. 牙醫助手
- attorney n. 律師	- drillmaster n. 教練
- baby-sitter n. 褓姆	- editor n. 編輯
- barber n. 理髮師	- editor-in-chief n. 總編輯
- bellhop n. 服務生 (=bellboy)	- fire fighter n. 消防員
- bricklayer n. 泥水匠	- florist n. 花匠
- butcher n. 肉販	- grocer n. 雜貨店老闆
- chef n. 廚師	- hairdresser n. 美髮師
- computer programmer n. 程式設計師	- hotelier n. 旅館老闆
- computer technician n. 電腦技術人員	- judge n. 法官
- concierge n. 門房	- letter carrier n. 郵差
- customs official n. 海關人員	- mason n. 泥水匠，石匠

- mechanic n. 技工
- medic n. 軍醫，醫學院學生
- mortician n. 殯葬業者，禮儀師
- monk n. 和尚，僧侶，修道士
- newscaster n. 新聞播報員
- nun n. 尼姑，修女
- obstetrician n. 產科醫師
- oculist n. 眼科醫生
- optometrist n. 驗光師
- orthodontist n. 齒顎矯正醫師
- orthopedist n. 整形外科醫師
- pastor n. 本堂牧師
- pediatrician n. 小兒科醫師
- pharmacist n. 藥劑師
- physical therapist n. 物理治療師
- plumber n. 水管工

- porter n. 行李搬運員
- priest n. 基督教牧師，天主教神父
- principal n. 校長
- prosecutor n. 檢察官
- realtor n. 房地產經紀人
- rector n. 教區牧師
- sanitation worker n. 垃圾清潔工
- seamstress n. 女裁縫師
- security guard n. 警衛，保全人員
- superintendent n. 警長
- TV personality n. 電視明星
- usher n. 引導員，招待員
- undertaker n. 殯葬業者，禮儀師
- veterinarian n. 獸醫
- vice-president n. 副總統，副總裁

★★★★★

2871 offender [əˋfɛndə]

    n. criminal

違法者，犯罪者

★★★★★

2872 penal [ˋpinl]

    a. of, relating to, or involving punishment

刑事的，刑法上的

★★★★★

2873 penalty [ˋpɛnltɪ]

    n. punishment

處罰，刑罰，罰款

★★★★★

2874 prosecution [ˌprɑsɪˋkjuʃən]

    n. the act or process of prosecuting

原告，起訴

★★★★☆

2875 search-warrant [sɝtʃ ˋwɔrənt]

    n. a warrant authorizing a search (as of a house) for stolen goods or unlawful possessions

搜索票，搜索令

★★★★★

2876 smuggle [ˋsmʌgl]

    v. import or export secretly contrary to the law

走私，非法私運

★★★★★

2877 suit [sut]

    n. litigation; lawsuit

訴訟，控告

❖ **Transportation** 運輸工具

2878	Her husband is a back-seat driver who endlessly tells her what to do while she is driving.	她先生喜歡越俎代庖，常在她開車時不停地教她該怎麼做。
2879	Could you call a cab for me?	你能幫我叫輛計程車嗎？
2880	The passenger next to me was carsick.	我身旁的乘客暈車。
2881	His car careened around the corner.	他的車搖搖晃晃地疾駛過街角。
2882	There was terrible traffic congestion on my way here.	我來的路上有大塞車。
2883	I pulled over to the curb and made a call to the customer.	我把車開到路邊，並打電話給客戶。
2884	Please drop me off at that corner.	請讓我在那邊街角下車。
2885	In this nation we should have emissions tested regularly.	我國應定期進行車輛排氣檢測。
2886	I can't start the engine.	我無法發動引擎。
2887	You've got an extinguisher? My car is on fire.	你有滅火器嗎？我的車起火了。
2888	I have a flat tire.	我的車爆胎了。
2889	Is there a gas station near here? I've almost run out of gas.	這附近有加油站嗎？我的車快沒油了。
2890	Please turn on the heater. I'm freezing.	請把暖氣打開，我好冷。
2891	We should not toot the horn when there are cows or dogs nearby. The animals tend to run into a car when scared.	牛群或狗出現在附近時不可按喇叭，以免動物受驚衝撞車輛。
2892	I think I'll have to open the hood and check the engine.	我想我得打開車蓋檢查引擎。
2893	Please hop in.	請上車。
2894	There was a terrible traffic jam on the highway.	公路上出現嚴重塞車。
2895	I got jerked on the bus.	我在公車上遇到路面顛簸。
2896	Do you happen to have jumper cables?	你剛好有跨接線嗎？
2897	Shall I give you a lift?	你要搭便車嗎？
2898	No littering!	請勿亂丟垃圾！
2899	I need to have the oil and water checked.	我需要檢查油水分離器。
2900	Please don't jump up the queue.	請勿插隊。
2901	Let's stop at the next rest stop.	我們在下個休息站停一下吧。
2902	Could you give me a ride to my house?	你可以載我一程回家嗎？
2903	No RV parking.	禁止停放休旅車。
2904	Please step on the gas.	請踩油門。
2905	They lowed away my car.	他們把我的車拖走了。
2906	Where do I have to transfer to the Metro Line?	我該去哪裡換車到地鐵線？
2907	A utility vehicle would be better for this kind of unpaved road.	多功能休旅車較適合這種未鋪柏油路面。

★★☆☆☆

2878 **back-seat driver** [bǽksɪt `draɪvə] *n. a passenger who is critical of the driver's driving skill or performance*	越俎代庖者，假裝內行的後座駕駛

★★★★★

2879 **cab** [kæb] *n. taxi*	計程車

★★★★★

2880 carsick [ˈkɑrsɪk]

a. affected with motion sickness, especially in an automobile

暈車的

★★★☆☆

2881 careen [kəˈrin]

v. sway from side to side

左搖右晃疾駛

★★★★☆

2882 congestion [kənˈdʒɛstʃən]

n. jam

壅塞

★★★★★

2883 curb [kɝb]

n. an enclosing frame, border, or edging

路邊

★★★★★

2884 drop [drɑp]

v. let fall

下車（註：和介系詞 off 連用）

★★★★★

2885 emission [ɪˈmɪʃən]

n. exhaustion gas

排氣，排出

★★★★★

2886 engine [ˈɛndʒən]

n. any of various mechanical appliances

引擎

★★★★★

2887 extinguisher [ɪkˈstɪŋgwɪʃɚ]

n. a portable or wheeled apparatus for putting out small fires by ejecting extinguishing chemicals

滅火器

★★★★★

2888 flat tire [flæt taɪr]

n. punctured tire

爆胎

★★★★★

2889 gas station [gæs ˈsteʃən]

n. service station

加油站

★★★★★

2890 heater [ˈhitɚ]

n. a device that imparts heat or holds something to be heated

暖氣

★★★★★

2891 **horn** [hɔrn]
n. a usually electrical device that makes a noise like that of a horn

喇叭

★★★★★

2892 **hood** [hʊd]
n. the movable metal covering over the engine of an automobile

車蓋

★★★★☆

2893 **hop** [hɑp]
v. leap; jump

跳上

★★★★★

2894 **jam** [dʒæm]
n. congestion; gridlock

阻塞

★★★★☆

2895 **jerk** [dʒɝk]
n. a single quick motion of short duration / *v.* make a sudden spasmodic motion

猛拉，顛簸 / 顛簸而行，突然移動

★★★★☆

2896 **jumper cables** [ˋdʒʌmpɚ ˋkeblz]
n. a pair of electrical cables with alligator clips used to make a connection for jump-starting a vehicle

跨接線

★★★★★

2897 **lift** [lɪft]
n. ride

搭便車，順便搭載

★★★★★

2898 **litter** [ˋlɪtɚ]
n. trash; wastepaper; garbage

垃圾，廢棄物

★★★★★

2899 **oil** [ɔɪl]
n. lubrication

潤滑油

★★★★☆

2900 **queue** [kju]
n. a waiting line, especially of persons or vehicles / *v.* wait in line

（人、車）行列，隊伍 / 排隊

★★★★★

2901 rest stop [rɛst stɑp]　　　　　　　　　高速公路休息站

    n. rest area

- broken line n. 虛線，分隔線
- car-pool lane n. 共乘車道
- cat's eye n. 反光路面標記
- crosswalk n. 行人穿越道
- divider n. 分隔島
- dirt road n. 泥巴路
- lane n. 車道，線道
- no U-turn sign n. 禁止迴轉標誌
- overpass n. 天橋
- ramp n. 坡道
- road sign n. 道路交通標誌
- school crossing sign n. 學校穿越道標誌
- shoulder n. 路肩
- sidewalk n. 人行道
- slippery when wet sign n. 路滑標誌
- solid line n. 實線
- speed limit n. 限速
- traffic light n. 紅綠燈

★★★★★

2902 ride [raɪd]　　　　　　　　　搭乘，乘坐

    n. lift

★★★★★

2903 RV [ˌɑrˋvi]　　　　　　　　　休旅車

    n. recreational vehicle

★★★★★

2904 step [stɛp]　　　　　　　　　踩

    v. press down with the foot

★★★★★

2905 tow [to]　　　　　　　　　拖，拉

    v. draw or pull along behind

★★★★★

2906 transfer [ˋtrænsfɝ]　　　　　　　　　換車 / 轉車

    n. a ticket entitling a passenger on a public conveyance to
continue the trip on another route / *v.* change from one
vehicle to another

★★★★★

2907 Utility Vehicle [juˋtɪlətɪ ˋviɪkl]　　　　　　　　　多功能休旅車

    n. a useful vehicle that can be used for various purposes

✤ Travel 旅行

2908 The explorer left a detailed account of his expedition. 探險家留下詳細的探險記載。

2909 One passenger got airsick during the flight. 一位旅客在飛行途中暈機。

2910 In Germany, there are many tourist attractions to visit. 德國有許多值得一遊的觀光景點。

2911 May I book a table for three? 我可以預約三人一桌的位子嗎？

2912 I'm just browsing. 我只是看看。

2913 We enjoyed a buffet lunch at the hotel. 我們在飯店享受自助午餐。

2914 Her father prevented her from going overnight camping. 父親不讓她去宿營。

2915 We needed to check out of the hotel before noon. 我們須在中午前退房。

2916 I rode the courtesy bus to the hotel. 我搭免費接駁巴士前往飯店。

2917 My grandparents went on a cruise for a couple of weeks. 祖父參加數周的郵輪旅遊。

2918 Let's dine out today. 今晚出去吃吧。

2919 Our class took an excursion to the historic city. 我們班到歷史古都遠足。

2920 I left a message at the front desk. 我在櫃檯留言。

2921 A globe-trotter is a person who takes a trip around the world. 環遊世界者是全球走透透四處旅行的人。

2922 A grand tour was an extended tour of the Continent that was formerly a usual part of the education of young British gentlemen. 歐陸壯遊是歐洲大陸旅遊的延伸，也是昔日英國上流社會年輕紳士的必要教育之一。

2923 The flight was almost hijacked. 班機差點遭到劫持。

2924 The exhausted traveller stuck his thumb up to hitchhike. 疲憊不堪的旅人伸起拇指想搭便車。

2925 The schedule on the itinerary was too tight. 旅行計畫上的行程表太緊湊。

2926 The Englishman made up his mind to lorryhop all over the country. 英國人下定決心在國內展開免費旅行。

2927 The guest left some money as a tip for the maid who cleaned his hotel room. 飯店賓客給打掃客房的女僕一點小費。

2928 The traveller found his destination on the map. 旅人在地圖上找到自己要前往的目的地。

2929 I'll ask them to give a morning call. 我要求他們早上叫我起床。

2930 During the summer break my roommate and I will take a motor trip all over the nation. 我和室友將在暑假展開全國汽車之旅。

2931 All third-class passengers in the forward berth are supposed to queue in this line. 所有前排座位的三等艙旅客應在此列排隊。

2932 Can you reserve a hotel room for me? 你可以幫我預約飯店客房嗎？

2933 Receiving room service was a fantastic experience. 享受客房服務是很棒的經驗。

2934 A: What's the purpose of your visit?
B: Just sightseeing. A：你此行的目的是什麼？
B：純粹觀光遊覽。

2935 Do you need a single or double bed? 你需要單人床還是雙人床？

2936 After brunch we went to a souvenir shop. 吃完早午餐後我們去逛紀念品店。

2937 A package tour led by a tour guide may be more enjoyable when we travel to a foreign country. 到國外旅遊時參加導遊帶領的套裝行程也許更能盡情享受。

2938 I have prepared all the documents to apply for a tourist visa. 我準備好申請觀光簽證的所有資料。

2939 The information center is a good place for you to get a tour map.	詢問處是個索取旅遊地圖的好地方。
2940 Before the overseas travel I contacted a travel agent for some information.	出國旅遊前我連絡旅行社代辦索取一些資訊。
2941 You could probably get some travel brochures from the travel agency.	你或許可以到旅行社索取一些旅遊指南。
2942 It's a good idea to carry traveler's checks instead of cash when traveling in a foreign country.	攜帶旅行支票而非現金出國旅遊是個好點子。
2943 Upon unpacking my luggage, I got out of the hotel.	我一打開行李後便到飯店外走走。
2944 Please give me a wake-up call at 6 o'clock.	請在早上六點叫我起床。
2945 A: May I help you?	A：我可以為您服務嗎？
B: I'm just window-shopping.	B：我只是隨便看看。
A: But this is a Chinese restaurant.	A：但這裡是中國餐館。
B: Really?	B：真的嗎？
2946 Can I get this gift wrapped?	能幫我把禮物包起來嗎？

★★★★★

2908 account [ə`kaʊnt]	記述，報導 / 解釋
n. *a description of facts, conditions, or events /* ***v.*** *explain*	

★★★★☆

2909 airsick [`ɛr͵sɪk]	暈機的
a. *affected with motion sickness associated with flying*	

★★★★★

2910 attraction [ə`trækʃən]	吸引人的事物
n. *something that attracts people*	

★★★★★

2911 book [bʊk]	預約，預訂
v. *reserve*	

★★★★★

2912 browse [braʊz]	瀏覽，隨便看看
v. *to look over casually*	

★★★★★

2913 buffet [bə`fe]	自助餐
n. *a meal set out on a buffet or table for ready access and informal service*	

★★★★★

2914 camping [`kæmpɪŋ]	露營
n. *living temporarily in a camp or outdoors*	

★★★★★
2915 check out [tʃɛk aut]　　　　　　　　　結帳退房
v. vacate and pay for one's lodging (as at a hotel)

★☆☆☆☆
2916 courtesy bus [ˋkɜtəsɪ bʌs]　　　　（飯店、機場等的）免費接駁巴士
n. shuttle bus provided as a courtesy

★★★★☆
2917 cruise [kruz]　　　　　　　　　　　搭船旅遊
n. a tour by ship

★★★★★
2918 dine [dɪn]　　　　　　　　　　　　進餐，用餐
v. eat

★★★★☆
2919 excursion [ɪkˋskɜʒən]　　　　　　　遠足，短途旅行
n. picnic; outing

★★★★★
2920 front desk [ˋfrʌnt dɛsk]　　　　　　櫃檯
n. the management desk in a hotel or motel lobby

★★☆☆☆
2921 globe-trotter [ˋglob͵trɑtɚ]　　　　　環遊世界者
n. a person who travels widely

★★☆☆☆
2922 grand tour [ˋgrænd tur]　　　　　　歐陸壯遊
n. an extensive and usually educational tour

★★★★☆
2923 hijack [ˋhaɪ͵dʒæk]　　　　　　　　劫持
v. commandeer (a flying airplane), especially by coercing the pilot at gunpoint

★★★★★
2924 hitchhike [ˋhɪtʃ͵haɪk]　　　　　　　搭便車
v. solicit and obtain (a free ride) especially in a passing vehicle

★★★★★
2925 itinerary [aɪˋtɪnə͵rɛrɪ]　　　　　　旅行計畫
n. a traveler's guidebook

★★☆☆☆

2926 lorryhop [ˋlɔrɪhɑp]
v. *hitchhike*

搭便車旅行

★★★★★

2927 maid [med]
n. *a woman or girl employed to do domestic work*

女僕

★★★★★

2928 map [mæp]
n. *a representation, usually on a flat surface, of the whole or a part of an area*

地圖

★★★★★

2929 morning call [ˋmɔrnɪŋ kɔl]
n. *wake-up call*

早晨以内線電話叫醒客人的飯店服務

★★★☆☆

2930 motor trip [ˋmotɚ trɪp]
n. *a trip using a motor*

汽車之旅

★★★★★

2931 passenger [ˋpæsṇdʒɚ]
n. *a vehicle such as a bus, boat, or plane is a person who is travelling in it*

旅客

★★★★★

2932 reserve [rɪˋzɝv]
v. *book*

預約

★★★★★

2933 room service [rum ˋsɝvɪs]
n. *service provided to hotel guests in their rooms*

客房服務

★★★★★

2934 sightseeing [ˋsaɪt͵siŋ]
n. *tour*

觀光，遊覽

★★★★★

2935 single [ˋsɪŋgḷ]
a. *designed for the use of one person only*

單一的，單人使用的

★★★★★

2936 souvenir [ˋsuvə͵nɪr]
n. *something that serves as a reminder*

紀念品

★★★★★

2937 tour guide [ˋtʊr gaɪd]

n. *a person who exhibits and explains points of interest*

導遊，領隊

★★★★★

2938 tourist visa [ˋtʊrɪst ˋvizə]

n. *a visa for a tourist*

觀光簽證

★★★★★

2939 information center [͵ɪnfɚˋmeʃən ˋsɛntɚ]

n. *a center which provides information for sightseeing*

詢問處

★★★★★

2940 travel agent [ˋtrævḷ ˋedʒənt]

n. *a clerk at a travel agency*

旅行社代辦

★★★★★

2941 travel brochure [ˋtrævḷ broˋʃur]

n. *travel pamphlet*

旅遊指南，旅遊小冊子

★★★★★

2942 traveler's check [ˋtrævlɚz tʃɛk]

n. *a check for travelers*

旅行支票

★★★★☆

2943 unpack [ʌnˋpæk]

v. *remove the contents of*

打開行李

★★★★☆

2944 wake-up call [ˋwekʌp kɔl]

n. *morning call*

早晨以內線電話叫醒客人的飯店服務

★★★★★

2945 window-shopping [ˋwɪndo͵ʃɑpɪŋ]

n. *look at the displays in retail store windows*

瀏覽商店櫥窗

★★★★★

2946 wrap [ræp]

n. *wrapping* / **v.** *cover especially by winding or folding*

包裹 / 包起來

✛ **Weather** 天氣

2947 The Beaufort scale was invented by Sir Francis Beaufort, and it is used to indicate the force of the wind.

法蘭西斯・蒲福爵士所發明的蒲福風級表可用來估計風力強弱。

2948 We had a blizzard last night.　昨晚暴風雪來襲。

2949 We took a walk in a fresh breeze.　我們在清新和風中散步。

2950 It must be over twenty degrees centigrade.　氣溫一定超過攝氏二十度。

2951 I feel a little too chilly. Let's turn on the heater.　我覺得有點冷，我們開暖氣吧。

2952 Heat travels by conduction and convection.　熱透過傳導與對流行進。

2953 Cyclones in the Indian Ocean cause great damage to coastal areas every year.　印度洋氣旋每年都對沿海地區造成重大災害。

2954 We had a downpour of rain last night.　昨晚下了傾盆大雨。

2955 It is easier to row the boat downwind.　順風划船較不費力。

2956 It's drizzling out there.　外面正在下毛毛雨。

2957 Please close the window. There is too much dust in the wind.　請關上窗，風中灰塵太多了。

2958 Dust devils are so called because the whirlwinds form in areas where there is much loose dirt to be carried by the whirlwinds.　形成於一區域並挾帶大量鬆散塵土的旋風稱為塵捲風。

2959 It has been over 100 degrees Fahrenheit for three consecutive days.　氣溫已連續三天超過華氏一百度。

2960 Foehn, or the warm and dry wind blowing down from a mountain, is prevalent in the east side of these mountains.　自山脈向下吹拂的乾熱焚風遍及山區東側。

2961 It fogs up.　起霧了。

2962 A front is the line where a mass of cold air meets a mass of warm air.　鋒面是冷、熱氣團的交界線。

2963 There was a heavy frost.　嚴寒來襲。

2964 The child's fingers were seriously frostbitten.　孩童手指嚴重凍傷。

2965 A strong gale did much damage to the crops.　強風對農作物造成重大損害。

2966 There was a violent gust of wind.　一陣狂風突然吹過。

2967 A hail is often called the White Black Death because of the damage to the crops it can cause.　冰雹因為會對農作物造成損害，常被稱為白色黑死病。

2968 We can often see a haze on a spring day.　春天常有薄霧出現。

2969 We have had such a long heat wave.　我們長期遭受熱浪襲擊。

2970 The temperature reached another record high this afternoon.　今天下午氣溫再創新高。

2971 It's pretty hot and humid today.　今天相當炎熱而潮濕。

2972 A hurricane is a tropical cyclone with winds of at least 74 miles (119 kilometers) per hour. It means that the wind exceeds 32.7 meters a second.　颶風是每小時風速至少七十四英里的熱帶氣旋，相當於每小時一百一十九公里，也就是說每秒風速超過三十二・七公尺。

2973 An isobar map is very important to learn about the weather.　等壓線圖對了解天氣狀況是很重要的。

2974 Lows will be 10 degrees centigrade.　最低溫將是攝氏十度。

2975 It is misting.　起薄霧了。

2976 In this nation we have a 3-month-long monsoon season.　我國雨季有三個月之久。

2977 The annual precipitation of this area is less than 1,000mm a year.　本區年降雨量低於一千公釐。

2978 We had a heavy rainfall in the latter part of last summer.　去年夏末有大量降雨。

2979 Because of a torrential rainstorm many streets were flooded.

一場猛烈的暴風雨導致許多街道淹水。

2980 The ridge is the high pressure area between low pressure areas.

低氣壓區之間的高氣壓區稱為高氣壓脊。

2981 We are having such a long scorching heat wave.

我們正遭受酷熱熱浪襲擊。

2982 I got caught in a shower on my way here.

我在過來的路上遇到一場驟雨。

2983 It sleets.

雨夾雜著雪一起落下。

2984 Last winter we had a heavy snowfall.

去年冬天我們受到大雪侵襲。

2985 It is expected that the temperature will soar this summer.

今年夏季氣溫預計將向上攀升。

2986 We have had a fine spell for several days.

好天氣持續數日。

2987 It is sprinkling. We'll need an umbrella.

下毛毛雨了，我們需要傘。

2988 A squall is a sudden violent wind accompanied by a rain or snow.

暴風雪指的是伴隨雨或雪的急速強風。

2989 A tornado is classified into five different types according to the Fujita scale.

龍捲風根據藤田分級制度可分為五種不同等級。

2990 According to the weather forecast, we are going to have torrents of rain tonight.

根據天氣預報，今晚會下傾盆大雨。

2991 The trade wind blows west along the equator.

信風沿著赤道向西吹拂。

2992 A low pressure trough is an elongated area of low barometric pressure.

低壓槽為狹長的低氣壓帶。

2993 A typhoon is a hurricane that occurs especially in the region of the Philippines or the China Sea.

颱風是主要發生在菲律賓或中國海域的颶風。

2994 The plane was flying upwind.

飛機正逆風飛行。

2995 People often set up a weather vane on the roof to know the direction of the wind.

人們常在屋頂豎立風向標以掌握風向。

2996 The wind veered clockwise.

風轉向順時針方向吹。

2997 Did you hear the weather forecast for tomorrow?

你聽了明天的天氣預報嗎？

2998 The weathercock on the roof is often shaped like a cock.

屋頂上的風向標通常形似公雞。

2999 A whirlwind whirling around usually raises much dust from the ground.

迴旋的旋風常捲起地面大量塵土。

3000 In Korea, especially in spring, there is too much yellow sand which is carried by the wind blowing from China.

源自中國的風，尤其是在春季會挾帶大量沙塵吹向韓國。

★★☆☆☆

2947 Beaufort scale [ˋbofərt skel]

n. a scale in which the force of the wind is indicated by numbers from 0 to 12

蒲福風級表

★★★★★

2948 blizzard [ˋblɪzəd]

n. a long severe snowstorm

暴風雪

★★★★★

2949 breeze [briz]

n. a light gentle wind

微風，和風

2950 **centigrade** [ˋsɛntəˌgred]

n. Celsius

攝氏

★★★★★

2951 **chilly** [ˋtʃɪlɪ]

a. noticeably cold

寒冷的，頗冷的

★★★☆☆

2952 **convection** [kənˋvɛkʃən]

n. the action or process of conveying

對流

★★★★★

2953 **cyclone** [ˋsaɪklon]

n. a storm or system of winds that rotates about a center of low atmospheric pressure

氣旋

★★★☆☆

2954 **downpour** [ˋdaʊnˌpɔr]

n. a heavy rain

傾盆大雨，豪雨

★★☆☆☆

2955 **downwind** [ˌdaʊnˋwɪnd]

ad. in the direction that the wind is blowing

順風地

★★★★★

2956 **drizzle** [ˋdrɪzl̩]

n. a fine misty rain / *v.* rain in very small drops or very lightly

毛毛雨 / 下毛毛雨

★★★★★

2957 **dust** [dʌst]

n. fine particles of matter as of earth

灰塵，塵土

★★★☆☆

2958 **dust devil** [ˋdʌst dɛvl̩]

n. a small whirlwind containing sand or dust

塵捲風

★★★★★

2959 **Fahrenheit** [ˋfærənˌhaɪt]

n. relating or conforming to a thermometric scale on which under standard atmospheric pressure the boiling point of water is at 212 degrees above the zero of the scale, the freezing point is at 32 degrees above zero

華氏

★★★☆☆

²⁹⁶⁰ **foehn** [fen]　　　　　　　　　　　　　　焚風
　　n. a warm dry wind blowing down the side of a mountain

★★★★★

²⁹⁶¹ **fog** [fɑg]　　　　　　　　　　　　　　霧，霧氣 / 被霧籠罩，起霧
　　n. mist / *v.* become blurred by a covering of fog or mist

★★★★★

²⁹⁶² **front** [frʌnt]　　　　　　　　　　　　　鋒面
　　n. the forward part or surface

★★★★★

²⁹⁶³ **frost** [frɔst]　　　　　　　　　　　　　霜，霜寒
　　n. ice particle formed from a gas

★★★☆☆

²⁹⁶⁴ **frostbite** [`frɔst,baɪt]　　　　　　　　使凍傷，使受霜害
　　v. affect or injure by frost or frostbite

★★★★☆

²⁹⁶⁵ **gale** [gel]　　　　　　　　　　　　　　強風
　　n. a strong wind

★★★★☆

²⁹⁶⁶ **gust** [gʌst]　　　　　　　　　　　　　陣風
　　n. a sudden brief rush of wind

★★★★★

²⁹⁶⁷ **hail** [hel]　　　　　　　　　　　　　　冰雹
　　n. precipitation in the form of small balls or lumps usually
　　consisting of concentric layers of clear ice and compact
　　snow

★★★★★

²⁹⁶⁸ **haze** [hez]　　　　　　　　　　　　　　靄，薄霧
　　n. fine dust, smoke, or light vapor causing lack of
　　transparency of the air

★★★★★

²⁹⁶⁹ **heat wave** [`hit wev]　　　　　　　　熱浪
　　n. hot spell

★★★★★

²⁹⁷⁰ **high** [haɪ]　　　　　　　　　　　　　　高峰
　　n. the highest point

★★★★★
2971 humid [ˋhjumɪd]
a. moist

潮濕的

★★★★★
2972 hurricane [ˋhɝɪ͵ken]
n. a tropical cyclone

颶風，熱帶氣旋

★★★☆☆
2973 isobar [ˋaɪsə͵bɑr]
n. an imaginary line or a line on a map or chart connecting or marking places of equal barometric pressure

等壓線

★★★★★
2974 low [lo]
n. the lowest point

最低點，最低數字

★★★★★
2975 mist [mɪst]
n. fog / v. be or become misty

薄霧，靄 / 使蒙上薄霧，起霧

★★★★★
2976 monsoon [mɑnˋsun]
n. rainfall that is associated with the monsoon

雨季，季風

★★★★★
2977 precipitation [prɪ͵sɪpəˋteʃən]
n. a deposit on the earth of hail, mist, rain, sleet, or snow

降雨量，降雪量

★★★★★
2978 rainfall [ˋren͵fɔl]
n. rain

降雨，降雨量

★★★★★
2979 rainstorm [ˋren͵stɔrm]
n. a storm of or with rain

暴風雨

★★★★☆
2980 ridge [rɪdʒ]
n. a raised strip

脊

★★★★☆
2981 scorching [ˋskɔrtʃɪŋ]
a. very hot

酷熱的

★★★★★
2982 **shower** [`ʃɑʊə]
n. *a fall of rain of short duration*

驟雨，陣雨

★★★☆☆
2983 **sleet** [slit]
n. *frozen or partly frozen rain* / *v.* *shower sleet*

霰，霙／下霰，雨與雪一起落下

★★★★★
2984 **snowfall** [`sno͵fɔl]
n. *a fall of snow*

降雪，降雪量

★★★★☆
2985 **soar** [sor]
v. *rise or increase dramatically*

猛增，暴漲

★★★★★
2986 **spell** [spɛl]
n. *wave*

（天氣等的）一段持續時間

★★★★★
2987 **sprinkle** [`sprɪŋkl]
n. *light rain* / *v.* *rain lightly in scattered drops*

毛毛細雨／下稀疏小雨

★★★☆☆
2988 **squall** [skwɔl]
n. *a sudden violent wind often with rain or snow*

暴風雪

★★★★★
2989 **tornado** [tɔr`nedo]
n. *a violent destructive whirling wind accompanied by a funnel-shaped cloud that progresses in a narrow path over the land*

龍捲風

★★★★☆
2990 **torrent** [`tɔrənt]
n. *a tumultuous outpouring*

（雨的）傾注，傾瀉（註：通常作複數形）

★★★☆☆
2991 **trade wind** [`tred wɪnd]
n. *a wind blowing almost constantly in one direction*

信風

★★★☆☆
2992 **trough** [trɔf]
n. *a long and narrow or shallow channel of depression*

槽

2993 typhoon [taɪˋfun] 颱風
n. a hurricane along the Pacific coast

★★☆☆☆

2994 upwind [ˋʌpˋwɪnd] 迎風地，逆風地
ad. in the direction from which the wind is blowing

★★★★☆

2995 weather vane [ˋwɛðɚ ven] 風標，風向標
n. wind vane

★★☆☆☆

2996 veer [vɪr] 改變方向，轉向
v. shift in a clockwise direction

★★★★★

2997 weather forecast [ˋwɛðɚ ˋforˌkæst] 天氣預報
n. estimate of weather

★★★★☆

2998 weathercock [ˋwɛðɚˌkɑk] 風向標
n. weather vane

★★★★★

2999 whirlwind [ˋhwɝlˌwɪnd] 旋風
n. a small rotating windstorm of limited extent

★★★☆☆

3000 yellow sand [ˋjɛlo sænd] 沙塵
n. yellow dust

Tea Time... ☕

<Greek myth> Titan **Any of a race of giant deities who were overthrown by the Olympian gods.**	〈來自希臘神話〉泰坦 希臘神話中被奧林帕斯諸神打敗的巨神家族。（註：本字的古希臘語為 Τιτάν，源自動詞 τιταίνω，帶有「伸長，巨大」之意。）

❋ **titanic** [taɪˋtænɪk] **a.** *gigantic; enormous; humongous; huge; colossal* | 泰坦巨神的，巨大的，力大無比的

This titanic ship has two swimming pools, a tennis court, and even a golf putting course. It is really gigantic.
這艘巨輪擁有兩座泳池、一座網球場，甚至還有高爾夫推杆練習場，真的相當龐大。

1 Complete each word by filling in the blank with proper spelling so that it has the same meaning as suggested. Then please write the meaning of each word in Chinese.

1. 颱風 = _ _ _ _ o o n
2. 等壓線 = _ _ _ b a r
3. 降雨量 = p r e _ _ _ _ t a t i o n
4. 旋風 = _ _ _ _ _ w i n d
5. 冰雹 = h _ _ _
6. 紀念品 = _ _ _ _ e n i r
7. 毛毛雨 = _ _ _ z z l e
8. 隊伍 = _ _ _ u e
9. 吸引人的事物 = a t _ _ _ _ _ i o n
10. 遠足 = e x _ _ _ _ i o n

11. scoop = _____
12. embark = _____
13. circulation = _____
14. editor = _____
15. follow-up = _____
16. astern = _____
17. cathead = _____
18. clipper ship = _____
19. deck = _____
20. bow = _____

2 Choose a word that best completes the sentence.

21. **The journalist was assigned to _____ the war in the Middle East.**
    (A) wrap　　　　(B) dispatch　　　　(C) unpack　　　　(D) cover

22. **One harpooned blue whale was said to drag a whaler's ship for 24 hours, even though the ship's engines were moving at half speed _____.**
    (A) astern　　　　(B) upwind　　　　(C) downwind　　　　(D) front

23. **The watchman on the _____ found an iceberg ahead and shouted a warning.**
    (A) bridge　　　　(B) ballast　　　　(C) anchor　　　　(D) draw

24. **When will this _____ heat wave end? I can't stand this heat any more.**
    (A) chilly　　　　(B) scorching　　　　(C) freezing　　　　(D) commercial

25. **We have had such a long cold _____ this winter.**
    (A) deck　　　　(B) gag　　　　(C) spell　　　　(D) gust

Practice Test 02

1
The highlighted word is closest in meaning to which of the following?

1. The **fog** was so thick that we could not see the vehicle coming toward us.
   - (A) feature
   - (B) mist
   - (C) current
   - (D) syndicate

2. Could you please give me a **ride** to the school?
   - (A) lift
   - (B) shower
   - (C) excursion
   - (D) extra

3. How often does your family **dine** out?
   - (A) hitchhike
   - (B) eat
   - (C) cruise
   - (D) hop

4. I feel a little too **chilly**. Isn't the window open?
   - (A) airsick
   - (B) hot
   - (C) cold
   - (D) humid

5. It must be over thirty degrees **centigrade**. It's too hot.
   - (A) monsoon
   - (B) sleet
   - (C) Celsius
   - (D) Fahrenheit

2
Please answer the following questions.

> **Comic Tale**
>
> Early in the afternoon, Charlie's father came back home from work. Charlie, a fifth grader, could notice a little different atmosphere was (1)_____ in the house. Father was hurrying and scurrying, helping Mother with (2)_____ chores. Judging from the atmosphere, Charlie could know that Grandmother, mother's mother, would visit them.

Whenever she comes to visit, strangely enough, Father is always on a kind of alert. Charlie wonders why Father always draws back in fear in front of her. Charlie thinks that it might be because Grandmother complains about their poor living conditions. Last time when Grandmother was visiting, she had an (3)_____ with Father over something which Charlie did not understand. Charlie does not like Grandmother, because she rarely treats Father nicely.

Early in the evening the door bell rang and Father was about to hide something which he did not actually own - his tail. Sure enough, Grandmother began to ask Father when they would move out of their (4)_____ two-room flat. Father only laughed.

As was always the case, Charlie had to yield his room to his Grandmother and sleep with his parents. The next morning at the breakfast table, Grandmother said, "Charlie, did you place a glass of water by my bed? I was extremely thirsty when I woke up during the night. It was very refreshing." Charlie (5)_____, "Did you gulp down my tadpoles?"

6. **What would be the most appropriate word in blank (1)?**

(A) efficient
(B) perpendicular
(C) mediocre
(D) prevailing

7. **What would be the most appropriate word in blank (2)?**

(A) domestic
(B) independent
(C) reticent
(D) tacit

8. **What would be the most appropriate word in blank (3)?**

(A) consolidation
(B) altercation
(C) merger
(D) compromise

9. **What would be the most appropriate word in blank (4)?**

(A) luxurious
(B) deluxe
(C) conterminous
(D) humble

10. **What would be the most appropriate word in blank (5)?**

(A) disclaimed
(B) exclaimed
(C) inspired
(D) curbed

Actual Test

Television

Since its inception , television has weathered the competition from other media, illuminating billions of world people by providing them with entertainment as well as information. Most especially, TV's amazing ability to relay live news on the spot has linked the world as a global village. TV's entertaining capability has also been almost matchless . No wonder then that an average American child will have spent 17,000 hours watching television by the time he becomes 18 years old.

However, despite its shiny accolade received as being as one of the most phenomenal inventions in the 20th century, TV has been accused of its addictive quality. In this matter, TV cannot find any pleas or excuses. Almost all family members squat themselves in front of a TV set as soon as they finish their supper. Their eyes stick to the TV screen, and all ears are directed towards the loudspeaker. Any interference from others is frowned upon. If the TV set were removed, all family members would do nothing but stare at the place where the TV set used to be. All the family members are spellbound and changed into statues. The difference between a father on Sundays and a Buddha's image is that there is no TV set in front of the latter. Actually, there is another difference: a Buddha's image does not have a remote control in its hand. Addiction is also responsible for inaction, or neglect of exercise. The recommended distance for watching TV compels us to sit motionlessly, depriving us of physical activities. We cannot do more exercise when we watch a baseball game than when we watch a golf game on TV.

TV is also to be blamed for its gratuitous violence. In many programs we can find characters whose first resort is to violence. If the real world is just like the one described in TV programs, people's average lifespan would be drastically reduced . Frankly speaking, violence is thought of by TV producers as an effective means of increasing the viewing rate. Some wrestling programs, for example, let us know that the Creator is amazing enough to create humans who are incredibly strong. Wrestlers survive a chair shot or a champion belt shot. The only consideration for young people is the simple sentence suggested on the screen: "Whoever you are, whatever you do, do not try this at home." What will young people do when they are away from home?

Some TV broadcasting centers cannot be exempt from blame in that they concentrate too much on earning easy money by focusing on TV personalities or celebrities. Some programs tend to last more than one hour, delving into TV personalities' houses or talking about their dates, spouses and even about their pets. Many audiences are sick and tired of these kinds of programs. TV broadcasting centers should not take advantage of so-called people's right to know for their purposes.

TV is surely one of the most phenomenal products in a civilized society, and it has contributed to cultures and civilizations. Its contribution in illuminating human beings is hard to beat. Because TV's influences upon human beings are so great, TV should be watched over closely, and not watched mindlessly.

1. The highlighted word inception can be replaced by which of the following?
   (A) conception
   (B) matriculation
   (C) advent
   (D) demise

2. The highlighted word matchless can be replaced by which of the following?
   (A) disparate
   (B) peerless
   (C) congruous
   (D) parallel

3. The highlighted word phenomenal can be replaced by which of the following?
   (A) flagrant
   (B) herbivorous
   (C) innate
   (D) remarkable

4. The highlighted word stick can be replaced by which of the following?
   (A) adhere
   (B) hesitate
   (C) kindle
   (D) heave

5. The highlighted word interference can be replaced by which of the following?
   (A) thicket
   (B) purview
   (C) meddling
   (D) probation

6. The highlighted word compels can be replaced by which of the following?
   (A) dissuades
   (B) urges
   (C) instigates
   (D) allures

7. The highlighted word gratuitous can be replaced by which of the following?
   (A) phlegmatic
   (B) sanguine
   (C) unwarranted
   (D) quixotic

8. The highlighted word reduced can be replaced by which of the following?
   (A) cut down
   (B) elongated
   (C) dragged up
   (D) hypnotized

9. The highlighted word exempt can be replaced by which of the following?
   (A) lethal
   (B) ambrosial
   (C) free
   (D) sophisticated

10. The highlighted word illuminating can be replaced by which of the following?
    (A) coveting
    (B) enlightening
    (C) mesmerizing
    (D) pasteurizing

Passage 2

Noah's Ark

Laymen often insist that the Bible is full of fiction, and thus the stories and events in it are difficult to believe. But these days some people try to verify them as truth. One of them is Noah's Deluge. In Genesis in The Old Testament, there is a story about a cataclysmic flood. It says that God found that the world was full of evil and violence. Therefore, He decided to destroy the people whom he created. However, God wanted Noah, with whom He was pleased, to be spared and ordered him to build a boat, or an Ark, out of good timber according to His instructions; the ship should be 133 meters long, 22 meters wide, and 13 meters high; the ship should have three decks, a roof, a door in the side, rooms, and should be covered with tar. Noah worked on the Ark for a hundred years, finishing it at the age of 600, when God told Noah to enter the boat with his wife, his three sons, Shem, Ham, and Japheth, and their wives, together with a male and female of every kind of animal, in order to keep them alive from the deluge which would start in seven days. The flood is said to have continued for forty days and nights, annihilating all the remaining living things on the ground. The water was so deep that it even rose seven meters above the top of the highest mountain in the world. One hundred and fifty days later the water went down, and the Ark came to rest on a mountain in the Ararat range.

Many laymens' suspicion focuses not only around the enormous lifespan of Noah - actually in the Bible the person who enjoyed the greatest longevity was Methuselah, who lived up to the age of 969 - but also around his feat of making such a gigantic boat with maybe primitive tools. However, there is an interesting thing much talked about. Mt. Ararat, which is located in eastern Turkey near the Armenian and Iranian borders, is 5,165 meters high and its hoary top boasts that it is a giant one. The upper third is covered with snow and ice throughout the year. It is a dormant volcano, which erupted on June 2, 1840. Ararat is a Turkish word for Agri Dagi, meaning a mountain of pain. Strangely enough, the mountain is said to be difficult to scale, and the first known ascent was made as late as in 1829 by Frederick Parrot, a German physician. There are many legends and witnesses' reports about the Ark which is supposed to have perched high on Mt. Ararat, but unfortunately there has been no conclusive evidence. It is said that only during short periods of time when some of the ice and snow melt, only the loftiest heights of the frozen peak allow explorers to have a glimpse of the remains buried deep in the ice and snow. A long time ago, Josephus, in about 70 AD, and Marco Polo, in about 1300 AD, mentioned the ship of the mountain, even though their insistence was based on others' accounts. Recently a certain alpine climber and his son insisted that they found the remains of a giant black object, which they believed was the Ark, and they even took a tiny piece of wood from the object as evidence. They also took some pictures. If they really found a giant object high on a mountain where there are no plants at all, what in the world could that be? Who could possibly have placed the giant object almost on top of the mountain? And for what?

11. The highlighted word verify can be replaced by which of the following?

(A) dovetail

(B) lionize

(C) aver

(D) reinforce

12. The highlighted word deluge can be replaced by which of the following?

(A) labyrinth

(B) iota

(C) masochism

(D) flood

13. The highlighted word annihilating can be replaced by which of the following?

(A) reproducing

(B) exterminating

(C) capitulating

(D) countervailing

14. The highlighted word suspicion can be replaced by which of the following?

(A) skepticism

(B) ostracism

(C) gamut

(D) chauvinism

15. The highlighted word enormous can be replaced by which of the following?

(A) infinitesimal

(B) teeny weeny

(C) gargantuan

(D) miniature

16. The highlighted word longevity can be replaced by which of the following?

(A) long lifespan

(B) intricate passage

(C) fauna

(D) flora

17. The highlighted word gigantic can be replaced by which of the following?

(A) humongous

(B) bacchanalian

(C) Machiavellian

(D) laconic

18. The highlighted word erupted can be replaced by which of the following?

(A) blurted out

(B) rebutted

(C) broke out

(D) abrogated

19. The highlighted word ascent can be replaced by which of the following?

(A) climb

(B) cupidity

(C) lethargy

(D) belligerence

20. The highlighted word tiny can be replaced by which of the following?

(A) limpid

(B) tantamount

(C) minute

(D) tantalizing

Building Vocabulary for
iBT, SAT, GRE, TOEIC, GEPT

01 | 02 | 03

04 05 Answers

Chapter 1-5 解答與中譯
- Review Test
- Practice Test
- Actual Test

Chapter 1

Review Test_01

❶ 第1到10題為「拼字題」，請根據中文意思完成英文拼字填空。第11到20題為「釋義題」，請根據英文字彙寫出中文意思。

解答 | 1. analysis 2. synthesis 3. anachronism
4. taxidermy 5. hypothesis 6. ecology
7. antagonist 8. concentrate 9. recession
10. retract 11. 過度熱情的，情感洋溢的
12. 輸血 13. 禁止 14. 會議，大會
15. 限制，受限於～
16. 扣除（額），減除（額）17. 懸掛，吊掛
18. 前言，序曲 19. 推翻，顛覆
20. 勤勉的，勤奮的

❷ 請根據句意，從底下四個選項中選出一個最能適切完成句子的字彙。

21. 當蚊子將吸血口針刺入嬰兒皮膚，幾乎沒有一個嬰兒不會哭鬧；同理，當護士使用皮下注射器刺入嬰兒皮膚，也沒有嬰兒是不哭鬧的。
(A) 皮下的 (B) 短暫的 (C) 公平的 (D) 懷舊的

22. 我們應全神貫注於解答數學問題，否則可能會出錯。
(A) 拔出 (B) 規避 (C) 逃避 (D) 全神貫注於

23. 這個商場的出口在哪裡？我想我迷路了。
(A) 沮喪 (B) 出口 (C) 假設 (D) 解剖學

解答 | 21. (A) 22. (D) 23. (B)

❸ 請根據句意，從底下四個選項中選出一個最接近套色單字意思的字彙。

24. 電影相當容易預測結局，許多電影迷看完開場白後，就知道主角和敵對者會發生什麼事，因此堅稱不必看完整部電影。
(A) 敵人 (B) 自私自利者 (C) 受扶養親屬 (D) 車掌

25. 我們將共同分擔珍的結婚禮物費用，每人各出十美元，從薪水中自動扣除。
(A) 期滿 (B) 減去 (C) 隔離 (D) 聚集

解答 | 24. (A) 25. (B)

Review Test_02

❶ 第1到10題為「拼字題」，請根據中文意思完成英文拼字填空。第11到20題為「釋義題」，請根據英文字彙寫出中文意思。

解答 | 1. suspect 2. retrospective 3. convivial
4. resurrection 5. recede 6. intermittent
7. elude 8. precocious 9. distract

10. distribute 11. 倔強的，固執的
12. 回到，回想 13. 公平的，沒有成見的
14. 禁止，使不可能，阻止
15. 呼氣，吐氣，呼出 16. 抗毒素
17. 冷淡，漠不關心 18. 大混亂
19. 漫無止境地，冗長地 20. 期滿失效，過期

❷ 請根據句意，從底下四個選項中選出一個最能適切完成句子的字彙。

21. 美國黃石國家公園以斷續噴出的泉水聞名，也就是間歇泉。
(A) 怡然自得的 (B) 間歇的 (C) 懷舊的 (D) 早熟的

22. 部長試圖介入以調停工會和領導階層。
(A) 退卻 (B) 解放奴隸 (C) 倒退 (D) 調停

解答 | 21. (B) 22. (D)

❸ 請根據句意，從底下四個選項中選出一個最接近套色單字意思的字彙。

23. 從事園藝必定會耗去大量水份，其中多半是汗水。
(A) 療養院 (B) 汗水 (C) 冷淡 (D) 吸引力

24. 布朗太太炫耀自己的兒子是早慧型天才，十個月大就會走路。懷特太太則表示兒子十個月大還要她抱。
(A) 過早成長 (B) 喜歡有人陪伴 (C) 時時發生
(D) 日以繼夜

25. 我們的雙眼瞳孔接觸到光線就會收縮。
(A) 杜絕 (B) 難倒 (C) 歸因於 (D) 收縮

解答 | 23. (B) 24. (A) 25. (D)

Review Test_03

❶ 第1到10題為「拼字題」，請根據中文意思完成英文拼字填空。第11到20題為「釋義題」，請根據英文字彙寫出中文意思。

解答 | 1. collaborate 2. eclectic 3. elaborate
4. conscript 5. diluvial 6. converge
7. divergent 8. inexplicable 9. preposition
10. omnivorous 11. 除草劑 12. 決定
13. 浸禮 14. 破壞的，滋生事端的
15. 了解 / 察覺意識到 16. 落葉性的
17. 讓渡，放棄 18. 虛偽，偽善
19. 交往，往來 / 使互相關聯
20. 淤積的，沖積的

❷ 請根據句意，從底下四個選項中選出一個最能適切完成句子的字彙。

21. 迷迭香經常和懷念聯想在一起，因為葉片被摘下後仍能長期維持翠綠。
(A) 破壞的 (B) 落葉性的 (C) 聯想的 (D) 衰敗的

22. 牛是草食性動物。據說如果餵食肉類給牛群吃，會使牠們變得瘋狂，最後更會感染狂牛症。
(A) 草食性動物 (B) 犯過者 (C) 偽善 (D) 浸禮

23. 弟弟認為只要是沒過期的食物，吃下去都對身體有益。我認為他可以<u>消化</u>任何食物。
(A) 消化 (B) 斷絕關係 (C) 分配 (D) 驅散

解答│ **21.** (C) **22.** (A) **23.** (A)

❸ 請根據句意，從底下四個選項中選出一個最接近套色單字意思的字彙。

24. 農夫葛林噴灑的是除草劑而非殺蟲劑，因此所有蕃茄都枯萎而死。
(A) 餵食各種不同食物 (B) 施行浸禮的行為 (C) 使植物中毒的物質 (D) 以植物餵養的動物

25. 一輛無法開動的車也能造成高速公路交通阻塞。
(A) 集中 (B) 徵召士兵 (C) 浸禮 (D) 壅塞

解答│ **24.** (C) **25.** (D)

Review Test_04

❶ 第1到10題為「拼字題」，請根據中文意思完成英文拼字填空。第11到20題為「釋義題」，請根據英文字彙寫出中文意思。

解答│ **1.** excavate **2.** concave **3.** upgrade
4. degenerate **5.** expatriate **6.** monarch
7. degradation **8.** upsurge **9.** resurgent
10. decrepit **11.** 休息，使休息
12. 干擾，妨礙 **13.** 埋葬 **14.** 中古世紀的
15. 青春期 **16.** 分子凝聚力
17. 固有的，與生俱來的
18. 侵略，入侵 **19.** 腦震盪
20. 適當的 / 足夠的

❷ 請根據句意，從底下四個選項中選出一個最能適切完成句子的字彙。

21. 我舅舅由於<u>與生俱來</u>的粗心大意，從來不是一名好駕駛。
(A) 中古世紀的 (B) 與生俱來的 (C) 衰老的
(D) 復甦的

22. 在<u>中古世紀</u>的封建制度國家，人們是靠左駕駛的。
(A) 中古世紀的 (B) 有黏性的 (C) 雙語的
(D) 使用多國語言的

解答│ **21.** (B) **22.** (A)

❸ 請根據句意，從底下四個選項中選出一個最接近套色單字意思的字彙。

23. 我們全班同學都異口同聲表示想開舞會，大家都很興奮。
(A) 與生俱來的 (B) 言行一致的 (C) 適當的
(D) 瀰漫的

24. 被馬克杯刺穿手掌的女子跑進醫院，她表示因為想用黏著劑把碎杯子黏起來，所以才會受傷。
(A) 黏膠 (B) 侵略 (C) 打擊樂 (D) 青春期

25. 父親在家中扮演多重角色，既是廚師、褓姆、裁縫，同時也是母親的按摩師。
(A) 各種不同的 (B) 同時代的 (C) 重婚 (D) 團塊

解答│ **23.** (B) **24.** (A) **25.** (A)

Practice Test_01

❶ 請根據句意，從底下四個選項中選出一個最接近套色單字意義的字彙。

1. 在美國早期歷史中，一場全國性的政治大會促使美式飯店的問世。
(A) 集會 (B) 輸血 (C) 經濟衰退期 (D) 脫離政黨

2. 據說不喜交際且內向的人需要的生活空間較小。
(A) 勤勉的 (B) 殷勤的 (C) 沉默寡言的
(D) 自我中心的

3. 男子喝醉了而無法控制自己。
(A) 倔強的 (B) 喝醉的 (C) 早熟的 (D) 謙虛的

4. 搬到我家附近的新鄰居是個相當古怪的人。
(A) 共同的 (B) 精心籌劃的 (C) 兼容並蓄的
(D) 奇怪的

5. 我患有消化不良的疾病，我想我的胃有很嚴重的問題。
(A) 全神貫注 (B) 反感 (C) 消化不良 (D) 無神論

解答│ **1.** (A) **2.** (C) **3.** (B) **4.** (D) **5.** (C)

❷ 請閱讀下面短文，並根據文意回答問題。

鮭魚

當太平洋鮭魚長到六足歲大時，就要開始進行交配和產卵，這意味著所有鮭魚都要逆水回游到出生地，也就是北美河川上游區。鮭魚群以氣味作為嚮導，憑著本能回游了大約兩千四百公里遠，到達其目的地。

鮭魚的逆水回游之旅充滿險阻。許多鮭魚成為熊類或其他掠奪者的食物而死亡，其他則因沿途逆流而上耗盡力氣而無法存活。

至於最終成功逆水回游到出生地的鮭魚，要在河床上挖開沙礫，築成產卵坑，準備安置成千上萬顆魚卵。一旦產下魚卵，鮭魚就會因為耗盡力氣、遍體鱗傷而集體死亡，完成一年一度漫長的生命循環。

6. 根據上述文意，回到一字最接近底下哪個選項的意義？
(A) 罷免 (B) 回到 (C) 懷疑 (D) 鄙視

7. 根據上述文意，死亡一字最接近底下哪個選項的意義？
(A) 死亡 (B) 扣除 (C) 禁止 (D) 規避

8. 根據上述文意，存活一字最接近底下哪個選項的意義？
(A) 後退 (B) 隱瞞 (C) 持續 (D) 撤銷

9. 根據上述文意，集體地一字最接近底下哪個選項的意義？
(A) 一起 (B) 易於 (C) 貿然地 (D) 非存心地

10. 根據上述文意，漫長地一字最接近底下哪個選項的意義？
(A) 過度熱情地 (B) 無窮無盡地 (C) 間歇地
(D) 不慎地

解答 | 6. (B) 7. (A) 8. (C) 9. (A) 10. (B)

✱Review Test_05

❶ 第1到10題為「拼字題」，請根據中文意思完成英文拼字填空。第11到20題為「釋義題」，請根據英文字彙寫出中文意思。

解答 | 1. epithet 2. hypothetical 3. magnificent
4. disperse 5. proponent 6. renovation
7. economical 8. disaster 9. prosperous
10. implicit 11. 移居，移民
12. 劃定界限，限定 13. 充氣，使膨脹
14. 報應，天譴 15. 熟練的，完美的
16. 配戴，使生色 17. 監禁，禁閉，拘禁
18. 使激發，爆炸 19. 工匠，手藝師傅，技工
20. 分給，給予

❷ 請根據句意，從底下四個選項中選出一個最能適切完成句子的字彙。

21. 伯朗先生有敏銳的生意頭腦，所以事業發展得很順遂。
(A) 順遂的 (B) 明確的 (C) 沮喪的 (D) 隱含的

22. 考古學家從古代墳墓中挖掘出許多手工藝品。
(A) 手工藝品 (B) 黨人 (C) 工匠 (D) 擁護者

23. 南亞災難大海嘯奪去成千上萬條人命。
(A) 擁立者 (B) 創新 (C) 災難 (D) 序言

解答 | 21. (A) 22. (A) 23. (C)

❸ 請根據句意，從底下四個選項中選出一個最接近套色單字意思的字彙。

24. 露營的第二天大人們笑問：「孩子們，你們比較喜歡吃什麼麵包？是牛油加沙子，還是蜂蜜裹螞蟻？」
(A) 較喜歡 (B) 使明顯 (C) 爆炸 (D) 打氣

25. 珍從考場走出來時神情沮喪，朋友們試著為她加油打氣。
(A) 氣餒的 (B) 不足的 (C) 莊嚴的 (D) 動人的

解答 | 24. (A) 25. (A)

✱Review Test_06

❶ 第1到10題為「拼字題」，請根據中文意思完成英文拼字填空。第11到20題為「釋義題」，請根據英文字彙寫出中文意思。

解答 | 1. impel 2. adduce 3. afford 4. effective
5. infect 6. protection 7. attaché
8. collateral 9. equilateral 10. provocation
11. 電療 12. 原生質 13. 動物學
14. 無定形的，難以歸類的 15. 判決，裁決
16. 暴動，叛亂 17. 迷信，迷信行為
18. 使再生 19. 祖先
20. 強索的，勒索的，貪婪的

❷ 請根據句意，從底下四個選項中選出一個最能適切完成句子的字彙。

21. 經驗豐富的飛機駕駛員對菜鳥飛行員說：「螺旋槳就像電風扇，如果它停下來，你就要冒汗了。」
(A) 抵押擔保品 (B) 螺旋槳 (C) 陪審團判決
(D) 原生動物

22. 請千萬不要提到她突出的下巴，我怕她會生氣。
(A) 突出的 (B) 認識的 (C) 被沒收的 (D) 起訴的

解答 | 21. (B) 22. (A)

❸ 請根據句意，從底下四個選項中選出一個最接近套色單字意思的字彙。

23. 地殼板塊相互碰撞時，支撐沉重海底岩層的板塊便陷落到海底深淵。
(A) 無底深處 (B) 暴動 (C) 降低身份 (D) 再次產生

24. 據說熱茶對預防感冒十分有效。
(A) 可推論的 (B) 貪婪的 (C) 熱塑性的 (D) 有效的

25. 史密斯法官無法達成判決，最後決定擇日再開庭。
(A) 法庭判決 (B) 祖先 (C) 暴飲暴食 (D) 叛亂

解答 | 23. (A) 24. (D) 25. (A)

✱Review Test_07

❶ 第1到10題為「拼字題」，請根據中文意思完成英文拼字填空。第11到20題為「釋義題」，請根據英文字彙寫出中文意思。

解答 | 1. educe 2. premise 3. prescribe
4. inscribe 5. constitute 6. destitution
7. precise 8. circumscribe 9. circumlocution
10. aggressive
11. 令人感到屈辱的，叫人生氣的 12. 驗屍
13. 來賓接待室，前廳 14. 雙邊的，有兩邊的
15. 四邊形的 16. 限制，監禁
17. 勸阻，阻止 18. 細讀，精讀 19. 原始的
20. 宣布赦免，免除

❷ 請根據句意，從底下四個選項中選出一個最能適切完成句子的字彙。

21. 教育的主要目的之一就是激發潛能。
(A) 提前發生 (B) 安撫 (C) 引出 (D) 勸阻

22. 該都市決定拆除年久失修的破舊建築物，並打造一棟新建物。

(A) 節制 (B) 拆除 (C) 說服 (D) 精讀

23. 牧師不喜歡主持婚禮儀式，所以當年輕人開始談論婚姻，他便設法岔開話題。
(A) 限制 (B) 赦免 (C) 主持 (D) 弔唁

解答 | **21.** (C) **22.** (B) **23.** (C)

❸ 請根據句意，從底下四個選項中選出一個最接近套色單字意思的字彙。

24. 企業主因財務危機而破產。
(A) 同時發生的 (B) 天生的 (C) 破產的 (D) 同步的

25. 瓊斯太太試著服用烤生薑來緩和害喜現象，因為親戚告訴她這樣做有效。
(A) 破壞 (B) 變弱 (C) 填入事後日期 (D) 強化

解答 | **24.** (C) **25.** (B)

Review Test_08

❷ 第1到10題為「拼字題」，請根據中文意思完成英文拼字填空。第11到20題為「釋義題」，請根據英文字彙寫出中文意思。

解答 | **1.** relentless **2.** reluctant **3.** faultless
4. overvalue **5.** overexpose **6.** entrench
7. retrench **8.** conjoin **9.** incessantly
10. depreciate **11.** 附上，附加，增補
12. 逼近的，即將到來的
13. 抨擊，對～表示懷疑
14. 無敵的，無法征服的 **15.** 副業的，次要的
16. 殘留物，剩餘，渣滓 **17.** 枯竭，耗盡
18. 維持生活，過日子 **19.** 星座，星群
20. 欺騙，迷惑

❷ 請根據句意，從底下四個選項中選出一個最能適切完成句子的字彙。

21. 貝克先生發現女兒遲歸後感到相當生氣，但後來態度就有點軟化了。
(A) 軟化的 (B) 假裝的 (C) 確定的 (D) 依賴的

22. 丈夫別無選擇只能屈服於妻子的心願。她想要搬到大都市居住。
(A) 屈服於 (B) 增補 (C) 包含在某範圍內 (D) 前導

解答 | **21.** (A) **22.** (A)

❸ 請根據句意，從底下四個選項中選出一個最接近套色單字意思的字彙。

23. 在第二幕和第三幕間的十分鐘換幕時間，傑克外出買飲料。
(A) 星群 (B) 曝光過度 (C) 研究生 (D) 中斷

24. 蚊子不停騷擾露營者，使他們難以成眠。
(A) 完美無瑕地 (B) 永久地 (C) 事先地 (D) 持續地

25. 人類應節省能源，否則自然資源的枯竭可能會像不請自來的賓客一樣，叫人措手不及。

(A) 增補 (B) 暫緩執行 (C) 耗盡 (D) 殘留物

解答 | **23.** (D) **24.** (D) **25.** (C)

Practice Test_02

❶ 請根據句意，從底下四個選項中選出一個最接近套色單字意義的字彙。

1. 自從他採用新裝配線系統後，生意就變好了。
(A) 詳盡的 (B) 繁榮興盛的 (C) 含蓄的 (D) 圓滿的

2. 學生考完試後感到很沮喪，因為他無法解答任何複雜數學問題。
(A) 不足的 (B) 莊嚴的 (C) 氣餒的 (D) 隨興而至的

3. 他簽完合約後決定不要購買房地產，因此失去保證金。
(A) 認出 (B) 失去 (C) 控告 (D) 斷言

4. 迷信的人不願從梯子底下走過，因為相信這樣會帶來厄運。
(A) 不願意的 (B) 不可避免的 (C) 無價的
(D) 產後的

5. 他別無選擇只能屈服於妻子的心願。她堅持要買一輛跑車。
(A) 增補 (B) 維持生活 (C) 讓步 (D) 抨擊

解答 | **1.** (B) **2.** (C) **3.** (B) **4.** (A) **5.** (C)

❷ 請閱讀下面短文，並根據文意回答問題。

地震

地震的發生幾乎是接連不斷的，然而大多數都不具有毀滅性，如地震學家稱之為微震的輕微地震，只能靠地震儀等高度精密儀器才能測知。然而恐怖的地震也不算少見，每年至少都會有一個非常強烈的地震發生在地球某個角落。最強烈的地震經常和地殼斷層錯動有關。大地震的威力能破壞都市、毀壞水壩、引起火山爆發，甚至能使整個湖泊消失不見。地震平均每年奪去大約一萬人的生命，當都市人口和住宅以前所未有的速度增加，預料因地震而造成的傷亡和財物損失也會隨之增加。有鑑於此，許多國家都致力於改善地震偵測方式，並強化地震預報系統，同時更建造耐震的建築物、橋樑和水壩。事實上許多環保運動者試圖勸阻科學家不要進行地下核武試爆，因為這類活動可能會刺激我們敏感而無價的地球。

6. 根據上述文意，強烈的一字最接近底下哪個選項的意義？
(A) 鍥而不捨的 (B) 強大的 (C) 動人的 (D) 熟練的

7. 根據上述文意，破壞一字最接近底下哪個選項的意義？
(A) 表現出 (B) 充氣 (C) 破壞 (D) 分開

8. 根據上述文意，致力一字最接近底下哪個選項的意義？
(A) 黨人 (B) 序言 (C) 努力 (D) 手工藝品

9. 根據上述文意，勸阻一字最接近底下哪個選項的意義？
   (A) 增補 (B) 維持生活 (C) 附加 (D) 阻止

10. 根據上述文意，無價的一字最接近底下哪個選項的意義？
    (A) 珍貴的 (B) 天生的 (C) 可取消的 (D) 逼近的

解答｜ **6.** (B) **7.** (C) **8.** (C) **9.** (D) **10.** (A)

⭐ Review Test_09

❶ 第1到10題為「拼字題」，請根據中文意思完成英文拼字填空。第11到20題為「釋義題」，請根據英文字彙寫出中文意思。

解答｜ **1.** transaction **2.** commute **3.** commotion
4. recess **5.** entomology **6.** epidemic
7. symposium **8.** default **9.** persecute
10. consecutive **11.** 接種疫苗，給予預防接種
12. 永久的，終年的，長年的
13. 使不安，使煩惱，使困擾
14. 切開，解剖，詳細研究
15. 擊敗，驅逐，瓦解敵軍攻勢
16. 牽連，連累，涉及 **17.** 減速
18. 有關，關於 **19.** 接受者
20. 犀利的，敏銳的，尖刻的

❷ 請根據句意，從底下四個選項中選出一個最能適切完成句子的字彙。

21. 部門經理被拔擢為總經理，所以我們一致恭賀他。
    (A) 切除 (B) 迫害 (C) 拔擢 (D) 取決於

22. 我打電話來確認預訂的機票。
    (A) 同情 (B) 安置 (C) 確認 (D) 鼓勵

23. 祖母剝去桃子的外皮，並切除蟲蛀的部分。
    (A) 保有 (B) 改變 (C) 保留 (D) 切除

解答｜ **21.** (C) **22.** (C) **23.** (D)

❸ 請根據句意，從底下四個選項中選出一個接近套色單字意思的字彙。

24. 勞軍茶點送到戰地軍事營區時，士兵們起了一陣極大騷動。
    (A) 休庭 (B) 情緒爆發 (C) 接受者 (D) 昆蟲學

25. 海軍擊敗從邊境入侵的敵軍部隊。
    (A) 切除 (B) 擊退 (C) 關於 (D) 停止

解答｜ **24.** (B) **25.** (B)

⭐ Review Test_10

❶ 第1到10題為「拼字題」，請根據中文意思完成英文拼字填空。第11到20題為「釋義題」，請根據英文字彙寫出中文意思。

解答｜ **1.** erode **2.** infuse **3.** contraction

4. vociferous **5.** invocation **6.** affection
7. deposit **8.** previous **9.** premature
10. immature **11.** 違背，脫離 **12.** 撤退
13. 相稱的，等量的
14. 不為情感所動的，冷靜的
15. 使中斷，使混亂 **16.** 爆發，噴出
17. 擦傷，磨損，侵蝕 **18.** 腐蝕，侵蝕
19. 道德淪喪的，腐敗貪污的
20. 打斷，插嘴，使中斷

❷ 請根據句意，從底下四個選項中選出一個最能適切完成句子的字彙。

21. 雄國王企鵝以慈祥的父愛聞名，牠們為了孵卵可以兩個月不吃不喝。
    (A) 鍾愛 (B) 祈禱 (C) 大量 (D) 密切關係

22. 祖母的痼疾使她變得虛弱，她已經病了很久。
    (A) 侵蝕的 (B) 相稱的 (C) 攔截的 (D) 長期的

解答｜ **21.** (A) **22.** (D)

❸ 請根據句意，從底下四個選項中選出一個最接近套色單字意思的字彙。

23. 侵略國入侵鄰國。
    (A) 侵入 (B) 遠足 (C) 傳染 (D) 擦傷

24. OK害蟲防治公司刊登一份報紙廣告，卻將「蟻群」誤植為「阿姨們」，以致整篇廣告變成：「別擔心您家的『阿姨們』，我們一定會徹底殲滅她們的。」
    (A) 減損 (B) 重新陷入 (C) 根除 (D) 光陰逝去

25. 由於年輕作家的早逝，其作品於身後出版。
    (A) 過早的 (B) 公正的 (C) 平靜的 (D) 腐敗貪污的

解答｜ **23.** (A) **24.** (C) **25.** (A)

⭐ Review Test_11

❶ 第1到10題為「拼字題」，請根據中文意思完成英文拼字填空。第11到20題為「釋義題」，請根據英文字彙寫出中文意思。

解答｜ **1.** avoid **2.** detain **3.** susceptive
4. multiform **5.** multiply **6.** intramural
7. intrastate **8.** compose **9.** effeminate
10. efficacious **11.** 身體畸形，殘缺，殘障
12. 撤退 **13.** 不可預料的，出乎意料的
14. 前任，前輩，祖先 **15.** 迫使，被迫，逼使
16. 詳細說明，辯明 **17.** 使暴露，露出
18. 令人沮喪的，沉悶的
19. （動物）肉食性的，食肉的，（植物）食蟲的
20. 兩黨的，兩黨人士組成的

❷ 請根據句意，從底下四個選項中選出一個最能適切完成句子的字彙。

21. 史考特太太匆忙為丈夫準備早餐，但餐點不見了，

原來被五歲的兒子狼吞虎嚥吃光了。
(A) 暴露出 (B) 推進 (C) 狼吞虎嚥地吃掉 (D) 起程

22. 我們將於本周五舉辦校內運動會。
(A) 校內的 (B) 容易接受的 (C) 合得來的
(D) 缺乏的

23. 老太太事實上想去找驗光師，抱怨幾天前拿到的眼鏡不好用，但卻誤入理髮店，完全找錯地方了。
(A) 瑕疵 (B) 驗光師 (C) 殯葬業者 (D) 左右對稱

解答 | **21**. (C) **22**. (A) **23**. (B)

❸ 請根據句意，從底下四個選項中選出一個最接近套色單字意思的字彙。

24. 兩國外交官都想建立永久外交關係。
(A) 發癢的 (B) 持久的 (C) 州內的 (D) 無法忍受的

25. 死亡和繳稅兩者皆不可免。
(A) 逃避 (B) 歸咎於 (C) 拘留 (D) 歸因於

解答 | **24**. (B) **25**. (A)

Review Test_12

❶ 第1到10題為「拼字題」，請根據中文意思完成英文拼字填空。第11到20題為「釋義題」，請根據英文字彙寫出中文意思。

解答 | **1**. compare **2**. fortify **3**. magnanimous
4. reverse **5**. appeal **6**. comprehend
7. composure **8**. proposal **9**. dissent
10. comfort **11**. 混合物，堆肥 **12**. 傳教士
13. 委託，委任狀，佣金
14. 外國傭兵，受雇傭工
15. 留宿，容納，收容，使適應，供應
16. 指控，控告，告發
17. 消耗，消費，花費，吃光，喝光，毀滅
18. 擔任，承當，假定，以為，假裝
19. 懸殊，不一致，差異 **20**. 贊同，同意

❷ 請根據句意，從底下四個選項中選出一個最能適切完成句子的字彙。

21. 我們這隊在上半場比賽落後，但下半場就扭轉比數。
(A) 顛倒 (B) 放大 (C) 同意 (D) 不同意

22. 近來人們消耗愈來愈多汽油，即使距離很短也習慣開車前往。
(A) 爭奪 (B) 增強 (C) 消耗 (D) 延長

解答 | **21**. (A) **22**. (C)

❸ 請根據句意，從底下四個選項中選出一個最接近套色單字意義的字彙。

23. 他具有自我犧牲的精神，並願意承擔這個重任。
(A) 充分了解 (B) 承擔 (C) 上訴 (D) 逮捕

24. 觀眾席上某位美貌女子轉移了演講者的注意力，使他開始變得言不及義。

(A) 分心 (B) 意見一致 (C) 答應 (D) 同意

25. 船隻相撞事故發生後，大型遠洋郵輪上的船務人員試圖讓乘客保持鎮靜。
(A) 冷靜 (B) 提案 (C) 譴責 (D) 主動表示

解答 | **23**. (B) **24**. (A) **25**. (A)

Practice Test_03

❶ 請根據句意，從底下四個選項中選出一個最接近套色單字意思的字彙。

1. 警方懷疑這起犯罪或許有其他共犯。
(A) 一時衝動 (B) 雙筒望遠鏡 (C) 共犯 (D) 醫務室

2. 十四世紀的歐洲有種流行的傳染性疾病，又稱為黑死病。
(A) 瘟疫 (B) 昆蟲學 (C) 縮影 (D) 行列

3. 聖海倫斯火山的爆發規模非常巨大，許多鄰近地區都被火山灰覆蓋。
(A) 密切關係 (B) 火山噴發 (C) 入侵 (D) 傳染

4. 友人山姆是仁慈的化身，我從未見過比他更仁慈的人。
(A) 觀念 (B) 化身 (C) 殯葬業者 (D) 配鏡師

5. 教室十分寬敞，可容納近百名學生。
(A) 可容納 (B) 爭奪 (C) 消耗 (D) 延長

解答 | **1**. (C) **2**. (A) **3**. (B) **4**. (B) **5**. (A)

❷ 請閱讀下面短文，並根據文意回答問題。

國王企鵝

在所有棲息於地球的動物中，哪種動物是以永恆的母愛著稱的呢？想必我們會毫不遲疑地回答：「人類。」但若被問到人類是否也具有最堅定不移的父愛，許多身為人父者則不免自問，自己是否也曾付出同樣的心力來撫育孩子。「當孩子發燒時，我曾和孩子的媽媽一同在病榻旁徹夜未眠地守候嗎？」「我曾經一晚起來兩、三次甚至更多，幫孩子換尿片嗎？」大部分的答案極可能都是否定的。因此最強烈的父愛化身似乎不是人類，而是國王企鵝。

國王企鵝多半在秋天交配，兩個月後雌企鵝便會生產。雌、雄企鵝成群結隊在南極洲的遙遠內陸地帶長途跋涉，以產下企鵝蛋。雌企鵝在生產過程需付出極大體力，包括長途跋涉至繁殖區的重擔，以及生產的辛勞等，生產完畢後體重通常會減少百分之二十，接著就潛入大海中覓食休息，而由雄企鵝肩負起孵蛋責任。

雄企鵝把蛋托在腳掌上，再用下腹部的外皮把蛋包裹起來，這層外皮內的羽毛會暫時脫落，就像個孵育袋一樣。這個由密布的血管組織構成的孵育袋可調節體溫，即使面對攝氏零下六十度的低溫環境，或每小時風速高達一百五十公里的強風氣候，都能成功孵化企鵝蛋。雄企鵝不吃不喝直接暴露在最惡劣的天候環境，就這樣屈身站立保暖著企鵝蛋，長達兩個月之

久。經過兩個月不眠不休和不辭辛勞後，企鵝蛋終於孵化，此時雄企鵝的體重已經減少了幾乎一半，剩下約三十磅到四十磅左右。當雌企鵝從海上歸來，形容憔悴的雄企鵝便出聲迎接。

6. 根據上述文意，永恆的一字最接近底下哪個選項的意義？
   (A) 永久的 (B) 兩黨的 (C) 肉食性的
   (D) 令人沮喪的

7. 根據上述文意，鍾愛一字最接近底下哪個選項的意義？
   (A) 女權運動 (B) 大量 (C) 鎮靜 (D) 愛

8. 根據上述文意，需要一字最接近底下哪個選項的意義？
   (A) 增強 (B) 改變 (C) 需要 (D) 放大

9. 根據上述文意，肩負起一字最接近底下哪個選項的意義？
   (A) 贊同 (B) 承擔 (C) 比較 (D) 顛倒

10. 根據上述文意，暴露一字最接近底下哪個選項的意義？
    (A) 迫使 (B) 裸露 (C) 光陰逝去 (D) 延長

解答 | **6.** (A) **7.** (D) **8.** (C) **9.** (B) **10.** (B)

✱Actual Test

Passage 1

鐵達尼號

　　一九一二年四月十五日凌晨兩點二十分，隸屬於白星航運公司旗下、為全球最龐大也最豪華的郵輪，且號稱「不會沉沒的」鐵達尼號沉入北大西洋的冰河深處。這場大災難共奪去一千五百條寶貴性命，同時也是人類史上在承平時期傷亡最慘重的船難。

　　鐵達尼號在註定失敗的處女航中，預定從英國南安普頓港出發，航向目的地美國紐約。總重高達四萬六千五百公噸的船艦，在深邃而平穩的海面上以時速二十二·五海里的速度全速前進。白星航運公司希望藉這次處女航，創下以最短時間橫渡大西洋的世界紀錄。此舉固然加速了鐵達尼號的航行速度，卻也使她快速奔向毀滅。四月十四日晚間十一點四十分，全長八百八十三英呎的鐵達尼號迎面撞上巨大冰山，開啟了她悲慘的命運。船橋上的守望員一看見前方出現巨大冰山便立刻高喊警戒，接著採取一切行動避開前方這個不祥的白色物體，但卻徒勞無功，鐵達尼號的船身已經被冰山劃開三百英呎寬的裂痕。撞擊意外發生後，高層船務人員想讓乘客保持鎮靜，於是告訴大家撞擊除了只造成些許延誤外，沒有任何嚴重問題，船上的交響樂團甚至繼續演奏流行音樂。但鐵達尼號的船頭吃水愈來愈深，船務人員只好下令乘客登上救生艇逃生。不幸的是，由於白星航運公司過於自負，認為鐵達尼號絕對不會沉沒，所以啟程時以準備了足夠半數乘客使用的救生艇。再者，有些乘客因過度自信

而拒絕逃生，他們相信以鐵達尼號如此龐大的客輪，不可能面臨真正危險。無論如何，撞到冰山後，鐵達尼號不出三個小時便消失在無底深淵的茫茫大海中。英國客輪卡柏菲亞號在接獲鐵達尼號的求救信號後，便啟程航向意外發生的大混亂現場，數小時後拯救了救生艇上的七百一十二條人命。

　　位於美國麻薩諸塞州的伍茲霍爾海洋科學研究所研究員達利·福斯特，在一九八五年靠聲納找到鐵達尼號沉船的殘骸位置。一年之後，該研究所的深海探測潛艇艾文號，潛入海平面以下一萬兩千英呎的深淵，讓世人得以一瞥鐵達尼號這艘幽靈鬼船的真正面貌。能夠下潛兩萬英呎深的法國最新式深海探測潛艇諾特爾號，於一九九八年肩負起歷史使命。諾特爾號使用內含三萬加侖柴油引擎的巨大浮力氣囊，將一件重達八噸的鐵達尼號船身殘骸拉出海面，這是號稱「重要船身碎片」的鐵達尼號殘骸在事隔八十六年之後首度重見天日。一項分析顯示，細菌導致鐵達尼號的船身鋼鐵產生微生物分解作用，鋼板上的硫化物含量過高，使其約只有現代船艦鋼鐵的四分之一堅固。一般咸信，這就是鐵達尼號禁不起冰山撞擊的原因。然而我們必須記住，鐵達尼號的大災難主要是因人類的疏失和錯誤判斷而引起的，倘若船務人員對鐵達尼號的無懈可擊性不曾過於自信，那麼今天鐵達尼號或許還能倖免於難；倘若船上的守望員未曾發現冰山或舵手不曾緊急轉舵，那麼鐵達尼號應該只會碰撞到前方的冰山而不至於被劃開巨大裂痕，以其特殊設計足以防止進水的水密艙壁，應該能夠勉強抵達目的地紐約，並安棲在自由女神的懷抱中。

1. 根據上述文意，套色單字豪華的可用底下哪個選項的意義來取代？
   (A) 奢華的 (B) 假設的 (C) 意見一致的 (D) 適當的

2. 根據上述文意，套色單字大災難可用底下哪個選項的意義來取代？
   (A) 聚結 (B) 侵略 (C) 大災難 (D) 青春期

3. 根據上述文意，套色單字加速可用底下哪個選項的意義來取代？
   (A) 黏著 (B) 淪落為 (C) 加速 (D) 挖掘

4. 根據上述文意，套色單字巨大的可用底下哪個選項的意義來取代？
   (A) 中古世紀的 (B) 巨大的 (C) 可推論的
   (D) 有效的

5. 根據上述文意，套色單字鎮靜可用底下哪個選項的意義來取代？
   (A) 身心折磨 (B) 冷靜 (C) 窮困 (D) 委婉用語

6. 根據上述文意，套色字詞無底深淵可用底下哪個選項的意義來取代？
   (A) 深淵 (B) 詔書 (C) 殘障 (D) 串通

7. 根據上述文意，套色單字大混亂可用底下哪個選項的意義來取代？
   (A) 瑕疵 (B) 懸殊 (C) 騷動 (D) 慰藉

8. 根據上述文意，套色單字殘骸的可用底下哪個選項的意義來取代？
   (A) 廢除 (B) 暗示 (C) 破碎的 (D) 校內的

9. 根據上述文意，套色單字顯示可用底下哪個選項的意義來取代？
   (A) 遵守 (B) 顯示 (C) 光陰逝去 (D) 撤退

10. 根據上述文意，套色單字引起可用底下哪個選項的意義來取代？
   (A) 徹底消滅 (B) 引起 (C) 延長 (D) 破壞

解答│ **1.** (A) **2.** (C) **3.** (C) **4.** (B) **5.** (B)
　　　6. (A) **7.** (C) **8.** (C) **9.** (B) **10.** (B)

Passage 2

雪崩

造成雪崩的因素很多，其中包括快速積雪或地震等，甚至一名滑雪者的重量也可能引起雪崩。有時一個小小的雪塊或冰塊從突出的岩石或樹枝上掉落，也會引發雪崩；甚至鳥爪輕輕一抓，也可能導致雪崩。此外，大量新雪初成後，若遇到溫暖陽光的照射或大雨沖刷而崩塌，也可能帶來雪崩。一堆積雪再加上大量新雪所造成的過度負荷，是非常不穩定的能量，脆弱的內聚力固然能將積雪穩定於一處，卻也可能在轉眼間輕易崩塌。起初雪板從斜坡層上斷落並滑下山腰，當雪板崩落時，可沿途積聚高達數百萬公噸的雪量。當下滑的速度增加，洶湧而至的大雪就像從天而降般，自空氣層上方幾乎是零阻力地猛衝直下，有時甚至可以約每小時三百六十公里的高速直衝而至，大約是高空跳傘者以自由落體方式落下速度的兩倍。

史上最具災難性的雪崩之一發生在一九七〇年的秘魯境內，地震引發的大雪崩，吞噬了整個雲蓋鎮。此外，一九一〇年同樣也有一場由地震造成的可怕雪崩，發生在美國華盛頓州史帝芬斯隘口不遠處的雪崩，導致兩列火車在雪堆底下起火燃燒，車上共有九十六名乘客，全部因走避不及而喪生。同年在加拿大，一場恐怖的雪崩困住了一群鐵路工作者，當時他們正在清理先前雪崩造成的鐵軌積雪。這場意外總共造成六十二人喪生。

目前估計光是在美國境內，每年就有超過十萬起雪崩意外。不幸的是，當愈來愈多人在冬季進入雪崩頻繁的陡峭山區進行冒險旅遊，因雪崩而喪生的罹難者即已超過五十年代以來的四倍以上。諸如滑雪、玩滑雪板、騎雪上摩托車、攀登高山等野外運動，在在吸引許多從事休閒娛樂活動者前往危險的雪崩地區遊憩，這些地區極有可能只因冒險者在山間一個輕微滑跤，就引發山腰旁傾瀉而下的雪崩。那表面上看來帶有柔軟觸感和脆弱外表的積雪，其實蒙蔽人類。猛衝而來的大雪帶有相當可怕的強大威力，根據估計每平方公尺的衝擊力約可高達一百四十五公噸，因此雪崩的擠壓威力通常是致命的。

在歷史上人類曾注意到雪崩的可怕威力，並將這股力量運用在戰場上。時間回到一九一六年，當時義大利和奧地利士兵互爭兩國邊界上的多羅邁特山脈控制權，雙方人馬都注意到可用砲火引發雪崩，再利用這股強大威力來攻擊敵軍。在為時四十八小時的戰役中，雪崩威力的確受到充分利用，雙方共有一萬八千名士兵喪生。

諷刺的是，過往的歷史戰役為現代的雪崩控制提供了一些觀念。時至今日人類常在積雪尚可控制時，利用加農大砲和炸藥來釋放大雪堆積造成的威脅，如果沒有這些方法，猛衝而下的駭人雪崩以其冰冷的強力一握，無疑將奪去更多生命。

11. 根據上述文意，套色單字堆積的可用底下哪個選項的意義來取代？
   (A) 包含的 (B) 堆積的 (C) 侵蝕的 (D) 綁架的

12. 根據上述文意，套色單字引發可用底下哪個選項的意義來取代？
   (A) 違背 (B) 引起 (C) 儲存 (D) 同情

13. 根據上述文意，套色單字一堆可用底下哪個選項的意義來取代？
   (A) 一堆 (B) 縮影 (C) 交易 (D) 勒索

14. 根據上述文意，套色單字高達可用底下哪個選項的意義來取代？
   (A) 達到 (B) 灌輸 (C) 打斷 (D) 腐蝕

15. 根據上述文意，套色單字災難性的可用底下哪個選項的意義來取代？
   (A) 連續不斷的 (B) 不能預知的 (C) 令人沮喪的
   (D) 災難的

16. 根據上述文意，套色單字每年地可用底下哪個選項的意義來取代？
   (A) 沒耐心地 (B) 每年地 (C) 永久地
   (D) 寬宏大量地

17. 根據上述文意，套色單字吸引可用底下哪個選項的意義來取代？
   (A) 吸引 (B) 放大 (C) 顛倒 (D) 增強

18. 根據上述文意，套色單字蒙蔽可用底下哪個選項的意義來取代？
   (A) 不同意 (B) 欺騙 (C) 慰藉 (D) 比較

19. 根據上述文意，套色單字致命的可用底下哪個選項的意義來取代？
   (A) 致命的 (B) 有推進力的 (C) 有自信的
   (D) 初期的

20. 根據上述文意，套色單字冰冷的可用底下哪個選項的意義來取代？
   (A) 鍥而不捨的 (B) 出生前的 (C) 星際的
   (D) 冰冷的

解答│ **11.** (B) **12.** (B) **13.** (A) **14.** (A) **15.** (D)
　　　16. (B) **17.** (A) **18.** (B) **19.** (A) **20.** (D)

Chapter 2

⭐**Review Test_01**

❶ 第1到10題為「拼字題」，請根據中文意思完成英文拼字填空。第11到20題為「釋義題」，請根據英文字彙寫出中文意思。

解答｜ 1. abbreviate 2. abominate 3. accompany
4. acknowledge 5. acquiesce 6. actuate
7. addendum 8. adjudicate 9. aftermath
10. aggravate 11. 聽從的，順從的
12. 修正，改良，改善，修正案
13. 使活潑，使有活力，激勵，賦予生命
14. 緩和，滿足
15. 適當的，合適的，恰當的，相稱的
16. 約定，指派 17. 軍備，軍事力量
18. 使慣於，使適合
19. 脊椎骨，分水嶺，書脊，中堅
20. 緩和，平息，減輕

❷ 請根據句意，從底下四個選項中選出一個最能適切完成句子的字彙。

21. 珍除了默許她先生的心願外別無其他選擇餘地，他想要搬到鄉間居住。
(A) 默許 (B) 滿足 (C) 撫慰 (D) 決定

22. 部門經理受到董事長的信任，接著又被指派為總經理。
(A) 收養 (B) 縮寫 (C) 指派 (D)承認

23. 抽煙加重了他的咳嗽。
(A) 使有活力 (B) 使惡化 (C) 無罪釋放 (D) 使難堪

解答｜ 21. (A) 22. (C) 23. (B)

❸ 請根據句意，從底下四個選項中選出一個最接近套色單字意思的字彙。

24. 女孩一想到要用老人剛剛舐過的杓子就感到厭惡，雖然她很喜歡吃冰淇淋。
(A) 不願意 (B) 判決 (C) 慣於 (D) 估價

25. 金錢並不是驅動工人展開行動的唯一因素。
(A) 退化 (B) 惡化 (C) 伴隨 (D) 促使

解答｜ 24. (A) 25. (D)

⭐**Review Test_02**

❶ 第1到10題為「拼字題」，請根據中文意思完成英文拼字填空。第11到20題為「釋義題」，請根據英文字彙寫出中文意思。

解答｜ 1. batter 2. beguile 3. belittle 4. beseech
5. bigot 6. blacken 7. blockade
8. bloodshot 9. bombastic 10. bossy
11. 恫嚇，叱責 12. 微積分
13. 笨重而不易搬運的，龐大笨重的，占地方的
14. 障礙，阻礙物，柵欄 15. 凸塊，鼓起之處
16. 使確信，使放心，向～保證
17. 牙牙學語，口齒不清地說話 18. 盆地
19. 故態復萌，墮落，退步
20. 禁止，取締，查禁

❷ 請根據句意，從底下四個選項中選出一個最能適切完成句子的字彙。

21. 懷特太太正在找一位能在她上班時幫忙照顧孩子的臨時褓姆。
(A) 牙牙學語 (B) 障礙物 (C) 臨時褓姆 (D) 盆地

22. 希望出國念書的學生應努力打破語言障礙。
(A) 連續猛擊 (B) 障礙 (C) 一營軍隊 (D) 低音樂器

解答｜ 21. (C) 22. (B)

❸ 請根據句意，從底下四個選項中選出一個最接近套色單字意思的字彙。

23. 女子搬著笨重的包裹上了火車。
(A) 大的 (B) 巨大的 (C) 請求 (D) 懇求

24. 老饕傑克到飲料免費續杯的餐廳用餐，當他第四度要求免費續杯，不堪其擾的女服務生對他說：「需要我給您一台電視機嗎？」
(A) 飲料 (B) 偏執狂 (C) 瘋子 (D) 狂熱份子

25. 請不要以為你跋扈的上司是全世界唯一一個雇主。
(A) 自負的 (B) 跋扈的 (C) 腫起的 (D) 心愛的人

解答｜ 23. (A) 24. (A) 25. (B)

⭐**Review Test_03**

❶ 第1到10題為「拼字題」，請根據中文意思完成英文拼字填空。第11到20題為「釋義題」，請根據英文字彙寫出中文意思。

解答｜ 1. commonplace 2. compromise
3. concentrate 4. condemn 5. confront
6. condensation 7. consolidate
8. contemplate 9. corny 10. correspond
11. 巨大洞窟，凹洞 12. 蛀牙，蛀洞
13. 結業證書，畢業證書，執照
14. 中止，中斷，停止 15. 喋喋不休，嘮叨
16. 倒塌，垮臺，崩潰，瓦解
17. 好戰的，好鬥的，鬥志高昂的
18. 憐憫，同情 19. 寬敞的 20. 清潔劑

❷ 請根據句意，從底下四個選項中選出一個最能適切完成句子的字彙。

21. 美國境內的謝爾曼將軍紅杉是世界上最高大的樹木，同時也是一棵結毬果的針葉樹。
(A) 針葉樹 (B) 弦外之音 (C) 形狀 (D) 外形

22. 董事們決定將兩家公司合而為一。
(A) 沉思 (B) 面臨 (C) 合併 (D) 面對

23. 你在教堂唱詩班裡唱聖歌嗎？我認為你有一付天生的好嗓子。
(A) 妥協 (B) 驚恐 (C) 違規者 (D) 唱詩班

解答│ **21.** (A) **22.** (C) **23.** (D)

❸ 請根據句意，從底下四個選項中選出一個最接近套色單字意思的字彙。

24. 據說該百貨公司是因本身重量而倒塌的，但我認為驚人的顧客量才是倒塌的真正主因。
(A) 崩潰 (B) 同情 (C) 攀爬 (D) 爬上

25. 露營者被告知如果在森林裡遇到熊要裝死。
(A) 凝固 (B) 面對 (C) 凍結 (D) 詮釋

解答│ **24.** (A) **25.** (B)

✳Review Test_04

❶ 第1到10題為「拼字題」，請根據中文意思完成英文拼字填空。第11到20題為「釋義題」，請根據英文字彙寫出中文意思。

解答│ **1.** covert **2.** creature **3.** criminal
4. crisscross **5.** crystallize **6.** culmination
7. cyclone **8.** daring **9.** debase **10.** deepen
11. 被告 **12.** 除霜，解凍，退冰
13. 意味，表示 **14.** 指定，指名 **15.** 蹂躪
16. 減少，縮小 **17.** 拋棄，丟掉，摒棄
18. 使氣餒，使打消念頭，阻止
19. 破壞，使大為遜色，使難看
20. 分割，瓜分，瓦解，解體

❷ 請根據句意，從底下四個選項中選出一個最能適切完成句子的字彙。

21. 他剛到教會時很難背熟《使徒信經》。
(A) 信條 (B) 釘死在十字架上 (C) 頂點
(D) 改革運動

22. 優勝者給了競爭對手致命的一擊。
(A) 給予 (B) 勸阻 (C) 使分心 (D) 阻止

解答│ **21.** (A) **22.** (A)

❸ 請根據句意，從底下四個選項中選出一個最接近套色單字意義的字彙。

23. 他阻止自己的妻子參加購物團。
(A) 荒蕪 (B) 蹂躪 (C) 阻止 (D) 厭惡

24. 疾病使他身體衰弱，什麼事也不能做，因為他太虛弱了。
(A) 延誤 (B) 拖延 (C) 耽擱 (D) 使失去能力

25. 醫護人員用過皮下注射器後就丟棄了。
(A) 拋棄 (B) 避開 (C) 生產 (D) 披露

解答│ **23.** (C) **24.** (D) **25.** (A)

✳Practice Test_01

❶ 請根據句意，從底下四個選項中選出一個最接近套色單字意思的字彙。

1. 詹姆斯對珍的迷戀是顯而易見的，他每次在她面前總顯得不知所措。
(A) 有錯誤的 (B) 明顯的 (C) 心愛的 (D) 跛腳的

2. 他犯了一個大錯，本來該向電腦公司訂購一百部電腦，卻訂成印表機。
(A) 錯誤 (B) 奴隸身分 (C) 違反 (D) 砲轟

3. 如果您能寄送足夠的小冊子，我們將萬分感激。
(A) 碰撞 (B) 教堂唱詩班 (C) 結業證書 (D) 小冊子

4. 如果本身的核燃料耗盡，星星可能因其重量而瓦解。
(A) 憐憫 (B) 攀爬 (C) 瓦解 (D) 譴責

5. 該國已推行節約能源改革運動。
(A) 罪犯 (B) 運動 (C) 僵局 (D) 被告

解答│ **1.** (B) **2.** (A) **3.** (D) **4.** (C) **5.** (B)

❷ 請閱讀下面短文，並根據文意回答問題。

（第一則喜劇故事）

　　鄧恩先生是個生性膽怯的人，他的智齒因為蛀爛所以痛了很久，然而一想到要去看牙醫，他就心生厭惡。某晚他痛到輾轉難眠，要靠服用阿斯匹靈來減輕牙痛，隔天早晨只好打電話到牙醫診所約診，最後前往診所報到。鄧恩先生坐在診療椅上，牙醫將椅子傾斜，他怯懦地緊閉雙眼，全身發抖。牙醫檢查過口腔後驚嘆地說：「哇，這是我這輩子看過最大的蛀牙！」鄧恩先生感到很羞辱，因為他聽到牙醫一再重覆著驚嘆聲，於是便向牙醫表達不滿，但牙醫堅稱：「我只提到你的蛀牙一次。」此時站在牙醫身旁的護士連忙補充：「那是蛀牙的回音啊！」

（第二則喜劇故事）

　　葛林農夫有六名年齡在十歲到二十歲之間的子女。某日他把所有子女都叫到面前來，想知道究竟是誰把農場外的廁所推到小河裡去的。他恫嚇、喊叫、咆哮、懇求，結果當然完全沒用。最後他開始跟孩子們述說美國開國總統喬治‧華盛頓的軼事，他說：「聽好！雖然喬治‧華盛頓砍倒父親心愛的櫻桃樹，但因為他站出來坦承是自己做的，所以不但得到父親原諒，還被稱讚。」此時，葛林農夫最小的兒子站出來承認是他做的，葛林農夫一聽到小兒子的招供，立刻開始打他的屁股。小兒子嗚咽地說：「爸爸，你剛才跟我們說，喬治‧華盛頓的父親原諒他，因為他坦承是他做的。那麼你現在為什麼還要打我呢？」葛林農夫大叫道：「華盛頓砍倒櫻桃樹時，他爸爸可不在樹上！」

6. 根據上述文意，厭惡一字最接近底下哪個選項的意義？
(A) 厭惡 (B) 減輕 (C) 臉色蒼白 (D) 貶值

7. 根據上述文意，減輕一字最接近底下哪個選項的意義？
(A) 減輕 (B) 惡化 (C) 啟動 (D) 採取

8. 根據上述文意，蛀牙一字最接近底下哪個選項的意義？
(A) 頂點 (B) 洞 (C) 中止 (D) 結業證書

9. 根據上述文意，恫嚇一字最接近底下哪個選項的意義？
(A) 碰撞 (B) 威嚇 (C) 相撞 (D) 擴張

10. 根據上述文意，心愛的一字最接近底下哪個選項的意義？
(A) 愚蠢的 (B) 棲息在樹上的 (C) 龐大笨重的 (D) 心愛的

解答｜ 6. (A) 7. (A) 8. (B) 9. (B) 10. (D)

Review Test_05

❶ 第1到10題為「拼字題」，請根據中文意思完成英文拼字填空。第11到20題為「釋義題」，請根據英文字彙寫出中文意思。

解答｜ 1. disorder 2. dispense 3. dissolve
4. dividend 5. dogged 6. downfall 7. drain
8. drought 9. dubious 10. durable
11. 持續，期間，持續時間 12. 居民
13. 厚顏，無恥
14. 窘困的，尷尬的，侷促不安的
15. 使深留，埋入，嵌進
16. 包圍，圍繞，包括，包含
17. 激勵，使精力充沛 18. 放大，擴大
19. 啟迪，啟發 20. 使生動，使活潑

❷ 請根據句意，從底下四個選項中選出一個最能適切完成句子的字彙。

21. 在長期乾旱期間所有田地都變得乾枯。
(A) 畜群 (B) 乾旱 (C) 大眾 (D) 一大群

22. 在印度，丈夫通常期望妻子帶來大批嫁妝。這筆錢的多寡常引發夫妻爭執。
(A) 嫁妝 (B) 傲慢 (C) 功效 (D) 厚顏無恥

23. 蜘蛛絲是世界上最耐用的物質之一，科學家正設法利用它來製造手術縫合用線、防彈背心、汽車保險槓，以及登陸錨鏈等。
(A) 可疑的 (B) 激動的 (C) 耐用的 (D) 不確定的

解答｜ 21. (B) 22. (A) 23. (C)

❸ 請根據句意，從底下四個選項中選出一個最接近套色單字意思的字彙。

24. A：我們要如何分辨可食用蘑菇和有毒蘑菇呢？
B：很簡單，吃吃看就知道了。
(A) 耐用的 (B) 激動的 (C) 有毒的 (D) 可食用的

25. 黃石國家公園是一座巨大的休火山，其岩漿庫長約二十公里，寬約四．五公里。
(A) 不間斷的 (B) 頑強的 (C) 潛伏的 (D) 持續的

解答｜ 24. (D) 25. (C)

Review Test_06

❶ 第1到10題為「拼字題」，請根據中文意思完成英文拼字填空。第11到20題為「釋義題」，請根據英文字彙寫出中文意思。

解答｜ 1. enumerate 2. equilibrium 3. erroneous
4. escapade 5. estrange 6. evanescent
7. exculpate 8. exorbitant 9. expenditure
10. fallible 11. 婚外的 12. 狂熱者，～迷
13. 兇猛的，殘忍的，野蠻的 14. 技巧，手腕
15. 浮誇的，炫耀的
16. 易燃的，可燃的，速燃的
17. 菜鳥，年輕而無經驗者
18. 有勇無謀的，魯莽的 19. 隊形
20. 偶然的，意外的

❷ 請根據句意，從底下四個選項中選出一個最能適切完成句子的字彙。

21. 懷俄明州給予婦女參政權，也就是選舉權，以吸引更多人前來定居。
(A) 參政權 (B) 兄弟關係 (C) 手足之情 (D) 艦隊

22. 這所學校的學生受到校方鼓勵，參加放學後的課外活動。
(A) 現存的 (B) 課外的 (C) 容易犯錯的 (D) 婚外的

解答｜ 21. (A) 22. (B)

❸ 請根據句意，從底下四個選項中選出一個最接近套色單字意思的字彙。

23. 這個容器裡的溶液十分易燃，你不可以在這附近吸煙。
(A) 草率的 (B)易燃的 (C) 衝動的 (D) 兇猛的

24. 對我來說，你的要求幾乎等於命令。
(A) 短暫的 (B) 艦隊 (C) 相當於 (D)經過的

25. 我們對於要負擔的過高金額感到很驚訝。
(A) 惡劣的 (B) 錯誤的 (C) 現存的 (D) 過度的

解答｜ 23. (B) 24. (C) 25. (D)

Review Test_07

❶ 第1到10題為「拼字題」，請根據中文意思完成英文拼字填空。第11到20題為「釋義題」，請根據英文字彙寫出中文意思。

解答｜ 1. fructify 2. fulfill 3. gainsay 4. gesticulate
5. ghastly 6. gigantic 7. glacier 8. glossy
9. grandiose 10. handy 11. 冰冷的
12. 怕老婆的，懼內的
13. 中空的，空的，凹處，洞

14. 合乎人道的，慈悲的，有人情味的
15. 僵局，死路，死巷
16. 無情的，殘忍的，毫不留情的，難以平息的
17. 無生命的，死氣沉沉的，無生氣的
18. 難以彌補的，積重難返的，無可救藥的
19. 控告，使負罪，牽連入罪
20. 不屈不撓的，勤勉不懈的，頑強的

❷ 請根據句意，從底下四個選項中選出一個最能適切完成句子的字彙。

21. 一九一二年四月，鐵達尼號沉入北大西洋冰冷的海底深處。
   (A) 巨大的 (B) 無邊無際的 (C) 冰冷的 (D) 微小的

22. 桌椅都是無生命的東西，它們是沒有生命的。
   (A) 缺乏的 (B) 無生命的 (C) 勤勉的
   (D) 難以彌補的

23. 鳥類擁有中空的骨骼，因為維持較輕的重量對飛行來說是極為重要的。
   (A) 中空的 (B) 可怕的 (C) 肌肉發達的
   (D) 最後面的

解答 | 21. (C) 22. (B) 23. (A)

❸ 請根據句意，從底下四個選項中選出一個最接近套色單字意思的字彙。

24. 許多人都認為經理自大傲慢。
   (A) 自大傲慢的 (B) 粗心的 (C) 不謹慎的
   (D) 怠慢的

25. 男子來自貧窮家庭，所以非常努力多賺點錢。
   (A) 不間斷的 (B) 窮困的 (C) 根本的 (D) 不適用的

解答 | 24. (A) 25. (B)

✦ Review Test_08

❶ 第1到10題為「拼字題」，請根據中文意思完成英文拼字填空。第11到20題為「釋義題」，請根據英文字彙寫出中文意思。

解答 | 1. infallible 2. infamous 3. infernal
   4. infiltrate 5. infinitesimal 6. inflammatory
   7. inflammable 8. initiate 9. inordinate
   10. insipid 11. 威嚇，脅迫，恐嚇
   12. 調查，審查，研究
   13. 無法挽回的，不能修補的 14. 投棄
   15. 滑稽的，愛開玩笑的 16. 法官的，司法的
   17. 明智的 18. 陪審員
   19. 親屬關係，血緣，家族 20. 跪下

❷ 請根據句意，從底下四個選項中選出一個最能適切完成句子的字彙。

21. 這道數學難題超乎我的理解範圍，無法解答。
   (A) 理解範圍 (B) 核心 (C) 物質 (D) 要點

22. 經過長時間的吃力工作，工人累壞了。
   (A) 可燃的 (B) 吃力的 (C) 微小的 (D) 可燃性的

解答 | 21. (A) 22. (B)

❸ 請根據句意，從底下四個選項中選出一個最接近套色單字意思的字彙。

23. 嘿，你這個動作慢的人，請快一點。
   (A) 危險 (B) 疲勞 (C) 風險 (D) 動作緩慢者

24. 我試圖將部分工作轉交新人以減輕工作量。
   (A) 排出 (B) 解放 (C) 減輕 (D) 使自由

25. 傑克以虛張聲勢恐嚇同學。
   (A) 分離 (B) 使恐懼 (C) 開始 (D) 使正式就任

解答 | 23. (D) 24. (C) 25. (B)

✦ Practice Test_02

❶ 請根據句意，從底下四個選項中選出一個最接近套色單字意義的字彙。

1. 據報澳洲這場久旱是史無前例的。
   (A) 乾枯 (B) 持續時間 (C) 居民 (D) 化身

2. 我不知道這是不是可食用蘑菇。
   (A) 窘困的 (B) 等值的 (C) 可食用的 (D) 錯誤的

3. 汽車保養維修費太高，以致貝克先生決定將車賣掉。
   (A) 婚外的 (B) 過度的 (C) 容易犯錯的 (D) 狂熱者

4. 他女兒對食物很挑剔，所以吃得很少。
   (A) 愛挑剔的 (B) 有勇無謀的 (C) 易燃的
   (D) 有光澤的

5. 由於辦公室的吃力工作，他回到家已精疲力盡。
   (A) 滑稽的 (B) 明智的 (C) 艱鉅費力的 (D) 合法的

解答 | 1. (A) 2. (C) 3. (B) 4. (A) 5. (C)

❷ 請閱讀下面短文，並根據文意回答問題。

（第一則喜劇故事）
紐奧良遭受惡劣雨季侵襲，大雨不停地下了四天，許多低窪地區一片積水。傑克村莊裡多數農舍都被雨水淹沒，村民們個個垂頭喪氣。最後雨勢終於減弱，疏散到鄰近小學避難的村民也在幾天後返回遭豪雨重創的家園。所有村民扶老攜幼合力重建倒塌住處，並重整凌亂農具。傑克詢問鄰居災情如何，鄰居回道：「該死的鯉魚竟然吃掉我種在後院的所有玉米，我還在閣樓上逮到幾尾！」

（第二則喜劇故事）
我把地鐵列車看成具體而微的世界，那裡有各種不同的人物個性，貪心、聒噪、好奇、為人著想，甚至挑剔都有。

我搭地鐵上班時，一個身穿雪白衣服的女士也上

車站在中年男子面前，而不坐在旁邊空位，然後立刻從手提包拿出純白手帕包住吊環，看來應該是不想碰觸表面。雖然不知道是什麼原因，但我猜她怕碰到細菌或吊環上黏有化妝品什麼的。坐在她前方的中年男子則正在打瞌睡。火車駛入車站時煞車突然失靈，最後終於勉強停下來，衝力使挑剔女士把手帕掉在中年男子的西裝領子上，再落到他褲子上，男子被緊急煞車吵醒，半夢半醒間發現一張白布就誤以為是自己的襯衫沒塞好，於是把它塞進褲子裡又立刻睡著了。

6. 根據上述文意，惡劣的一字最接近底下哪個選項的意義？
   (A) 幼稚的 (B) 可怕的 (C) 犯錯的 (D) 過高的

7. 根據上述文意，垂頭喪氣的一字最接近底下哪個選項的意義？
   (A) 沮喪的 (B) 心煩意亂的 (C) 每日的
   (D) 可食用的

8. 根據上述文意，疏散一字最接近底下哪個選項的意義？
   (A) 撤離 (B) 無能力 (C) 耗盡精力 (D) 點燃

9. 根據上述文意，有效的一字最接近底下哪個選項的意義？
   (A) 明智的 (B) 有知覺的 (C) 吃力的 (D) 無誤的

10. 根據上述文意，好挑剔的一字最接近底下哪個選項的意義？
    (A) 地獄的 (B) 罪大惡極的 (C) 無生命的
    (D) 愛挑剔的

解答 | 6. (B) 7. (A) 8. (A) 9. (D) 10. (D)

✱ Review Test_09

❶ 第1到10題為「拼字題」，請根據中文意思完成英文拼字填空。第11到20題為「釋義題」，請根據英文字彙寫出中文意思。

解答 | 1. licentious 2. lineage 3. linguistics
       4. longevity 5. lower 6. mammal
       7. masterful 8. maternal 9. merchandise
       10. mercurial 11. 不幸，橫禍
       12. 不適應環境者 13. 流動性 14. 國籍
       15. 駕駛 16. 極肥胖的 17. 天文台，氣象台
       18. 遠方可見之海面，近在眼前 19. 不祥的
       20. 產生，發生，發起，創始，起源

❷ 請根據句意，從底下四個選項中選出一個最能適切完成句子的字彙。

21. 新成立的政府正努力掃除前任政府留下的政治遺產。
    (A) 降低 (B) 駕駛 (C) 除去 (D) 帶領

22. 請冷靜下來，我不是有意要冒犯你。
    (A) 冒犯 (B) 產生 (C) 發起 (D) 引發

23. 蛋白石是不透明的，無法一眼望穿。
    (A) 及時的 (B) 不透明的 (C) 令人作嘔的 (D) 使人反感的

解答 | 21. (C) 22. (A) 23. (B)

❸ 請根據句意，從底下四個選項中選出一個最接近套色單字意思的字彙。

24. 胖女士在醫院量體重時，體重計顯示：「請把這個數字當成你的智商。」
    (A) 裝飾華麗的 (B) 不祥的 (C) 肥胖的 (D) 及時的

25. 警方無法斷定誰該為這起事故負責。
    (A) 意外 (B) 粗心 (C) 懶散 (D) 不履行

解答 | 24. (C) 25. (A)

✱ Review Test_10

❶ 第1到10題為「拼字題」，請根據中文意思完成英文拼字填空。第11到20題為「釋義題」，請根據英文字彙寫出中文意思。

解答 | 1. overwhelm 2. pallid 3. particle
       4. perfunctory 5. personnel 6. pestilence
       7. pinnacle 8. placebo 9. poignant
       10. prejudice 11. 第一的，首位的，首要的
       12. 原始的 13. 緩刑 14. 範圍，領域，視界
       15. 四重唱，四重奏 16. 問卷，調查表
       17. 徹底搜尋，尋遍 18. 折扣 19. 魯莽的
       20. 反責，反控

❷ 請根據句意，從底下四個選項中選出一個最能適切完成句子的字彙。

21. 我不喜歡這件洋裝的顏色，所以想退費。
    (A) 改革 (B) 療法 (C) 退費 (D) 剩飯

22. 請憑收據退費。
    (A) 偏見 (B) 折扣 (C) 緩刑 (D) 收據

解答 | 21. (C) 22. (D)

❸ 請根據句意，從底下四個選項中選出一個最接近套色單字意義的字彙。

23. 該國人民成功驅逐暴君。
    (A) 延伸 (B) 驅逐 (C) 延長 (D) 拖延

24. 她的仁慈使我大為感動。
    (A) 使透不過氣 (B) 排出 (C) 流放 (D) 驅逐

25. 我們駕車到郊外欣賞田園風光。
    (A) 部分的 (B) 零碎的 (C) 鄉下風光的
    (D) 非自願的

解答 | 23. (B) 24. (A) 25. (C)

✸ Review Test_11

❶ 第1到10題為「拼字題」，請根據中文意思完成英文拼字填空。第11到20題為「釋義題」，請根據英文字彙寫出中文意思。

解答│ **1.** renegade **2.** renew **3.** reparable
4. reproach **5.** resources **6.** retard **7.** rollen
8. semblance **9.** servitude **10.** shoplifter
11. 同時的，同時發生的
12. 散漫的，隨便的，草率的
13. 隨便的，潦草的 **14.** 懶人，遊手好閒者
15. 使窒息，使透不過氣 **16.** 快速的，迅速的
17. 主權 **18.** 不景氣的，蕭條的
19. 高峰會議，頂峰 **20.** 召喚

❷ 請根據句意，從底下四個選項中選出一個最能適切完成句子的字彙。

21. 人們常以人造奶油取代牛油。
(A) 毀損 (B) 聲明放棄 (C) 取代 (D) 更新

22. 基本上，我們的地球資源有限。
(A) 資源 (B) 必需品 (C) 脫黨者 (D) 叛徒

23. 樓上的女士以蛙叫般的聲音唱著聖誕頌歌，我發現她真是個音癡。
(A) 充裕的 (B) 廣闊的 (C) 寬敞的 (D) 音盲的

解答│ **21.** (C) **22.** (A) **23.** (D)

❸ 請根據句意，從底下四個選項中選出一個最接近套色單字意思的字彙。

24. 近幾年來我國經濟持續蕭條。
(A) 停滯不前的 (B) 寬敞的 (C) 迅速的 (D) 快速的

25. 冷凍肉品可減緩細菌蔓延。
(A) 揭露 (B) 翻找 (C) 使減緩 (D) 洩露

解答│ **24.** (A) **25.** (C)

✸ Review Test_12

❶ 第1到10題為「拼字題」，請根據中文意思完成英文拼字填空。第11到20題為「釋義題」，請根據英文字彙寫出中文意思。

解答│ **1.** totalitarian **2.** tycoon **3.** trealise
4. trespass **5.** turbulent **6.** trial
7. undergrowth **8.** upheaval **9.** uprising
10. uproot **11.** 預防接種 **12.** 激烈的
13. 復仇，報復，報仇
14. 致命的，劇毒的，充滿敵意的，惡毒的
15. 行蹤，下落，所在 **16.** 荒野，野外
17. 工作第一的人，工作至上者
18. 碼尺，量尺 **19.** 渴望的，沉思的
20. 狂熱份子

❷ 請根據句意，從底下四個選項中選出一個最能適切完成句子的字彙。

21. 大家都說嘗試錯誤是知識之源。
(A) 試驗 (B) 颱風 (C) 學術論文 (D) 大變動

22. 腐敗官員向她索取回扣。
(A) 私下的 (B) 有教養的 (C) 任性的 (D) 不孕的

解答│ **21.** (A) **22.** (A)

❸ 請根據句意，從底下四個選項中選出一個最接近套色單字意思的字彙。

23. 友人去世後，老人感到空虛。
(A) 自負 (B) 虛榮 (C) 空虛 (D) 復仇

24. 山姆送的玫瑰都凋謝了，因為她忘記放到花瓶中。
(A) 篡奪 (B) 連根拔除 (C) 滅絕 (D) 凋謝

25. 喬伊絲太太的休旅車維修費很高。
(A) 預防接種 (B) 動亂 (C) 維修 (D) 灌木叢

解答│ **23.** (C) **24.** (D) **25.** (C)

✸ Practice Test_03

❶ 請根據句意，從底下四個選項中選出一個最接近套色單字意義的字彙。

1. 新當選政府決定根除前任政府留下的政治遺產。
(A) 減低 (B) 產生 (C) 冒犯 (D) 根除

2. 她是很有勇氣的女士，不怕走在許多男子前面。
(A) 勇氣 (B) 不幸 (C) 流動性 (D) 疏忽

3. 洗完澡要花更多時間把自己弄乾時，你就知道自己變胖了。
(A) 貧窮的 (B) 許多的 (C) 鼻音的 (D) 肥胖的

4. 這座島嶼相當值得推薦給想欣賞田園風光的人。
(A) 部分的 (B) 鄉下風味的 (C) 公然的
(D) 裝飾華麗的

5. 我們要為媽媽舉辦一個驚喜派對，請不要洩露出去。
(A) 消失 (B) 洩露 (C) 平息 (D) 利用

解答│ **1.** (D) **2.** (A) **3.** (D) **4.** (B) **5.** (B)

❷ 請閱讀下面短文，並根據文意回答問題。

（第一則喜劇故事）

一對老夫妻走進寬敞的高級餐廳，在昏暗角落裡坐下，服務生詢問是否準備點餐，老夫妻對菜單挑三揀四了半天，最後決定點沙朗嫩煎牛排。食物才一上桌老先生就狼吞虎嚥起來，但老太太連叉子都沒有碰一下，只喝了點水解渴。服務生看老太太的樣子像是很餓，於是擔心地上前詢問是否餐點有問題，老太太回道一切都好，服務生只好退到一旁以免顯得多管閒事。最後老先生終於吃完了，接著悄悄遞了一樣東西給對面的妻子，原來是他的假牙！

（第二則喜劇故事）

一對新婚夫妻搭機度蜜月，新娘和新郎分別坐在靠窗和走道座位。由於兩人從未搭過飛機，因此從未見過許多新奇事物。飛機起飛後，近視頗深的兩人緊盯著地面景色，大約一小時後，新娘興奮地大喊：「吉米，快往下看，太讓人吃驚了，已經飛行了一個鐘頭，這個潔白海灘還看不到盡頭，真想不到會有那麼長的海灘。」新郎回答：「真的嗎？讓我看看。」他屈身向窗外望去，然後反駁妻子道：「胡說，這不是海灘而是機場跑道。天啊，真想不到會有那麼長的機場跑道！」此時止不住好奇心的空姐也靠近他們，並向窗外一瞧，原來只是機翼。

6. 根據上述文意，寬敞的一字最接近底下哪個選項的意義？
   (A) 寬敞的 (B) 平靜的 (C) 犀利的 (D) 瑣碎的

7. 根據上述文意，消解一字最接近底下哪個選項的意義？
   (A) 阻止 (B) 發生 (C) 侵占 (D) 解渴

8. 根據上述文意，許多的一字最接近底下哪個選項的意義？
   (A) 真實的 (B) 都市化的 (C) 許多的 (D) 散漫的

9. 根據上述文意，反駁一字最接近底下哪個選項的意義？
   (A) 模擬 (B) 駁倒 (C) 毀損 (D) 延長

10. 根據上述文意，止住一字最接近底下哪個選項的意義？
    (A) 冒犯 (B) 清償 (C) 平息 (D) 使窘迫

解答｜ 6. (A) 7. (D) 8. (C) 9. (B) 10. (C)

✱ Actual Test

Passage 1

黑洞

許多科學家堅稱某些太空區域具有強大重力，可吸噬時間、空間，甚至光線。強大吸引力會拖慢時間、拉長空間，並吞噬光線。由於光線逃不出去，所以這個區域是黑暗而不可見的。

美國物理學家約翰·惠勒將這些深不可測的吸噬空洞稱為「黑洞」。雖然還沒有具體發現能證實黑洞概念，早在一九一五年愛因斯坦提出相對論之際，部分科學家便已著手研究黑洞存在的可能性和成因。例如德國天文學家史瓦茲旭爾德便主張，與直徑一百三十九萬兩千公里的太陽同等大小的一顆星星，可以在一秒鐘內塌陷成直徑不到三公里，因為強大重力足以控制光線。一九三九年美國物理學家歐本海默和史奈德聲稱，一顆比太陽質量大三·二倍的星星一旦耗盡核燃料，就會因本身質量而塌陷變小。

一般公認包括太陽在內的許多星體都是透過核融合釋放能量，如果核燃料消耗殆盡，就會漸漸變小，

仰賴質量而存在的星體自此進入三種不同階段。不到太陽質量八倍大的星星會逐漸冷卻，最後因核燃料耗盡而成為白矮星；比太陽質量大八到十二倍的星星則因其核心質量而塌陷，中子核心壓縮導致大爆炸，形成超新星，並帶來半徑不到十公里、密度甚高的中子星；至於其他質量超大的較大星體也會塌陷，但不會爆炸，而是漸漸變小，在縮小過程中密度漸增，重力相對漸增，因此加速縮小，最後形成黑洞。

目前預估銀河共有一億個由塌陷星體形成的黑洞。一九九二年科學家利用哈柏太空望遠鏡觀測到極可能是約為太陽質量三百萬倍大的黑洞，此舉等於為將來一探黑洞奧秘而鋪路。

科學家同時也將注意焦點放在白洞上，因為相對於能吸入所有東西的黑洞，理應也存在能釋放所有東西的太空區域。此觀念源自相對論，約翰·惠勒將這條連接兩個黑洞的捷徑稱為「蟲洞」，暗示它就像條蟲一樣，連時間和空間都可「吞噬」。部分科學家認為人類可以超光速穿越蟲洞。

1. 根據上述文意，套色單字深不可測的可用底下哪個選項的意義來取代？
   (A) 無底的 (B) 好戰的 (C) 寬敞的 (D) 魯莽的

2. 根據上述文意，套色單字證實可用底下哪個選項的意義來取代？
   (A) 徹底搜尋 (B) 鎮壓 (C) 漫步 (D) 證實

3. 根據上述文意，套色單字塌陷可用底下哪個選項的意義來取代？
   (A) 召喚 (B) 窒息 (C) 崩潰 (D) 取代

4. 根據上述文意，套色單字消耗殆盡可用底下哪個選項的意義來取代？
   (A) 更新 (B) 耗盡 (C) 責備 (D) 驅逐

5. 根據上述文意，套色單字釋放可用底下哪個選項的意義來取代？
   (A) 易遭受 (B) 蒸發 (C) 取消 (D) 釋放

解答｜ 1. (A) 2. (D) 3. (C) 4. (B) 5. (D)

Passage 2

電影

看過榮獲一九六五年奧斯卡金像獎最佳影片《真善美》的人，一定不會忘記配樂〈Do, Re, Mi〉的優美旋律、片中孩童的逗趣對白、男女主角的羅曼史，以及緊湊懸疑的劇情。茱莉亞·安德魯斯飾演個性開朗但和修道院格格不入的修女瑪麗亞，被派往大家庭擔任家庭教師，從此一肩扛起照顧七名孩童的責任，不但陪伴他們嬉戲，當孩子們因父親嚴格管教而沮喪，也鼓勵他們振作。她教孩子們唱動聽歌曲，孩子們也深愛著她。瑪麗亞愛上並嫁給加拿大籍演員克里斯多夫·普拉瑪飾演的英俊男主人、海軍上校崔普。最後崔普和瑪麗亞決定帶著孩子們逃離納粹占領的奧地利。這部片長一百七十二分鐘的音樂片裡一應俱全

地涵蓋了喜劇、懸疑和愛情劇情等。

除了《真善美》之外，還有許多影評在吸引著電影迷。當我們沉醉於《齊瓦哥醫生》的雪景時，耳中還縈繞著〈拉娜的主旋律〉。喬治・盧卡斯自編自導的最佳科幻小說電影《星際大戰》帶我們一覽遙遠而奇異的銀河系。湯姆・漢克斯除了在《浩劫重生》裡教大家如何用冰刀拔蛀牙外，同時讓我們想像如果魯賓遜有威爾森牌排球在手，就算漂流到荒島也會喃喃自語個不停。從彼得・傑克森導演的《魔戒》中，我們發現只要有一枚戒指在手就能任由想像力馳騁，或如影片經典台詞「我的珍寶」般當成訂婚戒。

電影能讓電影迷雀躍不已，即使是不常看電影的人，只要一坐進電影院，也會焦急等待影片開演。漆黑的戲院讓大家毫無拘束地流露各種情緒。現在的觀眾大多不願流露感情，但過去的觀眾不怕笑掉大牙、哭腫雙眼、因恐懼而有意無意抱緊約會對象，甚至把嗓子都喊啞了。過去曾有過度投入愛情片或動作片劇情的觀眾心不在焉地把手伸進隔壁鄰座而非約會對象的爆米花筒裡。電影迷常會從電影角色中尋求認同感，例如看完阿諾・史瓦辛格或李小龍電影的男性觀眾，會挺著肩膀和脖子走出戲院。

自從盧米埃兄弟在咖啡廳地下室實驗第一部電影後，電影工業便如火如荼發展起來，並在電台、戲院，甚至電視的競爭下勝出。好萊塢備受尊崇的演員卡萊・葛倫曾說：「電影工作者在工廠裡製造產品，再以罐頭裝運出去。」無論如何，電影吸引電影迷猶如糖果罐吸引孩童一般。

6. 根據上述文意，套色單字沮喪可用底下哪個選項的意義來取代？
   (A) 沮喪的 (B) 龐大笨重的 (C) 每日的 (D) 謹慎的

7. 根據上述文意，套色單字沉醉可用底下哪個選項的意義來取代？
   (A) 著迷 (B) 頑強 (C) 可食用 (D) 逐漸消失

8. 根據上述文意，套色單字拔出可用底下哪個選項的意義來取代？
   (A) 放下 (B) 使無能 (C) 逐出 (D) 拔出

9. 根據上述文意，套色單字流露可用底下哪個選項的意義來取代？
   (A) 露出 (B) 訴諸 (C) 延長 (D) 加強

10. 根據上述文意，套色單字吸引可用底下哪個選項的意義來取代？
    (A) 終止 (B) 編織 (C) 吸引 (D) 枯萎

解答│ **6.** (A) **7.** (A) **8.** (D) **9.** (A) **10.** (C)

Chapter 3

✱ Review Test_01

❶ 第1到10題為「拼字題」，請根據中文意思完成英文拼字填空。第11到20題為「釋義題」，請根據英文字彙寫出中文意思。

解答│ **1.** acid **2.** acrimonious **3.** acetic **4.** adjoin
5. adjacent **6.** advent **7.** adjust **8.** adjunct
9. aesthetic **10.** agile **11.** 使敵對，使成敵人
12. 煽動，鼓動 **13.** 農藝學，農業經濟
14. 農業 **15.** 耕地的，農業的
16. 假名，化名 **17.** 高度表 **18.** 海拔，標高
19. 選擇，二擇一 **20.** 寬宏大量的

❷ 請根據句意，從底下四個選項中選出一個最能適切完成句子的字彙。

21. 足夠的財富使他可以環遊世界。
    (A) 足夠的 (B) 農業的 (C) 示愛的 (D) 模稜兩可的

22. 友人迷戀上同班同學，在她面前說話結結巴巴。
    (A) 充足的 (B) 迷戀的 (C) 外僑的 (D) 鄉土味的

解答│ **21.** (A) **22.** (B)

❸ 請根據句意，從底下四個選項中選出一個最接近套色單字意思的字彙。

23. 燕子是靈活而行動敏捷的飛鳥。
    (A) 連續的 (B) 鄰近的 (C) 尖酸刻薄的 (D) 敏捷的

24. 我別無其他選擇只能去看牙醫，因為牙痛使我整夜輾轉難眠。
    (A) 先兆 (B) 不在場證明 (C) 選擇 (D) 改變

25. 父親大力稱讚他在字彙測驗裡拿到七十%的成績。
    (A) 煽動 (B) 讚揚 (C) 喚起 (D) 引起

解答│ **23.** (D) **24.** (C) **25.** (B)

✱ Review Test_02

❶ 第1到10題為「拼字題」，請根據中文意思完成英文拼字填空。第11到20題為「釋義題」，請根據英文字彙寫出中文意思。

解答│ **1.** biennial **2.** centennial **3.** anthropology
4. misanthropic **5.** antiwar **6.** antithesis
7. antidote **8.** aquarium **9.** Aqualung
10. archetype **11.** 考古學家 **12.** 大主教
13. 熱烈的，忠誠的 **14.** 太空人 **15.** 星號
16. 觀眾席，禮堂 **17.** 可聽見的，聽得見的
18. 獨裁的，專制的 **19.** 自治，主權國家
20. 叛亂，反抗

❷ 請根據句意，從底下四個選項中選出一個最能適切完成句子的字彙。

21. 五歲大的傑克正在釣魚缸裡的魚，貓咪也非常興奮。
(A) 魚缸 (B) 抗體 (C) 年鑑 (D) 類人猿

22. 考古學家在巴基斯坦發現一些鯨化石。
(A) 天使長 (B) 無政府狀態 (C) 原型 (D) 考古學家

解答｜ **21.** (A) **22.** (D)

❸ 請根據句意，從底下四個選項中選出一個最接近套色單字意思的字彙。

23. 搬沙發到屋外是件非常費力的工作。
(A) 累人的 (B) 熱烈的 (C) 熱切的 (D) 百年一次的

24. 這條裝配線以機器人焊接零件和噴漆。
(A) 小行星 (B) 星號 (C) 機器人 (D) 慈善家

25. 該國無法和好戰鄰國和睦相處。
(A) 真正的 (B) 非偽造的 (C) 侵略的 (D) 聽得見的

解答｜ **23.** (A) **24.** (C) **25.** (C)

Review Test_03

❶ 第1到10題為「拼字題」，請根據中文意思完成英文拼字填空。第11到20題為「釋義題」，請根據英文字彙寫出中文意思。

解答｜ **1.** beneficial **2.** benefactor **3.** benefit
4. caloric **5.** chafe **6.** nonchalance
7. recalcitrant **8.** callosity **9.** candid
10. incinerate **11.** 激勵，刺激
12. 使入迷，使陶醉 **13.** 取消，宣布放棄
14. 懸崖，危機 **15.** 使陷於～，使突然發生
16. 投降，停止反抗 **17.** 主要的，根本的
18. 一致，和睦，友好協定 **19.** 食肉動物
20. 大災難，大慘敗

❷ 請根據句意，從底下四個選項中選出一個最能適切完成句子的字彙。

21. 坦白說，我並不滿意你的報告。
(A) 廣闊的 (B) 固執的 (C) 熱量的 (D) 坦率的

22. 兩鄰居和睦相處相互幫忙。
(A) 人頭稅 (B) 戒律 (C) 和睦 (D) 心臟病患

23. 電影鉅片使許多電影迷著迷。
(A) 投降 (B) 著迷 (C) 詠唱 (D) 宣布放棄

解答｜ **21.** (D) **22.** (C) **23.** (B)

❸ 請根據句意，從底下四個選項中選出一個最接近套色單字意思的字彙。

24. 請勿燒掉容器。
(A) 燒掉 (B) 背誦 (C) 扼要重述 (D) 誘捕

25. 我們須同意建議條款。
(A) 讓與 (B) 同意 (C) 正式放棄 (D) 著迷

解答｜ **24.** (A) **25.** (B)

Review Test_04

❶ 第1到10題為「拼字題」，請根據中文意思完成英文拼字填空。第11到20題為「釋義題」，請根據英文字彙寫出中文意思。

解答｜ **1.** insecticide **2.** concise **3.** incise
4. decisive **5.** incite **6.** recite **7.** disclaim
8. proclaim **9.** exclaim **10.** clamor
11. 下降，下跌，衰退 **12.** 隱士，遁世者
13. 結論，結局 **14.** 排外的，限制他人加入的
15. 合作 **16.** 巧合 **17.** 承認，察覺
18. 對抗，抵銷，中和
19. （地位、能力等）同等者，對應者
20. 偽造的，假冒的

❷ 請根據句意，從底下四個選項中選出一個最能適切完成句子的字彙。

21. 農夫噴灑一些殺蟲劑好除去作物上的害蟲。
(A) 背誦 (B) 編年史 (C) 殺蟲劑
(D) 高度精準計時器

22. 真巧，我也要去圖書館。
(A) 巧合 (B) 結論 (C) 上坡 (D) 喧鬧

解答｜ **21.** (C) **22.** (A)

❸ 請根據句意，從底下四個選項中選出一個最接近套色單字意思的字彙。

23. 老人因慢性病而變得虛弱。
(A) 簡潔的 (B) 長期的 (C) 簡練的 (D) 果斷的

24. 隱士過著隱居生活，避免與人接觸。
(A) 隱士 (B) 鑑賞家 (C) 對比 (D) 違禁品

25. 胖女士發現計程車司機忽略她後決定減肥。
(A) 知曉的 (B) 排外的 (C) 肥胖的 (D) 相反的

解答｜ **23.** (B) **24.** (A) **25.** (C)

Practice Test_01

❶ 請根據句意，從底下四個選項中選出一個最接近套色單字意義的字彙。

1. 隨著電腦的問世，現代人不用上圖書館也可以收集大量資訊。
(A) 附屬品 (B) 來臨 (C) 一致同意 (D) 先兆

2. 儘管似乎動作緩慢，北極熊其實是敏捷的掠食者。
(A) 毗連的 (B) 鄉下的 (C) 敏捷的 (D) 過度的

3. 她和弟弟間的爭吵起自她的謾罵。
(A) 海拔 (B) 爭吵 (C) 背誦 (D) 大災難

4. 使用殺蟲劑已對生態環境造成有害影響。
(A) 殺蟲劑 (B) 編年史 (C) 高度精準計時器
(D) 喧鬧

5. 與一般看法相反的是，飛機是最安全的交通工具之一。

(A) 同意 (B) 相反的 (C) 熱誠的 (D) 重要的

解答│ **1.** (B) **2.** (C) **3.** (B) **4.** (A) **5.** (B)

❷ 請閱讀下面短文，並根據文意回答問題。

（第一則喜劇故事）

大型油輪海鷗號的大副和輪機長一向不和，兩人脾氣都差，所有船員們都覺得他們水火不容。由於每次見面總是齜牙咧嘴，所以兩人可能最熟悉對方的牙齒形狀勝過其他一切。某日兩人間的仇視面臨一觸即發的緊要關頭，彼此爭論著誰在船上扮演的角色比較重要。吵了大概半小時後船長出面調停，叫兩人互換工作，看看誰更重要。大副下去機房控制引擎而對手輪機長則上去甲板掌舵。兩人角色剛換，大副就透過對講機叫道：「喂，在那邊的，所有引擎都突然故障了，我不懂為什麼啊！」輪機長回道：「船擱淺了！」

（第二則喜劇故事）

摯友送給吉米一隻大麥町幼犬當作生日禮物，他決定帶著可愛小狗到女友南西家讓她瞧瞧。南西也很喜歡牠，緊緊抱著牠親，叫吉米醋意大發。然而，小狗必定是對這種激烈的歡迎很反感，不但發出呻吟哀鳴，還伴隨著噪叫、嗚咽、吠叫、大吼，甚至怒號。這時外頭有人敲門，南西打開門一看，原來是帶著一臉笑意的祖母，她擁抱著南西並大叫：「我的寶貝，恭喜妳！吉米終於向妳求婚了！當年妳祖父向我求婚時也做了一模一樣的事。」

6. 根據上述文意，仇視一字最接近底下哪個選項的意義？

(A) 到來 (B) 麻醉藥 (C) 爭論 (D) 敵意

7. 根據上述文意，船長一字最接近底下哪個選項的意義？

(A) 總指揮 (B) 垂直面 (C) 受益者 (D) 海拔

8. 根據上述文意，對手一字最接近底下哪個選項的意義？

(A) 對手 (B) 屍體 (C) 食肉動物 (D) 鑑賞家

9. 根據上述文意，反感一字最接近底下哪個選項的意義？

(A) 反感 (B) 一致同意 (C) 農業經濟 (D) 緊要關頭

10. 根據上述文意，大叫一字最接近底下哪個選項的意義？

(A) 煽動 (B) 漫步 (C) 撤回 (D) 大叫

解答│ **6.** (D) **7.** (A) **8.** (A) **9.** (A) **10.** (D)

⭐ Review Test_05

❶ 第1到10題為「拼字題」，請根據中文意思完成英文拼字填空。第11到20題為「釋義題」，請根據英文字彙寫

出中文意思。

解答│ **1.** incredible **2.** discredit **3.** credit
4. credulous **5.** incubate **6.** accumulate
7. cumulative **8.** cursive **9.** precursory
10. cursory **11.** 貶值 **12.** 降級，降等
13. 使惡化，變壞 **14.** 誹謗，中傷
15. 慣用兩手的 **16.** 診斷書，診斷結果
17. 正相反地，完全地 **18.** 馴養，豢養
19. 有助於～，導致 **20.** 誘因，動機

❷ 請根據句意，從底下四個選項中選出一個最能適切完成句子的字彙。

21. 守財奴累積了大量財富。

(A) 懷疑 (B) 相信 (C) 累積 (D) 妨礙

22. 即使只是大略一瞥也可以看出他的報告寫得很好。

(A) 粗略的 (B) 有害的 (C) 靈巧的 (D) 精明的

23. 探險家並不氣餒，相信終能克服所有困難。

(A) 氣餒的 (B) 對角線的 (C) 熱心的
(D) 足智多謀的

解答│ **21.** (C) **22.** (A) **23.** (A)

❸ 請根據句意，從底下四個選項中選出一個最接近套色單字意思的字彙。

24. 父親想勸誘女兒用功念書，於是答應如果考高分就買手機給她。

(A) 原諒 (B) 誘使 (C) 捐贈 (D) 寬恕

25. 辦公室職員問他是否有興趣成為器官捐贈者。

(A) 依賴 (B) 信條 (C) 捐贈者 (D) 中傷

解答│ **24.** (B) **25.** (C)

⭐ Review Test_06

❶ 第1到10題為「拼字題」，請根據中文意思完成英文拼字填空。第11到20題為「釋義題」，請根據英文字彙寫出中文意思。

解答│ **1.** dyslexia **2.** dystrophy **3.** exemption
4. redemption **5.** ethnic **6.** ethnocentric
7. euphemism **8.** eulogize **9.** exodus
10. exotic **11.** 小說，虛構，想像
12. 傳染性的，傳染病的 **13.** 膚淺的，外表的
14. 使不能，使落空 **15.** 充分的，足夠的
16. 圓周，周長，周圍 **17.** 終止，斷絕，切斷
18. 冒泡的，起泡的 **19.** 使發酵
20. 忠實，忠貞，忠誠

❷ 請根據句意，從底下四個選項中選出一個最能適切完成句子的字彙。

21. 演員們常假裝流淚。

(A) 種族的 (B) 虛假的 (C) 不相干的 (D) 人種的

22. 關於安樂死或所謂的仁慈助死有許多爭議。

(A) 營養失調 (B) 贖罪 (C) 優生學 (D) 安樂死

解答｜ **21.** (B) **22.** (D)

❸ 請根據句意，從底下四個選項中選出一個最接近套色單字意思的字彙。

23. 我懷疑這個計畫是否可行，因為費用太高。
(A) 傳染性的 (B) 接觸傳染性的 (C) 可行的
(D) 膚淺的

24. 該國決定和鄰國斷絕外交關係。
(A) 煽動 (B) 中斷 (C) 反抗 (D) 徹底摧毀

25. 水族館裡有許多外來品種熱帶魚。
(A) 外來的 (B) 人工的 (C) 冒泡的 (D) 多管閒事的

解答｜ **23.** (C) **24.** (B) **25.** (A)

✳ Review Test_07

❶ 第1到10題為「拼字題」，請根據中文意思完成英文拼字填空。第11到20題為「釋義題」，請根據英文字彙寫出中文意思。

解答｜ **1.** infinite **2.** flexible **3.** reflection
4. floriculture **5.** affluence **6.** fluent
7. forswear **8.** forsake **9.** afford
10. fortification **11.** 零碎的，殘破不全的
12. 侵權，違反 **13.** 骨折，斷裂，裂縫
14. 冰箱 **15.** 冷淡 **16.** 逃犯，逃亡者
17. 起源，創始，發生
18. 異質的，由不同成分形成的
19. 當地特有的，土產的
20. 造成，引發，帶來

❷ 請根據句意，從底下四個選項中選出一個最能適切完成句子的字彙。

21. 簽署合約前，需仔細閱讀包括加註小字在內的所有文字。
(A) 細小的 (B) 如花的 (C) 體弱多病的
(D) 氣色紅潤的

22. 請站著別動，地板上有花瓶碎片。
(A) 逃犯 (B) 碎片 (C) 堡壘 (D) 軍事要塞

23. 儘管天生殘疾，她仍可望成為世界知名音樂家。
(A) 天生的 (B) 異質的 (C) 流暢的 (D) 零碎的

解答｜ **21.** (A) **22.** (B) **23.** (A)

❸ 請根據句意，從底下四個選項中選出一個最接近套色單字意義的字彙。

24. 中古世紀人們相信四種不同體液可決定人的個性和健康狀況。
(A) 變遷 (B) 骨折 (C) 液體 (D) 違法

25. 母親到郵局寄聖經給兒子，郵務人員問有無易碎物品交寄，母親便回答：「十誡。」（註：最早的十誡是上帝用手指刻在石板上的，但最後被摩西摔碎。）

(A) 易碎的 (B) 意氣相投的 (C) 坦率的
(D) 當地特有的

解答｜ **24.** (C) **25.** (A)

✳ Review Test_08

❶ 第1到10題為「拼字題」，請根據中文意思完成英文拼字填空。第11到20題為「釋義題」，請根據英文字彙寫出中文意思。

解答｜ **1.** grapple **2.** graphic **3.** monograph
4. bibliography **5.** calligraphy **6.** ingratitude
7. congratulate **8.** ingratiate **9.** gravity
10. grieve **11.** 違反，罪過 **12.** 進展，發展
13. 合計，總計的，集合 **14.** 聚集，人群
15. 群居的，喜群居的
16. 住處，住所，棲息地 **17.** 居民，居住者
18. 支持者，追隨者，擁護者
19. 遲疑，猶豫，躊躇
20. 異質的，由不同成分構成的

❷ 請根據句意，從底下四個選項中選出一個最能適切完成句子的字彙。

21. 學校牆上有許多塗鴉。
(A) 烹飪原料 (B) 接枝 (C) 組成要素 (D) 塗鴉

22. 經常成群結隊的野鵝是群居的鳥類。
(A) 群居的 (B) 重力的 (C) 免費地 (D) 感激的

解答｜ **21.** (D) **22.** (A)

❸ 請根據句意，從底下四個選項中選出一個最接近套色單字意思的字彙。

23. 多數孩子都不願受到雙親不必要的干涉。
(A) 感激的 (B) 寫實的 (C) 無稽的 (D) 活潑的

24. 如果沒有地心引力，學童就不需要花太多公車費。
(A) 悲傷 (B) 地心引力 (C) 違法 (D) 進展

25. 許多動物因自然棲息地遭到破壞而瀕臨絕種。
(A) 棲息地 (B) 聚集人群 (C) 專題論文 (D) 擁護者

解答｜ **23.** (C) **24.** (B) **25.** (A)

✳ Practice Test_02

❶ 請根據句意，從底下四個選項中選出一個最接近套色單字意義的字彙。

1. 即使粗略一瞥也可看出他的報告極需改進。
(A) 有害的 (B) 易碎的 (C) 身體虛弱的 (D) 倉促的

2. 她無法再忍受先生跋扈的態度。
(A) 熱情的 (B) 人工的 (C) 專橫的 (D) 充分的

3. 電視常播出許多不必要的暴力鏡頭，孩童過度接觸暴力肯定會有不良影響。
(A) 無根據的 (B) 感激的 (C) 極差的
(D) 支離破碎的

4. 美術系學生無法理解經濟學教授的解說。教授問紅色需求曲線遇到藍色供給曲線時會怎樣,學生回答:「變紫色。」
   (A) 引發 (B) 冬眠 (C) 理解 (D) 討好

5. 吉米獨自健行時遇到許多大麻煩,他在山巔跌斷腿。
   (A) 使不能 (B) 力足以 (C) 斷裂 (D) 擊敗

解答│ **1.** (D) **2.** (C) **3.** (A) **4.** (C) **5.** (C)

❷ 請閱讀下面短文,並根據文意回答問題。

無尾熊

澳洲特有的無尾熊只吃尤加利葉,成熊一天可吃掉一磅樹葉,特殊的盲腸功能可消化對其他生物有害的粗葉。幼熊七個月才斷奶,接著開始自行咀嚼樹葉。無尾熊從不離開尤加利樹,因此非常適應樹棲生活。無尾熊的食趾和其他趾相對,和人類一樣擁有可相對指頭,所以可抓取東西。無尾熊待在安全的樹上一整天下來,有四分之三的時間都在睡覺。

雌無尾熊以相當於一顆葡萄柚大小的育兒袋撫養幼熊,等幼熊大到育兒袋裝不下,就會爬到母熊背上,直到一歲左右才下來。幼熊兩歲大時已完全獨立,此時母熊才會再度懷胎。幼熊常坐在樹枝上將雙臂高舉過頭,模樣很像人類孩童被母親處罰,也許幼熊是因貪睡受罰吧。總之無尾熊最主要的日常活動就是睡覺。

6. 根據上述文意,特有的一字最接近底下哪個選項的意義?
   (A) 極差的 (B) 當地特有的 (C) 異質的 (D) 寫實的

7. 根據上述文意,有害的一字最接近底下哪個選項的意義?
   (A) 有害的 (B) 排外的 (C) 草率的 (D) 累積的

8. 根據上述文意,棲息地一字最接近底下哪個選項的意義?
   (A) 聚集的人群 (B) 棲息地 (C) 系譜學 (D) 片斷

9. 根據上述文意,抓取一字最接近底下哪個選項的意義?
   (A) 力足以 (B) 放棄 (C) 抓住 (D) 哀悼

10. 根據上述文意,主要的一字最接近底下哪個選項的意義?
    (A) 不屈不撓的 (B) 主要的 (C) 輕信的 (D) 種族的

解答│ **6.** (B) **7.** (A) **8.** (B) **9.** (C) **10.** (B)

★Review Test_09

❶ 第1到10題為「拼字題」,請根據中文意思完成英文拼字填空。第11到20題為「釋義題」,請根據英文字彙寫出中文意思。

解答│ **1.** hibernate **2.** posthumous **3.** humiliate
4. dehydrate **5.** hydrant **6.** hypersensitive

7. hypertension **8.** hyperacidity **9.** hypocrite
10. hypochondria **11.** 轉變,轉換
12. 特有氣質,癖性 **13.** 傻瓜,笨蛋
14. 火的,火成的 **15.** 點火裝置
16. 憤怒,憤慨 **17.** 關節炎 **18.** 注射,打針
19. 投影機,幻燈機 **20.** 少年的,年輕的

❷ 請根據句意,從底下四個選項中選出一個最能適切完成句子的字彙。

21. 懷特先生收到訃聞,得知友人伯朗先生已去世。
    (A) 慣用語 (B) 訃聞 (C) 行程表 (D) 打針

22. 電視機常被稱作傻瓜盒。
    (A) 傻瓜 (B) 點火裝置 (C) 關節炎 (D) 燃燒

23. 秘書因男同事的沙文主義情結而感到義憤填膺。
    (A) 憤慨 (B) 詐欺 (C) 變更 (D) 欺騙

解答│ **21.** (B) **22.** (A) **23.** (A)

❸ 請根據句意,從底下四個選項中選出一個最接近套色單字意思的字彙。

24. 董事長決定延會。
    (A) 憂傷 (B) 地心引力 (C) 延後 (D) 進展

25. 幾乎所有孩童都非常討厭打針。
    (A) 投影機 (B) 打針 (C) 偽君子 (D) 消防栓

解答│ **24.** (C) **25.** (B)

★Review Test_10

❶ 第1到10題為「拼字題」,請根據中文意思完成英文拼字填空。第11到20題為「釋義題」,請根據英文字彙寫出中文意思。

解答│ **1.** league **2.** legacy **3.** allegiance
4. colleague **5.** collection **6.** eligible
7. relentlessly **8.** alleviate **9.** literal
10. literary **11.** 新石器時代的 **12.** 巨石的
13. 使脫臼 **14.** 分配,配置
15. 多話的,非常健談的 **16.** 正式談話,討論
17. 發光的,明亮的 **18.** 半透明的
19. 滑稽的,可笑的 **20.** 錯覺,幻覺,假象

❷ 請根據句意,從底下四個選項中選出一個最能適切完成句子的字彙。

21. 史密斯太太從沒想過自己的兒子會是少年犯。
    (A) 清晰易懂的 (B) 有光澤的 (C) 透明的
    (D) 少年的

22. 空污問題的解決方案始終搖擺不定。
    (A) 多話的 (B) 新石器時代的 (C) 難以捉摸的
    (D) 文學的

解答│ **21.** (D) **22.** (C)

❸ 請根據句意,從底下四個選項中選出一個最接近套色單字意思的字彙。

23. 我相信申請者有資格擔任此職務。
    (A) 寬大的 (B) 有資格的 (C) 本地的 (D) 識字的

24. 大洪水過後一名受災戶在自家頂樓捕獲一條鯉魚。
    (A) 尾聲 (B) 沐浴儀式 (C) 洪水 (D) 配置

25. 同事的高大身材使我能輕易在人群中找到他。
    (A) 發現 (B) 挑選 (C) 以槓桿撬開 (D) 使脫臼

解答│ **23.** (B) **24.** (C) **25.** (A)

✱Review Test_11

❶ 第1到10題為「拼字題」，請根據中文意思完成英文拼字填空。第11到20題為「釋義題」，請根據英文字彙寫出中文意思。

解答│ 1. magnitude 2. malediction 3. malevolent
4. malcontent 5. malefactor 6. malnutrition
7. manual 8. manipulate 9. manufacture
10. pyromania 11. 偏執狂，狂熱 12. 竊盜狂
13. 大規模的，強大的 14. 中等的，媒介
15. 調停，斡旋，使和解 16. 愛管閒事的
17. 旋律，美妙音樂 18. 柔美的，圓潤的
19. 大赦，特赦 20. 潛入水中，潛航

❷ 請根據句意，從底下四個選項中選出一個最能適切完成句子的字彙。

21. 大部分人都反對在自家附近蓋工廠。
    (A) 詛咒 (B) 大部分 (C) 疾病 (D) 瘋狂

22. 我的電腦故障所以印出錯誤資料。
    (A) 操縱 (B) 浮現 (C) 故障 (D) 製造

23. 舅舅創辦一家電腦相關企業，並累積大筆財富。
    (A) 累積 (B) 干涉 (C) 仲裁 (D) 干預

解答│ **21.** (B) **22.** (C) **23.** (A)

❸ 請根據句意，從底下四個選項中選出一個最接近套色單字意思的字彙。

24. 健忘症患者去看醫生，醫生問怎麼了他卻不記得。於是醫生對他說：「請回家把它忘了。」
    (A) 追憶 (B) 健忘 (C) 仲裁者 (D) 手銬

25. 兩位企業主簽署合約將兩家公司合而為一。
    (A) 顯示 (B) 潛航 (C) 裝病逃避 (D) 合併

解答│ **24.** (B) **25.** (D)

✱Review Test_12

❶ 第1到10題為「拼字題」，請根據中文意思完成英文拼字填空。第11到20題為「釋義題」，請根據英文字彙寫出中文意思。

解答│ 1. prominent 2. imminent 3. minimum
4. dismiss 5. missionary 6. commit
7. admonish 8. demonstrate
9. monopolistic 10. mutable 11. 突變，變種

12. 產前的，出生前的 13. 否定，使無效
14. 負面的，否定的
15. 虛無主義者，無政府主義者
16. 有害的，有毒的
17. 無辜的，清白的，純真無邪的
18. 夜間活動的，夜間的
19. 初學者，新手
20. 創新的

❷ 請根據句意，從底下四個選項中選出一個最能適切完成句子的字彙。

21. 傳說烏鴉啼叫預告大雨來臨。
    (A) 微小的 (B) 凸出的 (C) 獨占性的 (D) 逼近的

22. 姪子的興趣是收集迷你模型車。
    (A) 即將發生的 (B) 迷你的 (C) 天然的 (D) 天賦的

解答│ **21.** (D) **22.** (B)

❸ 請根據句意，從底下四個選項中選出一個最接近套色單字意思的字彙。

23. 年輕人對新穎事物感興趣。
    (A) 誠實的 (B) 新的 (C) 負面的 (D) 無辜的

24. 女兒說：「爸爸最棒了，一定知道我要什麼，何不快點匯錢來呢？」
    (A) 寄送 (B) 押送 (C) 示範 (D) 告誡

25. 火山正噴出岩漿和火山灰。
    (A) 排出 (B) 否定 (C) 抗議 (D) 打消

解答│ **23.** (B) **24.** (A) **25.** (A)

✱Practice Test_03

❶ 請根據句意，從底下四個選項中選出一個最接近套色單字意思的字彙。

1. 小姪子很討厭打針，醫生只是提一下也會讓他大聲叫嚷。
   (A) 消防栓 (B) 傻瓜 (C) 槓桿 (D) 打針

2. 蚊子整晚嗡嗡叫個不停，露營者只好爬出帳外跳入水中。
   (A) 不斷地 (B) 局部地 (C) 字面上地 (D) 多話地

3. 蘇的營養失調肇因於飲食不充足和不均衡。
   (A) 瘋狂 (B) 營養不足 (C) 大多數 (D) 光輝

4. 國稅局注意到該富人多數財富都是透過土地投機買賣積聚的。
   (A) 減到最少 (B) 排放 (C) 累積 (D) 裝病逃避

5. 乘客決定勸告公車司機小心駕駛，於是起身走向他，此時司機卻突然加速行駛。
   (A) 犯罪 (B) 勸告 (C) 匯錢 (D) 潛航

解答│ **1.** (D) **2.** (A) **3.** (B) **4.** (C) **5.** (B)

② 請閱讀下面短文，並根據文意回答問題。

> **分享**
>
> 　　近年來印度某個小村落據報有多數孩童遭到狡黠的連續殺人犯殺害，村民連續好幾個月提心吊膽過日子，認為自己遭到惡靈詛咒。大家採取各種措施避禍卻徒勞無功，最後當幾乎所有孩童都慘遭不幸時，科學家進入村子裡展開持續調查。連續殺人犯之謎在一名孩童親眼目睹野狼攻擊自己的表弟後才開始逐漸明朗。孩童看到表弟被狼攻擊和拖行，便跑向狼，跟牠搏鬥，孤注一擲地想救回表弟，幸好兩名孩童都脫險了。村民和科學家終於知道連續殺人犯是一匹狼，同時也發現部分農夫曾因那匹狼毀壞穀物而放火燒掉牠的巢穴，把幼狼都燒死了。當然這是個特例，但我們也從中學到寶貴教訓，那就是人類不應獨占所有生物共享的自然環境。

6. 根據上述文意，多數一字最接近底下哪個選項的意義？
(A) 疾病 (B) 大多數 (C) 突變 (D) 通勤者

7. 根據上述文意，狡黠的一字最接近底下哪個選項的意義？
(A) 卓越的 (B) 少年的 (C) 難以捉摸的 (D) 有光澤的

8. 根據上述文意，有惡意的一字最接近底下哪個選項的意義？
(A) 微小的 (B) 夜間的 (C) 無辜的 (D) 邪惡的

9. 根據上述文意，持續的一字最接近底下哪個選項的意義？
(A) 不懈的 (B) 寬大的 (C) 合格的 (D) 本地的

10. 根據上述文意，獨占一字最接近底下哪個選項的意義？
(A) 壟斷 (B) 抗議 (C) 否定 (D) 出現

解答｜ **6.** (B) **7.** (C) **8.** (D) **9.** (A) **10.** (A)

✳ Review Test_13

① 第1到10題為「拼字題」，請根據中文意思完成英文拼字填空。第11到20題為「釋義題」，請根據英文字彙寫出中文意思。

解答｜ **1.** synonym **2.** onomatopoeia **3.** object
4. obstruct **5.** myopic **6.** optics **7.** oration
8. inexorable **9.** orthodox **10.** orthodontics
11. 超過，勝過 **12.** 比～長命 **13.** 以手勢示意
14. 萬靈丹 **15.** 比較，對照
16. 平行的，相似的 **17.** 無動於衷的
18. 愛國的 **19.** 無感覺的，無表情的
20. 父親的，由父親遺傳的

② 請根據句意，從底下四個選項中選出一個最能適切完成句子的字彙。

21. 他收到一封<u>不明</u>寄件人的匿名信。
(A) 傳統的 (B) 光學的 (C) 匿名的 (D) 客觀的

22. 小弟長大而穿不下外套，現在有意穿我的。
(A) 長大而不再～ (B) 比～長命 (C) 遣返 (D) 改寫

23. 國王企鵝以<u>父</u>愛著稱。
(A) 泰然自若的 (B) 父親的 (C) 冷淡的 (D) 愛國的

解答｜ **21.** (C) **22.** (A) **23.** (B)

③ 請根據句意，從底下四個選項中選出一個最接近套色單字意思的字彙。

24. 無情的酷熱沙漠迫使許多動物白天睡在土裡。
(A) 非正統的 (B) 不依慣例的 (C) 一視同仁的
(D) 不間斷的

25. 烏龜：你也知道據說我有個祖先勝過兔子。兔子：你也知道不是每隻兔子都會在賽跑途中睡著。
(A) 抗議 (B) 封鎖 (C) 領先 (D) 長大而不再～

解答｜ **24.** (D) **25.** (C)

✳ Review Test_14

① 第1到10題為「拼字題」，請根據中文意思完成英文拼字填空。第11到20題為「釋義題」，請根據英文字彙寫出中文意思。

解答｜ **1.** punctuate **2.** puncture **3.** pungent
4. acupuncture **5.** pedestal **6.** pedigree
7. pedestrian **8.** pendulum **9.** independent
10. perforate **11.** 使困惑，使混亂 **12.** 周邊
13. 能力，勝任，稱職 **14.** 食慾，胃口
15. 留聲機 **16.** 語音學 **17.** 複製品，模型
18. 開墾，開採，利用 **19.** 履行，實施，執行
20. 豐富的，豐產的

② 請根據句意，從底下四個選項中選出一個最能適切完成句子的字彙。

21. 小孩以大頭針<u>戳破</u>氣球。
(A) 不時打斷 (B) 沿街叫賣 (C) 戳破 (D) 阻撓

22. 攝影師將相機架在三腳架上。
(A) 三腳架 (B) 針灸治療 (C) 血統 (D) 鐘擺

解答｜ **21.** (C) **22.** (A)

③ 請根據句意，從底下四個選項中選出一個最接近套色單字意思的字彙。

23. 問題依舊懸而未決。
(A) 獨立自主的 (B) 未解決的 (C) 固執的
(D) 困惑的

24. 任性少年不聽父母勸告。
(A) 絕對的 (B) 充裕的 (C) 任性的 (D) 衝動的

25. 我想配這把鑰匙。
(A) 編辮子 (B) 複製 (C) 語音學 (D) 困境

解答｜ **23.** (B) **24.** (C) **25.** (B)

✲ Review Test_15

❶ 第1到10題為「拼字題」，請根據中文意思完成英文拼字填空。第11到20題為「釋義題」，請根據英文字彙寫出中文意思。

解答│ 1. ponder 2. repository 3. superimpose
4. posterity 5. postpone 6. omnipotent
7. potentate 8. pregnancy
9. comprehensive 10. apprentice
11. 堅不可摧 12. 壓力，壓迫，壓制
13. 印象 14. 初期的，原始的
15. 私人的，非公開的，機密的
16. 主人翁，倡導者
17. 必須做的，義務的，強制的
18. 連根拔除，消滅 19. 使著迷，使狂喜
20. 癡狂，滿心歡喜

❷ 請根據句意，從底下四個選項中選出一個最能適切完成句子的字彙。

21. 該國的軍事力量勝過鄰國。
(A) 儲藏室 (B) 勝過 (C) 戰後的 (D) 統治者

22. 父親在信件末尾寫上「兒子，請不要結婚」的附筆。
(A) 附筆 (B) 壓力 (C) 印象 (D) 匱乏

23. 男子別無選擇只能屈服於妻子的施壓。
(A) 壓力 (B) 學徒 (C) 主人翁 (D) 外交禮節

解答│ 21. (B) 22. (A) 23. (A)

❸ 請根據句意，從底下四個選項中選出一個最接近套色單字意思的字彙。

24. 為了後世福祉，我們應保護自然資源。
(A) 受訓者 (B) 君王 (C) 子孫 (D) 倉庫

25. 儘管看來行動遲緩，其實北極熊非常敏捷。
(A) 並列的 (B) 笨重的 (C) 萬能的 (D) 不起作用的

解答│ 24. (C) 25. (B)

✲ Review Test_16

❶ 第1到10題為「拼字題」，請根據中文意思完成英文拼字填空。第11到20題為「釋義題」，請根據英文字彙寫出中文意思。

解答│ 1. deride 2. ridiculous 3. corroborate
4. interrogative 5. abrogate 6. arrogant
7. sagacious 8. desultory 9. salient
10. salubrious 11. 致上敬意的，歡迎的
12. 公共衛生，環境衛生
13. 不衛生的，有礙健康的
14. 聖殿，教堂，寺院 15. 偽善的 16. 使飽和
17. 描寫，敘述，形容
18. 使隔離，使孤立，使隱居
19. 其後，隨後，接著 20. 交叉口，十字路口

❷ 請根據句意，從底下四個選項中選出一個最能適切完成句子的字彙。

21. 許多和愛迪生同時代的人都認為他實驗白熱燈泡是可笑的。
(A) 嘲笑 (B) 可笑的 (C) 奚落 (D) 偽善的

22. 請留意他有益的建議。
(A) 疑問的 (B) 自負的 (C) 有益的 (D) 強健的

解答│ 21. (B) 22. (C)

❸ 請根據句意，從底下四個選項中選出一個最接近套色單字意思的字彙。

23. 這家餐廳似乎不衛生，我們別在這裡用餐。
(A) 骯髒污穢的 (B) 神智清楚的 (C) 精力充沛的 (D) 派系的

24. 董事長厭惡總經理的阿諛奉承態度。
(A) 黨派性強的 (B) 卑躬屈膝的 (C) 偽善的 (D) 有幫助的

25. 部分美國作家指責清教徒的偽善態度。
(A) 荒謬的 (B) 不知足的 (C) 自以為正直的 (D) 可笑的

解答│ 23. (A) 24. (B) 25. (C)

✲ Practice Test_04

❶ 請根據句意，從底下四個選項中選出一個最接近套色單字意思的字彙。

1. 要成為博學而多才多藝的人，廣泛閱讀是很重要的。
(A) 廣泛的 (B) 萬能的 (C) 並列的 (D) 複雜的

2. 萊特兄弟製作的飛行器是現代飛機的原型。
(A) 特權 (B) 原型 (C) 困境 (D) 儲藏室

3. 飛機的噴射引擎推進力不夠強而有力，無法使飛機像火箭般升空。
(A) 行人 (B) 攻擊 (C) 用力推 (D) 誠實

4. 交喙鳥有非常強健的喙能啄開毬果。
(A) 結實的 (B) 可笑的 (C) 偽造的 (D) 笨重的

5. 被寵壞的小孩用鉛筆把妹妹的氣球戳破。
(A) 阻礙 (B) 刺穿 (C) 遣返 (D) 勝過

解答│ 1. (A) 2. (B) 3. (C) 4. (A) 5. (B)

❷ 請閱讀下面短文，並根據文意回答問題。

美國懷俄明州

懷俄明州是全美人口最少的一州，就連首都夏安也只有少數居民。一連數周漫步在人煙稀少的野地也不會遇到人。

為了吸引足夠移民以建立州地位，主事者便選用如黃石和風河等羅曼蒂克的地名。領地議會甚至在一八六九年採取以當時而言屬激進的手段，承諾給予婦女選舉權，只是懷俄明州的種種努力及其廣袤荒地

難以打動移民者。著名政治人物丹尼爾·韋伯斯特曾表示，懷俄明州只適合野蠻人、野獸、風沙和仙人掌居住。

然而時至今日懷俄明州因豐富的自然奇觀而被視為景色最優美的州之一，海拔一萬英尺以上的山脈由不毛冰原和長期風化侵蝕岩構成。

6. 根據上述文意，首要的一字最接近底下哪個選項的意義？
   (A) 主要的 (B) 私人的 (C) 偽造的 (D) 強制的

7. 根據上述文意，激進的一字最接近底下哪個選項的意義？
   (A) 貪得無厭的 (B) 根本的 (C) 衝動的
   (D) 長方形的

8. 根據上述文意，打動一字最接近底下哪個選項的意義？
   (A) 永恆的 (B) 使神聖化 (C) 深受感動 (D) 糾正

9. 根據上述文意，豐富的一字最接近底下哪個選項的意義？
   (A) 笨重的 (B) 恐懼的 (C) 豐富的 (D) 複雜的

10. 根據上述文意，侵蝕一字最接近底下哪個選項的意義？
    (A) 背叛 (B) 刻蝕 (C) 懷柔 (D) 驅逐

解答 | 6. (A) 7. (B) 8. (C) 9. (C) 10. (B)

Review Test_17

❶ 第1到10題為「拼字題」，請根據中文意思完成英文拼字填空。第11到20題為「釋義題」，請根據英文字彙寫出中文意思。

解答 | 1. supersede 2. obsession 3. sedentary
   4. sedimentary 5. senior 6. senator
   7. sentimental 8. presentiment 9. insensate
   10. sensitive 11. 消毒劑
   12. 拋棄，遺棄，離棄
   13. 分類，分級，使相配 14. 度假勝地，求助
   15. 多汁的，水分多的，美味的 16. 乾燥劑
   17. 孤獨 18. 決心，決定，解決，解答
   19. 夢遊症 20. 失眠症

❷ 請根據句意，從底下四個選項中選出一個最能適切完成句子的字彙。

21. 動物園管理員在搬運獅子前決定先用鎮靜劑使牠鎮靜下來。
    (A) 使鎮靜 (B) 憤恨 (C) 答應 (D) 順從

22. 你剛好有消毒劑可以治療這個傷口嗎？
    (A) 離棄 (B) 消毒劑 (C) 參議員 (D) 感覺

23. 這顆橘子水分不夠。
    (A) 腐敗的 (B) 無感覺的 (C) 水分多的 (D) 敏感的

解答 | 21. (A) 22. (B) 23. (C)

❸ 請根據句意，從底下四個選項中選出一個最接近套色單字意思的字彙。

24. 輿論一致認為稅負過高。
    (A) 意見一致 (B) 住宅 (C) 住處 (D) 補助金

25. 珍非常多愁善感，連看到落葉也會掉淚。
    (A) 可溶解的 (B) 容易感傷的 (C) 催眠的
    (D) 單獨的

解答 | 24. (A) 25. (B)

Review Test_18

❶ 第1到10題為「拼字題」，請根據中文意思完成英文拼字填空。第11到20題為「釋義題」，請根據英文字彙寫出中文意思。

解答 | 1. inspiration 2. aspirant 3. expiry
   4. tactile 5. speculative 6. respiration
   7. transpiration 8. sparsely 9. sprinkler
   10. prosper 11. 費力的，奮發的
   12. 限制，限定 13. 抑制，遏制
   14. 可勝過的，可征服的，可超越的
   15. 最好的，無與倫比的
   16. 超過，凌駕，非～能勝任
   17. 沈默寡言的，無言的
   18. 接觸的，鄰近的，相鄰的 19. 接觸傳染的
   20. 可觸知的，有形的

❷ 請根據句意，從底下四個選項中選出一個最能適切完成句子的字彙。

21. 他的事業前途一片光明。
    (A) 自動灑水裝置 (B) 蒸發 (C) 前途 (D) 噴灑

22. 價格標籤上顯示是六十美元含稅。
    (A) 價格標籤 (B) 接觸 (C) 海峽 (D) 呼吸

解答 | 21. (C) 22. (A)

❸ 請根據句意，從底下四個選項中選出一個最接近套色單字意思的字彙。

23. 將軍別無選擇只能向敵軍投降。
    (A) 使陷於困境 (B) 處理 (C) 屈服 (D) 期滿

24. 吉姆有個同事常在老闆面前流汗。
    (A) 處理 (B) 勝過 (C) 出汗 (D) 污染

25. 我不喜歡費力的運動，我認為步行就夠了。
    (A) 累人的 (B) 間歇的 (C) 至高無上的 (D) 一流的

解答 | 23. (C) 24. (C) 25. (A)

Review Test_19

❶ 第1到10題為「拼字題」，請根據中文意思完成英文拼字填空。第11到20題為「釋義題」，請根據英文字彙寫出中文意思。

解答 | 1. distend 2. extent 3. tortoise 4. attrition

5. extenuate 6. tension 7. tenuous
8. contentious 9. territory 10. terrain
11. 地下的，隱蔽的 12. 毗連的，相接的
13. 終點的，末期的 14. 神學 15. 溫度計
16. 分裂，二分法 17. 使扭曲，曲解
18. 懇求，乞求，請求
19. 有吸引力的，嫵媚動人的 20. 移植，移種

② 請根據句意，從底下四個選項中選出一個最能適切完成
句子的字彙。

21. 自然科學學生上神學課時適應不良，某次竟繳交打
    錯字的「原子與夏娃」報告。（註：誤將 Adam
    「亞當」拼成 Atom「原子」。）
    (A) 神學 (B) 分裂 (C) 終點站 (D) 終點

22. 山脈高處地勢被冰河覆蓋。
    (A) 神權國家 (B) 地勢 (C) 終止 (D) 終點

23. 醫生遲疑著不敢告訴病患他已病入膏肓。
    (A) 末期的 (B) 永恆的 (C) 熱的 (D) 有吸引力的

解答│ **21.** (A) **22.** (B) **23.** (A)

③ 請根據句意，從底下四個選項中選出一個最接近套色單
字意思的字彙。

24. 哲學家的思想深植於追隨者心中。
    (A) 使變化 (B) 懇求 (C) 深植於 (D) 抄寫

25. 對我而言準備考試常是一大折磨。
    (A) 扭力 (B) 痛苦 (C) 傳送 (D) 領土

解答│ **24.** (C) **25.** (B)

✱ Review Test_20

① 第1到10題為「拼字題」，請根據中文意思完成英文拼
字填空。第11到20題為「釋義題」，請根據英文字彙寫
出中文意思。

解答│ **1.** verbose **2.** verbalize **3.** reverberate
4. evasive **5.** invade **6.** veritable
7. wreck **8.** wrinkle **9.** advocate **10.** valiant
11. 喚起，引起 **12.** 古怪的，奇怪的
13. 精力充沛的，健壯的 **14.** 瀰漫，滲透
15. 歷歷在目的，栩栩如生的
16. 體弱多病的，無效的 **17.** 打擾，干預
18. 災禍，意外，不幸 **19.** 傳統的，保守的
20. 查證，核對，證實

② 請根據句意，從底下四個選項中選出一個最能適切完成
句子的字彙。

21. 我們無法逃避死亡或向國稅局繳稅。
    (A) 稅收 (B) 逆境 (C) 活力 (D) 體弱多病的

22. 老師的滑稽故事引起學生哄堂大笑，全班都笑翻
    了。
    (A) 引起 (B) 排除 (C) 移開視線 (D) 使多樣化

解答│ **21.** (A) **22.** (C)

③ 請根據句意，從底下四個選項中選出一個最接近套色單
字意思的字彙。

23. 工會成員聚集起來討論工作狀況。
    (A) 聚集 (B) 移開視線 (C) 離題 (D) 打擾

24. 該國採取精明手段阻止戰爭。
    (A) 逃避 (B) 防止 (C) 瀰漫 (D) 監督

25. 多數學生反對傳統測驗。
    (A) 能接納的 (B) 體弱多病的 (C) 精力充沛的
    (D) 傳統的

解答│ **23.** (A) **24.** (B) **25.** (D)

✱ Practice Test_05

① 請根據句意，從底下四個選項中選出一個最接近套色單
字意思的字彙。

1. 老人過著固定的生活，一年到頭都待在家裡。
   (A) 多愁善感的 (B) 固定的 (C) 剩餘的 (D) 衰老的

2. 我很難防止小孩拿糖果罐裡的乾燥劑來吃。
   (A) 溶劑 (B) 細目 (C) 乾燥劑 (D) 溝渠

3. 該書作者因讀者尖酸刻薄的批評而心煩意亂。
   (A) 嚴厲尖銳的 (B) 懺悔的 (C) 深奧難懂的
   (D) 平庸的

4. 湯姆是真正的朋友，每當我遇到困難時都能依靠
   他。
   (A) 保守的 (B) 真正的 (C) 精通的 (D) 精力充沛的

5. 許多智者都說節儉重要，因為未來可能遭遇窮困。
   (A) 體弱多病的 (B) 自願的 (C) 看不見的
   (D) 節儉的

解答│ **1.** (B) **2.** (C) **3.** (A) **4.** (B) **5.** (D)

② 請閱讀下面短文，並根據文意回答問題。

占星學

　　占星家研究天體運行以了解它對人類活動的影
響。雖然許多人認為占星學不過是種迷信，但有些人
面臨重大抉擇時的確會求助於占星家，更有些人深信
占星學能阻止災難發生或變得更有先見之明。最有名
的例子之一是前美國總統雷根的妻子。據說南西·雷
根因為受到一九八一年三月三十日刺殺行動的驚嚇，
轉而求教加州占星家有關總統任內處理重大事務的最
佳時間和日期、空軍一號最佳起降時間、能否簽署條
約、動手術、召開記者會等。

　　許多日報和雜誌都會刊登占星建議和預測，一般
咸信個人占星圖由出生時所有行星所在位置決定。占
星家將一年分成十二個均等的黃道帶，其中十二個宮
位分別是水瓶、雙魚、牡羊、金牛、雙子、巨蟹、獅
子、天秤、處女、天蠍、射手和摩羯座。占星學雖以
偽科學為基礎，許多人還是喜歡查閱每日星座運勢，
或出於樂趣，或尋求重要問題建議，或追求智慧。

6. 根據上述文意，種類一字最接近底下哪個選項的意義？
   (A) 事實 (B) 大道 (C) 吸力 (D) 種類

7. 根據上述文意，求助一字最接近底下哪個選項的意義？
   (A) 求助 (B) 移交 (C) 使變化 (D) 吸引

8. 根據上述文意，阻止一字最接近底下哪個選項的意義？
   (A) 防止 (B) 減去 (C) 搔癢 (D) 抄寫

9. 根據上述文意，有先見之明的一字最接近底下哪個選項的意義？
   (A) 鄰近的 (B) 透明的 (C) 有遠見的
   (D) 有吸引力的

10. 根據上述文意，決定一字最接近底下哪個選項的意義？
    (A) 離題 (B) 排除 (C) 入侵 (D) 決定

解答｜ 6. (D) 7. (A) 8. (A) 9. (C) 10. (D)

*Actual Test

`Passage 1`

百慕達三角洲

　　據說由百慕達群島、波多黎各和邁阿密、佛羅里達州等三點形成的百慕達三角洲是全世界最神秘的區域之一，由於許多船隻和飛機都神秘消失於此，因此此區被視為危險之地；莎士比亞名著之一《暴風雨》甚至以此地點為寫作背景。

　　謠傳許多船隻和飛機都毫無原因地神秘消失在百慕達三角洲，連失事殘骸都找不到。一九四五年十二月由五架美國戰機組成的十九號機隊從佛羅里達州訓練基地起飛，領隊只發出無線電訊號表示指南針故障後就消失無蹤了，前往搜尋的飛機也跟著消失；其中一名駕駛員返回基地後驚恐地表示自己遭綠皮膚生物綁架但幸而逃生。時間回到一四九二年，哥倫布宣稱見到詭異火光後指南針就故障了，就連龐大的伊麗莎白皇后號在一九七四年駛入此區時也失去電力。

　　現在許多人認為百慕達三角洲具有強大磁力，也有人堅稱三角洲內或許有第四度空間入口，消失的船隻和飛機就是經過這個入口進入另一個世界。然而最顯著的事實之一是迄今無人能解開謎團，而且許多飛行員和航海者都不願意冒險一遊。

　　似乎就連表皮無鱗又溜滑的鰻魚也難逃百慕達三角洲的神秘影響。據說一生都生存在淡水環境的美洲和歐洲品種鰻魚，會聚集成群一起游到三角洲產卵和死亡。為什麼牠們會聚集到該地並集體死亡呢？另一個有趣事實是歐洲鰻魚壽命比美洲品種多出一年，科學家懷疑那是因為前者比後者多需一年時間完成三角洲之旅。在三角洲深淵孵化成長的鰻魚會找到路回到上一代的棲息地生活，雖然牠們從未去過。部分科學家聲稱是磁力讓這些鰻魚回到上一代棲息地，又有人

爭辯牠們是直接靠嗅覺器官回到祖先居住地的，當然也有人主張新生鰻魚是利用群星排列成的星座位置找到回家之路。

　　許多謎團圍繞著百慕達三角洲和成群前往該地死亡的鰻魚，儘管許多人努力解開謎題但似乎不易解答。無論百慕達三角洲的神秘起源於何處，似乎都跟永恆的三角習題一樣難解。

1. 根據上述文意，套色單字地點可用底下哪個選項的意義來取代？
   (A) 地點 (B) 終止 (C) 終點 (D) 地形

2. 根據上述文意，套色單字故障可用底下哪個選項的意義來取代？
   (A) 使孤立無援 (B) 故障 (C) 戲弄 (D) 減少動力

3. 根據上述文意，套色片語進入可用底下哪個選項的意義來取代？
   (A) 進入 (B) 剝奪 (C) 認真思考 (D) 反對

4. 根據上述文意，套色單字死亡可用底下哪個選項的意義來取代？
   (A) 嘲笑 (B) 證實 (C) 下決心 (D) 死亡

5. 根據上述文意，套色單字聚集可用底下哪個選項的意義來取代？
   (A) 削減 (B) 抑制 (C) 聚集 (D) 理解

6. 根據上述文意，套色單字完成可用底下哪個選項的意義來取代？
   (A) 調整 (B) 完成 (C) 毗連 (D) 反駁

7. 根據上述文意，套色單字棲息地可用底下哪個選項的意義來取代？
   (A) 踏板 (B) 不斷改變 (C) 三腳架 (D) 棲息地

8. 根據上述文意，套色單字祖先可用底下哪個選項的意義來取代？
   (A) 整形外科醫師 (B) 後代子孫 (C) 原型 (D) 祖先

9. 根據上述文意，套色單字居住可用底下哪個選項的意義來取代？
   (A) 廢除 (B) 居住 (C) 使飽和 (D) 使鎮靜

10. 根據上述文意，套色單字永恆的可用底下哪個選項的意義來取代？
    (A) 最好的 (B) 多汁的 (C) 超自然的 (D) 永遠的

解答｜ 1. (A) 2. (B) 3. (A) 4. (D) 5. (C)
　　　 6. (B) 7. (D) 8. (D) 9. (B) 10. (D)

`Passage 2`

紅杉

　　世界上最高的活生物是紅杉，在約兩千年的壽命中可長到四百英尺高，其近親巨杉可活三千年，高度可超過兩百五十英尺。紅杉種子大小不超過一枚大頭針，最後卻長成巍巍大樹，大約四百年後樹幹便有二十英尺寬，不過直徑三十五英尺的巨杉比起來還是小巫見大巫。

一般咸信世上最巨大的樹木是位於加州紅杉國家公園裡的謝爾曼將軍紅杉，估計已生長約兩千七百年，底部直徑超過三十五英尺，光是支幹直徑就有足以讓人橫躺的七英尺寬度。謝爾曼將軍紅杉應重約六千一百六十七噸，如果砍下來，需要三百輛載重二十噸的巨大卡車合力才能一次搬運。

長久以來人們很好像紅杉這麼巨大的樹木要如何將水分輸送到頂端，就連植物學家也認為這是個謎。已知氣壓能支撐水柱到十公尺高，但紅杉卻另當別論。有些人堅持是根壓將水分輸送到頂端，又有些人主張是活細胞負責輸送水分。然而紅杉屬針葉樹，根壓相對較低，即使是死木也能輸送部分水分到一定可見高度，就是一大反證。近來才發現表面張力也是原因之一，水分從葉面蒸發，使紅杉內部柱狀體呈現負壓。令人吃驚的是，小小孔管內的溶液柱狀體張力幾乎和相同直徑的金屬線張力一樣強。

紅杉和巨杉都是結毬果的針葉樹，如海綿般吸水性強的樹皮常可達十二英吋厚。過去尤羅克族印第安人利用傾倒的紅杉建造獨木舟和屋舍，尤羅克族人敬畏樹木，相信印第安神瓦皮科梅噴灑神奇湯藥在樹上，所以可以防火。無論如何，紅杉不但能抵擋森林大火，也不怕蟲害或疫病侵襲，即使是好幾百年的死木也不會腐爛。時至今日紅杉木不但常用來製作家具、屋瓦和嵌板，更可見於木工和一般建物，主要是因為它紋理精美又輕巧，容易製作。

今日紅杉可見於加州到南奧勒岡州的海岸地帶，至於巨杉則限於內華達山脈西坡一小塊區域。目前將近七十％獨具特色的巨林都受到州政府或國家公園保護，高聳入雲的巨木深受廣大參觀者的讚佩、撫摸和擁抱。

11. 根據上述文意，套色單字巨大的可用底下哪個選項的意義來取代？
(A) 發狂的 (B) 巨大的 (C) 一年一次的 (D) 短暫的

12. 根據上述文意，套色單字直徑可用底下哪個選項的意義來取代？
(A) 統治者 (B) 口是心非 (C) 寬度 (D) 鐘擺

13. 根據上述文意，套色單字主張可用底下哪個選項的意義來取代？
(A) 認為 (B) 憎恨 (C) 流汗 (D) 折磨

14. 根據上述文意，套色單字針葉樹可用底下哪個選項的意義來取代？
(A) 多年生植物 (B) 闊葉樹 (C) 落葉樹 (D) 針葉樹

15. 根據上述文意，套色單字反駁的可用底下哪個選項的意義來取代？
(A) 語言的 (B) 假設的 (C) 反駁的 (D) 空虛的

16. 根據上述文意，套色單字溶液可用底下哪個選項的意義來取代？
(A) 新手 (B) 液體 (C) 基因 (D) 固體

17. 根據上述文意，套色單字噴灑可用底下哪個選項的意義來取代？

(A) 使飽和 (B) 焚化 (C) 同意 (D) 噴灑

18. 根據上述文意，套色單字蟲可用底下哪個選項的意義來取代？
(A) 隱士 (B) 蟲 (C) 喧鬧 (D) 慣例

19. 根據上述文意，套色單字限制可用底下哪個選項的意義來取代？
(A) 包括 (B) 下降 (C) 降級 (D) 限制

20. 根據上述文意，套色單字廣大人群可用底下哪個選項的意義來取代？
(A) 創舉 (B) 人群 (C) 地心引力 (D) 依靠

解答｜ **11.** (B) **12.** (C) **13.** (A) **14.** (D) **15.** (C)
16. (B) **17.** (D) **18.** (B) **19.** (D) **20.** (B)

Chapter 4

✱ Review Test_01

❶ 第1到10題為「拼字題」，請根據中文意思完成英文拼字填空。第11到20題為「釋義題」，請根據英文字彙寫出中文意思。

解答｜ **1.** alumnus **2.** anthology **3.** applicant
4. assessment **5.** attend **6.** award
7. background **8.** appointment **9.** brochure
10. bulletin **11.** 證書 **12.** 畢業典禮
13. 能力，勝任，稱職 **14.** 指導老師，顧問
15. 學分，歸功於～ **16.** 宿舍
17. 為應考倉促用功 **18.** 母校 **19.** 考古學家
20. 試鏡，試音

❷ 請根據句意，從底下四個選項中選出一個最能適切完成句子的字彙。

21. 好餓喔，我們隨便去吃點東西吧。
(A) 咬 (B) 版權 (C) 課外作業 (D) 選集

22. 你的書在我背包裡。
(A) 背景 (B) 背包 (C) 能力 (D) 學分

23. 我正在讀富蘭克林自傳。
(A) 男校友 (B) 評分 (C) 自傳 (D) 答辯

解答｜ **21.** (A) **22.** (B) **23.** (C)

❸ 請根據句意，從底下四個選項中選出一個最接近套色單字意思的字彙。

24. 畢業典禮將於四月十五日舉行。
(A) 抄襲 (B) 場地 (C) 顧問 (D) 畢業典禮

25. 本英文測驗目的在於評估學生英語溝通能力。
　　(A) 能力 (B) 行政 (C) 作註解 (D) 答辯

解答│ **24.** (D) **25.** (A)

✳ Review Test_02

❶ 第1到10題為「拼字題」，請根據中文意思完成英文拼字填空。第11到20題為「釋義題」，請根據英文字彙寫出中文意思。

解答│ **1.** elective　**2.** eligibility　**3.** enroll　**4.** evaluate
　　　　5. excerpt　**6.** expulsion　**7.** faculty　**8.** failure
　　　　9. feedback　**10.** final　**11.** 翻閱，翻頁
　　　　12. 兄弟會　**13.** 大一新生
　　　　14. 詞彙表，專業辭典，術語彙編　**15.** 體育館
　　　　16. 校內的，校際的　**17.** 授課
　　　　18. 文學，文學作品　**19.** 樂透彩券，抽籤
　　　　20. 大學入學許可

❷ 請根據句意，從底下四個選項中選出一個最能適切完成句子的字彙。

21. 教授將評量學生的英語口說能力。
　　(A) 入學 (B) 評量 (C) 接電啟動 (D) 摘錄

22. 學費超過我能負擔的，實在太貴了。
　　(A) 兄弟會 (B) 梗概 (C) 退學 (D) 學費

解答│ **21.** (B) **22.** (D)

❸ 請根據句意，從底下四個選項中選出一個最接近套色單字意思的字彙。

23. 這張身分證無效，你該補辦新的。
　　(A) 無效的 (B) 期末考 (C) 主修 (D) 到期的

24. 學生會將於本周六集會。
　　(A) 集會 (B) 誹謗 (C) 能力 (D) 年級

25. 我非常喜歡唐納遜教授的授課。
　　(A) 合格 (B) 詞彙表 (C) 課 (D) 意見回饋

解答│ **23.** (A) **24.** (A) **25.** (C)

✳ Review Test_03

❶ 第1到10題為「拼字題」，請根據中文意思完成英文拼字填空。第11到20題為「釋義題」，請根據英文字彙寫出中文意思。

解答│ **1.** participation　**2.** pastime　**3.** permit
　　　　4. piracy　**5.** presentation　**6.** proctor
　　　　7. reevaluate　**8.** registration　**9.** prerequisite
　　　　10. recruit　**11.** 離開，放棄，停止
　　　　12. 休息，不工作，停止　**13.** 校稿，校對稿
　　　　14. 租用　**15.** 獎學金　**16.** 保全，保安
　　　　17. 上課時間，學期，集會　**18.** 翹課，未出席
　　　　19. 姊妹會　**20.** 班級舞會

❷ 請根據句意，從底下四個選項中選出一個最能適切完成句子的字彙。

21. 想申請職務空缺者，只要寄履歷到公司即可。
　　(A) 履歷 (B) 成績 (C) 筆記 (D) 姊妹會

22. 監考老師不可怠忽職守，學生才不會考試作弊。
　　(A) 上課時間 (B) 監考老師 (C) 校稿 (D) 校園導覽

23. 部分學生強烈主張應將獎學金提供給清寒學生。
　　(A) 著作權侵害 (B) 消遣 (C) 許可證 (D) 獎學金

解答│ **21.** (A) **22.** (B) **23.** (D)

❸ 請根據句意，從底下四個選項中選出一個最接近套色單字意思的字彙。

24. 學生正在進行田野調查。
　　(A) 重修 (B) 研究 (C) 保全 (D) 成績

25. 優異的考試成績對申請獎學金而言是重要的。
　　(A) 成績 (B) 推薦信 (C) 翹課 (D) 拒絕

解答│ **24.** (B) **25.** (A)

✳ Review Test_04

❶ 第1到10題為「拼字題」，請根據中文意思完成英文拼字填空。第11到20題為「釋義題」，請根據英文字彙寫出中文意思。

解答│ **1.** transcript　**2.** transfer　**3.** undergraduate
　　　　4. anthropologist　**5.** corridor　**6.** courtyard
　　　　7. fireplace　**8.** insulation　**9.** facade
　　　　10. lodge　**11.** 鐵窗，格板　**12.** 家教
　　　　13. 磚，磚塊　**14.** 小屋　**15.** 橫樑
　　　　16. 席間走道，通道　**17.** 屋簷
　　　　18. 地下室，地窖　**19.** 打字排印錯誤，誤植
　　　　20. 教學大綱，課程大綱

❷ 請根據句意，從底下四個選項中選出一個最能適切完成句子的字彙。

21. 他整個上午都在上網。
　　(A) 上網瀏覽 (B) 家教 (C) 鐵窗 (D) 橫樑

22. 約翰交報告前得仔細閱讀，裡面都是打字錯誤。
　　(A) 課程大綱 (B) 塊 (C) 打字排印錯誤 (D) 走廊

解答│ **21.** (A) **22.** (C)

❸ 請根據句意，從底下四個選項中選出一個最接近套色單字意思的字彙。

23. 聽說你要搬家，東西都打包好了嗎？
　　(A) 轉校 (B) 東西 (C) 拱門 (D) 圓頂

24. 我肯定珍有音樂天份。
　　(A) 小屋 (B) 天份 (C) 塊 (D) 磚塊

25. 這棟建築物的原始藍圖是屋主繪製的。
　　(A) 草圖 (B) 拱心石 (C) 部落 (D) 後代子孫

解答│ **23.** (B) **24.** (B) **25.** (A)

Review Test_05

❶ 第1到10題為「拼字題」，請根據中文意思完成英文拼字填空。第11到20題為「釋義題」，請根據英文字彙寫出中文意思。

解答│ **1.** pillar **2.** skyscraper **3.** steeple
4. abstract **5.** composition **6.** tepee
7. movement **8.** perspective **9.** aggregate
10. collide **11.** 展示會，展覽會，展示，陳列
12. 彗星 **13.** 日暈，月暈 **14.** 碎片
15. 晝夜平分時，春分，秋分
16. 占星術，星象 **17.** 流星
18. 天體運行軌道，環繞軌道運行
19. 窪地，凹地 **20.** 爆炸

❷ 請根據句意，從底下四個選項中選出一個最能適切完成句子的字彙。

21. 太陽最外層的光環稱為日暈。
(A) 油畫布 (B) 畫風 (C) 日暈 (D) 表現

22. 人造衛星環繞月球運行。
(A) 聚集 (B) 環繞軌道運行 (C) 碰撞 (D) 表現

23. 多數門外漢很難了解抽象畫。
(A) 抽象的 (B) 風格 (C) 欄杆 (D) 黃道

解答│ **21.** (C) **22.** (B) **23.** (A)

❸ 請根據句意，從底下四個選項中選出一個最接近套色單字意思的字彙。

24. 這幅畫的所有色彩都是陰鬱的。
(A) 色彩 (B) 窪地 (C) 星雲 (D) 監測

25. 原住民的住所是以泥巴建造的。
(A) 陽台 (B) 柱子 (C) 欄杆 (D) 房屋

解答│ **24.** (A) **25.** (D)

Practice Test_01

❶ 請根據句意，從底下四個選項中選出一個最接近套色單字意義的字彙。

1. 教授將於所有學生演講結束後填寫評分表。
(A) 評價 (B) 行政 (C) 學費 (D) 課程大綱

2. 本測驗成績的效期為兩年。
(A) 校內的 (B) 原始時代的 (C) 有效的
(D) 族長制的

3. 研究生正在撰寫有關全球暖化效應的論文。
(A) 大廈 (B) 走廊 (C) 論文 (D) 家教

4. 要及格須有百分之八十以上的出席率、繳交學期報告，並參加兩次考試。
(A) 重修 (B) 租用 (C) 參加 (D) 入學

5. 我今天沒去上伯朗教授的課，有課外作業嗎？
(A) 獎學金 (B) 成績 (C) 家庭作業 (D) 班級舞會

解答│ **1.** (A) **2.** (C) **3.** (C) **4.** (C) **5.** (C)

---

❷ 請閱讀下面短文，並根據文意回答問題。

> 大學新學期開始，伯朗教授像往常一樣既興奮又熱情。如同許多以個人職業為榮的老師一樣，他一定要記住學生的名字，所以一開學便要求學生繳交護照尺寸照片並附上姓名，然而這學期卻出現一張嚇人的年輕學生照片，不但是黑白照而且還很模糊，照片清晰度也很差。於是伯朗教授找學生來問為什麼會這樣，學生膽怯地笑答：「我沒時間去拍照。」教授又問：「那你是從哪裡拿到這張照片的？」學生低頭說：「我把臉貼在影印機上。」

6. 底下哪個選項最適合填入空格(1)中？
(A) 學期 (B) 窪地 (C) 柱子 (D) 構圖

7. 底下哪個選項最適合填入空格(2)中？
(A) 原始時代的 (B) 校內的 (C) 熱情的 (D) 抽象的

8. 底下哪個選項最適合填入空格(3)中？
(A) 職業 (B) 爆炸 (C) 活動 (D) 遠近畫法

9. 底下哪個選項最適合填入空格(4)中？
(A) 碰撞 (B) 繳交 (C) 租用 (D) 重修

10. 底下哪個選項最適合填入空格(5)中？
(A) 表現 (B) 清晰度 (C) 尖塔 (D) 浮雕

解答│ **6.** (A) **7.** (C) **8.** (A) **9.** (B) **10.** (B)

Review Test_06

❶ 第1到10題為「拼字題」，請根據中文意思完成英文拼字填空。第11到20題為「釋義題」，請根據英文字彙寫出中文意思。

解答│ **1.** perigee **2.** planet **3.** pulsar **4.** quasar
5. rotation **6.** satellite **7.** solstice
8. arthropod **9.** biome **10.** capillary
11. 天頂 **12.** 細胞 **13.** 無性繁殖 **14.** 細胞質
15. 腹足動物 **16.** 學名 **17.** 共生 **18.** 催化劑
19. 酵素 **20.** 動物群

❷ 請根據句意，從底下四個選項中選出一個最能適切完成句子的字彙。

21. 行星地球繞著太陽轉。
(A) 行星 (B) 波霎 (C) 類星體 (D) 近地點

22. 巨星大爆炸產生超級新星。
(A) 天頂 (B) 至 (C) 超級新星 (D) 動物群

解答│ **21.** (A) **22.** (C)

❸ 請根據句意，從底下四個選項中選出一個最接近套色單字意思的字彙。

23. 有人堅稱人類可以超光速穿越蟲洞。
(A) 自轉 (B) 速度 (C) 近日點 (D) 托勒密的

24. 肥胖者相當討厭油脂。
(A) 油脂 (B) 地衣 (C) 蕨類植物 (D) 爬蟲類動物

25. 葉片表面有許多氣孔。
(A) 界 (B) 毛狀體 (C) 小孔 (D) 寄生蟲

解答｜**23.** (B) **24.** (A) **25.** (C)

✴ Review Test_07

① 第1到10題為「拼字題」，請根據中文意思完成英文拼字填空。第11到20題為「釋義題」，請根據英文字彙寫出中文意思。

解答｜ **1.** inorganic **2.** molecular **3.** oxidation
4. conservation **5.** proton **6.** ecosystem
7. assess **8.** auction **9.** barter **10.** bidding
11. 荒漠化，沙漠化 **12.** 可回收資源
13. 帳單，支票 **14.** 餘額，結存 **15.** 債券
16. 商品，日用品 **17.** 合併 **18.** 需求，要求
19. 貶值 **20.** 福利，社會救濟

② 請根據句意，從底下四個選項中選出一個最能適切完成句子的字彙。

21. 這個塑膠容器可回收再利用。
(A) 特價品 (B) 盟約 (C) 可回收利用的 (D) 上漲的

22. 我必須背書支票，以支付所選商品。
(A) 徵稅 (B) 背書 (C) 債券 (D) 繁榮

23. 這本書何時到期？
(A) 到期的 (B) 有機的 (C) 預算 (D) 要求

解答｜**21.** (C) **22.** (B) **23.** (A)

③ 請根據句意，從底下四個選項中選出一個最接近套色單字意思的字彙。

24. 所幸意外造成的損失極小。
(A) 通貨緊縮 (B) 傷害 (C) 水藻 (D) 拍賣

25. 部分專家將評估對環境造成的影響。
(A) 合併 (B) 掠奪 (C) 影響 (D) 均勢

解答｜**24.** (B) **25.** (C)

✴ Review Test_08

① 第1到10題為「拼字題」，請根據中文意思完成英文拼字填空。第11到20題為「釋義題」，請根據英文字彙寫出中文意思。

解答｜ **1.** fiscal **2.** forgery **3.** interest **4.** intangible
5. lending **6.** merger **7.** teller **8.** vault
9. withdrawal **10.** welfare
11. 票面價值，面值 **12.** 海灣 **13.** 礦物
14. 幾何的 **15.**（功的單位）爾格 **16.** 大草原
17. 完全失敗 **18.** 群島，列島 **19.** 供應過剩
20. 火山灰

② 請根據句意，從底下四個選項中選出一個最能適切完成句子的字彙。

21. 礦物（註：如媒、石油等）燃燒造成嚴重空污問題。
(A) 塌陷火山口 (B) 海底平頂山 (C) 火山碎屑
(D) 化石

22. 位在華盛頓州喀斯開山脈的聖海倫斯火山在一九八零年爆發。
(A) 爆發 (B) 間歇泉 (C) 海角 (D) 火山口

解答｜**21.** (D) **22.** (A)

③ 請根據句意，從底下四個選項中選出一個最接近套色單字意思的字彙。

23. 土地太乾燥不適合發展農業。
(A) 乾燥的 (B) 礦物 (C) 橢圓形的 (D) 多邊形

24. 地質學家分析土壤構造。
(A) 構造 (B) 浮石 (C) 石英 (D) 沙岩

25. 密西西比河沿岸大草原常在夏季氾濫成災。
(A) 石灰 (B) 花崗岩 (C) 頁岩 (D) 草原

解答｜**23.** (A) **24.** (A) **25.** (D)

✴ Review Test_09

① 第1到10題為「拼字題」，請根據中文意思完成英文拼字填空。第11到20題為「釋義題」，請根據英文字彙寫出中文意思。

解答｜ **1.** taiga **2.** tropical **3.** trace **4.** accent
5. nonverbal **6.** phonetic **7.** abrasion
8. bandage **9.** administer **10.** antacid
11. 音節 **12.** 使痛苦，折磨
13. 齒顎矯正器，牙套 **14.** 不足，缺乏
15. 分娩 **16.** 牙線，用牙線潔牙 **17.** 發燒
18. 雙母音 **19.** 辭典，語彙 **20.** 字首

② 請根據句意，從底下四個選項中選出一個最能適切完成句子的字彙。

21. 近北極區針葉林帶有許多針葉林。
(A) 凍原 (B) 針葉林帶 (C) 鹽沼 (D) 鋸齒狀山脊

22. 造訪語言不通的國家須仰賴非語言溝通。
(A) 辭典 (B) 口腔的 (C) 字首 (D) 非語言的

23. 他罹患不知名疾病。
(A) 內視鏡檢查 (B) 疾病 (C) 紗布 (D) 幻覺

解答｜**21.** (B) **22.** (D) **23.** (B)

③ 請根據句意，從底下四個選項中選出一個最接近套色單字意思的字彙。

24. 帶給他諸多病痛的疾病最後終因新藥問世而得到控制。
(A) 劑量 (B) 繃帶 (C) 疾病 (D) 傷口

25. 他因為沒戒煙導致情況惡化。
(A) 折磨 (B) 開藥 (C) 出院 (D) 惡化

解答｜**24.** (C) **25.** (D)

❶ 第1到10題為「拼字題」，請根據中文意思完成英文拼字填空。第11到20題為「釋義題」，請根據英文字彙寫出中文意思。

解答｜ 1. malocclusion　2. mitigate　3. operation
4. stethoscope　5. inertia　6. measure
7. quantum　8. aristocracy　9. deputy
10. consul　11. 外傷，傷口，創傷
12. 病房，防止
13. 打預防針，接種疫苗，種牛痘　14. 離心的
15. 扭矩，轉矩，扭轉力　16. 內閣，全體閣員
17. 領導權，支配權　18. 議會，國會
19. 現狀　20. 精神分裂症

❷ 請根據句意，從底下四個選項中選出一個最能適切完成句子的字彙。

21. 醫學的發達使醫師能在沒有切口的情況下進行手術。
(A) 無黨籍人士 (B) 本我 (C) 自我認同
(D) 手術切口

22. 總統於元旦正式就任。
(A) 防止 (B) 減輕 (C) 使正式就任 (D) 測量

解答｜ 21. (D)　22. (C)

❸ 請根據句意，從底下四個選項中選出一個最接近套色單字意思的字彙。

23. 詹姆斯仿效其他成員脫離工會，最後導致工會瓦解。
(A) 本能衝動 (B) 脫離 (C) 刺激 (D) 資本主義

24. 暴民試圖推翻政府。
(A) 推翻 (B) 正式批准 (C) 臨時替代 (D) 選舉權

25. 工廠毒氣為鄰近環境帶來有害影響。
(A) 擔架 (B) 官員 (C) 精神錯亂 (D) 有毒的

解答｜ 23. (B)　24. (A)　25. (D)

⭐Practice Test_02

❶ 請根據句意，從底下四個選項中選出一個最接近套色單字意思的字彙。

1. 島國採取各種措施保護沿海珊瑚。
(A) 礁 (B) 前線 (C) 針葉林帶 (D) 遺跡

2. 鄰近工廠排放的有毒氣體導致居民皮膚過敏。
(A) 灰塵 (B) 氣旋 (C) 疾病 (D) 放射

3. 年邁體弱者即使得了普通感冒也會變得虛弱。
(A) 致命的 (B) 虛弱的 (C) 易患的 (D) 航海的

4. 城外的騷動來自想親自面見市長的暴民。
(A) 騷動 (B) 角 (C) 西裝 (D) 處罰

5. 小孩常會弄混自己的母語和正在學習的外語。
(A) 領導權 (B) 本國語 (C) 特徵 (D) 充血

解答｜ 1. (A) 2. (C) 3. (B) 4. (A) 5. (B)

❷ 請閱讀下面短文，並根據文意回答問題。

喜劇故事

在教會主日學校裡，牧師正在教導一群小學生。他要大家改掉壞習慣，尤其是不可以罵髒話。他對孩子們說罵髒話會被上帝懲罰，聖誕老人也不會送他們精美禮物。等到他開始佈道，一隻小蟲卻一直在他身邊嗡嗡叫，最後還停在他鼻子上。他好幾次扭曲著臉想趕牠走，但小蟲一直在他臉上飛旋，弄得他很煩。最後他使勁用手掌打自己的鼻子，但敏捷的小生物竟逃過致命的一擊。牧師喃喃自語：「祈禱吧，可愛小蒼蠅快飛走吧！哎喲，不是蒼蠅，天啊，是蜜蜂！該死！」

6. 底下哪個選項最適合填入空格(**1**)中？
(A) 有毒的 (B) 虛弱的 (C) 致命的 (D) 基礎的

7. 底下哪個選項最適合填入空格(**2**)中？
(A) 使正式就任 (B) 發表 (C) 測量 (D) 減輕

8. 底下哪個選項最適合填入空格(**3**)中？
(A) 減輕 (B) 扭曲 (C) 折磨 (D) 正式就任

9. 底下哪個選項最適合填入空格(**4**)中？
(A) 致命的 (B) 易受影響的 (C) 易患的 (D) 航海的

10. 底下哪個選項最適合填入空格(**5**)中？
(A) 正式批准 (B) 防止 (C) 委派 (D) 喃喃自語

解答｜ 6. (D) 7. (B) 8. (B) 9. (A) 10. (D)

⭐Actual Test

Passage 1

仿生學

人類常常吹噓自己的身體機能是地球所有動物都比不上的，然而這種自誇只在效率上說得通，因為還有許多不同種類的動物機能勝過人類。

螞蟻能夠回到自己遠在兩百公尺外的聚居地。蒼蠅只需要不到一公釐的起降帶就能起降自如。沒有孩童被蚊子叮咬或護士打針時不會哭鬧。眾所周知，蝙蝠的聽覺比雷達或聲納還要敏銳，能發出四萬八千赫茲的超音波以找出獵物位置，並利用回音避開途中障礙物。人類曾研究測試蝙蝠利用回音鎖定物體的能力，先在暗室中以不規則的方式懸吊二十八條細金屬絲，再用七十個喇叭放大類似蝙蝠超音波的音量，蝙蝠仍能在細絲間穿梭，完全不會碰觸到線。眾所周知，貓即使以頭下腳上的姿勢落下，也能在半空中自我翻轉。就算沒有施以扭轉力，靈活自如的貓也能前後翻轉，再以四腳安全著地。據說狗能分辨並記住大約五十萬種不同氣味，與人相比之下，多數狗具有無可匹敵的敏銳嗅覺。狗的鼻子能有效感知氣味，並讓空氣在鼻內循環，直達感覺中樞。狗鼻通常都是濕潤的，能將氣味微粒溶解在鼻分泌物中。被馴服的狗因

嗅覺靈敏精準，常協助嗅出毒品、槍枝、炸彈，甚至分辨可食菌類。

　　另外還有一種動物製造的物質同樣被視為成就非凡。蜘蛛絲經過適當合成，其拉力強度據說大約是相同直徑鋼線的五倍。蜘蛛絲比尼龍有彈性，如果可立即量產，將會是完美原料。許多科學家一直努力想找出構成蜘蛛絲的基因之謎。蜘蛛絲可取代目前用來製造汽車保險槓、韌帶、手術縫合用線，甚至航空母艦登陸錨鏈的原料。

　　隨著愈來愈多的動物非凡成就呈現在世人眼前，人類更加渴望了解動物及其驚人機能和構造物。仿生學作為新的科學分支，專門分析動物神奇構造物和行為，再應用在科學發展上，現已日漸學有所成。現在正是我們向大自然學習的時刻。

1. 根據上述文意，套色單字比不上的可用底下哪個選項的意義來取代？
(A) 顯眼的 (B) 無敵的 (C) 著名的 (D) 奢侈的

2. 根據上述文意，套色單字勝過可用底下哪個選項的意義來取代？
(A) 愛國的 (B) 無動於衷的 (C) 勝過 (D) 否定

3. 根據上述文意，套色單字找出可用底下哪個選項的意義來取代？
(A) 營救 (B) 沉著的 (C) 出席 (D) 找出

4. 根據上述文意，套色單字懸吊可用底下哪個選項的意義來取代？
(A) 懸吊 (B) 釋放 (C) 重新開始 (D) 棲息於

5. 根據上述文意，套色單字放大可用底下哪個選項的意義來取代？
(A) 座落於 (B) 放大 (C) 遵守 (D) 冬眠

6. 根據上述文意，套色單字有效地可用底下哪個選項的意義來取代？
(A) 無情地 (B) 明智地 (C) 有效地 (D) 大量地

7. 根據上述文意，套色單字溶解可用底下哪個選項的意義來取代？
(A) 改述 (B) 累積 (C) 溶解 (D) 減輕

8. 根據上述文意，套色單字可食的可用底下哪個選項的意義來取代？
(A) 複雜的 (B) 可食的 (C) 夜間活動的 (D) 豐碩的

9. 根據上述文意，套色單字合成可用底下哪個選項的意義來取代？
(A) 補充 (B) 製成 (C) 蔑視 (D) 遵守

10. 根據上述文意，套色單字製造可用底下哪個選項的意義來取代？
(A) 製造 (B) 恢復 (C) 創新 (D) 破壞

解答│ **1.** (B) **2.** (C) **3.** (D) **4.** (A) **5.** (B)
　　　 6. (C) **7.** (C) **8.** (B) **9.** (B) **10.** (A)

迷信

　　有些美國人不喜歡從梯子底下經過，因為擔心搖晃的梯子會突然倒塌嗎？恐怕不是。主要是因為迷信。迷信的人認為從梯子底下經過會帶來惡運。迷信無法明確解釋，也無法透過科學驗證，常起源於宗教或文化。

　　世界上有太多迷信例子，似乎人類擅長製造迷信。美國人相信如果左手癢就會收到禮物。有些年輕美國女子會在五月一日將戒指穿過蛋糕後再放在枕頭底下，她們相信這樣做就能在夢中見到未來老公。對數字十三的恐懼來自聖經，因為「最後的晚餐」有十三個客人列席，包括猶大在內。許多高樓不為第十三層樓編號而直接從十二樓跳到十四樓。許多迷信的西方人相信如果黑貓從自己面前走過就會帶來不幸。中古世紀時期認為邪惡女巫能化身成黑貓。打破鏡子被認為會帶來七年惡運。有個喜劇演員曾說過一則笑話：高齡九十的老翁早起梳洗打扮，不慎打破鏡子，於是樂得手舞足蹈。古羅馬人相信鏡子反映人的靈魂，如果不慎打破鏡子，要花七年的時間才能使靈魂復原。義大利人相信只有在滿月的時候才能殺死蛇，因為部分義大利人深信滿月時殺蛇會醉倒在葡萄園裡的葡萄上，如果在蛇沒喝醉時殺牠，不幸就會降臨在自己身上。有些東方人會威嚇孩子，如果晚上吹口哨會引來蛇；或跟女兒說如果坐在桌角會變成嫁不出去的老處女。中國人送禮從不送時鐘，因為時鐘和死屍的發音相近。

　　人們同時也認為透過迷信方式能夠「更積極地」保護自己免遭不幸。據說做飯時打翻鹽罐會招來惡運，相信這種說法的人如果灑了鹽罐就要抓一小撮鹽往自己的左肩後方丟去，以驅逐據稱正站在那裡的惡靈。做惡夢的人只要敲敲木頭就能避免壞事發生。抱著新娘跨過門檻和在新婚夫婦的轎車後方繫上金屬罐頭的習俗，很可能是希望藉此阻止惡兆發生或嚇阻惡靈。避邪護身符和幸運符咒常被用來擊退惡靈。在美國，也可攜帶兔腳或馬蹄鐵作為幸運符使用。在韓國，從寶寶第一件衣服上剪下的一小塊布、米糕和偶數叉子可用來祝福考生考運亨通。在日本，折一千隻紙鶴可滿足心有所求者的願望。

11. 根據上述文意，套色單字倒塌可用底下哪個選項的意義來取代？
(A) 調整 (B) 寬恕 (C) 有助於 (D) 瓦解

12. 根據上述文意，套色單字解釋可用底下哪個選項的意義來取代？
(A) 暗示 (B) 解釋 (C) 誹謗 (D) 勸誘

13. 根據上述文意，套色單字驗證可用底下哪個選項的意義來取代？
(A) 減少 (B) 貶值 (C) 證實 (D) 降級

14. 根據上述文意，套色單字擅長可用底下哪個選項的意義來取代？
(A) 氣質 (B) 膽量 (C) 愛好藝術者 (D) 才能

15. 根據上述文意，套色單字邪惡的可用底下哪個選項的意義來取代？
    (A) 偽善的 (B) 憂鬱的 (C) 壞心腸的 (D) 仁慈的

16. 根據上述文意，套色單字沒喝醉的可用底下哪個選項的意義來取代？
    (A) 認真的 (B) 不喝醉的 (C) 重大的 (D) 不小心的

17. 根據上述文意，套色單字死屍可用底下哪個選項的意義來取代？
    (A) 褻瀆神明的 (B) 死屍 (C) 防禦 (D) 鑑賞家

18. 根據上述文意，套色單字不幸可用底下哪個選項的意義來取代？
    (A) 烹飪 (B) 僵局 (C) 改革運動 (D) 災禍

19. 根據上述文意，套色單字驅逐可用底下哪個選項的意義來取代？
    (A) 驅逐 (B) 蹲伏 (C) 使結晶 (D) 重擊

20. 根據上述文意，套色片語擊退可用底下哪個選項的意義來取代？
    (A) 制止 (B) 保護 (C) 評估 (D) 使有活力

解答│ **11.** (D) **12.** (B) **13.** (C) **14.** (D) **15.** (C)
    16. (B) **17.** (B) **18.** (D) **19.** (A) **20.** (A)

Chapter 5

✱ **Review Test_01**

❶ 第1到10題為「拼字題」，請根據中文意思完成英文拼字填空。第11到20題為「釋義題」，請根據英文字彙寫出中文意思。

解答│ **1.** carousel **2.** cart **3.** cockpit **4.** departure
    5. landing **6.** porter **7.** tailwind **8.** burrow
    9. dormant **10.** hibernate **11.** 鼯鼠，田鼠
    12. 騾子 **13.** 繁殖 **14.** 偽裝，掩飾
    15. 晝行性的，日間活動的 **16.** 飛禽
    17. 水獺 **18.** 姿勢，姿態 **19.** 繁殖
    20. 野生動物

❷ 請根據句意，從底下四個選項中選出一個最能適切完成句子的字彙。

21. 你什麼時候回來的？時差調過來了嗎？
    (A) 護照 (B) 時差 (C) 降落 (D) 起飛

22. 能不能請你幫我把這件行李放進頭頂上方置物櫃？
    (A) 頭頂上方置物櫃 (B) 緊急應變計畫 (C) 順風
    (D) 繁殖

23. 哺乳動物以肺呼吸，魚類則用鰓。
    (A) 上頜骨 (B) 鰓 (C) 鰭 (D) 視網膜

24. 臼齒是用來咀嚼磨碎食物的。
    (A) 門牙 (B) 瞳孔 (C) 虹膜 (D) 臼齒

25. 他的煙癮過大引發部分呼吸道疾病。
    (A) 營養 (B) 腺 (C) 道 (D) 膽汁

解答│ **21.** (B) **22.** (A) **23.** (B) **24.** (D) **25.** (C)

✱ **Practice Test_01**

❶ 請根據句意，從底下四個選項中選出一個最接近套色單字意思的字彙。

1. 我們應攝取足夠食物以獲得充分營養。
   (A) 營養 (B) 腎臟 (C) 開胃菜 (D) 視網膜

2. 冬眠的動物須在秋天攝取足夠食物。
   (A) 繁殖 (B) 冬眠 (C) 規定 (D) 環繞軌道運行

3. 電影劇本是由國際知名小說家撰寫的。
   (A) 道具 (B) 字幕 (C) 劇本 (D) 影像

4. 該國許多年輕人強烈反對嚴格的電影審查制度。
   (A) 紀錄片 (B) 影片 (C) 蒙太奇 (D) 言論箝制

5. 釣線的尾端繫著魚餌。
   (A) 籠子 (B) 魚鰾 (C) 餌 (D) 釣客

解答│ **1.** (A) **2.** (B) **3.** (C) **4.** (D) **5.** (C)

❷ 請閱讀下面短文，並根據文意回答問題。

喜劇故事——積習難改

　　從前在懷俄明州的小村落裡住著三個年輕農夫，互為好友的他們喜歡互相幫忙農事，常一起播種，一起收割。奇怪的是，三人各有一個怪癖。最年長的約翰喜歡搔頭，連一分鐘也停不下來，沒人能阻止他。常流鼻水的尼克總是用袖子擦鼻子。至於年紀最小的亨利則喜歡搔背和肩。

　　某個夏日三人坐在樹蔭下乘涼休息時，決定來打個賭，誰能不依賴自己的習慣並維持最久，誰就獲勝。於是三人面面相覷，想忍住衝動。

　　約翰還不到五分鐘便打破沉默：「上周我在這附近看見一頭大鹿，牠這裡跟這裡長著很漂亮的鹿角。」約翰邊說著「這裡」，邊用姆指搔著自己的頭。

　　此時尼克馬上接口：「真的嗎？如果我看到鹿，一定會用弓箭像這樣射死牠。」他邊說邊用袖子擦鼻子。

　　亨利逮到機會衝口而出：「如果我也在場，我一定會把死鹿扛在肩上。」他一面說著一面搔著自己的肩膀。

6. 底下哪個選項最適合填入空格(1)中？
   (A) 引誘 (B) 阻止 (C) 釋放 (D) 勸服

7. 底下哪個選項最適合填入空格(2)中？
   (A) 適應 (B) 調節 (C) 報導 (D) 依賴

8. 底下哪個選項最適合填入空格(**3**)中？
   (A) 侵蝕 (B) 挖掘 (C) 忍住 (D) 推翻

9. 底下哪個選項最適合填入空格(**4**)中？
   (A) 有毒的 (B) 巨大的 (C) 終點的 (D) 食肉的

10. 底下哪個選項最適合填入空格(**5**)中？
    (A) 取代 (B) 流產 (C) 搔 (D) 勝過

解答| **6.** (B) **7.** (D) **8.** (C) **9.** (B) **10.** (C)

✱ Review Test_02

❶ 第1到10題為「拼字題」，請根據中文意思完成英文拼字填空。第11到20題為「釋義題」，請根據英文字彙寫出中文意思。

解答| **1.** typhoon **2.** isobar **3.** precipitation
4. whirlwind **5.** hail **6.** souvenir **7.** drizzle
8. queue **9.** attraction **10.** excursion
11. 獨家新聞，最新內幕消息，囂起，搶先報導
12. 上船，登機 **13.** 發行量，銷售量
14. 編輯，報章專欄主筆 **15.** 後續報導
16. 向後地 **17.** 繫錨架 **18.** 快速帆船
19. 甲板 **20.** 船頭，鞠躬，低頭

❷ 請根據句意，從底下四個選項中選出一個最能適切完成句子的字彙。

21. 記者負責報導中東戰事。
    (A) 包裹 (B) 新聞稿 (C) 打開行李 (D) 報導

22. 即使捕鯨船以半速後退，據說仍遭被魚叉叉中的藍鯨拖行二十四小時。
    (A) 向後地 (B) 逆風地 (C) 順風地 (D) 鋒面

23. 船橋上的守望員發現前方有冰山便高喊警戒。
    (A) 船橋 (B) 壓艙物 (C) 錨 (D) 平手

24. 酷熱的熱浪何時才會結束？我再也無法忍受酷暑。
    (A) 寒冷的 (B) 酷熱的 (C) 極冷的 (D) 商業的

25. 我們經歷了一段漫長而寒冷的冬天。
    (A) 甲板 (B) 言論箝制 (C) 一段時間 (D) 陣風

解答| **21.** (D) **22.** (A) **23.** (A) **24.** (B) **25.** (C)

✱ Practice Test_02

❶ 請根據句意，從底下四個選項中選出一個最接近套色單字意思的字彙。

1. 霧太濃了使我們無法看見迎面而來的車輛。
   (A) 專題報導 (B) 霧靄 (C) 水流 (D) 報業聯盟

2. 你可以載我一程到學校嗎？
   (A) 搭便車 (B) 驟雨 (C) 遠足 (D) 特刊

3. 你的家人多久外出用餐一次？
   (A) 搭便車 (B) 用膳 (C) 搭船旅遊 (D) 跳上

4. 我覺得有點太冷，窗戶不是打開的嗎？
   (A) 暈機的 (B) 炎熱的 (C) 寒冷的 (D) 潮濕的

5. 這一定超過攝氏三十度，太熱了。
   (A) 季風 (B) 霰 (C) 攝氏 (D) 華氏

解答| **1.** (B) **2.** (A) **3.** (B) **4.** (C) **5.** (C)

❷ 請閱讀下面短文，並根據文意回答問題。

喜劇故事

查理的爸爸一到下午便下班回家，五年級的查理感覺得出家裡瀰漫著一股不尋常的氣氛。爸爸匆忙地幫媽媽打理家事，查理從家中氣氛研判是外婆要來探望大家。奇怪的是，每當外婆來時，爸爸總是提心吊膽。查理不明白為什麼爸爸在外婆面前老是害怕退縮，他猜想可能是因為外婆抱怨家裡生活條件不好。上次外婆來訪時還跟爸爸吵了起來，查理不知道兩人在吵什麼，但他不喜歡外婆，因為她很少對爸爸好。

傍晚一到門鈴就響了，爸爸就像想藏起自己沒有的尾巴般侷促緊張，外婆自然又開始問爸爸何時才要搬離這個簡陋的兩房公寓，爸爸只是笑而不答。

就像往常一樣，查理得把自己的房間讓給外婆睡而跟父母擠一晚。隔天早晨吃早餐時外婆說：「查理，是你在我床邊放一杯水的嗎？我半夜起床時好渴，喝完以後覺得真是神清氣爽。」查理聽了大叫：「妳把我的蝌蚪喝光了嗎？」

6. 底下哪個選項最適合填入空格(**1**)中？
   (A) 效率高的 (B) 成直角的 (C) 中等的 (D) 普遍的

7. 底下哪個選項最適合填入空格(**2**)中？
   (A) 家事的 (B) 獨立自主的 (C) 沉默的
   (D) 不說話的

8. 底下哪個選項最適合填入空格(**3**)中？
   (A) 鞏固 (B) 爭吵 (C) 合併 (D) 妥協

9. 底下哪個選項最適合填入空格(**4**)中？
   (A) 豪奢的 (B) 奢華的 (C) 毗連的 (D) 簡陋的

10. 底下哪個選項最適合填入空格(**5**)中？
    (A) 放棄 (B) 大叫 (C) 激勵 (D) 遏止

解答| **6.** (D) **7.** (A) **8.** (B) **9.** (D) **10.** (B)

✱ Actual Test

Passage 1

電視

電視從一開始便擺脫其他媒體的競爭，並藉由提供娛樂和資訊的方式來啟發全世界無數民眾。最特別的是，電視現場直播的驚人能力將世界連結為一個地球村。電視的娛樂功能幾乎是無可匹敵的，難怪美國孩童到了十八歲時，平均每人收看一萬七千小時的電視節目。

然而儘管世人盛讚電視為二十世紀最傑出的發明之一，電視使人上癮的特性常成為眾矢之的。在這點上，電視是難辭其咎的。全家人幾乎一吃完晚餐就窩

在電視機前看電視，眼睛直盯著螢幕，耳朵只朝著喇叭，並對旁人的干擾表示不悅。如果電視機被搬走，全家人就會凝視著原本擺放電視機的地方，其他什麼事也不做。每到周日待在家的爸爸跟一尊佛像間的差別，只在於佛像面前沒電視。事實上還有另一個差別，那就是佛像手裡沒有拿遙控器。對電視的沉迷也導致不愛運動。收看電視的建議距離迫使我們坐著不動，連身體活動也被剝奪。不管是收看棒球還是高爾夫球比賽，同樣無法運動。

電視也因不必要的暴力鏡頭遭到詬病。許多電視節目角色第一個憑藉的手段就是暴力。如果現實生活就像電視節目描繪的一樣，那麼人類的平均壽命將會大為減少。坦白說，暴力鏡頭被不少電視製作人當作提高收視率的有效工具。例如有些摔角節目讓我們知道造物者的神奇，竟能創造出如此強壯無比的人類，摔角者無論被椅子丟到或被冠軍腰帶打到照樣能活。這類節目唯一考量到年輕觀眾的一點只是螢幕上簡單的一句話：「無論你是誰，不管你做什麼，請勿在家中嘗試。」但離家外出的年輕人會做什麼呢？

部分電視公司把焦點放在電視明星身上，專門賺取不義之財，因此難辭其咎。部分節目播放超過一小時，專門刺探明星居家情形或談論其約會對象、配偶，甚至寵物。許多觀眾對這類節目倒足胃口，電視公司不應濫用所謂人民知的權利來遂其私利。

電視無疑是文明社會最了不起的產物之一，無論對文化或文明都有貢獻。電視對人類的啟發是難以匹敵的，正因為電視對人類影響甚鉅，所以我們更該仔細收看，而非不假思索。

1. 根據上述文意，套色單字開始可用底下哪個選項的意義來取代？
   (A) 觀念 (B) 大學入學許可 (C) 到來 (D) 終止

2. 根據上述文意，套色單字無可匹敵的可用底下哪個選項的意義來取代？
   (A) 不同的 (B) 無可匹敵的 (C) 一致的 (D) 平行的

3. 根據上述文意，套色單字傑出的可用底下哪個選項的意義來取代？
   (A) 公然的 (B) 食草的 (C) 與生俱來的 (D) 非凡的

4. 根據上述文意，套色單字黏住可用底下哪個選項的意義來取代？
   (A) 緊黏 (B) 猶豫 (C) 點燃 (D) 舉起

5. 根據上述文意，套色單字干擾可用底下哪個選項的意義來取代？
   (A) 灌木叢 (B) 範圍 (C) 干預 (D) 鑑定

6. 根據上述文意，套色單字迫使可用底下哪個選項的意義來取代？
   (A) 勸阻 (B) 迫使 (C) 慫恿 (D) 引誘

7. 根據上述文意，套色單字不必要的可用底下哪個選項的意義來取代？
   (A) 多痰的 (B) 樂觀的 (C) 沒有理由的
   (D) 不能實現的

8. 根據上述文意，套色單字減少可用底下哪個選項的意義來取代？
   (A) 減少 (B) 拉長 (C) 提出 (D) 使著迷

9. 根據上述文意，套色單字免除的可用底下哪個選項的意義來取代？
   (A) 致命的 (B) 美味的 (C) 免除的 (D) 老成世故的

10. 根據上述文意，套色單字啟發可用底下哪個選項的意義來取代？
   (A) 貪圖 (B) 啟迪 (C) 迷惑 (D) 加溫殺菌

解答｜ 1. (C) 2. (B) 3. (D) 4. (A) 5. (C)
        6. (B) 7. (C) 8. (A) 9. (C) 10. (B)

Passage 2

諾亞方舟

一般人常堅稱聖經裡全是虛構故事，裡面的傳說和事件叫人難以相信。然而近來有些人試圖證實其所言不虛，其中之一就是關於諾亞時代的洪水。《舊約聖經》裡的《創世紀》有一則關於大洪水的故事，據說上帝發現世界充滿邪惡和暴力，於是決定毀掉自己創造的人類，但祂希望自己喜歡的諾亞能夠倖免於難，於是便命令他依指示選用上等木材建造方舟。方舟長一百三十三公尺、寬二十二公尺、高十三公尺，共有三層甲板、一個船頂、一道側門和幾個房間，另外還要塗上焦油。諾亞花了一百年建造方舟，完工時已高齡六百歲，此時上帝指示他和妻子一起進入方舟，以免在七日內即將發生的洪水中喪命，同行的還有閃、含、雅弗等三對兒媳，以及所有動物雌雄各一對。據說洪水日以繼夜地持續了四十天，徹底摧毀地面所有剩下來的生物，洪水泛濫高度比世界最高峰還要高七公尺，一百五十天後洪水才完全退去，至於方舟則停放在亞拉拉特山上。

一般人的懷疑不只來自諾亞的高壽，事實上聖經裡最長壽的人是活了九百六十九歲的瑪土撒拉，同時更來自他以簡單工具打造大船的技術。然而，這裡有件流傳已久的趣事。位於東土耳其靠近亞美尼亞和伊朗邊境的亞拉拉特山高五千一百六十五公尺，白靄靄的山頂在在證明這是座高山，有三分之一的山脈頂端終年被冰雪覆蓋，這座休火山曾在一八四零年六月二日爆發過。亞拉拉特是土耳其語「阿特」，意為「痛苦之山」。奇怪的是，據說這座山很難攀登，直到一八二九年才由德國內科醫生弗雷德瑞克．派諾特完成史上首度攀登。關於棲息在亞拉拉特山上的方舟有許多傳說和目擊報告，只可惜缺乏決定性證據。據說只有在部分冰雪消融的短暫片刻，探險家才能登上最高峰一瞥深埋在冰雪堆中的方舟遺跡。很久以前，西元七零年的猶太歷史學家約瑟夫和一三零零年的義大利威尼斯探險家馬可波羅都曾提到有關山上之船的傳說，雖然他們也是道聽塗說的。近來某對登山父子檔堅稱找到黑色龐然大物的遺跡，父子兩相信這就是諾亞方舟，甚至還帶回極小片木頭作為佐證，並拍照存證。如果他們果真在寸草不生的山頂上找到龐然大

物，究竟會是什麼呢？是誰能把這龐然大物放在山巔上？目的何在？

11. 根據上述文意，套色單字證實可用底下哪個選項的意義來取代？
(A) 楔形榫頭 (B) 捧為名人 (C) 證實 (D) 增援

12. 根據上述文意，套色單字洪水可用底下哪個選項的意義來取代？
(A) 迷宮 (B) 極微小 (C) 被虐待狂 (D) 洪水

13. 根據上述文意，套色單字徹底摧毀可用底下哪個選項的意義來取代？
(A) 繁殖 (B) 消滅 (C) 投降 (D) 對抗

14. 根據上述文意，套色單字懷疑可用底下哪個選項的意義來取代？
(A) 懷疑 (B) 放逐 (C) 整個範圍 (D) 沙文主義

15. 根據上述文意，套色單字龐大的可用底下哪個選項的意義來取代？
(A) 極微小的 (B) 很小的 (C) 龐大的 (D) 迷你的

16. 根據上述文意，套色單字長壽可用底下哪個選項的意義來取代？
(A) 長壽 (B) 迷宮 (C) 動物群 (D) 植物群

17. 根據上述文意，套色單字巨大的可用底下哪個選項的意義來取代？
(A) 巨大無比的 (B) 飲酒作樂的 (C) 不擇手段的 (D) 簡潔的

18. 根據上述文意，套色單字爆發可用底下哪個選項的意義來取代？
(A) 衝口而出 (B) 反駁 (C) 爆發 (D) 廢除

19. 根據上述文意，套色單字攀登可用底下哪個選項的意義來取代？
(A) 攀登 (B) 貪心 (C) 昏睡 (D) 好戰

20. 根據上述文意，套色單字極小的可用底下哪個選項的意義來取代？
(A) 清澈的 (B) 同等的 (C) 極小的 (D) 誘人的

解答 | **11.** (C) **12.** (D) **13.** (B) **14.** (A) **15.** (C)
16. (A) **17.** (A) **18.** (C) **19.** (A) **20.** (C)

五大考試單字速記手冊－十倍速提升字彙力 2011
Building Vocabulary for iBT, SAT, GRE, TOEIC, GEPT 2011

編　　　　著	Dr. Park Jong Hwa
發　行　人	Isa Wong
主　　　編	李佩玲
責 任 編 輯	鄭安致
封 面 設 計	黃聖文
美 編 印 務	楊雯如
行 銷 企 畫	楊震宇
發行所／出版者	台灣培生教育出版股份有限公司
	地址／台北市重慶南路一段 147 號 5 樓
	電話／02-2370-8168　　傳真／02-2370-8169
	網址／www.pearson.com.tw
	E-mail／reader.tw@pearson.com
香 港 總 經 銷	培生教育出版亞洲股份有限公司
	地址／香港鰂魚涌英皇道 979 號(太古坊康和大廈 2 樓)
	電話／(852)3181-0000　傳真／(852)2564-0955
	E-mail／msip.hk@pearson.com
台 灣 總 經 銷	創智文化有限公司
	地址／23674 新北市土城區忠承路 89 號 6 樓（永寧科技園區）
	電話／02-2268-3489　　傳真／02-2269-6560
	博訊書網／www.booknews.com.tw
學校訂書專線	02-2370-8168 轉 8866
版　　　次	2011 年 8 月二版一刷
書　　　號	TT179
I　S　B　N	978-911-000-305-7
定　　　價	新台幣 700 元

★資料請填寫完整，才可參加抽獎哦！

讀者資料

姓名：＿＿＿＿＿＿＿＿＿＿＿＿ 性別：＿＿＿＿ 出生年月日：＿＿＿＿＿＿＿＿＿.

電話：(O)＿＿＿＿＿＿＿＿ (H)＿＿＿＿＿＿＿＿ (Mo)＿＿＿＿＿＿＿.

傳眞：(O)＿＿＿＿＿＿＿＿ (H)＿＿＿＿＿＿＿＿.

E-mail：＿＿＿＿＿＿＿＿＿＿＿＿＿＿＿＿＿＿＿＿＿＿＿＿.

地址：＿＿＿＿＿＿＿＿＿＿＿＿＿＿＿＿＿＿＿＿＿＿＿＿＿.

教育程度：

☐國小 ☐國中 ☐高中 ☐大專 ☐大學以上

職業：

1.學生 ☐

2.教職 ☐教師 ☐教務人員 ☐班主任 ☐經營者 ☐其他：＿＿＿＿＿

任職單位：☐學校 ☐補教機構 ☐其他：＿＿＿＿＿

教學經歷：☐幼兒英語 ☐兒童英語 ☐國小英語 ☐國中英語 ☐高中英語
☐成人英語

3.社會人士 ☐工 ☐商 ☐資訊 ☐服務 ☐軍警公職 ☐出版媒體 ☐其他＿＿＿＿.

從何處得知本書：

☐逛書店 ☐報章雜誌 ☐廣播電視 ☐親友介紹 ☐書訊 ☐廣告函 ☐其他＿＿＿.

對我們的建議：

＿＿＿＿＿＿＿＿＿＿＿＿＿＿＿＿＿＿＿＿＿＿＿＿

＿＿＿＿＿＿＿＿＿＿＿＿＿＿＿＿＿＿＿＿＿＿＿＿

＿＿＿＿＿＿＿＿＿＿＿＿＿＿＿＿＿＿＿＿＿＿＿＿

＿＿＿＿＿＿＿＿＿＿＿＿＿＿＿＿＿＿＿＿＿＿＿＿